Boots, Bikes, and Bombers

T0308766

Boots, Bikes, and Bombers

Adventures of Alaska Conservationist
Ginny Hill Wood

Edited by Karen Brewster

UNIVERSITY OF ALASKA PRESS
FAIRBANKS

© 2012 University of Alaska Press
All rights reserved

University of Alaska Press
P.O. Box 756240
Fairbanks, AK 99775-6240

Library of Congress Cataloging-in-Publication Data

Wood, Ginny.
Boots, bikes, and bombers : adventures of Alaska conservationist Ginny Hill
Wood / edited by Karen Brewster.
    p. cm. — (Oral history series)
Includes bibliographical references and index.
ISBN 978-1-60223-173-3 (pbk. : alk. paper) — ISBN 978-1-60223-174-0
(e-book)
1. Wood, Ginny. 2. Wood, Ginny—Travel. 3. Women conservationists—
Alaska—Biography. 4. Conservationists—Alaska—Biography. 5. Women
adventurers—Alaska—Biography. 6. Alaska—Description and travel.
7. Camp Denali—History. 8. Wilderness areas—Alaska. 9. Alaska—
Environmental conditions. 10. Oral history—Alaska. I. Brewster, Karen.
II. Title.
QH31.W67A3 2012
639.9092—dc23
[B]

2011033346

Cover design by David Alcorn
Cover photo: Ginny Wood hiking to McGonagall Pass in Denali National
Park, 1961: "doing what I loved best." Courtesy of Ginny Wood.
Back cover photo: Camp Denali today, © Ralph A. Clevenger.

This publication was printed on acid-free paper that meets the minimum
requirements for ANSI / NISO Z39.48–1992 (R2002) (Permanence of Paper
for Printed Library Materials).

To my mother, Renate Brewster,
who supported my own desire for adventure.
— KNB

To Celia Hunter, a friend who
was always there to share in the adventure.
— GHW

Oral Biography Series
Edited by William Schneider

Books in the Oral Biography Series focus on individuals whose life experiences and personal accomplishments provide an intimate view of the events, personalities, and influences that have shaped Alaska history. Each book is created through a collaborative process between the narrator, an editor, and often other community members, who record the oral history, then transcribe and edit it in written form. The result is a historical record that combines the unique art of storytelling with literary technique and supporting visual and archival materials.

Contents

Map of Alaska by Dixon Jones.

Acknowledgements

I would like to thank Susan Grace, Roger Kaye, Pam Miller, Keith Pollock, and Frank Keim for helping conduct the oral history interviews; Ginny's daughter and son-in-law, Romany Wood and Carl Rosenberg, for their support of this project; Ginny's friends for their enthusiasm and encouragement about the importance of this project and for allowing me and Ginny undisturbed time to review the draft manuscript together; the devoted team of amazing caregivers who provide Ginny laughter and comfort and make it possible for her to remain living in her home during her final years; the reference staff at Elmer E. Rasmuson Library, University of Alaska Fairbanks, for helping me locate obscure references and navigate the foreign world of government documents; Dixon Jones, graphic artist, Elmer E. Rasmuson Library, for creating the maps (maps of Denali and Katmai National Parks were adapted from National Park Service source files); Kathryn Myers, museum curator, Katmai National Park and Preserve, for photographs and references; Amy Johnson, Wally Cole, and Ramona Finnoff for the use of photographs; the Alaska Humanities Forum for funding a portion of my early interviewing and transcription work; Dr. William Schneider for his encouragement, guidance, and reviews; Elisabeth Dabney for her editorial talents and enthusiastic support of this project; and my family and friends for their love, support, and acceptance of my self-imposed isolation while I tried to complete parts of the manuscript.

Finally, I am grateful for my friendship with Ginny Wood and thank her for the opportunity to get to know her during these last five years. She has inspired me and enriched my life in ways too many to name.

Karen Brewster, November 2011

Ginny and Karen Brewster,
August 2010.
Photo by Amy Johnson.

Ginny Wood with her dog, Sheenjek, December 2009. Photo by Amy Johnson.

Prologue:
The Unexplored Life
By Ginny Wood[1]

One cannot help but ponder what motivates an individual now entering the sunset of her allotted years on this planet to want to chronicle the interlude between her arrival and her impending departure from this world—especially when few will notice the exit. This would-be author, who wrote little of note in her lifetime, would actually prefer to spend her remaining years doing more of what she always has instead of writing about it.

Perhaps it is mostly a matter of ego after all? One can accept the inevitability of one's demise, but not its anonymity. Like the ubiquitous folk-soldier of World War II who marked his passage with the inscription "Kilroy was here" on public places everywhere GIs served, I wish to inform passersby in a book rather than on a tombstone: Ginny Hill Wood was here!

Then there is the matter of one's progeny. We make wills to instruct the distribution of our worldly estate—providing providence and the Internal Revenue Service allow us some to leave. But what of the essence that was you—the thoughts, reactions, and encounters along the way that shaped your inner self? Offspring, after the age of twelve, are wont to find their parents rather a disappointment, if not an obstacle. Youth are too absorbed in their own adolescent vicissitudes to wonder very much about their immediate antecedents' lives while they are extant. No longer do I have an elder or a sibling to ask "Remember when?" or to query about an incident or connection in our family's history. Perhaps a bit of the impetus in attempting an autobiography of sorts is wanting to tell our offspring all the events and thoughts we'd like them to know about, about which they never asked. It is akin to leaving notes and directions around the house to remind your kids about matters of importance to you when you are leaving the place in their care while you are away traveling for a time.

But overriding all these rationalizations is for me a desire to take stock of the greater part of an extraordinary century I've had the privilege to encounter. A matter of self-appraisement, a summing up to find out who is this person that I turned out to be. Would that girl who was me at eighteen approve of what she had become? Did I let her down? How do I perceive myself as a little girl growing up in a small western town? As an adolescent during the Great Depression? As a ferry pilot for the air force during World War II?[2] As a student roaming Europe in the war's aftermath? What did my vagabond spirit find in Alaska that caused me to put down the roots that held me here for the remainder of my life?

Most of my life I seemed to have been deciding what I wanted to be when I grew up. Now is the time to ask myself: Who did I become? What have I learned? What values did I choose to live by? How did I get from there to here? What and who has given my life meaning and direction? What was the importance of being me? What of the legacy that defines the person I have become? What were my perceived triumphs? My disappointments? My sorrows?[3]

Perhaps it is another adventure in discovery—one of the spirit of rediscovering yourself, the places you have been, how you interacted with events of history, and the people you met and loved along the way. There are many episodes I'd like to live over, and some I'd wish to be able to amend—or forget. But in the final summing up it seems I was always the right age, at the right time, in the right place.

1

Introduction

I was the right age, at the right time, in the right place," replies Virginia Hill Wood, known to her friends as Ginny, when asked about events that have shaped her life. Ginny is self-effacing and shuns suggestions that she has led a remarkable life or is a role model for others. She is quick to say that there were plenty of other people doing exactly the same things. With such humility, you would think Ginny shy. Far from it. She is an animated storyteller, captivating her audience with tales of a time and way of life that have long since disappeared. Her blue eyes brighten, she smiles, and her speech revs with feverish excitement when a visitor stops by her small log house in the hills above Fairbanks, Alaska.

At five feet, four inches tall and skinny as a tent pole, Ginny appears frail. She moves more slowly than she used to, but despite appearances is determined to remain as independent as possible. She dresses in a classic casual style that looks like she walked right out of an L. L. Bean catalog—jeans and a fleece jacket for home, brown corduroys with brown-toned windowpane plaid shirt and Fair Isle sweater when dressing up for an event. She ties back her thin gray hair into a small ponytail with bobby pins on the sides to keep flyaway ends out of her face. She flits about in a constant whir like a bee jumping from flower to flower to gather pollen. She talks fast, like a squirrel chattering from the treetop at an intruder.

Like Ginny, her house has a rustic, simple quality. The main room has a maple syrup–like glow produced by the dim lamplight reflecting off the log walls. Handmade wooden chairs, stools, table, and bench are scattered through the room. There is no big-screen TV, no computer, no overstuffed leather couches, no plush carpet, no coffeemaker, no bread machine, no food processor. The only hint of modernity is a small thirteen-inch television and stereo system hidden away in the corner. The TV is rarely turned on—only to watch PBS. A woodstove sits at the back of the room encircled by boxes of kindling, burnable paper, and a stack of wood waiting to be made into a warm fire. Old photos, environmental posters, scenic paintings, and knickknacks from a world of travels cover the walls. Almost every flat surface—the butcher-block square in the middle of the kitchen, the eating table, and the window seat—is covered with piles of paper, papers in boxes, and newspaper clippings in triangular magazine boxes like those found on a library shelf. A forbidding turn-of-the-century cast-iron wood-burning cookstove stands as a sentry in the corner of the kitchen, partially blocking the entrance to the hallway that leads to the rest of the house.

Sitting in this house rich with Fairbanks history, it is easy to fall back in time and in step with Ginny and her stories. You can see the people sitting here forty years ago scheming conservation strategy. You can imagine Ginny tapping away at a manual typewriter, writing newsletter editorials or magazine articles. You can hear the friends laughing together at potlucks. You feel a living connection to the past.

Ginny's Gab Group

The winter of 2005–2006 was an anomaly. At age eighty-eight, Ginny had injured her back the previous summer and was forced to take things slower. She was not driving, she was not skiing, and she was staying home more. This confinement meant she had time to record some of her memories and stories.

In March 2006, I and three of Ginny's friends (Susan Grace, Roger Kaye, and Pam Miller) began weekly evening visits to record her stories. "Ginny's Gab Group," she called it. The idea started when Roger mentioned to me in passing one day that someone should write down Ginny's stories. Roger has known Ginny since 1974, when he came to work for her at Camp Denali, and he interviewed her extensively for his own book about the history of the creation of the Arctic National Wildlife Refuge.[1] "Me, me, it should be me," I called out, waving my hand in the air like a schoolkid wanting to be called on by the teacher. I only knew Ginny in passing. She was a familiar figure in town, with a reputation as a strong, outspoken woman who had led an interesting life and played an important role in Alaska's history. I had conducted oral history interviews with her in 2000 and 2002 for a project I was doing about pioneering women through my job as a research associate with the Oral History Program at the University of Alaska Fairbanks, and I felt drawn to her by common interests. And after living in Alaska for close to twenty years and having worked as both an environmentalist and an oral historian, I was confident that I knew enough to understand the context of what Ginny would talk about. When I met with Ginny's friends, they agreed an oral history project should be done and that I should be involved.

We made each interview a social affair. We gathered at Ginny's house, with the friends bringing dinner and taking care of cleanup so as not to burden Ginny as hostess. We sat at her long wooden table in front of the windows looking out on her yard of birch and spruce trees towards a view of the Alaska Range. We happily chatted about our lives and current political and environmental issues as we ate. After dinner, we relocated to the group of chairs in front of the woodstove for video recording. Ginny's friends did the interviews, since they knew her better than I and already had questions they wanted to ask or specific stories they wanted to hear. I, the outsider and the professional, operated the video camera and chimed in with questions or to help move the conversation along. Ginny sat in her rocking chair with the old, worn, and faded beaver pelt hanging over the back. It was an intimate, cozy, and informal setting.

After three recording sessions at her house, Ginny complained of the pressure of having to "clean up" for us. She used her table to sort piles of junk mail, articles she clipped from the newspaper, and bills she had to pay. Having to move her piles upset her system and routine. Also, having guests, especially ones who were videotaping, made her self-conscious about the cleanliness of her home. So, we took turns hosting the weekly gatherings at one of our homes. Since Ginny did not drive, one of us would pick her up and take her home again while another played host. We continued the potluck format and emphasized to Ginny that all she needed to bring was herself and her memories. Summer is a hectic time for Alaskans, who try to make the most of the short season of warmth and sunshine. Our group was no exception, so we took a hiatus. And anyway, Ginny was too busy with gardening to make time for recording.

Despite Ginny's grumblings about time, she enjoyed our evening gatherings. As a social person, she enjoyed the company, especially that winter when her activities and outdoor travels were limited and she felt cooped up and perhaps a bit lonely. And as a storyteller she relished having an audience.

As Ginny tells a story, she starts and stops regularly, interrupting herself with a digression of extra background, context, or detail that she deems relevant to understanding the topic and essential to the point of her story. Once Ginny gets started on a subject, it is difficult to insert a comment or question of your own. Nowadays, her stories sometimes follow a circuitous and redundant route as she works to mine her memory for forgotten details. But if you are patient, or can help push her along, she eventually winds her way through to the end.

Ginny speaks in half sentences and assumes you are keeping up and have the background to understand what she is talking about. "I don't want to start with Adam and Eve," Ginny complained once about being interviewed by people who had not researched their subject well enough. In this project, since it was friends interviewing Ginny, she did not have to explain every detail and was free to speak in her normal uninhibited flow. And with my background in history and anthropology and our common interests in conservation and a love of the outdoors, she began to trust that I, too, knew what she was talking about.

The Art of Storytelling

Ginny Wood frames her life in terms of moments and memories that are retold in fragments of stories, not as reflections about personal motivations or philosophical meanings. As she said, "I see my life as a story, with the people in it like characters in a book."[2] Storytellers like Ginny create their storied world using the tools of fiction. They employ dramatic style, build suspense, pick and choose details, mix time frames, and insert characters as they are relevant. As a raconteur, the flow of the story and what it represents takes precedence for Ginny over the accuracy of the details. For instance, her standard story about me is: "She is from the archives. She came out to interview me once and I was mean. Now she's one of my best friends." My memory is that Ginny put me off because she was busy with gardening but that I was not offended. For an oral historian, persistence and patience are essential tools of the trade. Finally in winter, when life slowed down, Ginny agreed to be interviewed. No matter how many times I offer my interpretation of these events, and that I did not feel she was mean, it falls on deaf ears. As a typically welcoming and friendly person, putting me off made Ginny feel mean. Her created memory based on these emotions is what has become true for her. Her version shows her emotional shift from seeing me as an intruder to accepting me as a friend, which is more important to her than are "the facts."

Ginny reshapes the past based on the present.[3] This is what David William Cohen has called "the production of history."[4] Our tellings of the past are not stagnant single repetitions of fact but are stories based upon a continual re-layering of meaning as we are influenced by audience, setting, current events, or interests.[5] Because of these varying influences, we all tell stories in different ways, even if about shared experiences.

Our telling about the past is also influenced by memory. Some people remember facts, figures, and details from long ago with accuracy. Some of us cannot remember the name of someone we just met. The retelling of memory is a personalized art form. As fiction writer Isabel Allende says:

> Memory is fiction. We select the brightest and the darkest, ignoring what we are ashamed of, and so embroider the broad tapestry of our lives… In the end, the only thing we have in abundance is the memory we have woven. Each of us chooses the tone for telling his or her own story. [6]

Cohen also reminds us that memory is as much about forgetting as it is about remembering. Making these decisions about which facts to leave out and which to put in means there is a difference between "history as lived" and "history as recorded."[7]

Ginny has told her stories so many times that they have become her reality, whether that is how things really happened or not. Her stories are her memories now, her connections to the past. She connects to these memories through a set repertoire of stories that are triggered by certain topics. These standardized tellings are similar to what William Schneider calls "signature stories":

These are accounts that play a primary role in the teller's life and are retold often to interpret and emphasize important themes. The hallmark of signature stories is that the narrator retells them often and relates them to core values in his/her life.[8]

In comparison, Ginny's stories appear to be reflexive responses triggered by certain topics instead of platforms for conveying life lessons. The same story has been told so many times and for so many years that it sounds as if she is reciting a rehearsed presentation. I do not know if Ginny talked about her experiences in different ways when she was younger, or if because of failing memory she sticks vigorously to her pre-prepared and prescribed palette, but it appears that for her, the story is not the story if it is told in a different way. It has to start at a specific place and the details have to be told in a particular order. If she is interrupted, she is not dissuaded. She will stop and start over from the beginning. As her friend Bob Weeden observed, "It is like a spider who must spin anew when its web is damaged."[9] In this way, these are her signature stories and are what she is known by.

Ginny has used her stories to create a public persona for herself. She is the pilot, the founder of Camp Denali, the wilderness adventurer, and the activist. She is not the divorcée, the mother, or the frail elder. It is difficult to break through this wall of signature stories to get at her inner feelings. In this way, Ginny protects her privacy and does not have to talk about things she is uncomfortable with. But as she herself has reflected in her own writings:

Life is more than what you do. It is what you thought, who you became, who you really are. I'm still on my quest. One conclusion I've come to is that you are many you's. The you, you think you are. What you were to all the people you have met and treasured. What you were to those who didn't like you much, to those you loved and hurt. To your progeny, to "your public." You are many you's. As Alfred Lord Tennyson says, "I am a part of all that I have met."[10]

Alessandro Portelli and Ronald Grele, among others, consider the telling of a story to be a created negotiation between narrator and oral historian,[11] with the constructed narrative being influenced by the experiences, ideas, and biases the researcher brings to the questioning and his or her responses to the narrator.[12] While the general subject of a conversation with Ginny was determined by the interest of the interviewers, Ginny's reliance on signature stories often guided the course of the discussion more than our questions did. In the sense of "shared authority" as defined by Michael Frisch,[13] we allowed Ginny to focus on what she was comfortable sharing. As her friends, we did not want to ask questions that might cause her discomfort, such as the more private and emotional parts of her life like her marriage, her divorce, raising her daughter, or the deep connections of friendships.[14] In this way, our lack of questions also helped construct the narrative.

It is interesting to note that Ginny Wood's life history does not focus on topics like motherhood, family, nurturing, or gender roles, which some might expect a woman's life history to include.[15] There are a few possibilities as to why. First, these are not subjects central to Ginny's identity, so she would not voluntarily bring them up. As Ginny has said, "I was not a feminist. I just did what I wanted to do and I happened to be a woman. I was lucky that I never had any trouble." Second, these were not themes that those of us doing the interviews were particularly interested in or thought to ask about. Similar to oral histories that have been done with female public figures,[16] Ginny's stories focus on her public life. This is what she is comfortable sharing with a broad audience.

Myriad Voices

Transcribing or summarizing thirty-five tapes, combining various versions of Ginny's stories, and editing for redundancy has been a long and arduous process. It has been over four years of fits and starts. I started by transcribing our 2006, 2007, and 2008 interviews, then integrated transcriptions of previous interviews Ginny had done that are housed at the University of Alaska Fairbanks Oral History Archives.[17] Given Ginny's reliance on signature stories, it is not surprising that she told the same stories in different interviews. In order to get the best possible rendition, with the most details and the least redundancy, there are places where I combined pieces from different tellings into one presentation of the story.[18] They are all Ginny's words, so it did not matter to me which interview they came from. Therefore, I have not indicated the precise locations of the merging. The other benefit of turning to previous interviews was that by the time Ginny's Gab Group was recording, Ginny's memory was beginning to fade. I discovered that some of the details she left out were well stated in an earlier telling of the same story.

In keeping with the notion of shared authority and what David Dunaway calls an "oral memoir," where a narrator tells his or her own story and a writer adds explanation and footnotes,[19] you will find my words interspersed throughout Ginny's stories. A different font is used to distinguish between my writing (Garamond) and the transcription of Ginny's words (Optima). I have done this for two reasons. First, as editor, I need to create context and transition to promote understanding for the reader and foster overall narrative flow.[20] Second, as oral historian, it is my responsibility to provide historical background and make connections between Ginny's life and broader subjects.[21] This is what Tracy K'Meyer and Glenn Carothers call a co-created document, which "combines the narrator's version of his or her story with the results of the historian's effort to illuminate the context of the narrator's life and the connections between his or her story and broader historical themes."[22]

Typically, a life history is based on oral narrative. However, throughout her life Ginny has been a prolific and talented writer. Having access to this written legacy offered a chance to let Ginny speak for herself on a variety of levels: as narrative storyteller, as author, as activist, as advocate. Therefore, I have incorporated excerpts of her writings into her stories to fill in missing details and provide richer descriptions. For particularly long passages, I have footnoted sources.

In this same way, I have interwoven commentary from other people. Memory can be a fickle thing, so I found it interesting to hear what other people had to say about some of the same circumstances Ginny discusses. Such as Ginny's former husband, Woody. Or her longtime friend Celia Hunter. Or Bob Weeden, who worked with Ginny and Celia to start the Alaska Conservation Society. I included their words side by side with Ginny's in places where I found they provided richer detail than she gave or could help paint a fuller picture of the events described. There are other comments that I instead included as notes, because they disrupted the flow of the narrative or were less critical to understanding the story. It is interesting to note where some of these descriptions vary from Ginny's memory.

Ginny has made several previous attempts to write her autobiography.[23] She collected scraps of paper with lists of stories and subjects, inspiring quotes, photos, or ideas she did not want to forget. She wrote bits and pieces in her frequently illegible scrawl on scrap paper, on lined yellow pads of paper, or in spiral-bound notebooks.[24] Many of these stories are similar to the ones she tells in this oral history, although sometimes the written versions are more descriptive and show Ginny's poetic skill with language—the process of writing being different from telling a story out loud. Where possible, I have incorporated elements from her writings into the stories in this book, but mostly her written stories were too long or too similar to what was told orally so space limitations prevented fuller use of the material. Despite her best efforts, Ginny never completed the project. She was too busy with other things, like gardening, preparing for winter, doing house chores, or hosting visitors. As she wrote in one of her notebooks:

Often friends and causal acquaintances had advised, "You should write a book about your life." My flip answer had always been "I haven't the time. I'm still living it." Besides my religion prevents me from sacrificing the trees for the paper it would take to write it and leave a record of some sort—the woof and warp of one's life— if only for one's offspring other than an epitaph on a headstone.

What would pen produce from looking backwards on seven decades of tasting, exploring and ruminating about being on this earth, compared to the one who saw and lived it from the me that had only two decades of being on it? What had she lost? What had she gained? What has she learned? A fresh fall of October snow, the first of the season, beckons me onto my skis and off through the trail through the woods and hills that surround my log cabin home. Have I the incentive, the sacrificial time, or talent to attempt to find out?[25]

The Friendship

As Ginny and I spent more time together, our relationship changed from interviewer and interviewee to friends. I stopped by for dinner on a regular basis where we just chatted as any two people getting to know each other would. I told her about my growing up in California in the 1970s, what my family was like, and getting my bachelor's degree in environmental studies from her good friend Dick Cooley at the University of California, Santa Cruz. She'd tell me about her childhood, her sister, her parents. She'd tell me about running Camp Denali or about some wilderness adventure. And I'd talk about the latest stress or bureaucratic frustration of my job at the university; "I'm so glad I worked for myself," she'd always say. She'd ask me what it was like when I lived in Barrow from 1989 to 1997. I'd ask her about bicycling through Europe in the 1930s and '40s. We'd talk about the latest politics of the day, our reactions to news stories, or what other people we knew were up to.

We found that we had much in common. "I wish I had known you when I was younger and more active. When I was still skiing or biking or hiking. I bet we would have had fun together," Ginny would say to me with regret and frustration. And I came to see aspects of myself in Ginny: fiercely independent and refusing to ask for help; set in her ways—there being only one or "right" way to do something; and worrying about a never-ending slew of details about house maintenance, seasonal chores, and time management. Interestingly, I ended up learning how difficult some of these traits can be when experienced from the other side and have tried to change them in myself.

Some oral historians warn against becoming too involved in the lives of their narrators.[26] I disagree. I believe friendship is critical to something as personal as a life history. With friendship comes trust. And with trust comes an intimacy and an ease in sharing memories that would not otherwise come out. As a type of participant-observer, I am able to share someone's stories from the unique position of both insider and outsider. I can see through the biases from a sense of internal understanding while also relating elements to larger social, cultural, and historical contexts. As a friend, I feel a specific sense of responsibility in how I retell the stories, thereby driving the type of collaborative life history it will be.[27]

Ginny's and my friendship deepened in the summers of 2007 and 2008 when I had the great fortune of accompanying her to Camp Denali. Hiking the trails she carved from the wilderness, picking blueberries with her, and feeling

Ginny outside her garden, which she humorously dubbed "Fort Vamoose," circa 1980. Courtesy of Ginny Wood.

her sense of connection to this place created shared experiences. We now had present memories to talk about, instead of me just listening to her tell about the past.

I finally felt that I gained Ginny's trust when in the summer of 2008 she allowed me to help in her garden. Ginny is an expert gardener who takes great pride in her plants and harvest success. Digging in the dirt gives her great pleasure. She spends much of her summer outside in the garden. Ginny's hip pain was getting worse, but she refused to let it slow her down. I did not like to hear how long it had taken her to do a chore or that she'd been in the garden until late at night. I offered to help. I have never had much interest in gardening, but when I moved to Fairbanks from Barrow in 1997, I felt obligated to garden since everyone else was doing it. I merely dabble at my house: a couple of tomato plants in barrels on the deck, a few lettuce plants and potatoes in raised beds. So my offer to help Ginny was based more on wanting to help an elder friend in need than it was on a desire to garden.

Ginny is very protective of her garden and adamant that it be done a certain way. She had always rejected assistance: "That person doesn't know how to do it right." There is the classic tale of her replanting potatoes because she felt the person who planted them had not done it properly—"they weren't deep enough." Of course, my help was rejected, too. But I would not take no for an answer.

I kept asking. Although I was careful in what I pushed for. I did not want stories of doing things wrong following me around. Ginny finally agreed to let me help dig up the soil and pull out the big roots.

Ginny had always just grown vegetables in her large garden; "things you could eat," she said. Flowers were a waste of time. Suddenly, one day she said to me, "Maybe it would be nice to have some posies in that patch in front of the garden so I could see them out the window when I'm doing dishes?" I dug out weeds, worked the dirt, and planted an assortment of colorful flowers— pansies, petunias, snapdragons, and nasturtiums. Ginny was thrilled and dubbed it "Karen's Garden." She continues to reserve that space for my flower planting only—making sure everyone else knows—and I indulge her. To her surprise, she enjoys seeing the colored flowers and thanks me as if it had been my idea in the first place.

In the summer of 2009, Ginny worked the soil in her entire garden herself by crawling from plot to plot since getting up and down with a bad hip was increasingly difficult. It must have taken her nearly a month. This year, she was more willing to accept my help. I was nurse to her doctor. She did the planting. I carried the plants or seed packets to where she was. I passed her the bucket of manure or the watering can when they inevitably were on the wrong side of the plot or out of reach. I got up to refill them when they were empty. I sat across from her and took the small seed spreader from her hand to finish sprinkling seeds, so she did not have to get up to complete the row. I copied her as she planted one row of peas and I another. The opportunity to learn was not lost on me, so I picked her brain about what she was doing and why. In 2010, when Ginny was no longer able to garden, I planted solo—confident that I now knew her way. She did not protest.

Reading Stories

In the fall of 2009, Ginny fell and broke her knee. This, in combination with increasing deterioration of her hip, led to reliance upon a walker and increased caregiver presence at her home. Ginny was doing less and less. That summer, I had restarted the life history project after feeling pressured by Ginny's friends, who kept asking, "How's the book coming?"

When we began the interviewing, I always had the idea of doing a book in the back of my mind. However, every time I mentioned it to Ginny, she was against it. She always had an excuse: "I haven't done anything that important";[28] "Who would be interested in the stories of some old lady?"; "It will mean lots more people are going to want to come visit me and I don't have time for that"; "I'm too old to go on a book tour now"; "I started to write my own life story and want to finish it"; "I don't trust that someone else can do it right." I tried to encourage a positive response. I'd say, "Well, this is like you've written it, only you wrote it orally and all I'm doing is putting it on paper. It's all your words." My attempts at persuasion failed. I respected Ginny's privacy and did not want to go against her wishes, so I would drop the subject. But I kept working on it without telling anyone. That is, when I could find time amidst my busy life. Eventually, I stopped working on it because I didn't want to put all the time into it if Ginny wasn't agreeable to publication and decided I preferred to spend my limited free time focusing on Ginny instead of sitting alone in front of the computer. I realized I would hate to have missed out on getting to know her. But by 2009 it was time to get back to it. With Ginny turning ninety-two that October, we were running out of time.[29]

One evening in February 2010, I once again broached the subject with Ginny about publishing her stories. This time I had to remind her about the recordings we did three and four years earlier. "You agreed to put those tapes in the oral history archives at the university," I said. "That means anyone can go and use them and write whatever they want." Ginny flinched. "But they won't do it right." I suggested, "Would you feel more comfortable with publishing your stories if you can see what I've written?" I had wanted Ginny's involvement from the beginning, but she kept putting me off. This time she liked the idea of reviewing what I'd written and having a chance to make corrections. I returned the following weekend with the childhood chapter. This time, I realized that reading it to Ginny, instead of leaving it for her to read at her leisure, would provide instantaneous feedback on whether she liked it. Thus began our regular story sessions.

I am not the first to attempt this type of collaboration. Sally McBeth worked closely with Esther Burnett Horne to record, write, and collaboratively edit her life history, *Essie's Story: The Life and Legacy of a Shoshone Teacher*. McBeth explains some of the benefits of this approach:

> From the outset, a life historian must concern herself with the fact that moving from interview to published account involves countless decisions. Even though each of these decisions affects the tone and often the very meaning of the final account, few life historians discuss this concern in the context of their work. Collaboration on some level with informants thusly becomes essential to ensure that the presentation of the life represents the individual's experiences and interpretations. The partnership method allows the subject of the document a role in presenting the text in its final form and receiving authorship credit.[30]

Ginny's short-term memory was faltering. Some days she was not able to keep focused. But other times she was alert and attentive when I read to her. "Wait," she'd say, "that was redundant." Or "I don't like that word." One time she smiled and said, "Oh, you got that part right." I laughed as I reminded her that those were her words I was reading to her. Sometimes she was correcting her own stories, sometimes she was correcting my words. I did not care. This was the first time I had read the chapters out loud, so I was finding plenty of awkward sentences or redundancies of my own that I had not noticed when staring at the fragmented pieces on a computer screen. We truly were creating a shared representation of her life.

Ginny enjoyed our story sessions. She said, "When I listen to you, I see pictures in my head. Of the people. Of the places. It's like watching a movie." As the weeks passed, Ginny began to associate my visits with reading stories. "Well, let's get to it," she'd say when I was just chatting or dilly-dallying with the dishes. It is funny that when she told other people what we were doing she said we were going through something she'd written a long time ago. I didn't bother to correct the confusion. If she so clearly heard herself in what I read, then I figured I had achieved my goal of blurring the boundary between the oral and the written. And after so much cajoling, I was thrilled that she was now so engaged in our project that she was taking ownership credit for it.

Finally, when I asked again in May 2010, Ginny agreed that I could pursue publication. She was beginning to accept her own limitations and mortality: "I realize that writing my own book just isn't going to happen now. There isn't enough time left for me to do it." But she wondered who the author would be. "Both of us," I said. "This is a collaboration." "Oh, you mean like an 'as told to'?" "Exactly," I replied, excited to have Ginny on board as a partner.

This collaboration was rewarding on many levels. It gave the product a true sense of shared authority "not only in the production of the interview, but in the interpretation and presentation of the material to scholarly and public audiences."[31] It provided me a live audience to read to with a built-in editorial function. It gave Ginny the chance to determine how her stories would be presented. It strengthened our ties by giving us a shared project to work on together. And it allowed Ginny to be present in her past once again. As she said to me one night, as I was helping her get in to bed, "Thank you for doing this. Some of these are things I haven't thought about in a long time or I don't remember anymore. It brings back good memories."

2

Childhood: The Foundation of an Adventurous Life

It seems like from the time I was about ten years old until I was ready for college that we always had a Depression and Roosevelt was always president.

Ginny Hill Wood was born in a small rural town southeast of The Dalles in north-central Oregon not long after the United States officially entered World War I in April 1917. The draft was in full swing to enlist as many American men as possible to fight in Europe. Ginny says, "I kept my dad out of the war." Recently out of college, Charles Edwin ("Ed") Hill was working at a government-operated experimental farm developing ways to improve soil conditions for better harvest productivity after years of drought and soil loss. This work to improve domestic food production was considered part of the war effort, so he did not have to go fight. When Ginny was to be born, her mother's mother came from California to help around the house and cook for the family.

I was born on October 24, 1917, at the tail end of World War I. I was the first one born in our family. I have a sister, Marjorie, three years younger than myself. I was born in my family house in a little town of three hundred people called Moro, Oregon. It was hardly a wide spot in the road. My father was assistant superintendent of an experimental farm there.[1] I was born at home because my parents had been told not to go the hospital in Portland because of the flu. The hospital was full of people with the flu and they didn't want more people to get it. I was born while my grandmother held a kerosene light while the doctor delivered me because the lights were off in the town. Electricity in this small town was furnished by a community generator, which was turned off at midnight. My mother was worried about my father getting hurt walking around town on the boardwalk sidewalks in the dark to go get the doctor. He had to go get the doctor because there was only one phone in town and it was turned off when the electricity went out. I was born at four in the morning. My mother said when she saw me, "That's not my baby." She was Scandinavian and everybody

L: *Ginny's father, Charles Edwin "Ed" Hill, date unknown. Courtesy of Ginny Wood.*
R: *Baby Ginny with her mother, Edythe Brunquist Hill, circa 1917. Courtesy of Ginny Wood.*

was blonde, and I had coal black hair. She was sure her baby had died and they had gone out on the nearby Indian reservation, picked up an Indian kid, and were trying to pass it off as her baby.

According to Ginny, her father left the East Coast riding freight trains and ended up in Oregon, where he studied agronomy at Oregon State College in Corvallis. He had a successful career working on experimental farms in Oregon and Washington. Ginny's mother, Edythe (Brunquist), born October 4, 1890, was the youngest of five children from a Swedish immigrant family who settled near Boston. Edythe's oldest brother, Albert, had four children and owned an apple orchard in Oregon, where Ginny helped pick apples after World War II when he had a hard time finding workers. Edythe's oldest sister, Harriet, never married and taught school in Berkeley, California. Their brother Ernest was married and a professor in Denver, Colorado. Ginny says they didn't see him much but she remembers that he liked to hike. And then there was Lea, the youngest, who also never married, sold insurance, and lived in Oakland, California with her sister Harriet. Eventually, their mother moved in with the unmarried sisters. Ginny recalls visiting her grandmother and aunts in California when she was a child: "My Aunt Harriet was born an old maid. She was what you'd call 'old-fashioned.' My sister and I used to

L: *Ginny's grandmother, Julia Brunquist, date unknown. Courtesy of Ginny Wood.*
R: *Virginia "Ginny" Hill, age three, with her mother, Edythe Brunquist Hill, and her grandmother, Julia Brunquist, circa 1920. Courtesy of Ginny Wood.*

laugh about it. My grandmother came to live with my Aunt Harriet and Aunt Lea to cook for them. My grandfather had died so she moved to be closer to her children, who were all in the west by then. But the question became, who was really taking care of whom?"

Both my mother and father were from New England. They were both born in Massachusetts, but they didn't know each other there. My mother was a Bostonian. She grew up in a town south of the city, where they would take a streetcar into downtown.[2] She was of Swedish background, but she always had a Boston accent. She was from a very poor family because her dad, Eric Brunquist, had come over from Sweden. He was a master cabinetmaker who found employment at a major piano manufacturer in the outskirts of Boston soon after arriving.[3] He worked for the Pickering piano company making the wood pieces for the pianos. So he was not just a carpenter. He did very fine woodworking. My grandmother, Julia, became engaged to him when she was fifteen. But then he went to California, which would have been about in the gold rush days. He wrote her every day. I have a whole bag full of letters that my grandfather wrote to my grandmother before they were married. His writing is very clear. It's not in that script style. But it's all in Swedish. He was there for ten years and came back and married her and they had five kids. My mother was the last one.

Ginny's grandfather, Eric Brunquist,
date unknown. Courtesy of Ginny Wood.

But my grandfather Brunquist died from some contagious disease like pneumonia and left his wife to bring up five children. My mother grew up very frugal, but being only four when her father died she was spared a lot of the hardship. Although my grandfather did not leave them much in terms of material wealth, he left them with a legacy of a taste for good music and liberalism, and at a time when all Swedes were born Lutheran he became a Unitarian. In America at a time when working men's children were fortunate to finish high school, all except one of those five children went to college. This was due in no small part to the industry and resourcefulness of my grandmother, Julia. She did piecework for a jewelry manufacturer working from home, having help from all members of the family, including her own widowed mother. My uncle, Ernest Brunquist, worked his way through a succession of universities to earn a PhD in psychology. For years he taught at the Denver University Medical School. On the side, as a hobby, he became such an outstanding botanist that he was given a private office for his research collections at the Denver Museum of Natural History.[4]

My dad was from a very wealthy, well-known family from Springfield, Massachusetts, whose ancestors had landed on the shores of America in the early 1600s to colonize what became the state of Virginia. The story of the more recent generations was that my grandmother, Josephine Garfield, was from a rich family and my grandfather, George Hill, was poor. He grew up on a farm in Vermont, enlisted to fight for the North in the Civil War, and never returned to rural life. The family story was that George came shoeless from Vermont to Springfield. But I think that was just an exaggeration, that it probably was more

Ginny's father, Ed Hill, with his parents, George and Josephine Garfield Hill, date unknown. Courtesy of Ginny Wood.

like maybe toes sticking out of his shoes. He was pretty much a self-made man, though. After returning from the war, he landed a job at the ice cream soda fountain of the main drugstore in Springfield. A few years later he owned the store. He met my grandmother, Josephine, his future wife, when she came to have a soda. She was very wealthy. She was a cousin of President Garfield. My grandfather did not marry her for her money, but for her charm. He rose to become a well-to-do prominent citizen in his own right. They were both in their eighties when they died, and still very much in love.

After my Hill grandparents died, my parents were sent a copy of one of those books that traces a family's lineage for those for whom such things matter and can pay the price. This volume included a chapter on the Hill ancestry. It read a bit like the Genesis chapter of the Bible, full of begats of which I was the last noted. Only the successful and illustrious members of the tribe were included, obviously, as I am sure is the case for most every family who succumbs to this ego-enhancing scam. This began with a Hill who sat in the House of Burgesses, the earliest representative legislative body in the new world, apart from the Iroquois Nation. It was formed in 1619 in the colony of Virginia. Perhaps this is where my parents got the name they gave me but never used, except when I misbehaved. As a young girl perusing this family genealogy in our library, I often speculated how much more interesting my ancestral history could have been if it had traced and recorded all the ruffians, outlaws, and nonconformists in our family tree.[5]

Both my parents came west for various reasons. They met in college at the annual freshman dance at Oregon State College. It is now Oregon State University in Corvallis, Oregon. They were both older students, in their mid-twenties, both having done other things instead of going to college right after graduating from high school. The instant glue, I gather, was during their first waltz together they discovered they both were born and bred in Massachusetts and probably were the only students in their class who didn't grow up on a farm or cattle ranch in the West. Although my mother always claimed it was his good looks and dancing ability that swept her off her feet.

My father had gone to sea with the marine equivalent of the Massachusetts National Guard at age eighteen for several summers and had wanted to join the navy, but that didn't work out. After completing high school and failing to qualify for Annapolis, he eschewed Ivy League academic institutions, which would have benefited his parents' economic and social status in Springfield, and opted for the vagrant life of an itinerant tree surgeon up and down the East Coast for a company that rejuvenated ailing trees for the wealthy on their estates. Having tasted a traveling lifestyle, he decided he wanted to go west. He didn't buy a ticket on a train, he rode freight trains. He hopped from train to train. He was on a train somewhere out west, and the only other person in the boxcar was another young guy, who said he was headed to Oregon to enroll in the state's agricultural college. That sounded like as good an idea and destination as any, so Dad got off the train and enrolled, too. He got a degree in agronomy in 1915 from Oregon State College with honors. His life took him into very small towns where he was superintendent of experimental farms, which was work that he found very interesting.

After high school, my mother took up one of the few careers open then to female high school graduates. She became a schoolteacher. Her first job took her to Illinois. She came to the realization that this was not how she wanted to spend her life. The alternative, a marriage proposal from one of the town's leading eligibles, was not who she wanted to spend it with either, even if he did own one of the few automobiles in the community. In the meantime, her oldest brother, Albert, had migrated west to seek his fortune. He had just bought an orchard in the Hood River valley of Oregon. It included a large log house, a barn, a young orchard, pastures, timberland, and a magnificent view of Mount Hood. He sent for his mother, his maternal grandmother, and his youngest sister to manage the domestic part of the farm operation until he could find a wife. This included the poultry, milk cows, and garden. My mother helped cook for the fall harvest crew. Realizing that life on a ranch was not my mother's idea of a future either,[6] Albert offered to pay tuition for her first year of college instead of paying her wages. So she went to Oregon State, where she met my dad. My mother graduated with a degree in home economics. But my mother didn't work after she was married and had kids. She became the autocrat and intellect of their partnership. Dad was more a man of the soil. He always said he got his degree in dirt.

Shortly after I was born, my family moved to Waterville, in Central Washington, because my father was promoted to be superintendent of the experimental farm there.[7] Waterville was a little town of nine hundred people. Our house was a two-story yellow clapboard bungalow that had two bedrooms upstairs with a room in the middle that my father made his office. My sister, Marjorie, and I shared one room. My parents had the other bedroom. Our house was three miles from the farm, a distance that seemed very far off then. Even though Mother and Dad had college educations, that wasn't the way people talked in this small, rural town. So, I had two languages. One was where you split infinitives and used the wrong gender and wrong tense and all that stuff. Talked like the town folks. The other was that of my parents. Even after moving west, my mother never lost her distinct Boston accent. And despite her immigrant background, she was ever an aristocrat, not as a snob, but in her sense of good taste, graciousness, and propriety. Dad wanted to blend in, in speech and manner, with the rough-cut fabric of the rural west, so he adopted a rural western twang. Much to his mother's dismay.

Waterville was in the high-plateau Big Bend country of eastern Washington. The state research station where my father was working was for dry land farming. The Big Bend country was mostly wheat land with coulees of sagebrush. Intensive farming and overgrazing during World War I had reduced the once rich loess soil to the status of a dust bowl. Dad's challenge was to develop cultivation practices and cover crop that would re-enrich the soil, stop the erosion, and conserve the moisture. Among my early childhood memories was accompanying him in the station's old Model T Ford pickup when he drove the rural countryside gathering seeds from the indigenous weed plants that grew along the roadside strips below the dusty roadbed and the barbed-wire fence that enclosed the wheat fields and livestock pastures.[8] We would bump along the roads and he would stop to collect plants. I would hold the little paper sack while he put the seed heads he'd gathered into it. In trying to improve agriculture in the area, his whole idea was to develop summer fallow, to let part of the land lay unused for a while and then sow these seeds in from these plants that he had collected.[9] He would test them to see what the nutrients were. Much, much later, after his death, I learned that from those seeds he collected, he developed a strain of wheatgrass that was sown, grown, then plowed under in a crop rotation program that did bring back rich soil that stayed in place when the wind blew. It rejuvenated dry land farming in the area.[10] I don't think the community appreciated his work at the time. They viewed this "college/government feller" with a certain amount of skepticism and headshaking, but it was tempered by a western big-hearted tolerance of "but at least he's a hard-working, honest sort of guy." His fame was buried in the unheralded government reports of

The experimental farm's Ford pickup truck, 1928. Courtesy of Ginny Wood.

his experiments that go unnoticed by the press and the public at large—at least in those days when the science of agronomy was some mysterious alchemy not a concern for daily living.[11] When the station was abolished in a sudden political decision to do away with government frills during the Depression, his ongoing experimental plots were destroyed along with data he had so painstakingly compiled for over twelve years.[12]

Ginny's father died of cancer in December 1958 at sixty-nine years old, as a result, she believes, of the poisons sprayed on the fields he worked in. Her mother was ninety-four years old when she died on May 4, 1984, outliving all her siblings, despite, as Ginny says, "having never been of robust health." Ginny's younger sister, Marjorie, who also died of cancer, was married to Bert Dennis and lived in Coeur d'Alene, Idaho. She passed away in 1978. Ginny has said that because she and her sister had diverse interests and different personalities they did not always get along with each other, and as adults were not particularly close. However, some of Ginny's earliest family memories relate to her sister.

The first childhood memory that I am really aware of is from when I was three. It is like snatches of a vague dream that is too ephemeral to relate in sequence. I can recollect standing by the open curtain in a large living room watching my father's black Model T Ford drive up to our house and my mother handing my dad a pink bundle while she climbed out of it. I have no memory of seeing what was in it, only that from then on I shared my parents' adoration with a baby sister, in what from my viewpoint appeared to be decreasing proportions. My responsibility for her welfare was soon made clear. My mind's eye can clearly recall the time when I was scolded because she got into the strawberry patch, a deed I was supposed to have prevented.

My sister was slow to start walking. She could sit and pull herself to a standing position, but even after eighteen months she was still reluctant to take her first steps unaided. She had learned to fulfill her desire for locomotion by scooting on her bottom from a sitting position with remarkable speed—even out to the strawberry patch. My mother solved the problem of wear and tear on my sister's pants by placing her on a pie tin. My mother didn't seem bothered by Marjorie's ambulatory retardedness. No doubt after having experienced the mischief and life-threatening situations I, her firstborn, had gotten into when learning to walk before my first year, she was in no hurry to encourage my sister to walk any sooner than necessary. On the other hand, our neighbor, Allie, was worried. She took it upon herself to get my sister walking. Allie was a cheerful, neighborly soul who didn't recognize the word "impose." So she came over one day determined to get Marjorie to walk. She stood Margie in one corner of the kitchen while she stood in the opposite one with a cookie in her hand. First Margie slid down to her scooting position, but Allie sharply admonished her and stood her upright. This was repeated three times before Margie walked steadily and unwaveringly the twenty feet across the room to retrieve her reward. She never did resort to her scooting maneuver again.[13]

And then there was the time soon after Margie learned to walk when I was again supposed to be watching her while my father briefly left the room. He was left in charge of both of us for an afternoon while my mother was out doing something else. My sister chose that moment to toddle up to the metal woodstove that was heating our living room, lose her balance, and fall against it head-first. She burned her scalp, which left a small fifty-cent-piece-sized bald spot under her hair for the rest of her life.

Were she still alive today, I am sure Margie could recount the time I set a trap for the boy down the street by digging a hole in the path he used to our back door, covering it with cardboard, then a layer of dirt over that. It was my sister who fell into it, letting the neighborhood know about it with loud shrieks of distress—promptly followed by my own when I was summarily spanked for this dastardly prank.[14]

My mother sang in the choir when I was growing up, because she had a beautiful voice. She sang in different choirs in town for church and for funerals. We went to church regularly because my dad went to go hear her sing, not because he wanted to go to church. In Waterville, there were three or four churches—Catholic, Episcopalian, Presbyterian, etc. My sister and I went to Sunday school. We went to the Presbyterian Sunday school because I think it was closest to our house. We learned all the little fables and said our prayers at night. But I wouldn't call it growing up very traditional in terms of religion.

When I was in junior high school maybe, I decided I should read the Bible. So I started in with Adam and Eve. Adam's rib made Eve. Then you go into it and they begat and they had two boys and one of them killed the other one, and I decided this was the first dysfunctional family. So, that's as far as my religious training went.

At Christmas we went to the Catholic church. My mother was Swedish and had been raised Catholic so she wanted to celebrate the special holidays that same way. My mom told me about one of my early Christmases. I must have been about two years old because that would be about when parents would be excited about Christmas with a child and when a child would be old enough to remember. My parents had ordered a Santa suit from the Sears and Roebuck catalog. My father came downstairs dressed in the suit. Apparently, I said, "Why is Santa wearing Daddy's shoes?" I guess I was pretty observant even then.

I must have been of school age when I was taken to my first motion picture show at Waterville's only cinema, the Nifty Theater. It was a Tom Mix western. Motion pictures were silent then. Someone, usually a woman, played the piano with tunes appropriate to the story on the screen. She also usually chewed gum at a tempo to match. I still always associate the William Tell Overture with scenes of the good guys at full gallop heading the bad ones off at the gap still used in many westerns today. I also remember being shushed when my level of reading couldn't comprehend the captions that flashed on the screen. "What's that man saying, Mama?" would boom out over an audience enraptured by a tender love scene. In a hushed but stern tone I would be threatened with banishment to the "crying room" if I couldn't be quiet. The crying room was a semi-soundproof enclosure in the balcony with picture windows facing the screen. Mothers were instructed to take their wailing infants there so both she and the audience could enjoy the film. This is a convenience lacking in theaters and auditoriums today.[15]

Looking back on it, my recollection was I had a great childhood. One of the advantages of growing up in a small town of nine hundred inhabitants in those days was that all of it, including its adjacent environs, was accessible by foot. Chauffeuring offspring was not then a necessary part of parenting. And I think that anybody who wasn't born on a farm or in a small town had a deprived childhood. The whole town parented you. Every adult citizen was a concerned parent, even the village reprobates, as far as children were concerned. You could be assured that if you fell down and scraped your knees roller skating, banged yourself falling off your bicycle, or sprained your ankle falling out of a tree anywhere in town, some adult would pick you up, bandage your wound, dry your tears, and see that you were transported to your own household. I'm not so certain the townspeople were always this solicitous of each other. I recall conversations I overheard among adults about "those people" or about "Mrs. So-and-So." But I don't remember any of them shooting at each other or any crimes of violence.

The Hill family on vacation, Cannon Beach, Oregon, July 10, 1923. Courtesy of Ginny Wood.

Acts of child molesting, kidnapping, or the like were not concerns—"perhaps in Chicago or New York, but never in our town."[16] It was a very good way to grow up. And there was no danger that I knew of. It was just "Be careful, dear, when you're jumping off barns into the hay. There's a pitchfork down there." Something like that. You weren't afraid of people or of trying any physical activity. As a child, everybody took care of you and they were good to you.

Up until I was a teenager, I would go out to the experimental farm with my father whenever I could. When I was a little kid, the foreman—Cassius "Cash" Bartholomew—had a lot of kids, so there was always one my age to play with. Cash was a lean, unshaven man with thinning, unkempt grey hair and cross-eyes. According to town folklore, his only accomplishment before this job was the siring of nine children, all of them "pretty good kids." His wife was a slight, dark-haired lady, then probably in her mid-forties, but with hands already misshapen from rheumatism. She still exhibited vestiges of the beauty she must once have been. I never learned from Dad why he had chosen Cash for the job. Perhaps there were lesser apparent choices? But perhaps he sensed a latent quality of loyalty, willingness, and sense of responsibility that defined his reputation as the town's best-known indigent who lived on his wife's income as a seamstress.

I don't remember my father ever complaining about Cash's work, but I still recall Cash extolling the virtues of "Mr. Hill" to my mother when he delivered our milk and how "him and Mr. Hill was experamentin" on this and that project. My father had bought a Jersey cow out of his own pocket, which was kept on the farm to be milked by one of the older Bartholomew boys. Under this arrangement, they kept all she produced except for the two quarts a day that went to us.

During the winters, my father had to go east to Washington, DC to write reports. He left us in Cash's care as far as snow shoveling, coal hauling, keeping chunks of ice in our refrigerator, and delivery of the milk. Cash took the responsibility of our welfare with pride and diligence.

My mother often hired Mrs. Bartholomew to make or alter dresses for us. Standing still while she took my measurements or pinned new hemlines was not one of my favorite ways to spend time. Much more to my liking was putting on a pair of overalls to go out to the farm to play with her offspring.[17]

There was always something fun and interesting going on at the farm. There were horses to ride. They had hay lofts to jump in. A barn full of wonderful hiding places for games of hide and seek. You had all these farm animals to help feed. Or cows to milk. They made their own butter from the milk from the cows. My dad said he never knew where to find me when it was time to go home, so from a young age he put me on a horse, because he said it was easier to catch the horse than it was to find and catch me. There'd be a bunch of horses running loose in the pasture and he'd put me on one. I rode hanging on to their little mane. When I got bigger, I would ride on the great big black workhorses my father used for plowing his study plots. For the studies, my father would plant small plots with all kinds of different seeds, harvest them, and then weigh all the contents from the different experiments to see which was most productive. When they unhitched the four big Percheron horses, I took them back to the barn. Or that's what I thought I was doing. Of course, the horses were all headed for the barn anyway because they were going to be fed. I had nothing to do with actually driving them in. But I was so excited thinking I was controlling those horses. Later on, when I was older, I did ride them. I rode a lot at the farm. I guess that's what got me liking horses.

What I comprehended from Hollywood's portrayal of the Wild West was that real cowboys did not ride draft teams. They rode saddle horses—and so

Ginny driving the horse team on the experimental farm, circa 1925.
Courtesy of Ginny Wood.

would I. The farm's equipment did not include a saddle, much less one to fit a very small girl on a great big Clydesdale. But my father rigged up a cinch that went around the big animal's middle holding a saddle blanket on top, and shortened a pair of draft horse driving reins. With no stirrups to assist me to climb on the big black stud, I was dependent on someone to lift me aboard. I could dismount by myself by just swinging both legs on one side and sliding to the ground. As I extended my rides farther and farther afield, remounting alone became a problem when the necessity to answer nature's call became an emergency. When the situation became a choice of riding back to the farmstead with wet pants and the shame of it all or coping with the problem of getting back on my horse, I chose to cope. I well remember those attempts to position my mount close to a gate or fence from the top of which I could leap onto his back. Often I was successful after repeated tries. But more than a few times my now un-trusty steed, having had enough of this saddle horse role, would choose to move aside just as I was poised for the jump. I can still feel the humiliation and frustration of that tear-streaked little self of long ago trudging the long miles back to the barn with my reluctant "cow pony" in tow. Eventually, I grew up to ride many real cow ponies, having acquired riding skills without the benefit or expense of proper riding lessons.[18]

And then I had my own farm in the backyard of our house—my bottle horse farm. I collected bottles of all different colors and shapes and put them out in a dirt lot that was behind and beside our house. Different colored bottles were for different colors of horses. Another color was for cows. The short, stubby Finlax bottles were pigs. A Log Cabin syrup can was the farm house. I had other cans for the barns. I used an old eggbeater for a windmill. Eventually, that lot got plowed under so that was the end of my farm. But I sure had fun playing in it, setting up the "horses" and everything. I thought everyone had a bottle horse farm. Maybe not?

When I became a few years older, the farm offered an opportunity for us to make some pocket money. This was before the days of child labor laws as applied to farming; the institution of parental allowance to their progeny for discretionary spending needs; or laws of nepotism and the taking of government property for private profits. Wheat yields and forage crops were not the only subjects of Dad's scientific investigations. The possibilities of peas as a viable commercial crop for the Big Bend country was also one of his experiment projects. All that the Department of Agriculture was interested in at the time was the comparative yields of the different species that he planted. What became of the pods after the results were tabulated was not a matter of concern. We picked the pods for science to record, at no expense to the taxpayer. In return, we got them back to peddle for whatever profit the market would bring—mostly from our neighborhood at ten cents a pound, as I recall. My share usually was spent on my current object of longing in "The Great Wish Book"—the Sears and Roebuck catalog, which arrived by mail semiannually. I'm sure the Bartholomew kids' return had to go towards new shoes for the beginning of the fall school semester.

My other source of revenue was from three pie-cherry trees that grew in our backyard. I was considerably daring in the tree climbing and ladder work connected with this enterprise, but a complete coward when it came to ringing doorbells to sell our product. For this part of the operation, I enlisted my younger sister—I'd do the high picking if Margie would do the selling—the proceeds to be divided equally. This phobia of mine has persisted to this day. As a member of several nonprofit organizations and boards, I have volunteered to lick many stamps, testify at numerous hearings, and produce bowls of potato salads for annual meeting potlucks rather than endure the agony of making telephone calls or in-person appeals for fundraising campaigns.[19]

Growing up, we had a dog, Bobby. He was a beagle. My sister and I wanted a dog but our parents kept saying no. Finally, one day we found a stray kitten in the open field that we had to cross to get to school on the opposite side of town. It was lost and crying. We brought the kitten home, figuring if our parents would not let us have a dog, at least they wouldn't take the cat away. We thought if we just arrived home with it, then they'd have to accept us having a pet. My father did not like cats. That cat was a female and it had male visitors all night long. He said he'd take the cat out to the farm where it would have a good home and lots of room to play and it could chase mice from the barn, which is what he thought a cat was supposed to do. Not just be a house cat. My mother said to him, "Well, Ed, if you're going to take their cat away, you have to replace it with something else. You'll have to get a dog." He agreed, but said it had to be small because there already wasn't enough room in the car when we went to the cabin at Lake Chelan, especially when my sister and I each brought a friend. And it had to be short-haired. So my sister and I scoured the big massive encyclopedia that sat on a wrought-iron stand in our dad's office on the top floor of our house. It had a section of full-color pages of pictures of different breeds of dogs. I insisted on a dog that had its own ears and tail that hadn't been trimmed or cut. We went back and forth for a while—I wanting one kind, she another. But finally, I made my sister want what I wanted. I persuaded her that we wanted a dog that hadn't been altered. We were finally able to agree on a beagle. My sister and I looked through the listings for dogs for sale in the Spokane newspaper, which we got daily. Waterville only had a monthly paper. Finally, there was a listing for beagles. We sent for one and it cost five dollars. They brought the dog on a stagecoach. The driver had taken the dog out of the box and had it up front with him and was feeding it milk. We named the puppy Bobby, because at the time there was a book we really liked called *Lochinvar Luck* by Albert Payson Terhune,[20] who wrote dog stories, whose main character was named Bobby. Both my parents ended up falling in love with Bobby. He was the greatest dog. Years later, he got run over by a car when we lived in Pendleton.

Ginny was twelve years old in 1929, when the US stock market crashed, throwing the country into an economic depression that lasted until World War II. Families across the country lost their life savings when banks failed and many others lost jobs, making it hard to put food on the table or keep a roof over their heads. While Ginny's memories of the Depression are those of a child, she reflects clearly on its impacts and how it influenced the rest of her life.

The Depression was very hard on my family, because my dad lost his job. The Depression didn't just happen in one day. He had his money in three different banks and they all failed. There was no compensation. There wasn't any protection for that sort of thing like you have now. Now you have bank insurance. It was only the beginning of the Depression, and we were comparatively well off because my dad had a high position as superintendent of the experimental farm. But then the government discontinued the experimental farm in Waterville. They just took it out. So we went to being just broke. Dad had to go out then and find a job right in the middle of the 1930s, when things were the worst. My father didn't get any government relief or anything. Just one day he's on the experimental farm and the next he's on the street looking for a job. That's why he just got a day laborer job, to do manual labor, to keep food on the table. Because he was an agronomist, he thought he could learn the fruit culture. We moved to Wenatchee, Washington, where he tried to get a job at one of the American Fruit Growers orchards. But of course they didn't want this college guy getting their jobs. He ended up working in the orchards picking apples or spraying, when before he'd been superintendent of a whole big operation up in Waterville. This was a big comedown for him. He did a lot of the spraying. He never did anything but lug spray hose around. He would come home covered with white stuff, pesticides, they put on the orchards. There was no protection or anything. That's what killed him. The pesticides.

I guess we were pretty poor, but I never thought about it because we had enough to eat and the things I liked to do were free. I never felt deprived. But it was very hard on my folks. I think my mother and father had a lot of sleepless nights wondering how they were going to pay the bills. I think it was a matter of pride. My dad felt a college man should have a good job and put away money for his kids' education. It was a lot of anxiety for him and for my mother.

My mother was an excellent seamstress. She could take any old piece of clothing and fix it up with a few ribbons and a needle. So we always had nice clothes to wear that she made. But she didn't do mending and sewing for other people. My dad wouldn't allow it. That would have killed him. He was the head of the household and he was the one who was supposed to provide for his family. It was very hard on my dad psychologically. Dad worried because I think that he felt he'd failed as a man, that he wasn't a man if he couldn't support his family, send his kids to college, or buy his wife a new dress.

For my mother, she wondered if we were going to have enough money to buy food. My mother was very frugal, and she was always very conscious of what we ate because of her knowledge of nutrition, having graduated from college in home economics. So we were very well fed. We never went hungry. There was always food on the table. But I know there were things that we didn't get because it was too expensive, like steak. We ate what was cheap. We didn't eat meat very often because we couldn't afford it, but we had very delicious food that was well cooked and very, very healthy. I think she worried very much, only she didn't complain about it.

I did feel sorry for my folks during the Depression. For instance, when I was in high school in Wenatchee, the football team was playing over at Everett and people were going over in a car and staying overnight in a hotel to watch the big game. I couldn't go, because I didn't have the money to pay for it. My mother said, "Now, don't tell them that you can't afford it. You tell them that you're doing something else with your folks that weekend." Not being able to afford it was a reflection on my dad's ability to take care of his family.

I was twelve when we moved to Wenatchee. I had one year of junior high in Waterville and then I finished junior high and part of high school in Wenatchee.[21] Then Dad got a job with the Soil Conservation Service that took him to Pendleton, Oregon. One night, Mother said that we were having a very important man for dinner. She said that when they introduced him, my sister and I were not to laugh, and to not say anything after that. That Dad may have a very important job, rather than just working in an orchard. The government had just started the Soil Conservation Service, and the head of it, Mr. Lowdermilk[22]—that's why we weren't supposed to laugh—was coming to dinner. He knew of Dad's work with plants and soil. Dad was one of the first people hired to work for the Soil Conservation Service.

When we lived in Pendleton, that was when we felt "rich." Dad had a good job that he loved. We knew we were going to be able to pay the rent for the house. And my mother didn't have to worry about how they were going to buy groceries next month.

I look back and realize for me, as a kid, I didn't notice the Depression as much as my parents did. I had a wonderful childhood. I always found a way to have a good time. Gosh, in Waterville, the edge of town was right there. We could go ice skating on the frozen ponds or the flooded tennis court, which the town turned into a skating rink. It seems like it was free to skate there, or maybe you paid a little bit, maybe two dollars for the season. Or we could go skiing, horseback riding, swimming at the town pool with a five-dollar season pass, anything we wanted to do. There was no charge connected with things. It didn't cost any money to do most of the things we were doing. I got my first bike when I was eleven. It was a secondhand bike that cost seven dollars. And I always could go hiking. We still had our cabin up at Lake Chelan and I had a little sailboat that I bought with my own money that I sailed around in.

The other thing is that we didn't have TV. We did have radio, but I don't remember listening to it that much. So we used our imaginations and pretended. One day we were Indians, and another day we were cowboys. Then we started reading books, and would go out and pretend what we had read about, emulating some hero or heroine.

I was an avid reader. I just started reading what I could get at the library. I read Nancy Drew or the Bobbsey Twins or some of those stupid books. I thought, "Well, that doesn't sound like much fun," so I read the ones for boys. I liked what the Rover Boys did best, or the ones Clarence Budington Kelland wrote. Or the novels of Zane Grey, James Oliver Curwood, or Ernest Thompson Seton's stories—*Rolf in the Woods* and *Two Little Savages*.[23] Oh, they just had the most wonderful adventures!

We never said to our folks, "I'm bored. There's nothing to do." Or expect they were supposed to provide something for us to do. The only thing is that they made you come home and go to bed and get some sleep, and have a meal. In Waterville, the vacant lot adjoining my parents' house, the old barn and empty woodshed on our property, and the rolling field that began at the end of our street were transformed into any scenario we dreamed up. We would be Lewis and Clark making our way over the Rockies with Sacajawea played by me because I was the only girl. We played Tarzan of the Apes swinging through the African jungles with his primate companions with the ropes we hung from trees. I think Dick Berg always got the Homo sapiens role. Or I was always with Scott going to the South Pole when I stepped into my wooden toe-strap skis dragging a toboggan behind to glide off across the snow-covered fields adjacent to town. The next day, armed with bows and arrows, we were Robin Hood's merry band roaming through Sherwood Forest.[24] Guess who was Maid Marian? I didn't think she was very interesting.

One of my favorite things to do in the winter was to go sledding, or what we called "sliding." There was a hill called Roger's Hill in the middle of Waterville that we used. On Saturdays, the road to the top was closed to traffic by the town fathers to be used exclusively for coasting. We didn't just slide down it, then walk back up dragging our sled for another run. We devised a game of cops and robbers with street rules and protocol for participants. It was a game to see who could go down the fastest. We'd run and jump flat onto our sleds. The robbers were allowed to take only three steps from the starting line before slamming belly down on their sleds. The cops started their run as soon as the robbers were horizontal, but they could run as far as they wanted to before taking to their sleds. The object was to overtake the "culprit" before their sled came to a halt at the bottom, grab their rudder, and try to upset or derail them into a snowbank, which constituted an "arrest" and elimination from further competition.[25] You would try to catch up and beat the one that had gone down before you. When you got up next to someone, you would reach over and push their steering bar to send them off into the ditch or push them off their sled. I had a fast Flexible Flyer sled. I rarely got pushed off.

One side of the hill went down to an ice rink. One time I remember not being able to stop and going down onto the rink in the middle of a hockey game. The boys got mad and threw my sled into the ditch. I went home crying. So my mom suggested getting ice skates as an alternative activity. My parents skated a lot. They grew up in New England, where they did a lot of skating on frozen rivers and ponds. My mother was not athletic, but she ice skated. From then on, in the wintertime, I was always ice skating. The skating rink was where "our gang" gathered after school. One of the diversions from just plain skating was a primitive form of ice hockey called "Skinny." The puck was a tin can and our sticks were old brooms worn down to the nubs. I don't know if the rules were introduced from elsewhere or if they had evolved locally. Crack the whip was another team sport when we children could get the rink to ourselves. We would all join hands in a line with the strongest skater on one end in the center of the rink and the faster skaters near the outside end, then we would start skating, turning like the sweep hand of a clock around the pivot person. When the outside skater had reached critical speed, he (or she) let go, letting momentum catapult them off to the edge of the rink to the snowbank at the side. The object of this maneuver was to see who could use this centrifugal force to leap the farthest out over the bank into the snow beyond.[26]

The ice rink was also where you had all your love life. When you started going with boys. They'd come up and ask to skate with you. I was a pretty good skater, if I do say so myself. And we'd dance on skates together. I won an ice dancing contest at a winter carnival when I was in college at Washington State in Pullman. I remember Dick Lavin was a boy who asked me to skate with him. We got pretty good at it. They had the skating rink going on at night. I had to be home by nine o'clock. He walked me home one time, and right out in front of my house at night he tried to kiss me. It was his first kiss, I think. It was certainly mine. I had my skates around my neck and he had his skates around his. We were just going to kiss and our skates came together. Clatter! And he ran. Then my dad came and turned the porch light on. I said, "Dad, you scared him away."

The only thing I remember about the Depression was I thought, "Boy, I am never going to let money be the object of my life," because I saw what it did to my folks. Heaven knows my father was working as hard as he could, but he was only being paid thirty cents an hour for it. That didn't go very far even with all his education and everything. So, I thought I wanted to not let the standard of living be the criteria of how you enjoyed life. I would always like to be able to do things, but my pride was just not seeing how much money you could make or your standing. I always thought that if you had enough to eat and you weren't suffering, that was enough. Some people did suffer, but I never did. To me, money wasn't the main thing, or how much money you made or what part of town you lived in or how well furnished your house was. I felt that those things weren't the important things. For some people my age who lived through the Depression, they would come out never wanting to be poor. For me, I came out believing that I never wanted to be someone that losing money ruined my life. If you didn't have any, you couldn't lose it. My sister was the opposite. She said she was never going to be poor, so her goal was to marry a rich man, someone who would see that they always had enough money.

I also have evolved a kind of philosophy that is: what you don't spend, you don't have to earn. I didn't want to go into something where you have to put your nose to the grindstone just to have to live. There were so many things that you could do that didn't require too much money and were fun to do. You could get jobs that were fun to do, not ones that you did just to earn money to save up for your old age and you were waiting to do things when you retired. Then, something could happen like a depression and take all your money so you didn't have any fun with it anyway. I guess that's what I got out of the Depression.

Ginny's experience as a child growing up in small towns and on farms inspired an early love of the outdoors. As she has said, she didn't think about wilderness, it was just going out to the edge of town and playing in the woods or the fields. She credits the development of her adventurous spirit to her supportive parents, her curiosity to want to know what was over that hill, and having childhood playmates who were mostly boys she had to keep up with or else be left out of the fun.

I suppose I was an adventuresome girl. From the time I was a little kid, Mother always said I had the wanderlust. I always wanted to see what was over the hill. According to her, I hadn't much learned to walk when one day she couldn't find me. I guess I had been out on the lawn playing and wandered off. She found me under a team of horses parked near a house down the street a ways. In this little small town of Waterville, Washington, people that came in from the farms, especially when it was muddy or snowy, still came in with horse teams. She couldn't believe I'd gotten that far from the front door, since I had just learned to walk. She used to tell that story all the time. I don't remember it.

My mother said I also ran away from home once. I was three and was mad at something and I imagine I was a strong-willed little kid, and I said, "I'm gonna run away from home." So my mother said, "Well, I think you should have some lunch with you. You'll want to take your raincoat. And you'll probably want a hat." So my mother packed a little bag for me. She found me about two blocks down the street bawling my head off.

People ask me where did I get my feelings for wilderness, and I don't think I had any concept of wilderness when I was a kid. I lived in small towns where the wilderness started at the edge of the last house. There wasn't any city around. Spokane was at one end of the state of Washington and Seattle at the other, and we were in the middle. If you just stepped outdoors and went half a mile from town you were in sagebrush. There were no people. It was just cattle country and farming country.

I don't know if I was an exceptional girl. How would I know if I was different than most girls my age because I didn't know what I was supposed to be? I didn't know I was not a "normal" girl. I grew up playing with the boys, because it just happened that the three families that my folks chummed with had boys. The Bergs, the Zentners, the Winstanleys. There weren't any other girls, so when the families did things together, I played with the guys. The Bergs had two boys: Howard, whom everyone called Ole, who was six months younger than me; and Dick, who was a year older than me. They were my playmates. We went exploring together all the time; whatever the Berg boys thought up, I did it with them. I guess I must have unconsciously figured it out that I wouldn't be asked to do the things they liked to do if I wasn't a pretty good sport about it. I think I sensed without even really knowing it, that if you wanted to play with the boys then you better not want any special treatment because you were a girl. That you don't say anything, don't be afraid, and just do what they want to do. But I never consciously thought, "I want to be a boy."

I remember one time the boys said, "Let's go clear across town and never walk across a street. Go crawl under the culverts." That sounded like an interesting thing to do, and so we did it. I don't imagine we went into details explaining to our parents how our overalls got so dirty. Waterville in the 1920s was in the transition from the age of the horse and wagon to that of the internal combustion

Ginny in her preferred outfit when growing up, 1922.
Courtesy of Ginny Wood.

engine and the kilowatt. Artifacts from the former era still existed, such as the old livery stable, now vacant, which provided an afternoon of challenging "I dare you's." One was to walk the beams twenty feet above what had been the wagon and buggy room.[27]

It was lots more fun than the girls playing with dolls. Until I got to be a teenager, and then I thought, "Boys are kind of nice, aren't they?" If there had been girls around, I probably would have played with dolls more. When my sister was growing up there were more girls in the neighborhood, so she grew up playing with dolls and liking girly things. So I think that there was always this interest in adventure long before I had any concept of conservation or any kind of environmental feelings.

It was because of the Bergs that I got a pair of skis when I was ten years old. Mr. Berg was an old Norwegian and he always skied. His kids always skied. I came home crying once because I couldn't follow them playing because I didn't have skis and I felt left out. So my mother bought me a pair for ten dollars from the Sears catalog. She thought it was another good way to make use of the snow and hills we had, besides sledding, and to have something that not many of the other kids had. I contributed some of my own money, too. We didn't have fancy bindings then, just a single toe strap. So the Berg boys and I would go on "expeditions." They lived on the other side of town so I would only usually see them on Saturdays. Our close companionship disintegrated with puberty and high school, although our parents kept in touch. Dick became a physician serving in the Army Medical Corps, but was never sent overseas during World War II. Ole was drafted and was a private who returned unscathed.[28]

Waterville also provided more passive pursuits. The five-block walk from our home on the eastern outskirts of the town to its center took one past the blacksmith's shed. His door, large enough to roll a wagon in, was usually open so you could stop to watch him at his forge fashioning horseshoes and shoeing horses, re-welding broken tools, or fashioning items to repair farm machinery. Stripped to his underwear tops, he would alternately hold a piece of iron in his tongs over the hot coals until it glowed red hot, then holding it on a huge anvil he'd take a hammer in the other hand and beat it into the desired shape in a flurry of red sparks.

A half a block beyond, across the street and down an alley, you would come to Bunce's saddle, harness, and shoe repair shop, an annex to the hardware and building supply store in front. Bunce—we never knew him by any other or more names—was the village pied piper, only he couldn't walk very well. A bachelor with a badly shriveled leg (from polio, I surmise), he hobbled with a cane from one of his machines to the other mending and fashioning anything that had to do with leather. I can still conjure up the aroma of the leather that pervaded his shop. And he loved and attracted kids. We'd gather at his shop on Saturdays, sitting in the saddles stacked on sawhorses that awaited repairs, while we recounted the week's events at school, or sought his opinion on all manner of subjects. Sometimes when there were no more than three of us present he would give us bits of leather, rivets, and waxed thread to fashion what we willed using some of his simpler and safer tools. I still have the quiver he helped me make for my arrows. More often than not, he would reach into his till as we left, tossing us a nickel apiece for an ice cream cone at Mitchell's drugstore. Sundays, which usually meant Sunday school and the Presbyterian church for me as my mother sang in the choir, Bunce would load up his open touring car with kids, mostly those whose parents couldn't afford cars, and drive with them around town—perhaps to give them status equal to those of us whose parents could and did.

Down the alley from Bunce's was the Waterville Hardware's lumber yard, where we would go next to ask for any old scraps of wood for some building project we had in mind. Seldom did we come away empty-handed.

Despite its name, Waterville, alleged to have been chosen because of the quality of its well water, there were no large streams or bodies of water nearby. We learned to swim on family picnics down to the Columbia River, about twenty miles and a couple of thousand feet of drop down off the Big Bend plateau, and on summer outings to some lakes within a day's driving distance. I don't remember ever being taught to swim—my mother had never learned—but somehow by imitating other bathers or experimentation at the age of six I was dog-paddling out over my head, and by the age of ten I had to be called in to shore for lunch, having been immersed in water since the customary wait of an hour after breakfast (the specter of being immobilized and drowned by cramps if we swam right after eating was impressed on us upon the acquisition of our first bathing suit).

Roads, all except the major ones, were not kept plowed of snow during the winter. Although the Model T Ford was the forerunner of the Jeep as far as navigating snow, mud and rutted roads went, many farmers in the outlying areas put their wagons on sled runners in order to come to town for supplies. Many a winter Saturday, a gang of us would assemble with our Flexible Flyer sleds and a long rope on the outskirts of town waiting for one of these wagon/sleighs to start the return trip to a ranch. With a nod of assent from the driver, we would tie the rope to the back of the wagon. Then sitting single file behind on our sleds, we would hang on to the rope to be pulled as far out of town as we dared go and still be able to catch another team headed back to town.

To the youth of today living in snow country, spending a day being hauled at a horse's pace along a country road would be the epitome of boredom. They are off over fields and country lawns (and often suburban lawns and gardens) on their ear-splitting snowmachines and four-wheelers spewing fumes and consuming gasoline at breakneck speeds. But if fun could be calibrated, I doubt theirs could exceed ours then.

Summers seemed endless and euphoric. We discarded our shoes after the last day of school at the end of May and never put them on again except for Sunday school and invitations out to dinner until after Labor Day when school started again. My time was spent "helping out" at the farm and the diversions my buddies and I thought up to do around town. I suppose we were "street kids" of the late 1920s, except our escapades were looked upon with benign tolerance by our superiors. Our activities were never motivated by malice, destructiveness, or anger—only by our imaginations.[29]

For me, all this pretending in childhood was just magic. It was fun to invent your world. You didn't watch somebody else be that character, you were that character. I think that nowadays kids who grow up watching TV or playing their videos or their computer games, they watch somebody else have adventures. Our imaginations just went wild. I think if they'd taken me to a child psychiatrist, they'd have said this kid is out of touch with reality. But my mother didn't think there was anything wrong with me. That just was my fantasy world.

Even when I was an adult, I found myself pretending. I always thought I'd liked to have been the gal on that trip with Lewis and Clark, so when I was out hiking, I pretended I was. But I don't think I'd have wanted to lug a baby all that way. Wherever I was, I was exploring a jungle, climbing Mount Everest, was with Mallory on his first ascent of the Matterhorn, or was one of the pilots in those Jenny biplanes in aerial combat. I knew that wasn't true, but I could feel myself doing it.

I don't know at just what age psychiatry now decides one is out of touch with reality if you still live in a world of "pretend." I only know that much of the magic goes out of living when you grow up to live in what grown-ups call the "real world." I confess to a delayed adulthood in this respect. Something seems lost, I am convinced, when one reaches so-called maturity and the realization that you are only what you are instead of whomever you choose to pretend to be in whatever world you decide to conjure up. Having long ago left behind that stage of "make-believe," I have often speculated if the "real world" isn't actually the *Alice in Wonderland* one.[30]

When we lived in Waterville, my parents had a chance to buy a lot on Lake Chelan, which was a sixty-mile-long lake. It was a fjord really. It started at the town of Chelan and then wound up sixty miles into the mountains. Wherever there was a place where a stream came down it would make a kind of a fan, and there would be cabins. They bought land at Granite Falls and built a summer cabin there. We called the cabin "Kenjockety." It was named after a cabin my mother's family used to go to when she was growing up in New England. I must have been about ten. During our first summer there, we lived in tents and cooked outdoors under a tarp while my father and a hired carpenter built a rustic cabin with a wide screened porch (where my sister and I slept) and a huge stone fireplace from local granite.[31] During the Depression, the cabin was one thing we had. My dad didn't sell it. Then the next year, the Berg family built a cabin just across a ravine on a lot next to ours.

I was fortunate enough that my folks had that very modest little cabin on Lake Chelan. It wasn't like a second home like people have there now. For the next seven years, we went up every weekend during the summer and for vacations. As soon as Dad got off work, we'd have the car all packed and take off. It was about thirty or thirty-five miles. That was considered a long way in those days. It took about two to three hours to get there in our family Chevy from Waterville. It depended on which side of the river the ferry was on when we got there. This barge, common then along the unbridged rivers of the Northwest, could carry up to six automobiles at a crossing and was propelled solely by the force of the current and the pulley system that ran along the cables stretched above the water from bank to bank, setting the angle of attack of the ferry to the water rushing against it.[32]

At Lake Chelan, we learned to sail and swim, and very soon I liked the woods and hiking. I liked camping, exploring. I guess I must have liked rural life but not farming or anything like that, because that was sort of dismal in the 1930s. Farming was sort of a depressed occupation then. Some of the kids that came to school from the farming country in those days often did not even wear shoes. Nowadays, the farm people are the wealthy people and the town people are the poor people.

For us children, our activities at "The Lake" were mostly aquatic, except for forays up the steep slopes that rose behind us to explore the ponderosa pine forest that covered them. First came a rowboat I purchased with my cherry picking savings, then a very unstable canoe that Ole Berg fashioned out of canvas stretched over a barrel stove. We painted the canoe green and dubbed it *Spareribs*. Keeping it upright was akin to balancing peas on a knife. Upsets, especially paddling with the waves before the wind, were frequent. I don't remember ever owning, much less wearing, a life preserver, but by this time we were as much at home in the water as river otters.

Ole and I thought it delightfully devilish to paddle *Spareribs* around to the resort side of Granite Falls, purposely tip it over just in front of the rental cabins there, then stay under the overturned hull just to alarm the guests. Most of them didn't realize there was adequate oxygen in the airspace between the water and the bottom (now the top) of the craft. Then we would emerge just when we were sure rescue attempts were under way. It never occurred to us that someday we might really need assistance after one of our accidental dunkings and no one would pay attention anymore.

Ole, Dick, and I had another scam. Lake Chelan, being on the dry side of the Cascade Mountains, was rattlesnake country. That we went bare-legged and shoeless most of the time, yet never in our many encounters with these poisonous reptiles were we ever bitten, should have dispelled the myth that all sighted should be killed. But like the wolf, the coyote, and black bears in many locales today, rattlesnakes are considered varmints, a mistake of the creator, and a threat to mankind. So mankind, particularly males, no longer having dragons or real live beasts that are actually threatening their hearths, have to go out and find whatever critter that is the substitute in their local mythology to slay to prove their manhood. So our father killed rattlesnakes if he came upon them near the cabin. We children would then take the limp carcass around to the resort to swing it conspicuously before the guests, knowing the manager would offer us ice cream cones for the deceased rattlesnake, so it wouldn't frighten away customers. We also soon learned we shouldn't flood the market if we wanted a continued offer of ice cream for dead snakes.[33]

As she grew older, Ginny's curiosity, wanderlust, and love of the outdoors deepened. She attributes it to reading and the influence and support of her family.

Those types of adventure books that I read may have contributed to my sense of adventure. And in school, my favorite thing was geography. I was fascinated to learn about other countries and different ways people lived and the food they

Ginny in her canoe, Spareribs, *on Lake Chelan, circa 1932. Courtesy of Ginny Wood.*

ate. In fact, my teacher took my geography book away from me because I always had it out and was reading it when we were supposed to be doing other lessons, so I wasn't learning spelling and other things. That's maybe why I'm not a very good speller!

But I do know that I got things from my family. I don't know as my father encouraged me to be adventurous, but he did take me up in my first airplane when it was barnstorming near the experimental farm. But my mother was more likely to say yes to things I wanted to do. My dad was usually the one that said no because he'd done it. Like having climbed Mount Hood with college chums knowing little about alpine mountaineering. He knew what to worry about. My mother wasn't athletic. She didn't like to camp. It was too dirty. She liked things that were cleaner. She'd say things like, "Why can't we just stay home and eat instead of going on a picnic or camping?" But she loved nature. She had an appreciation of music, art, and nature. And she really had an appreciation of scenery. She knew how to row a boat and to ice skate, but other than that she didn't do that sort of thing. She loved to get in the rowboat at our summer cabin up at Lake Chelan and just look at the mountains. But she would never think of climbing or hiking or anything like that. She would just go out and sit in the rowboat and say, "Oh, I love it up here." But she was wonderful about anything I thought up to do. She'd say, "Well, I think you can do that. But we won't tell your father, until I've talked to him." She felt that if I wanted to do it, I must be good at it. And it must be okay. She wouldn't want to do it, but it was okay for me.

Ginny had a slight advantage when her formal school education began. She had been exposed to reading from an early age by her college-educated parents, who were avid readers. Wanting to know what words on a page meant, she would ask, "What's it say, Daddy?" Ginny claims that she did not do well in school.

My formal education began in the first grade when I was seven years old, pre-schools and kindergartens being unavailable as part of the school system then. I had just missed starting a year earlier because of my late-fall birthday. However, I spent only a few months in the first grade before I was put in the second. I don't remember if this was because I already knew my numbers, the alphabet, and had a rudimentary knowledge of reading, or because there was a shortage of seats in the first one. My mother always claimed that my lifelong deficiency in spelling was because I missed phonics. Late in my life I came to realize I actually had a mild form of dyslexia, which I compensated for by learning to gulp the meaning of full sentences without digesting each word. I am eternally grateful that my academic education occurred before I learned I had a "learning disability." I accepted my D's in spelling along with my B's and A's in other subjects as not having too much importance in my pursuit of knowledge or my life's agenda. Thus I never considered my problem a hardship. I probably have the dubious distinction of being the only student to enter Washington State University who was required to take a "bonehead" spelling program at the same time as I was in an honors freshman English class as a result of my entrance examination.[34]

Although I was an A and B student in school, I was always getting in trouble and being sent to the cloakroom because I'd done something I shouldn't have. There's a story my mother always told about an incident when I was about in the third grade. I was sent to the principal's office because I hit a little boy. His name was Willis. We were playing marbles at recess and I accused him of stealing one of my "steelies," a special silver-colored marble. I felt that he cheated, so I hit him. He went crying to the teacher. The teacher took me up to the principal. She gave me a talking-to about little girls that fought with little boys. The principal asked me, "Why did you hit Willis?" "'Cause he doesn't play fair," I answered. "What do you think we should do with little girls who hit little boys?" "Well, I suppose you could let him hit me back," I reasoned. Many years later, when I was probably eighteen, when I again met the woman who had been principal, she said, "You know, I had to be stern then when the teacher brought you to my office to be reprimanded because you had started a fight on the schoolyard. But when I found out what you'd done, I wanted to hug you and slap you on the back and say, 'Good for you, girl.' I never could stand that mean, sneaky boy." What I didn't know at the time but found out later was that Willis was a difficult child and had been in trouble before. So secretly the principal probably was glad that I hit him and didn't really want to have to punish me.

I didn't really get into trouble at home as a kid. If I did, I would be spanked as punishment, but I don't remember it happening too much. I do remember one time when my dad and I were mad at each other. He was trying to catch me and couldn't. I think it might have been about me not finishing a chore. Or maybe it was for saying something mean to my sister. But he couldn't catch me to spank me.

I graduated high school at age seventeen. When we moved to Pendleton, Oregon, after my junior year, they discovered that in Wenatchee I had already taken all the courses for senior year. The schools offered classes in a different order so I'd already taken what was required in Pendleton to be a senior. So after one month of being a senior, they decided I was eligible to graduate. I then went to Washington State College in Pullman, Washington.[35]

I think I assumed I would go to college, because in my family that was what you were supposed to do. I think that's what worried my father about losing his job, was how they were going to send me to college. But then, when it got down to the time for going, he had a break. He'd gotten the job with the Soil Conservation Service, which had a good salary, so he could afford to send me to my first year. While my dad was working for the government, he said that there was all sorts of hanky-panky going on that was fraud. He was a Republican, but he would think honesty above all was the most important thing. I think that was a time when both "conservative" and "liberal" were good words. But then, these political things within the Service made him decide that he didn't want to be in it anymore, so he quit and went to Seattle.[36] He had a hard time. This was just before World War II and things were still pretty bad.

During her teenage years, Ginny applied her developing interest in the outdoors and wilderness experience to summertime work at camps and dude ranches. She explains how she ended up doing this type of work:

One thing I was able to do to help our family during the Depression was when I was in my teens I could get jobs in the summertime at summer camps or dude ranches. I started out as a junior counselor when I was fourteen. I wasn't paid, but there were lots of benefits, like I got to go to camp for free. Then I got older, in high school and then in college, and got jobs in different parts of the West—the Cascades or the Sierras—just so I could see new country. Because the Depression was still on I couldn't have afforded to go to those places otherwise. I didn't make much money, but they paid my way. I got hired because I was pretty good at outdoor things, I liked to hike and backpack and knew how to sail, and I'd grown up riding horses. Since usually horses were involved at these camps, I got out of having to take care of kids. I would be in charge of the riding program. This gave me a chance to see the country on horseback trips and camping out, which I liked to do anyway.

Ginny on horseback as a teenager, circa 1932. Courtesy of Ginny Wood.

My first experience with camps was when I was twelve years old and I went to a Campfire Girls camp on Lake Chelan. My father said, "Why does she have to go to camp? What's the matter with the lake here at our cabin?" My mother said, "No, she needs to mingle with other children." So I went to the camp. Later when we moved, I went to another camp for kids that they started on Lake Wenatchee in Central Washington. I think, to be truthful, by the time I was fourteen, I was such a little devil thinking up ways to sneak out of camp in the middle of the night or raid the pantry or do something devilish, that they made me a junior counselor just to keep me out of trouble. That made me very authoritarian, to make those kids shape up. You know, "Where's your buddy when you're swimming?" For safety, you were supposed to always be near a buddy when swimming. And "You're supposed to be quiet after Taps." You were supposed to be in your bed after Taps. You know, I must have been a martinet. I was bossy.

One particular trip that I remember from one of those camps was one that I was in charge of along with an older woman. She was the older counselor, but she didn't know anything about horses. We took a trip from Lake Wenatchee on up the trail that now goes all the way over to the Seattle country. It went up through the mountains. Well, the horse I was riding fell down. We were going across a ridge and there was a rock there and the horse slipped and fell. My foot got caught underneath it and it kind of smashed it, banged it up. But since

I was in charge, I still had to take care of the horses and keep on going. It didn't hurt too bad. I could ride all right, but I couldn't walk very well. I could ride, but someone had to lift me on the horse and help me off of the horse. This was until I got down to where I could go to a doctor. I don't know how many miles it was. It was three days, I think. So that was kind of an interesting trip. I was young and healed fast.

After I got older, when I was eighteen, I worked at dude ranch–type places and resorts taking riders out on trail rides and then overnight trips and then weeklong trips. I started with an outfit in California called Sierra Camps, Incorporated. They were running short of cowboys, because World War II was beginning and their men were getting drafted. Finally, the owners said, "Would you like to take charge of all the pack trips that go out?" They would go out riding and camping for three, four, or five days. I said, "Yeah." Another girl and I took over all the work at the corrals. An old packer had told me how to throw a diamond hitch and how to pack a packhorse, and I had enough experience in packing food, so that was enough to lead trips. In terms of bringing food, the cowboys just went to the kitchen and had the cook do it. We found out that we didn't need to take as many packhorses if we took just the amount of jam or the amount of pancake flour we needed for the trip, instead of taking a number-ten tin of everything.

Sierra Camps, Incorporated, was off Echo Lake, in the Sierra Nevada Mountains in California, which is off of Highway 50 that goes over to the foot of Lake Tahoe. But you're way high. There's upper and lower Echo Lake. The camp was at the foot of the lower lake. You had to go in by boat to the lower lake, and then there was a trail you could go on to the upper lake. For the winter, they kept the horses pastured down in the lowlands somewhere near Lake Tahoe. A lot of people that had resorts and so forth kept their horses down there. So in the beginning of the season, you'd go and pick out the horses you wanted for the summer. We'd go down and pick out a whole bunch of them, about thirty or forty, and drive them all the way back up to the camp. I used to like to do that. But I loved going out on the trips. It was wonderful country. I thought that camp would be all summer homes by now, but I've heard they've now made it wilderness forest.[37] It's wonderful country for hiking. For a while it was great, because they needed workers. All the guys were getting drafted. Then they closed up entirely. They didn't even try to run it during the war.

Camping was more primitive when I was a kid than it is now. I didn't even own a sleeping bag. We used two blankets. One went this way, another that way to make like an envelope. And you carried it in a U-shaped roll around your neck. That's how you went backpacking. And we'd make a bough bed to sleep on. You chopped boughs off a tree. You'd pick the ones that were fuller and fluffy. Kind of curved. You laid them on the ground overlapping and interlaced with each other with the natural arch of the bough curving upward to make a springy mattress. You didn't want anything sticking up to poke you. It was an art to making a bough bed. Then you would roll your bedroll out on top of your bough bed. If it was raining you made a lean-to shelter. People don't do this anymore.

But that was wonderful having worked at camps and exploring the back-country. I think that's when I started to get interested in different habitats, different wildlife. That's where I got my taste of wanting to get in the wilderness. I didn't think about wilderness then. It's a name that didn't mean anything to me. But just exploring the country interested me.

L–R: *Myra Francisco, Joan Wickersham, and Ginny in Copenhagen, Denmark, wearing matching shirts hand-sewn from towels they took from the freighter ship on which they sailed to Europe, 1938. Courtesy of Ginny Wood.*

3
Europe by Bicycle

> We had selected bicycles as a means of transportation not as a stunt but
> for economy. We would remember countryside through which we had pedaled
> long after those through which we had been whisked by train were forgotten.
> These were treasures that would be kept forever in that storehouse
> called memory, safe from fire, robbery, poverty, or wars.

As a young woman growing up in small towns in Washington and Oregon, Ginny Hill differed from her friends and classmates. She had a desire to see other countries, to meet new people. Perhaps this was fostered by her love of reading, her interest in geography in school, or her parents' college-educated background. Perhaps it came from hearing the stories of her parents' own journeys west to Oregon from Massachusetts. Or perhaps her Swedish ancestry influenced her to want to see that country. Upon graduating from high school in Pendleton, Oregon, Ginny knew she did not want to marry a rancher and live there the rest of her life like her classmates. As she explains:

By the time I was in high school, I knew the things that I didn't want to do. I remember that I made a list of what and where I wanted to experience before my life ended. At that time, thirty-six seemed a good age; it seemed to me that after that people got old and feeble, especially women. I don't remember everything that was on the list, but I do remember mushing a dog team in the Arctic, climbing the Matterhorn, sailing a sailboat on the high seas, tramping through exotic lands. I guess I wanted to see as much of the world as I could. Mostly people stayed where they were born in those days, and I wanted to see what Europe looked like. I wonder if getting halfway up the Matterhorn, ascending fourteen-thousand-foot Mount Rainier, visiting Nepal, Ethiopia, and the Sahara Desert, hiking the tracks of New Zealand, biking three thousand miles through fourteen countries of war-torn Europe, and spending two years ferrying fighter planes for the air force during World War II fulfill my dreams and aspirations of youth? I don't know what I thought I wanted to do for a living then. But as it turned out, I didn't have to worry about that much because things sort of took care of themselves.

Ginny enrolled at Washington State College at Pullman (currently known as Washington State University) but her tenure did not last long. She saw an opportunity to fulfill her dream of traveling and took it. It would be years before she earned her bachelor's degree.

I spent one year at Washington State College in Pullman, Washington, and then instead of going to my sophomore year, I went to Europe. This was just before World War II and the economy was still pretty bad. It didn't look like I was going to make enough money that next summer to go back to college for my sophomore year. But about that time, my grandmother died and left me five hundred dollars. She left all her grandchildren five hundred dollars and you were supposed to invest it for your education and your future. But because of what had happened to my dad's investments during the Depression, I didn't think much of that, so I took mine and went to Europe, which was something nobody from Pendleton, Oregon, ever did. I said, "Now I know what I'm going to do with mine." My dad tried to tell me to invest it and it would accrue interest. My mother said to me, "Well, you know, if I were you, I'd do that, too. Go to Europe." Mother never did anything adventurous like that in her life. But she told my dad, "Well, what did you do when you got out of high school? You hopped freight trains all the way to Oregon."

I had read about youth hostels in some magazine. Maybe it was a time when I was trying not to have to write the term paper that I was supposed to write. You know you get diverted by anything. I came home to my sorority house and said, "Do you know what I'd like to do? I'd like to go to Europe and take a bicycle and stay in youth hostels. You can do that for twenty-five cents a night." It was started back right after World War I by an Englishman who thought that poor people should be able to travel, too, not just rich people.[1] So they started this youth hostel system. I decided that sounded like a good place to go, and on a bicycle. When I said, "That's what I'm going to do," Myra Francisco and Joan Wickersham, two seniors living at my sorority house, said, "We'll go, too." Well, I thought they were kidding. But they finally convinced me that they really did want to go.

We picked our departure date based on the end of the school year and when they were graduating. We decided we could take a freighter to Europe. Joan found an advertisement for a freighter, so we sent our money in to go and the boat was leaving in May. We decided that would be a good time to start out on our bicycles. It was the beginning of May 1938. Joan in the meantime had gotten herself engaged to Bob, who was also a senior. He was taking his first job and he wanted to get married. Joan said, "No, I'm going with Ginny Hill to Europe." He thought she was kidding. She said, "I'll marry you when I get back, but I want to have my trip first." We were all three different. Joan was from Spokane. She was very good-looking, very effervescent, and had been secretary of the student body. Myra was from a big cattle ranch down in Pomeroy, in southeastern Washington. She was laid-back and talked real slow. She drawled. She was a very nice-looking gal but always talked very slowly. Joan talked very fast and was into everything and had more dates than she could possibly go out on.

We took the train to Chicago. Bob had gone back there to take a job, so he met us there to drive us up to Montreal, where we were to catch the boat. We met up with Bob and two other guys in Chicago and went out dancing. We stayed at a YMCA that night. Then we drove on to Montreal where we stayed at a small hotel. We left our big tin suitcases in the car. We only had the dresses we were wearing, our toilet gear, and our passports and money with us. In the morning, we found everything was stolen out of the car. My mother had made a nice, beautiful knit suit for me and that got stolen. Our boat was leaving at four that next afternoon, so we went shopping. We went to one of those cheap places, a secondhand place like the Salvation Army, where you buy cheap clothes, and we spent ten dollars apiece for our wardrobe. We each got a pair of slacks, a pair of shorts for bicycling, pants that came down to midcalf and were pleated and looked like a skirt so you could wear them in town, and a jacket. We still had our pajamas and our underwear and our passports and our money. Just what you'd take into a hotel room. Then we got aboard the boat with only minutes to spare. But due to foggy weather, the boat didn't end up leaving until four in the morning. Bob was on the dock as we were leaving, saying, "Joan, change your mind? It's not too late to change your mind." She kept saying, "After I get back, Bob. After I get back." The irony of it was that at four a.m. when we finally left, he was the only one around so he was the one who undid the rope on the dock that turned the ship loose.

Ginny has previously described this European journey in a book titled "Once Upon a Time" that she wrote after their return to the United States.[2] As she explains:

I turned twenty-one years old abroad in Europe and had a great time there, so I wanted to get back there. I had this idea about writing a book about our trip, so I could make money to go back to Europe. I just really wanted to go back, and look up some of the people I'd known before and see some of the places that I missed, because Myra and Joan didn't want to see them. I got to New York and I got a job there because I didn't have any money. I can't remember keeping a journal on the trip, but my mother saved all my letters that I had written home. And the trip was still very much in my mind. I could remember things then like I don't now. A friend took my material to a publisher. The editor liked it and agreed to publish it. But when the war started, he turned it down. He said they couldn't publish it because they couldn't sell a book about three girls batting around Europe when everybody was now marching through it. Nobody would buy it. It was out of date. So my book never was published.

A few years ago, I was rooting around in the attic of the garage trying to find something and found a box instead which had this book in it. Imagine, so many years later, reading what you wrote when you were twenty-one, and how you looked at the world and how you looked at yourself. It had little philosophical things in it. It was Europe when the evil war wasn't on yet and I was traveling and in youth hostels with these people from all different countries. With Germans, English, Dutch, mainly. And a Dane that I kept in touch with until he died just a couple of years ago. It was fascinating for me to read. I was laughing about it. I thought it was interesting being in my eighties and looking back at what I wrote when I was in my early twenties. To me, it was fascinating. To everyone else, they thought it was just a damn good yarn. They thought it was great. So some friends decided it should get printed. Their daughter saw someplace that a mountaineers' association was looking for manuscripts that had to do with bicycle trips. She asked if I minded if she sent it in. I said, "If you want to." It came in second. So, it's not ever going to get printed. It's not destined to. First it was a war that stopped it, and now I imagine they thought anyone who's that old probably isn't going to be able to go around on a book tour and give signings. Which is true. I wouldn't want to do that.

Ginny has a heart-hitting way with words when she describes and reflects upon her 1938 European experience that puts the reader right there in the middle of it. Many of the stories she shared in 2007 when reflecting back upon that trip are also included in her book, however in well-crafted prose versus the off-the-cuff verbal telling, and often with more detail. Since the written descriptions are so rich and were created closer to the time of the actual events, some of them have been woven into the following account of her trip. For example, Ginny began her book by saying:

> This is a story of Europe, but not the Europe of today, and perhaps not the Europe of tomorrow. It is about the Europe that I saw in 1938 with two companions in months of bicycling around the British Isles and the Continent.
>
> As I write this, youths are marching over Europe in uniforms, with tanks and trucks, carrying bayonets and hand grenades, living in trenches and underground fortresses, intent on destroying one another. Two years ago youths were wandering over Europe. They wore shorts, traveled on foot and on bicycles, carried rucksacks and cameras, lived in youth hostels, and they traveled together in friendly comradeship, singing and laughing as they went.

It is of the latter that I write, for we were among them. This is the story of the things we saw, the things we did, and the people we met. The Europe that we knew is gone, but I recount our adventures in hopes that it will soon return. And until the day when those youths can again take to the road in lighthearted comradeship, can again gather around in the common rooms of the youth hostels of Europe to seek understanding and appreciation of one another, my wish is that this heritage that has been passed on to the Americans who have been privileged to share it over there, can be kept alive in the youth hostels of this country—lest Europe forget.[3]

So begins the story of a six-month bicycle adventure through Europe, experiencing different countries, learning new things, and meeting new people. And seeing a Europe on the brink of war.

We sailed out of Montreal, up the St. Lawrence River, and then out across the Atlantic Ocean. The ship was the *Brookwood*. We called it the *Driftwood*. It was built in 1909 and had been left over from World War I. It had survived a world war and all those sinkings, and had been badly damaged but patched together again. It went very slowly. It took about fourteen days to go straight across the Atlantic. People went on freighters in those days. There were about twelve passengers altogether. We could run all over the boat. Folks would play bridge with the captain. He was an ace at it. I've never liked playing bridge so I usually read a book. But Joan, she was a shark at bridge. She was just stunningly vivacious. She had a way of just flirting without being a flirt. She just had a twinkle in her eye and always got a lot of attention from men, including from the captain and the crew on the ship.

Our boat had originally been scheduled to dock in London. But three days from shore a message was received that the cargo had been sold in Antwerp, so we landed in Belgium. The freight company paid our way back across the English Channel. We went by train to Brussels in thirty minutes, and then on to Ostend to meet the midnight boat across the Channel. We went aboard fast and got nice seats outside. It was cold and dark. It was miserable. We eventually had to go inside and there wasn't any room because everyone else was there, too. They had all gotten there before us because they knew it would be too cold outside.

Once in London, we stayed at a rooming house. The next day after we arrived was going to be the "Trooping the Colour" celebration.[4]

In her book, Ginny provides more details of this event:

We had the good fortune to be in London for the "Trooping the Colour," a ceremony of pageantry and military revue given in honor of the King's birthday because it isn't his birthday. King George VI was born in December, but winter is a cold month in which to hold a parade, and past British monarchs had obligingly been born in summer, so this ruler must celebrate his natal day in June. For weeks practice and preparation had been under way. Finally the day arrived and even the sun decided to shine for the occasion. After days of previous contemplation and careful scrutiny we had come to the conclusion that the best point for observing the affair would be from the Victoria Monument in front of Buckingham Palace. When we arrived on the scene we discovered that half of London had apparently decided this too. It was useless to try to find a place to sit on the steps; we could only stand for the two hours until the ceremony began, and then for two hours more until it ended. However, it proved a small price to pay for what we were privileged to witness.

The entire path of the procession, from Buckingham Palace down the Mall to the Horse Guard's Parade, was lined with Coldstream and Grenadier Guards. The Queen Mother and the two Princesses were first to leave the palace, their carriage accompanied by an escort of White Horse Guards, steel vests and helmets glistening in the sun. Then came the King mounted on horseback wearing the uniform of his regiment. Male members of the royal family rode behind him and their wives followed in carriages. Next rode military commanders and the military attachés of foreign powers. The procession continued with columns and columns of Horse Guards, bands, and the infantry of the Coldstream, Grenadier Scotch, Welsh, and Irish regiments, distinguishable only by the small emblem on their busbies.

An hour later the procession returned to the palace. The royal family assembled on the balcony above the courtyard, the colorful regiments filing in to stand at attention below. Then King George VI, sitting erectly on his mount in the archway of the palace gate, climaxed the ceremony by giving the royal salute. Although their hearts were bursting with pride, in a typical display of English emotion, the crowds uttered faint and stilted cheers at this gesture, which completed the program.[5]

The poor king. He'd only been king a few months. His brother, who was king, gave up the title to marry an American divorcée.[6] So he obviously didn't want to be king. There was all this pomp and stuff. There were all these guys with their big hats and all this parade that went by. You could see he wasn't comfortable. This older gentleman who was standing behind us explained what was going on. He said, "Well, you see, he never planned to be king, and this is the first time that he's had to do this. Now, you see that guy coming up on horseback, he's telling the king what he's supposed to do now." Queen Elizabeth and her sister, Princess Margaret Rose, were just little girls then. The oldest one was seven and the youngest one was four.[7] They came by in a carriage. I could have reached out and touched the one that became queen.

After they'd had all this and it was breaking up, the nice gentleman standing behind us introduced himself as Mr. Morgan and asked, "Now, girls, where are you staying?" We told him. Then we said that we had to buy bicycles and asked where would be a good place. "Well, I can tell you the best store. Where you'll get the best deal. Well, I can take you there." So he did. It was a big department store, and we bought bicycles. They were men's bicycles. They looked sturdier. We also bought saddlebags for them. Then he said, "Now, how are you getting out of London?" We said, "Well, we hadn't thought about that, but we guessed we'd bicycle." He said, "Have you had much experience on bicycles?" I said, "Oh, I've had one ever since I was ten years old." So had Joan. Then he asked, "And you, Myra?" She said, "I've never been on one." Joan and I were surprised at this news. Myra had never mentioned this before. He said, "Tomorrow morning I will meet you. I will come to the place where you are staying and I will escort you. Put your bikes on a train and take you to the outskirts and see you off. Because I don't think you should start in London."

We put our good clothes, dresses, and everything that we weren't going to need when bicycling into our tin suitcases that we bought in Montreal and stored them in London. Mr. Morgan arrived early the next morning. He was a very fatherly type of person. We drove to the outskirts of London and then we were headed for the first youth hostel. That's when we found out that Myra really didn't know how to ride a bicycle. We thought she was kidding, or just hadn't ridden for a while. Just getting her started was the hardest part, 'cause she'd keep falling. She hadn't realized that balance would be such a problem. And she hadn't figured out yet that you had to get your momentum up. But she was a good sport about it. When she would crash, she would just say, "Oh, my." She'd pick herself up and we'd get out the first aid kit and patch her knees or elbows.

As Ginny explained in her book:

> Joan and I would steady the vehicle while Myra climbed on, and with our hearts in our mouths would watch her weave across the road narrowly missing cars to collapse in the path of an oncoming bus. Miraculously she escaped injury. After numerous episodes of this sort, we came to the conclusion that she bore a charmed life and left her to master the art of equilibrium by herself, closing our ears to the repeated crashes that announced she was in the middle of the road with a bicycle on top of her again.[8]

We were in the outskirts of London and we were looking for the first youth hostel to stay in. I think it was near Windsor Castle. We stopped to ask a "Bobby" for directions. The policeman obviously had been watching us approach. He said to me, "I would suggest that you, young lady, go in front, and you [pointing to Joan] go in the back. And put her [Myra] in the middle. Otherwise, I don't think you're going to make it." Bobbies were very interesting people. Sometimes we'd just ask them questions to see their responses. Anyway, we did wobble along and made it to the first hostel. I don't know how many times Myra fell down. She was pretty good once she got going, but she usually stopped by falling off of the bicycle. And getting on it took several tries before she'd get enough momentum to stay upright. She did this half the way of the trip. She never really did learn to ride very well. She had a few accidents and scratches and things but she survived.

We started out from London, not really sure where we were going. We just went from youth hostel to youth hostel. At Manchester, we did put our bikes on the train to get around the industrial area. We went up as far as Edinburgh and made a circle and came back down to London. At one point, we kept running into these same three guys at the youth hostels. I went off with them for a day to climb a mountain, Ben Nevis. I wanted to do that, but Joan and Myra didn't, so we split up and met again at the next youth hostel. We hitchhiked on trucks, with our bikes, to get all the way back down to London to that same hostel where we started. We were gone about a month.

On our way back to London, we were having an intense discussion trying to decide where we'd go next. Joan wanted to go to France because she spoke French. She'd had four years of French. I wanted to go to Scandinavia. Myra just wanted to go someplace that was flat. We were sitting by the side of the road having our lunch and here went this cute blond guy going by on a bicycle. I'd seen this guy at the youth hostels who had always been looking our way, but I had never talked to him. He rode by and said, "*Tak for mad.*" That means "hope it tastes good" in Danish.[9] So we held up our sandwiches or whatever we were eating. We'd buy food and fruit and whatever. We said, "Come on. You want some." That was Ib Larson, Ibby. He came from just working class in Denmark. His mother and father had died in the flu epidemic after World War I, so his grandmother raised him. She'd brought him up, and he loved her dearly. I was nineteen then, and he was too. He had just worked down on the waterfront, or sweeping out streetcars at night to earn money. And he'd earned enough to go traveling. He was on his way back to Denmark, just coming back from having pedaled for five months all through the mainland of Europe and staying in youth hostels and visiting. He listened to us argue whether we were going to go to Germany or France first. I can still hear him now. He said, "Ladies, ladies, ladies, Ibby will solve it for you. You will come with me to Copenhagen and we will eat our way to my grandmother's and my dear sweet grandmother will have the most wonderful meal you have ever eaten in your life." He spoke English quite well. He learned German, French, and English by going down to the docks and talking to the sailors.

Ibby Larson, 1948.
Photo by Ginny Wood.

Myra, Joan, and I took his advice and followed him. We took a boat from Harwich, England, and went with him all through Denmark. We stopped at his grandmother's. Oh, she was a sweet old lady. We went all the way up to Frederikshavn and got the boat over to Norway and stayed about two weeks just around Oslo and hiking up in the woods. We then took a boat back to Denmark and took another boat to Sweden, and then took a boat that goes through the canal to Stockholm. When we came back to Copenhagen, we went to see the play *Hamlet* right in the castle of Hamlet.

From Copenhagen we took a boat to northern Germany. That's where, when we stayed at a youth hostel there, in the morning the guy came in and said, *"Heil Hitler. Alles Aufstehen.*[10] Everybody get up. Heil Hitler." We were sleeping. We didn't like being woken up that way. So starting from that time, whenever we were faced with "Heil Hitler" we'd always say back, "Heil Roosevelt."

When we were getting our mail at the American Express office in Berlin, Joan started talking to these two American guys. They had a car and they were going to drive over to the Rhine River. Well, they said, "Why don't you ship your bicycles ahead over to the Rhine and come with us in the car?" We'd been biking enough by that time, and thought that sounded pretty good. So that's what we did. They were enamored by the Nazis. They just thought that was the coming thing for Europe. Myra, Joan, and I often discussed amongst ourselves how it was possible that these Americans could swallow the Nazi propaganda. It showed us how easy it is to get people to fall for things like that. We could see how everyone in Germany was falling for this. They'd been through World War I and were very poor, so were taken by the new way touted by Hitler.

While we were with these guys we visited German work camps for the men and *Hitlermädchen* camps for girls, that would be like the Girl Scouts. We realized that these two guys must've had friends in high places, because majors and so forth in the German army would take us around a camp. They were proud to show us the Nazi way. We weren't in the war yet, but these two guys were really hooked on the Nazis.

In her book, Ginny provides a vivid account of visiting these German work camps:

Posing as social workers deeply impressed with modern Germany, we obtained passes to inspect several of the Arbeitslager in the environs of Berlin.... Every boy between the age of eighteen and twenty-five was required to serve six months in the labor service at one of the one thousand, five hundred camps located throughout the country. At the time of our visit, labor service was compulsory only for girls wishing a college degree.

Our guide was an official in the Arbeitsdienst.... The labor camps, he told us, were a nonmilitary institution with purely a leveling or socialization goal.... Civilian clothes were taken away from them on arrival, and their sole wardrobe for the duration of their term was the rough uniform of the service. They received no pay, only a twenty-five pfennig (about ten cents) allowance a day for beer. The men were given a five day vacation during their half year and they were free from duties Sunday afternoon and evenings.

The entrance to the first camp was guarded by a sentry armed with a shovel, the symbol of the labor service. He presented arms with it in a brisk salute as we passed by. Two leaders of the camp, themselves only in their middle twenties, appeared in immaculate uniforms and polished black boots to escort us around the establishment.

The two hundred men were quartered in an old farmhouse that had been revamped for the purpose. The rows of double-decker bunks were made in precise order. At the foot of each bed stood a tin washbasin that had been polished to shining brilliance. A wardrobe locker completed the equipment for each man. Rough benches and long wooden tables were the dining room furnishings. In the kitchen we were allowed to read the menus that had been made out for each meal of the month.

All the food had been calculated down to the last calorie, and only the amount required by each man for a reasonable healthy existence was served. The diet consisted of plain substantial food, devoid of any gastronomic frivolities such as desserts, salads, or baked dishes. Potatoes, soup, bread, and cabbage formed the bulk of the meals.

We were shown the daily schedules of the men. Their day began at five o'clock in the morning when they arose, went through gymnastics, ate a light breakfast, then went into the fields. A few hours later a second breakfast consisting of coffee and bread was served them at their work. Five minutes of rest was allowed every hour, and an hour was given them at noon for lunch. Afternoon activities included an hour's drill with shovels when said implements were shouldered, presented, aimed and all but fired.

"Nothing militaristic, girls. Absolutely nothing militaristic," Joan mimicked under her breath.

After supper the men had an hour of educational enlightenment. We noticed that all the textbooks were such volumes as "The History of the National Socialist Party," the Führer Hitler's "Mein Kampf," etc.

Other men's camps we visited were similar to this. Most of them had been constructed especially for barracks, however, and resembled in appearance the wooden structures of our CCC [Civilian Conservation Corps] establishments. Our guide explained the work done by the men in the camps included road work, land drainage, tapping trees for turpentine and rosin, reforestation, and crop cultivation.

... We arrived at the women's camp just in time to eat supper which consisted of pudding and black bread. Their routine was similar to the men's except that militarism is confined to a few marching drills and vigorous "heiling." Only thirty to fifty girls were quartered at one camp and their accommodations were more homelike with a few feminine flourishes added to their barren dormitories. Their work consisted of helping neighboring farmers in their fields and assisting the farmer's wife with household duties and care of the children.

Each girl worked for one family for two weeks then went to another. The girls took turns with the cooking and cleaning at their camp. For the first three weeks after her arrival a girl was not allowed to leave or see anyone outside the camp group. This was because she didn't have her uniform, which consisted of an olive-drab wool skirt, a plain white blouse, a swastika pin brooch, flat shoes, and cotton stockings.

After the meal the girls put on a program for the families from the surrounding farms. A play, *Rumpelstilzchen*, was presented, the characters rigging themselves up in costumes that had been assembled with ingenuity typical of impromptu productions. Charades were the next

thing on the program. Then the evening was thrown open to folk dancing and singing. Gaily we joined them, whirling and stamping to the
lively rhythm of the folk songs.

It might have been a scene at a girl's summer camp, except that on
the morrow the girls would arise at five o'clock to go into the fields and
kitchens of the farms to work all day. At night they would sit down to
another repast as meager as the one they had shared with us. And while
they toiled so that Germany might have food, we would be on our
lighthearted way, free to wander where we chose. And on our way we
would pass corps of army trucks, units of marching men, and overhead
fighting planes would roar. While part of the nation slaved to squeeze
the last ounce of efficiency from their country's resources, the other part
marched and drilled.[11]

The guys were okay, they didn't make any passes or anything, but they
weren't very good drivers. And they drank a lot of beer. We didn't think much
of all this driving sometimes. Finally we said, "Let's dump them." Even though
it was nicer to ride in the car again instead of having to bicycle everywhere. So
as soon as we got over to the Rhine we got out of the car. We said, "We think
we'll just get off here."

We went down the Rhine River to Heidelberg. That's where the University
of Heidelberg is, which is famous because it's where the operetta *The Student
Prince* takes place. It wasn't a big town, but the college was there and they had
a lot of students. The whole old town is very picturesque. It's a very nice place.

Ginny has a favorite story about their time in Heidelberg. Apparently, Myra, still
not a very competent cyclist, had quite a time negotiating the streetcar tracks on
the narrow streets. Ginny laughs heartily when telling this story. Her best rendition appears in her book:

The main thoroughfare running through the heart of the city from one
outskirt to the other has the town's only streetcar track. The street is so
narrow that the trolley almost brushes the curb on one side. If a cyclist
is caught between two streetcars going in the same direction, he must
either hop quickly off his vehicle and drag it up on the sidewalk to let
the streetcar behind pass, or take a chance with the oncoming traffic and
circle out around the trolley ahead of him. Myra could do neither. She
was unable to get off her bicycle fast enough to get up on the curb, and
crossing tracks was always a disastrous enterprise for her. She invariably
caught her wheel in the groove and she and her bicycle would part company very quickly. Therefore, poor Myra had only one alternative—to
stay between the cars until they stopped at the end of their run on the

edge of town. I wish I had counted the number of times Myra traversed Heidelberg. Holding our sides in hysterics, Joan and I, safe on the sidewalk, would watch Sister Francisco frantically pedaling down the street with the streetcar chasing her.

"Going somewhere, Myra?" we would call out to her tormentingly.

"Laugh, you idiots. This isn't a bit funny," she would gasp as she tore past. A half-hour later she would pass by again in the same predicament, going just as fast in the opposite direction.[12]

Traveling in Europe in 1938 gave Ginny and her friends a unique opportunity to witness the expansion of Hitler's regime and see changes that not many Amtericans were fully aware of yet. It was not until later that Ginny realized the historic significance of her experience.

Everywhere you went in Germany, you saw this "Heil Hitler" stuff. When we were on the train, the German troop trains would come along and our train would be sidetracked so they could go by. They'd go by with all the guys hanging out the windows waving, and we were hanging out the windows of our train waving, and they're waving back at us. On our way from Munich to Salzburg, Austria, we saw a group of men training for fighting fires using a fake fire. It was well organized. Everything was done in cadence, by the numbers: one, two, three, hep, hep, hep. And this German kid said in English to us, "That's the way we do everything now. We march to orders. That's Hitler's government. That's Germany now. That's what's become of our country." We talked to him for a while. That would happen to us quite often. Especially in Austria, people would come up and talk to us. Hitler had just come into Austria a few months before we were there.[13] There were big Nazi flags flying everywhere and everybody saying "Heil Hitler." But people had mixed emotions about it and talked to us.

When we were in Munich, we went to get mail. We did this about once a month, whenever we hit a big city. We were sitting in a park that was around the American Express office and reading our mail. Here was this American woman, corpulent kind of motherly type, who came out and said, "Do your folks know where you are?" We said, "Well, sort of." "When did you last write?" "Oh, we sent a postcard about a month ago." You see, you didn't make long-distance phone calls in those Depression-ridden days unless it was an emergency. She said, "Do you know there's going to be a war? As soon as you can, you get right to a boat and get booked home." She said, "There's going to be a war." We said, "Huh?" Well, we each had one hundred dollars left and weren't about to leave.

We found out that Chamberlain, who was the prime minister of England, had flown over to Germany to "make peace in our time." And he did. Hitler had gone into the Sudetenland, which is part of Czechoslovakia, which he claimed belonged to Germany. The agreement was that England wouldn't start a war over the Sudetenland if Germany would not invade England. That was the peace Chamberlain made. Then things kind of got worse. Well, you know, looking back now in history, it looks like Chamberlain kind of sold out to Hitler. But if he hadn't done that, Hitler would have gone into England first. We had just been in England for a couple of months and could see that they weren't anymore ready for war than the United States was. They had had enough of war in World War I. They didn't want anymore of that stuff. They didn't have an army or an air force and they didn't have much of a navy. They had more of a navy than they had an air force. So to me, Chamberlain's a hero, because of what he did then.[14]

Hitler went into Russia first instead of attacking England. He made his big mistake, just like Napoleon did, to go into Russia first. That was his undoing. He should have known better. He was probably like our President George W. Bush and had no sense of history. Doesn't know that whatever you do, don't go into a foreign country. No matter how backward they are, you are on their land and everybody's going to fight you. And that's what happened. Hitler got bogged down. That's how he got in touch with the Finns. Because he wanted the Finns to fight with Germany against Russia to get their land back which had been taken by the Russians before. And the Finns said, "We'll do that, but when we get to the border of what used to be our land, we're not going any farther." They all knew that the Finns were good fighters in the winter. Then the Germans turned on the Finns and fought them. They burned everything that was made of wood.[15] The poor Finns, no matter what they did they seemed to be at war.[16] The thing was, that held up the spread of the war because the Germans were stuck over there in Russia.

But it was just by luck we happened to be there in Munich at that time. We were in the middle of history. But we still didn't think of it much. For us, the trip was about the adventure of it. We weren't there for education or anything else.

So, Joan, Myra, and I decided we wouldn't go up to Prague, since that's where Hitler seemed to be headed. We went down to Italy because we figured they wouldn't get in the war for a while. They don't like wars. Anyway, we put our bikes on a train and went to Venice. Then we went to Florence. We then got off the train to find a place to eat and a place to sleep in the town of Sienna. If you've ever been to Sienna, you know it's a very old town and they have the big square where they used to have horse races. Well, we were there going to all those little stores seeing where we could get something to eat and where we could stay that was cheap. All of a sudden, the doors opened and everybody rushed out in that square. They were dancing and singing and laughing and clapping hands. We were just trying to find out what was going on. Finally, someone spoke English and said, "No war. No war. Chamberlain's made a deal with Hitler." We stopped in Rome and went down as far as Naples. We hiked up Mount Vesuvius and saw in a museum there at Pompeii all the bodies that were there from when the volcano exploded. And we went out from Naples to the island of Capri and stayed there a couple of weeks. It was wonderful swimming and they had a youth hostel there.

Ginny's description of her time in Capri is one of the most moving passages in her book:

Perhaps the walks that will linger in our memories the longest are the moonlit nights we wandered along the path on the southern side of the island when the palms, cypress and cacti lining the way stood silhouetted against the sky and the moon washed the world with silver. Coming to a stop on the bluff overlooking the Faraglioni we could look down on the nuptial arch of the sirens. Nor will I soon forget the night I followed the little dirt trail which descended down to the sea at the Porto di Tragara, a natural harbor sheltered by rocks where once the Romans moored their triremes, and intoxicated with ecstasy, flung off my clothes and plunged into the scintillating waters to swim down the silver pathway towards the moon.

One day we walked up the road to Anacapri, followed a stony path through vineyards and orchards to arrive on the bank overlooking the Grotto Azzurra, the Blue Grotto. Outside the entrance to the cave bobbed the tiny rowboats of the guides who were always ready to take the sightseer inside—for a substantial fee. We scrambled down the bank to the water's edge to bargain with the men. They wanted thirty lire; we would give but ten. Much dickering ensued and one oarsman came down to twenty-five and we went up to fifteen. Then we retreated up the hill for a huddle, and he rowed out on the water to put his head together with those of his cohorts. He weakened to twenty-two, and we to nineteen, then with an air of "that's my last price, take it or leave it" each party stood firm. The argument developed into an endurance contest, we sitting invulnerable on the steps at the top of the bank, and he smirking up at us from his boat. The pirate had the advantage for he knew that no one would leave Capri without seeing the grotto, and the only way to get in was by boat—or was it?

In a moment of sudden inspiration I dashed to the nearest bush and in its seclusion tore off my clothes and put on my bathing suit. Then with nose elevated, I flounced down the stairs, dove into the water, and swam through the opening in the Cave.

At first thought I was floating on some ethereal substance unknown in earthly mediums. The sapphire water glowed as if a giant blue light burned on the bottom. Outside the sea had been rough, waves dashed against the rocky shore, but inside, the surface was smooth, disturbed only by the ripples the movement of my body sent out. The walls of the cavern seemed glazed, and as my eyes grew accustomed to the dark I could make out caves and indentations that led back through the rocks above the waterline. In sheer delight I dove beneath the surface into the translucent depths expecting any moment to see a siren pop out at me. No wonder these golden-haired damsels fought so ferociously against the monster Tritons for possession of the grotto. If it were mine, I'd fight for it too. My voice echoed and re-echoed in a strangely hollow tone when I laughed and shouted. To get out of the grotto it was necessary to wait for a wave of the right size that would carry you through the opening without scraping my knees, and yet not so large that I would bump my head on the top or be of such force it would be impossible to swim against it.[17]

Bicycling around Europe for six months on a tight budget can be a stressful situation even for the best of friends. Ginny knew Myra and Joan in passing from living at the same sorority house, but since they were seniors and she a freshman they had not been particularly close. They were brave to take this journey together without really knowing each other well. Fortunately, it all went smoothly. As Ginny discusses, the three of them got along well, each brought something different to the team, and they were able to do things separately or together depending upon each woman's interest.

We got along fine together. Joan was for cities, culture, art, music, and literature. And "the places you should see" in Paris, London, and Munich. Myra just wanted to get there. To get off the bicycle. She would just say, "How far is it that I've got to ride?" But she hung in there. And I wanted to go up in the Alps. Joan brought lots of things into our lives that I might not have otherwise known. I think we all enriched each other.

They were good companions. We got along pretty fine. But we were all different. Quite often the three of us would split up. Often we'd be in a youth hostel and I'd meet some folks who were going someplace that I wanted to see and Joan and Myra met somebody else, so we split up for a couple of days and then would meet again at a certain youth hostel. Or Joan and Myra wanted to stay in a city more and I said, "Well, I want to go climb a mountain, so we'll meet at the next hostel." But mostly we were together.

In her book, Ginny explains this difference in their views on mountains, which explains why Joan and Myra rarely accompanied her on these forays:

Our opinions on mountains differed. They liked to view theirs from the bottom; I liked to look down on mine from the top. To them, mountain climbing was an insane waste of time and energy, a form of self-inflicted torture, for no purposeful reason. You wore yourself out struggling to the top, then turned around and came back down. If one liked to go up and down, why not do it in an elevator?

My version was something like this. One might forget a mountain viewed only as a thing of scenery, or pausing momentarily to reflect on its beauty, soon lose that imprint in the maze of impressions that fade into the black of forgetfulness when new ones come along. But one could never forget a mountain up whose slopes he had struggled, each step an agonizing effort and a thrilling accomplishment. And once on the highest pinnacle, above the mundane cares and smallness of the world below, could one ever forget the surge of exultation that comes when he has conquered the peak that once had challenged? The challenge had not been a taunt, but rather an invitation to a rendezvous with blue sky, white clouds, strong cold wind, and rocky heights. Impressions are fleeting, but experience lingers forever in the memory always ready to be conjured up and relived again.[18]

We lived very frugally on the trip. One dollar a day is the most we ever spent. In places that didn't have a youth hostel, we'd find an inn or something and say, "*Guten tag. Wir schlafen alles drei in ein bett. Haben sie ein gross zimmer und gross bett?*" That was our bargaining. "Do you have a great big room with a great big bed, and we'll all sleep in it together? The three of us will all sleep in one bed."

A lot of good things happened to us. Like we got a ride for a long time in a car down to the Italian border. Then we started hitchhiking. We hitchhiked a lot, and that's kind of nice. But if you'd been a young girl alone, I don't know if that would have been possible. Sometimes it took two of us. We would split up in the day quite often, but it seemed better to hang out together. It didn't seem like there were many other women doing this type of traveling when we were there. There must have been some. But it certainly didn't make much of an impression on me. When I look back at it now, it seems like if there was a girl, she was with her brothers or her family or as husband and wife.

After Capri and hiking Mount Vesuvius, Ginny, Myra, and Joan traveled north, finally ending their journey in Belgium, from where they returned to the United States.

Then we went into France. We went to Paris. That's where I came of age. I turned twenty-one in Paris. We climbed the Eiffel Tower at night when it was closed with three guys from the youth hostel. They boosted us up so we could get up on to where the cement stops, which is the second story, and then you can crawl through and get on the stairs. We went all the way to the top, sat there, and saw

L–R: *Joan, Myra, and Ginny on a truck that picked them up near Zurich, Switzerland, when they were struggling with a flat tire on one of their bicycles. Courtesy of Ginny Wood.*

Paris at night. We did it this way for free. Otherwise you had to pay to go to the top. By this time we had to think of every penny.

Joan wanted to stay in Paris. She really liked the culture and she spoke French. Myra wanted to stay with her. But I'd met this guy at the youth hostel who had just finished kayaking down the Danube, and he was on his way back home biking to Belgium. So he and I biked together. We planned to meet Joan and Myra a couple of weeks later in Bruges. He and I biked through all those old World War I battlefields. We were making seventy and eighty miles a day. This was November, so by then most of the youth hostels were closed, but we'd crawl through [the windows] and stay in them anyway. Antwerp was great, wonderful. And so was Bruges. Joan and Myra came by train. They decided to sell their bicycles. They didn't want to take them home. I went down to sell mine and said no. I just couldn't do it. I was not going to sell my faithful bicycle "Constantine." Their bikes were named "Modestine" and "Josephine." These were the bikes we bought in London. I took my bike home and rode it again through Europe ten years later when I went back to school in Sweden.[19] Then I sold it to a guy there who was a student.

In her book, Ginny paints a touching picture of the bond she developed with her bicycle, Constantine:

> The best offer was one hundred and fifty francs apiece for them. Myra and Joan agreed to the transaction and I almost did. In fact, I probably would have, had I not taken a last look at Constantine reclining against the wall in the corner of the shop.
>
> "For six months we've been together," she seemed to say, "and I've carried you through fourteen countries, taken you to places you had never seen before and may never see again. I've carried you through rain, hail, and sunshine. How much trouble did I give you? Four flat tires, three broken carriers, a burned-out headlight, and a broken gear. Is that so bad for three thousand miles? And now you would sell me for a paltry five dollars!" Even her handlebars drooped in sadness.
>
> Sell Constantine! What was I thinking of? Why, I loved every inch of her rusty frame from her mud-splattered tail light to her bent front fender. The shopkeeper was already taking the money out of the cash register, when I stopped him.
>
> "How much would you charge to take the gears off of my friend's bike and put them on mine?"
>
> For a long time he didn't answer and I hopefully fingered my last one dollar bill. Then he said, "Twenty-nine francs."
>
> Exactly one dollar. I hurried out of the store and had the bill exchanged into Belgium currency. Thus instead of emerging from the shop with no

bicycle and a pocket full of money, I emerged with a rejuvenated wheel and no money at all.[20]

Joan, Myra, and I got another freighter back home from Antwerp, the *Jean Jadot*. It was fancier than the one we took over to Europe in May. It was a Belgian freighter, but everybody spoke English. It was November. It was cold, and the sea was rough. Lots of people were seasick. It was more formal than the other boat. We had more like staterooms rather than bunk rooms, and this time they didn't let us help paint the ship like they did on the other one. The trip took two weeks. We got to New York City just before Christmas. I had a cousin that lived in New Jersey who met us.

I hardly saw Joan and Myra again after we returned from this trip. Joan did marry Bob. He was in the military for five years. He got sent to the Hawaiian Islands. He hadn't been in combat. But he came out a captain. I visited them once when they lived in a little town in the middle of Washington. I stayed overnight with them. They had two children, a boy and a girl.

I stayed back there in New York City and worked a year because I didn't have any money left to pay for getting all the way back to Seattle. I wanted to earn enough money to go back to Europe or return to the mountains I'd known. A gal that I knew who had been a counselor when I was a junior counselor at a camp at Lake Wenatchee in Washington, she had married and lived in New York. She married very well, upper crust. At that time, upper-crust young ladies were supposed to do something for the good of the community. Give themselves away, volunteer, for a good cause. Her thing was Campfire Girls, because she'd been one when she was a girl in Seattle. I looked her up and she said they're looking for an executive at the Campfire headquarters. I'm telling them you're twenty-five, so don't tell them any different. In those days, you could get away with that. I was just twenty-one. I'd just had my birthday in Paris in October. So I stayed there and worked for Campfire Girls, and then that summer I was an assistant director of a Campfire Girls summer camp on this little puddle of a lake in upstate New York with what must have been six other youth camps. It was not much of a wilderness experience. Their idea of camping was not very primitive compared to what I did as a kid. When we were closing the camp in September 1939, that's when World War II started.[21] We did escape it on our trip, but I was home less than a year before war broke out.

I found New York City more bizarre and as foreign as any country I had just cycled through and certainly a milieu far from that of Waterville and Wenatchee, Washington, or Pendleton, Oregon, where I grew up surrounded by open fields, forests, and mountains. Navigating its streets and subway systems presented little problem. I knew how to read maps and a compass, a skill unknown to New Yorkers. But there was the human comedy of watching so many assorted human beings get themselves on and off subways—a whole new social specter for me. I wondered how many of these millions I encountered hurrying to work or home ever walked on anything but cement or encountered trees, mountains, or wild things in their lives? I wondered why New York City was such a mecca for success of one kind or another for so many of the young in those days.[22]

That fall of 1939, while I was living and working in New York, I got word from my mother that the woman of the family next door to them was waiting for her daughters to come back from Europe. My family had moved to Seattle while I was in Europe. This woman, Mrs. Dunham, had two daughters that were bicycling and youth hostelling in Europe. They were in Poland, and she was worried about if they could get out because Hitler invaded Poland. It was October and she had gone to New York to wait for her daughters to come back. She was worried because they'd been born in Canada by American parents, and she didn't know if they had used Canadian or American passports. If they had Canadian passports, they would've been interned in Poland, because England went into the war and at that time Canada was a colony of Britain. It would have meant they had an enemy passport, as far as Hitler was concerned. Fortunately, they had gotten American ones. They were put on the last train that left Poland and arrived in New York safely.

Mrs. Dunham got in touch with me, and asked did I want to drive the car with them back to Seattle? Her one daughter was going to stay in the East. She could get a job there with the youth hostel association. They were just starting the youth hostels up in New England. Mrs. Dunham didn't drive or didn't like to drive. And her younger daughter, Pat, was eighteen and could drive but she didn't have a license yet. So we drove together all the way across the United States to Seattle by way of the Smokies and the Southwest.[23] We went by way of Albuquerque, stopped at the Grand Canyon, where Pat and I hiked down to the bottom, and then went over to where I had relatives in California. We stayed with them, and then drove up the Pacific coast to Seattle. So that was kind of a neat trip. Mrs. Dunham didn't camp, so we'd find places that had cabins. They did not really have many motels then. Pat and I would just unroll our sleeping bags and sleep outside, since that's what we had been doing in Europe.

I came back to Seattle in late 1939 and lived at home where my family was now living, and had a part-time job clerking in a sporting goods store, so I could afford to enroll at the University of Washington to finish my college education. But I was no longer the co-ed I had been two years before at Washington State College, concerned primarily with dating, dances, and sorority affairs. My European exposure had changed my scholastic focus. I had developed a thirst for knowledge for its own sake instead of making good grades in required courses just for a diploma. I became interested in so many things that I took all kinds of courses. And that's why I had a hard time getting a diploma.[24]

Ginny and Pat Dunham change a tire during their cross-country odyssey as Mrs. Dunham looks on, 1939. Courtesy of Ginny Wood.

By my junior year, when I was supposed to have settled on a major, they said, "What are you majoring in? Will you make up your mind?" In those days, cross-discipline degrees were jealously frowned on if you wanted a career or even a job when you graduated. They looked at all the things that I had taken and decided how they could be combined into something that I could graduate in. You always had to take certain subjects, but if I didn't like them, I didn't take them. I took something else. There was so much to learn, so much that I wanted to know, that I kept changing subjects. I had signed up to be a journalism major, with visions of being a foreign correspondent. But one's junior year in journalism required a course in advertising and typewriting. Can you believe that now, given my poor typing skills? And an internship in a downtown newsroom. Instead, I chose to take Russian history since the revolution, history of the Balkans, Spain during the Civil War, a survey of European architecture, and a German language class. I refused to take a required physical education course on Saturday. I went skiing or mountain climbing on weekends instead.[25]

Finally, when I got near to getting a degree, I found out that the English department didn't want me because I was too much journalism. And for journalism, I hadn't completed the half-year that you were supposed to go work for a newspaper as a fieldwork type of thing. Then the war came along and they needed pilots so I did that instead. I went without a diploma for a long time because they said I had never fulfilled the two credits of freshman physical education requirement and that in order to graduate I'd have to return another semester to complete them. I wasn't going to do that. For a long time, I didn't bother doing the paperwork to see if I could get that waived. Finally, after living in Alaska for a long time I applied and got my credits. I finally got a degree from the University of Alaska Fairbanks in journalism.

As a woman in her nineties, Ginny reflects back on her experience in Europe as a young woman nearly seventy years earlier and what it meant to her personally:

I guess I knew one thing when I got back from being in Europe that first time: I was very glad I was born and raised in the United States. Because especially as a woman, we had more freedoms to choose our occupation, or to marry or not to marry. In Europe, "a woman's place is in the home" was more of the sentiment. But I also came away with the thought that we Americans don't always do everything best. Every country does something better than we do. I mean, no matter what it was. Whether it was technology or whether it was just custom, or whatever. I learned, "Oh, that's a sensible way to do it." By staying in youth hostels and biking or hiking with all different nationalities where we shared food and sang together, we developed connections between people from lots of other countries and gained a better understanding of the world. I became a citizen of the world. I know from then on I never thought of myself as an American. But on the other hand, I realized how lucky I was to have grown up in a small town in a very rural community. I just had the best of all worlds.

Growing up in a small, rural town, not everyone was well educated or spoke proper English. So dump me down in Europe, which was very sophisticated. It was very different for me. What impressed me was when we'd go to a youth hostel in like Paris, London, or Copenhagen, the American kids all went out for a beer and the European kids went out to the opera. There was always a place you could go very cheaply to watch a performance. You might have to stand, but they went anyway. They went to art galleries. Anyone from Wenatchee wouldn't want to go to an art gallery. It was, "Oh, have you seen this building, the architecture?" I realized how little I knew about architecture. I came back and took a course in architecture. Just because I didn't know this was German or this period. It made me be interested. I developed an appetite for things that I wouldn't have ever been interested in if I'd stayed in the Northwest.

I'm just so grateful that my grandmother left me five hundred dollars and I had enough sense to go spend it. Then I think of the places I've been, and the adventures I've had, and the people I've met, and I just think, "Wow." I can't complain about anything.

Ginny reflects on the impact that being in Germany just before the outbreak of World War II had on her own life and beliefs. As she says, "It was interesting to see Europe on the eve of the war." First, as she wrote in her book, there was what she witnessed in Germany:

The scene was the Munich youth hostel on September 22. It was night and inside, the main room was filled with noise and gaiety. To the accompaniment of a guitar and two accordions, one group was engaged in a lively folk dance. Every one was lifting his voice in rafter-ringing song. Suddenly the music stopped and we all rushed to the window. In the streets below were marching columns of soldiers headed for mobilization on the Danube, thirty miles from the Czechoslovakian border. For a few minutes the German youths leaned out of the open windows, cheering and heiling, their eyes sparkling with enthusiasm at the stirring sight of the marching men. After a while they returned to their dancing and singing. Late into the evening the festivities continued, the rhythm of their music and dance synchronizing with the tread of the marching feet, the clatter of horses' hooves, and the rattle of machine guns and ammunition wagons as they passed into the night.

The accent in Germany was on youth. They were kept marching and singing inspired by the words of their leader Adolf Hitler, who said to them, "I put the destiny of Germany in your hands. I know that you will not fail me!" It did not occur to them that perhaps their destiny was in Germany's hands. The German youth did not question why he was marching or where he was going. He only knew that his companion next to him was marching too, and when one is young, it is fun to march and sing.

They were all marching in Germany, but some marched out of step. We didn't see it by watching them, for to the eye there was about as much individuality in their movements as in those of the Radio City Music Hall Rockettes. We wouldn't have seen it if we had gone to Germany as the average American tourist staying in the best hotels, ordering the four-mark meals. We wouldn't have seen it if we had stayed only a few days or a few weeks. We wouldn't have seen it if we had tried too hard, for it wasn't with their feet that they faltered; it was with their hearts. Nazi regimentation kept them marching, and fear of a concentration camp kept them smiling, but neither of these forces could control their hearts. We didn't discover the dissenters by seeking them out. They betrayed themselves by a few words that escaped their lips in a burst of bitter rebellion, by a chance gesture, or a casual inflection in their voices.[26]

Second, there was the effect this European experience had on Ginny's own thoughts and reactions after she returned home and World War II officially began in the fall of 1939:

Hitler, when he invaded Poland, he just marched right straight through it. Then everybody else got in the war, too. But I won't go into that. You can read that in a history book. In the United States at that time there was just about the same atmosphere that there is now about going into Iraq. Wondering whether we should or shouldn't have done it. We don't get into other people's wars. We're not going to go to war. At that time, you see, everybody was looking back at World War I and saying, "Should we get involved again or not?" Asking, "What did we get out of World War I?" The sentiment was you don't go to war; people die in wars. Even though no one thought much of Hitler or that regime, people were asking, "Why are we getting into European fights? We've got an ocean on both sides. We don't have to worry about being invaded. Why don't we stay out of this war? Let them fight it out." At the time, you didn't hear much about the Jews. You didn't hear about what he'd been doing to them. I don't remember that crossing my screen. So, the people that were pro-war realized we were going to get in it sooner or later. England was our ally, so we'll always get into anything England does. Canada will be in it, too. And they're our neighbors. Sooner or later we're going to get involved and we don't have an army, and we don't have any air force to speak of. So the powers that be then started to build things up. And of course, if the Japs[27] hadn't bombed us, I don't know whether we would have gotten into World War II.

I wasn't paying much attention to the war stuff, except I knew this was debated a lot. My folks didn't talk about military things or war very much. They weren't very patriotic about it. But having been in Europe for a year, all I could think of was, "You mean all those nice little German boys and English boys, they're going to be killing each other? That doesn't make sense. Why, I bicycled and youth hosteled with them and know all of them." I just couldn't imagine people killing each other. So I was very anti-war.

During World War II, there was rationing here. It wasn't like Europe, but it was tough. My dad got only enough gasoline to go to work. They closed down all ski resorts, golf courses, anything that used gasoline. People that had resorts just closed up. I never heard anybody kick about rationing. Nobody complained or was bothered a bit about being rationed with gasoline. People just wouldn't do it now. What would people say if they were told, "You can't run your snow-machine race to Nome,[28] it uses too much gasoline"? Or be told you can't do anything that uses gasoline. What would they do? They don't know what it was like. And we weren't even in a bombing war like Europe, where you had to take your kids to the subway during the bombing. But a lot of things were rationed.

Ginny, age twenty-six, upon graduating from the Women Airforce Service Pilots training, August 1943. Courtesy of Ginny Wood.

4
Flying and the Women Airforce Service Pilots

And when peace comes, and sugar and silk stockings can all be bought, then we'll be glamour girls, we'll be glamour girls, and oh boy will we be hot! (WAFS song)

As a child, Ginny was exposed to airplanes and flying like many other boys and girls of her generation. There were the great aviators, like Charles Lindbergh and Amelia Earhart, who captured the world's imagination as they pioneered equipment and air routes. And there were the classic barnstormers, landing in rural fields across America who attracted attention like the circus coming to town; often it was someone's first or perhaps only airplane ride. Ginny explains her first exposure to flying:

I think I had an interest in flying because of Charles Lindbergh's pioneering solo flight across the Atlantic to Paris when I was about ten years old, and Amelia Earhart of course, and Richard Byrd's aerial explorations of the South Pole. All that sort of thing.

The first time I ever was in an airplane I was sitting in my father's lap in the rear of an open-cockpit World War I biplane that was barnstorming. I was with him in his little Ford Model T bouncing out to the experimental farm in Waterville. We saw this airplane fly over and he said, "Oh, he's going to land near here. He's barnstorming." And I said, "What's barnstorming?" He says, "Oh, that's someone that bought an old World War I plane and was going around to small towns and landing in a field. They buzz the town and people come out, and for five dollars they can get a ride." He said, "Would you like to go up in that?" I nodded my head and said, "Oh yes, Daddy." He said, "You won't tell your mother?" I shook my head and said, "No." So for thirty glorious minutes we climbed, circled, and dived over my hometown and the wheat fields and sagebrush that surrounded it.

Ginny, age fourteen, in her flying hat and goggles, 1931. Courtesy of Ginny Wood.

After that, I always thought it would be neat to fly myself, but I didn't know how I'd do it because I didn't have any money. Then, see, events always took care of me.

Although Ginny does not recall specifically dreaming of becoming a pilot when she was a child, she believes she must have had some inkling because of what she and her playmates did when all the news was about Charles Lindbergh flying solo across the Atlantic:

We went out and got some old discarded lumber and put together an airplane in my backyard. You'd go down to the lumber company and they'd give you old lumber, you know, scrap pieces. Other things we collected from the town junkyard or were donated by neighbors. We used old canvas to cover the fuselage and wings. It had fore and aft cockpits that we sat in and controls and everything rigged up. It had wings with ailerons that you could make flap up and down.

I think they both went the same way. And a tail assembly with a movable rudder and elevators. I remember we had an empty apple box on the front for the engine. We went to the dump and just got a lot of old pieces of machinery and junk—nuts and bolts, wheels, pipes, wire, and an assortment of tubes, auto parts, and other assorted discarded paraphernalia—that we threw in there. And we had a propeller we'd hand-hewn from a two-by-four that you could spin. To "start" the engine, we'd swing the propeller and loudly yell, "Contact!" We controlled the ailerons and rudder with a stick in the front cockpit.

The boys got to fly in front, but I was usually relegated to the rear cockpit because I was a girl. I was the navigator, or the gunner, or the observer, or the ground crew. But the plane was in our backyard, so I could be the pilot when nobody else was around.

We even fashioned a parachute from canvas and old ropes. We made Ole Berg test it by jumping off from the roof of our chicken coop. Luckily, he survived with only a sprained ankle. We got scolded and spanked for that.

We used to spend hours in that plane until my father made me take it down because "it was an eyesore." We logged hours of "flight time" pretending to be flying over the Atlantic, being in aerial dogfights over France in World War I, going to the South Pole, flying the mail, or barnstorming with passengers. I always thought it funny that neither of the Berg boys ever learned to fly an airplane, but I did.

Ginny was attending college at the University of Washington in Seattle in the early 1940s when she learned of an opportunity to advance her fledgling interest in flying. It was the Civilian Pilot Training Program (CPTP). The US government established the CPTP in 1939 as an initial way to get trained pilots for military service, even though the country was not yet involved in World War II. The program was run through universities and was under the command of General Henry "Hap" Arnold. Arnold was commissioned to build an air force in anticipation of the United States becoming involved in World War II, where air power was going to be critical for success.[1] The training was open to all, with one woman accepted for every ten men.

The Civilian Pilot Training Program was started because the government realized that the United States didn't have much of a backlog of pilots. We didn't have much of an army and we certainly didn't have an air force. We weren't in the war yet and there was a lot of feeling that we shouldn't be, and they didn't have a draft for anything like that.

The CPT program was peddled as a way to boost civilian aviation. That it was not a war thing. The government thought if they allowed women to take the program that would shut up the people saying this was to get us into the war. A lot of times women were afraid of flying and airplanes. My mother wouldn't fly in those things. My dad thought it was great when he had business to do and to go back east to see his relatives. But my mother would say, "I wouldn't get in one of those things." The government thought if they let women in the CPT program then the women wouldn't be afraid to fly with their husbands when they wanted to use airlines for business or something. And also it would encourage people to buy airplanes.

Ginny had wanted to learn to fly before, but had not been able to afford it, so she applied for the Civilian Pilot Training Program. It only cost forty dollars for a lab fee.[2]

I read about this CPT program when I was in my senior year of college. They awarded some of the training opportunities to universities so that that many more people could learn to fly. The university would be given so much money for training so many people to fly. To get their private pilot's license. When I heard about this program, I saw it as an opportunity to learn to fly. Ten percent of the quota for each university could be women. And the University of Washington, where I was in school, got fifty people, of which ten percent could be women. So that meant five women.

You had to pass the same military physical as fighter pilots or as West Point cadets, and that eliminated a lot of people. You had to have good eyes—twenty-twenty eyesight—and I just by luck happened to have good eyes. I had twenty-fifteen vision. You had to be within a certain weight-height range and I just happened to be. I didn't have anything wrong with me. I had very good health. That was a matter of no talent of my own, but just good genes! That eliminated an awful lot of girls who tried. Wiped out a lot of people who wore glasses or if you had a heart murmur or anything like that.

Then it was competitive on grades. They took you on your grades. I wasn't a scholar but had about a B-plus average. Because I was really majoring in skiing by that time. The physical plus the grades got me in, so eventually I got one of those five spots for women. I entered the CPT in the fall of 1941.[3]

The training was very programmed. You didn't just go like you do now. Go find someone to teach you to fly and as soon as you've soloed say, "Well, I don't want to pay anymore." Whatever we had was the exact routine they did for training the guys. To get your private pilot's license, there was a ground school class that you had to attend and pass exams, and thirty-five hours of solo flight training. The first eight hours were dual, with the instructor sitting next to you, then you soloed. After soloing, flight training consisted of alternating an hour of flying maneuvers alone to practice all the things that you'd learned, with an hour with the instructor to catch any bad habits, with a few check rides in between to hone your proficiency.

My flight instructor was a tall, lanky, initially taciturn man, too young to have flown in World War I, but too old to serve in the military if we were to get involved in another war. During our association in the air, I learned offhand in bits and pieces about his soldier-of-fortune career, which included barnstorming, flying freight into primitive jungle airstrips with old Ford Tri-Motor aircraft for mining operations in South America, and "bush" flying in Alaska. I sensed he had taken on this job of teaching a woman to fly as just another challenging adventure—a bit less life-threatening and nerve-wracking than winter flying out of Juneau, Alaska, his last home base. He was a great instructor. I was to be eternally grateful for his innate patience, and savvy and quiet confidence-building demeanor combined with a "practice until you get it right" insistence that was to stand me in good stead in my future flying career.[4]

Ginny was an independent thinker who did not feel constrained by societal pressures regarding women's roles, so learning to fly did not seem unusual to her. As she tells it, she always just did what she wanted to do in life and never found being a woman to be an obstacle. She also was fortunate to have a family that gave her the freedom to be herself.

Amelia Earhart was a person I very much admired. But we didn't think in terms of gender. We admired some of the things that men did, too. But I guess I had decided that most women didn't live very interesting lives. That most women's professions weren't very interesting: schoolteachers, nurses, or secretaries. I just had a lot of things that I wanted to do. It just never occurred to me to think that I would not be able to do them because I was a woman, neither did I ever feel discriminated against particularly. I guess there were things that you did that you always had to do a better job, to prove that you could do it. You somehow had to prove yourself. When I was young, I was always welcome in the neighborhood gangs to do what the boys were doing, so I guess it didn't occur to me that there were differences. I realize now that there were sort of subtle rules. Don't suddenly be female on 'em, you know, and try and want special consideration. As I grew into high school I found it could be pretty neat. You could be a woman and go on dates and have fun as a woman, but on Saturday you could go and do something with the boys where they wouldn't always take other girls because they'd want special consideration. I think that's what's good about today. I don't think that women ask for that.

Ginny recalls her first solo during her early flight training:

My first time taking the controls of a plane by myself was in a two-seater, sixty-five-horsepower Taylorcraft on floats on Lake Union in the heart of Seattle. I was twenty-three years old. My instructor sitting beside me had made the takeoff run and took the small plane up to two thousand feet, heading out over Puget Sound. Then he turned to me and said, "Okay, it's yours. Easy does it! Move the rudder and the stick gently to get the feel of what they do. Gently." I was half scared and half elated. I mean, I'd had my first eight hours of dual instruction that was required, and besides you have check rides all the time, but this was different. You soloed after eight hours or you flunked out of the CPT program. I put my feet on the rudder and my hand on the "stick." The plane was no longer an object but started to be an extension of myself, responding to my slightest movement of its controls. The first rush of exhilaration was soon replaced by the concentration of being completely absorbed in the mastering of a new dimension—the up and down, the left and right of flight. I thought all that experience I'd had as a kid flying our homemade airplane in our backyard meant I knew what the stick and rudder controls did and how to handle a plane. Instead, it was like trying to balance a ball on a two-by-four.

Perhaps the most important, but almost the most ephemeral, moment in a pilot's life, no matter how long her or his flying career, comes when the instructor climbs out of the cockpit of the aircraft and says, "Okay, I'm getting out. Take 'er up. Practice a few stalls, then shoot a couple of landings and takeoffs. And don't forget to look out for other traffic. Have a good time!" I will wager that even the most self-assured and cocky, who felt the last couple of hours of their instruction were redundant, experience similar feelings in the pit of their stomach. That no matter how strong the anticipation of this moment, when they taxi out for their first solo flight, never is another person so conspicuous in his or her absence than your instructor.[5]

You didn't fly that far away, like to Mount Rainier. No, you practiced maneuvers. You practiced landings and takeoffs. I had my first one hundred hours on floats before I ever got in a plane with wheels. I always looked for a big lake to land on. I had an awful time trying to get a plane down on a little airport. In a plane on wheels, if you can get it on the ground, you have it made, even if the wind's blowing, or whatever, or your engines quit, or anything else. With a floatplane, it's different. Your big problems are when you get on the water. If a storm's come up and there's waves, it's very easy to get your wing up a little bit when you're downwind and get flipped over by the wind. When you're in a land plane you can push it, or put the brakes on and get out of it. When you're in a seaplane you have to get it docked, and you have those wings out, and you have trees and docks. It's like you've got a boat to take care of. So, it's entirely different. On the other hand, if you're anywhere near the water, you'll make it. In a wheeled plane, you better be within the bounds of the runway and the airport.

First thing, my instructor took me up and went through acrobatics. I didn't upchuck 'til I got out of the airplane. Ran over to the bushes. I think my instructor brought us in prematurely because he noticed the pallor of my face and tight-lipped, tense reaction to anything other than mild banks and straight and level flight. And I thought, "Oh God, if I have to do this all the time." I figured that while I might master these maneuvers, my stomach would flunk me. Having been rather contemptuous of others who got car- or airsick, I was as embarrassed by my own weakness as I was discouraged about my chances for any future as a pilot. But after a short time on the ground, my airsickness symptoms disappeared, leaving only the memory of exhilarating moments of taking off, landing, and just of flight itself. Any tendency toward airsickness went away after a couple more sessions.[6]

They teach you to do spins and stalls and Immelmanns. An Immelmann is a looping-type turn where the aircraft is upside down at the top of the maneuver and then you turn right side up as you flatten out at a higher altitude. It isn't anything that's very exciting as an acrobatic maneuver. Not like what we did when we got in the air force. Eventually, I began to look forward to doing these out-of-the-ordinary flight maneuvers, especially spins. Doing a spin called for climbing several thousand feet, pulling the nose of the plane up into such a steep angle that the plane stalled, interrupting the normal airflow over the contour of the wing which allows aircraft to literally float. Just at the point of stall, one kicked hard on the rudder, causing the aircraft to become just a tumbling object subject only to the laws of gravity rather than the physics of flight. Recovery back to flight was accomplished by a sudden thrust forward on the stick to break the fall into a controlled dive and recovery back to normal flying altitude.[7] I wondered, "Now, why do they do that?" I mean, what use is there for knowing how to spin? They wanted you to know how to get out of a spin or a stall in case it accidentally happened to you. Or more importantly, they wanted to teach you how to not get into a spin in the first place or to use the stalling and falling technique for controlled emergency landing when you're close to the ground. I have never really been convinced why practicing this maneuver was an integral part of flight instruction any more than practicing parachute jumping would be. But I enjoyed doing it.

The only practical use I ever found for learning to do spins was in getting even with a boyfriend who had come by the hangar to give me a ride home. He had expressed disapproval of my learning to fly, and while he was most anxious to marry me, had expressed uneasiness with ever going up in an airplane with a woman pilot. I had recently climbed Mount Rainier with him, and at his insistence descended over a route that called for more expertise than I was comfortable in doing.[8] I knew he would be on the dock watching my yellow seaplane as I circled up to three thousand feet, nosed it up steeply, then kicked it into a spin. This time I held it for six gyrations before executing a recovery. When I taxied up to the wharf, he was the one who was green. He said, "Don't ever, ever do that again. Now I know that I would never want to ride in an airplane you were flying." "That's how I feel about mountain climbing with you!" I replied.[9]

You would have a check ride about every ten hours, and at thirty-five hours, as long as you passed everything, you got your license. And usually the guy that owned the flying service was your private instructor, and saw that you passed, because he wouldn't have got his money if you had flunked.

In February 1943, Ginny entered the Women's Auxiliary Ferrying Squadron (WAFS) of the United States Army as a civilian pilot. The WAFS was established in September 1942 to assist the Ferry Division of the Army Air Force's Air Transport Command (ATC) with delivering airplanes from factories to where they were needed for pilot training or overseas combat.[10] The use of women pilots was the brainchild of Jacqueline Cochran, a successful racing pilot.[11] In 1942, Nancy Love, another well-known female pilot, was hired to oversee the Women's Squadron. At the time, Cochran was in England with the first twenty-five women hired; they were training with the British Air Transport Auxiliary, which had already been using women pilots. The WAFS women served as civil service employees with a monthly wage of $250, plus per diem. This was six hundred dollars less than the civilian men in the division made.[12]

Women were eager to serve their country during wartime, so they came from all across the United States to serve in the WAFS. Entry requirements included being between the ages of twenty-one and thirty-five, having a high school education and letters of recommendation, having a two-hundred-horsepower rating, taking a test flight, and passing the air force's physical.[13] Initially, women were required to have a minimum of five hundred hours of flight time, but this was changed because they were not able to find enough eligible women.[14] The women who were accepted into the WAFS were issued standard gray uniforms of slacks, shirt, jacket, cap, and leather flying jacket adorned with the Ferry Division patch and wings of a civilian pilot.[15]

Ginny already had an instructor's rating when she was accepted into the WAFS' Class 43-W4, the fourth group of 1943. She was sent for her military flight training to Houston, Texas, and then on to Avenger Field in Sweetwater, Texas, which had been commandeered specifically for the WAFS. As Ginny says, "I had to go learn to fly all over again, this time the military way." She explains the path that led her to the WAFS:

After CPT you got your private license, and then what do you do with that? I figured I needed to get my commercial license so I could get paid for piloting a plane. This seemed the only way I'd be able to keep flying. You needed a minimum of two hundred logged hours of flying to even apply for a commercial license, and renting an aircraft to do this was beyond my means. I still had college to finish. So, while I was going to school and on the ski patrol on the weekends, I was also working part-time at Kurtzer Flying Service on Lake Union—a floatplane service in Seattle—just to earn money to buy flying time to build up time to get a commercial license. They were a small company that had had the contract for my CPT training. You had to work an awful lot of hours for one hour of flying time. It came out to a salary equivalent of four hours of grand labor for one hour of flight time. I did everything from record keeping in the office, to sweeping out the hangar, to gassing and washing planes and windshields, to helping with the launching and docking of rental planes, to hand propping the engines to get them started for customers. Back then you didn't have self-starters, so you had to start a plane by spinning the propeller. Going out to spin the propeller for the pilot was called propping. For the floatplanes, you stood on a pontoon behind the propeller to yank it. But earning two dollars an hour to pay for renting an airplane that cost five dollars an hour meant it was going to take forever to get my two hundred hours of required flight time. With interruptions to work at summer camps in the Sierra Nevada Mountains leading horseback trips and weekends in the winter being on the Mount Baker ski patrol, I managed to build up ninety hours of flying time.

Then came December 7, 1941, and the Japanese bombing of Pearl Harbor. It had been the first big snow of the season. A bunch of us on the ski patrol at Mount Baker had just started up the mountain. We were just up about one thousand feet when we heard somebody call up and say, "Hey, the Japs have just bombed Pearl Harbor." I remember standing there, and Otto Trott,[16] the guy that I'd been going with, who was a German, an excellent skier, and a medical doctor, said, "Let's go up Shuksan Arm and down the other side. This may be the last time we ever ski together."[17] He was interned shortly after that. Just for being German. He ended up in the American Army after two years of being incarcerated.[18]

They stopped all civilian flying within two hundred miles of the Pacific coast. Because the Japs came out of nowhere and bombed Pearl Harbor and they also bombed Dutch Harbor in the Aleutian Islands in Alaska. The United States thought, "Oh my, when are they going to come to the Pacific coast?" So the War Department issued an order that any aircraft that was not a scheduled, identified airliner was to be shot down.

They said all private planes have to be flown away from the coast. They had forty-eight hours to get them inland two hundred miles. Most of them didn't have radios and they didn't know where the Japs would strike next, so they didn't want a lot of these puddle jumpers flying around with no radio contact. But you had to get away or else any planes that were left within two hundred miles of the coast would be grounded for the remainder of the war. The whole flying service I was working for moved east of the mountains. Kurtzer's picked Walla Walla, Washington, as their new base of operation. A lot of them didn't even have enough time to take the floats off the planes and put wheels on them for inland use. They just flew them over and landed them in plowed fields to get them out of the water, otherwise they'd be grounded for the rest of the war.

So that meant I couldn't work for the flying service in Seattle anymore while I was finishing school. I accepted a job at Mount Baker ski lodge as a permanent duty ski patrolman and truck driver to haul supplies from Bellingham twice a week, as much of their manpower was drafted or volunteered for military duty.

I still was owed fourteen hours of flying time that I'd earned by working that I hadn't used, so I went over to Kurtzer's in Walla Walla the next fall to use up those hours. I had never flown a wheeled plane. I'd always been on floats. So I got checked out on that there.

While I was over there in Walla Walla, I heard they were starting another program. It was called the War Training Program to train flight instructors. They took the people who had been in the civilian pilot training program if you had eighty hours, which I had built up working doing odd jobs. It was for people who already had a private license who wanted to upgrade to a commercial license and a flight instructor rating. The idea was to get a lot of flight instructors to train people to fly and to get more pilots for the Army Air Corps.[19] I was attracted to the program as a way to earn my instructor's rating.

It never was really said in black and white whether the trainees could be men or women. They'd farmed them out to little flying services, private outfits, out in the middle of the state of Washington, out in the wheat fields. I applied to one, and I said, "Do you take women?" And he said, "Nobody said I couldn't." I think they wanted the students, because they got paid per student by the government. So I applied and got in. There were five other women who had been accepted. The rest were mostly middle-aged men too old to go into the air corps but who needed a commercial license with an instructor's rating to train cadets. It was based in Lind, Washington, a small town of about six hundred people east of the mountains in southcentral Washington. Three months later I had my instructor's rating, my commercial license, and 160 hours of flying time.

Our regime was several hours in the air practicing the same maneuvers we had learned for our private license, except this time we flew from the right-hand side of the dual-controlled plane with our instructors as "students." There were also many hours of ground school, although it was more advanced than we had for our private tickets. I recall we received a small stipend or per diem for board and room. At the beginning of the program, we were assigned to private homes for rooms, and board was at the town's only eatery—a greasy spoon–type diner. In the interests of our pocketbooks and our digestion, me and three other women elected to rent a two-bedroom accommodation with a kitchen at the only motel in town. Besides, we needed the camaraderie of each other to lighten the otherwise rather grim isolated existence.

My instructor was an intense, earnest young man who displayed an apprehension about women pilots, especially about me. Our planes were two-place Porterfields, which had a reputation for a tendency to flat spin and to have other unreliable attributes. I wonder if this may have been perpetuated to inflate male courage and egos. The chemistry between me and my instructor did not improve. One of my piloting weaknesses was simulated "dead stick" landings. Your instructor would suddenly yank the throttle all the way back, which would reduce the engine speed and windmill the propeller. He'd say, "Okay, where are you going to put it?" This usually occurred when all your attention was on another maneuver. With the propeller barely windmilling, you had to immediately push the nose down to keep flying speed up before the plane stalled. Then you had to pick a place you could possibly land. Of course, you were supposed to always fly with a possible landing place below you, in case this might happen. We had the same training in our CPT course, but then I was flying floatplanes. One was rarely out of glide distance to a lake or Puget Sound. But you had to deal with landing in rough seas, strong winds, or shores with steep cliffs, which could still make for an exciting situation. In this case, with a whole landscape below me of wheat fields, avoiding fences was the only obstacle to a forced landing. But it was like trying to land on a baseball field. My planned maneuver to glide just over a fence usually put me fifty feet short. In disgust, my instructor would slam the throttle forward so we could pick up speed to gain altitude. As we neared the date when an inspector from the Civil Aviation Authority would give us all our final check ride for that coveted commercial license and instructor rating, confidence in my ability, especially in forced landing maneuvers, was rapidly waning.

The day for my check ride arrived in early January. It was clear, calm, and cold with snow deep on the fields, except for the cleared airport runway. The inspector, a tall, lean middle-aged man with a strictly business countenance, climbed into the plane beside me. With no words of encouragement from my instructor, I taxied out for takeoff. In my mind, the future of my flying career was in question. My inner automatic pilot took over to perform the similar stalls, spins, and lazy eights around pylons that I had been practicing for 160 hours. Then he called out, "Dead engine. Take her down for an emergency landing." Automatically, I pushed the stick forward to keep from stalling, felt the plane increase buoyancy as I put it in a glide to keep up my flying speed. I chose a snow-covered field then planned a flight pattern for the final approach that would just use up my altitude. My heart was pounding the closer and closer we glided towards that snow-clad field on a final approach. We had just passed over the fence when he shoved the throttle forward and we zoomed over the field and started climbing. "Good job. Now take me back to the field and do three short field landings." I had just touched down within the proper bounds for the first one and began to push the throttle forward for another go around, when he said, "That's okay. You've done very well. You don't need to do it again." Perhaps the cold was getting to him. He would never know that it was just luck rather than my skill. If I had done it again and not done it right, he could have flunked me.

Only once in my twenty years of commercial and private flying did I actually have to do a real "dead stick" landing. I was flying back to Portland, Oregon, from having delivered two passengers to Seattle in a four-passenger Fairchild, which I had never flown before. The tank had plenty of gas for a round trip, but on the return, at four thousand feet over heavily timbered mountains, my engine coughed twice then stopped. Dead silence, not the idling of a simulated "dead stick" maneuver. I checked my tank gauge—still half full. The only possible safe landing field was a cow pasture just beyond the Columbia River straight ahead. I had no idea what the glide angle would be for this aircraft. I'd only just made a power landing at a big airport near Seattle. There was no real panic. It was more of a, "Well, I wonder how this will turn out?" There was just the silence. I thought to myself, "Hey, this must be like being in a glider. But updrafts won't help me here!"

I kept my flying speed just above stalling to stretch my glide. Safety lay in that lone field just across the Columbia River. I passed over it with just enough altitude to make a standard flight pattern around the field, dissipating my remaining height. It looked rain soaked, but at least it wasn't trees. The cows in it were off to one side. I was about fifty or one hundred feet above the ground lined up on a final approach for a landing that I was pretty sure would clear the fence at the end, when suddenly the engine coughed, sputtered a couple of times, and burst into a roar. The windmilling propeller whirled into full revolution. For the first time since the engine had died, sheer terror invaded my being. Now I was in a dilemma! I had to make a decision. If the engine kept going, I could get back to my home field at Troutdale that was a half hour away. If the engine quit again, I'd be over the Colombia River or the city of Portland, neither of which would make for a good landing place. Instinct prevailed. Or my past training kicked in. I'm not sure which. But faster than today's computers could calculate, I cut the switch and dropped the plane, keeping the tail low, into the mud below me. The plane only rolled a few yards before I came to a sudden stop without the nose going up and with the tail staying down despite the soft field. This was much to the amazement of two nearby cows!

All I got from my boss at the company I was flying for was a reprimand for not having topped off the gas tank in Seattle. No one had told me when I was assigned this plane for the first time that it was prone to vapor lock in the fuel line when the gas tank got below half full. The long glide of the forced landing had probably cooled the fuel line enough to clean out the vapor lock, which is why the engine sputtered and started again. But I did not know this at the time. I received not even a word of commendation from my male fellow pilots either for not damaging the plane or myself! But I knew that I had justified that earlier flight examiner's faith in me.[20]

After finishing the training program in Lind, Washington, we were supposed to be flight instructors, but I wasn't sure that's what I wanted to do. After being a student pilot in a rigid prescribed flight curriculum, my enthusiasm for a flying career as an instructor with students as inept as I sometimes saw myself began to fade. I wasn't so sure about riding around hour after hour teaching others to do the same thing, having to balance wanting to take the controls for your own safety against letting a student learn from their mistakes as long as they weren't life-threatening. I thought if everybody had done the dumb things I had done, then I didn't want to be an instructor.

They militarized the guys that came out of the program. They were automatically drafted to be flight instructors at army bases. But no one knew what to do with the women who went through the same program. They had no way to make you do anything as a woman. They couldn't draft you into the military like they'd done with the men. By then they'd started the WAFS program, but you had to have two hundred hours to get into that.

When I was in Lind, a friend of mine, BJ [Barbara Jane] Erickson, wrote me from back east, where she'd joined this first WAFS group of twenty-five women, to tell me that the Army Air Corps had just hired a woman named Nancy Love to be in charge of recruiting women pilots. I first met BJ when she was a new instructor hired at Kurtzer's Flying Service when I was a CPT fledgling being trained there. She was a former CPT student who had just passed her commercial/flight instructor's examinations. She was a vivacious, attractive, self-assured but not cocky young woman in her early twenties. She then followed Kurtzer's when they moved to Walla Walla to continue her flight instructing. This allowed her to earn the six hundred hours required to become part of that first group of WAFS. She was on active duty delivering training planes to military cadet bases for the Second Ferrying Division of the Air Transport Command at Newcastle Army Air Base in Delaware. Of the eighty-three women who had met the age, height, and flying experience qualifications for the WAFS, twenty-five were selected to be the first to fly military aircraft, be it only primary training planes within the borders of the United States. Pilots were needed to fly planes coming off assembly lines, and there were people who felt these shouldn't be men trained for combat. But this first selection had just about drained all the women with over five hundred hours on two hundred horsepower who could pass the rigid air forces' flying officer's physical and wanted to leave hearth and home responsibilities for the demanding schedule of military life, especially the air forces.[21] In her letter, BJ told me to build up my flying time and to get a commercial rating so that I could be eligible. Well, I hadn't had one hundred hours yet and I was still trying to build up my flying time by working, and it cost quite a bit. Only two dollars an hour then, it was still a lot. The dollar was a dollar in those days. She said, "Get your flying time in as fast as you can, because I think this outfit is going to go a different direction."

They decided that with those first twenty-five gals, that most of them had been from wealthy families that had bought them an airplane, and after they soloed all they did was fly around and sightsee or take friends for hops. We called them "country club flyers." They had little experience in flying a variety of planes. They were no good at going to another type of plane different from the one they owned. They'd been accepted just on the number of flight hours. They had no check rides to learn what they might be doing wrong and to improve their skills. Love's recruiting had just about scraped the bottom of the barrel of qualified women pilots who could meet the WAFS requirement and could accept the regimented, spartan, and demanding routine of military life.[22] The CPT people were taught to do a lot more. It was a very rigid regime of check rides and frequent tests that we had to pass to stay in the program. If you failed, it was called being "washed out." We were taught to be comfortable moving from one type of plane to another. That a plane's a plane. If you fly one, you can fly any of them. That you get to know the cockpit, get the feel of it.

Then they decided the women in the WAFS program would do exactly the same course as the male cadets. It would be a five-month program with frequent test rides. This program eventually became the WASPs.[23]

Before I got frozen in a job where I would have to be a flight instructor for the rest of the war, I went up to Spokane, Washington, with my friend Eileen Roach and took my physical and turned in my application for the WASPs. Because of the 160 hours I had and those two ratings, I was able to get into the program. All of this interrupted my academic career at the University of Washington. I was just a few credits short of getting a BA. I said to heck with a degree and went off to ferry combat planes.

It was only a few months after Pearl Harbor when I went into the WASPs. After Pearl Harbor, everything sped up real fast. I would say I was about twenty-five at the time. I know from then on it seemed like I was in an airplane all the time.

After getting accepted into the WASPs, we went down to Texas and I spent five months learning to fly all over again—"the air force way." You went right through the cadet program as if you had never flown before in your life. I was flying A-26s, Bamboo Bombers, you know, twin-engine planes. You stayed on the base and went through exactly the same flight-training program as the guys did except for combat training. We had some good instructors, but we also had some lulus of instructors that hadn't had as many hours of flying as I had. Any guy that was any good as a pilot, they put him in the air forces instead of being an instructor. Some girls got killed because of these guys who weren't good instructors.

Ginny describes few details of day-to-day life during the months she spent training in Texas from February to August 1943. In passing, she mentions daily calisthenics, long waits for an available airplane and instructor, and carrying the heavy parachutes to and from the planes. However, there is one aspect that stands out in her memory. She explained that every day as they left the mess hall the women had to open their mouths and have a salt tablet laid on their tongue,

Carrying her parachute, Ginny boards a military plane to fly to her assigned destination, circa 1943. Courtesy of Ginny Wood.

"like a communion wafer." This was the military's attempt to ward off dehydration in the dry desert environment of Texas. Ginny laughs when she says she would spit out her tablet as soon as she got out the door because she couldn't stand the saltiness.

Upon graduation from the WASP training program in Sweetwater, Texas, Ginny was assigned to the Sixth Ferrying Division in Long Beach, California. BJ Erickson was her squadron leader. Other women were stationed with the Second Ferrying Division at Newcastle Army Air Force Base in Wilmington, Delaware; the Third Ferrying Division at Romulus Air Base in Romulus, Michigan; and the Fifth Ferrying Division at Love Field in Dallas, Texas.[24] The women's squadron was one of many on base, the others being all male. According to Ginny, the women were assigned to fly all types of airplanes as they came from the factories, just like the men were, and they flew everything given to them. Apparently, this had not been the Ferry Division's original plan: "Due to the scarcity of seasoned pilots, these women ferried basic and advanced trainers from the first, even though this was against the Ferry Division policy, which restricted the WAFS to primary-type aircraft."[25] Ginny recalls that the only time she did not take an assignment was during the transition to getting to fly the bigger planes. She was required to remain on base while completing this extra training.

By October 1943, there were 275 women pilots in the Ferry Division.[26] Some military bases were more accepting of the women than others, but the difficulties that the skeptics had originally predicted regarding male-female relations proved to be relatively rare occurrences.[27] The women proved to be an asset.

However, conflict and politics played out behind the scenes. Jackie Cochran wanted the women to do more than ferry airplanes and to be certified with a military rank. And she did not like that another woman, Nancy Love, was in charge of the WAFS. Cochran pressured the top ranks of the military and Congress. To appease her, they created the Women's Flying Training Detachment (WFTD) under her command as a separate program to train additional women pilots.[28] In August 1943, the WFTD and the WAFS merged to become Women Airforce Service Pilots (WASP).[29] In early 1944, the women finally were issued formal Santiago blue uniforms, which gave them a more professional, organized, and militarized appearance than the previously used oversized gray coveralls jokingly referred to as "zoot suits." However, Ginny tells of being in a women's restroom during a fueling stop in Alabama and another woman giving her money because in her WASP uniform she was mistaken for a restroom attendant.

During her tenure in the WASP, Ginny crossed paths with both Cochran and Love and had the following to say about them:

Jacqueline Cochran was perhaps the most well-known aviatrix since the death of Amelia Earhart (if not, she intended to be), setting speed and altitude records one after another. Her flying was supported by her husband, Floyd Odlum, a wealthy financier who had connections in high places in the Roosevelt regime. Jackie herself had had to fight her way up from poverty and being an orphan to afford her first flying lesson. If she appeared to be sometimes ruthlessly aggressive, she had to be to accomplish her goals. Odlum, who met her when she was a rising success in her beauty products business, admired her drive and guts. Theirs was a long and devoted marriage.[30]

I give Jacqueline Cochran credit. She had to fight all the way up from the time she was born. She hadn't even finished high school, I don't think. But she married a very wealthy guy, so she had plenty of money. Before the war, she already had a private airplane that he'd bought her. And she was in races. You have to give her credit and admire her for getting where she was. But I don't admire her as a person or the methods that she used. She told me personally once that she had something on Hap Arnold, who was head of the Army Air Forces. She told him, if she wasn't made a full colonel and the WASPs had equal standing with the WACs [Women's Army Corps] and the WAVs [Women in the Navy] and the other, she could fix him. Or another time she said to me, "If your squadron leader, BJ Erickson, doesn't shape up, you guys are going to be in trouble. If you stick with me, I'll make sure you have a good job after the war."

Nancy Love was the first one that was directly in charge of the WASPs. Two more opposite individuals in background, demeanor, and appearances could hardly be imagined between her and Cochran. Nancy Harkness Love, still in her twenties, came from a privileged family that furnished her a private school education. She was trim and strikingly attractive with prematurely graying hair; intelligent but unassuming, but with a streak of quiet determination and independence. She earned her private pilot's license when she was sixteen, and while at Vassar College as an undergraduate passed the commercial pilot's examinations. She left college to become an aircraft saleswoman when she met and married Bob Love, also from a prominent family. He was a graduate of Princeton and had an Air Forces Reserve Commission. Soon they were operating their own flying service.[31]

Jackie Cochran was a very aggressive person; she demanded attention. You could see this when she was coming into base with her plane. She got a command car to come and meet her. A lot of people didn't like her for that. In contrast, Nancy Love was just as common as the rest of us and was a neat person. She didn't put on airs. She never asked for any special attention or favors. You didn't even know she had landed until she trudged in with her parachute over her shoulder and closed her flight plan. Then she would come in and sit down with us.

Cochran had no use for Nancy Love. Love was supposedly head of the WASPs and Cochran was head of the whole program. Cochran thought using women pilots was her idea so was not happy when Hap Arnold started the

WASPs and put Nancy Love in charge. She was very resentful of Nancy's husband, thinking he'd used his position as colonel to get Love her command. But he wasn't pulling any strings. Nancy was just an ordinary person who was a very excellent pilot. She earned and deserved her position.

But for the inauguration of the CPT program, I might have been working in aircraft factories building airplanes instead of flying them. And if it hadn't been for Jackie Cochran's brassy persistence that she be put in charge of a cadet training program that would produce a large pool of women pilots, even with a commercial license and instructor's rating and my 160 hours of logged flying time, I might have been doomed to spend the war riding behind or beside air cadets, training them to fly the military aircraft I would never be allowed to fly. Endeavoring to help them learn by all the same mistakes I had made without letting those mistakes kill both of us.[32]

Ginny flew airplanes from factories to where they were shipped by boat to Europe for combat duty, to training facilities in the Midwest, and she left them in Great Falls, Montana, for male pilots to fly to Alaska as part of the Lend-Lease program, in which the United States military supplied fighter planes to the Russian army for battling Hitler on the eastern front. American pilots delivered the planes to the US Army's Ladd Field in Fairbanks while Russian pilots arrived to fly them back to Russia. Ginny talks about how she flew across country, the routes taken, and stopping at military bases along the way to refuel and rest, but she never had a problem with a plane, crashed, or found herself in an emergency situation.

I was lucky to have been assigned to the Ferry Command Base in Long Beach, California, to the Sixth Ferrying Group, where I spent two years ferrying all the airplanes that were made around there. There were more varieties of planes built around there than anyplace else: North American, Douglas, Vultee. Boeing's were made in Seattle. The WASPs were just one squadron on the base. We did the same things as the guys. They wanted to get as many fellows overseas to combat as possible. If they had to stay home and ferry airplanes, they weren't out fighting the war, so they had us women do it. It worked out very well. It was really neat.

We started out ferrying training planes because that was the baby carriage of the air for the women. Then they got short of pilots for the next step of a plane—twin-engine and instrument rating—so they'd take a few women and put them through what they called transition, a training program, and find out that the women could fly any plane, without any problems. They said, "Well, I'll be darned, they can do it as well as men; there's no difference." That plane became like the family car of the air and the boys went off to fly something bigger. Finally, after you had enough experience, you were sent down to Brownsville, Texas,

Ginny as a WASP pilot, 1943. Courtesy of Ginny Wood.

into pursuit flight school. This was to learn instrument-rating flying of fighter planes. It kept on like that, and by the end of the war there wasn't anything that was made that the women didn't fly.

You just took a plane to where you were told it was supposed to go. And most of the fighter planes went to Newark, New Jersey, where they put them on boats and sent them over to Europe. Some of them went to San Francisco to the Asian war. Fortunately, most of our planes were fighter planes and their limit was about three and a half or four hours before they needed refueling. You weren't up in the air that long. This gave you a chance to use the restroom. Although I have some hilarious stories about gals that had to and tried using the relief tube, they called it. With varying success. After we delivered a plane, we might pick up another plane to ferry to another base, or we'd fly back to our home base either on a commercial flight or with the Military Air Transport Service (MATS), depending on where there was space for us. MATS were regular large airplanes, but they were used to transport only military personnel around. On a commercial flight, we could bump anybody except Mrs. Roosevelt for a seat.

They had no way of militarizing women except through the WACs or WAVs, which would have put us in a chain of command with people who didn't fly,[33] so they wanted us directly in the air forces. They didn't know what to do with the women, so we were just put in as an unclassified unit. We had no rank. You were just a name on a card who was qualified to fly lots of different airplanes. What planes you were checked out to fly in were listed on that card. When a plane came up to be delivered, they just took the card with the right qualifications that was on top of the pile. When you delivered the plane, your card went to the back of the stack, and it moved up as you kept delivering planes. They didn't know when they pulled the card if you were male or female. They didn't even look at what sex the pilot was. There was no distinction made. Men and women had equal assignments.

They found out that it made no difference if they used male or female pilots. They couldn't find any difference in our flight skills. And they discovered that actually women took less time off for health reasons than they had expected. This really threw the men, because they thought that one week out of the month we shouldn't or couldn't be flying. The flight surgeon would come down and he'd say, "Now ladies, whenever you don't feel like flying, when it comes to that time of the month, I'll put you on sick call." This idea of women not being any good one week out of the month was a lot of hooey. The thing was, nobody could tell when that was. And none of us ever told! Because we knew it didn't make any difference. The doctor said: "You gals never come up to get on sick call. You know, if you don't feel like flying, you should just come up. You know, guys do it all the time." For a lot of guys that was a neat way to get off flight duty if they wanted to loaf for a while, just have a cold or something. We were damned if we were gonna be put on sick call! We weren't about to let them have an excuse to throw us out of the WASP. But you would get kicked out if you were pregnant.

They also found out our accident rate was lower. It was not because we were better pilots. I think it was because women were more inclined not to fool around and do something dumb. For instance, all the fighter planes had on the throttle a wire that kept it from being pushed past the point where there was a supercharger that gave the engine an extra boost. It was only good for about three minutes. It was meant to only be used in combat, if somebody was on your tail. You give it a kick in the pants if that's the only chance you have of getting out of a tight spot in combat. We didn't get in those tight positions so we didn't need the boost. I hardly knew any male ferry pilot that hadn't pushed the throttle past this point to see what it felt like. Girls never did. They were always thinking that their boyfriend or their brother or maybe even their father would be flying that plane in combat. Why should I deliver a plane to some guy that may save his life and I've already ruined the engine? The women were probably less aggressive and more careful, because we thought we were on the spot and wanted to have a good record.

By the end of the war, about a thousand women were trained as ferry pilots. Women ferried about thirty to forty percent of all the fighter planes in the United States, because they fitted the cockpits better. To be a fighter pilot a guy had to be under six feet, one inch tall. Mostly the girls were smaller. The fighter planes were built for a guy to be in combat for less than an hour. Ferrying them, we'd be in the planes much longer. They found that since women weren't as cramped in the cockpit we didn't get as tired. Also we were trained to be able to go from one type of plane to another. Guys that were in combat were very good at one plane and knew it just like the inside of their pocket. They were meant to go up for a short time and have people shoot at them. We weren't trained for that. The men weren't used to adapting to planes of different sizes and with varied horsepower, like we were. One time I flew ten different planes before I got back in one that was the same as one I'd been in before.

I did get checked out in a B-17, and I delivered two of them during the whole war. Later, they had the women doing other things, towing targets, flying military personnel around in Military Air Transport planes. I had MATS training with a guy who'd been a commercial pilot and had been drafted into the military but was too old to be a fighter pilot. He was a good trainer. He treated me like his daughter. He had no ego. He just wanted you to get the best training you could have. They also had two girls stationed at the experimental stations for experimental jets.[34] They just wanted to find out what women could do if they had to scrape the bottom of the barrel if the war had lasted longer. Just to see what the potential was. Nobody knew how long the war would last.

We didn't get paid very much in the WASP. If you were a guy ferrying planes and you were a second lieutenant you got 250 dollars a month. The women got

150 dollars. The girls got six dollars per day per diem. The men got seven dollars. When we were off delivering planes and had to spend the night along the way, if you stayed on base, you could stay for one dollar and fifty cents a night in the barracks. If you went to town, it would cost you five dollars to stay in a hotel. That's what most girls did. They'd never been away from home and they thought, boy, they wanted to live it up. They'd take a taxi, eat meals out, go to the bars, and spend all their money. I'd stay in the barracks and eat in the enlisted men's mess for fifty cents, which I could do, instead of going to the officer's club, which was more expensive and where you had to wear a dress. Nobody knew quite what we women were supposed to do, so we could go to either place. Not only did I save money by staying on post, but I could get up in the morning, get down to the airfield early to have the first ground crew start my plane, and I'd be at the next stop before those women who were in town got a taxi, came back to base, and waited for a ground crew to come and start their plane.

Ginny rattles off a list of military planes she flew during World War II like it's her daily shopping list:

There were three planes that were made during the war that were probably equal: the Mustang, the British Spitfire, and the German Messerschmit. As far as being a pilot's plane, I think the Mustang was probably by far the best. They weren't up for a long time—most of them were used in dogfights over England or the English Channel—and they didn't want the weight, so they trimmed them down as much as possible. Anything that was superfluous had been taken off. It was just pure poetry. Like having wings. These Mustangs, they just never let you down. They were fun to fly. What I used to like to do with these planes was to find some clouds—a lot of the nice cumulus clouds—and then play in them. You could fly right through them if you wanted, but there were places in the cloud formations where you could really maneuver around and pretend it was a canyon.

My favorite airplane would have been the P-51 [Mustang]. They just were a dream. Everything in the cockpit was logical. If your gear went up, your toggle switch went up. The first plane I soloed was a P-40, and the switches and levers were spread out all over the cockpit so you're trying to find what you need next. You were doing gears over here, and gas over there. And if you wanted to make this gear go up, this switch would go down. Anything that North American made was just beautiful; it was like playing an organ. You started in one place and went around the cockpit and did everything you needed to do in order to fly the plane.

We did lose thirty-eight women pilots all together during the war.[35] Most of them were not the women's fault. The P-39 and the P-61 were bad airplanes. We had a song for one: "The P-39 kills them all, kills them all. The long and the short and the tall. I've a notion, I'll never cross the ocean. The P-39 kills them all." But it was the easiest plane to bail out of. Like getting out of a car, you just pulled a latch and the door fell out and you just fell out, too. You didn't have to worry about climbing over the cockpit or hitting wires. Fortunately, I never did have to bail out of an airplane. But I sure had some that had some queer things happen with them. Like once, when I was flying a P-51 fighter plane I couldn't get the coolant shutters closed. I went back to the airfield; I wouldn't want to try to fly all the way to Newark that way. This plane was going overseas to Europe for combat so I wanted to be sure it was working properly. It turned out the problem was a hair curler blocking the shutter so it wouldn't close all the way. The curler had rolled down under there and gotten stuck. It wasn't my hair curler!

I know another funny story about a friend of mine who was ferrying a Bell P-61. We called them Bell Boobytraps. She was at one thousand feet and her engine quit. The plane started going this way and that way. There was a guy flying behind her who saw black smoke just pouring out. He was yelling at her, "Jump. Jump. Just get out of there!" She waited until the last minute. In fact, her parachute opened and there was one swing and she was on the ground. Well, it turns out that she waited that long because she had black underwear stashed in the ammunition compartment that she didn't want to burn up. We were wearing these mechanic suits that were the most unglamorous things you can imagine and she just wanted to feel sexy, so she'd gone out and bought black underwear at her last stop. When they finally got to her, they found her going through the wreckage seeing if she could find it.

You stuffed your unmentionables in the ammunition compartment because there wasn't any room in the cockpit. You couldn't take anything but what you were wearing and what you could sit on. As soon as you landed in Newark, where a lot of the planes were taken to be shipped to Europe, you hardly had put the plane down, were just writing in your little logbook, and there was a tractor coming out to get the plane. They were already hooked on the plane and you were running alongside trying to get the Dzus fastener on the compartment open so you could get your toothbrush, Kotex, or anything else out. They wanted to get the plane out on a ship right away, 'cause it wasn't doing anybody any good until it was in combat. And they had to "pickle" the planes before they put them on the boats. The planes were too big to put in the hold of the ship, so they carried them on deck. They put a preservative waterproofing material onto the planes to keep the saltwater from ruining them. We called it "pickling."

The WASP training program did not last long. By mid-1944, the need for fighter pilots in Europe was shrinking and trained male pilots were returning to the United States in need of jobs. The women who had previously been essential were now thought to be taking jobs away from the men. The WASP was officially deactivated on December 20, 1944, just over two years after women were first authorized to fly for the military. The women were sent home with a certificate of service, their pilot qualifications, a set of insignia, and their uniform.[36]

They disbanded us five months before the end of the war. It was a fight between Jackie Cochran and General Hap Arnold. It was all politics. The guys back in Congress decided, well, women, you know, they're kind of flighty, not good for one week out of the month anyway, and why are we spending money on salaries when guys are coming back from the war who need jobs. Well, that didn't mean that those guys knew how to fly the planes we did.

One day we were flying any type of military-made plane, and the next day we couldn't even get on the base. It just happened that fast. We were disbanded, because the military felt they had enough pilots. Well, really, they didn't. They had a lot of planes that needed moving. And the guys that came back from the war, they may have been pilots and they probably were good pilots, but they didn't know how to fly the variety of planes that needed moving. And they weren't very good flying all the way across country. In combat, they flew in squadrons, with a lead pilot, so they didn't know anything about doing their own navigation. So that was kind of sad. That was not the air force's fault. They didn't want this. It was Congress that decided. When they decided they were going to get rid of us, those of us in the Long Beach bunch offered to fly for a dollar a year since they still had planes that needed moving. They rejected our offer. Well, it didn't bother me, because I wanted to get back to skiing.

I remember the last flight I took. I think it was a P-51. I just remember that all those guys in my ground crew lined up and saluted me. They didn't have to do that. I didn't care about that military stuff. I knew some gals that just used their rank as pilots to get their way. But I never pulled rank on anybody. Supposedly, we had the rank of a second lieutenant, but we didn't wear any rank on our uniforms. We got paid as civilians and didn't get quite as much money as the male second lieutenants did. But I thought that was pretty neat what my ground crew did and I felt very good about that.

When I got out, I was given a chance to be a first lieutenant at a desk job. I turned it down. I wanted to keep flying. I was a pilot, for goodness sake! And I didn't want any more war stuff. I was by instinct a Quaker, I think. It just bothered me some. I guess I rationalized, well, you know, what's the difference between flying airplanes and making them? Just be grateful you got good eyesight so you get to fly. You have a privilege a lot of people don't.

In the twenty-seven months of service in the ferry division, WAFS/WASPs flew seventy-seven types of aircraft on 12,560 missions, covering 9,234,000 miles. They had flown more than sixty million miles, averaging thirty-three hours of flying time each month.[37] Ginny notes that despite their dedicated service during the war, the WAFS/WASPs did not qualify for the GI Bill like their male counterparts, so they were not able to take advantage of educational and other opportunities provided to male soldiers after the war. On November 23, 1977, President Carter signed legislation that finally certified WASP pilots as military personnel, which is what Jacqueline Cochran had wanted all along.[38] Ginny did not care about this newfound military status. Her years as a WASP had been long ago and she had gone on to do many other things. She had not cared about military rank during the war, so she certainly did not care about it thirty years later, especially when it provided her no benefits.

You wouldn't have known the difference that we weren't militarized during the war. It wasn't until retroactively that they gave us honorary military status.[39] I guess that means you can be buried in a military cemetery or something. It gave us a rank equivalent to what we did in the WASP. It doesn't make any difference. I'm sure I won't get invited to the next war. You didn't get any of the privileges—you know, free education and the GI Bill and all that. All those were outdated. All it did was recognize that we were serving as equal to the men who were military.

After the war, some of the women wanted to go home and have babies and some of them never touched an airplane again. They'd had plenty of it. They were women first and pilots incidentally. They wouldn't have given anything to trade their experiences, but that wasn't what they wanted to go on being. What it gave me was a profession. I could get a job flying and I could get more money flying than doing anything else. That's what I did, and I learned that that affected my education after I went back to college. I didn't have to take anything that I was taking because it was part of a curriculum that led to a career. I just took what interested me. That was good or bad, depending on your perspective. Flying just happened to be a trade for me.

Ginny has tried to describe the sensation of flying and why she loved it so much.

Rumbling down a runway with two to six thousand horsepowers responding to your hand on the throttle, you feel the thousands of pounds of aircraft is ready to leave the surly bonds of earth to be airborne. Your air speed and RPM indicators confirm what is actually an ineffable feeling in your gut as you pull back on the stick or the wheel and lift this lumbering hulk into the air. The airfoil, an engine, and very little physical exertion has transformed this immobile assemblage of metal and plastic into a world that only the birds have experienced. Does a duck or a goose experience this transformation? Or does the physical exertion involved in the transmigration transmit different signals to its pectoral muscles? It would take me little physical exertion to climb thousands of feet in a few minutes in an airplane, while it took me eighteen hours of exhausting energy to climb on foot from bare ground over the snow-covered slopes, up the steep pitches, and across the icy crags of the glaciers to reach the fourteen-thousand-foot summit of Mount Rainier.[40]

Ginny receives her Congressional Gold Medal from Alaska Senator Lisa Murkowski, April 2, 2010. Photo by Amy Johnson.

I think why I loved flying is because I began to see the earth from another perspective. That always stayed with me. When I was ferrying planes, the one thing you were supposed to do was to stay over flat lands so if you had an emergency, there were fields you could land in. But I didn't do this. I went exploring. I can remember flying P-51s and P-38s that had never been in the air before and taking them over the Sierras and over the red rock country in New Mexico. I was always looking down to find places that I'd want to go hiking when the war was over. I did go back later and find some of those very places I had looked down at.

In July 2009, the approximately three hundred surviving members of the original 1,074 women in the WASP were given the Congressional Gold Medal to honor their service.[41] In response Ginny said, "Why now? What I'd like to have had is the same thing the guys did at the time the war ended—the GI Bill with its free tuition."[42] A formal ceremony for all medal recipients was held on March 10, 2010, in Washington, DC, but Ginny and her WASP roommate Nancy Baker, also living in Fairbanks, were unable to attend. On April 2, 2010, Alaska Senator Lisa Murkowski personally delivered the award to Ginny. Despite their political differences, Ginny was very touched by the senator's visit. Ninety-year-old Nancy Baker received her medal at a public Veteran's Day event later that day.[43] When handed the bronze duplicate medal, Ginny commented with her typical wit, "Oh, it's heavy. It will make a good paperweight." Ginny concludes her reflection on her wartime experience as a WASP pilot by saying:

It's interesting to have lived through that part of military history. At that age, having spent a year batting around on a bicycle with all those different nationalities and then to see war. This is when the role of women changed, because all of a sudden they had the draft, which took all the men. So if you were a woman, there weren't many men around, unless they were unfit. Even people who were not too physically fit could get a wartime job. Women were driving trucks, taxis, making airplanes. I think women built more Boeing bombers than men did.

As I said, if I hadn't been flying airplanes, I probably would have been making them. I felt sorry for the enlisted men who were doing the ground crew for the planes we were flying. You didn't just get in and start them yourself. It was standard operation to be started by a big outside machine that was brought up to the plane. The outdoor crew plugged it in and started it. After they started it up, you called the tower for takeoff. Then you went just as fast as you could go to the starting line to get to takeoff. I used to look at those guys and here I'd be flying this P-51, P-38, B-17, and the only reason that I was sitting in the cockpit and he was outside doing it was because I had better eyesight.

I don't think I was any more important than a nurse. Or the people that were making the planes. Or the people that were in communications. It was just one of those things. I was the right age at the right time. Just had lucked out. I passed all my tests and had good eyesight. I wouldn't say I was a hot pilot. I was just a safe pilot.

Celia Hunter when she was a pilot for the Women Airforce Service Pilots, circa 1944. Courtesy of Ginny Wood.

5

A Lifelong Friendship: Meeting Celia Hunter

I think you make friendships with people that you do things with
or are thrown together with.

A fter the war, Celia Hunter became a key figure in Ginny Wood's life.
They became close friends, had many adventures, operated a business together, and eventually in later life even shared a house. Their
friendship had its ups and downs and they did not always agree on how things
happened when retelling their memories of past events, but after fifty years a
close bond had developed. Celia was a calming, levelheaded counterbalance to
Ginny's whirlwind.

After the war, I had a job ferrying old surplus airplanes. That was how I met
Celia Hunter. She was from Everett, Washington, which is fifty miles north of
Seattle. We'd both been in the WASP, but we hadn't been in the same class going
through training and we hadn't been at the same base. Celia thought she lucked
out because she was in the second ferrying group, which was in Delaware,
because she had never been East.[1] She could go to New York and see a play, or
do all these things that she had never done in the West. We just knew of each
other, because we were both from the Northwest and she knew BJ Erickson, who
was from Seattle and was my squadron commander and a personal friend. Once
in a while, I saw Celia when we'd be at the same place at the same time having
just delivered planes. She was good on the P-47 Thunderbolts. It was a bright,
big, everything plane. It was a pursuit plane. In fact, she delivered three or four
a day. You know, we'd just see each other in passing. Like I would meet her in
Newark, and we'd just say hi. She'd say, "Say hi to BJ for me." Because they
were friends. Every once in a while she'd show up in Long Beach, having just
delivered a plane there. After the war, I think I met her at a concert or something
and I knew she'd been in the WASPs.

Celia Hunter was born in 1919 in Arlington, Washington.[2] She grew up on a small farm and was raised as a Quaker. Her father also worked in the nearby logging industry. She graduated as salutatorian from Marysville High School in Everett, Washington, in 1936 and entered business college. She worked at the Weyerhaeuser Timber Company as a secretary for three years, then attended Linfield College until 1943, when she entered the WASP. After the war, she completed one semester at the University of Washington before being lured away by the excitement of a flying job. It was at this time that Celia and Ginny began to develop a friendship:

It wasn't until about three months after the WASPs were disbanded and we were wondering what we were going to do with the rest of our lives and missing what we'd been doing and trying to figure things out, when I got a call from BJ. She said, "Hey, they're looking for pilots to fly surplus airplanes that are kind of discarded, that have not been flown because they have been sitting on the ground for a year. There's an outfit in Portland, Oregon, that's reconditioning them and selling them privately.[3] And they're looking for pilots to go pick up these planes that are lying in fields all over the country and fly them into Portland, where they'd fix them up and sell them. Are you interested?" She had gotten married, and so wasn't looking for a job. The company was called Reconstruction Finance Corporation. It was partly a government thing where they were getting old army surplus airplanes that had been stacked up, and partly private where they were buying from the military to resell these old airplanes. It's not that the planes were decommissioned from active service, it's just that they'd been sitting around and not flown for a year, so were in questionable operating condition.

I said, "Yeah." BJ said, "See if you can find Celia Hunter. I think she's in Everett." So, I spent the day trying to find her name or her folks' name, and they weren't listed. We were supposed to be in Portland at eight the next morning for this job. And it was already late in the day. The last bus left, I think, at nine that night, which if we could catch it meant that we could still get down to Portland in time to be hired for the job. I almost quit trying. I said, "I don't know about finding her. I don't have time to keep doing this anymore. I've got to get my own stuff packed." But I finally got Celia on the phone. She said, "I'll be there." Celia drove up just about as the bus was about to leave.

We did that for five or six months. We were based out of Troutdale, Oregon, which is just outside of Portland. They had us pick up these old beat-up planes that were getting full of dust. Talk about old clunkers. We really had some lulus then. We didn't take these planes too seriously. We thought we were such hot pilots after flying P-51s and P-38s and Boeings, that these were just toys. We thought if we could fly all those big planes, what's the problem with these little puddle jumpers. They were kind of trainer planes. Stearmans, and Ryans, and

PT-19s. Those were the ones that they could fix up and sell. A PT-38 would be kind of expensive. It would cost too much just for the gasoline alone.

We thought, "Well, gee, in the WASP we put the first hours on these airplanes that were ever put on after they rolled out of the factory." They had things wrong with them and we survived. And these ones didn't have all that horsepower or other stuff that those fighter planes we'd flown had. These just seemed more like a kiddie car. Looking back on it now, I realize we could have gotten ourselves killed. We were pretty cocky after what we flew during the war. You didn't really think of it as being very daring. It was just a lot of fun! It was a good way to make a living. It was a job, and jobs, especially as a pilot, were hard to come by after the war.

You started these old planes up and the dust came up in your face. One time there were five of us that were flying Stearmans. I'd never even been in one before. The closest ones I had been in were PT-19s, which I'd had my training in. Anyway, here we were droning across the Midwest and we were playing follow the leader just out of sheer boredom. The gal that was flying out in front put her plane over on its back. Then the next person did the same thing. Then there was me, and I did the same thing. And all that dirt that had been accumulated in the plane fell into my eyes. You see, I didn't have my goggles down. I couldn't tell if I was up or down. Celia was flying behind me and she said I was going all over the place, up and down, side to side. I was going through all these gyrations. She was saying, "Hell, for Christ's sake, get that thing right side up."

We finally decided that the planes were in such bad shape that we had to fly with a buddy, so if your engine failed they'd know where you went down. Because we were both Hs—I was Hill and Celia was Hunter—alphabetically we got put together. We started out on a flight course together so we'd come back together. Then we'd be sent out together again. As soon as you got the planes back, then you went out for another one. So we kind of got thrown together. Then we got weathered in together places, or mechanicaled in—something that was wrong that needed fixing on the airplane. So I got to know her pretty well.

I remember one time when Celia's plane was flying ahead of me and all of a sudden I saw this black smoke come out of the engine, the exhaust. We'd been flying over flat land, Nebraska. Celia was sort of slumping over. Not sleeping, but it's not like driving a car where you have to be paying attention all the time. All of a sudden I see her head come out of the cockpit. We were in open-cockpit planes with goggles and all that stuff. I think that happened to be a PT-19. Celia's head had been down and all of a sudden she says, "Ah!" And points down with her hand gestures, shrugs her shoulders, and points down again. We didn't have any radio communication. Then the plane starts going down and down. I thought, "Gee, whiz. I can't leave her." Luckily, it was over Nebraska and there was a farming field. If it had been another hour we'd have been in the Rockies.

I thought, "Well, I just can't leave her there. I'll go down, too." So I went down and landed in this pasture with some cows and horses. We almost killed ourselves getting over the power lines. Then behind me came two other planes in our group. We hadn't seen each other since we'd taken off that morning. They came down and landed, too. Then came another two and they came down and landed. We didn't know how we were going to take off again, but we decided we better stick with Celia until we found out what happened. There were five of us down in a mud field in Nebraska! And then came the guy who was the mechanic that was supposed to stay with us, and he said, "Did you all have to go down and land in this pasture?" Eventually he fixed Celia's plane. Did a whole engine thing. Then we all had to take off in a very short field.

Then one time we were in Wyoming. It was cold and we had to get these old planes started. We didn't have any ground crews. We had to do it ourselves. We got everyone's started but Celia's and mine. She told me later she did it on purpose. She said, "Well, I thought you were an interesting person and if I was going to be stranded, have to stay over because we couldn't get a plane started, you'd be the one I'd want to have to be stuck with." That's really when we started to get acquainted.

Another thing that kind of drew us together was that everybody else would pick up these planes in the Midwest, and knowing they were in pretty bad shape they would stay over flat farmlands. I liked to go see mountains. I wanted to find places where I wanted to hike. Celia thought that was fun, too. So we both did that since we had to stay together flying.

I remember one time I was going over the Blue Mountains and it was fogged in. You knew that it wasn't really bad weather, but the mountains were in the clouds and you'd have to find a valley and scoot through it. My compass didn't work, and my engine would just start missing every once in a while and I'd have to move the throttle around until it would run a little better. I had to just stay on Celia's wing. We knew how to fly formation, because that was one of the things that you were taught to do in the WASPs. There's a little knack to that. I called on her wing and she took me right over the bad mountains. My life depended on her; it was just a matter of trusting her. I think you make friendships with people that you do things with or are thrown together with, but I think this was more like combat where you know your life depends on another person's judgement. When you're flying over mountains and might have to make a forced landing, your life depends upon another person's judgement, so it's important to have someone there that you trust. I think building this trust is especially hard if you've always been sort of independent, and had a sense of "I know what I'm doing." Celia and I had several incidents like that. That's where we really bonded.

At the end of the war, when they were disbanding the WASP, I wanted to get back up to Mount Baker to go skiing again. All these guys that I used to be on the ski patrol with who were still in the military and waiting to be released were writing to me, "Get up to Mount Baker and save us a cabin." There were just

Celia Hunter driving a dogteam, circa 1960. Courtesy of Ginny Wood.

these little wooden cabins that had been summertime things. I thought it would be nice to have company up there, to have somebody else to ski with. If you're out skiing in the mountains, it's better to have a buddy or someone who knew where you were. It wasn't safe to be all by yourself doing that. No one would ever know if you went down and broke your leg or something. I was thinking about all that, and said, "Well, I wonder if Celia would be interested?" Celia didn't even know how to ski. I said to her, "Would you like to learn to ski? Come up and live in this cabin at Mount Baker until the guys get back?" She said, "Well, I never thought about it." Celia was from a very poor family. What you'd call on the other side of the tracks. But she was the smartest person that ever graduated from high school in this very small town. She knew how to spell everything. Her mother had kind of a chip on her shoulder. She had a fit, she said, "Hunters don't go skiing."

I encouraged Celia to come along, and she said, "Oh, it sounded like fun." So we bought some surplus skis and I taught Celia to ski. For a while she wasn't so sure if that was a bad bargain. She learned pretty fast. It was mountain-climbing skiing, downhill. And mostly just cross-country skiing, exploring.

This was in the spring of 1946. You see, they had closed the hotel at Mount Baker during the war and they hadn't reopened it yet. The war was still on. They had a new manager of the hotel but he didn't know where everything was. He didn't even know where the cabins were under the snow. There was thirteen feet of snow. But I knew where all the cabins were and I knew where the firewood was stored. I had to dig down eight feet to get to the chimney. So we made an underground tunnel to get to this cabin that was full of firewood. And then as the guys came back, we started to have a whole gang up there. Eventually, there were eight of us in the cabin. This time together helped me to really get to know Celia more.

Celia was ebullient. She was friendly and laughed a lot. She had a hearty laugh. Her father was a logger. Her mother had a high school education. I don't think her dad had gone past the eighth grade, if that much. But he was the salt of the earth, a wonderful guy. She had grown up on a farm. During the Depression her dad had gone broke. So, they went down and bought a chicken farm down in southern Washington. Then I guess they had a problem with someone stealing his chickens. They had a really rough time. So for a while during the Depression they had to go on relief. She had two brothers and then there was a sister that came along a long time afterwards.

Celia was a born leader. She loved being out in front. She didn't step on anybody to get ahead, but she enjoyed it. Anything she did, she did well. She had a high IQ. Her family couldn't afford to send her to college but her father worked double-time as a logger to pay for business college, so she went for one half year. Celia learned to fly out of a small airfield near Everett, Washington, with electrical wires and a ditch that had to be navigated through. She was working for Weyerhaeuser then, making fifty dollars a month, and she didn't like it. She didn't know you could just do things without money or you didn't have to be born into it. You don't have to have money to do the things you want. You just have to have time and goals. And you don't do it by cheating anybody. I always thought money was something that you just earn enough of to do what you want to do and then you tighten your belt. What Celia got from me was just decide what you want to do and do it. There's a way you can. She was a can-do person. It's just that she had to get over the idea that Hunters had to stay poor.

Ginny at the helm of her sailboat, the Flying Dutchman, *1946. Courtesy of Ginny Wood.*

6

A Summer Under Sail

The sea and the wind and the tides; all that was your life.

As part of her childhood love of the outdoors and adventure, Ginny took an early interest in sailing. Reading books about great sailing expeditions sparked her enthusiasm for doing her own such trips one day. Not only did she learn to sail as a child but she even managed to save enough money to buy her own little sailboat.[1]

I first learned how to sail at our summer cabin at Lake Chelan. I'd had a rowboat and I'd read books, but there was a guy on the lake that had a sailboat. One time he took all us kids for a sail in it. And I thought, "Wow." After that all boats were only poor substitutes for those under canvas. In the meantime, I'd been reading a lot of adventure books, all kinds of books on sailing and how to sail. I read the one called *Sailing Alone Around the World*, written in about 1898 by a guy named Slocum.[2] And I thought, "Ooh, wouldn't that be fun to do." I remember being in school and deciding that I would like to do that. I probably was about twelve then. I'd planned this trip where I wanted to sail to, but then who would be my mate? Who would I take along? I'd take Ole and Dick Berg. And then another girl, her name was Margie Dalkie. I'd take her.

But before that we used to float on logs on Lake Chelan. We each had a log. And we had a cave that we'd found up the beach, which you couldn't get to except by water because it was too steep. That was our secret cave. Those logs were our boats. And we would go on those logs, just using them as surfboards. We sort of pushed them ahead. Now they'd have all kind of flotation gear for people to have. They didn't have those then. We just had our logs that we hung on to and then kicked with our feet to push ourselves along.

When I was older, maybe fifteen, the guy that owned that first sailboat I went in was making his annual drive over the Cascade Mountains to Seattle to get equipment and supplies for his boat. I had accumulated fifty dollars, thinking maybe I could buy a little sailboat. I asked if he would look around the boatyard for any small sailboats for sale in our price range. On his return he brought the news that not only had he seen one but had taken a picture of it. It was a fifteen-foot open-cockpit centerboard sloop with a mainsail and a jib. It was decked in. It was all mahogany. It needed some work on it, but it was basically sound. Moreover, he would be returning to Seattle the next weekend with a boat trailer and could tow it back for me if I wanted to buy it. I certainly did![3]

But it cost seventy-five dollars. I only had fifty dollars. But I conned my sister into donating twenty-five dollars of her own. I told her, "If we have this boat, then we can be eligible to use the facilities of the Lake Chelan Yacht Club. Wouldn't that be nice? Go to the dances and stuff." The yacht club was located about five miles north of Granite Falls, where our cabin was. Margie thought that sounded good. So we bought the boat. My father was out of town when I bought it and our neighbor towed it home for me. I bought it when it was up on the dock and it needed the seams caulked, so I had it in the garage when my dad got home. He said, "She'll kill herself." Previous mentions of a desire on my part to own a sailboat had been met with a negative response. Sailboats were dangerous and he didn't want to see me drowned; winds were too tricky and unpredictable on Lake Chelan's sixty-mile-long waters, which snake between tall, steep, cliffed mountains with few sheltered harbors; and sailboats were expensive—I needed to save my money for my future.[4] When I told my mother my plan, she said to my father, "You know, Ed, she's put her own money in that sailboat." As Dad usually did, he acquiesced. With the help of boys like the Bergs, I sanded, caulked, and revarnished the shabby old mahogany hull of that boat.

The great launching day came in early May when the boat was towed to Lake Chelan. Everyone in residence at their cabins on our point was invited to the ceremony—a bottle of grape juice, speeches, and the official christening in true nautical tradition. Rides for all in my sailboat and afterwards weenies, beans, and marshmallows around our campfire.

The hull, all shiny under coats of varnish, was lifted from the trailer cradle and carried down to the beach. Then the mast was put up, the shrouds tightened, and the sails furled along the boom after it was attached to the mast. Then the jib was hooked on the front stay and the rudder and tiller put in place on the stern.

With cheers from family and friends assembled and an "I here christen you *Scamper,*" my sailboat was pushed out into the water and tied to the buoy we had anchored with an old road grader wheel fifty feet offshore. An hour later, *Scamper* had settled in water down to her gunwales, much to my chagrin and disappointment. No one had forewarned me that a month in "dry dock," while we scraped, sanded, and varnished her, would open seams I couldn't have seen in our dark garage. This denouement, in spite of all our work, was normal, a kind neighbor with lots of boat experience assured me. The water would soon swell the planking and she'd be a tight ship in a few days.

Ginny's first sailboat, Scamper, *on Lake Chelan. Courtesy of Ginny Wood.*

I pumped her dry, set the sails, and made my maiden voyage all alone early in the morning before anyone else was up, just in case there were more mishaps to learn about. I learned a lot with that little boat. I did have to promise never to sail out of sight, which gave me about a ten-mile range up and down the lake and two miles across.

There was room for a sleeping bag on the floorboards on each side of the centerboard well. We could lash a canvas tarp over the boom for shelter if rain was a possibility. We also had a small Sterno stove on which to heat a can of beans or soup. So with all our "stores" aboard, Margie as first mate and I as captain, with our dog, Bobby, the boatswain, we would set sail for "distant shores." This meant we could explore our circumscribed water world as long as we returned to tie up at night to our home buoy just off our dock.

More than one windy night as our moored vessel was being tossed by waves, much to our delight—a storm at sea! Have to ride out a South Pacific gale!—my mother would come down to the dock in her raincoat over her nightgown, lantern in hand. She'd call out, "Ahoy there! Are you girls all right? Are you warm enough? Do you want your father to row out and bring you in?" Of course we were all right. Couldn't she see our hatches were all battened down, our storm sail keeping us into the wind? And besides, we were riding out a storm off Tahiti, and she was spoiling it all by even suggesting we be rescued!

My sister was never as interested in the act of sailing as in the prestige of owning a "yacht." Her favorite "voyage" was to sail up the lake to tie up among the other boats at the yacht club there. Our junior membership also gave us the privilege of attending the summer monthly yacht club dances. As both my parents were graceful ballroom dancers, my dad had early coached me through the waltz, the two-step, and whatever else was in fashion on the dance floor then to the music of records on our wind-up Victrola. Ole's folks didn't dance, as I recall— at least they never taught him to, so I tried. I wanted a partner for those dances. Thus on Saturday night we stumbled around together to the music in awkward, stilted conversation, playing the role of "dating." On Sunday morning we would be back in jeans, shorts, or bathing suits interacting much more comfortably as buddies and partners in pranks again.[5]

Well, you know, later on, I started going away in the summertime working on dude ranches and summer camps, so I didn't use the boat much. My father became curious about my sailboat stored away under the porch of our cabin at Lake Chelan. Being always of an adventurous nature himself, he decided perhaps he should try his hand at sailing. Not having sailed it before or having previous book knowledge of the art of small sailboat handling, he learned vicariously. Of course, he tipped it over and the neighbors had to go rescue him. It became the standard joke among the summer residents on our point whenever he took *Scamper* out: "Somebody better get their outboard ready to go. Ed Hill is taking that sailboat out again." While I had never tipped it over,

Dad had an upside-down boat and had to accept a tow to shore several times before he got the hang of it.[6] Anyway, that was my beginning of sailing and what I learned to sail in. But I finally sold that boat while I was in the WASPs, because it was just drying out from not being in the water. The wood was shrinking and cracking from dehydration, which ends up leading to leaks in the seams of a boat.

When the federal government suddenly disbanded the WASP flying program in December 1944, many women were left with unsure futures. Some happily returned to their previous lives to become wives and mothers. This was not enough for Ginny. Flying provided her a sense of thrill, excitement, and adventure that she craved more of. She found work after the war as a flight instructor in the Seattle area, but she was always making bigger plans. She pursued her childhood dream of taking extended trips on a large cruising sailboat.

I came out of the war with about two thousand dollars. I had saved all the money that I made during the war so I could buy a sailboat. I wanted a bigger one than the little open-cockpit one I had as a teenager. In the fall of 1945, I bought this sailboat that had been laid up during the war for eighteen hundred dollars. That took all I'd saved. It was a wonderful twenty-six-foot yawl. A sailboat is either a yawl or a ketch rig. A yawl rig has the jib in front, then the mainsail, and then the mizzen sail behind the steering post. If the mizzen is in front of the steering post, it's a ketch. The neat thing was in really stormy weather—and we had some—we could take down the mainsail and furl it, and just go under power of the mizzen and the jib. They would be balanced and we could go zippity, as fast as we wanted to go. And the motor we had on it was an inboard.

The name of the boat was the *Flying Dutchman*. It came with that name. Right after the war, it was found drifting in Puget Sound without sails up and with no one aboard. Whoever rescued the boat, they called it the *Flying Dutchman*, because in early myths of the sea there is a story about a boat found abandoned and that is its name.[7] There's also an opera by Wagner called the *Flying Dutchman* that is about a boat found sailing empty.[8] The opera is based on that same myth. With my boat, they think that the guy who owned it committed suicide. That he jumped overboard and left it drifting in Puget Sound. He could have just fallen overboard. Anything could have happened. But the rumor was that he wanted to make it look like he just fell off the boat.

In the summer of 1946, my plan was to sail to Alaska. I was working as a flight instructor. That can get kind of boring after a while, so the idea was, let's go up to Alaska and get jobs flying there. I asked Celia Hunter, whom I was friends with by this point, if she wanted to be my first mate or chief engineer. I didn't know anything about engines and I knew that she knew how to fix engines. She had two brothers, so anything they did, she did too, including taking engines

Ginny's sailboat, the Flying Dutchman, *1946. Courtesy of Ginny Wood.*

apart and putting them together again. Celia would always say, "I can do anything that Hill thinks up."

The boat was all wood. Wood boats take a lot of work. So for two months after I bought the boat, all we did was work on it. We took the rigging down and we found out that the mast and the boom, the spars, what you call the bright work, was all mahogany and it had been painted orange. So we stripped it all, sanded it off, and varnished it. Celia just about quit me as crew then. She said, "I thought we were going to go sail this thing."

Once we got the boat all fixed up, that fall we took a couple of trips down the Inside Passage over to Whidbey Island and so forth to test its seaworthiness. I took my mother and dad out in the boat. My dad thought it was great. My mother wasn't so sure. Then we laid it up for the winter.

In the spring, we had to finish painting it. We had it at a dock at Lake Union while we worked on it. We raised it up so we could get underneath it. There was an old-timer who sat there with his pipe in his mouth and said, "A boat ain't nothing to ride on, just something to work on." .

When Celia and I came back from one of our run-down cruises on Puget Sound after we finally got the boat all painted and fixed up and everything, here was Pete. She was another gal that I'd flown with during the war in the WASP and who had been in my class at training camp in Sweetwater, Texas.[8] Her real name was Isabelle Madison, before she got married, but everyone called her Pete. She'd been instructing flying at a girls' school in Missouri and her boyfriend that she was supposed to marry came home from the war and said he was marrying someone else. She said, "I thought about taking my plane up to ten thousand feet and jumping out of it, but I just bought a brand-new suit and I'd get it all messy. I thought, well, I bet Ginny's doing something more interesting than this. So I think I'll find out what she is going to do for the summer. She's always talking about getting a sailboat and sailing to Alaska." So Pete decided she was going to come and go on this cruise with us. She just arrived. Well, maybe she told me she was coming? But I didn't believe her. She was from Crystal City, Missouri, and she'd never been in anything except one day in a rowboat on the Mississippi River. That was the only nautical experience she'd ever had, but she came with us. She brought this suitcase full of all these outfits that she'd bought. Yachting clothes. And she brought a deck chair. I said, "You get one pair of jeans, two shirts, shorts, sweatshirt, and rain gear. That's all, because that's all the room we have to stow it in."

The boat had two bunks inside. The bunks were seats by the table. The table came down; it was on a swinging thing and you could take it off and store it. All three of us could stay in the cabin if somebody slept on the floor, or one of us had to be outside on the deck. Very often we'd have one or two of us who would row ashore or go to an island with a tent and sleep out, because it was pretty and it was too crowded on the boat. The others would stay on the boat.

L–R: *Pete, Celia, and Ginny in the dinghy* Me Too, *1946. Courtesy of Ginny Wood.*

We only had a space of six feet on the deck of the boat for storing a dinghy. So I had to have a dinghy specially built so it would fit. They guy who built it said, only put one person in it. We put three. We called the dinghy *Me Too*. We always towed it. We'd put it up on the deck when we were at anchor. You see, it would have been in the way of the sails and the boom if it had been on deck while we were sailing. Sometimes Celia and Pete put me out in the dinghy because I was the captain and I was getting too bossy. As it was being pulled behind the sailboat, standing up in that was kind of like surfing. It was fun.

The three of us spent a whole summer—four months—sailing together. We had a ball. We really did. I was captain under sail. Celia was captain under motor. Pete didn't have any sailing experience but she wanted to be in charge of something too, so we named her captain of the head. She was very proud of this until somebody else told her what it meant.

Pete was from a good Catholic family. I think there were nine kids in her family. Any time we anchored, she'd have to get in my rowboat to go find a church. She'd say, "The Pope wouldn't like it if I didn't go to church." But she was lots of fun. She was very good-looking and attracted men everywhere we went. Celia and I would go ashore with the little dinghy to get some food or something and we'd come back and there was no Pete on the boat, even though we'd left her to stay on it. Then from the fanciest yacht that was parked anywhere near us, we'd hear this "Yoo-hoo! The guys say to come on over for dinner." Or then we'd have times when she said, "When's the next tide that we can get out on? I've got to get out of here before they wake up!"

Ginny, Celia, and Pete enjoyed getting to know the inland waterways, mountains, and people of southern British Columbia. They lived frugally. They learned new sailing skills. They showed that as three women they could do a trip like this by themselves. Ginny loved showing off by coming into a mooring under sail, instead of by motor, which requires quick maneuvering to line up the boat properly. Most importantly they remained friends throughout the long journey of living together in close quarters.

We left Seattle in May. We had everything fixed just perfect, because here we were just three gals. We spent the whole summer going from Seattle up the Inside Passage on the mainland side of British Columbia, going up all the little inlets. We were going to sail to Ketchikan, but we found out that every time we came to an inlet, one of those fjords, we wanted to go up to the head of it to explore it. We explored everything we came to. Or sometimes we'd throw the anchor down and stay awhile just to fish and hike. Or we'd meet some people that had a cabin there. Or we'd meet people with another boat that was sailing somewhere and we'd sail with them for awhile. We had all kinds of adventures.

I had wanted a big sailboat because I wanted to sail to the Hawaiian Islands or something like that. But on this trip, I found out that what I really liked to do was to go ashore. Sometimes where we'd go there was a dock. Sometimes you just anchored out in a sheltered inlet. And other times we tied up to log booms—a bunch of logs tied together. We didn't have any radio or anything, and we knew the reason they were tied up was because they had word that a storm was coming and if they were towing logs they'd lose some of their logs. In reverse, we knew the weather was going to be good when we saw the tugs pulling a log boom along; we knew they wouldn't be out on the water if there was a storm coming.

There also were resorts and little towns. One of the places where we stayed over we stayed for about a week because we liked going ashore and hiking and visiting with people that lived there. The reason we were waiting at this one place was because they were going to have a dance. But they have to have the dance on a neap tide so it comes when the tide's right for people to get there. So they said, "Stay over." They needed more women. So we stayed.

Sometimes you went into an inlet and there were a lot of other boats there. So we had quite a social life there. Particularly because of Pete. Or sometimes we stayed at a place three or four days and people that lived along there came to visit us. There was no road north of Vancouver then. And so all it was were people who would go by boat. They'd say more than just "Come and have a cup of tea." They'd say, "Help yourself to our clams. Help yourself to our oysters or

L–R: *Ginny, Celia, and Pete aboard the* Flying Dutchman, *1946. Courtesy of Ginny Wood.*

our berry patch. Come and get something out of our garden." They were just hungry for people. Now they have roads up there on both sides, so it wouldn't be like that anymore.

There was one time when we couldn't get our boat started at all. Even though Celia was good with engines. We happened to be near a little, small village and a guy came down to help us, to see if he could get it started. He said, "Look, I can tow you around to the other side of the island and there's an old Swede over there working for a lumber company and he can fix anything." So he did that. The old Swede was the cook. So while he fixed our engine, the three of us took over the kitchen and cooking and made the meals for the crew that was logging. We were there for three days.

Sometimes we'd just find a little cove in an inlet and we wouldn't see another person or another boat for three or four days. If it was a sunny day and it was a good place to do it, we'd wash our hair in a bucket on deck. Or we'd go skinny-dipping. To bathe or just to cool off. We wore swim caps when we were swimming because we all three had long hair and we didn't want our hair in our mouth. We did have sunny warm days, so we had good tans by the time we got back. We had tan lines from our shorts and shirts. So when we went skinny-dipping we were quite the sight! But we had rainy days, too. And windy days, too. But I just remember the sunny ones.

Another place where we stayed for a week was where everybody came to catch big fish. I finally caught one. From that little dinghy of ours. It was a king salmon. It was fifty-five pounds. We decided, well, we can't eat it all, so we'll build a fire to smoke it. So that's what we did. Even though it was now smoked, that fish only lasted for two days. It wasn't that good. We got most of it eaten by that time. The rest we threw overboard. We couldn't eat it all. That was too bad.

Another place we went was where you have to go up the Yuculta Rapids, which are pretty tough.[10] The rapids are in the narrows. There are quite a few of them like that. There's the Dodd Narrows,[11] and then there's one that's famous for wrecks. Everybody camps there to wait to go up the rapids, because you have to go through exactly on the neap tide, the low tide, when it's calm. And you've got about fifteen minutes or half an hour to make it through before you can't go any further because the tide's against you. It's one of the places where all the boats gather up because they're all waiting for low tide. Anytime there's a storm, you can't go through at all.

Washing day aboard ship. Photo by Ginny Wood.

Malibu Club of Canada in Princess Louisa Inlet [upper end of Jervis Inlet] was a very fancy resort that we went in. To get into the inlet, you have to go through a little narrow stream that you can only go through at low tide [Malibu Rapids]. So you have to wait. Once you get in, it's an inland lake with real steep sides. And down at the end of it, there's a resort where everybody parked.[12] I think we stayed there a week. There were lots of big fancy yachts. Gosh, we met a lot of round-the-world sailors. And people who had just come in from the Hawaiian Islands. We met an awful lot of interesting people who were yachting people that did nothing but just go around the world in boats. And the Seattle Yacht Club was on their annual cruise. So we got invited to board all these fancy yachts. Then we spent a whole two days hiking up in the mountains. This is the place where Pete said, "When's the next low tide so we can leave? This is getting too serious." There were a couple of guys with a boat up there and they thought she was pretty neat. So we had to get up at four o'clock in the morning to get out of there. They were nice guys, but she thought it was just getting a little bit too much.

We lived off of fish. We caught oysters and clams and lobsters. And we'd often go ashore and have a campfire. There was plenty of water. You could always find streams that came down. We had about a ten-gallon tank that we could carry with us to fill up. It must have been under one of the bunks or something. I can't remember where it was. But I know we had a little pump.

Getting gasoline wasn't an issue. Do you know how much we used for the whole three months? Thirty gallons. There was a tank for the gas outside of the boat's cockpit. You could fill up at some of these small villages, but I don't think we did. We didn't use much. We prided ourselves on just staying under sail. It's really tricky to anchor under sail, especially where there are lots of other boats anchored. But we got good at it. You have to throw the anchor, and then you have to back off so you seat the anchor. It's easier to control when you take the mainsail down and you just use the jib and the mizzen. You have less power. Us three gals would sail in where there were lots of other boats anchored and do that. It was very unusual to see three women. They'd say, "Where's the guys?" We said, "We don't need them."

Ginny, Celia, and Pete were having so much fun on their journey that their northern progress was slow. Ginny's desire to sail all the way to Alaska did not work out as planned.

By September we hadn't even made it to the north end of Vancouver Island. Then I happened to look at my insurance on the boat and found out it wasn't any good after you went past the head of Vancouver Island. I couldn't use it if I went into open ocean, and there's that crossing at the north end of Vancouver Island where you have that one day of open seas.[13] It's about sixty miles. It's open water to the Pacific Ocean, with all those storms. And we were starting to get the fall storms. And besides it wasn't fun once it started getting dark. So we turned around and went back to Seattle.

When we came back down, we went to the opposite side of the Inside Passage along the coast of Vancouver Island and stopped at all the little places and towns there. The other side didn't have many towns. On the way back, we stopped at Victoria, Canada. Going up we were more on just islands that hardly had any people. In Victoria harbor, we were parked right under those fancy buildings. Then this big yacht came in with all these guys on it. They were on a company cruise. They invited us over. And they had lots to drink. *Lots* to drink. Both Pete and Celia had too much to drink, and I had to get them home in that little dinghy when they were both roaring drunk. When I started to get aboard, they said, "We don't like our captain anymore." And they pushed me off. I had on my leather flying jacket because it was cool out and it was dark. Actually, I was sinking because my big, heavy jacket was filling with water. I said, "You guys, I'm drowning. Let me back in the boat." They said, "She's drownding! Do we want her aboard?" I said, "Throw me a rope, for crying out loud!" I couldn't keep my head above water anymore. And they finally did. That sobered them up very fast. They really had realized that they almost didn't have a captain.

On our way home we stopped at Bellingham and hitchhiked up to Mount Baker because I wanted to show Pete where I had skied. Celia already had been up there with me. We went out to the San Juan Islands from there. In the San Juan Islands, we met this couple, June Burn and her husband, Farrar. They were in this old lifeboat. She was doing a story for the Seattle newspaper, "One Hundred Days in the San Juan Islands."[14] I knew of her because she had written this book about living there on a little island.[15] They wanted to homestead somewhere on the water and they picked this little dot of an island.[16] There wasn't anyplace nearby. They had to row about an hour to where he could get some work at a mine on another island. She wrote a very good book that tells about meeting him and living on that island. I remember one story where they were trying to get to a doctor, but it was too rough and they couldn't get across to the main island, to San Juan Island. We traveled together for several days.

Then there was a family on a fancy yacht that we met. And this guy, he thought it would be more fun to be on a sailboat, so we traded. He joined me on my boat, and the girls went on his boat. Celia and Pete found out the man and his family were leaving the next morning for Seattle. Pete said that she wanted a ride because she had to get back for a job. With Celia and me, it was going to be at least another week before we got home with the boat.

So we left Pete in the San Juan Islands. Celia and I brought the boat home. We got back in October. It was getting kind of bad weather and rainy. We parked it at a place on Lake Washington in Seattle. I paid to have it stored there.

It was a worthwhile expedition. I wrote an article about the trip for a yachting magazine. It was called "Three Maids Before the Mast."[17]

When we came home we thought about driving up to Alaska. Neither one of us owned a car, so we bought this old army surplus car. Our folks had a fit. They thought that was awful. The Alaska Highway at that time was in bad shape; you practically had to have a duplicate engine to put in, a lot of spare parts, and you had to carry a lot of gasoline. So we didn't go.

Unfortunately, Ginny never made that sailing trip to Hawaii that she had dreamed of as a youth, or to anyplace else for that matter. This maiden voyage of *The Flying Dutchman* turned out to be its only voyage.

When we got back from the trip, I tied up my boat and I never sailed it again. I came to Alaska later that fall thinking that it was for a short visit and I'd be going back to Seattle. I intended to sail a lot on Lake Washington and then maybe on the saltwater. I had it moored and was paying for it, and my dad went down to check on it. Finally, he said, "You know, every time we have a storm, I have to go down and rescue your boat. I'm tired of having to do this because it broke loose and was banging against the dock. Are you coming home to take care of your boat?" He said, "If you want to sell it, I know somebody that wants to buy it very badly." I said, "Sell it." That was probably after being in Alaska a couple of years. By that time, I decided that I probably wouldn't go back to Washington. I just figured that this was a whole new life up here. I was flying, and going to all the villages. I was living in this wonderful little town. It was either Alaska or my sailboat. I thought, well, that one sailing trip probably was my adventure. Just like during the war it was ferrying planes. And before that it was working on dude ranches with horses. I never did any of them again. You know, it's just sort of, as I say, I was the right age at the right time and had the right skills.

I've never really sailed a boat since. Well, except for trying it on Wonder Lake in McKinley Park in a little boat we had down there for a while. When we first had camp, when Pat Pyne was working for us and she had three kids, you could get a sailboat if you had the labels from a whole big carton of cigarettes. So we bought one carton to sell at Camp Denali, just so I could have the ends off of each pack. And Pat did the same thing. So we got three of these boats. They were made out of fiberglass. They had a little sail that was just cat rigged. And we sailed them on our little pond at Camp Denali [Nugget Pond] and we'd take them down to Wonder Lake and sail them. They handled nicely. They didn't have a jib, they just had a mainsail. It didn't have any deck, it was just open. But it is very tricky air coming down Wonder Lake. You had to be on your toes to bring it up into the wind. I thought I was pretty good at it.

Then I did buy another boat that had a little cabin on it. I was going to have it so we could trailer it to the saltwater at Valdez.[18] We had it at Camp Denali and I did sail it on Wonder Lake a few times, but you always had to have time to go down to rig it and that wasn't always possible. When we sold Camp, we brought the boat home. Later, I traded it to Kent Pyne, who helped me build my porch [arctic entry] on my house. He towed it to lakes and stuff, but I don't know what became of it. I hardly sailed it enough to get used to it. I never took it down to sail in Prince William Sound as I had hoped. We were running Camp Denali then, and it ran from May into October by the time we got it closed up and got home. Then we were building the house and all those things, so I had no time.

Of all the dreams I had as a kid, all the books I read about sailing and people that had sailed around the world, I always intended I would have some kind of sailing adventure like that. When I traded that boat to Kent Pyne, that was the end of my sailing.

That's the way life comes. And then along the way, you know, I got married and had a kid. And I wouldn't have wanted not to have done that. That was an adventure, too. At least I can look back on some wonderful memories. And not only because I did it. It was because of the people I met and the life I led doing it. You know, horses, skiing. And I always had a skill so I could get paid for what I did, or at least not have to pay. I was on the ski patrol at Mount Baker and I got free tows and free skiing. And hauled in a lot of people with busted legs. And I went with a guy for a while who was German who liked to climb mountains. So I climbed Mount Rainier and I climbed Mount Baker and I climbed Mount St. Helens when it was a lot taller than it is now. And each time brought a way of life and an adventure.

Ginny and Celia stop over in Watson Lake, Yukon Territory, on their flight to Alaska, December 1946. Courtesy of Ginny Wood.

7

Alaska: The Early Years

I've been at the right place, at the right time, at the right age.
I think I've been very lucky. I just had an appetite for seeing new country.
And life. As a whole, I haven't any regrets.

When Ginny delivered fighter planes to Great Falls, Montana, for World War II's Lend-Lease program, she heard stories about Alaska from the male pilots who had been up there. These tales piqued her curiosity. Her lifelong interest in exploring new places made her want to see it for herself. So, in 1946, when an opportunity arose for Ginny to go to Alaska, she jumped at the chance.

One day, months after we returned from our sailing trip in the fall of 1946, I got a call from Celia Hunter. She called up and said that a friend of hers who had been a pilot in the war had started a business selling secondhand surplus military airplanes like the ones we'd been ferrying. He said to Celia, "Hey, there's a guy down from Alaska who bought a couple of beat-up old airplanes that he wants delivered to Fairbanks and he asked me if I knew of any pilots that would be interested in taking them up. Are you interested?" So Celia called me to see if I would I be interested in the job. I said yes.

The guy was Gene Jack. He ran a trading post in Kotzebue and had these two old military planes that he had bought privately and wanted delivered. They weren't fighters, they were kind of puddle jumpers. At that time, I was instructing flying on Lake Union in Seattle for a flying service that had just started up and I was the chief pilot. Celia was flight instructing north of Everett, Washington. We just left our jobs for a week to ferry these planes to Fairbanks.

We did it because we wanted to see where this place was that these guys were talking about during the war. We flew the Alaska-bound planes to Great Falls, Montana, and turned them over to pilots who would fly them up to Fairbanks. They wouldn't let the women fly to Alaska. They said there were no facilities for women. But I think they could have added them if they wanted to. They made places for women on all the other bases we flew to. So I've wondered if it was just that they wanted someplace that women couldn't go or because they considered it too dangerous for women to fly across all that uncharted territory in Canada?

The guys we met in Great Falls talked about flying north with a B-25 as their guide that they just had to follow. When you ferried a plane up to Alaska, you had a lead plane and then the fighter planes would be going along in formation. When these pilots landed they had ground crews to look after the planes. If you went down, right away they would know where you were and there would be a rescue plane right there. The guys would talk about Watson Lake, Whitehorse, and Northway, and all these names became sort of mythical places or magic places. They'd talk about Fairbanks and watching the Russian pilots come in to pick up the planes, and all the women pilots that would come over to fly these planes all the way to the Russian front. One guy said he asked one of the women how many flying hours she had and she said, "Twenty-seven." "In this plane?" he asked. "No, altogether," she replied. And here we thought we were pretty brave just to get them across the United States.

Celia and I took off for Alaska on December 6, 1946. We thought it would take one week to get those planes up to Fairbanks from Seattle and then we'd go home. But it was horrible flying weather. It took us twenty-seven days to get from Seattle to Fairbanks. We flew the only four days that were flyable. A lot of it was just because of bad weather, like fog, freezing conditions, or storms.

Celia was flying a bigger and faster plane than mine. It was a seven-place civilian plane, a Stinson Gullwing, that had been used for training navigators.[1] I had an L-5. It was an old one that had been used as an ambulance plane to carry a single patient. It was made for picking up wounded soldiers. They made it so a stretcher would go in back, so it didn't have a bulkhead. We put our skis in there instead. I couldn't go flying to where there was snow without bringing my skis! My plane only had a 190-horsepower engine. It didn't have a fuel range of more than an hour and a half. In order to be sure I could make it to the next gas stop, we put an auxiliary tank in the cabin that you had to pump by hand to pump the gas up into the wing tank.

When we were first hired in November, these two surplus airplanes weren't even rated as flyable. My plane had been so poor—the fuselage had too many holes in it—that it didn't even check out for being flyable under the X rating, which is where you can ferry but not take passengers. We only could get it out of Boeing Field if it would pass the test just for ferrying. The fabric was so rotten on my plane that Gene Jack, being a typical Alaskan, cut a little piece out of the plane's fabric right under the fuselage, right under where you sit, where it doesn't get much weathering and wear, and then cut another piece just like it off of the leading edge of the wing, which does get a lot of wear. He turned in the one from under the fuselage as if it were the piece from the wing, since he knew it would test out strong enough to pass for the X rating. They tested the pieces and the fuselage one was the one that just barely tested positive. The wing certainly wouldn't have. Then he got the plane repainted to cover up the fact that the fabric was so bad, so it looked new. So I got to know that type of Alaska "businessman."

Despite this funny business with the fabric, Gene Jack paid us everything he promised to us and he was a gentleman. He hired us because the last three male pilots he'd hired had gotten drunk on him and couldn't fly. So he thought he'd try women and see if that worked better. It turned out that Gene Jack had bought three airplanes and was planning on flying one himself. Although he'd never flown a twin-engine plane before. He didn't have a twin-engine rating. He was using our twin-engine ratings to get permission to fly these planes to Alaska. So he needed us. We had to teach him to fly the twin-engine. Celia checked him out in a Bamboo Bomber, which was a training plane, so he could fly that third plane up to Alaska with us. Once he got in his plane, he never let us touch it again because, he said, "That's a man's airplane."

By the time we got the planes all ready to go, we didn't get out of Seattle until the first of December. Even though we'd been hired in November. We waited for six days trying to get good weather to fly out of Seattle heading north. It just wasn't minimums. We finally flew south to Portland, up the Columbia River gorge, and then up around to Spokane following the river because we couldn't go over the mountains because of the weather. Well, that was the start of it. It kept that way all the way up to Alaska.

After Spokane, the first place we were cleared to fly to was no problem. I didn't like the looks of the weather report but we went anyway. Gene learned to fly up here in Alaska. He never looked at a weather report or anything. He'd just stick his head out the window and say, "Looks good to me. Let's go." That takeoff was the last time I saw him until I got to Fairbanks. He was in a faster plane.

I got across the border and started up Crowsnest Pass in Canada. It's a narrow opening in the mountains, just as you cross the border. It's like a trench. I hadn't seen Celia since we got gas at a little town near the border and had taken off. She was in a faster and more comfortable plane. It had a good heater. All I had was holes in the fabric. It was very cold. I called it "Little Igloo." I saw Celia and Gene going into the pass. I didn't like the looks of it, but I flew in. I thought, this is not for me, not with this plane. I know my fabric doesn't even test right because we cheated on that. I don't want to be just flying a fuselage with no fabric on it. I saw where there was a little radio station and an emergency landing field below, so I said, "Well, I'm a sissy. I'm landing here." So I landed there. I thought, "Well, I'll have to go all the way to Fairbanks by myself, because I'm a sissy," and I turned back. I was just putting my plane to bed, just closing my flight plan, and looking for a ride into the little town. At least they had a hotel.

And I heard a little *putt, putt, putt.* I looked up way in the sky and saw a little black dot. Out of the clouds comes Celia with her plane. And she landed. She said, "Boy, I had decided they've all gone without me since I couldn't see where you were, but I went up into Crowsnest Pass and I wasn't going to fly in that stuff." Gene Jack went on through. He got to Calgary and called the Canadian Air Force to see where we were. You see, then you had to get permission from the Canadian Air Force to be flying in Canada. They were in control of who went over that area so they knew everybody's flight plans. Probably for safety, to report a crash, or something. Anyway, they said to him, "No, their flight plan has been closed. R-O-N." R-O-N means remaining overnight. They told him where we had landed. He phoned us at the hotel and said, "What made you go back?" We said, "What made you go on?"

We got to Grand Prairie and gassed up, and after that he got ahead of us again and he just went straight on to Fairbanks. There was a big storm that came up. He didn't know how to read a weather report. He didn't know you could look at that and tell what the weather was going to be. And knowing that my wings weren't very good anyway, I wasn't anxious to be brave. Celia stayed with me. We turned back. Gene had a mechanic with him, who was supposed to take care of our planes, too, except they separated from us, so we never had the help of that mechanic. He knew how to firepot. We'd never heard of firepotting. But they'd put one in our planes. They told me, "You don't need to know how to run it because the mechanic that's with Gene, he knows how to do that. He'll take care of that, with all the ground stuff." Well, we never saw either of them again until twenty-one days later.

We flew on the only four flyable days in December. At that time the Canadian Air Force wouldn't let you clear for takeoff if there was fog anywhere. Fog over the Alaska Highway, which we were following, or anything, you wouldn't be given a flight plan. It would just be patchy stuff but we wouldn't be allowed to fly. You couldn't just fly when you wanted to. You know, we had instrument ratings and could look at a map and read a weather report and see what it was doing. We could tell if you could fly through or over that—you don't even have to fly in it—but they wouldn't clear us for takeoff or even let us submit flight plans. We overnighted for several days in Edmonton to get something fixed on the plane. We spent several days at Dawson Creek when it was too cold; when the temperature got below zero we needed heaters to start our planes. From Dawson Creek we followed the Alaska Highway as our navigational aid. We had Christmas in Fort Nelson. There was a small contingent of the Canadian Air Force and the American Air Force still there after the war, so we had to eat two dinners to be equal to both. The next stop was Watson Lake. We were weathered in there for five days and we had our skis, so we skied down to an Indian village. That was exciting. There were sled dogs that howled like wolves and people who didn't speak English. That was fun. Then we made the next hop to Whitehorse. We had lunch there and then went on. We usually made only one stop in a day, but we made two stops that day. Whitehorse was very cold. My feet were frozen since I didn't really have heat in my plane. I stood over a heat register to thaw them out before we took off again. After Whitehorse, we landed in Alaska, at Northway, on the last day of 1946. We stayed in the barracks there. There were still some US Army guys stationed there after the war. They would only give us a heater if we went to the dance that was being held that night. It was New Year's Eve. We went to the dance and celebrated New Year's, and then got up early the next morning to try to get to Fairbanks in one day.

We followed the route that the military used when they flew the planes to Alaska for the United States and Russian Lend-Lease program. They followed the Alaska Highway. The reason the highway was built was to be able to gas those planes up along the way. People get our flight mixed up with that. Even though I'd flown the same planes during the war as a WASP, I didn't fly them to Alaska. The plane I brought to Fairbanks was a secondhand plane that had been a war plane, but it was not part of the Lend-Lease program.

We followed the Alaska Highway as a navigational aid because we didn't have radios. Well, we did have radios, but mine would only receive and Celia's would only send. So we'd have these signals back and forth to be able to better communicate with each other. We got to the beginning of the Alaska Highway at Dawson Creek and got weathered in. It hadn't been too cold before we arrived, but then it went down to fifty degrees below zero. We got out these firepots that were in our planes that Gene's mechanic was supposed to take care of and tried to figure them out. We couldn't get them to work, so we finally hiked to town and found a plumber. He said, "These never would have worked, because they were made wrong." So he fixed them. Finally, we got down to where we only had one battery that was working between the two planes. We'd get one started, then get the other started, but you had to stand in that cold blast of the other plane while you got the second one going. By this time it was into the middle of December and that was the first real cold weather we had. I had on my big heavy leather flying stuff that I had from the WASP, but I was still really miserable. We had never had to take care of a plane before. In the WASP, the ground crew did all that for us. On this trip, we had to get gasoline, get a ladder, and get up and pour it into the plane from five-gallon buckets. You know, we'd never done that before. If they'd let us do this trip as part of the Lend-Lease program, we'd have had ground crews and our planes would have been in hangars at night. But these weren't.

In the morning, when we were leaving Northway heading toward Fairbanks, we looked at the weather report and it was terrible, but we said, "Let's get these things delivered." We'd been in the planes so long. We took off from Northway in clear weather. But the weather reports were getting worse and worse as we flew north. So we came over Big Delta, what we now call Delta Junction, and using our hand signals, I pointed down to indicate to Celia that I wanted to land at Big D. She shook her head to say, "No way." And pointed her finger forward and wiggled her hand to say, "Keep going." So we did. Celia got the weather report for Fairbanks and they said there's a snowstorm coming in and there's about three miles and about a thousand feet visibility. So I wiggled my wings, "Yeah, let's go for it." We finally went over 26 Mile Field, that's what we called it then, it's now Eielson Air Force Base. But you couldn't land there because it was military. Then we were able to follow the railroad tracks from there into Fairbanks. We figured we'd know when we got to Fairbanks because that's where the tracks ended at the station. The weather and visibility were really bad. By the time we got to Fairbanks, it was "one-one"—one thousand feet minimum and one mile visibility. You wouldn't pick it as the time or place to land, but where do you go, there was nothing beyond Fairbanks. Except if you wanted to fly to Russia, and we didn't have that much gas.

We got to where we thought Fairbanks was, but we couldn't see the field. At that point, we were milling around trying to find out where the hell's the airfield. Ladd Field was the main airfield for Alaska. It was even bigger than Anchorage at that time. But we couldn't find the airfield for town, Weeks Field. Celia was ahead and finally she wiggled her wings indicating, "Oh, I've got the field in sight." So we got into formation flying where you're taught what to do if you're on instruments with another plane. You fly at a certain air speed and altitude so you always see the other plane and you won't be milling around hitting each other. I got on her wing so that we wouldn't run into each other, because it was snowing hard, and we could just see straight down. We couldn't see very far ahead. We kept going lower and lower. We were maybe thirty feet off the ground. All of a sudden I looked down and thought, "That's no airfield!" Turns out it was the field at Creamer's Dairy.[2] We thought the silo was the tower, and it was the only field we could see. So we pulled up real fast. We couldn't land in that field. We were on wheels, not on skis. Up in the air again, we started around, staying in this combat formation so we wouldn't hit each other. All of a sudden through the haze of the snow and fog, we could just faintly see this green light, red light, green light, red light. This was at Weeks Field.[3] The tower had us in sight and knew our flight plan and was trying to get our attention. Weeks Field was just a narrow field on the edge of town and it didn't have much of a tower to speak of. It was smaller than that cow pasture "field," which just stood out alone out on the edge of town that had looked like the landing field.

Celia landed first. Hers was a heavier plane. She got it off the runway and then I came in. It had been snowing and there was about ten inches of fresh snow. When I landed, I felt the tail start to lift as the wheels plowed through the unplowed landing strip. Fortunately, I had done a real tail-dragger landing because I knew that this plane was pretty light and most of the gas was gone. And I thought, "Oh, no, no, not having come all this way and now this thing is going to go over on its back at the end." As I felt the tail going up and up, I did the last thing you can do, I gave the throttle a quick thrust. You give it a blast with your engine to see if the sudden burst of air over the tail surface will put the tail back down. It worked. I felt the tail settle back down. Then I could slowly taxi off the field towards the hangar. But it came so near to going over, because the snow was so deep.

The four hours of daylight on New Year's Day was fast dwindling. A figure loomed out of the dusk as I approached the hangar. I heard a voice call to me, "Just shut it off and park it here." It was Gene Jack. He had got back up to Alaska before us and I guess he told everyone about these two lady pilots who were bringing up his airplanes. It seems that on the radio every night they had a position report. It got on the news every night of where we were, and so there were lots of spectators waiting for us when we arrived. He was especially anxious to see that we arrived. After our long journey, I was grateful to be in Fairbanks. "Fairbanks at last and mission completed! Intact!" I thought to myself. I suppose I expected some sort of warm acknowledgment of our accomplishment from Gene, but all he said was, "You took twenty-seven days to get here. And you have to land here on a weekend and a holiday to boot. Now I have to pay three times the regular rate for customs clearance!"

So, that was how we got to Fairbanks. We arrived on 1/1 with "one-one" visibility. And I have been here ever since.

Early January in interior Alaska is not the ideal time of year for visitors. It can be a brutal season. Temperatures hover between twenty and sixty degrees below zero. Snow and hoarfrost coat the trees, rooftops, and railings with a fluffy jacket of white, like a downy snowy owl chick. Although the sun is higher than on December 21, the shortest day of the year, there are still only about six hours of daylight. People tend to stay close to home and hunker down around warm fires. Amidst all this, Ginny describes her early impressions of Fairbanks:

We arrived in Fairbanks on New Year's Day, January 1, 1947, having left Seattle on December 6, 1946. Of course, that was the darkest time of the year and the coldest time of the year. My first impression of Fairbanks wasn't much. The weather was so bad you couldn't see very far ahead of you. It had sidewalks, but only a few blocks of paved streets. We went to the Nordale Hotel. They put us up there. There were some Pan American pilots that heard that there were two women pilots in the place, and they were banging on our door wanting us to go down to the bar to have a drink with them. We were exhausted and just wanted to go to bed. So we didn't go. Then in the middle of the night all of a sudden I woke up to Celia trying to crawl across my bed to get to the window. I said, "What are you doing?" She said, "We're on fire." Actually, the building across the street from the Nordale Hotel was burning up and the flames were dancing on the wall of our room so she thought our building was on fire. We looked around in the hotel room and all they had for a fire escape was a rope they had on the second floor. Pretty soon we figured out what was going on and went to watch the fire department spray water from their hoses onto the fire. That was our first night in Fairbanks.

The deal was that Gene Jack paid us a ten dollar a day per diem for flying up to Alaska and our expenses home. But when we finally delivered the planes to Fairbanks, the temperature dropped to between fifty-five and sixty-five degrees below zero for three weeks. The winter of 1946–1947 was one of the coldest winters. Pan American was the only scheduled commercial carrier flying into Fairbanks at that time, and it came in three times a week. It had just a DC-3 propeller ship, and they can't fly when it's that cold. Neither could we in smaller airplanes. So there wasn't anything flying. We were stuck in Fairbanks.

Finally, the temperature rose to twenty above and the weather was clear. Gene Jack said, "Hey, you gals are still around? I have a bunch of cargo to fly out to Kotzebue. Would you like to fly a load out for me?" We thought, "Ooh, Eskimos, Bering Sea, Kotzebue. Ooh, that would be nice, we'd get to see the rest of Alaska." So we did.

This time Gene put the larger of the two planes on skis. It was an old war plane with two engines—a Bamboo Bomber. He said, "Which one of you wants to take it?" We said we'd both take it and fly for half the pay as we both wanted to see Kotzebue and since we figured it would take two of us to handle that ski plane. He took us out and checked us out on skis, since we had never been on them before. We learned later that this plane was one of the hardest to fly on skis, as it had a huge tail. The wind would catch the tail and whip it around. We also found out later on that flying on skis wasn't all that hard. But we spent a lot of time pushing that plane out of snowbanks when we'd land!

Galena was our first stop and it got cold again, down to fifty below, so we were there for eighteen days. Gene Jack was paying us so many dollars a day, so we were making quite a bit of money even just sitting in Galena. It was great because we were living on the military base there. The old base was being renovated for civilian use. There were just a few maintenance men on base. Also, that was our introduction to the Athabascan village. We got very well acquainted with people there. There was this fascinating couple that ran the trading post, Millie and Wy Speeks. Every night we'd go down to their trading post and Millie would make coffee and dessert. We'd sit there and listen to Wy tell his tales about Alaska, early days of flying up here, etc.

When the weather finally warmed up and we got to Kotzebue, the next hop was to Selawik, where we were the only white people. We stayed with Hadley Ferguson, who was a delightful Eskimo woman who ran the trading post and operated the short-wave radio station, and where we got gas. She'd been married to Archie Ferguson.[4] She was just a wonderful person. We were stuck there for three days because of high winds. We got to know the Eskimo way of life and the people. We were just fascinated by the Eskimos. They were just such jolly and intelligent people. Just great. When we were ready to leave Selawik the Eskimos prepared the plane for us. They skillfully firepotted the engine, scraped frost off the wings, and poured gas through a chamois-covered funnel to strain out the water and ice. Never had we had a more capable and diligent ground crew.

We went back to Kotzebue in a wind that most other pilots wouldn't have flown in. We landed there on the sea ice. Male pilots in Kotzebue waiting for the weather to change were teased that here they were waiting and two women had just landed. It was easier to land than take off, because we knew exactly which way the wind was blowing since we'd been out in it. Because we came in in that weather, we got the reputation for being pretty good pilots. Really, it was that we didn't know what to worry about. We didn't do it to be smart or to be daring. It just happened that we didn't particularly have any problems with what we did. Then the weather went bad with a blizzard. We were there at Kotzebue for a week. They didn't even have scheduled airlines in there yet at that time. Well, we learned a lot about the Eskimo culture on that trip, and we saw a lot of Alaska.

I must say, that was the best introduction you could have to Alaska, to be weathered in at those villages with all those characters and to get to know the Natives. They were the most outgoing, friendly, cheerful, tolerant people. They were nice to us because we didn't know what we were doing. We bumbled around. We were invited into their homes. And one night in Kotzebue they had an Eskimo dance that they gave in our honor.[5] They made up a dance called "lady pilots." I remember the skin on one guy's drum broke and he said, "Oooh, engine stop." They had such a good sense of humor. While we were grounded in Kotzebue as the weather got worse, folks from Noatak were coming down to have dog-team races with people in Kotzebue. It wasn't for tourists, it was just a homegrown thing.

By the time we got back to Fairbanks it was February and the days were getting longer and warmer, so we decided that we might as well stick around and see what the summer was like. Having been out that long delivering cargo, we had quite a pile of money, and by this time we'd been gone so long from home that we'd lost our jobs in Washington. We'd been flight instructors, and they'd replaced us. We thought Fairbanks was a pretty interesting town. We got to know a lot of kids from the university, including the guy that I eventually married.

I met my future husband, Woody [Morton Wood], shortly after arriving in Fairbanks. Like other guys, he came on the GI Bill to finish his college degree while having his Alaska adventure.

There were all these GIs here at Ladd Field waiting for their discharge, so they were trying to get skiing going to give them something to do. They had put a

Ginny and Morton "Woody" Wood, 1948. Courtesy of Ginny Wood.

little rope tow in pretty near what is now Birch Hill. Most of these guys had been through the thick of it. They were tired of uniforms, they were tired of fighting. They just wanted to get home and be a civilian. The military thought to ease it a little bit, until they could get them all released, that they would have something fun for them to do. Celia and I saw a little notice that was posted on a board at the USO saying that girls were wanted to go out to the base to ski. It didn't say "Women Wanted," but they were trying to make it more of a civilian and community recreation thing so everybody out there wasn't in uniform. They sent free buses in to get girls, and Celia and I had our skis with us, so we went.

According to Ginny, she and Woody met when he stopped next to her on the slope and commented on her old military-style ski boots: "Where did you get those boots?" "They were selling them as army surplus," she replied. He said, "Well, when I was in the army we never got such nice leather boots." Apparently, they'd never been issued to the GIs.

Born in January 1924, Woody grew up in Freeport, Maine, in a big stone house on Casco Bay. His father was a successful businessman working for the American Hoist and Derrick Company. While Woody developed a love of nature and hiking and honed his outdoors skills in the woods of Maine, he also lived in

France for a period in his youth, where he learned to speak French and appreciate European culture. Woody had completed one year of college when, at the age of eighteen, he was drafted. He served in the Tenth Mountain Division during World War II, hoping he would get to ski and climb mountains. Instead, he was stationed in Italy, where he saw horrible combat at Lake Garda and in the Po Valley. He was one of the few men in his unit to survive. This was a traumatic event for a man who did not want to kill people.[6]

Woody was going to school at the University of Alaska Fairbanks and living on campus. He would cross-country ski or walk the three miles to come downtown to take me out to dinner. Following the railroad tracks was the most direct route.[7] Or we'd gather with friends at one of their cabins for a meal and lively conversation. Or we'd go folk dancing at the university in the old gym. Oh boy, was he a good dancer!

So, my staying in Fairbanks was a bit of an accident. I have yet to meet anybody who would say, "I am going to move to Alaska and spend the rest of my life there." It takes a long time before you make that decision. They came up for the military, to look around, to climb a mountain, as a tourist, or just for a summer job. They came because the rest of the world was too crowded, or the opportunities were shrinking where they were, or just for the adventure of it. Or they were running away from families. They didn't have to be outlaws to be running away from something. A lot of them came just to get rich and then go back to where they came from. You don't really know you're Alaskan until you have left Alaska and you say, "Oh, ye gads. There is just no place like Alaska; no place that is as exciting, where you get to know as many interesting people." Each person seems important because there aren't so many of us.

Celia and I just ended up staying in Fairbanks because we got stuck. By the time we came back from flying cargo to Kotzebue, we began to see that Fairbanks at least had civilized things. If the planes had been flying, then we would have gone back to Washington, because we left jobs and families and boyfriends. And I always thought if you couldn't go downhill skiing in the wintertime on Mount Rainier and Mount Baker or something, then you weren't living. You looked around Fairbanks and there wasn't much. But I realized these people here in this faraway place were happy. That they were very able to take care of themselves. I was just intrigued by that. I never would have picked Fairbanks as the place to spend the rest of my life. If we were to live anywhere in Alaska, we thought it would be Anchorage, because we'd have better skiing, be near the mountains. Of all the places in Alaska to live in, Fairbanks is the least dramatic when you first look at it. If you just came in, it looks like a dumpy, cruddy little town, but it turns out to be one of the neatest places to live. I just started meeting people, a fascinating bunch of people. It was just a very stimulating and exciting place to be. I just am grateful and kind of awed at how it all just happened right.

Ginny describes what Fairbanks was like when she and Celia arrived:

A lot of GIs had come up to Alaska right after they had got back from the war and decided they didn't really like life in the Lower Forty-eight. They were kind of lost, you know. They went to war over there in Europe when they were little boys, saw an awful lot of bad stuff, so came back as men. They had been through a lot. I think they came back from the war and weren't satisfied anymore. Decided they really weren't happy, you know, they couldn't live with their family. They wanted to see something else instead of just settling down back in their hometown and taking over their father's business. Have that as the reward of life. So instead, they said, "Oh, I think I'll go to Alaska." It was the same thing that drove a lot of people west with the covered wagon, to go out to California and look for gold, or to go to the Northwest and log. All the things that said itchy feet. So there was a whole flood of guys up here when we got here who had just got back from the war and felt, well, if they had all their arms and legs and their sight, "Wow. Boy, were they lucky!" They were thinking, "I don't want to go work in an office." They had the GI Bill, so the University of Alaska was just flooded with guys that were in their mid- or later twenties. It was a very interesting group of young men up here at that time. They were older than the average college boys and they had seen a lot of fighting, seen a lot of life and death. They were anxious to get on with their lives and knew what they wanted to do.

In those days, everybody went to the university in the winter because that was the cheapest place to get housing and food and warmth and to wait for jobs to open up in the spring. There was quite a collection of characters there, because they were either guys who had been out in the bush working in the goldfields or working in the summer for Fish and Game or working somewhere else seasonally, and were just waiting for jobs to open up again in the spring. Or they were GIs that were on the GI Bill.

Oh my goodness, some of the lifestyles some of the people lived! People were living in Quonset huts, barabaras and whatnot, just hovels. Trapping rabbits just to be able to stay in school. Mostly, though, we all lived on the same economic level. There might have been people who made it rich, but I don't think anybody got real rich on gold like they did in the Yukon. People treated each other well. Even the people who were dead set against what you believed in still were your best friends.

On Thanksgiving or Christmas the Salvation Army or the Red Cross, or whoever the do-gooders were, had a hard time finding who it was that needed help. Everybody already helped each other. This is what you did in a small town in the frontier where everyone depended on each other. The kids going to the university that were just living in old cabins and some of them in tents, they'd benefit from these services. They'd say, "Hey, guess what? I'm on relief. Somebody left this turkey. If we can just get the cabin warm enough to thaw it, we'll cook it."

Fairbanks was a very interesting place fifty years ago. This was an entirely different community. Everything was a mom-and-pop business. Every store, the owner owned it. It wasn't part of any big corporation at all.[8] It wasn't until the pipeline came in that we got anything like that. We had more grocery stores then than we do now. More choices than we do now with everybody having bought out each other. Now, we only have Fred Meyer and Safeway.[9]

Coming from Seattle and all of a sudden you come to this small town, it was a big change. The Alaska Highway wasn't even open to civilian travel yet in early 1947 when we arrived. That didn't happen until the next summer. And to just find this comfortable little town of about five thousand year-round residents living on this river in log cabins, who had all this strange way of living because it's cold, and yet they all seemed to be happy. They didn't have indoor plumbing, but if you went into their houses you'd see all the books they read, and they all had nice paintings on the walls. I just was intrigued by the people. Impressed by the people. People that lived very happily, had a nice social life, despite living in this small, remote, and cold place. First thing I did was I joined a great books club. We read great books and then sat around and talked about them and had something to drink afterwards. Down in Washington, I'd grown up in a small town. But they had small thoughts, too. Good, hard, wonderful, and honest people. But you didn't have a great books club. I was just intrigued with the quality of people in Fairbanks when I got here, whether it was intellectual or it was just real honest. There was joy in living here. It was a small town without the usual smallness of a small town.

When we hit town, most of the places didn't have plumbing. The N.C. [Northern Commercial] Company had put in sewer pipes next to the buried heat steam pipes to have a sewer system, but anything that was beyond Sixth Avenue wasn't on that system, so nobody's toilet flushed. Everybody had honey buckets and I think they were all dumping them in their neighbor's yard. Or else you got up and ran clear downtown to go to the hotel where you could go to the john if you could hold it.

Then in the summer, down below the bridge, everybody was loading their boat to be gone for the summer, looking for gold, I guess. You'd see them all getting ready, putting on all their gear and stuff. And then, of course, I was flying for a living and getting weathered in all these little villages. If I'd stayed in Washington, I probably wouldn't have been flying for a living. I wouldn't have been interested in doing it. I had other things to do then, like ski.

Ginny and Celia settled into a small cabin on Ninth Avenue in downtown Fairbanks and looked for work. As Celia said, "At times we were holding down two jobs: working in the office of a travel bureau during the day and instructing flying out at Weeks Field in the lingering twilight of the Arctic summer for another six hours or so."[10] The travel bureau was Arctic Alaska Travel Service, which was

L–R: *Ginny, Chuck West, and Celia at Arctic Alaska Travel Service office, Fairbanks, 1947. Courtesy of Ginny Wood.*

owned and operated by Chuck West. Chuck had been a pilot for Wien Airlines, flying cargo flights throughout the Arctic, who saw the potential for tourism in Alaska. When Sig Wien was not interested in tourism, Chuck started what he considered to be the farthest north travel agency at the time.[11] Ginny and Celia inspired Chuck to run tours of Fairbanks and helped organize the first guided tours of Kotzebue.

Chuck West, who had a radio program called *Wings Over the North*, interviewed us when we first arrived in Fairbanks, and asked me and Celia to come work for him in the tourist business he was starting. But he couldn't pay us very much. Any time he didn't have money to pay us, we'd work as flight instructors. Like at night in the summer while there was twenty-four hours of daylight. Or we would fly a charter flight somewhere. Neither place knew that we were working someplace else too. Celia and I even would trade off jobs, so one of us covered for the other. One guy never knew that both of us weren't really working for him. It didn't matter as long as the job got done. This travel service office that Chuck had was an old tin shack down on First Avenue that was so cold that winter that Celia put the typewriter on top of the stove and typed there. When it got down to twenty degrees below zero Fahrenheit, it was so cold that we just couldn't keep the place warm. We'd go out flying for a living until it got warmer.

When the summer came, the first tourists started coming over the Alaska Highway. It had just been opened to the public after originally being built for the military.[12] One day some people that had just come over the highway walked in and they wanted to know if there were any tours they could take around Fairbanks. We said, "Well, could you come back this afternoon?" Chuck was out for lunch, and when he came back, we said, "Chuck, if you had a better car than your old beat-up Plymouth, we could take these people and show them some sights around here! Take them on tours around Fairbanks." He said, "You didn't tell them no, did you?" We said, "No, we didn't. We told them to come back." He said, "Well, I'll see what I can do." So he was on his way to the bank to see what he could borrow to buy a car, and up drove this big eleven-passenger limousine. They asked, "Hey buddy, know any place I could sell this rig?" Chuck said, "Well, step into the bank." Next thing you know here's Chuck outside the office beeping on the horn. He said, "Will this do?"[13] Then he said, "Okay, you girls, you go out and make up a tour." We made a banner, put it out front of the office, and did tours for the rest of the summer with that rig.

Then Wien Airlines started flights out to Kotzebue for the tourists to see an Eskimo village. Wien Airlines just provided the flights and Chuck had to do the rest. Celia and I worked on this starting in the summer of 1949. We mostly were tour guides. The tourist passengers sat in bucket seats in the DC-3 airplanes that flew out on weekends. We would be the flight attendants on the plane, serving food and drinks. As hostesses, we sat in the back of the plane on laundry and made peanut butter sandwiches for them for lunches. We would take a turn at the controls if the pilots needed a rest. Then we'd be the guide in Kotzebue.[14] We'd take care of the people. We'd show them Kotzebue, tell them about life in an Eskimo village, and find places for them to stay.

At the beginning, we put people up at Archie Ferguson's roadhouse and fed them at Beulah's restaurant, the only places in town. Later, there was a conflict with Archie so instead of stopping the tours, Chuck West decided to convert an old three-story building out there that had previously been owned by Gene Jack into a hotel. Celia and I were put in charge of the conversion and of taking care of the people who stayed there. We were only given about a week to get everything ready. When I flew out with a plane-load of army cots, mattresses, blankets, pots and pans, dishes, and other equipment to get the place set up for our first guests, Wien bumped it for cargo that they thought was more important, so that made it even more of a scramble. I found some local Eskimos to help me clean up the place, put in an oil-burning kitchen range for cooking, set up chemical toilets, and arrange partitions and blankets to create separate sleeping rooms for men and women. At the last minute, I discovered the range had no oil drums to supply it, so I ran out to borrow a two-burner Coleman stove from an Eskimo man named Abraham Lincoln who lived next door. His family was using it to fix their lunch, but he just handed it to me still lit. Amazingly, I managed

Ground transportation used for the Kotzebue tour—back of a truck, 1950. Courtesy of Ginny Wood.

to have hot soup and drinks ready for the passengers that Celia was bringing in. As the passengers wandered the beach and went for skin boat rides that we had arranged, Celia and I finished the makeshift rooms. We had an Eskimo handy-man, Levi, who had just finished painting the rooms where the toilets were. I asked him to make a sign warning people of the wet paint. He proudly made a sign that said "Fresh P." I tried to explain to him that this would not work and he made another sign that said "Wet P." It was pretty funny what we got into in those early days. We had to deal with things like the weather being bad and our guests being unable to leave and the new ones not getting in, running out of water and the delivery truck being broken, or running out of fresh meat and supplies.

So that's how we started the first Wien Kotzebue Roadhouse—the farthest north tourist accommodation at the time. We jokingly dubbed it "The Last Resort, Kotzebue-by-the-Sea," which had a double connotation, not only geo-graphically but quality of the facilities. It could handle twenty-five people if the employees, namely me and Celia, slept on the floor. Celia and I alternated with one in Kotzebue as a tour guide and the other in Fairbanks meeting trains and planes and driving tour passengers on local sightseeing trips. We brought the sheets back and forth to Fairbanks to be washed. We had a team of Eskimo girls and women who helped us make up all the beds when the clean sheets arrived. Celia and I prepared the meals, sometimes wandering the beach looking for a sheefish from a local fisherman to serve for supper. Sometimes with a loaf of bread under each arm for bartering purposes. In the evening, we'd arrange for an Eskimo dance to be held to entertain the tourists. York Wilson was one of the leaders of the dance group whom we often would ask, "You will dance again tonight, won't you? Another plane is coming today with white people to see the Eskimos dance. Promise you and Chester and Lester and Abraham and Lucy will be there tonight at nine o'clock." He always told us, "Don't worry so much." We tried to protect the Eskimos from being exploited or cheapened, like we told the tourists that they should request permission before taking pictures and should not enter a village home unless specifically invited to do so. We wanted people to understand that the Eskimo were a proud and competent people.[15]

Fairbanks was a much more slower-paced community when I got here. There were fewer people and everybody was more important. Everybody wasn't in such a hurry. In those days people had more time, and more time for each other. Winter came and people slowed down, waiting for summertime to get going again. The town sort of settled down to a peaceful communal-type thing. I guess Fairbanks has always had a boom and bust economy, but there was a much more live-and-let-live feeling when we first got here than now. Every time we had a boom, like the first building boom during the Korean War when they were making all the DEW Line military installations [Distant Early Warning Line],[16] we got the first rush of people coming up to get rich quick, but they sort of left with the termination dust (that's snow) in the fall and Fairbanks would go back to being just a little old sleepy town. People always had opinions and there were always factions. But it was more of a family-type quarrel; now there seems to be polarization. Whether you're talking about the game or the land, or whatever it is. There are just more and more people wanting the same things. Wanting it to be the way it was in the early days. That won't work anymore. There are too many people. You can only cut a pie so thin. It is just that we happened to come to Fairbanks at the right time when it was just growing enough to be interesting and not so isolated as to be far away from everything. It had a university and a plane to Seattle three times a week. I think that Fairbanks is still overall a little small town on the outskirts of a frontier, but it is more sophisticated now.

The frontier is an interesting concept. I think it was Wallace Stegner who said that progress spoils what makes a frontier attractive. Frontier is another name for transition. I think a lot of people come to a frontier place feeling temporary. That this is as far as you want to go for now. You didn't come to this frontier place as a destination. It was just a jumping-off place for people that were going out further. That was part of the mystique and part of the adventure of it. You know, the idea that if we got a boat, we could go down this river. Or when snow comes, we could get a dog team and go out into the country.

And when the snow melts, you know there was always the thought that maybe we could walk somewhere.

You had to have a reason for coming to a frontier. Often it was to exploit a place, take it over from the Indians, to get rich, find new beginnings, or you were running away from something at home. Maybe the law even? So you got the best and the worst of civilization. You may have come as a settler to farm or to raise cattle, but you didn't come to just stay there the rest of your life. A lot of it was just to make it rich and then go back to marry the person you left at home. Usually, it was just a staging place; a stopping point to explore the next frontier.

But a frontier society is something that only exists until you get what you came for—growth and prosperity. As soon as you get there, you want to have everything like it was in the place where you left. But bigger and better. Progress, it's called. Some people would say then that progress corrupts the frontier that they came to. But for others they see it as an opportunity. It's whatever your value system is. I'm sure that all the women that came to the frontiers thought it was great when they finally got running water and electricity because it made life a little easier. Then they got schools and they didn't have to home school their children anymore. I think for them that was progress. The thing is, where progress becomes what changes, takes, or spoils what you came for, then you don't realize it until it's happened. It's like the Renaissance. I'm sure that one day somebody didn't wake up and say, "Oh, this is the first day of the Renaissance." It's when you look back and analyze it that you say, "Oh, this is what was happening." At the time, you're part of something and you don't see it the same way.

But then some come to the frontier to make a new place for themselves. Frontier towns become communities when you're not just people like Lewis and Clark or people with the covered wagons—you know, just passing through—but when everybody wants to farm, to get somewhere where they could own more land, or have a chance to do something with their lives. A frontier community is a place where everybody is interdependent. People may have come from cities where they felt they had a community with a small group of people. Where it was one segment of society that was their community. Or if the parents had lived there a long time, maybe it was a larger segment. But here in the frontier of Alaska, nobody knew who was who, what anybody's background was. You didn't know whether they came from the wrong side of the tracks or what their education was. What their families did. Even what their religion was. Everybody would just take you for what you were because no one knew your background. This was perfect for people that wanted to make a new start or be accepted for just who they were for now. They lost those labels up here. People became liked and accepted not because they were from Back Bay, Boston, or the upper classes of Philadelphia, but because they were somebody that you knew you could depend on. To some extent that's still true in Alaska.

When we came to Fairbanks in 1947, it was almost still the frontier. The Alaska Highway was not opened yet to civilian traffic. And scheduled flights to the Lower Forty-eight only came in three times a week on Pan Am Airlines. There was a railroad that went to Seward and boats that connected with that. But it really was kind of isolated. You could get land cheap. You could either homestead it, or like we did, buy it for one hundred dollars an acre. That's what everybody was doing. And you could cut your own logs. There were no rules and regulations particularly. You don't need them until you get what you wanted: more people, growth, and prosperity. Then you've lost all those opportunities that you could just go out and do things. You don't need rules and regulations and restrictions as long as there are very few people. And I think that's one of the things that the Republicans partly don't understand yet—that you can't have growth without regulations. Where there are very few people you kind of make your own rules and you're ostracized if you don't shape up, if we don't like you. The community kind of sets the tone. It's just a matter of saying that things are not done this way here, but this is how we do it. You can't afford to be an outlaw or be outside the group, because you're dependent on the group. Then when you make it big and you've built your big home, that kind of isolates you. You separate into hierarchies of wealth and power. You lose that feeling of freedom, independence, and the frontier that you had when nobody else was here.

Celia (left) and Ginny (right) with their heavily loaded bicycles in northern Norway, 1948. Courtesy of Ginny Wood.

8

Returning to Europe

**It was two different eras: after the war and before the war.
I saw war in Europe. I saw the aftermath of war in Europe.**

Ginny's plan to return immediately to Europe in 1938 by earning money
from the sale of a travel book she wrote did not materialize. World War II
and a variety of other adventures got in the way. Her long-lost dream of
visiting Europe finally happened in 1948, when she and Celia went to Sweden as
exchange students from the University of Alaska Fairbanks.

It was coming up on our second winter in Fairbanks, and Celia and I decided
we didn't want to fly in the winter anymore. It's hard work flying a small plane
in Alaska in the winter. You have to drain your oil and bring it inside so it doesn't
freeze overnight. You spend more time on the ground trying to get the plane
going in cold weather than flying it, and there's a lot of bad weather that's
always grounding you. So we signed up for courses at the university. At the time,
European universities had set up these programs for veterans to come and take
courses. They knew we had the GI Bill that gave American soldiers who had
been in the war five hundred dollars month for college tuition and five hundred
dollars for room and board,[1] so they were trying to take advantage of this opportunity. They had these courses in England, in France, in any place that wasn't so
bombed out that they had room to put the students.

Even though as WASPs Celia and I didn't get the GI Bill,[2] we had money
from our flying jobs in Alaska to pay for college. We signed up to be students
in the special course for Americans at the University of Stockholm in Sweden.
I chose Sweden because my mother and grandfather were Swedish. My mother
knew some Swedish, but I only knew the bad words or things like "I have to go
to the potty." I wanted to learn more. Plus, I had been in Sweden only a short
time on my 1938 bike trip and wanted to go back.

Celia Hunter wrote a column for her hometown newspaper, the Everett Daily Herald, to finance her part of the European schooling and travels. The paper published the letters she sent to managing editor, Mr. A. M. Glassberg, which describe in prosaic detail day-to-day life in Sweden, their traveling adventures, and her observations on life in postwar Europe. Ginny explains that Celia bought a lightweight Swiss typewriter, which she carried in the bottom of her rucksack, and that when they returned home "we had to smuggle it through US customs because to bring things like that back, you had to pay a large duty fee." Celia was paid $2.50 per column[3] and was given a press pass that once in Europe gave her preferred access, free tickets, etc.[4]

Celia wrote eloquently of the destruction and hardship she witnessed. Of finding pleasure in traveling with few belongings and having the freedom and flexibility that bicycling or hitchhiking allowed. Of meeting new people and learning about new cultures. Of political changes in countries after the war. And of appreciating both being American and coming to understand Europeans. Many of the following stories Ginny tells also appear in Celia's columns. Since they were written at the time the events happened, they often contain more detail than Ginny's retelling sixty years later, when memories had begun to fail.[5] The combination of these tellings provide a richer view of what Ginny and Celia experienced. Quotes from Celia's columns are interwoven with Ginny's stories, or appear in endnotes as verification.

We went over in the fall of 1947 on a boat where everybody else were ex-GIs.[6] In Sweden, Celia and I both stayed with different people who knew that there were American students coming over and had chosen us from a list.[7] The one that I stayed with was a neat lady.[8] Celia stayed with a family that lived about nine miles away from town.[9] The course that they put together was on Swedish culture. You took two hours a day of Swedish language. Then the rest of it was the history of Sweden, their economy, their art, their literature.[10]

Ginny goes on to explain how their study abroad trip turned into a yearlong bicycle tour of Europe:

Instead of paying five hundred dollars tuition and room and board for a second semester, I said to Celia, "Let's go traveling by bicycle." I wanted to see more of Europe and go see some of the people I'd met before, like my friend, Ibby, in Denmark. I talked Celia into it. So we used that money for traveling instead of for school.[11]

As skiers, Ginny and Celia were given an opportunity in early March that they just could not resist. It proved advantageous for launching their tour of Europe.[12] As Ginny explains:

At the same time when I was suggesting the idea of a bicycle trip to Celia, students from the Austrian Student Union at the University of Vienna invited students from Sweden to come to Austria for a month of skiing with them at special areas in the Tyrol. They had a hostel that they were renting for a month to ski in one of the really well-known places. This was downhill skiing. I had brought my skis with me from Alaska because I figured I'd use them in Sweden. So we went as Swedish students, part of the "studenten cap." We paid in German marks. You could get a handful of them. Marks were nothing. We went down on a train that went through Germany.[13] You were allowed to take the train all the way to Salzburg as long as you didn't get off the train. The train didn't stop. Germany was so bombed out, they didn't want any company. You'd go through towns and there wasn't anything standing. They didn't even have enough to eat. They had some youth hostels that were open, but the thing was the police came every night—whether you were in a hostel or you were staying in a little room—they came every night to check your passport. To see who was staying there. Because they were flooded with people that had just escaped, like from Latvia, Estonia, Lithuania, whose countries had been occupied and they couldn't go home.

Celia writes about her impressions of their cross-Germany trip:

> The ruined cities of the Third Reich passed in review. It's one thing to see them in pictures—even motion pictures—and quite another to meet them face-to-face. The effect is simply complete depression, so that you long to see a whole city once again. The few untouched cities along the route, like Heidelberg, the famous university town, are restful. Hamburg we couldn't see, for it was night, but Hannover [sic], which we passed in the early morning, showed acre after acre of blasted, shattered dwellings, and buildings. People still live in the habitable rooms in the ruins. The stations' once vaulted arches of steel with thousands of glass windows, are open to the weather now, not a single piece of glass left.
>
> The faces of the Germans have a lean, drawn, hungry look, and they are dirty. Food and soap are scarce in post-war Germany. Children beg for oranges, cigarettes, and candy at trains at the stations.[14]

And we went to two different places in Austria to these ski camps for Swedish students. The first was Gries, a little village in Brenner Pass. That sounded like a good place to ski. There was a hotel run by a family, called Gasthof Weisses Rossl ["inn of little white horses"].[15] It was about eighty or ninety miles south of Innsbruck. I traded my skis to the man of the family because he had broken his skis and had no way of buying a new pair. He was a beautiful skier.

Ginny enjoying the skiing and scenery in Austria, March 1948. Courtesy of Ginny Wood.

According to Celia, these ski areas and hostels were full of international students, not just those they had come with from Sweden. After Gries, Ginny and Celia went on to ski in Saalbach and then traveled to Salzburg. They spent about a month total in Austria.

Instead of returning to Sweden with the student group, we snuck into Austria, which you weren't supposed to do. You had no way of getting any rations unless you lived there. So you had to live on whatever you could get. We'd be staying at these ski hostels and have to translate the care packages that came from the United States. Explain what it was and how to cook it.

One time Celia and I were walking down the streets of Salzburg, talking to each other, and this woman in a WAC [Women's Army Corps] uniform, a captain, said, "It's good to hear English. Could I ask what you girls are doing here?" We said, "Well, we've just been to one of the ski camps, downhill skiing." We went to two different camps and we were between camps. She said, "I bet you'd like to have a hamburger and a milkshake." We said, "Oh, yes." "Well," she said, "I'll give you a permit to go to the American PX." This was after the war, but we were still an occupying force. We went to the PX to get our hamburger. Boy, was that wonderful!

A captain who was sitting with his girlfriend at one of the booths called over to one of the enlisted men and said, "I want you to kick out those two Krauts that are sitting over there. They shouldn't be here. Go ask for their passports." He came over and told us the captain said he wanted to see our passports. I said, "What for?" Of course we were wearing these shabby clothes. We'd patched our pants, and patched our pants, and we'd patched the patches. Because you couldn't buy anything new. We would just go off in the woods somewhere and take off our pants and sew them. We had started out with ski pants that came down to the ankle, so we would use all the leg parts for our fanny, which is where you wore it out the most, and patched them.[16] We showed him our passports and he went back over to the captain and said, "Sir, they're Americans." The captain comes over and says, "What in the hell are you wearing all those Kraut outfits for? Can't you get decent clothes?" I said, "I'm sorry, sir. We can't buy them here."

These were the American troops that hadn't fought in the war. You found out in the youth hostels and places wherever people were together that anybody that had been in the war, no matter which side they were on, had a camaraderie of understanding. Americans talking to Germans, they'd say, "You were in that campaign? Oh my gosh, you were giving us hell. That was the worst. Wow, wasn't that hell?" They didn't care what country you were fighting for, they knew what you'd gone through.

But the new ones who had come over later, that had never been in the war, they were just throwing their weight around. You know, crowding the Germans off the street. Calling them Krauts. I was ashamed of their behavior. One time when a guy was telling us to get off the street, I said, "Why?" He said, "Well, aren't you a Kraut?" I said, "No. And I wouldn't get off for you anyway. I'm ashamed of you. You get off the street! This belongs to the Germans." It was so different from the feeling in the youth hostels.

Then we went on to Italy and spent a month there.[17] We bought bicycles when we went through northern Italy, which they tried to take away at the border when we left. You were supposed to have gone through customs for that, and they said we didn't have a permit. Well, I said, "They sold us the bicycles." So I kind of dickered with them and let a few little tears drop and they said, "Oh, go on." These were good Italian bicycles. They had gears and were light and fast.

In her May 4, 1948, column, Celia tells the story of buying their Italian bicycles in Como, Italy. Here we learn that they named their new bikes Guiseppe and Garibaldi. And that Ginny and Celia were stopped by a border agent at the town of Chiazza, Italy, on their way to Lugano, Switzerland, for not having the permit for their bicycles. As Celia explained, "Italy had recently passed a law forbidding any foreigner from taking a bicycle out of the country without a special export permit issued from Rome. The dealer had forgotten to mention this."[18]

While Ginny does not elaborate on the Italian portion of their journey, Celia does. For example, in one column Celia mentions their stay in Venice. It rained the entire time and she was dismayed by the dirtiness of the city that she had heard was one of Europe's crown jewels. She goes on to explain:

> We had a map of the city, but we soon found that navigating a plane over the trackless wastes of Alaska was child's play compared to reaching a given destination through these tangled thoroughfares. And you can imagine the two umbrellas trying to pass in a space no more than four feet wide![19]

After World War II, there was a great need for reconstruction assistance throughout Europe. It was obvious that heavily bombed countries like Germany, France, and England needed help, but there were also relief efforts directed toward the smaller but equally damaged countries, such as Finland. Finland had fought three wars: the Winter War of 1939–1940 against the Russians; 1941–1944 when the Germans attacked Russia, the Russians moved into Finland, and the Germans sent troops after them; and in the fall of 1944, when the Finns gave in to Russia and under the terms of the peace treaty were forced to turn against the Germans, their previous allies, in order to drive them out of Finland.[20] The result was a scorched-earth campaign where the Germans burned everything in their path as they retreated.[21] In 1946, the American Friends Service Committee organized work camps in Finland to help reconstruct homes. The workers were volunteers who received food and lodging and travel expenses in exchange for their service.[22] Ginny and Celia found themselves working at one of these camps in northern Finland.

I stopped in Paris to see a gal that I knew who was from Seattle. Her name was Pat Dunham. She was head of the work camps for the Quakers that were helping to rebuild in countries devastated after the war.[23] She said, "Would you like to work in Finland?" I said, "Yeah." She said, "Well, they need some more students up in northern Finland." So Celia and I were on the train the next day and stayed up there a month. It was a town called Lokka. It was way north of the Arctic Circle.[24]

We were building log houses. There were Germans and French and several English there, too. They were all college-age kids. We lived in tents that had been given by the army, and ate rations that you wouldn't believe.[25] We were hungry all the time. But those Finns could work. They had a word they would say, *sisu*, which meant being able to go on against all odds.[26] And boy did they.

There was another American, and she was black. That was the first time I'd ever been around or known a black person. There wasn't a black in Waterville.

L–R: *Toni Sander, Ginny, and Celia Hunter chinking logs on a new home in Finland, August 1948. Courtesy of Ginny Wood.*

I'd never associated with a black before. Her name was Toni Sander. She was from Chicago. Her father had been president of a black university. She was hilariously funny, a riot, and just a neat person. She was the favorite person of the Finns and anybody who worked there.

When we were building these foundations for the cabins, they'd have the pile of gravel over here, and over there would be the cement sacks you had to fill, and down there were the footings where you were to pour the cement.[27] Celia, myself, and Toni—the Americans—we said, "Look, why don't we move the piles closer together, and then you only have to wheelbarrow just that one into the other? That would save three processes." Ken, the young Finnish guy that was the head of our program, who was an awfully nice guy, replied, "You Americans, what do you do with the time you save?" I always remember that.

Those Finns would work hard day labor.[28] And then dance all night. We were just exhausted. And I was pretty skookum in those days. I don't remember the songs, but maybe it's because I didn't know Finnish, so I wouldn't have learned any words. It seemed that there was always a dance that went on until four in the morning.[29] And then at six, you were up mixing cement.

The sound of the music awakened me. The haunting notes of an accordion filled the night, bittersweet like those of a gypsy violin, yet with a hint of the lilting tempo of a Swedish polka. I could hear the rhythmic clump of dancing feet hitting the floor like the percussion instruments of an orchestra.

I lay in my bunk in the tent. The soft warmth of my down sleeping bag urged my aching body to stay, while the haunting melody beckoned my feet to join the music and the dancing. Weary with eight hours of mixing and pouring cement for the new homes we were helping to build in this war-devastated village of Finnish Lapland, I had declined the invitation to join my fellow work campers at the dance the villagers were holding in our honor. But the call of the accordion was stronger than the balm of my bed.

The frosty chill in the air was a harbinger of the fact that, although it was still mid-August, winter would come early to this settlement two hundred miles north of the Arctic Circle. I shivered into my clothes and stepped outside the tent.

My watch showed the hour to be almost midnight, but faint streaks of light still colored the sky to the north silhouetting the tall pine trees creating the effect of perpetual twilight. A few weeks ago the sun had merely dipped to the horizon in acknowledgement of night, then started back its climb overhead. The village lay still and ghostly in the half light, blackened chimneys of burned-out homes stark against the sky, newly built log structures nestling in the pine clearing nearby. And everywhere the squat round hut of the sauna, the steambath house, that every Finnish family builds before he lays a log of his house or barn.

A fog was rising from the river surface and starting to creep up the bank toward the village. As I started down the path toward the water a Lapphund bounded out of an open doorway, his curled bushy tail standing out like a question mark. A few sniffs at my feet satisfied his curiosity and he jogged back to his bed.

I shoved the upswept prow of the boat into the stream, seated myself at the oars and pulled through the mist towards the opposite bank and the music beyond.

The orange glow of a campfire illuminated the dance platform and the perimeter of trees bordering the clearing. A log railing had been erected around the floor but only the sky served as a canopy overhead.

Perched on a corner of the rail was an orchestra, a lone man with the accordion, his booted foot beating out time against a log. Couples swirled and stamped to the somber folk music that seemed part Slavic and part Scandinavian, yet somehow intrinsically Finnish. There was no seeming gaiety and abandon in this group as there had been in similar groups I had watched Schottisching and Hamboing outdoors under the Norwegian and Swedish midnight sun.

Their movements were graceful and coordinated, but their expression seemed more like the dedicated seriousness of a Hopi ceremonial than a social festivity. The minor key of the music, the somber mood of the dancers, and the grey sky outlining the vast deep forests around seemed symbolic of the very history and soul of Finland. As I joined the onlookers hunching their backs to the warmth of the fire, I imagined I could hear the overtones of a Sibelius symphony.

A stocky blond man clad in a rough shirt, breeches, and knee-high black boots approached me and nodded towards the platform. I smiled my acceptance and took my place with my partner among the dancers.[30]

Of anyplace that Hitler had marched through or we had been in war-torn Europe from England to France to Belgium, I admired the Finns the most. The Finns suffered a lot of destruction and still had to pay war reparations, because they had fought with the Germans for a while. The Finns had the attitude that when they got through rebuilding their country, then it would all belong to them and they'd be a prosperous country again. The hard work was worth it to them and was seen as giving them training. They always would see the bright side. They never complained. They talked about it as a learning experience, saying, "We'll be better for it when it's over."

Ginny's bicycling through Europe with two other women in 1938 seems quite unusual for that time period. Most women then would never have even thought of such a journey, much less attempted such a journey. When asked whether women traveling alone were more common on this second trip ten years later,[31] Ginny said:

Isn't that funny, but I never saw it through that lens. We just had fun. Celia and I did have some very interesting experiences, which you might not have had as a woman alone. Like, we were hitchhiking more. Even hitchhiking with bicycles.

Oh, there was one interesting thing when we were staying at one hostel. This German gal came in who was kind of surly. She just had a chip on her shoulder. We learned that she had grown up in Berlin, and when it was being bombed she had to go down in the subway overnight to get out of the bombing. When the Russians were coming into Berlin at the end of the war, she knew it wasn't very good to be a German woman there, so she ran away and hid at night so as not to get caught. When she got to a river she swam over to the American side, leaving all her clothes behind, because she just didn't want to be in German territory. She knew what would happen being a blonde woman with Russian soldiers coming. Then she had worked in Switzerland on a farm. She had just gotten paid for working and was going back to Germany on a bicycle. She spoke English pretty well, so she asked us a lot of questions. We said, "Why don't you come bike with us? We've got some money. We'll pay for your food." We wanted to hear more about her experience. When we got back to the States, we gathered up a lot of clothing and sent it to her. We kept in touch with her for a long time.

It is informative to compare Celia Hunter's description of this same incident:

We met a German woman at the youth hostel in Lugano—"Jugen-herberge." Her name was Margund. She was twenty-four years old and a student at Gottingen University near Hamburg. She had poor clothing and shoes, and she didn't even have a pair of pajamas.

Under a special arrangement with the Swiss universities, groups of students from different German schools were permitted to come to Switzerland to work for a short period.

Margund had worked for three weeks on a farm in the French section of the country, near Solothurn, and was now traveling before returning to her classes in Germany. A friend of her father's, a Swiss, had loaned her a bicycle, and with this, she was traveling into every part of the country, pushing it over the high mountain passes because she had not the money for train fare.

Like almost every German, her adventures during the war sounded like fiction. She had fled from her home north of Berlin when the Russians reached it. With many other young girls from her school, she hid in some woods. Eventually only herself and a small handful of girls elected to chance the hazardous trip into American-held territory, fleeing by night and hiding by day, and at last swimming a lake in order to get there.

This trip to Switzerland has been her first experience in visiting a foreign country, and finding out how Germany and German aggression are viewed outside of the country. She had not realized how much Germany is hated by the nations it attempted to subjugate.[32]

Ginny was clearly aware of the differences between her first trip, when Hitler was expanding control and amassing troops, and this trip, when Europe was undergoing postwar recovery and reconstruction. It provided a rare opportunity for comparison.

Celia and I were on the road for a year and a half. Some places were just so devastated. And it was hungry. I know what it's like to be so hungry you just can't think of anything except food. Because we didn't have any way of getting ration points, we had to take anything that wasn't rationed. In summertime, locally you could buy things directly from the farms, and you could get sweetened canned condensed milk. That wasn't rationed. We'd buy it and that was our sweets. And usually you could get bread. You couldn't buy butter, so we'd buy a can of that milk and spread it on our bread and that was yummy. People would ask us, "Do you eat that in America?" "No," we'd say. "How can you stand it?" "Well, it tastes good and we're hungry."

A lot of the youth hostels served food. I remember one that served a cauliflower dish. All they had was cauliflower and some cheese, because it was rural. They probably made cheese there. It was delicious. I don't like cauliflower, but I learned to like it then. It was okay if you mixed it with potatoes. There were always potatoes. In some places the food wasn't bad. Like in France, it didn't matter what it was, it tasted good. I mean, they could do anything with anything and make it taste good. Anything the English did tasted terrible. They didn't have their usual roast beef so they didn't know what to do. They hadn't learned foreign cooking.

In Germany, you see, you weren't even supposed to be there. When we went on the train through Germany to Austria for the ski camp you couldn't get off the train, so you took stuff to eat with you. There just wasn't enough food to go around. You saw kids begging for food along the way. I don't know what we weighed, but we must have been terribly skinny. I remember I was so hungry that all I could think about was food. And then we'd come to a place where there was a market, and you usually could get bread. There was this peasant bread that we loved, but everybody else wanted white bread.

It was an interesting time to have been there. To know what it's like to be hungry, and know how wonderful people can be. Even though some others were not. But it was safe. We never had one unpleasant incident. All the biking we did, nothing was ever taken off our bicycles. It was a different world then. It was two different eras: after the war and before the war. I saw war in Europe. I saw the aftermath of war in Europe. And I was in the war here. Not the shooting part, but I knew what the world was like. When I first went to Europe there were the peasants and the people who were wealthy. This class thing was very apparent to us that don't have classes. I grew up in Waterville, and there were people that probably were the upper crust and there were the peasants, if you wanted to try to put them that way, but you just all lived in Waterville. After the war, in Europe everyone was more even. Everybody was rationed.

But it was interesting talking to people of different nationalities and their different view of things and how the war had been for them. I just thought there's this great big world out there. It's all different. And we aren't the best in everything. I think that without having gone to Europe the first time, I would've stayed in Waterville and married a rancher or something, maybe. I don't know. I think that probably the most interesting for me was to have seen Europe just on the brink of war from eleven different countries, and then to go back ten years later and do just about the same again with a bicycle and see some of the same people. Because you stop with a bicycle. You get off a bicycle and look. You don't stop a car.

I think it's just a different world nowadays. Everybody is going faster. There were no cars in Europe when I was there. I mean, bicycles could go anywhere because hardly anybody had a car. I don't think kids traveling today could have the same experience. I think that what they do is that everybody has too much money. For example, I know one young woman who has traveled a lot and gone and had some wonderful experiences, but she had Daddy's checkbook. She's never known what it was to be on the road in a country where people don't have any money, or don't have much food, and to be hungry. And you don't have much more yourself. Having to be self-reliant and finding creative ways to find food and shelter. And being with people that are on the same level.

Lunch break in a hay field, 1948. Courtesy of Ginny Wood.

Yet it isn't like going where they're poor or uneducated. Everybody that travels now has a credit card.

It was interesting for Celia, who had never been abroad before.[33] She grew up on the wrong side of the tracks and knew what it was like to be hungry during the Depression. This was all new to her.[34]

Some of our experiences were different because there were two of us. Celia would catch things that I wouldn't. There were little nuances that one of us would catch and the other one wouldn't, especially with the language. Like when we were in Ireland. We hitchhiked around Ireland because our bikes were in such bad shape after we'd gone through northern Norway.[35] We left our bicycles in London to have the rims redone.[36] They just needed whole new spokes and we didn't want to wait around for them to get finished. That was an interesting country to be in. Sometimes we'd sit by the side of the road waiting for a ride and all that would go by were people with burros. Sometimes you might not have taken the ride alone but with two of us, you would.

Celia and I would maybe split up in a town and do different things. But we didn't split up for long periods like I did on my first trip with Joan and Myra, because this time we were in war-torn Europe and it was very difficult. There were a lot of things that we did together, like deciding we wanted to go up the

Repairing flat tires was a recurring theme of the bicycle trip. Courtesy of Ginny Wood.

Gornergrat to see the big high place in Switzerland where there's a big fancy hotel at the top.[37] This guy that I had been going with in Seattle before I moved to Alaska was German. His father had come over to visit and he knew I was going to go to Europe, and he said, "You must go up to the Gornergrat and say I sent you. You have to do that." It's where a train winds up this mountainside in Switzerland.[38] We got there and found out it was very expensive. So we took the time table and decided we could walk up, as long as we knew when the trains were going to be on it. All the way up we'd see workmen and they'd say, "*Das ist verboten.*" And then we'd speak Swedish to them and they'd give up.[39] It was a very handy language to know just when you were doing something you shouldn't. Celia and I wrote my friend Otto a postcard from the top. It said, "Mission Accomplished." Otto said, "Mission accomplished. What does that mean?" His father explained it to him. His father loved that we'd done this. He would tell people that story all the time.

Or I remember one time coming over the mountains in southern France. We'd gotten up real high and we saw this big thunderstorm coming. It was near a place that had a ski tow in wintertime. There was big thunder and lightning; being up so high was a bad place to be. So we left our bicycles and went up and crawled up into the place where the ski tow turns around and goes back down again. It was covered. It wasn't luxurious, but at least we were dry. I'd never been in the middle of a storm like that.

Celia also mentions this thunderstorm in her column. She tells us that it happened in a mountain pass in the eastern Pyrenees Mountains called Col de Puymorens along the Spanish-French border:

> We found a hut designed to house ski tow machinery, and the whole back was open. It offered protection from the rain, at least. Closer inspection disclosed an attic, where we would be sheltered from the wind as well. We were snug and protected so much so that we made ourselves at home and cooked supper over our primus, but at the same time we were just a little apprehensive about what would happen if the lightning should hit the metal cables stretching from the big metal drum beside us on up the hill. We felt as exposed as swallows perched on a lightning rod, until our particular storm took itself away from our hill and died grumblingly away in the distance.[40]

After working in Finland, Ginny does not say much about the rest of their journey. However, by reading Celia's columns, we discover that they went on to Norway, and then Belgium.[41] From Antwerp, they got a ride on a small freight steamer across the English Channel, which they later discovered had a reputation for smuggling. After hitchhiking around England and Ireland, they went to Paris.

We met our friend Woody in Paris in October 1948. When Celia and I went to Sweden, he'd gone to Grenoble, France, for a year of college on the GI Bill so he would speak French fluently.[42] We managed through letters to say, "Let's meet in Paris at the American Express office on such and such a date." Celia and I went, and there was no Woody. We were just going out the door and here he came. His train was late. So we all went around Paris together for about a week. Celia very conveniently disappeared, even though by that time Woody was engaged to someone in San Francisco. I rode on his handlebars all around Paris. I was just thinking how I'd love to go to some of these cute little French restaurants with a guy, when he said, "Hungry? Would you like to eat?" I answered, "Yep." I was excited, thinking we'd go to one of those outdoor restaurants we'd been passing, when he brought out a loaf of bread from his pack and offered me some.

Woody delayed his return to Grenoble to join Ginny, Celia, and two guys (Brian Arnold and Frank Hotchkiss) they had been running around Paris with, for a week of hiking in Switzerland.[43] It was now early November and time for Ginny and Celia to return home. They had to go back to Sweden to retrieve belongings they left behind and then find a ship home.[44] In Oslo, they found an oil tanker

Woody and Celia in Paris, October 1948. Photo by Ginny Wood.

"It was harder getting rides hitchhiking with the boys than it was with just us gals," Switzerland, October 1948. Courtesy of Ginny Wood.

called the *Nordanger* heading to Curaçao, an island belonging to the Dutch off the coast of Venezuela, that was willing to take them as passengers. They were expecting a sixteen-day trip. Instead, because of stormy weather and rough seas, it took twenty-five days and they landed in Aruba. Fortunately, in Aruba they were able to gain passage on an American oil tanker called the SS *Strathmore*. After eight more days of sea travel, Celia and Ginny arrived in New York City. While glad to be back on American soil, they still had to find an inexpensive way to get home to Seattle. After over a year of traveling in Europe, they had little money left. According to Celia's column, they drove an old jeep from Hackensack, New Jersey, arriving in Seattle on December 23, 1948. They drove continuously for six days, with one sleeping in the back while the other drove. They only stopped for gas and oil, and to cook one hot meal a day on their Primus stove.

Ginny explains how she felt upon returning home from her second European trip:

When I came back from a year and a half of being in Europe, I thought I'd left Alaska for good that time. I thought Alaska was a great place with wonderful people, but who wants to spend the rest of their lives there. I was home in Seattle about one month and I decided I wanted to come back here to Fairbanks. I just didn't like what people were doing out there in the Lower 48. I just didn't like the milieu. I wanted to go back to my friends in Alaska.

In the fall of 1949, after Celia and I came back from Europe, we were looking for something else to do instead of flying. So we decided to buy up all the mukluks at the trading post in Kotzebue and drive around in my old Jeep station wagon to sell them at ski resorts in the Lower 48. It was a way to pay for a skiing trip. We sold them all and then decided we'd go on to Mexico.

On our way down to Mexico, we met Woody at the Sierra Club's Clair Tappaan Lodge in the Sierra Nevada Mountains in California. After skiing together, Celia and I went back down to Berkeley with him. I had relatives down there in Oakland I was staying with. One day he called up and said, "Can I see you before you leave for Mexico?" We went for a walk and ended up at Indian Rock, which is a large rock outcropping up in the hills with a view of the San Francisco Bay.[45] It's a pretty spot. It was about sunset time. He was acting very funny. Like he had something on his mind. I said, "Well, I guess you'll be married when I come through here on the way back?" He said, "Not really. I just called it off." I said, "You did?" He said, "Yeah. I want to marry you." I said, "When?" And he said, "Tomorrow."

Upon first meeting Woody in 1947, Ginny was attracted by his worldly experience, by the fact that he had spent time in Europe as a child. Plus, he was nice looking and a skilled outdoorsman. Ginny had had her share of boyfriends in her youth, some of whom wanted to marry her. When asked why she never accepted

Ginny's new jeep station wagon, December 1948. Courtesy of Ginny Wood.

any of the proposals, she says she was not ready to settle down yet. She had too many things she still wanted to do. When Woody transferred to the University of California, Berkeley to finish his degree in forestry, Ginny had thought she would never see him again.[46] So his proposal was especially surprising.

I thought it was a good idea to marry him, but I had to think it over. Besides, it was kind of sudden. I thought, "Does he really mean it?" So, I said, "Well, you know, I'd planned this Mexican trip with Celia and I can't let her down. And besides, I can't do this to my folks. It really would be terrible to just go off and get married. Plus I'd promised Wien Airlines that I'd run their Kotzebue operation this summer. So before we can get married, I've got to find somebody to take my place. I promised them and they're counting on it."

On our way back from Mexico, Celia and I stopped at Palm Springs to see my friend Nancy Baker from the WASP. She was flight instructing there.[47] Nancy said, "I'm getting sick of this place. I don't like the person I'm working for. Where's that place you guys work?" Nancy never knew geography. She grew up in New

York so that meant down south there was Florida and there was Boston. During the WASPs, she knew how to get places, she could navigate, she never was lost, but she never knew what state she was over or what state was next to it. I said to Nancy, "I may have a job for you." She quit her job, met me in Seattle, and we drove up, camping all the way. I introduced Nancy to Sig Wien and I don't think he knew to the day he died which one of us was which. And I don't think he cared. Anyway, Nancy really enjoyed the work and stayed in Kotzebue for many years. She just really loved it.[48] I knew my job would be well filled by her. I hadn't let Wien down.

I got married in Seattle in July 1950. Woody came up from Berkeley. And his mother and his aunt came to the wedding. We had a wedding and a reception that my mother took care of. She was satisfied that she saw me married, and my dad was tickled to death. He was wondering if I ever was going to get married, while my mother fell in love with every boy I ever went with. One of them was Tom Stewart—Judge Tom Stewart from Juneau who worked for the Alaska Constitutional Convention when they were working for statehood in 1958.[49] He was part of my skiing crowd when I was a senior at the University of Washington. He was a beautiful skier, wonderful skier. We were on the ski patrol together and we dated a few times. My mother would say, "Where's that nice little Stewart boy that used to come around?"

As soon as Woody and I got married, I got him a job up at Mount Baker, because from skiing up there I knew the guy that was head of the Forest Service. Woody and his buddy got a job for the summer inspecting all the logging operations for complying with regulations[50] while I got the job up in the lookout tower—spotting for forest fires.[51] After having been up in Alaska and Kotzebue, and all the adventures I'd had, I had to just go up and sit all alone in the tower. I climbed one hundred feet up this ladder every day and sat there. It was a nice view, but there weren't any fires. I never saw a fire! But I had to be on duty. So I did lots of reading. One of the things I read was Henry David Thoreau. Thoreau's *Walden* was one of Woody's favorite books, so I decided I would read it.[52] I knew of him, but this was the first time that I really read it and got into his philosophy. Aldo Leopold, too. Then Woody would come back and tell me all about the neat places he'd seen while he was out inspecting.

That fall we went back to Berkeley for Woody to finish his senior year at Cal. He thought learning how to fly might be a good thing to do. He could do it on the GI Bill and I was working as a flight instructor, so I taught Woody and his best friend, Robin Welch, to fly at Buchanan Field in Concord. They were very good students.[53] Woody went on to get his commercial and his instrument rating. Then we bought a Ragway 170 Cessna airplane for two thousand dollars.[54] That was a lot of money back then. I think we were living on eight thousand dollars [a year]. I guess we afforded it by eating less. It didn't take much to live back then. I was always good at saving money. I was never good at making it.

Ginny and Woody get married on July 20, 1950, in Seattle, Washington. Courtesy of Ginny Wood.

The fire tower that Ginny climbed every day and the little house she and Woody lived in near Demming, Washington, during the summer of 1950. Photo by Ginny Wood.

But I always could earn enough to eat. And Woody got a sum of money when they discharged him from the army, as well as the five hundred per month for tuition and five hundred a month to live on from the GI Bill.

Woody and Ginny focused their attention on creating a life together in a new place and enjoying the varied outdoor activities available to them, like hiking in the nearby hills or skiing in the Sierra Nevada mountains. Woody soon would be finished with his forestry degree, and would have to think about what to do next. As Ginny explains, returning to Alaska was the furthest thing from their minds:

When I left Alaska to marry Woody, we both thought we would not come back. There was lots of the rest of the world to see or sample. And Woody thought, "Well, you know that time in Alaska had been great, but you wouldn't want to spend your life there." As it turned out, I was only out for one winter. I remember going to a play or a concert in San Francisco, and we got held up on the San Francisco Bay Bridge by an accident. We were getting tired of sitting in the traffic. Suddenly, Woody said, "Would you like to go back to Alaska?" Without hesitation, I said, "I sure would." That was only nine months after we left.

With Woody's graduation coming up, we had started to say to each other, "Well, what will we do for the summer?" Woody had been applying around for a job and he had an offer to go to Juneau with the US Forest Service. But he didn't like rain. In the meantime, he'd gotten this letter from Grant Pearson, who was superintendent of McKinley Park.[55] He knew Woody from when he was climbing around there and liked him. He said, "There's a job opening for just a workman for a couple of months, but then we'll need another ranger. Are you interested? I'll hold it for you, if you'll be here." When Woody was a student in Fairbanks, he and three others had gotten up to seventeen thousand feet on Mount McKinley but hadn't made the top. So that was sort of unfinished business for him. He just wanted to be near that mountain. So all of a sudden sitting there in traffic, we just said, "Well, let's do that!"

Woody didn't even stay to get his diploma. We had our plane all packed and ready to go, and after graduation we took off that same day to fly back to Alaska.

A steaming fumarole in the Valley of Ten Thousand Smokes, 1951. Photo by Morton and Ginny Wood. Katmai Administrative Records Collection, Accession Number KATM-283, National Park Service, Katmai National Park and Preserve.

9

Exploring Katmai National Park

All we had were maps that said "unsurveyed."

In 1951, when Woody Wood was hired by the National Park Service at Mount McKinley National Park (now Denali National Park), Superintendent Grant Pearson also had administrative oversight of Katmai National Monument, located at the head of the Alaska Peninsula in southwestern Alaska. Katmai National Monument was established in 1918, after the 1912 volcanic eruption of Novarupta near Mount Katmai, which spread ash for miles and left a deep crater in the mountain, attracted scientific interest in this geologically unique area. The first National Park Service ranger was stationed at remote Katmai in 1950. In 1980, the area became Katmai National Park and Preserve under its own management regime.[1] Woody was expecting his first Park Service assignment to be the Wonder Lake Ranger Station, but a young biologist named Les Viereck had been given the job as temporary ranger for the summer.[2] (Later, Les, Woody, and Ginny would come to be very close friends.[3]) Instead, Woody was sent to Katmai in June of 1951 with the mandate to explore it for recreational opportunities.[4] Ginny went with him.[5]

We went kicking and screaming down to Katmai because we wanted McKinley Park. That's why Woody went into the Park Service in the first place. He went down to Katmai in late June and I joined him about the first of July. I flew down with our plane. I was going to fly it all the way to King Salmon, but the weather was bad, and the motor was missing a little bit, so I left it in Anchorage. I took a commercial flight over to King Salmon, and then a hop with a floatplane that came and got me. We were to be there all summer, until around the first week of September. They told us they would come and get us in September on a certain date. We were so disappointed not to be in McKinley Park. I'm used to alpine stuff—glaciers and trees. But we realized, when we were coming back, we said, "Where on earth nowadays could just the two of us have been alone in all that wilderness with our mission being just to explore it? Where would you ever have the chance to do that?" Looking back on it, I think where could you ever be plunked down like that, unless you'd been born a hundred years earlier and then you wouldn't have had an airplane.

We were the second ones down there at Katmai for the Park Service. The year before they'd sent Bill Nancarrow, who was a ranger at McKinley Park,[6] down with his wife, Ginny, to go down and build a cabin so you'd have someplace other than a tent to sleep in.[7] They built two six-by-twelve tent-frame cabins. One to keep their gear in, and another one to live in, to cook in and sleep in. And they'd left some gear there. They'd left a small motorboat there. It was just an overgrown rowboat with a probably twenty-five horsepower motor on the back. They didn't do much exploring. We had to make sure to keep the little motorboat going because the only other transportation we had on the lakes down there was our Folbot collapsible kayak. So the first thing Woody did was bring the motor into the house and take it apart. He said, "If I can take it apart, I can put it together again. But I don't want to do it for the first time out in a storm in the middle of the lake in waves. I want to practice on it first, on my own terms." Woody had a sense of how things worked. It wasn't something he did as a kid or wanted to do. That didn't appeal to him. But he had a wisdom of how it had to be.

Our mandate was to explore as much as we could for recreational opportunities.[8] That was our mission. It was pretty well surveyed in the area around Lake Grosvenor, but on the map the rest just said unsurveyed. So maps didn't do us any good. It was just the two of us, and the only thing to go by was a compass. Luckily, Woody was very good at navigating. Parts of this area had been explored and written up by the National Geographic Society. They had sent a team in around 1917 after the volcano blew.[9] They sent in teams two different summers.[10] One to explore from the ocean side up over the top and down into the Valley of Ten Thousand Smokes, and then one up into the valley. They wrote it up, and Woody and I had a copy of that edition of *National Geographic* with us.[11]

We spent a couple of weeks at what we called "park headquarters," where the two tent cabins were. There's a place there that's been used by the Natives. Every fall they'd come in there to get fish and hunt. You could see the racks where they hung their fish and everything. But we were the only ones down there. Brooks Camp, where the lodge and visitor center are now, is in a different place. There are two lakes, which are about a mile and a half apart. And we cut a trail between the two of them. Over on Brooks Lake, the Fish and Wildlife Service had some biologists,[12] so we'd hike over there—by trail it was about two miles—because the Fish and Wildlife Service flew wonderful food in for them. They had fresh food, steaks, and vegetables and stuff. We just had canned goods and dried stuff.

Before we decided to explore Katmai by rivers and lakes, Woody and I made a hiking trip into the Valley of Ten Thousand Smokes. Not many people

Map of Katmai National Park by Dixon Jones.

had been in there, because you had to go across the Ukak River. Grant Pearson, when he was a ranger in 1945, he and another person had tried to cross it and it was just too deep and fast to get across.[13]

Woody and I took the park's motorboat down to the head of Iliuk Arm and left the boat there. We bashed through the brush, but there wasn't any river. It had changed since Grant had been there. About two or three miles up, the main channel of the Ukak River now made a right-angle turn, which ended up putting all the water higher up into the Savonoski River instead. The map showed the river in one place, but now it was in another. This left a dry riverbed for us to cross. Grant had told us to take along waterproof bags and a rope to pull ourselves and our gear across the deep river, but we ended up not having to do that.

We took three days, camping and I wouldn't call it hiking but stumbling into the valley. We started to follow the Ukak River to go into the Valley of Ten Thousand Smokes, but we found out that was bad because we kept running into quicksand on the river. It was a helluva place to walk in. We were used to hiking in McKinley Park. Sure, they have rough going there, but you get so you can spot it. You botanize with your binoculars. You can tell by the trees, by the

Campsite near the mouth of the Ukak River, 1951. Photo by Morton and Ginny Wood. Katmai Administrative Records Collection, Accession Number KATM-283, National Park Service, Katmai National Park and Preserve.

vegetation, whether it's good walking or not. If you get up high, on the ridges, anywhere you just see green grass, that means it's good walking. So we thought at Katmai if we went high where we could see green meadowy stuff, we could get out of this bad stuff. But up along the ridges it was just as bad or worse. Because of the volcanic explosions the brush had buried logs and stumps in it. It was just dense brush that you can't ever find a way out of. The rocks don't bother you as much as the shrubs. They are from a foot up to three feet high and you stumble over them. They have thick trunks. There's no nice tundra. It wasn't smooth walking. It was very uneven. You don't take a real step, you stumble. If you had a stream to cross, you had to deal with rocks. But the rocks floated. They were volcanic.

Finally, after days of stumbling we came out on the valley. All of a sudden it thins out and you see these stumps of big trees just sticking out of the sand. They'd been sheared off. You can tell that's where the foot of the flow from the explosion had come to. They had weathered down, but you could see that the trees probably were originally cut off at about six feet high. It was fascinating.

We were reading the *National Geographic* to help guide us. We went about two miles up the valley along the edge of Mount Griggs until we got to the last stream where you could still get fresh water. So we could get drinking water. After that, the streams aren't clear and they just sink underground beneath all

Stumps and cut-off trees at the edge of the Valley of Ten Thousand Smokes, 1951. Photo by Morton and Ginny Wood. Katmai Administrative Records Collection, Accession Number KATM-283, National Park Service, Katmai National Park and Preserve.

the ash cover. We made a base camp there to explore the valley from. We had five days of food with us for the whole trip, but we'd already used up two getting in there.

We wanted to try to get as far up into the Valley of Ten Thousand Smokes to where we could see the smokes. But there are two streams that run right through the valley that you have to cross, and they'd cut down about fifty to seventy-five feet straight down. When we got to the first stream, we followed along it until we finally found a way that we could let ourselves down and cross it and then climb back up the other side. It was like mountain climbing. Woody was very sure-footed. He had done a lot of climbing. I'd done some climbing myself at Mount Baker, and in 1940 I climbed Mount Rainier.[14] The two sides of the cut down are so close that you almost think you can do a running jump, but if you didn't make it you could fall some fifty to seventy feet. So we didn't try that. We crossed both Lethe River and Knife Creek. We had the rope we were going to use to get our stuff across the Ukak River, so we used it for climbing down into these creeks instead.

Once we got in the valley, it was just rocks. It's not like seeing the Grand Canyon for the first time. They're very dull rocks. They aren't pretty at all until you pick them up and turn them over and then they're all kinds of colors. The rocks were dull because I think it had just been blown over so much. So in

The upper part of Lethe Creek canyon, 1951. Photo by Morton and Ginny Wood. Katmai Administrative Records Collection, Accession Number KATM-283, National Park Service, Katmai National Park and Preserve.

our notes that we were supposed to make, we made the suggestion that if they stationed a ranger there that one of his duties was before the tourists came to go and turn the rocks over. They were a brilliant color.

We did get up to where we could see the smokes. We didn't see ten thousand smokes. We only saw seven smokes, so we called it the Valley of Seven Smokes. The steam comes out in puffs. It doesn't blast out like at Yellowstone. It wasn't too dangerous to walk right up to them, but it was a matter of time and food. We only had food for three days of exploring after we got into the valley.

We never saw any sign of any man or anything. We never saw another person. No flowers in there. We didn't see any animals. But we did see very old bear tracks.

The Park Service was talking about putting a road through or building a lodge out there, and we said how nothing would stay there. We really expressed that. Because there usually are big winds. Griggs's book told about terrific winds in the valley, and these rocks flying through the air. We were lucky to not have any wind the whole time we were in there. If we had, we wouldn't have been traveling. Since then I've read the accounts of scientists who had helicopters taking them in and they remarked on the wind and the bad weather. I thought how we were just babes in the woods. We didn't even have radios back then, walkietalkies or anything like that, in case the weather got bad or we had needed help.

We came out of the valley on one little pack of rye crisps, a can of sardines, and a candy bar. That's all we hiked out on for two days because we wanted to stay up there as long as possible. It was our food that was limiting us. Coming back out, we found a place to cross those creeks that looked like a sand bridge, so we didn't have to climb way down the sheer drop-offs and back up again. Woody went up and he said, "I think we can get across here. Gee, it looks solid."

Bridge of snow and sand across Knife Creek, 1951. Photo by Morton and Ginny Wood. Katmai Administrative Records Collection, Accession Number KATM-283, National Park Service, Katmai National Park and Preserve.

It was ice with about five feet of sand on it, and so we walked across. That saved us a bunch of time. When we got back to our base camp at Mount Griggs, we were out of food. We were very tired and a little hungry, because we had made food for three days last us for six. We stayed in the valley extra, because every day we spent up there, we saw something else interesting we wanted to look at.

We went out to where we'd left the boat in two days of continuous walking night and day, because we didn't want to make a camp. Well, it's not like we were going to starve to death, but we were hungry. We were anxious to get to a can of peaches we'd left in the boat. When we got there, we were so hungry that all we could think about was getting to eat those peaches, so we just threw our packs down in any old place, and threw the gun over someplace else. The Park Service had insisted that we carry this gun. I think it was an old World War I gun. They said, "You'll be in bears all the time. Don't go anywhere without this. Take it with you if you go to the john." It was horrible, having all that weight all the time. And Woody was sick and tired of guns by that time, having been in the war. So here we were sitting down in a little hollow to get out of the wind and were just going to town with that can of peaches. All of a sudden, Woody says, "Look up." Here's a grizzly bear, about ten feet away, looking down at us. Woody said to the bear, "Do you want it?" Offering it the can of peaches. "Because I'm either going to throw it at you, or if you want it, I'll give it to you." The bear turned away. In the meantime, the gun and our movie camera and our other 35 mm cameras were all thrown around every which way, so we never even got a picture of this bear. Later in the summer, we saw lots of bears. But we never had trouble with them.

After we made our trip into the Valley of Ten Thousand Smokes, we decided we wanted to get into Lake Grosvenor, so we went around into the North Arm of Naknek Lake with the motorboat towing our kayak.[15] There was a trapper's cabin where there was supposed to be a trail going over to Lake Grosvenor.[16] But we couldn't find it. We'd been there almost a week and we'd eaten up all our grub and hadn't gotten anywhere, so we decided we'd cut our own trail to portage all our gear and the Folbot over to Grosvenor. It was about two and a half miles. Then we could go to the head of Lake Grosvenor. Also we could go down to the foot of it, which goes into Lake Coville. We did that and we came back up, and Northern Consolidated Airlines had a plane stationed down there and a guy and his wife living there on Lake Coville.[17] The little stream that goes between Grosvenor and Coville lakes can't be more than half a mile, and when we went down it all the salmon were facing one way. We stayed overnight and went back the next day, and the fish were all facing the other way. The current had changed. The reason it changes is because the wind is so strong that it piles up the water in Grosvenor and it all flows into Coville. Then the wind changes and it all goes out of Lake Coville and flows back into Lake Grosvenor. It's just a very short distance. When you saw the fish doing this, it made you wonder why are they this way, and why are they that way. It made you think about what nature was doing. Anyway, those are some of the neat things you see.

Then we paddled the whole of Lake Grosvenor, and that took several days. It's a big lake, so you can get very big waves. You get to shore quickly if that happens. At the head of Lake Grosvenor, we camped for about three days. We watched bears fishing for salmon about a quarter of a mile away where a river came into the lake. We hadn't seen many bears before this because the salmon weren't running. Then we got into the Folbot that we'd backpacked over and went down this very nice little river that took us into the headwaters of the Savonoski River. We had tried once before to get up the Savonoski River from the Iliuk Arm side where we'd been living, but the salmon were going ashore, it was upstream, and it was rocky. There was no way we were going to get a motorboat up there.[18] So that's why we said, "Well, what if we went around?" At the end of Lake Grosvenor was Grosvenor River, a channel of the Savonoski River. The idea was to go around from this side and come down the Savonoski. We had never been down there before, so we didn't know what it was like. I don't think we even had life preservers because we wouldn't want to pack them out. I'd done some river rafting before, but not much. I mean, I knew how to paddle a canoe, but mostly on lakes. And to sail. In those days, when people first came up here, nobody had any training in anything they did. Neither did we. But we had been around water.

When we were partway down the Savonoski River, I had to go to the johnnie, so I went ashore. There was lots of quicksand. I went right over my boots right away as I stepped out of the boat. I just stopped and Woody came up and threw some oars over it so I could get out of that. When I got over to shore, here was a whole graveyard with the Russian Orthodox double crosses. Turned out that was the old Savonoski village site. They left when the volcano was erupting. I don't know if the people survived the eruption. They had trails that went all the way from saltwater on over to the Interior. The Park Service seemed to have no idea that place was there. So we did tell them about it.

Basically, the only people we saw all summer were us. Except the Fish and Wildlife Service guys at their camp near park headquarters, and that man and his wife at Lake Coville. And we saw a few other people that summer who were flown in by the Park Service. I remember George Collins in particular.[19] We were down at the foot of the Savonoski River with our Folbot, fooling around, because it was real interesting. Whenever they had a storm there'd be all these rocks floating and all the logs sinking, because they were all full of sand and stuff that sank. George Collins was brought in there and dropped off because he was doing a survey for the Park Service about the recreational possibilities at different parks.[20] In the meantime, Celia was over in Kotzebue, running the roadhouse for tourists for Wien Airlines, and she'd met George over there and told him that we were in Katmai and to look us up. The Park Service had been told to find us to work with George. We were told to take him by motorboat wherever he wanted to go. So we did that with our boat. He stayed over at the Fish and Wildlife camp. He was just exploring the potential for hiking. He was interested in knowing that we'd walked into the Valley of Ten Thousand Smokes. We got to know George real, real well later on. He was a hilariously funny man, really interesting, very well informed.

Once in a while a plane flew in on floats. People came in to fish for the day. We'd see someone get out and pull in a big fish. Our tent cabin headquarters was about a mile from where the planes landed. They'd land there because it was very good fishing. That's why the Natives all came there to get their salmon. The scaffolding that the Natives used to dry fish on were still standing around there. We didn't fish much ourselves. It's kind of messy with the fish in a Folbot. I just remember that we were focused on exploring.

Another one of our missions was to try to find out a good way to put a road in if they could get in. So we went down to Old Creek—it has another name now—and surveyed that to see if that would lead over to the Valley of Ten Thousand Smokes. But when they finally did put in a road, they did it from Brooks Lake. It doesn't go where we went. The road goes around and you get up on a high point where you look down on the valley, on where we were hiking. That was quite an experience to ride up on a bus with a bunch of tourists twenty years later, when I went back to Katmai on a trip hosted by the Alaska Conservation Foundation, and look down on where Woody and I had been plodding, stumbling, and never knowing where we were going to put our feet. He and I never had any glimpse from high up so we could chart a route. Like you do in the Brooks Range, where you just get up high and can see the area and go, "Yeah, that's where we want to go." It was a thrill to be able to see exactly the route that Woody and I had come in on.

The Park Service told us they would come and get Woody and me in September on a certain date. We had to get everything put away to dry by then. We took down the tent, put away the boat, stored all the food, and packed everything away in the cache down near the park headquarters. We sat on the beach on our sleeping bags that were all packed in duffle bags to wait. We sat there and sat there and sat there, and nobody came. Finally, a plane flew over and it turned around and came back. It landed on floats and they said, "Are you people all right?" I said, "What do you mean, are we all right?" They said, "Well, we just saw you sitting on your gear and wondered why you were waiting." I said, "Well, the Park Service said on this date, if the weather was good, they'd come get us." The weather was fine, and we'd been waiting and nobody was coming, so we were just about ready to say, "Well, geesh, should we get out our pup tent?" That pilot said, "Well, we don't know anything about that, but we're flying on over to King Salmon. We'll take you." So we took it. We only went to Anchorage, because I'd left our plane there. We didn't have cell phones or anything like that, so we couldn't call to see where the Park Service plane was. Turns out the Park Service got mixed up on the dates. Anything this government is going to do gets fouled up. They tell it to somebody and they forget to tell somebody else. That's life. It's always going to be that way.

We did write up our findings. I wrote it for *Alaska Sportsman* magazine.[21] Woody wrote it up as a ranger report to the National Park Service.[22] And we have photos and movies that we took. I don't know if he told them they should turn the rocks over. He did tell them that it should be called the Valley of Seven Smokes. And how we got down in the valley by finding those places where you could climb down. And how on the way back we found an ice bridge with sand on top and we just took off our packs and Woody went across first and pulled the packs across. And we did recommend that they go in and get those crosses at Savonoski village and keep them, because they were going to have recreational people who were going to pack them out. But nobody went there in those days. I can say what's it like to be where nobody else has walked. And to have to find a way in. We never felt lost. We just felt this is not much fun walking. Now they go into this area by helicopter.

Woody as a ranger at Mount McKinley National Park with one of the park's sled dogs, 1952. Photo by Ginny Wood.

10

Finding a Place to Call Home

You have a certain security,
if you aren't caught with your standard of living too high.

After Ginny and Woody's great adventure of exploring Katmai National Park, they returned to Mount McKinley National Park, where Woody continued his employment as a park ranger. They spent the winter of 1951–1952 living in a small cabin by park headquarters. They became close friends with Bill Nancarrow, the other main ranger, and his wife, Ginny. And they enjoyed exploring the winter wonderland of the park's backcountry on dog-team patrol trips. This was the start of Ginny's deep love of and connection to the place.

The whole next winter we were living at McKinley Park. Woody was very good at handling dogs, so we took a lot of wonderful dog-team trips together.[1] I wasn't really supposed to be with him, but they didn't have any other ranger that liked to be out roughing it and it was safer to have two people. We were living in a little small one-room log cabin at headquarters, and it was the same type as the patrol cabins, so it didn't matter if we were back at the base or were out on the trail. We just liked to be out away from all the things you had to do when you were around headquarters. I remember a great trip we did by dog team over Christmas and New Year's. Celia came down from Fairbanks and we went out to the Savage River cabin. Woody came out and met us after he got off of work. That was one of the best New Year's that I had.

Then there was a dog-team trip Woody did with Bill Nancarrow.[2] At the time, the Park Service had been experimenting with using these tracked vehicles. It's something that came out from World War II. It was not like the snowmachines they have today. It's tandem, but enclosed.[3] The park had two of these things. Two guys sit inside, one in front of the other, and they put a drum of gasoline on the back. Typical military thing, typical Park Service–type operation.[4] They used dog teams to stash gasoline at patrol cabins and used the vehicles to bring out the dog food.

Woody on dog-team patrol in Mount McKinley National Park, 1952. Photo by Ginny Wood.

Two of these vehicles had gone out on a trip and one broke down, so they left it behind. The track had broken and the vehicle was stuck by McGonagall Pass. They had removed the broken track and tried to fix it but couldn't, so they just left it on the snow. It needed a new track. So Bill and Woody went out there with two dog teams to deliver and install a new track and retrieve the vehicle.[5] They'd gone all the way up there and couldn't get the darn thing on. They said, "No more. We'll stick with dog teams."[6] Woody and Bill were camped out there for a long time, so Bill's wife, Ginny, and I thought they might like something fresh to eat. It was Easter and Celia came down to visit us where we were living at park head-quarters. We said, "Let's make a salad," and Ginny Nancarrow said she'd make a pie, and we'd go out and drop it to them from the airplane. We made a little parachute. And it worked. They held up the pie and the salad to show they had survived the drop intact. That's what you really call a "tossed salad."

Then they wrote in the snow, "WL, Sunday." This meant that they wanted us to meet them two days later at Wonder Lake. So Celia and I went up to Lake Minchumina to borrow Dick Collins's airplane because ours was on wheels and we needed a plane with skis on it to land on Wonder Lake. Dick Collins worked for the CAA [Civil Aeronautics Administration, now the Federal Aviation

Administration (FAA)] over at Lake Minchumina and was a friend of ours. We could land on Wonder Lake then, when there were fewer people in the park. In fact, there were several different winters when we landed on Wonder Lake ourselves, and Dick Collins and his wife, Jeanne, would fly over and land their floatplane in the summer and come up to visit us at Camp. Then the Park Service said no more landing on Wonder Lake.[7] Woody, Bill Nancarrow, Celia, and I all had a wonderful rendezvous at Wonder Lake and stayed overnight at the Wonder Lake Ranger Station. The warm spring weather made the snow soft by the middle of the day. Traveling through this soft snow was hard on the dogs and slowed the team down. This meant it would take the guys longer to get back to headquarters. In the morning, Celia and I said we'd do the dishes and close up the cabin, so Bill and Woody could leave early while it was still cool. After Celia and I packed everything up, we tried to take off in the plane, but couldn't. It had gotten too late in the day and too warm, and the snow on the lake was now too soft to take off in. We went back to the cabin to wait for the cooler nighttime temperatures to firm up the snow. While we were waiting and having some dinner, all of a sudden we heard footsteps. "My gosh," we wondered, "who could that be?" It was Bill and Woody. They had turned back on the trail because the dog teams just kept bogging down in wet and soft snow. They decided to come back to the cabin and wait until it got cold that night. Finally, later that night Celia was able to get the airplane in the air by not having a passenger. I was left behind at the ranger station waiting with Woody and Bill. I told them that I was fine, that I would take care of the dinner dishes and closing up the cabin, and that they should leave while it was cool because they had a long trip to make. Then all of a sudden Dick Collins showed up to get me. I had to rush out of there and leave the guys to do dishes after all.[8]

Later that spring, while there was still snow on the ground, somebody else went out and retrieved that tracked vehicle. Woody and Bill had left the new track there with the broken machine. These other guys knew more about this type of equipment and were able to put it on and drove it back out to headquarters before all the snow melted.[9]

In the spring of 1952, the Park Service decided Woody should go to Yosemite to get more training on how to be a regular ranger.[10] He said, "I didn't come back to Alaska to go back to Yosemite. I know Yosemite Park. I don't want to be a ranger there." So, he decided to quit. He realized he didn't really want a career in the Park Service.

In an oral history interview on May 23, 2007, Woody explains this decision:

> After a year working with the National Park Service as a temporary ranger and later a ranger, I decided that it was too much like the military, in that they can send you wherever they want you to go. But I had long ago

fallen in love with McKinley Park. I wanted to live there. I didn't want to go to the Statue of Liberty or Mammoth Cave or Death Valley. And also at the same time, Ginny and I both had the thought of finding some way to get people out into the park so they could enjoy it instead of just staying at the park hotel and spending their time at the bar. So I quit.[11]

One of the immediate impacts of Woody leaving his job at Mount McKinley National Park was that he and Ginny no longer had a place to live. They had been residing in National Park Service housing. It was not a problem for the summer, because this was the first season of Camp Denali, a wilderness camp lodge they founded outside the park's boundary at the far end of the ninety-three-mile park road. They happily lived in a wall tent. However, at the end of the tourist season and as winter approached, they needed something more permanent. They went to Fairbanks to find a home.

We built our first cabin in the fall of 1952. We came back to Fairbanks after the first summer of running Camp Denali and started to build a house to live in that winter. We had to fly up to Fairbanks and start to find someplace to live for ourselves at the end of the season. Woody flew up on September 2 to start building us a cabin and I stayed down at Camp to close it up for the season. I got snowed in for five days from about September 4 until the ninth. They finally did get the park road open again, so I got the jeep out. I had to take the jeep out because that was the only car we had. It wouldn't have been much good building a cabin if I couldn't have gotten the jeep out for the winter. Woody had flown out in our airplane. At that time, almost everybody was flying up here. We almost had to have a plane then. It only took us about an hour and fifteen minutes to fly to Fairbanks from Camp, but it would have taken us two days to drive out the park road and then take the train to Fairbanks. The train to the McKinley Park entrance only ran three days a week. You couldn't drive the whole way until the Denali Highway was built in 1957.

We went down to the land office in Fairbanks to see if there was any homestead land left. The ones they had were way back off the beaten path and you'd spend all day just to trying to find where the boundaries were. Then you'd have to build a road to it if you were going to live there. Well, we ran into Gordon Herreid, who was camping down on the Chena River with his wife, Marilyn, and their little baby. Gordon Herreid and Woody had become friends when they were both students here at the university. They had both been in the war in Italy in the Tenth Mountain Division but hadn't known each other then. Gordon had done the same thing as Woody, where he'd come up to Fairbanks for a year and then decided you wouldn't want to spend the rest of your life here and went out to another university, two of them, in fact.[12] But then he decided, "Oh, I think I'll go back to Alaska."

Gordon said to us, "Oh, why don't you come down and have dinner with us? I just put down money on 160 acres on the dog-team trail north of the university. You all can build yourself a cabin there if you want, but don't ask me to survey it. I've got to get a cabin of my own up quick before the winter comes."

Gordon bought that land from Judge Bunnell, who was the old university president.[13] Bunnell used to get land from people who were prospectors. They would get a grubstake, and then the thing was, you put up your land as collateral. If you couldn't pay back what you borrowed, you gave up the land. Bunnell gave miners money for the land so they could leave when they hadn't struck it rich. He collected a lot of land this way. He wasn't a scrooge. This was a fair trade. The story was that Judge Bunnell would never let go of any of his land, but he liked Gordon, and when Gordon asked Bunnell about buying some land he said yes. Gordon said, "I want a piece out there at the end of the dog-team trail," and the judge said okay. Gordon got 160 acres. I guess that's the most the judge would part with.

Gordon's philosophy of zoning was, you make someone buy a big enough piece of land so they have to live in the middle of it, then I don't have to see their junk and they don't have to see mine. He only sold enough land to pay back the four thousand dollars it cost him to buy the land in the first place. He said, "Uh, it's crowded enough. I don't want to sell any more." And he never did. In the meantime, our kids have come and there's other people that have built their own cabins, too, on neighboring properties. So there are a lot more little cabins around here than there used to be.

We got eight acres from Gordon. We paid a hundred dollars an acre for it. We didn't pay that off for about three or four years. Gordon said, "Oh, I don't need any money right now. Why don't you save it for awhile. I'll come and ask you for it when I need it." Finally, we said, "Hey, why don't we just pay it off."

We needed a home over our heads quickly. We put up a sixteen-by-sixteen-foot cabin in six weeks. It's the little one at the front of my property.[14] We lived in a tent while building the cabin until it got down to nine degrees and pretty cold. We were trying to get the roof on the house so we could move in. We just got it closed in and with a door, and built a fire and were warm, but we were a long time in making it a house. We got it finished just as it was starting to get cold and snowy.

That's what we could afford. But we weren't trying to prove anything and it wasn't a cult. Everybody around us was doing the same thing. Why do you want to have anything fancier than what you need? I'm not for freezing to death in the dark, but when we were there, we thought, "Wow, we got a house that's warm. It's not like the tent with all this frost covering us every time we moved. And we can be warm." I don't know if there's a way of measuring happiness or satisfaction or feeling secure, but if you could measure it, would it be any more back then than now when I have running water? Now I think it's nice to have running water, and it's nice to take a shower, and it's nice to know that you don't have to go out and use the outhouse. But I still have the outhouse. You know, all you have to do is have the power go off and then you don't have anything. You have a certain security, if you aren't caught with your standard of living too high.

The Herreids and the Woods were the first to settle in what is now known as the Dogpatch neighborhood of Fairbanks.[15] It is a quiet and secluded haven located amidst rolling wooded hills about five miles north and above the campus of the University of Alaska Fairbanks. It is a close-knit community of like-minded folks who enjoy nature's space and quiet living. They have maintained large lots to protect from noise and to provide viewsheds between homes. They established a neighboring one-hundred-acre park with an extensive network of crisscrossing and winding cross-country-ski trails where motorized access is prohibited. Except for the widening and paving of Ballaine Road, with its fifty-five-mile-per-hour speed limit, that bounds the western edge of Dogpatch, the neighborhood seemingly has changed little since Ginny and Woody arrived. Although Ginny is quick to counter this view: "We had to fight to keep our walking trail along the side when they widened Ballaine Road two different times. Now the snow-machiners are driving on our walking trail at high speeds and it's dangerous. I've almost been hit at least a few times."

When we moved out here to Dogpatch, Ballaine Road was just a dog-team trail and then later a jeep trail. But sometimes we could barely get our jeep up it, even with chains. Sometimes we had to leave the jeep down by where the golf course is on Farmer's Loop Road and hike in. That's about two miles. It was especially bad during breakup. In the summertime, it got so muddy sometimes that we still needed to use chains. We didn't have telephones. We didn't have mail service. We didn't have electricity or running water. At the time we bought our land, everybody else was on the same economy. Although there were people that lived better in town. Every time we got invited by somebody that lived in town, we'd take all our laundry and our dirty selves and get a shower. They knew that was likely to happen when they invited us. They'd say, "The bathroom's free." There were so many people doing that and we didn't feel like we were doing it to prove anything or feeling envious of somebody else. No, I just feel, boy, great, that we could afford it. If I had to buy this place now I couldn't afford what the borough says it is worth per acre. Living the way we did, in a small cabin without running water and electricity, made it possible for us to afford it.

I had a friend who was with the university and he made this wonderful observation about life in Fairbanks in the early days. He often was on sabbatical at other universities abroad, and one night at a party he said, "Well, you know when you're in a group of people in New England, they talk about their ancestors. If it's in England, they talk about their history. The French talk about their women. But I got back to Alaska, and everyone talks about their plumbing."

After about two years, Woody decided he needed a place for a shop because we just had a one-room log cabin. So in 1954, he built the place where I now live, what we call "The Wood Shed." We made it into a house later on after our daughter was born and we needed more space and running water. We moved in here about 1957. At the time, this place didn't have a basement like it does now. We just dug a hole in the loess soil, and then one summer years later, one breakup, water came in and went under the house, so that part ended up being just in the air. Then we had to prop it up and make a basement. That's not the way to build a house. You should build a basement first.[16]

Woody and Ginny settled into the routine of life in Fairbanks. They enjoyed a community of close friends. They appreciated the cultural offerings of a university town. They had found a place to call home. Nevertheless, they remained attached to Mount McKinley National Park. Which is why in 1953 they jumped at a chance to run a winter recreation program at the Mount McKinley Park Hotel.[17] It was also a way to help a young married couple make ends meet. According to Ginny, the hotel, which had previously been run by the Alaska Railroad, had recently been turned over to McKinley Park Services and was being managed by Bud and Ella Lauesen.[18]

They had closed the hotel down for the winter but were using it for the military as a rest camp.[19] Bud Lauesen hired me and Woody to come down and run a program, like take them skiing and things like that. The military even got hold of an old ski tow, a little rope tow, that they put up at Mount Healy. But it didn't run very long. We were hired to lead winter activities for them, to take them on snowshoe trips, ski trips. But whoever was in charge of the military said we couldn't go outside if it was colder than ten degrees above zero. Well, that was when it was zero most of the time. So nobody was allowed out of the hotel most of the time we were there. You know, how were they going to fight a war if they didn't know about the cold. But Lauesen's kids thought it was great, and I took them out skiing. It was fun. They did have a gal there at the hotel who liked folk dancing. So we did have a wonderful time folk dancing with the military. We had good dances. I never sat out a dance. There weren't many women there.

Bud Lauesen was a character; he was a riot. He was a great type for managing a bar. He would tell people anything. If a hotel guest was complaining about having a rough trip and a poor lunch, he would say, "But you got lettuce in your sandwich." Bud finally got kicked out. Mardy Murie would have had a good way of describing him, like, "He was an interesting thief who was a good guy." He was just one of those characters you find in the Old West.

L–R: *Celia, Woody, and Ginny at the Camp Denali signpost, 1952. Courtesy of Ginny Wood.*

11

Establishing Camp Denali: Alaska's First Wilderness Camp

The country told us what it wanted to be and we had to listen.

The concept of ecotourism is so commonplace in modern parlance it has almost become cliché. Remote and rustic accommodations with an appreciation for and educational orientation about the natural world are easy to find. Eco-lodges meet the needs of baby boomers seeking more adventurous lives than their parents led. They are the poster children for the current generation's mantra of "living green." However, in the early 1950s when Ginny and Woody and their friend Celia were exploring Mount McKinley National Park, things were quite different. Camping in a tent or staying in an expensive resort-style luxury hotel were the only options. These three young friends with a love of the outdoors and hiking were inspired to do something new. They established the first remote wilderness camp in Alaska. It was located ninety miles inside Mount McKinley National Park, and they called it Camp Denali.

The story of the founding and running of Camp Denali is not Ginny's alone. It was a shared partnership amongst Ginny, Woody, and Celia. Unfortunately, Celia is no longer alive to add her memories to the discussion. But Woody is. He is in his late eighties, still has a full head of thick white hair, remains fit and active, and is an accomplished folk musician. He lives in Seattle with his wife, Martha. Woody's memories remain strong. Comments about Camp Denali that he shared in two interviews conducted in 2007 have been incorporated below with Ginny's stories or as endnotes. Sometimes Woody's stories add more detail to Ginny's presentation, while other times they offer a contrasting perspective.

The story started in the summer of 1951. Before we left for Katmai, where Woody had been assigned for the summer, we were living at the east end of McKinley Park at park headquarters. John Rumohr was the chief ranger.[1] We knew him real well. He was an old Norwegian. He was taking a young lad out to establish him as the temporary ranger at the Wonder Lake Ranger Station for the season. That

Morton "Woody" Wood, April 2007.
Photo by Karen Brewster.

young college kid was Les Viereck. John Rumohr wanted to know if Celia and I wanted to ride out with him. To bring our sleeping bags and stay for a few days, and then Woody would bring our airplane out on the weekend when he got off of work and pick us up and fly us back.[2] We didn't have a car then, we only had an airplane. In the meantime, we'd have a couple of days out there.

Celia was living in Fairbanks at the time, working for Wien Airlines. They got the idea that if they could get a place near Wonder Lake they could host people there. There was the hotel way out by the railroad station, but there was nothing inside the park. So she actually came down looking for an area for Wien Airlines that they might develop for a tourist place, like had at Kotzebue. Celia and I had both been very active in getting Wien's tourist business established out at Kotzebue, so that is why she'd been given this mission.

They wanted an area where they might build a lodge, but they wanted an airstrip nearby which they could use to bring people in. Celia was sent out to see if there was such an area outside the park boundary in the Wonder Lake area of McKinley Park that they could use for an airstrip. At that time they were flying DC-3s, which could get in and out of short strips. So she wanted to go out to Kantishna to see if there was an airstrip there that had enough room to get a Doug [DC-3] in there so they could bring in tourists. This all was outside of the park then, a mile over the boundary.

Celia and I went with John Rumohr, and Woody flew out later. The next day, after Woody got there, it was lousy weather. And the next day was lousy, too. And that was our weekend. We couldn't fly home on Sunday because it was just too overcast. It was pouring rain with clouds sitting right down on the mountains, so we couldn't get through the passes with the airplane to get back to headquarters. John had already left by car. It was raining, but Les, Woody, Celia, and I decided to go for a hike anyway. We had to stay below the clouds, so we went up the ridge along Moose Creek. We got up to this little pond. It was time to eat lunch, so we sat there under our raingear. It was just kind of drizzling. We said, "This would be a nice place to have a cabin. I wonder if you could see the mountain [Mount McKinley] from here?" Celia said, "Gee, I'm supposed to find something down there at Wonder Lake, but you know, this would be a perfect spot. Especially if you could see the mountain." The next day, Monday, was good weather and we flew out.[3]

When Woody and I were at Katmai, we kept thinking about that spot at McKinley. We liked Katmai, but we didn't like the weather much. So we thought, when we got back from our assignment why didn't we go back out there by Moose Creek and see what it was like. All Woody and I were interested in was a spot that he and I could build a cabin on to come out to on weekends from the other end of the park. In the meantime, we had asked Les if on the first time that they had clear weather, completely clear, would he hike up that ridge where we'd been and see if he could see the mountain from there.[4] Particularly from that little pond where we had our lunch. We got a postcard from him and all it said was "Wow!" That told us what we needed to know.

When Celia was running the roadhouse for Wien Airlines over in Kotzebue, she had met George Collins, who worked for the National Park Service.[5]

View of Nugget Pond and Mount McKinley from Camp Denali. Photo by Ginny Wood.

He was staying there and she got chatty with him. He told her it would be nice if there was someplace in McKinley Park except that "damned big hotel." He said that all the Park Service thinks about is getting up another big hotel. He felt that there should be some place where people could stay out in the wilderness longer, not for just a one-night stand. Of course then, the concept for hotels in national parks was to have a band, tennis courts, and a golf course to entertain you while you were there. It was sort of the European idea of the spa. George didn't think that was the way to go, but at the same time he felt that there should be some facilities in the park, mainly so that people would stay in one spot and then explore it on foot. And take it as it comes, you know, the weather and whatever.

Celia did stake an area down below for a landing strip for Wien Airlines' tourist operation, but you can't see the mountain very well from there. And Wien Airlines never did go through with that plan, because their operation in Kotzebue kept them so busy that they didn't ever follow up on it. Probably, it's a good thing. It wouldn't have been a very good airstrip. And then they stopped using the types of airplanes that they were planning to use on that airstrip and started using bigger airplanes that wouldn't have fit.

The ideas George Collins had been talking with Celia about resonated with her, Woody, and me. Woody and I had already been thinking, "Well, gee, there's nothing here for anybody in the park, except for the little bus trip out to Polychrome Pass. There's a hotel from which you can't even see the mountain, and it isn't even part of the park. It isn't tundra." We decided that why should Wien bring all those people to a big hotel in that little area by Wonder Lake? And why didn't we just make a little camp there for backpackers and for people who wanted to hike, not tourists? It would be for people that were interested in hiking and camping and backpacking and wanted to just be out in the wilderness.

So Celia, Woody, and I decided why didn't we stake this land and just start a small campground with some tent cabins and some camping sites? All we envisioned was some kind of a business that would enable us to live on the boundary of McKinley Park and wander around the park all summer. We were very naïve about what this would be. So Celia went ahead and staked the land as a homestead lot. This was still when we were the Territory of Alaska and it was BLM [Bureau of Land Management] land. It was all public land, and you could homestead it. We paid two hundred dollars an acre for that, and it was a hell of a lot of work to prove up on it. In those days they had this whole Homestead Act.[6] You could have a home site, five acres, which could be your home. You could also have a homestead that was mostly for farming. There was also a little something in small print that said it could be a commercial thing. It was for logging or mining camps so people who worked for that company could have a place to live permanently. It was called a trade and manufacturing site, and it was eighty acres of land that you could have as a business, provided you were using it all for that purpose.[7]

And that's what we staked. Of course, the program was soon discontinued, but we got in on it. We had five years to prove up on the property. That meant we had to use the whole eighty acres for what we had claimed it for. Which we did. BLM sent someone out there and they said they don't give eighty acres for tourist things. They came out to tell us they weren't going to give us all eighty acres, because they didn't know how we could possibly use that much. Then they saw the place and realized we had used all the acreage. They let us stay there. It was just a half-mile outside the park boundary. Later on they enlarged the park so it's now inside the park boundary, but it has grandfather rights.[8]

At the time we started all this, Woody was still working for the Park Service, so he couldn't stake public land right on the boundary of the park. Celia put the land in her name. This was in the summer of 1951.[9] All Woody and I wanted to do originally was to build a cabin out there. We didn't care what Celia wanted to do as long as we had a cabin. Woody and I had had all summer at Katmai to think about what we wanted to do with our lives. He wasn't that sure about the Park Service. He got his degree in forestry but the trees weren't all that good up here. There wasn't a forest industry at that time. Trees in interior Alaska were used as firewood or to build a cabin, not for lumber.

We came back to McKinley Park from Katmai in late September or October. We were living by park headquarters. We started just to go out to help Celia. Woody still had to work, so he came out on the weekends, on his days off. It was a late winter, so Celia and I spent two weeks out there at Camp Denali. Woody flew us out. And then he was making trips back and forth with the park truck to close up the Wonder Lake Ranger Station for the winter. To get all the food out and everything. So we'd see him about every two days. In the meantime, I cut the first log at Camp. We put up a tent and a cache. We just put up the logs and platform so we could lash our ten-by-twelve canvas tent up on that for the winter. There were two snowstorms while Celia and I were out there and we thought we wouldn't get out, but Woody was able to come with the plane and he got us out. Woody and I spent our winter living at the park and exploring it while he was a ranger. He was making benches and things, so we were stockpiling furniture and stuff for Camp Denali's first summer season.

During that first winter [1951–1952] Celia was up in Fairbanks and we were in the park. All of us were kind of separately thinking, wondering what we would have Camp Denali be. We didn't really know what we were starting or what it was. All three of us had spent time in Europe, bicycling and staying in youth hostels and mountain huts, and had come to the same conclusion. We had all come away with the impression that Europeans, when they take a vacation, they go to the mountains or the seashore, take the whole family, and go where they'd gone when they were kids, to where their parents and grandparents had gone. Whereas Americans got in the car to see how many miles they could make. We wondered why Americans get in cars and drive as far as they can and then stay

Ginny cutting down the first tree at Camp Denali, 1952. Courtesy of Ginny Wood.

overnight in a tourist cabin in the mountains or by the seashore somewhere or a resort, and then the next morning they get in their car and do the same thing? And the farther they've driven, that meant it was the best vacation they'd had. We wondered why the Americans didn't do it like the Europeans and go to one place and stay there for a week.

Up until World War II, they didn't have cars in Europe. You took a train or a bus with your family, and you stayed in a little inn. They didn't have the concept of tents so much. They had hut systems in places like Switzerland and Austria. You walked, and you stayed in the huts. These were sometimes nothing but a great big bench with straw in it and everybody just slept in their sleeping bags. They were not fancy places. They would hike, get to know the country, just explore the region. You walked a lot. They stayed in one spot where nature predominated. You touch it, you feel it, you smell it, and you hear it. And not as a scientist. It was just something that you grew up doing. Especially the British and the Germans, Austrians, the Swiss, and the Scandinavians. This is what they did. It may be crowded over there in Europe, but still to them their vacation was something that should be entirely different from the way you live.

So we thought, why wouldn't there be Americans who would do this? Where they have a vacation in depth at one place. We were curious. We started Camp Denali because we wanted to be out there. It was just a nice place for us to spend the summer. And we wanted our guests to do what we liked to do, and that was go exploring. We'd been in Alaska for a number of years and were anxious to know the animals and the plants. I think my original thing was just a curiosity and a sense of wonder about the place. Woody wanted to be out there because he wanted to be around Mount McKinley, to just see it. He still wanted to climb it and was drawn to it. Having been in the Tenth Mountain Division during the war, he had just fallen in love with mountains. Celia, who was working for Chuck West in the tourist business, decided she'd like to spend her summers seeing more of Alaska than just being on the other side of the desk from the tourists.

We didn't even think about whether Camp Denali would be a viable business. If we could actually make money. We didn't know what we were doing. We were just like kids going out to play in the woods. We didn't really have a grand plan for Camp. We had an idea about a place where you came for vacation, not just overnight. Our vision was a little like the youth hostel system they had in Europe that was primitive and then you explored country from there, mixed with the mystique of homesteaders and miners in Alaska. We wanted a place that you could come to and immerse yourself into a place where you lived rather simply, and in McKinley Park, in the Kantishna area, where there wasn't anything like that, and to see what happens. There weren't any examples of what we wanted to do in other national parks in the Lower 48. We used to think that we needed to develop McKinley Park because there were no facilities for people. There wasn't anything. Then we began to ask if we really wanted to do that. It began changing. Our concept was that this is a place where you can make a headquarters and stay and get immersed in what's out there. We decided not to have TV. Not to have a bar, to not sell beer. This was not because we were teetotalers. We could have made a lot of money. We needed money badly. But mainly it was because we didn't want to see beer cans strewn all the way back along the road.

We decided we didn't want to be a hotel. I think the nature and our staff told us what we should do. And the camp itself told us what it wanted to be. The country told us what it wanted to be and we had to listen. When we didn't listen, we learned the hard way. Our wilderness here in Alaska can be pretty rugged. The weather and the bugs, bears, and so forth. Nature was telling us what we were doing wrong. I always remember Conrad's writings of the sea, saying that the sea is not for you or against you, it's just very unforgiving of errors.[10] We found out that you better be aware of nature and work with it, because if you don't it's going to give you your comeuppance.

We took our jeep up on to what was then a treeless ridge. Now a lot of small spruce trees have grown in around Camp. But mostly it was just open when we started. You got a sweeping view of the mountain with a little pond in front. Since we didn't have a forest right in back of us, we took our jeep over the tundra up the hill into the woods to snake down logs for our first buildings. And pretty soon we discovered that as soon as you cut the tundra and get down to mineral soil, that it melted the permafrost. We had a stream coming down into camp, which we had to divert. We realized you don't do that.

You learn about the country, a lot about permafrost, a lot about what you can do and what you can't do. You learn that you have to adapt to the conditions of nature. You can't just go pushing your weight around. You learn that you have to work with weather, things like permafrost, even the animals, instead of shooting them all off. And you just kind of have to outwit the bears. Like you just learn what to do and not to do with garbage. You remember that they were there first. You have kind of a coexistence. In fact, that is one of the reasons you're there, to see the country, to see the animals, and to see Alaska as it is instead of seeing how much you can rearrange the scenery and how much you can change it so that you are living just like you do at home out there in the Lower 48. We did improve things, but we never improved them so much that the camp didn't keep its individuality. It sort of evolved. We didn't have any idea that this was what we were gonna do, but this is what happened.

The thing we learned was don't intrude on nature anymore than you have to to be comfortable and be able to stay in business. We learned from experience and just noticed things around us. I think that's why Camp Denali survived. You learn you don't leave any garbage around so you don't have any bear trouble. You go to a lot of trouble to do that, to take care of your garbage. And like the miners did, you don't leave things hanging out that would attract the bears. And then your next step is that you just realize how everything is connected to everything else. And then the final thing that you learn is that here's this whole system. Sure, something eats something and it's nature—it's seldom mild. But as an ecosystem it all works. Until we come along and muck it up. Just being out there and having to make a living there and having to survive, you begin to see that.

You realize that it is bigger than you. You're part of creation and evolution. Whatever your thoughts or your feelings are about that. That here are these animals, that have had to survive on their own instincts. Then you see them with their offspring, and they have to survive. It's not something you just cross off of your list—I've seen a moose, I've seen a bear, I've seen the mountain; I can go on now. Everybody has to answer for themselves and has a different feeling, but I think there is a feeling of, look, maybe we'd better pay attention because we're mucking things up a lot and maybe we're like the dinosaurs, we've outrun our usefulness. Or maybe it's just one part of a wonderful thing that happened in our lives and we got to be human beings so we could get to appreciate it and take care of it.

At the beginning, we were desperate for money. We were just doing it on our own. We couldn't start a camp with no money, so we tried to borrow money. But the banks said no. They said, "You don't have any collateral." And we said, "We have Camp Denali." They said, "Oh, that will never be worth anything. Who'd ever want to go out there? That won't be a successful business." So they didn't want to loan us money. They couldn't understand why we had all these little cabins scattered around. Why we didn't put them in a row. That this was not very efficient. That it cost too much money to build that way. We said we did it so everybody thinks they're all alone in their own little cabin in the woods. They don't have to hear the talk that's going on in the next one. That you could look out from your cabin and just see nature. You'd look at the mountain and not see anything else. This is a nice little valley. It's got everything you'd want. For a long time, until very recently, we were the only ones out there. The fact that the banks wouldn't loan us any money was a good thing in the end, because we never were in debt. We just built what we could afford to build. If we didn't have the money, we didn't build it. We built everything ourselves with the help of a lot of friends and the staff. We never had to pay back anybody. We never owed any money longer than until the fall. We might have been running a bill from May to September, but we always paid our bills in October from what we earned during the summer.

I guess you'd call Camp Denali a tourist operation. Or a way of life. It is pretty hard to describe. It was sort of unique. It was something that sort of had to be, and we just happened to be the custodians of it. It sort of expressed itself. It was kind of a combination wilderness resort and retreat. It was a northern version of a dude ranch, except you didn't have horses. We had activities that were more related to Alaska. It was sort of a total experience, but we didn't plan it that way. It evolved that way.

We called it Camp Denali because Bobby Sheldon had come out into the park as far as Savage River and set up a tent camp operation there. It was called Camp Savage. And then he'd set up another one called Camp Eielson, which was near where the Eielson Visitor Center is now, back around Mile 66 on the park road.[11] Another guy had a tent camp at Igloo Creek. So we decided we were Camp Denali, since Denali was the name of the mountain, and we were located way out near it.

Before her death in December 2001, Celia Hunter also spoke and wrote frequently about the founding and development of Camp Denali. In a 1984 interview, she summarizes the beginnings:

Our original idea was for Camp Denali to be a place for people to come where they would do their own cooking. Our first guests were on what is called "The American Plan." But we realized we were stuck with feeding people because we were so far out the road. Eventually, we picked people up at the park's railroad depot, drove them out the ninety miles on the park road to see wildlife and the park, and gave them an interpretive program, offered guided trips, and used planes to take people flight-seeing around Mount McKinley. We offered simple solid comfort, good food, and privacy, but not luxury. People were thinking we were nuts to go out on the other end of the park road and set up facilities for tour-ists. Yes, the first two to three years were tough. We all three worked in the winters to support Camp in the summer. We put all the money we earned back into Camp. To build cabins. We were not making any mon-ey. Eventually, as more people came out to Camp, we prospered by word of mouth. Also, Ginny and I had both worked for Chuck West when he first was starting his travel agency in Fairbanks, and so he gave us a spot advertising Camp Denali in his Westours brochure.[12]

Finding the spot for Camp Denali and staking claim to the land turned out to be the easy part. Ginny, Woody, and Celia now had to do the hard physical work of making their dream a reality. Of creating their paradise in the wild subarctic tun-dra wilderness. They cut a trail and road by hand up the ridge to the pond where the base of Camp would be. They began to build tent cabins and dig outhouses to accommodate guests. They carried lumber and building supplies up the ridge on their backs. And eventually, as Camp Denali became more popular and their yearly guest population increased, they built a large log structure as a central gathering place. Ginny, Celia, and Woody all were involved in the construction of Camp, as were friends, visitors, staff, and even sometimes the guests. Accord-ing to Ginny, Celia was a good carpenter, having learned from her brothers. Nevertheless, Ginny credits Woody, a skilled woodworker, as the central figure in the building of Camp Denali when she says, "Celia was the businessperson of our group. She was the bookkeeper. She handled the money. Woody built the place. And I thought up things to do."

The summer of 1952 is when we started really building. The previous fall, we had put up three platforms for cabins. We'd cut the trees and made the base parts. We had to put the cabins and outhouses on good ground, but that was limited because of all the permafrost. There was a lot that was swampy that we ended up hauling gravel in to use as fill. We had an old truck with a dump on it that we would use to haul the gravel in. We'd go prospecting for gravel in Kantishna.

That first summer we got out there as soon as the road opened so we could bring in supplies and start building right away.[13] We had an airplane so we could fly in in the spring, before the park road was plowed and opened for the season, and land at the airstrip at Kantishna, which was four miles away from

The first season of Camp Denali, 1952. Photo by Ginny Wood.

Camp. The park road from headquarters went over four-thousand-foot passes, so sometimes it wouldn't be open until June because of the snow. We didn't even have a car at that point in our lives. But we soon got an old truck that the Park Service was auctioning off. We got it for two hundred dollars. It was an old Ford truck. It could carry a lot of stuff. We sent in lumber and stuff down on the train from Fairbanks to the park headquarters area, so once the road was opened we could use the truck to haul it along the park road out to Camp.[14]

We'd been out there only three days and Les Viereck came to help us. Les was working for the Alaska Department of Fish and Game studying beaver or marten. He was going to be at a lake way in the western part of the park working for the summer.[15] He could work with us until they came and picked him up with a plane to fly him out there. He was around for about a month. He stayed all summer at that lake and ended up walking all the way back from the west end of the park instead of being picked up by plane.[16]

We built the first tent cabins out along the ridge that drops off steeply to Moose Creek about one thousand feet below. We wanted to get up high on the ridge, because from there you got one of the most breathtaking views of Mount McKinley. You couldn't see another manmade thing, and there was this nice stream, really a river, below us. Our first cabin was where the trees were. We named it "Discovery." Our idea was instead of having cabins like people were used to staying in in those days, where you could hear everything, like the wife yelling at the husband next door, we wanted it so you didn't hear or see anyone else and everyone had a view of the mountain. So we built the cabins staggered. You looked out and you felt like you were alone. Everyone had a view of the mountain, even from the outhouse. Not only do you see Mount McKinley, but you see all the other mountains in the Alaska Range over fourteen thousand feet. I call them Mount McKinley's neighbors. And if they were anywhere else, they'd be pretty spectacular just by themselves.

At the start it was just me, Woody, Les, and Celia. We started by putting up a wood frame for the cabins. We had all our tent cabins on log platforms. The first year we were building, before the road went all the way up, Grant Pearson brought out the head of the National Park Service from Washington, DC. At the bottom of the hill we had a lot of lumber stored. The unspoken rule was that no one was supposed to come up without bringing along at least one piece of wood. And Grant told the head of the Park Service you're supposed to bring up a piece of lumber when you go. And he did. Grant liked to bring people out to show them Camp Denali. He thought it was pretty neat. He was an old-timer. He had been a dog-team driver, had taken the mail. He knew this country.[17]

After a while, people just wandered in. Mostly hitchhikers and campers would come in. Anybody that came to Camp had to work. We'd feed them and they'd help us build. Ted Lachelt was one of these helpers in our first year. He was studying wolverine in the park and built his own cabin up the hill behind Camp. Friends also often came to lend us a hand. And even some paying guests pitched in to help build Camp in those early years. By the end of that first summer, we had three tent cabins and a couple of regular cabins. We kept it simple. Along the lines of, this is what it was like in the old days with miners and prospectors. You had a tent cabin and you lived off the land. You were comfortable. We built a foundation and had wood siding along the bottom part, like wainscoting, that went up so far. Then we put canvas that came down from the top. Each cabin had windows, a screen door, and a Yukon stove—a woodstove—in it. We furnished wood for people. And there were bunks. We bought these from army surplus. We had some honeymoon couples the first year and we just let them figure all this out for themselves. Each cabin also had a washbasin and "running water." We ran a rubber hose three-quarters of a mile up the hill to a spring and had big barrels up the hill behind camp to collect the water. Hot and cold running water was furnished by one of us hauling water in buckets. Later there was a hose outside each cabin.

Our idea was that guests would do their own cooking; so we had housekeeping cabins. We hadn't even thought about cooking until the first guests came and they said, "Oh, we didn't bring any food. We're on a vacation. We want to be fed." So Celia set up a kitchen in the little tent in which we were living. Since we had to go collect all of our own wood, we couldn't waste any wood on where we were living, so by making it the kitchen too it served double duty. We had to saw our own firewood. We didn't even own a chainsaw until later when we built the lodge. In fact, the kids on the staff made up a song about how they didn't even have heat in their cabins.

The first thing we did was to build a three-quarter-of-a-mile-long road to get up high enough on the ridge to where we wanted to build more of the cabins. There was an old Italian miner who was through mining in the Kantishna. It had been a big mining place; there once were several thousand people living there.

A completed canvas cabin at Camp Denali, 1952. Photo by Ginny Wood.

We used to take people to go visit the old cabins, the old mines.[18] It's interesting history.[19] This miner was leaving the country for good and taking his equipment out on the train to go elsewhere in Alaska.[20] And he said he'd give us ten hours before he took his bulldozer out. He was a nice guy. Woody had done some engineering—the only good thing he brought home from World War II—so he surveyed where the road would go. He had put in another switchback on it, but it was getting late in the season and the guy didn't have anymore time. He had to walk the bulldozer all the way to the railroad station, ninety miles away. So he took out one of the switchbacks at one place where it's very steep now. We had to be careful or he'd just put the blade down and give it the gun and start pushing. "Oh, no, no, no," we'd say. He'd say, "Oh, you're one of those crazy guys, you don't even want to hurt a blade of grass. When you want a road, you want a road."

That road only went as far as the upper landing, where the current garage is.[21] That's as far as he got before he ran out of time. It was more of a trail than it was a road. But we could get our jeep up if it wasn't too muddy. Our jeep had a

Ginny carrying a surplus window from Camp Eielson up the hill to Camp Denali, 1952. Courtesy of Ginny Wood.

winch and we'd drive it as far as we could and then winch lumber and stuff up beyond that. We had to pull up everything over the tundra until you got to where the garage is, then we started hauling everything from there up on our back.[22] The boys devised a way of hauling lumber by carrying several lengths in teams of two, with the planks tucked under their rucksack frames. The groceries arrived and we carried them up the ridge a case or two at a time.[23] Then we decided we better build the rest of the road. We wanted this place to be away from it all. But when you start hauling in groceries and everything by hand, you start changing your mind about stuff. So from the garage to the cabins at the top, that's the part of the road that we built by hand. That was hard work. Muddy work. Women as well as men did time on road work. Even after we got a "road" carved out of the tundra on this upper part, we had to constantly be ditching along the edge, especially when it rained, to keep the water running downhill. Over the years, we did have some washouts along different parts of our road that required a lot of work from the staff to repair. Maintaining that road was a constant effort.

Ginny working on the road to Camp Denali, 1952. Courtesy of Ginny Wood.

In a 2007 oral history interview, Woody Wood adds details that help clarify this story of building the road up to Camp Denali:

> The miner agreed to bring his bulldozer up and try to scratch us out a road leading to this little pond up on the ridge, on the bench. And he did. He just started zigzagging up. Nobody ever surveyed it. It's an eighteen percent grade. It's really steep and he just scraped the tundra off and scratched out a path until he got to a place below the pond, the actual site of Camp. And there he saw there was a swamp. And he said, "I'm not going to drive my bulldozer in there." He knew enough that he realized he would get it stuck. Now, some of this area was permafrost. But much of it was an exposed south slope so it was dry. Gravel underneath, so you didn't have to worry about permafrost. But when he reached this flat spot—which incidentally is the place where the garage and all the oil barrels and stuff are stored for Camp Denali and where the buses park.

That's the spot from where we had to build that road by hand. From there on. And that was a chore.

Ginny and I had differing ideas about finishing that upper part of the road. One of us thought we should pile more tundra into it and the other thought no, we should scrape it out, let the sun melt the permafrost. And it definitely was permafrost there. We had a little military-style jeep that we had bought in 1952 that had a power takeoff winch on it. From the very beginning we had to winch the jeep up there to get it through the tundra. The only way we could come up from this swampy area to the actual site of Camp Denali where it is today was by burying logs—what is called a deadman—about every one hundred and fifty feet. You'd bury this crossways and then you'd hitch your winch cable to that. And then you could make it so the jeep would be able to pull itself up through this quagmire of chopped-up tundra.

The tundra eventually got all chopped up. Okay, that exposed the gravel. Exposed it to the sun. It started thawing. So instead of having a level tundra-covered slope, you had tundra and a trench three feet deep. We hated to chop up the tundra like this. But it was the only way you could do it. If you moved around into a different path every time, pretty soon you'd end up with a total mess. Which is of course what the Cats do up in the Arctic a lot and they really tear up the terrain. We preferred to tear up one little section really badly, open it up, let the sun hit it. We knew this would sink, because when the permafrost melts of course it contracts and leaves you a big ditch. We tried to drain it as much as we could. We did a lot of our work with picks and shovels ditching that thing along the side so the water would not wash out the road too badly but would go along the side of it. At one point, we found an old culvert back in the park somewhere that the road commission had tossed over the edge, and we salvaged that and put that in to keep that road a little better.

Eventually, it thawed and we got down to gravel and we were able to pull the jeep up with a lot of work. Gradually the road got better. But the road is still to this day way down below the level of the tundra that surrounds it, but it's a good road. We did all that work by hand until we got that little Oliver tractor.[24]

And we made mistakes. Like taking that jeep up over the tundra. We didn't have bulldozers and we didn't have very much money. So we had to do it. If you look at how the upper road goes, part way up there's this flat plain and after that there's this big four-foot dip. That's where it was a swamp and permafrost melting and where the jeep got stuck and did a lot of damage.[25] It's all vegetated again and looks natural. But you can see it if you know why it happened. We learned from those mistakes.

Even though there's a road now, no car goes above the garage except a camp rig. You'd go up with a camp rig, do what you're doing, drop off things or people, and you brought it right back down. This is so you don't look out of any cabin up top and look at a car. We didn't want people driving in and parking in front of the mountain. We didn't want the noise of cars coming in and out. We wanted to preserve that feeling of remoteness and having a sweeping view of Mount McKinley.

By November 1953, Camp Denali had been operating for two summers. In that month's edition of *Alaska Sportsman*, Ginny Hill Wood describes this new tourist facility within Mount McKinley National Park as follows:

Though we subscribe to the view of keeping the wilderness unspoiled, we reflected upon the irony of building a road through a wilderness placing a luxurious hostelry at one end, then providing no facilities the rest of the ninety-three miles. The hotel, operated by the Alaska Railroad, offers comfortable rooms with baths, a fine dining room and bar. But it is a hundred miles away from Mount McKinley and twelve miles from the first point along the road from where the mountain can be seen.

In an effort to provide physical comforts for its guests, the railroad has lost sight of the fact that many people come to McKinley Park to see its mountains, glaciers and wildlife.

We mused on the trend current in Alaska at present. Awake to the tremendous tourist potential promoters are keen to develop tourist attractions. But most of the plans call for making living in Alaska just as comfortable and convenient as it is in the States.

Did the public really want to travel all the way up here to have everything just as it is at home? we wondered. Surely there were many, we thought, who were seeking experiences genuinely Alaskan—who would like to go home feeling as though they'd gone a little sourdough, caught the spirit of the bush country, even if it meant living without running water and electric lights, and taking the mosquitoes along with the scenery.

Here was the ideal spot to find out. We'd provide tent cabins with wooden floors and sides, put canvas roofs with flies overhead to keep them cool in warm weather and warmer in cooler temperatures. We'd supply bunks and down sleeping bags. Yukon stoves would furnish the heat, and Coleman stoves would be used for cooking. We would locate every unit with a full view of the mountains, but we'd scatter them around the ridge so each had space and privacy. We'd equip them with housekeeping, so guests could economize on meals and live independently of set schedules. We'd have a complete stock of groceries on hand.

We would make our tent-cabins clean and comfortable, but the emphasis would not be on comfortable living. The cabins would serve merely as shelter from which to explore the surroundings.[26]

In her oral history storytelling, Ginny goes on to explain Camp Denali operations and serving their first guests.

Once we had these first tent cabins built, we put out our shingle at the bottom of the hill. It was a sign that said Camp Denali three-quarters of a mile up that way. Woody made the sign. It was at the bottom of the hill and then you turned and went up about four switchbacks. Later on we installed an old army field phone down there which visitors could use to call us up at the top of the hill to tell us they had arrived and to ask for a lift.

Our first visitors came to Camp Denali in June 1952.[27] We were not expecting them. We had built one tent cabin, but we hadn't finished the johnnie yet. And we were fighting over who would be the first to get to sleep in that first cabin. Then one day a pilot dropped a note from a plane flying overhead. We used toilet paper rolls so when you threw it out of the plane it would unravel as it came down and you could see where it landed and then find the note. It said, "I have three live ones for you. I'm leaving them at the airstrip. Come and get them." It was three girls from Juneau who had been traveling in the Interior and were looking for something else to do. They had gone flying and were talking to their pilot about wanting to find a place to go, but they did not want a hotel.[28] I'd flown with this pilot so he knew about us and told them about us. But they didn't bring food. They thought they could buy food at Camp. Since they wanted food, Celia used our primus stove inside our plain white tent pitched on the ground and cooked meals for them. Woody and Les spent the rest of the night making an outhouse to go over the hole we had just dug. We were in business![29] We hadn't finished the other platforms and tent cabins yet, but by the end of the summer we had five of them.[30] I can't remember how much we charged our first guests. But we had eighty to ninety people who came that first summer.[31] Mostly people who knew us in Fairbanks. They were used to going out to Wonder Lake or Moose Creek to fish and now they realized, oh, there was someplace to stay. They were used to roughing it. Camping. At that time, Camp Denali was still pretty rough.

We didn't have any communications. Celia had a ham radio, which was used in an emergency, but otherwise there were no telephones or anything. You were just on your own. We did have our airplane, so we could fly back if we had an emergency, some mechanical part that we needed to get or something. And of course there were the trains, but the trains only came through McKinley Park three times a week to start with. Then later they started having daily ones.

One of the fun things we did in the early days of building Camp was have

Celia at the Camp Denali phone at the bottom of the hill. Photo by Ginny Wood.

privy parties. In the early days of the park, there were a number of tent camps run by concessionaires. By our time, the tent camp at Eielson was abandoned. The old tin shack that they had for a dining room had been torn down, but that's where we went to get windows and johnnies. What was happening was that people were camping out there, and the Park Service wanted to get rid of it because people were leaving garbage and it was becoming a mess. In the summer of 1954, Superintendent Grant Pearson had orders to remove all the buildings at Camp Eielson, to burn them down. He said to us, "I'm supposed to clean it up, get rid of it." You weren't supposed to give away government property. The park had the government mentality that if something of government property was thrown away in their landfill and you took it, you could be apprehended. Now Grant was an old ranger and knew that everything has time and place utility. That anything that could be used by anyone—didn't matter if you were a Park Service person or not—anything that was useful, you didn't throw it away. You put it to one side at the dump. To hell with that thing about not being able to use public property. So he told us we could take whatever we wanted from Camp Eielson. He said, "Whatever you kids take, take it all so it doesn't show. Don't leave any residue. Don't leave any cabins half taken. Take it so no one can see that you've taken something. Take everything. Take it all so it looks like there had not even been a cabin there." So we got lots of windows, lumber, and outhouses from there. We'd go drive out to Eielson with our jeep and tow an outhouse behind on a trailer and haul it back up to Camp Denali. By that time we'd bought a little Cat and used that to bring the outhouse building up the hill and put it in place until we had time to build a nicer one. We'd call them "privy parties." We sure had fun with that.

We also helped ourselves to other surplus things we found. Like we used lots of people at Camp once to help us carry old mattresses from Red Top Mine, near Kantishna, which had been abandoned.[32] Or in the summer of 1954, we retrieved an old 1915 horse-drawn road grader abandoned on the Red Top Mining Road. For years, we pulled that grader behind our Cat to grade and keep our gravel road in shape. It's still sitting out there at Camp—getting rusty and with weeds growing up around it.

Every time we built a cabin we had to dig a hole for an outhouse. We had outhouses because we couldn't see any point in having flush toilets in permafrost. Every cabin had a private path to its own outhouse. They were the fanciest outhouses you ever saw. Every one has a view of the mountain. The first one happened this way because we'd built the outhouse but we hadn't built the door yet. The first guest had to use the outhouse, and it was facing the mountain, and they said don't ever put a door on it. The view was so nice. Then we'd have other guests come and say they wanted that cabin with the outhouse that didn't have a door on it. So we decided not to put doors on any of them. But we did put up a life list for birders, so you could bird from there if you wanted to.

We built a cache that first year so we could put our stuff up and the bears wouldn't get to it. Celia, Nancy Baker, and I worked on that. Woody wasn't around. We didn't have any advice. We had a heck of a time trying to figure out how to get the four posts equal distance and make the structure work right. We couldn't figure out how you figure equidistance from each of the posts. There's a formula, but we didn't know it. We had the posts, but this one is equidistant from that, and equidistant from the other, and then this hypotenuse has to be this way in order to make it square. I have a hilarious picture of us hanging off it and trying to figure that out. We didn't finish it until 1953. Wally Taylor, who was a big-game photographer and lecturer, helped us finish it. He was a bit of a loudmouth. But we kept him around until he helped us finish the cache. The next year we built a little log cabin on top of it for more secure storage.

In later years, we hauled those initial tent cabins down to lower acreage and made them permanent buildings. Gradually, we found out that making things out of canvas was a pain, even though we would build wood frames partway up which made them rather attractive. Those canvas tent cabins used up a lot of canvas from always having to repair them. When they were just canvas on top

Dragging a surplus outhouse back to Camp Denali, 1952. Courtesy of Ginny Wood.

Grading the Camp Denali road with the Little Oliver OL3 Cat pulling the circa 1915 road grader. Ginny walks behind carry a shovel, and Woody and Ginny's daughter, Romany, rides in the bucket with a friend. Camp Denali, 1964. Courtesy of Ginny Wood.

Ginny on the now abandoned old road grader, Camp Denali, May 2007. Photo by Karen Brewster.

they leaked, so one year we tried sheet tin roofing so it would be waterproof and help the canvas last longer. But that looked hideous and it made a lot of noise in the rain. So we put this little cap of metal roof on the top and that looked nice. It kept it cool when the sun was out and it protected the canvas. But it still meant they would only last about three years and then you'd have to get new canvas and that's not cheap. Plus, it was also a lot of extra work because we had to take them down every winter since they weren't sturdy enough to withstand the harsh winter conditions.

At one time, we even had spots for people to put up their own tents. But we stopped that after one year. We had swarms of people, and they took up all the best seating room in the mess tent and were always in the kitchen.

We never did get running water. Eventually, we found a natural spring up the hillside and we put in a mile of plastic pipe to bring the water down into Camp, but it was not hot and cold running water. We had five big heavy aluminum barrels behind Camp that we used for collection storage. Before that we hauled water from the pond. We used two old Blazo cans attached with rope to each end of a wooden yoke that you put around your neck. We had a constant problem with porcupines chewing that pipe. The staff loved getting the assignment to climb up the hill to go and splice the damaged pipe and put in a new coupling so we could get water again. It gave them the chance to get out away from the main Camp area.

Celia, Ginny, and Nancy Baker having fun with cache construction, 1952.
Courtesy of Ginny Wood.

The men help complete the cache, 1953. Photo by Ginny Wood.

After the Denali Highway was opened in 1958, and we started to get more visitors driving in, the health department decided they needed to check on us. They would send a health inspector to check on us and places in Kantishna. They were surprised by how primitive we were. But I think they were just looking for something to catch us on. We had three basins for washing dishes like you were supposed to have. But the hose could drip from one to other, and so they cited us. They also didn't like that we kept lids in cardboard boxes, saying it was unsanitary. We were sanitary in comparison to those shabby places that had just opened on the Denali Highway. They had a hard time finding something wrong, but they had to catch us for something. They brought up the question about water supply. It was a mile up the ridge, piped in from a spring. We'd dug out a rock area, put a screen over it, dropped the water into camp, and stored it in galvanized drums. It was pure water. Although a porcupine might chew the pipe or late in the season it might freeze. When a health department guy was sent out to check our water supply, he had to walk up a mile through brush to get there to check it, so he didn't really inspect it. Finally, a different guy came out, a young man named Stan Justice. He was a mountain climber, really fit and active, so he was not bothered by the hiking conditions. He really checked it and said we had to chlorinate. Before this, nobody had ever gotten sick from that water.

As the years went by, word spread about Camp Denali. They advertised as any tourist business would. They wrote articles to promote their business. But many people heard about it from previous visitors or staff. This increased popularity meant Camp Denali had to increase in size.

Camp Denali gradually grew. From everybody that came, by word of mouth. It attracted people from all over the world. People who liked to go to the mountains, who didn't want a touristy thing. And it got all kinds of individuals, families, lots of repeat business. It grew from just being tent cabins and rather primitive, where you do your own cooking, to having a twelve-by-fourteen dormitory cabin, a separate kitchen and mess tent, and a trading post cabin where we sold a few groceries and supplies and that was used for recreation and get-togethers. We pitched plain, white, wall tents on the ground; equipped them with Yukon stoves, beds, and mattresses only; and offered them for a dollar a night. For each paying guest we had another who hiked or hitchhiked in to offer labor in exchange for shelter from the elements.[33] We eventually changed the tent cabins to be permanent wooden cabins. But we didn't change our philosophy, which was that Camp Denali was a place where you could sleep under cover, out of the bugs.

At first we didn't have a garden. We just started having compost to get rid of all our vegetable matter and so it wouldn't attract bears. We were just putting the waste in the soil, digging it in, and turning it over. But during the winter, all that heating around the rocks churned it up. And pretty soon we said, why don't

Permanent cabin at Camp Denali, circa 1960. Photo by Ginny Wood.

we just put some lettuce and radishes there and see if it will grow? And it did. So that's how we started growing our own vegetables that we served at Camp.

We couldn't have built Camp Denali without an airplane. There was no road connecting McKinley Park to Fairbanks. There was no road that went all the way from Anchorage to Fairbanks.[34] The only way to the park then was by train from Anchorage or Fairbanks. You'd put your car on the train and take it off at the park's depot, and then you could drive it through the park. But we didn't have much traffic. I can remember we'd been in business about five years when Woody came back and said, "Guess how many cars have come in the park this year? One hundred." That's how many they'd had all year. Private cars that had gone over that road. Mostly, our guests came on the train and then we went in and got them. That was the only way you could get there.

But then when they started to build the highways, that was different. When people from Anchorage and Fairbanks could get in there by car.

In 1958, the Denali Highway was opened from Paxson to Cantwell.[35] It was 450 miles to Fairbanks. This meant people now could drive from Fairbanks to McKinley Park. We were expecting changes from this. We expected a lot more people than we'd had in the past, so our main goal was to move tent cabins down the hill below the garage. We knew we would have people coming in trucks with campers that would want to do more of their own camping, and we would have to take care of them. The tent cabins had full cooking facilities. We wanted to separate those doing their own cooking from those eating at the lodge. So the lower camp was housekeeping and the upper camp wasn't. And we built the

Celia gassing up an airplane at the Kantishna airstrip, circa 1960. Photo by Ginny Wood.

trading post as a permanent building because folks got out there with nothing and we ended up selling them stuff out of our warehouse, which was hard on the cook. We even ended up selling people our own gasoline. We got all the tent cabins towed down to the bottom of the hill in 1957. Tourism was running low that year, so we could transition the tent cabins down the hill. We did have a large USGS [US Geological Survey] party staying with us, though. After we moved the tent cabins, then we began to build walled cabins. And every year after that we converted tent cabins to permanent cabins.

It wasn't until they built the Parks Highway in 1971 that they started to get the traffic on the park road. Camp changed when the cars came in. We still kept the cars parked down below and brought people up to Camp in our jeep. We still didn't have drive-in trade ever and kept that remoteness and kept it from being a roadside attraction.

Then it changed again when they closed the park road to private cars.[36] Then you wouldn't need to have housekeeping cabins. Before, when they would come in with their own cars, we thought we should have something fairly simple, you know for backpackers, so we had "Bedrock." It was basic tents for people like that. It was cheap. Kind of like a youth hostel. We thought we really ought to do that, because that's how we traveled around Europe. We remembered when we were students and when we camped and we didn't have any money, and felt we had to pay our dues to the club so we just pitched tents on the ground. Bedrock was furnished with beds and a woodstove; that was two dollars a night. The other one was just a tent with a bunk with a mattress on it;

that was one dollar a night. These were for the hitchhiking crowd, people who couldn't afford or didn't want more. They had probably been sleeping in their own tents and were wet, and would call up on the phone at the bottom of the hill and ask if there was a place they could stay to dry out.

Visitors to Camp Denali get a breathtaking view of Mount McKinley when the mountain decides to throw off its cloud shroud and reveal its full glory. An added attraction is the reflection it makes in the calm, clear water of the small pond that sits in the middle of Camp. According to Ginny, she chose the name Nugget Pond and says that it really is a tarn, with permafrost being the only thing that holds the water in. They realized this one day when they discovered the pond empty of water. A moose had broken through the lower bank, which acted as a dam. All the water flowed out, and with no incoming water source, the pond was dry. They got their pond back by fixing the hole and building up the bank with rocks and mud. She also laughs at how many photographers through the years have taken photos of the mountain's reflection in this water and pawned the images off as "reflection in Wonder Lake." Alongside Nugget Pond with its spectacular view— and where Ginny, Woody, Les, and Celia had stopped for lunch in the rain on their first visit to the area—is where Woody and Ginny built the lodge.

The first lodge was just a big tent cabin. We ate in the lodge. It was a place where we all sat around and visited, hung out. We had a woodstove in it. Then we built the log lodge building.[37]

We cut all our own logs for the lodge down by Carlo Creek in 1953. Way at the east end of the park, outside the boundaries. We were camped there in tents in September while we were cutting the logs. It was beautiful fall colors. Bill Nancarrow helped Woody cut the logs. They'd get logs and haul them across Carlo Creek. And in those days women's work was peeling them, so that's what I did. Peel logs, that's what you do up here if you're a wife. You promised to love, honor, and obey. Peel logs. And cut your husband's hair. We finally got a little Cat. We bought it for four thousand dollars. That changed our lives when we stopped having to do everything by hand. We first had the Cat at Carlo Creek for logging, and then we took it into Camp to use on our road and build the road on up to the upper landing.

We let the logs weather and dry at Carlo Creek and then began to truck them into Camp the next summer [1954]. It was three years until we got the last log in. We had this old 1935 Ford truck—I think we bought it from the Park Service for two hundred dollars—in which we could carry three logs at a time. But the logs were forty feet long and they would stick out over the cab and over the back. There was so much weight on the back with some of them that the front end would come up and it was hard to steer. You had to put a big weight on the front bumper to hold that down, so Woody built this little platform out the front where he would put

Ginny peeling logs at Carlo Creek, 1953. Courtesy of Ginny Wood.

a drum of gasoline. This was enough weight to bring the front end down so you could steer. So every time one of us had to go in to the train station by park headquarters, we'd bring a log or two or three back with us. Woody did most of that. At that rate it really did take three years from the time we cut the first logs.

Woody adds his description of cutting and hauling those logs for the lodge:

> We bought a little crawler tractor that same year we started cutting logs. The little Oliver OC-3. We bought it from Harold Herning, who'd been a miner. It had a loading bucket in front. That tractor was a lifesaver. With that we were able to pick up dirt and move it around. We were able to hitch on with a cable and pull a tent cabin to a new site when we finally would build a good decent wooden little house to replace it. They were all built on skids, of course. We'd haul the tent cabins down the hill the farthest so they'd be additional housekeeping cabins. We got a lot of use out of that tractor.
>
> We also had that little tractor down by Carlo Creek, where we cut good, nice straight spruce logs. We dragged the logs over the creek and we'd load these things onto old Jumbo, the truck. Well, the longest ones,

if I remember correctly, were about forty feet long. Well, you couldn't load those logs on the truck and have that much sticking out behind without having the front wheels of the truck go up in the air. Which they did. I'll never forget that.

We'd load it until we thought it was safe enough. But we had to carry more logs than that. So what we ended up doing was tying a fifty-gallon drum on the front bumper of the truck. How on earth did we do that? I don't remember what we had in that for weight. Whether we put rocks in an empty drum or whether we were carrying a drum full of gasoline. Anyway, it worked. We chained down the logs with chains and chain binders in the front end of the bed, but they were sticking way out in back. And we'd haul these logs out, load after load, all the way through the park.[38]

Before we could build the lodge we had to move what was the trading post down the hill to a new location. This was the store we set up to sell groceries and basic personal necessities once we realized that guests were coming without these things. That building is now down by the garage and is being used for some other purpose. Woody and I stayed in after the season was over in 1954 to work on the lodge. We laid the new foundation after Labor Day, after everyone else had left camp and the park road was closed by snow. We had our airplane down at the landing field at Kantishna. The highest pass in the park on the road is just under four thousand feet and the airstrip is only at seventeen hundred feet, so we could still fly out to the north, where there are lower elevations, even though the road was closed. So we stayed in for a month and got the logs up to the top plate log for the lodge, up to the ridge poles. Woody and I got it up this high, and Ted Lachelt would come down and give us a hand sometimes. He was building his cabin up on the hill behind Camp. He was going to be in for the winter so he was busy trying to finish his place, but he came and helped us some. By October the pond was frozen over and it had snowed twice—there was about six inches of snow on the ground. It was getting to be hard to work. It got so cold you had to wear gloves with everything. Everyone would ask Woody how he learned to build a log cabin like this, and he said, "Living in a tent when it's getting to be zero. You learn fast." So it was time to leave. We flew out in our plane.[39]

Celia couldn't stay out to help us. She had to go back to a job. Somebody had to make money out of this triumvirate. She gave us a chainsaw as a present.[40] Up until that time we just had handsaws and an ax, and did everything by hand. And the darn thing didn't work! It broke after a few days and we never could keep it running. We spent two days trying to fix it. Obviously, we couldn't take it back. We couldn't go buy a new chainsaw. Later, we found out that chainsaw hadn't even been put together right. There was a part missing. But we had no way of finding that out back then.

Building that log lodge was all done by hand, with primitive tools. We didn't have any electricity. It was not a big deal. That's how people used to do it. We bored all the holes for the spikes with a hand drill, an old ship auger. And Woody used a chisel to make the notches. You lift the logs using ropes and pulleys. You make like a pulley system where you wrap rope around the logs and pull on the ropes and it would make the logs go up. You get somebody on each end and then pull. Woody had to notch each log and hope it would fit. We did the ridge poles the next year when we had more people. We got the roof on in the summer of 1955. You always make a double roof for insulation, and there's an art to that because you have the wind up here. It can be a hundred miles an hour in the wintertime in that gap where Camp Denali is. But not in the summertime.

As the main carpenter on the lodge construction, Woody adds the following details:

The trouble was I didn't put up enough rounds of logs. I should have put one more round and then the two cross logs. It would have been higher and there would not be the problem of everybody hitting their heads in there now. Those log beams are just plain too low. But I guess we were

The completed lodge at Camp Denali, circa 1955. Photo by Ginny Wood.

getting pretty tired and pretty discouraged and we wanted to get that roof on for the next season. And it was getting towards winter.

I remember when we bought the big windows for that lodge. We had to get those shipped down on a train. We picked them up with this big old 1935 flatbed Ford truck that we had bought surplus from the Park Service. I had to tie those windows against the stake sides and bring them down. And then we hauled them up here to the lodge. I think we had a road by that time, although I don't think the truck was able to make it. We may have had to haul those windows up by hand.[41]

So the lodge became everything. When it was finished, we made a little kitchen partitioned in one end, had a woodstove, three tables for eating by the windows, and had a fireplace and a gathering area. We could have twenty-four people in there. That was a full house. That's when Liz Berry came out and started cooking for us. Guests and staff would get together in there in the evenings to play music and sing. Now you have performers, but back then we all participated. Some people sat around after dinner and talked. Or it was a good place to sit and read or play games on a rainy day.

Staff singing around the woodstove, circa 1952. L–R: Les Viereck, Ginny, Ted Lachelt, Joan Hessler, Celia, Woody. Courtesy of Ginny Wood.

To save money on trips to Fairbanks, large shipments of food were brought in to Camp once a year and stored for the season. In those days, the food they served was not the gourmet fare it is today, where they even grow their own vegetables in a greenhouse. It was No. 10 cans of beans or veggies, canned ham, fifty-pound sacks of flour or rice, and large jars of peanut butter. There was homemade bread, cookies, and jam. The cooks did the best they could with the supplies at hand and remote conditions to make hearty but healthy meals. A small warehouse was built to store the large quantity of food needed to feed a staff of ten people and from twenty to forty guests a day for a three-month summer season. It was an aluminum-sided wood-frame building. It stood out as one of the larger structures at Camp Denali. This is why it was shocking to find it missing one year.

One spring, our friends the Collinses, who lived at Lake Minchumina, had been flying over the area of Camp Denali and told us they thought a bear had been around there. It looked like it had been in different cabins and pulled a bunch of stuff out. We said, "What about the warehouse?" That's where our food and mattresses and other supplies were. It was bearproof, we thought. "What warehouse?" they replied. Woody and I were Outside [in the Lower Forty-eight states], bringing a car up for Camp. So Celia got in our airplane that was on wheels then and flew down to Camp with a girl who was teaching in Fairbanks but had worked at Camp—Allison. They flew around and looked and looked, and the more they looked the more the warehouse wasn't there. Celia flew over Wonder Lake so she could land and hike up to Camp to see what was going on. It was black ice. It was spring and it had thawed some, but it was still frozen. So she thought she could land on it. She knew we weren't supposed to land on the lake, but that was with floats, so since she was on wheels she figured it would be okay. She came down and tested it and thought, "Oh my goodness, I think it's solid." So she went up around again and landed and walked up to Camp to do a check. To see how much damage had been done by the bear. To see what we needed to fix, and what extra supplies we might need to bring in. To see what we were facing before Camp opened up.

It turned out that the bear had gone and burned up the warehouse. That's why nobody could find it. We thought it must've been miners from Kantishna who stole the warehouse—all that metal on it. But when we went into Camp in the spring, you could tell where it started burning and you could see the bear's paw prints.

We built that warehouse out of metal and with cables around the whole thing to make it bearproof. The ramp you used for getting up into the building in the summertime pulled up into a solid wood door over the entry when it was all closed up for the winter. Then we pounded spikes through that door. We put three layers of cables around the building and put turnbuckles on them to keep it as tight as possible. The bear had used his claws to grab up and under those cables and turned until each one fell down. We figured this happened in the fall.

The original aluminum-sided warehouse at Camp Denali, 1953. Photo by Ginny Wood.

We could see the bear prints where he'd gone into the warehouse. He'd gone in one side just pulling down cans and hams, the jams we'd made, and honey. Other things were pulled outside. There was one case of something that must've been yummy, but he did not digest well. It had gone right through him. The only thing left of that case was a box with advertising on the side that said "Let's eat outdoors." We gathered up all the feces and put it in a box and sent it to our friend, Dr. Fred Dean—a bear specialist—to be analyzed. In his scholarly manner, he sent back a hilarious letter analyzing the excrement of this bear.

We figured out that the warehouse burned down because we kept the cases of strike-anywhere matches up above where we kept the jam. From that point, everything was charred in place. Where it had been in a cardboard box. As a kid, did you ever take a box of strike-anywhere matches and throw them on the sidewalk to see what happens? We used to. The box explodes. So that's what started the warehouse fire. The matches fell to the ground when he was pulling things off shelves and caught fire. It must've been fun to see him try to get out of that place.

Near the warehouse was where we stored three fifty-five-gallon drums of gasoline so that we would have gas for our Camp rigs when we came in with the plane to open Camp before the road opened. The drums were bulged, but luckily hadn't exploded. If they had, it probably would've taken out the cook-house. And if the cookhouse burned, it would've taken out the lodge. All those buildings are clumped close together. So we built a new warehouse with better bear protection.[42] There are still spikes on the door.

The day-to-day operations of Camp Denali appeared to run like a well-oiled machine. Ginny and Celia had a specific routine established for both guests and staff. Breakfast was served in the lodge, food was put out for people to make their own lunch for hiking, and dinner was a grand affair of sharing and storytelling of the day's hikes, wildlife sightings, and adventures. Transportation for group backpacking trips and to the railroad station was a highly choreographed logistical affair. Although it was not fancy, Celia and Ginny made every effort to make Camp Denali a comfortable and enjoyable place to stay. This meant a long list of daily chores for the staff following a rigid daily routine. Ginny was definitive about how she wanted things done and made this clear to her employees. Everyone had a job, knew what it was, and knew exactly how they had to do it. Usually that meant doing it Ginny's way.

The job had to be done because everybody depended on it. If you don't bring in wood for the stove, the cook doesn't get breakfast. If you don't gas the car and it runs out of gas, somebody misses their train. You just learn that you're more than just yourself. We liked kids that came from farms, because they always knew if you left the gate open the cows got in the oats or the wrong animal bred with the wrong animal or ran away. Kids don't learn that anymore. But these kids did.

Segregation of tasks occurred on the owner level as well. Ginny and Celia took responsibility for different aspects of the business, each according to her personal talents and interests. Their varied skill sets complemented each other and may have been one of the reasons they were able to successfully run Camp together for so long.

Celia handled the money. She was the bookkeeper. She was the businesswoman. She had had a year at business college. She focused more on logistics, like getting people to and from the train, and maintenance. She had a lot more mechanical savvy than me. If there was a problem that we had, or a mechanical thing that I didn't quite know what to do with, she was the person I'd call on to pick up the other end. Woody built things. He was a fantastic carpenter. And I thought up things to do. I focused on the programs and the visitor experience. I led the overnight trips. I don't think we ever sat down to say, this is what we're each going to do, or this is what we each wanted to do. I think each one of us added something, while also maybe we were each weak in other things. It was a real team effort, the three of us together. Things just happened and you coped with it. But there were a lot of awful good things that happened, too.

Or as Woody explains:

> Ginny was the dreamer. She came up with the ideas. And Celia and I were the ones who in many cases kind of put them into effect in a practical sense. I was good at the building and the planning of things: of getting material out there. Finding ways to get it up the hill. Celia was excellent at doing the paperwork. She could keep records of things, records of expenses, costs, and income. That was her strong point. She was organized. Neither Ginny or I was well organized about anything. But actually, the three of us worked very well as a team. Perhaps because our skills did complement each other. And we were able to do a lot of good stuff there. Those years were very productive in terms of actually building that place, getting it going, figuring out the physical problems and the logistics.[43]

In those early years, we thought we were full when we had about twenty guests. I guess our peak at that time would be once in a while we could gather up as many as forty. We had a staff of about ten. We did everything ourselves. We went back and got the people at the train, brought them through the park, and took them out on trips. You had to take care of your own cars, you know. We had to do all our own mechanical work. We did our own washing in a 1930 Maytag gas-powered washing machine and hung things out to dry on the line. There was no mechanical means of doing dishes. We used to have to haul water by hand, then we got that plastic pipe running down from the spring. We didn't have electricity, so things were done rather primitively. But that was kind of interesting too, because people had forgotten how to do things this way. There was a woodstove in each cabin and people had to build their own fires. A lot of people thought this was neat and it reminded them of their childhood when they used to do that kind of thing.

The gals did dishes and chopped wood. The guys just chopped wood. Now everybody does everything. We had a head cook and the rest were assistants. Nancy Bale[44] was one, she made all the bread. We had a wood range that we cooked on as well as a propane one. The old tent cabin where the cooking and baking was done was called "Potlatch." Eventually, that's where all the meals were served, too.

Hanging laundry out to dry, Camp Denali, 1956. Courtesy of Ginny Wood.

Woody explains a bit more:

> We would serve these meals that were like casserole dishes. It was good, healthy food. But we didn't have fresh vegetables then, unless someone flew to Fairbanks. It was pretty basic stuff because we would get a shipment once a year in spring from West Coast Grocery. They'd ship it up to the park on the freight train and we would go in with the old truck we had, load it from the freight car onto the truck, and that was our supplies for the summer. Period, pretty much.
>
> Sure, occasionally people would go up to Fairbanks with the airplane. You might come back with fresh lettuce, but you always brought ice cream. You could fly pretty low and slow and drop things out of the plane, which is always a fun thing to do. Camp was in a perfect spot for this, because it was on a sort of a saddle of a ridge, so you could fly in and just skim over the ground and there was a drop-off to Moose Creek on this side and a bigger drop-off on the other side so you never had to worry about getting caught in a downdraft or anything.
>
> You'd fly as low as you could over Camp and the staff would all be out there lined up like a flank across the ridge there, and you'd come in and you'd push the door of the plane open and then push the ice cream out of the door, which would be wrapped up in a sleeping bag to keep it from melting. The kids would all race for it and grab it. That was a big treasure. That was fun. I remember doing that so many times. One time I did that, I got too close to the buildings and I guess the sleeping bag

Ice cream air drop, circa 1956. Photo by Ginny Wood.

unrolled or something and ended up getting fouled up in the wires that held the chimney for the lodge. Somebody had to climb up on the roof and untangle that.[45]

Over the years we had an assortment of different vehicles that we used for various things. At one time, we had a Volkswagen van that carried eight people. That was economical to run and we used it for our adventure trips. We also had an old World War II army surplus six-by-six truck. One thing we used it for was to collect alders and willow and deadwood along the road for firewood.[46] This was outside the park boundaries then so we could do this. When we first got that big truck, I drove it alone over the Denali Highway when it was first opened to the public. At the beginning of the season, Woody asked if I wanted to fly our plane to Camp or drive the truck. I said I wanted to drive to see all that new country. He packed it as full as he could with lumber and supplies that we'd otherwise have to pay to send by train since it was stuff too big for our plane. It was a heavy load. Well, it was a rough road and eventually my load began to shift. It was too heavy for me to work with. So I'd back up to an embankment at a turnoff along the road and slowly bump up against it to shift the load back into place. I had to do this more than once. It was a long drive. It took two days. I slept on the ground under the truck. I was out of the rain, I didn't have to bother with a tent, and I had more room to stretch out than staying in the cab of the truck.

We always kept a gun around Camp for bears. Woody was a good shot. But we never served game meat. It was against the law to serve game for commercial purposes. And of course, we wouldn't have done that anyway. You are on the

The Volkswagen bus Camp Denali used to transport guests, 1956. Photo by Ginny Wood.

boundary of a national park and the reason you're there is to see the animals. You can't shoot 'em and look at them at the same time. I am not against hunting. In fact, I like moose and caribou, but you couldn't very well shoot a big bull that you had watched and photographed all summer, or a cow and a calf that you watched develop into a bull and come back next year and shoot him. We had other ways to get meat. You could drive ninety miles back to the railroad and bring food in. It wasn't as if we were way out and had no other choice. Also, the hunting season came in September, after Camp's season was mostly over. We usually closed down about the first of September. The only food from the land that we served were blueberries and cranberries. And we had a little token garden so we would have some fresh stuff at the end of the summer when visitor numbers declined and we weren't going back and forth to the railroad as often and couldn't get any fresh stuff in.

I sound like a purist against hunting and that's not it at all. I have a respect for people who are really on a subsistence living. But to see some of the hunters that would show up, who would shoot something way back in the boondocks and then couldn't figure out how to get it out. We had to help pack out all kinds of meat. They'd come and want to borrow our truck. The first thing was we didn't want the truck going across the tundra anyway and getting bogged down somewhere far back. So we'd often say, "We'll get the staff together. We'll help you pack it out." Usually three-quarters of the staff would be girls. Sometimes the hunters would get so they'd get trigger happy and fire away, blast away, so that the meat wasn't good for much. We knew these animals, you know. You got to know their families and a lot about 'em and you just didn't want to go kill them, that's all.

A unique feature of Camp Denali was the annual newsletter that Ginny and Celia put together highlighting events of the previous summer season. Every Christmas it was mailed out to former guests, staff, and friends of Camp—everyone who had signed the guestbook. According to Ginny, she mostly wrote the newsletters, and Celia used her secretarial experience to type them and correct spelling and grammar. These newsletters provide a vivid account of life at Camp Denali while simultaneously serving as a record of who came to Camp, what the weather and environmental conditions were like from year to year, and activities occurring within Denali National Park. For example, the 1952 newsletter tells us:

> Breakup came late to Kantishna and so did we. Arriving behind the snow plow that blasted through the last drift on June 13. The road was impassible for a week even for the "Indomitable Jeeper."...It was the worst crop of mosquitoes and wettest summer on record. By the end of the season, we realized our sourdough tent cabins worked for those who wanted to be warm and comfortable with all the necessities, but we needed a different type of accommodation for backpackers on a shoe string budget who were prepared to rough it but not to extent of sleeping on the ground with mosquitoes. So we established "Bedrock" and "Hardpan." These were tents on the ground instead of on a platform with Yukon stoves and mattresses. We charged $1 per night. You could rent cook gear and sleeping bags if you needed to.
>
> Camp closed on September 2, sooner than expected. We got "Jumbo," a surplus truck from the National Park Service. Les and Woody flew to Fairbanks to build a cabin for us to live in. Ginny drove "Jumbo" back to Camp to store it for the winter. At Savage she started to get snow. At Stoney Pass drifts obliterated the road.[47]

One of the hardest things about running Camp Denali probably was compressing everything into the short season we had. It was usually three months at the most. It made for a busy time. Every day you had to get all the guests fed and get them to where they wanted to be. It was a lot of coordinating people's schedules, because their whole vacation would be made around their jobs that they had to get back to. In the third year we were there, all the bridges on the park road washed out except one. And we had to ford all the rivers when driving our guests to meet the train. The drivers all wore hip boots. So the trip took longer than normal. You had a lot of emergencies that happened like that, which you couldn't plan for.

Woody adds his own thoughts on the difficulties of running Camp Denali:

> There was good and bad, as there is in every enterprise. There were times when the weather could be absolutely merciless out there at Camp.

You'd look out and it would be sleet or rain going horizontally across, so you'd think, "Why would anybody ever want to come out here?" And then maybe at two o'clock in the morning the storm would blow away and all of a sudden here's the sun on the Alaska Range and you'd be just, "Oh, wow, I had no idea it was like that." There were times like that. And there were times when the weather would stay socked in for a discouraging length of time. Other times when the mountain range would be out absolutely cloudless for a week or two in summer. Both extremes happen. It is a land of extremes. Always has been.

Well, we had a lot of things that were real obstacles other than just the insecurity of the road. You never knew how well that road was going to hold out. Whether you were going to be able to make that train appointment. The train came in at a certain time and you had to be there to pick up those people.

I remember once I had a flat tire on that little jeep station wagon out by the Savage River. Boy, I never changed a tire so fast in my life. And the guests were out there helping me, too, and we managed to get those people in there to get them on that train to go up to Fairbanks. And picked up our new guests.

There were times like that where there were physical problems, but the isolation was difficult. We didn't have cell phones, we didn't have radio. I'll never forget one time we made the horrible mistake of buying a Volkswagen Combi Bus, as they were called in those days. They were a little hopelessly underpowered Volkswagen bus, which was never designed for the kinds of roads we coped with. They were maybe fine in Germany on the Autobahn, but not in McKinley Park. Sure, they held a lot of people, but they looked like a great big loaf of bread, but with this tiny little engine.

You didn't know when one of our vehicles was going to break down on you. There was a lot of tension that way.[48]

Eventually, Camp Denali's influence spread to the park entrance area. Over the years, Ginny and Celia realized that they needed a cabin near the entrance to help support the operation. In 1970, they built a cabin at Deneki Lakes, a series of small, idyllic lakes about ten miles south of the park entrance on what is now the Parks Highway. Their friend Bill Nancarrow had a cabin nearby. This new cabin was used to stockpile supplies needed for Camp. They put guests up there who missed a train or Camp bus connection. They enjoyed it as a stopover to break up the long drive from Fairbanks to Camp. Although the cabin wasn't far off the main road, it was still a dirt road. It was not yet the speedway between Fairbanks and Anchorage that this route is today.

We built that cabin at Deneki Lakes because we needed to have two things. First, a place at the other end of the park because we were beginning to explore the Yanert River area. We started having our wilderness workshop, where people would come and they'd have the option to stay for three or four days and we'd come back to the park and stay overnight just so people got off the road. We needed a place for them to stay in transition or when waiting for a train.

And second, we had to send a crew in to go unload a freight car with our groceries, and they needed a place to stay. During the construction of the Trans-Alaska Pipeline in the mid-1970s,[49] the railroad was so busy hauling stuff to build the Haul Road [Dalton Highway], and then the pipeline, that they wouldn't stop at the park station to unload unless we had a freight-car load. Well, we weren't that big. We didn't intend to get that big. Before that, the freight got unloaded for us. It didn't matter how much we had. It finally got so bad that we ended up having to come up to Fairbanks to do our own buying. All the places where we got our wholesale supplies, they all were working for big contractors for the pipeline. We had to buy a car—we bought a little pickup truck—just to come up to buy groceries. The pipeline was a big headache for us. I didn't make any money off the pipeline like others did. It meant making extra trips up to Fairbanks. And then there were no more guys in the warehouse shop to tell us about products. We used to call in an order from Camp and if they didn't have a fifty-pound bag of what we ordered they would send two twenty-five-pound ones. But then with computers, they don't know to do that. It's changed. In ways, the improvements to life after the pipeline made our lives simpler, but not everything. When dealing directly with people, we would get things sent down to Camp that we could not get now because it wasn't in the computer.

Johnny Parker helped us build that Deneki Lakes cabin. He must've been about sixteen then. His mother, Marge Parker, was a friend of mine in Fairbanks, and she came and cooked for us at Camp for many years. She would use her vacation time to come down when we were first opening up Camp for the season. She loved it. She stayed only until guests came and then she turned over the cooking to someone else for the rest of the summer. She always brought one of her kids with her. One year it would be Johnny, the next it was her daughter, Carolyn, and so forth. As a fourteen-year-old Carolyn was a big help. I think she was bucking to get a job at Camp. Her mom would joke about whether she would still do the things once we agreed to hire her.

The narrow gravel park road winds its way through Denali National Park, date unknown. Photo by Ginny Wood.

12

Driving the Denali Park Road

We sure had some adventures all those years of driving the park road.

onstruction of the ninety-mile road through Mount McKinley National
Park began in 1923 and was completed in 1938.[1] The narrow, winding
gravel road remained primitive and remote during the more than twenty-
five years that Ginny drove it.[2] After so many trips to and from Camp Denali,
she knows the road intimately. At every bend there is a story. At every valley
or ridge there is a good hike to be pointed out. Or an observation about how
things have changed. As the miles tick past on the long, slow, dusty, bumpy ride,
adventures are replayed through Ginny's memory bank like an old-fashioned
flip-card book.[3] In 1972, she even submitted an article to *Reader's Digest* about
McKinley Park written from the perspective of journeying along the hazardous road.[4] Ginny's experiences along the park road not only show the ways in
which she and guests at Camp Denali enjoyed the park, but provide insight into
changes over time within Denali National Park. The uncertainties of the road
were just another part of what made life at Camp Denali challenging.

On the fourth of September 1952, we got caught out at Camp by an early snow.
We'd finished closing up for the season, bearproofed the warehouse, and Woody
and Celia had flown out. I'd been left behind to drive the jeep out the park road.
That's all we had in the way of rolling stock, and how could we build a cabin in
Fairbanks without it? I didn't even get to Eielson Visitor Center area before I was
stopped by drifts. I could bust through on the downhills, but on the tight turns I
couldn't do it uphill. I returned to the Wonder Lake Ranger Station because the
Park Service said they'd only make one try at getting through the road, otherwise
we would have to be evacuated by helicopter and leave our equipment behind.
Elton Thayer was a college student who had worked at the ranger station that
summer and he had a beat-up Park Service pickup, so we figured we could
travel together. We were stuck for days before they opened the road. We thought
they weren't even going to attempt to open the road at all.[5]

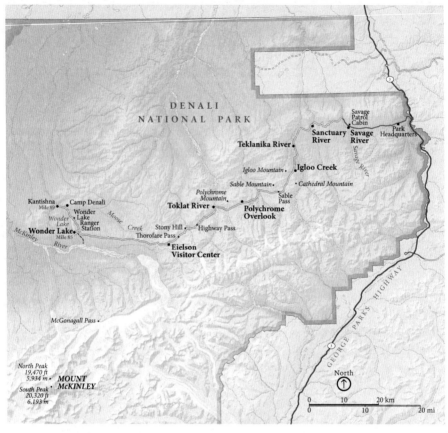

Map of Denali National Park by Dixon Jones.

The only thing that got us out of there was a U.S. Geodetic Survey team that had a camp with crew stationed below Camp that were trying to get out the road, too. They kept trying and kept getting turned back. They had a radio and were able to make contact for help. The national head of the Survey said, "Get that road open. Get my ground crew out. We've got trucks and camping gear we want out. Tell the Park Service to do it." They had helicopters, so they could have flown their people out, but they wanted their equipment out, too, which wouldn't fit in the helicopters. The Park Service came from one direction and me and Elton started out to try to meet them. We got three miles before where Eielson Visitor Center is and we could hear bulldozers. All of a sudden, Ted Lachelt came hopping over all the drifts blocking the road. He was going to stay in all winter at the cabin he'd built and had been to Fairbanks to buy groceries and was trying to come back in. He'd gotten a ride in with the bulldozers. He said it would take them about another hour to get to us. So, luckily we got out.

After that first year, we left our truck at Johnny Busia's place across Moose Creek in Kantishna. We would fly our plane in before the park road opened to get the truck out across the ice before the river melted. In 1953, when we flew down in April to get our truck, we discovered there was an underground spring seeping all winter, so the whole road from Kantishna to the Camp Denali turnout was covered with overflow. It was ten feet thick of ice at a steep angle down the hill-side and across the road along a quarter-mile section. We needed to get through this spot to go back out to the entrance as soon as the Park Service cleared the park road and get lumber we'd shipped in. So we chopped trenches in the ice with mattocks and tried to make it more level. We put ash down to help with traction and to help the ice thaw in the sun. We put a winch up on a tree and used a block and tackle and cables to belay the truck and keep it from sliding down the hillside as we inched it along across the overflow. We spent a whole week doing this. Finally, we got the truck through it. It left big ruts in the ice.

Since we had an airplane we weren't completely reliant on using the park road to get to and from Camp. We could fly in earlier, before the road was open in the spring, and stay later in the fall after snow had closed it. The airstrip at Kantishna was about two thousand feet in elevation and the highest passes on the road were up at four thousand feet. In the fall, when the snow was coming and could close the road at any time after the first of September, we would drive out any vehicle we were going to need for the winter in Fairbanks. When the road

Negotiating treacherous overflow on the road between Kantishna and Camp Denali, April 1953. Photo by Ginny Wood.

closes, you can't go back, so you have to take out everything that needs repairing. We closed Camp by then, because we didn't want a lot of people out there that we might not have a way to drive back to the railroad station. Sometimes we would fly back to stay longer to work on repairs and maintenance at Camp.

We had some wild river crossings on the park road. In the summer of 1953, we had rain, rain, rain, and every bridge went out, except the Teklanika River Bridge that had just been newly rebuilt. Savage River Bridge was okay. And little streams were passable. But the Stoney Creek Bridge was out. It got so bad that the Park Service came in with bulldozers to evacuate all the people from the park. Everybody was going to be towed out or their passenger car was going to be put on a truck. They even had to pull some cars through the high water. We even had to evacuate everyone from Camp.

Then, for the next two years, you wore hip boots and drove a four-wheel-drive vehicle until they rebuilt all the bridges. The highway department had camps at each one of those crossings, with crews rebuilding the bridges. Where they didn't have a bridge finished, every morning they'd bulldoze a route through the water, supposedly to take out the boulders. It took them three years to get all the bridges rebuilt. When the Little Stoney Creek and Big Stoney Creek Bridges went out that wasn't so bad, because those rivers are shallower and easier to find your way across. At the East Fork of the Toklat River, there were times we thought we wouldn't make it through, but we never missed meeting a train to pick up or deliver guests.

Then there was the time I navigated the Toklat River in a jeep. I'm the only person I know to have floated the Toklat! I had taken some guests out to catch the train out of the park. It turned out there was no train because the track between Anchorage and the park had been washed out. I left those guests at the hotel to wait and I drove back to Camp alone. It wasn't too bad of a drive. It had been a nice day. I had to drive through the rivers, but they were low. By the time I was leaving the train station it began to rain and was raining harder and harder, which would make the rivers rise.

When I got to the East Fork of the Toklat River it was probably six o'clock at night. The highway department crew still had one bulldozer out there blading the boulders out of the way. Since they bulldozed there every day, you didn't have to fight going across. They waved, "Come on, come on." I looked at it and thought, "That water is higher than my wheels." They said, "Lady, step it up." I went out and sure enough it came through the floorboards and the engine stopped. The jeep was being pushed downriver by the current. They were out in the middle of the river with a bulldozer and saw me floating away but they didn't have anything to pull me with. So I got out of my car and crawled on the hood and reached down to where I had a winch. It was under water, but I was able to unlock it. These guys in the bulldozer started yelling, "Lady, don't jump. Don't jump. We'll save you." Oh, you guys, I thought. I got the cable loose from

Crossing the Toklat River by jeep, 1953. Photo by Ginny Wood.

the winch and was waving it and said, "Here, come and get me." So they did and I got across.

There was always something like that which would make life interesting. At that time, people were always doing things like that all over Alaska. When I stop to think about it, people were mining, hunting, living off the land, prospecting, and their lives were just a series of things like that. Everyone across Alaska had adventures like that. It wasn't a big deal.

Woody had his own adventure at Toklat. He was bringing in a bunch of tourists, and there again it was a big rainstorm. At that point there still was a bridge, but it had collapsed into sections, so he had to take the car through the river. To be safe, he didn't want to take passengers. The bridge structure was down, you couldn't take a car over, but it hadn't washed away so it was okay for people. After Woody got the jeep across the river, he crawled back over the structure and helped the guests one by one get over it. He didn't get them back to Camp until eleven at night. And we all were having an uproarious party. We thought since Woody wasn't back, "Well, we aren't going to have any guests, so let's have a party." Woody phoned from the bottom of the hill and whoever answered was a bit drunk and said, "Sorry, we're not taking any customers tonight." He said sternly, "Well, this is Woody." So we quickly had to get things ready for those guests. Poor guy, he had spent all day fording rivers only to be treated like that at Camp.

Woody provides his own memory of this adventure on the park road:

There was one year, which I will never forget, in which they had bad floods. There were a lot of floods. It was in the 1950s. All the bridges washed out. The East Fork Bridge was demolished. The Toklat Bridge, which is a long, kind of a causeway, except at the very eastern end where the river goes right up against the cliff and it's deep and fast and black water, that got wiped out. And we had guests we had to get out to Camp. How on earth did we do that?

I remember driving a load of schoolteachers in the little jeep four-wheel-drive station wagon. I picked them up at the train station and we drove out. We forded the East Fork River, and that was no problem because it was broken up into a lot of braided branches and streams. You could pretty well figure out where the deepest water was not going to be and so where you'd be able to make it across. So we went up on the Polychrome Pass and on down into the Toklat, but then it was, "What do you do when you get to the Toklat?" Here's this roaring river and no way to get across it. But I can remember driving down off the road onto the river bar and driving fairly far, oh, probably maybe a quarter of a mile, up along the braided branches of this stream. Finally, you eventually came to the main part of the river and you had to guess whether you could make it or not.

I remember disconnecting the fan belt of the jeep, because it looked as though it would be too deep. When you're fording a river and the water gets up to the level where the fan can hit it, it will blow a spray back onto the engine and then just kill your engine because the spark plugs are shorted out. In those simple cars in those days, you just released the generator strap and that disconnects the fan. But you've still got to figure out how to get across this river. I remember driving into that water pointing at an angle downstream, and it got deeper and deeper and finally the water is getting into the floorboards and you realize you might be in trouble. You just hope and pray that engine keeps going. And it did.

And we pulled out on the other side and I can remember a feeling of relief. But what a crazy thing to do. I never should have done that. We could've been stranded there and then God knows what could have happened. This brown water, you know, you can't see anything because it's glacial melt. It takes my breath away when I think about that. But then we were able to hitch up the fan belt again, and pick our way across the smaller streams, and come up on the other side. Highway Pass and the rest of the road was just fine from then on. But, phew, I will never forget that experience![6]

In July 1953, we were driving on the park road and saw where a whole hill-side had slid across Stoney Creek and formed a lake. We called it Quake Lake, because we'd felt an earthquake two days earlier. There were big blocks of black ice made up of rocks and sand that had just cut off the flow of Stoney Creek and backed it up into a lake.[7] The USGS came out to find out when that happened. They asked us if we felt an earthquake, because they had no record in their seismic information of an earthquake. We said, "Yes, we did feel one." And they said, "What time?" I told them, "Well, I know we were eating lunch so it was sometime between twelve and one." They wanted the exact time. So I said, "Well, Brad Washburn was up on Peak C and he measures everything. He would tell you." And it turned out that, yes, he had it in his notes, the exact time of the earthquake. Brad Washburn was staying at Camp after his climb, and of course he went out and measured Quake Lake. He sounded for the depth and made a map of it.

It was a neat place to go with our guests, so we picnicked and camped there, and paddled around the lake with canoes. We would go down there and climb around in all the ice and stuff that slid down. We had grayling from the creek. There were also beaver there. Most people know it as Bergh Lake. That was named after a guy who was flying low over it, tried to land, and his plane cartwheeled and he died.

It had been a big lake reaching all the way to where the bridge across Stoney Creek had been. About a month later, the water reached the top of the dam that had formed and only a small remnant of the original lake was left. The lake slowly had less and less water until it finally washed out. It took about fifteen years for the lake to disappear.[8]

Then there's the issue of the traffic on the park road. We still own property by Camp Denali, so the Park Service gives us permits for six private-car trips into the park a year. Everyone else has to go in on a bus. When we ran Camp, we tried to be careful about the number of bus trips we made on the road. We only had transportation going back and forth a few days a week, coordinated with the train schedule. But now there are all these other businesses out there at Kantishna who have a lot of buses going back and forth every day. I don't think that should be allowed. It's too much dust and noise and impact to the wildlife. I've noticed a reduction in wildlife along the road since I started driving it in 1951. There is pressure to open up the Kantishna end even more to big tourism by building a road or railroad to it from the north side. We don't want another road coming into Kantishna so you can pour more people in. You'll have another Glitter Gulch all the way out there. Just like they have along the Parks Highway by the entrance. People just want to get more money and they get greedy. They want to make a profit. That was something we weren't focused on with Camp.

I also don't like the idea that you should straighten the existing park road and make it a sixty-mile-an-hour road so more people can get in to see the

Camp Denali guests stopping to admire the view at Stoney Hill along the park road, 1954. Photo by Ginny Wood.

mountain and out again. You know, when you come to a mound, get a bull-dozer and go through it instead of going around it! That's what the chamber of commerce would like. No, I think that road should be kept the way it is. This is my lecture. Like you keep an old building, it should be a monument to what roads were like when Henry Ford made it so a car could be within everybody's budget. The park road is what roads were like when I was a little kid, and when I first learned to drive when I was fifteen. Thirty-five miles an hour was about top speed; maybe you got it up to forty once in awhile. It was gravel roads. You had to be careful. If a road had lots of curves in it, you didn't take a bulldozer and take them out, you just went slowly. They should keep this road the way it is, as a historical artifact. Just fix it when it washes out or gets dangerous, or something. I don't want to see it become a thing where it's just trying to see how many more people you can pack into the park or onto the road.[9]

Originally, Camp Denali was located just outside the boundaries of Mount McKinley National Park. Nevertheless, as Ginny's tales will attest, they still dealt with the National Park Service. Whether it was as friends with the super-intendent or rangers. Obtaining permits for Camp's overnight trips into the backcountry. Keeping up with the rules of landing an airplane on Wonder Lake. Or their use of the park road, the only ground-based access to Camp. Maintaining good relations with the Park Service was essential for Camp's continued well-being. The quality of the relationship waxed and waned through the years, depending upon the superintendent and the rules and regulations being applied. Relations with the National Park Service became even more important after 1980 when the Alaska National Interest Lands Conservation Act (ANILCA) expanded the park's northern boundary and Camp Denali suddenly found itself within the confines of the national park. As an existing landowner and commercial operation, Camp Denali was grandfathered in as an inholding, but they still had to follow the park's rules about use of the road, obtaining permits, and being a good steward of the land. Building positive working relations with the Park Service continued to be both important and challenging.

Ginny and Celia stayed informed about what was happening in Denali National Park, and freely commented on park management issues, such as road use, visitor capacity, wolf control, wilderness management, tourist development, or a northern access road through Kantishna. For instance, in 1973 Ginny wrote an essay regarding construction of a new hotel after fire destroyed the original building, recommending that the park be managed as a wilderness area and that new tourist accommodations be constructed outside the park boundary.[10]

When we started Camp, the Park Service didn't seem to mind us. They mostly thought it was a good idea, because they had nothing else out there at that end of the park. They liked that there was a place for tourists to go. The main three people we had to contend with in the early days that affected our operation were the superintendent, the railroad, and whoever ran the park's hotel. The hotel and the railroad and the Park Service were all run by the Department of the Interior. Always one of them was good and the others were a pain in the neck for us. It seemed that we never got the three of them together on an issue.

Like for a while we had good relations with the hotel. We could hide our guests' luggage there. That's how we met Wally Cole.[11] He was just a kid, bell-hopping at the hotel. In those days people came up to Alaska for a month and they would have their good clothes and their city clothes all with them in their suitcases. Those were the days where you dressed up for dinner in a good hotel or resort. You didn't come to the table unless you were dressed. It was a different world then. Well, they didn't need all this at Camp. So, Wally would let us keep the extra luggage at the hotel while these people came out to Camp, so we didn't have to carry it back and forth. That worked fine as long as nobody found out. Wally got fired once when they discovered he'd hid our luggage for us. But they couldn't find a replacement for him so he went back. Later, he ended up running the hotel, I think. We had to stop doing that when the hotel changed management. I think it was something about helping out a private business in the park that wasn't allowed.

Guests and staff at Camp Denali on a backpacking trip, 1961. Photo by Ginny Wood.

13

Exploring Mount McKinley's Backcountry

Every day we had a hike leaving for someplace.

O ne of the special features that Camp Denali offered were guided hikes and camping trips. Mount McKinley (Denali) National Park's back-country is rough and wild country comprised of rolling hills and ponds, glaciers and roaring rivers, mountains and tundra terrain. There are no trails to follow. It can be a harsh and unforgiving place. Not one recommended for the inexperienced. Ginny Wood developed the outdoor programmatic aspects of Camp Denali. The trips she led offered visitors a rare opportunity to experience the raw beauty and wild ruggedness of Alaska in a safe and protected way. But these were not just your normal, everyday hikes. They were learning experiences. Ginny shared her favorite spots, taught people about the plants and animals they saw, and offered an everlasting example of finding connection to a place and the importance of conservation and preservation.

All my life I'd done these fun things. It wasn't just go out on a toot. It was curiosity, and I loved being outdoors. I loved hiking. So at Camp Denali we started having it be that everybody that came there went on hikes. When guests first arrived, I took them on a hike to what I called the "clover ponds." They spent the day just going from pond to pond and seeing what was in them. It was not a hard hike, and you were walking on tundra. I'd point out things like, "Where you are walking, that's one of our willows under your feet." And mainly it was to give them a sense of the tundra. I found out that what was the lure of the tundra was that there weren't any trails except animal trails. It wasn't like down in the States, where there was a good trail everywhere. The thing that I liked about being up in Alaska was there were very few trails. Everywhere you were, you were someplace. Because you weren't always sure of your destination. Then you begin to notice natural features. You know, tundra. These little tiny willow trees that are only a few inches tall. What the birds are doing. What the animals are doing. It just becomes a part of your life the same way as you would have a certain sense of cities if you lived in New York and had to use the subways and buses and use elevators to get to where you're working or something. You'd have a lot of savvy about that.

At Camp Denali we were out all the time. That was the whole purpose. To get everybody out. Every day we had a hike leaving for someplace. We usually had one guided trip and also had maps for people to go off on their own. We even had canoes or Klepper folding boats on Wonder Lake for people to use for the day. We never served lunch. Instead, we'd have our guests make their own sack lunch from ingredients put out on the table after breakfast. We put out homemade bread and lots of spreads and lots of things to go with it. This way everybody got the amount they wanted to eat and what they liked. They wouldn't be stuck with a lunch they didn't like or were allergic to or something. And then we'd be gone for the day. Or they could go anywhere they wanted to on their own. But most people didn't know where to go or what to see, so we had three types of hikes that we led. We didn't want to spoon-feed people, but we always wanted to get people out. We called them the "Gung Hos," the "Ho-hums," and the "Posey Sniffers." And one of them—the Gung Ho—was to go up on the ridge. That's an all-day trip. Or we'd go over to the glaciers. Or just

Canoeing on Wonder Lake, 1959. Photo by Ginny Wood.

go out along the roads. The weather planned programs for us. We had several hikes we'd scouted out already that we could rotate through depending upon the weather and what people wanted to do and were capable of. And you make it so people have a feeling that you're all exploring. This wasn't planned ahead of time, particularly; I mean, you may have known the trail you were taking a group on, you may have been in that area before and know certain things about it, but usually we just let things happen. And then there were always some people who just wanted to rest. We always had coffee or tea on for people who wanted to stay in Camp.

One year a woman named Louise Potter came to stay at Camp and she said, "If I was younger, I'd apply to work here." And we said, "Why don't you anyway?" So we hired her. But she insisted on at least paying for her food. We said, "All right, nine dollars a day for one room." And she said, "Okay." She knew the flowers. She taught botany at the University of Alaska Fairbanks and wrote the premier guidebook at that time for flowers along Alaska's roadways.[1] She said, "Nobody's got a book about the flowers here. I guess I'll write one." And she did.[2] She would take the older people or the people who just wanted to go more slowly and look at flowers—we dubbed her trips the "Posey Sniffers." It was the same way with birders. The "Lifelisters," I call them. And then you have people that want to climb

Guests getting up close and personal with the tundra, circa 1960. Photo by Ginny Wood.

Guests panning for gold at Friday Creek in Kantishna, 1960. Photo by Ginny Wood.

a mountain or walk on a glacier. People just told us what they wanted to do, and wanted to see and know more about.

And then we added gold panning on Louise Gallop's claim at Friday Creek. It happened because there was a guest who arrived late, because she missed the train and got stuck, and we went to the depot to get her specifically. It turned out that she was not built for hiking. We suggested gold panning instead. She loved it. She even panned on her cabin steps. We nicknamed her "Kantishna Lou." Celia, Woody, and I had no interest in gold panning, so it was something that we really didn't do. But it turned out it was fun for the guests, so after that we kept returning. When Roger Kaye worked for Camp, one of his jobs was to take people gold panning.

In 1953, I started guided camping tours based out of Camp Denali. It was a one-week, all-expenses trip in a station wagon, which included camping and hiking at Igloo Creek, an overnight at Moose Creek, a day at Kantishna, hiking at Wonder Lake, an overnnight at the McKinley Bar cabin, and up Summit Glacier. It was three nights at Camp Denali and four in other parts of the park. In those days, people would come to Camp and stay for a week. People took longer vacations than they do now. They would come to Alaska and stay for a month. I think because it took so much longer to get here back then. People just kind of came and lived the Alaskan way for a week or two.

Then we started having overnight backpacking trips in the park. We'd just pick a spot and head for it. Like we did overnights at Cathedral Mountain or Muldrow Glacier. And you had to wander up and down the streams to figure out the best way to cross. You didn't have bridges. You might be on a good animal trail, but they usually weren't bothered about hip-deep water. You learned to kind of prospect for your route. You'd look at a ridge in the distance with your field glasses and look at the vegetation and that would tell you what the footing was going to be like—whether it was soggy or boggy or brushy. When you're hiking, you begin to notice where you want to hike and where you don't. You're able to judge by the vegetation what's going to be good walking or not. Like if you look on the side of a hillside and there's a lot of brush, you avoid it. But you look over there and there's a bare ridge that would offer better walking. The reason that brush is there is because in the wintertime the snow blows in a low spot so it gets damper, and that allows vegetation to grow. On the ridges the snow gets blown off and there is less vegetation so the exposed ground is usually smoother and easier walking. I mean, this is just a general statement, but after

Hike to McGonagall Pass, 1961. Courtesy of Ginny Wood.

awhile you just start noticing things like that. You just become aware. Like the old woodsmen or the early explorers in the West did in the old days. You know, like Daniel Boone and Lewis and Clark, how did they get across the country? They weren't backwoodsmen, they had to learn. They got a lot of knowledge from the Indians that guided them, but they learned a lot themselves, too. No one told Lewis and Clark to take this route or that. The West was not won by an unregistered gun, it was won by people, backwoodsmen who learned from the Indians and learned from experience and just noticed things.

We did these kinds of trips for twenty-five years. At the time we started doing backpacking trips we were the only ones in the park, so we were allowed to do them. There was no law against it. We had the whole park to ourselves. We hardly ever saw anybody in the backcountry. The Denali Highway didn't come through until 1958, and the Parks Highway to Anchorage didn't come through from the north until 1971. So in between those times we had the park to ourselves. But by the time we sold Camp, there were so many people in the park, so many hikers coming, that they decided that they wouldn't give commercial permits for overnight trips anymore. They could do day trips and take people out as an educational part of their program, but no overnight trips. The Park Service decided that there were enough people getting into the backcountry. And if an organized trip like we used to do got a permit, then every commercial outfit would want a permit to do the same thing, and then you would have commercialization of the wilderness. As it was, it didn't matter when we did it, because at the time nobody else was using the park but us.

We could use Igloo Creek Campground for our guests because nobody else was using it. It wasn't developed. It had pit toilets and that's all. The surroundings there were entirely different from at the other end of the park where we were, so it was very interesting to show our guests this. Within walking distance there was a lot of variety of different things to see and learn about. Adolph "Ade" Murie, who was the ranger/biologist stationed at Igloo Creek Ranger Station,[3] would come down and talk to us around the campfire at night. Or else sometimes I would stop in and see him and ask him questions. He was always very friendly. Or we'd see him when we were hiking around Igloo Mountain. We'd see that head of white hair and we'd go over there to talk to him. One time there was a Dall sheep[4] lamb that had just been killed by an eagle. We went over and in his very kindly way Ade gave a little talk about predators and prey.

For me, one of the most gratifying parts of running Camp Denali was being able to live out there and run backpack trips and hiking trips and natural history trips. And the guests we got. They were good. People would ask me, "How could you stand tourists?" Some of them were a pain in the neck, but very few. Mostly we got people that were very interested in nature and in learning about the park. I met some of my best friends through Camp Denali, and people who were experts in their field who I could learn from.

Wading the McKinley River, circa 1960. Photo by Ginny Wood.

Well, you know, we had an educational thing going on while you were out on a hike. It was very important to us that we were educating people, so we never told anybody a lie about what we were seeing. We found out that you never tell somebody about something you don't know. To try to pass a parkie squirrel[5] off as another kind of animal, to say it was something different. Don't ever bluff it. Because you may have a guy who got a PhD in that particular flower, that particular animal, that particular part of nature, or in that question that somebody has asked. So you say, "Does anybody here know?" That's how we learned. You could always learn something from the guests. I learned as much from guests as I taught them. We had some very interesting people come through Camp who were tops in their field, and they were the ones that taught me. That's when I started thinking about the science of wilderness.

I found joy in going out and discovering and learning new things together with our guests. I wanted people to understand the little things. They all thought you had to see a wolf and a bear and a caribou migration, and then you could go on to the next thing. That they had been there and done that. Or if they didn't see these, then they thought the place wasn't all it was cracked up to be. I used to tell people to just go out, and sit down, and search with binoculars to see what there was to see.

We made a trail around by Camp that we called "Walkabout Trail" because we went up it so many times. And we made a trail up to the top of the ridge behind Camp. A lot of the trail was cut by women and children. But we also spread out and let people find their own little goodies. We'd usually ask guests, "Why did we go this way and not that way?" You get to know things, but not trying to be an academic or not trying to be a know-it-all. It's just a way of learning how to enjoy. Or to go out and say to the guests, "What do you think this place looks like in the wintertime?" To get them to think. I mean, there are just so many things you learn yourself. And that without giving a lecture or being a smarty-pants, you just get people to more than just see how many miles they can hike in a day.

Our main program was to get people walking, since that's what we liked to do. We thought, well, we'll just cater to people who are interested in that. You know, we got involved ourselves, and I guess that led to a curiosity about the natural history around us. So we also started specialized programs. We had a program called Wilderness Workshop, which was ten days of natural history in early June. And then another one that we called Tundra Treks, which was our outdoor program and included hiking and backpacking trips. People could come to Camp and either stay in Camp, or for the same money they could go out on two- or three- or four-day backpack trips. And then there also was Shutter Safari, at the end of August or early September, which featured wildlife photography.[6] In 1974, the energy crisis and the Park Service's new backcountry use permit requirements made us focus our activities on nature walks, day hikes, and backpacking trips of two to five days. The Park Service had already cut the number of people they would accept on each expedition to eight.

One of Ginny's most frequently told stories about hiking at Camp Denali was an incident with a bear. Fortunately it did not happen when she was leading a guided trip, but instead when she was just on a day hike with her good friend Barbara Powell. Barb first came as a guest to Camp Denali in 1971, when she was nineteen years old, on a summer adventure during college. She returned in 1972 and 1974 as an employee. After completing law school, Barb made Fairbanks her home. She and Ginny continued to hike and ski together and remain close friends to this day. Barb brings dinner and visits with Ginny every Saturday night.

I'm the only one at Camp that ever got treed by a bear. After twenty-five years at Camp, with all the people we had on hikes there or working there, everybody has a bear story. A time where you came pretty close to a bear or you were picking berries on one side of a hill and the bear was on the other side and you went over and said, "Oops." But nobody had ever had a close call in the twenty-five years we were running Camp.

It happened about two years before we sold Camp.[7] It was after we had had one of our campouts at Igloo Creek campground and I'd sent one of our staff members back to Camp with the people in the car, and I kept the truck and all our gear. Over by Double Mountain there are a bunch of lower peaks, some rocky peaks, some very interesting formations. I thought, "Gee, that looks like neat hiking country. I'd like to go explore it before I take people there." So I asked Barbara, "Do you want to stay and help me close up our base camp, take down camp and we'll get it all packed, and then do this hike?" So that's what we did. If you're coming out into the park, we were where it's just before you come down to the Teklanika River Bridge. After you've passed the Teklanika campground. And just before you turn the corner to go down to the bridge, there's kind of a little draw that goes up towards the mountain. We parked the car there and hiked up that draw. And then we got up on the hillside, going up towards Double Mountain. We were just above timberline. There were just a few trees, probably half a dozen, before we were going to be completely above the trees.

We saw three bears coming down the Teklanika River. They were at least a half a mile away, if not more. And they were running. And we said, "Oh, they're chasing something. Maybe they're going to make a kill?" And so we sat down to watch them. And they kept coming, coming, and coming and coming. The Teklanika River goes one way and we were going the other. Yet those bears were still coming. All of the bears were the same size, so obviously it was third-year cubs that were still staying with their mom. We'd been sitting down watching them, and I said, "Maybe we'd better get up near those trees?" There were still a few spruce trees nearby that were about thirty feet tall. Barb picked one tree and

I picked another. I left my pack at the bottom of one tree. As we were climbing them, I said, "Isn't this silly? You know, they can't see us, they don't hear us. We aren't threatening them at all. We're not even on their course." But they kept on coming towards us. Barb's tree was probably about twenty feet from me and I said, "Do you see them anywhere?" She said, "One of them's here. At the bottom of the tree. And he's growling." We waited about twenty minutes. And she said, "They've gone. But I don't know where." We knew where we were going, but we didn't know where they were going.

So after another twenty minutes, I said, "Well, there's no use in both of us getting mauled." I said, "You stay in the tree so you'll know what happened. And I'll go down and see if I can see anything." I felt responsible for her. I couldn't imagine having to call her folks to tell them I'd let their daughter be attacked by a bear. So here I am on my stomach like in World War I going through the trenches through the brush. I would raise up my head and look around, and finally I could see them and they were going away from us. They were all three together. But every once in awhile, this one bear would go out and hit a stump and knock it over. Or he'd come to a pond and he'd get in and just splash, splash, splash. And then he'd go over and get his brother and push him. He was what I'd call a hyperactive kid. He was always fighting something.

I said, "Well, Barbara, I think we're safe. You can come on down." The funny part of it was I swore that when I went up my heart wasn't even beating fast. I thought, "This is silly. You know, this is ridiculous. Is this necessary?" But when I tried to descend, I had so many branches to climb through that I had a hard time getting down. And Barbara had a hard time finding handholds. So obviously I had been more panicked than I realized.

We watched those bears go all the way down to the road, go over to my truck, and one of them stood up and was swaying back and forth and probably growling at it. Then they all three disappeared down to the Teklanika River. We went ahead and did our hike. And when we were driving home that night, we said, "You know, what if we hadn't had any trees?" I'm sure we could've bluffed them. I mean, what had we ever done to annoy a bear? I've met lots of bears. You know, it isn't something that's that unusual. But we hadn't done anything wrong. It didn't make any sense. I don't think we really needed to climb those trees, did we?

Then about two days later, word came back that the ranger had been giving his talk on bears to people at the Teklanika campground, and across the Teklanika River they watched three bears come out of the woods and chase two hikers. These were the same bears that chased us. We thought we were pretty safe up in those trees, because I thought grizzlies couldn't climb that far. But maybe we weren't. We heard the story about how one of those bears climbed up a tree until it got to this one guy. He took off his jacket and threw it over the bear's head, and the bear went down. But the bear was aiready up to the guy's boot. The ranger went to the Igloo Creek Ranger Station to get a gun, because there wasn't a gun at the Teklanika station. He came back and no bears. The Park Service sent out patrols for a month. If they could have found that bear, they would have killed it. But they never did find it. And the next spring, they went out again and they never caught him. Nobody knows where he went.

Camp Denali staff, 1974. Courtesy of Ginny Wood.

14

Camp Denali Staff and Friends

Some of my best friends are people I've met at Camp.

While Ginny, Celia, and Woody were the ones who thought of Camp Denali and kept it operational as a business, Ginny is quick to praise the multitude of staff and friends who contributed. They helped build new structures and were vital for keeping the day-to-day operations going, from cleaning cabins to doing laundry, cooking meals, and hauling firewood to helping lead hikes. Camp Denali had to do little actual recruiting of staff. Word spread quickly that it was a fun place to work, the people were nice, and the location was spectacular. The staff was typically young, often college students looking for a summer job. Ginny calls them kids. Some folks hitchhiked or otherwise just showed up and volunteered to work in exchange for room and board. Others wrote asking for a job. Some had been guests who returned the following year as an employee. And others were recommended by friends or previous employees.

Many Camp staff members returned year after year. There was something about Camp Denali that promoted closeness amongst the workers. Perhaps it was that Ginny and Celia created a supportive and fun atmosphere. Or that as the owners they did not put themselves above the staff, but considered everyone equally important to making the operation function. Or that there was a sense of family, of camaraderie, out there in the remote wilderness.

The wonderful part of running Camp Denali was the young people who came to work for us. They were just the neatest and most marvelous, wonderful kids I've ever known. I call them kids, but really we were all kids together in those days. We were kids ourselves when we started. Sometimes it was hard to tell who ran Camp Denali, but after twenty-five years, we got so we were older than most of our staff. They arrived by car, plane, horseback, or their own feet. Many of the people that worked for us were just backpackers and mountain climbers that came in and stayed to help us because they loved the area and wanted to spend the summer there. Camp Denali was a labor of love. When we started, we didn't pay our help much. We just paid room and board. And we had plenty of people who worked for nothing. Then, it became room and board and their transportation expenses. If we had anything left over at the end of the season we'd divide it up. In the later years we paid folks some salary, but it wasn't much.

Our first worker was Joan Hessler, who had come along with a group of mountain climbers from the Harvard Mountaineering Club that drove up to Alaska in an old hearse and climbed Mount McKinley from Wonder Lake.[1] She was to find some place to stay with the car in the lowlands until they got back. While she was waiting, we captured her. She wanted to be sure that she was the first woman this one guy saw after he got off the mountain. And she was. He proposed to her in our cache, and they got married.

Overall, in all our years at Camp, we had little trouble with staff. We had a few losers, but very few. We only had one person quit, and we had a couple we had to fire because they were doing things we didn't like. Or we had some we didn't keep, because they just didn't fit in. Like one kid who rappelled down to an eagle's nest, we sent him packing. Or another guy who was delivering the woodstove supplies that you find in each cabin, and instead of soaking the sawdust used for fire starter in kerosene, he was pouring gasoline on it. He wasn't paying attention to what he was doing and got it out of the wrong tank. He said, "Boy, that would sure give them a bang, wouldn't it?" Like it was funny or he didn't care much. I said, "And you're going back on the next airplane."

We did have a few problems with the hippies. There was an issue about why they couldn't take over the lodge after the guests left in the evening. And you know, boys being boys and girls being girls, there were always relationships starting. We said, "Look, we're not going to have a bed check, but for gosh sakes don't do it in the lodge." "Well, why not?" the staff said. I said, "Because the guests get up at three in the morning to take pictures of the mountain and they come in here to get warm. And that's not what they want to be seeing." The staff said, "Well, let them be shocked." I said, "Look, these people are paying a lot of money to come here. And you don't have to shock some poor little old schoolteacher who is spending her life savings to do this. Now, just be a little considerate."

What we did with the staff was that tipping didn't go to any one person. We told the guests that we have a pot for tips. So if you think you'd like to give something to the help, to please put it in the pot. We divided it up at the end of the season. Otherwise, then what you'd get is the cute girl that serves your meals gets tips and the person that's on duty to clean the outhouses doesn't. We wanted to even it out. Make it more fair for everybody that was working hard, whether they interacted with guests or not. Sometimes for people that we knew had really gone all out, Celia and I would give them some extra money at the end of the season from what we had made.

One thing was that you were independent at Camp. Out there, we were like a little country. There was nobody that you could hire to come fix anything or do anything. You were on your own. If something broke, you either replaced it because you had a part already, or you made it. You were completely dependent on each other. That everybody did what they were supposed to do. That we had to put up with each other. And learned to deal with each other. We were like a family. Anything that happened, we had to take care of it. Nobody else was going to rescue us or take care of us or get us out of the predicament we got ourselves into. The country had a lot to teach about Alaska. And you never knew what was going to happen next.

The other thing was a complete respect for other people. If the road washed out, we all got together, the miners and us. If the tourists wanted to help, yes, fine, we'd get out and fix the road or put in a culvert. We took care of anything that had to be taken care of. If a car went off the road, we all went out and helped push it back on. Even the Park Service—they just had a ranger at Wonder Lake and he didn't have a radio, so the Park Service couldn't tell him what to do or how to do it. So, we just all did what needed to be done.

It was our camp. It wasn't the staff's or the management's, it was our camp together that we were building. A lot of the camp that was built was an extension of the staff—a little bit of everybody that worked there became a part of the camp. Maybe it was just a bridge somebody built over the creek, or maybe it was some type of a little finishing touch on a cabin or old seat that somebody made with an axe from a log, but there were always different contributions. It became sort of an extended family, because now we have kids all over the world! Anyone who has ever worked at Camp Denali can go and visit anybody else who worked there. It's a fraternity; it's family, you have to take 'em in. So that was a very warming experience.

Many of the people who worked at Camp stayed on to live in Alaska, and then some of their kids have come back to work at Camp, too. I'd say fifty percent of our close friends came to work at Camp Denali.

Like Bill and Liz Berry. We'd met Liz when Woody was finishing up college at UC Berkeley. I met her when I went on a field trip with Woody up in the hills to look at California quail.[2] He was going for a weekend, and we were just married and I didn't like him going away for that long, so he said why didn't I come too. Aldo Leopold's son, Starker Leopold, was the professor. There were about fifty people. There was this cute little blonde girl that I was walking beside, and it was Liz Berry. We later found out that she and a girlfriend only lived two blocks away from where Woody and I were living. So we started going skiing with her at the Sierra Club's Clair Tappaan Lodge in the Sierras.

Liz met Bill later. He was a wildlife artist, and one year they decided to drive up to Alaska to visit us. But they never made it. They stopped so often for him to do drawings that they never got out of Canada. But the next year, 1954, they made it

Liz and Bill Berry at Camp Denali, 1954. Photo by Ginny Wood.

up. They loved it at Camp Denali. Bill could observe real animals for his drawings. While Bill sketched, Liz took notes on the wildlife behavior. Liz helped at Camp. She was very sociable, talented, funny, and opinionated. She was an incurable naturalist. One year, she had a red vole she named Imitrude, who raised a large family in a cage. And another time she had Clementine the ptarmigan.

Liz was really good at leading early-morning bird walks. She had a rollicking sense of humor. Even when she led hikes in the rain, she managed to convince everyone that they had had the time of their lives. Bill hauled wood and water for Camp when he wasn't out drawing. Bill and Liz stayed on to live in Fairbanks and we were good friends. One year, we realized we needed a cook, so Liz came and did that. She was our cook for a number of years. She wanted to make it possible for Bill to be out there working on his drawings. In fact, the 1955 Camp Denali brochure featured his drawings.[3]

Another of our great staff was a guy named Garry Kenwood. He kind of just showed up there. This was after the Denali Highway was open, because Woody and I drove in to Camp with our big six-by-six truck—"Jumbo"—loaded with lumber for the summer's building activities. Celia had flown her own plane in earlier with another woman to start working on opening up Camp for the season. Woody and I arrived late at night and went straight to bed. When we awoke in the morning to a man's voice, we were a bit puzzled. We knew there weren't any men. It turned out to be Garry. Celia said to me and Woody, "His name is

Garry Kenwood, circa 1960. Photo by Ginny Wood.

Garry Kenwood, and we're keeping him." Garry had grown up on a horse ranch in California and had been in the Korean War. After the war, he decided to get away and come explore Alaska. He'd found Camp and offered to help Celia with building some of the cabins she was working on. He was absolutely one of the finest human beings I've ever met. He liked animals, and while at Camp he became a wildlife photographer and filmmaker. Camp Denali changed his life. He later went on to become an animal handler and worked on some Hollywood films. Like he handled the wolves in *Never Cry Wolf*, or the big bear in *Big Ben*. He had this amazing connection with animals. Eventually, he moved to a ranch in California, and died of cancer at age seventy.

Woody has his own different memories of Garry Kenwood:

> Garry Kenwood became a very important person in our lives. He was a guy who had just gotten out of the Korean War, in the Marines. And he was a wonderful guy from Three Rivers, California, down there at the foot of the mountains and the giant sequoia park. He'd grown up on a ranch, but at a very young age he was taking packhorses and was leading fire crews and trail crews in the mountains. One day a friend said, "Let's go up to Alaska." Okay, they made an agreement, they'd go up. Of course, his friend backed out at the last minute. That didn't bother

Garry. He had an old jeep pickup truck and said, I'm going anyway. So he drove that truck up to Alaska. I guess he drove out the park road and he realized there was a cabin over there across the river, and I guess he pulled himself across the river and was talking with Johnny Busia. Celia happened to be flying down from Fairbanks at that time with a load of stuff in her little white Piper airplane and she landed at Kantishna. She stopped at Johnny's cabin and here was Garry Kenwood. She said, "Well, you want to come up and help us build Camp?" "Okay, might as well." So he ended up staying all summer and building a number of buildings there. He built the first garage. All the storage for the car parts and gasoline and things.

Garry was an absolutely amazing character. He had this foghorn voice. He was a naturalist. He knew a lot about nature that he had just taught himself. And he learned about photography. We had a lot of photographers up there all the time. They would bring these tours up and they had beautiful cameras. And Garry was just fascinated and he'd learn all about these cameras by asking people about them. He got to be a good photographer. He eventually ended up taking wildlife movies. And got very good at it. He had a natural, almost uncanny, ability to handle animals. And he eventually was working for the game farm out at Sequim, Washington, that had a lot of animals used for movies. He did a lot of movies with these animals. He brought up some geese from the very time they cracked out of the egg. The geese bonded with him. He'd be in a wetsuit right down in the water. He made a beautiful black-and-white movie about them called *Wild Goose Calling*.[4]

In addition to the staff, Ginny, Woody, and Celia made friends with other people in the area, residents and visitors alike. There was Johnny Busia, the last remaining resident of the former mining town of Kantishna, about four miles farther out the road. There was Dick and Jeanne Collins at Lake Minchumina, about sixty-five miles northwest by airplane. There was Fred Dean, a neighbor in Fairbanks, who based his research on bears in the park out of Camp Denali, while his wife, Sue, stayed there with their children. Or Les and Teri Viereck[5] who were doing fieldwork for their PhDs[6] and would come in from their campsite by Muldrow Glacier to get a good meal at Camp Denali.

We met Johnny Busia in 1952 when we had our first season.[7] At that time, he was the only person who still lived in Kantishna year-round. He was from one of the Slavic countries. Croatia, I think. His father had come into the Kantishna country to mine in 1910. And then in 1914, when Johnny was eighteen or twenty, he'd come over and gone out to visit his father. His father had left, but Johnny stayed.[8] He lived in a cabin across the river, so you had to pull yourself across

Johnny Busia, 1957.
Photo by Ginny Wood.

Moose Creek by a little cart on a cable.[9] He was the guy to visit there. Everyone went across and signed his guest book.

Johnny spoke very poor English. He was hard to understand, but if you asked him a specific thing, like when was the latest that Wonder Lake froze up, the coldest it got, the latest thaw, the first bird, he'd tell you very plainly and you could understand him. He had a great memory, so if you asked him a specific question like this, his answer was always right.

If Johnny started drinking his beer and telling stories it was half in Croatian and half in English. He made his own beer. He was known for his homemade beer. But he didn't like drunks. Johnny would tell people from Camp to come down and have a beer. He knew when we had guests that hadn't come to see him, and he would say to us that they hadn't come to visit. He wanted to share his beer. He liked company.[10]

By the summer of 1957 more private cars started coming in, and the Denali Highway was being built and proposed to open soon. We knew this meant more people would be coming out to Kantishna. We tried to warn Johnny. We said, "Johnny, you better move all your gear that's over the other side by

Moose Creek, where your other cabin is. Because cars are going to start coming in. More people will be here." He said, "Well, if they need something give it to them." We said, "No, they'll take it." We couldn't convince him that they were a different kind of people.

He hadn't been to Fairbanks in who knows how long.[11] He hadn't been to park headquarters since 1948 or 1949. He had an old Ford pickup that he drove around the Kantishna area. The way he got supplies was that he just made a list and Grant Pearson, the superintendent, saw that he got the things.[12] Johnny thought that was just how it worked. He didn't know he hadn't paid for it. Grant just said, "No, at your age, this is what people give you." Like it was social security or a pension. And we always air-dropped packages and food to him at Christmas.

Johnny died in August 1957.[13] I think it was his kidneys. He'd always been there alone for the winter, but that last year when we were getting ready to leave at the end of the season, we knew he was dreading being there alone. He got sick that fall and we knew he didn't want to face the winter. That and he was just living on his beer. I think he decided to die. He didn't want to go through another winter alone. Before that he was active, had a dog team, got his own moose, kept busy. We tried to get him to go to Fairbanks, but he said, "Johnny not leave. Be with dogs." He wanted to be buried where his dogs were. We knew he was dying and we had an airplane, so we offered to fly him out, but he'd rather die there as the mayor of Kantishna than as a pauper in the hospital in Fairbanks.[14] And we thought, "Why drag him up here to the hospital in Fairbanks where he was nobody?" He wouldn't take a dime if he thought he hadn't earned it. He got a regular check in the mail that he thought was his payment for taking care of Kantishna, but it really was government welfare. We never told him.

So Woody went down with his sleeping bag and slept there for three nights to be there with him. He died when Woody was down there. He didn't want to die alone.

We had a little ceremony for Johnny. All the people that lived around the Park, even the chief ranger, came up for it. We had a little service and buried him over by his dog graveyard in Kantishna. He was 63.[15] He's still there. We later salvaged logs from one of his old cabins—"drunk cabin," he called it—that was falling into Moose Creek and re-used them at Camp. The guestbook that was in his old cabin disappeared. I suspect it was taken by campers who had driven in when the Denali Highway first opened and his place was empty.

Then there was Ted Lachelt, who built the cabin up the hill from Camp that he called the "Eagle's Nest." He would walk down to help us with a project or just to visit. He was a handsome guy. He didn't like wars so had become a conscientious objector. He did his time and then came up to Alaska. He went to the University of Alaska in Fairbanks. He was studying wolverine.[16] He really was a physicist, but

Ted Lachelt, circa 1952.
Photo by Ginny Wood.

decided for one year he'd study wildlife. Nobody knew much about wolverine at the time, so that's what he was going to do. It was a challenge.

The last addition to the Camp Denali family occurred in 1956, when Ginny and Woody had a daughter, Romany. This did not stop them from continuing to focus on the growth and development of Camp Denali as a successful tourist operation. Romany grew up immersed in Camp Denali, spending every summer there until her teenage years, when she preferred to stay in town with her school friends. Ginny recalls the challenges of handling a baby while still running Camp and keeping track of a young child in their wilderness setting:

Romany wasn't born at Camp Denali, but she was conceived there. She was born at St. Joseph's Hospital in Fairbanks in May. At this time of year, with

Six-week-old Romany Wood arrives at Camp Denali, 1956. Courtesy of Ginny Wood.

breakup, Ballaine Road, our main access route to town, could be completely muddy, deeply rutted, and impassable. Luckily, I went into labor at five o'clock in the morning and an unusual cold snap caused the nighttime temperature to drop low enough that the road had frozen overnight, so Woody could get the jeep up to the cabin from the golf course where we had left it the day before because the road was impassable. Otherwise, I would have had to walk the two miles down to the bottom of the hill.[17] Romany wasn't born until four o'clock in the morning the next day. After hours of being in labor and not getting much attention, Woody finally asked a nurse when she thought the baby was coming because he wanted to go back home to finish putting the roof on our cabin. If it was going to be a long time, he'd leave and come back. The chief doctor, who was dressed in a tuxedo for going to a party, overheard this and said, "Get that woman to a delivery room immediately. That baby should've been out of her a long time ago!" I spent three days in the hospital before I could go home. It wasn't like nowadays, where mothers and babies go home the next day.

I first brought Romany to Camp Denali when she was six weeks old. Woody had already flown down to Camp to start getting ready. The road wasn't open yet, but he went in early by landing our airplane at Kantishna. He went in to get the crew started. To fly in some of the supplies and things that were needed. To start building what we were going to build that year. He came back to Fairbanks to get me and the baby and put us on the train to go down. I had the diapers and

Ginny carries baby Romany in her backpack "papoose board," 1956. Courtesy of Ginny Wood.

the bottles and me—I was mostly breastfeeding—and her. Everything that she needed was in a diaper bag. As the train pulled out, I realized I'd forgotten the bag. And here was Woody running alongside the train with it in his hand. I cried out, and the guy who was the conductor asked what was wrong and I said it was all my baby's diapers. He just reached up and pulled the cord and stopped the train. Woody was able to hand me the bag. They wouldn't do that now.

Two days before this, Woody had put our car on the train in Fairbanks so that it would then be down by park headquarters waiting for me when I got there so I could drive it into Camp. Woody was going to fly our plane back down. As my train was leaving the freight yard in Fairbanks, I saw that our car was sitting there on a flat railcar. It hadn't gone down ahead of me. So there I was going to arrive at McKinley Park without my car waiting for me there. So that trip didn't start out the best. Luckily, our friend Ginny Nancarrow happened to be at the McKinley Park train depot when I arrived, so she took me and the baby to their house at Deneki Lakes south of the park entrance, where I waited for three days for my car to arrive.

Woody made a backpack papoose board out of wood as a way for me to carry the baby when I went hiking or was doing something around Camp where I needed my hands. You could strap diapers and a bottle to it. It was great, but boy was it heavy. One of the first times I used it Romany got all sunburned sitting there on my back facing the sun as I walked. I hadn't thought about this.

*Ginny and five-year-old Romany on the tractor grading the Camp Denali road, 1961.
Courtesy of Ginny Wood.*

But it came in really handy one time when I was hiking and all of a sudden a big thunderstorm and hailstorm came up. I placed the papoose board on the ground and turned it upside down so Romany was facing the ground and protected underneath the big board part. She never even got wet.

It was okay to have a baby there at Camp, until she got older. Once she started walking I had to worry about things like Nugget Pond, her getting run over, or wandering off. When Romany started walking I used to put her up on the Cat when I was driving it to grade the road or haul stuff. This way I knew where she was. I didn't have to worry about backing over her. There was always a lot to worry about with a kid at Camp. Like the one time when she got stuck in the outhouse when the latch turned. I spent a lot of time on the outside of that outhouse door explaining to her how to undo the latch. She always had plenty of playmates at Camp. Friends would come out with their kids. Or other staff or guests who had kids. They all always had a great time running around and exploring and playing in all that open country. Like this one time when Romany was about two and there was another mother there with a two-year-old and suddenly we couldn't find the kids. We had everyone looking for them. Finally, we found them on the road to the Wonder Lake Ranger Station. They said they were going back to headquarters to get ice cream.

CAMP DENALI STAFF AND FRIENDS

Camp Denali's spectacular location and the outdoor-based vacation opportunity it offered attracted a variety of interesting guests—from the college kid backpacking through Alaska, to famous mountaineer and photographer Brad Washburn, to the Rockefellers, to wildlife filmmaker Herb Crisler, who was shooting a movie about wolves in 1952.[18] And in the summer of 1963, the Wilderness Society held their annual meeting at Camp Denali.[19] Camp Denali provided Ginny and Celia an opportunity to meet people from around the world, both the common and the elite, and build connections and lifelong friendships that would later prove useful later in their environmental conservation and advocacy work.

Camp Denali became quite a well-known place. The guests were special people, people looking for something off the beaten track. The repayment we got from Camp was the fantastic people we met that came there.

Ginny with her Cessna 170 airplane, 1954. Photo by Les Viereck. Courtesy of Ginny Wood.

15

Flying Search and Rescue

I got involved with doing searches,
just because I had an airplane and they needed help.

G inny has said that they could not have run Camp Denali without an airplane. In those days, having an airplane in Alaska was more critical than having a car. There were few roads and flying was the best way to access the vast expanse of the territory. By having an airplane so close to the north side of Mount McKinley, Ginny found herself called into service as support for mountain-climbing expeditions and for their search and rescue.

I wasn't in the business of doing searches, but we had the only airplane out there at Wonder Lake. And we often knew some of the people who were on the climbs. I was on an early rescue in 1954.[1] It was for an expedition that was organized to make the first ascent of the north peak of Mount McKinley via the so-called Cook Route, the northwest buttress. It was led by Dr. Don McLean, who was a physician in Fairbanks, and the party included Bucky Wilson, Captain Bill Hackett, Fred Beckey, and Henry Maybohm. They had hired Dick Collins of Lake Minchumina to land them on a frozen lake at the base of Straightaway Glacier, from where they would snowshoe up to Peters Basin and the start of the climb. McLean claimed to have permission from the Park Service for Dick to land the grub, extra equipment, and high-altitude climbing gear in Peters Basin after they arrived there.[2] Well, they found out later that he didn't. Dick had advised McLean to package their supplies in small bundles that could be airdropped out of the window of the plane in case he was unable to land. This request was ignored, and the supplies were shipped to Lake Minchumina in large duffle bags too bulky to airdrop.

In order to travel fast and light, the climbers took only a minimum of food and stove gas for the trip in to their base camp at Peters Basin.[3] They had gone in with just enough food for four days, figuring the plane would resupply them

Dick and Jeanne Collins, circa 1954. Photo by Ginny Wood.

with the rest of their food and high-altitude climbing equipment. On the fourth day after leaving the climbing party on the glacier, the weather forecast predicted the approach of a storm front. Despite strong winds and turbulence in advance of the front, realizing that a delay might mean the climbers would run out of food and gasoline, Dick and his wife took off to deliver a load of groceries.[4] There was not a good place to land on the glacier. McLean had marked a landing strip, but it was much too close to the northwest buttress for a safe approach. While they were making a look-see pass overrun of another site, a downdraft from the changing weather conditions caught the Collinses' plane and forced a hard emergency landing at a spot over a mile from the climbers' camp. In landing, a ski was caught on an ice hummock and ripped off.[5] Our good friends Florence Weber and Florence Rucker[6] had a little lightweight plane, and they were good friends with the Collinses, so they went down just for fun to fly over them while Dick did this glacier drop. They ended up seeing him have the accident. They saw both Jeanne and Dick get out of the plane and wave they were all right. Both plane and pilots were intact, but without survival gear, for Dick had removed theirs to make room for the climbers' gear, in order to lessen the number of trips in light of the approaching storm. So there they were.

L-R: *Florence Rucker Collins and Florence Robinson Weber, circa 1954. Photo by Ginny Wood.*

Stranded. With the wind rising, the climbers were inside their tent brewing tea and had not heard the plane over the roar of the primus stove and flapping tent.[7] So the Florences were the only ones that knew the Collinses were there.

Dick and Jeanne walked over to the climbers' camp. They did it without any rope or anything. They didn't even know enough about glaciers to know that they should be scared. They later said, "Oh, my foot went through once and there was a hole down there, but it was no big deal." Since the climbers didn't know about the plane accident and that Dick and Jeanne were nearby, you can imagine their astonishment when Dick and Jeanne walked in. Jeanne had said, "I don't think they'll even have the teapot on." Those guys tussled out of the tent and were pretty surprised. They retrieved one load of food from the plane and tied the plane down to the rest of the gear, then all spent the next three days pinned down by the storm at base camp.[8]

The Florences flew back to Fairbanks and told me about what happened. Florence Weber had to go Outside on business, so she couldn't go back to the mountains. So I took my plane down with Florence Collins to take part in the air rescue attempt. I was a close friend of the Collinses and several of the climbers. The violence of the ensuing storm prevented air rescue attempts. We stayed in

Mount McKinley as seen from Eielson Visitor Center, August 2007. Photo by Karen Brewster.

Dick and Jeanne's house at Minchumina, where the climbers' stuff was. While grounded there, Florence and I took the liberty of repackaging the rest of the climbers' supplies according to my own priorities—first the stove gas and some more grub, and then enough climbing gear so establishing camps up the northwest buttress could begin.[9] We decided what they needed real badly, what they had to have for climbing, and what they could do without. Like one of them didn't need three pairs of underwear. And I eliminated some of Captain Hackett's extra clothes. Although a very able climber, he was well known for never forgetting his appearance as an officer and a gentleman, even at high altitudes. Their high-altitude climbing gear is what they really needed. They were at the base of a mountain and couldn't go anywhere until they got this equipment and food. We went through and sorted it all out so it was a smaller load. We had it all packed in my four-place airplane. We were all ready to go. We made three attempts and we kept getting stopped by the wind. The turbulence was so bad we couldn't even get near the mountain. This happened for four days. Then on the fourth day at four o'clock in the morning, Florence knocked on my door and she said, "Hey, the wind's stopped!" I said, "Let's go."

In the meantime, the word was out and it was big news on the radio and in the papers: "Plane crashes on McKinley. Climbers without food. Pilot and passenger marooned." So here comes the military. They flew in with all these little planes. The guys were all wearing their street shoes and light jackets. They said, "Well, we're not going to land on the glacier. We're just going to drop stuff." So they were all still asleep when Florence and I took off and went in. I had the door off the plane. Florence was in the back. I said, "Get everything out as fast as you can. 'Cause I don't like it in here. We're beginning to get some downdrafts." There was a little cirque in there and the wind was funny, but it was pretty good weather. We flew over and found because of the storm Dick's plane was flipped on its back with a wing strut broken.

We got the drop out, but I forgot to reel in my aerial that was used for radio communications so that got damaged. Then I turned the plane to go home and Florence was just grinning. She said, "I got everything." Well, it turned out that included my sleeping bag, which I had in there for safety purposes.

Just before we made the drop, here came the military planes. They were in the air milling around everywhere. I picked up the radio and said, "Would you please stay out of here until we complete this drop?" Because it was hard enough to get in there and out of there without those planes all around. They were sightseeing, taking pictures.

It turned out that McLean and Bucky left the other two climbers at camp and hiked out with Dick and Jeanne to Straightaway Lake down in the tundra at the base of the mountain. They said, "The helicopter flew over the night before and we had made a big fire on the tundra, but the pilot didn't even look down. He was taking a picture of Mount McKinley as it was a beautiful clear night." But the next day the air force helicopter picked them up.

I couldn't drop the gasoline for their stoves, because I looked at that wind and it had swept off all the snow so it was just ice. I knew the gas would spill when it hit that. So I went back to the military. They were going to pull out now that everything was over and Dick and Jeanne were picked up. I said to the military, "Hey, guys. They still have to have their gasoline. They can't make the climb without it. You can't cook any food if you don't have gasoline. I can't drop it because of the ice. But you guys have chutes. You could put a parachute onto the cans." Well, they weren't very interested. That wasn't what they were supposed to do. I said, "Well, you came down here to rescue people. Everybody will need help if they can't get water and if they can't make food, because they haven't any gasoline." I had to really talk them into that. Finally, they did it.

Dick lost his plane and he and the others could have lost their lives, all because the leader of the expedition chose to ignore the pilot's request that the gear be packaged properly for airdropping, instead of risking a landing, and in not taking in sufficient grub to allow for a storm.[10]

I was also involved in the search for the Thayer Expedition that Woody, Elton Thayer, Les Viereck, and George Argus were on in 1954.[11] They made the first traverse of the mountain by going up one side and down the other.

Elton Thayer had been a student at the University of Alaska in Fairbanks and had lived as a ranger down at McKinley Park. When I first got to Fairbanks, I worked with him on the night shift at the laundry downtown. While we were folding laundry, we'd get into these great, long philosophical discussions about climbing and the wilderness and things like that. I really enjoyed talking with him. He was very interesting. But boy did we shrink a lot of sweaters! We sure weren't paying attention to what we were supposed to be doing.

Woody went along on this trip, because he thought, "I don't know as I'll be any good at the top. But I'll go and help lug your stuff in." They were all students at the university, although Argus was in the military stationed at Big Delta, and were close friends. Woody said, "You know, everybody climbs to the top. Why don't we just go in to where we can say no one has ever stood in this place before and we will see a side of the mountain that has never been explored?" So that was their main goal. Elton planned it. They were going to get off the railroad at Curry, which was a railroad stop south of Cantwell. From Curry, they were going to snowshoe up to Ruth Glacier. They had to haul all their gear for miles, so we were going to do an airdrop at the big amphitheater of the Ruth Glacier. But they had to get up there first. We were trying to fly in, and when we got there we saw that they were way behind, because they had a big warm spell and their snowshoes kept clogging up. They'd take two steps and they'd have to hit them to clear them off. They were about two days short of where we were to give the

Members of the 1954 Thayer Eexpedition. L–R: Woody, Elton Thayer, Les Viereck, George Argus. Courtesy of Ginny Wood.

airdrop. So they wrote in the snow, "Come back Saturday." That was on April 24. We dropped four hundred pounds of equipment.

From there on, it was all unknown. They wanted to get up over the head-wall of the Ruth Glacier and then go up along the Southeast Buttress. No one had ever tried to do this route before. They just wanted to see what it was like. An early explorer who had been with Cook when they had gone up the Ruth Glacier had written that this route was impossible, that no one would ever climb that area of the headwall of the Ruth. That intrigued Elton.

There was an old log cabin down on the Chulitna River, and they said after a certain date I was to come over and if they were there to drop them an axe and some wire because they were going to have to build a raft to float down when they finished climbing. They figured it would be a month before they came out and by that time it would be May and the river wouldn't be frozen anymore. There would be no way they could get across the river at that time of the year. The plan was if they made the top and came out the other side, they'd go down the Muldrow Glacier and there was an old Park Service cabin at the edge of the McKinley River that they could use. By that time, they figured, the park road would be open and they could get a ride back to headquarters.

Although Ginny was not part of the expedition, she goes on to talk about the climb itself—the route the climbers took, their successes, the hardships they faced, and the climb's tragic ending. Woody has told and written about the details of this climb, as has Les Viereck,[12] so Ginny's secondhand telling will not be repeated in its entirety. It is most appropriate to hear about her involvement in the search and rescue operation. It is a part of the story that has not otherwise been told.

They found that getting up the headwall actually wasn't too hard. It was like a cornice that had got a lot of rain on it, so it was just ice. Then they were on the long ridge of the Southeast Buttress for about two weeks. Once they got on the ridge, they'd find places where they'd say, "Hm, I guess this is it. I don't know if we can go farther." Always whoever of them felt up to that particular challenge would say, "Well, I'll give it a try." By that time, you couldn't tell who'd had the most experience or who was the leader. They just took turns. At one place they had to cut a thousand steps to get up it. They called it the Lhotsa Face. Somebody would stay in camp and rest, and the other three would go cut steps. And then they'd trade.

They got to seventeen thousand feet and decided, "Well, why should we go to the top? We've now made it so we're looking down in the Muldrow. So why don't we just go home?" Well, it was a nice day. There wasn't a breath of wind. And they said, "Okay, let's go for it." So they did. They made it to the top and they just sat out there and ate their lunch and took their pictures. There wasn't anybody tired, there wasn't anybody who had any problems. They'd been on that mountain so long that they were well acclimated.

They came down Karsten's Ridge. They hadn't seen anything but snow and ice now for over a month, so they wanted to get off the ice. Elton was the one who had the most experience and had done several first ascents, and he was the last one in the line. He's the one who fell. The three others were on a fixed belay, while he was moving down. When Elton fell, he just swung down and went over a ledge. That pulled off Argus. Then the two of them pulled off Les. Woody was the last one. They tumbled down about a thousand feet. Les went into a crevasse, which stopped Elton and is what broke his back. He was dead. Les probably broke a few ribs, but his going into the crevasse stopped the rest of them. Argus was stopped, but was badly injured. Woody was the only one that was not injured.

Les and Woody went around picking up gear. They found one tent and some food bags. They had a primus stove. They found one gallon of gasoline and sleeping bags for three of them. Woody even found the little sack that had his exposed film in it. They all had their mittens tied behind them, like what dog mushers do, so none of them lost their mittens, which meant nobody got frostbite. They got the tent up, got Argus in there in a sleeping bag, and got the primus going. He wasn't able to walk or move. They were up there for six days.

All of this time, I was searching for them with our airplane because they were overdue. I wasn't just sitting and waiting. Celia came with me, and one time Elton's wife was with me. We flew over where they would have come out at the McKinley River at that cabin, but there were no tracks. I'd fly up to Karsten's Ridge looking for tracks along there to see if they'd come down that way. I could only get up to ten thousand, almost eleven thousand feet. The place where they fell was just a little higher up than that, but I didn't know that at the time. When I didn't see any tracks on Karsten's Ridge—and I was only about four feet over the ridge—then I'd fly all the way through those mountains over to the Ruth Glacier to check for them on that side. To find out if they had gone back the way they came. Then I did it again on the next two days.

Woody heard me on one of those flights. He tried to get out of the tent to get my attention, but couldn't in time. Another time, he saw me go over; I was practically right over them. But I wasn't looking that way. I was looking for somebody on Karsten's Ridge and they'd fallen a thousand feet down. It's especially hard to spot someone when you're trying to get the plane as close as you can to the ridge. Woody had a signaling mirror, but he couldn't quite get it on me, he said, until I was flying away from him. I had Elton's wife with me on that trip. If I hadn't had the extra weight of her being with me as a passenger, I might have gotten up another five hundred feet and seen where they fell. But I didn't. I just barely got over the ridge as it was.

After all this, Woody and Les decided nobody could come up to help so they'd better get Argus off the mountain themselves before an avalanche struck. By that time George could sit up and eat and he could run the primus stove. It turned out he had dislocated his hip, and had a very badly sprained ankle. They figured they could lower George down a route along the Harper Ice Flow using their ropes and wrapping him in the tent. Les and Woody soon realized that George was too heavy and just the two of them couldn't drag him down. Argus's life was at stake, so they decided to leave him and walk out to get help.

They went all the way down the Muldrow Glacier. It was into May and the crevasses were opening up, so they had to be really careful. If one of them fell in, the other one wouldn't be able to get him out. They got out to McGonagall Pass and hiked all the way out to the park road. They did all this in two and a half days from the time they left Argus. But the road was not open yet for the summer. So they left their packs at the Wonder Lake Ranger Station and hiked down to Kantishna, because Johnny Busia stayed there all winter and he had a radio that he used to keep in touch with the Park Service. When they got there, they found out the radio batteries were dead. Then they thought, "Oh, my gosh, we've got ninety miles to hike to headquarters for help. Or to wherever the road crew is working." By that time they were pretty discouraged.

Then they heard a voice yelling. It was Superintendent Grant Pearson and Assistant Superintendent Oscar Dick. They knew the group was overdue and were a little worried, so they went out in the car looking for them, shoveling their way out the road. When they got to the ranger station, they saw the two packs and thought, "Something's happened. Let's go down to Kantishna." Grant figured the only place they'd be would be at Johnny's. They took Les and Woody back to headquarters. Then of course we got a phone call.

We were just back from doing the last search trip when I heard the news. We had asked the military for a higher-altitude search. We said they must be above ten thousand feet, because we've covered that mountain from ten thousand feet down with no luck. But we can't get any higher with our little airplane. We knew a guy who was a geologist at the university who knew the mountain well and had a lot of ins with the military,[13] so we were finally able to get the military standing by for a search. It was that night when we heard word that Les and Woody had gotten back. So then we notified the military that this was now a matter of rescuing an injured man.

This was the same military outfit that I'd worked with before on the Peters Basin accident. They were going to set up their headquarters at the McKinley Park landing strip because of the radio contact. I said, "You can't even see the mountain from there. You can't see where the guy you need to rescue is. You've got to fly all the way to the mountain, and the weather's different and everything. Go to Lake Minchumina." That's where I'd been on that previous rescue. One of the guys who had been the helicopter pilot on that earlier rescue said, "She's right." So they did move over to Lake Minchumina.

The helicopters couldn't go above five thousand feet, so what the military decided to do was to land them at McGonagall Pass and all their men would then climb up to rescue Argus. After two days they hadn't moved very far, so they decided they wouldn't carry sleeping bags or food in order to move faster. They planned to fly in every night and drop the men new food and gear they needed. But, you know, the weather could be bad or something, anything, and they wouldn't get their stuff. Woody flew over with them and showed them where the tent was. They said, "Well, there's no sign of activity. There's no sign of life." Woody was so frustrated by how long it was taking the military that he got help from two friends of his who had climbed the mountain before.[14] He told them, "Don't stay with the military. Just keep going. I'm worried about George running out of gasoline. If he can't cook, he can't eat, and he can't melt water." They were on skis. The military guys were on snowshoes. The military kept saying, "He's dead." And Woody said, "He'll have tea ready for you when you get there." And that's what happened. The mountaineers, Freddy and John, got there and said to George, "Hey, you know what, there's a whole military down there coming to get you because you're AWOL." George did have tea ready for them. And they did get him off the mountain.

I also used our airplane to do airdrops for climbers. I did one for the group in 1962 that were the first ones to ski all the way in from park headquarters and went to the top of Mount McKinley.[15] The group was Anore Bucknell [Jones], Keith Jones, who's now her husband, Garry Kenwood, Howie Kantner, Paul Dix, and Jim Mack. Anore was the second woman that ever climbed the mountain.[16] My daughter was very young then, maybe five years old, so before I did the airdrop, I flew over to Lake Minchumina to leave her with friends. For some reason, there wasn't anybody home to leave her with, so I took her with me. She had a little rubber dolly with her when she got in the plane. I didn't even know she had it in her hand. When we dropped the gear, she dropped her dolly along with it. Those guys found it among their supplies, so they took it to the top of the mountain with them. They got a picture of it strapped to a pole up there. She loved seeing that.

And I flew for USGS expeditions that were doing geological studies and tri-angulation things on the mountain. I flew out a guy that froze his feet. He came down off the mountain with frozen feet and we picked him up to get him to a doctor. And we did a lot of flying for Brad Washburn.[17] Celia did a lot of that. Also, she's the one that flew for the USGS guy, Austin Post, who's written a book about the glaciers of Alaska.[18] He's the guy who knows more about glaciers than anybody else I know. He was also an old boyfriend of Celia's. Anyway, she did the airdrops for him on those little cirque glaciers that are in Polychrome Pass. That was something, because it's easier to drop onto the Ruth Glacier or the Muldrow Glacier than it is to drop on those little ones. And we did a lot of reconnaissance flying for people who wanted to fly over the mountain before they climbed it. I don't remember how many of those there were.

We sold our airplane in about 1964. By then, driving back and forth to the park became easier, and owning a plane was getting too expensive.

Ginny and Celia with the Cole family (Wally, Jerryne, Land, and Jenna), 1975.
Courtesy of Wally Cole.

16

Selling Camp Denali

Selling Camp Denali was a hard decision.

Camp Denali is a different place today than when Ginny, Celia, and Woody built the first tent cabins in 1952. By the mid-1970s, Ginny and Celia were getting older and realized that they could not keep running the place forever. Camp Denali was a lifestyle and had been the basis of their identity for many years. Selling it was not an easy decision to make. Certainly, they had to find the right buyer. They found that person in Wally Cole and his wife, Jerryne. Wally came from Maine in 1959 to work as a bellhop at the McKinley Park Hotel and would come out to visit Camp on his days off. According to Wally, he often hitchhiked out to Camp and would get in after midnight so would throw his sleeping bag out on a couch in the lodge, careful to be out of there before the guests arrived in the morning.[1] Wally later became the hotel manager and in 1967 hired Jerryne Berglund, a newly graduated nurse, as a tour guide. They were soon married and eventually joined the staff at Camp. According to Woody, "Wally shared our love of the park. He understood what we were trying to do."[2] As former Camp staffers, Wally and Jerry understood Ginny and Celia's philosophy and connection to the place.

The Coles retained Camp Denali as a remote wilderness lodge with an environmental ethic. They continued to lead hikes, teach their guests about the plants and animals of Denali National Park, and pass on an appreciation for the beauty that surrounds them. Under their tutelage, Camp Denali has become a bit more upscale. They converted the tent cabins into permanent structures, they serve gourmet meals, and they have a guest speaker series. But the staff is still mostly young people looking for a summer of adventure, and they have maintained the family atmosphere by passing the business on, in 2009, to their daughter and son-in-law, Jenna and Simon Hamm.

Camp Denali Generations. L-R: *Simon Hamm with baby, Danika, Jenna Cole Hamm, Wally and Jerryne Cole, Woody Wood, Ginny Wood. Camp Denali, August 2007. Photo by Karen Brewster.*

We ran Camp Denali for twenty-five years. It grew from just being tent cabins and rather primitive. But then everybody that came told everyone else, and it gradually grew by word of mouth. But we didn't change our philosophy, which was that Camp Denali was a place where you could come to relax.

Nineteen seventy-five was the last year we had Camp. Selling Camp Denali was a hard decision. Celia was on the Federal-State Land Use Planning Commission that was selecting lands after the Alaska Native Claims Settlement Act (ANCSA) leading up to the Alaska National Interest Lands Conservation Act (ANILCA).[3] She spent two summers being mostly gone, flying all over the state attending public hearings. She'd pop in for two weeks and be off for two weeks. I was left to run Camp mostly on my own. That got kind of old. So we were trying to decide what to do. She had so many opportunities, and we wondered, "Did we want to run camp any longer? But what do we do with it?" It was like having a bear by the tail. If we could see that whoever bought it, or if we bequeathed it, that we could ensure that it never could be anything more than what it already was, except to maintain it. That the place couldn't be changed. Then we wanted to do that. But we found out that we couldn't even give it to the Park Service, because they'd probably put a maintenance station there, a road crew at least, and get gravel out of our place. We certainly didn't want that.

Ginny sharing memories while hiking at Camp Denali, May 2007. Photo by Karen Brewster.

If Wally and Jerry hadn't come along and made the offer, I don't know what we would have done. They had worked for us, and we knew who they were and we knew their ethics. Wally was perfectly capable of doing it and would do a good job. We would never be ashamed that we sold to him. I think that Wally came around just at the right time. Camp needed a new, different, more professional approach. Wally and Jerry were able to improve on things that we should have started improving on earlier. Wally had grown up on a farm. Any kid that grows up on a farm can do a lot of handy things. No matter what goes wrong, he's not gonna moan; he just fixes it. And his mother would cook in restaurants in the East and brought him along as a little kid to be the helper, so he knew about cooking. Plus, he also had gotten a degree in hotel management. We knew that they had basically the same value system we did. Now that place is worth so much that no one could afford to buy it except for maybe Princess Tours. But Wally would never sell it to them. Someone would put a hotel there.

Celia and I kept twelve acres with two cabins so we'd always have a place where we could go in the park. We sold Camp to Wally for no money down and twenty years to pay, so that if he didn't make it, it wouldn't go to the bank and then Princess Hotels would have it or something. We took as a down payment two rocking chairs made from wood and rawhide lashing, like snowshoes, that Wally made. They're still in my living room.[4]

By the mid-1960s, Woody and Ginny were divorced, and he was no longer involved with Camp Denali. He moved to Seattle to earn a degree in foreign languages, and spent the rest of his career teaching at Lakeside School. However, like Ginny, he had been attached to Camp Denali and all it represented. His time in McKinley Park had a permanent impact on him:

> Eventually, I realized I loved teaching. The reason I knew this was because of a real joy that came in building Camp. And in going back over this remarkable ninety-mile stretch of road to headquarters picking up our guests from the train who'd flown up from the States and didn't really know what to expect. We'd have these people in this old jeep station wagon—later we had Travelall station wagons, which were a little more roomy—and we'd drive them out this five-hour trip over the tundra, up over the mountains, down across the rivers to Camp, all the time teaching them about this country that we were traveling through and which we loved. We loved that part very dearly. The whole country meant so much to us. Every river and all those wild animals we would see. Going up over Sable Pass. And Igloo. It was a unique experience. An experience that not many people can say they have had. I suppose it's a little the way people feel who have been to Africa and seen the migrations there.

We did have the experience of watching the caribou migrate. It used to happen every year shortly after July 1. It was a deeply emotional experience. I don't think I'll ever forget it. Everybody would be at Camp and somebody would come riding in in the middle of the night, and say, "Hey, the caribou are migrating!" People would get into any old type of vehicle they could and we would drive back to Stoney Hill and Highway Pass and you'd watch these animals gathering from the snowfields up above and they would just come down with their calves and they would start moving west along the route of the park road. Then they'd go from Stoney down onto the flats of Thoroughfare Pass and go by the Eielson Visitor Center.

I'll never forget lying under a bush in the brush there on the way to the Toklat River up towards Highway Pass, and just lying there with a camera and listening and watching these animals as they would come past me. You could hear their hooves clicking. And you'd hear them snorting. And the little ones would be running along with them. It was absolutely a deep emotional experience that few people have had. It doesn't happen anymore. The caribou are taking a different migration route now.[5]

Despite selling Camp Denali, Ginny never lost her connection to the place. When I went there with her in 2007 and 2008, her deep love of the place oozed from every pore. She was energized by the surrounding tundra, by the stunning view of Mount McKinley, by her memories of good times and hard work there. She was so in tune with the routine and the pace it was as if she had never left. Although in pain, she had to walk her beloved Cranberry Ridge one more time and pay homage to Celia, whose ashes had been spread at a memorial cairn there. And she enjoyed talking with the guests. She reveled in the attention they paid her, in how they hung on her every word.

View of Mount McKinley across Wonder Lake, circa 1960. Photo by Ginny Wood.

17

Preserving Alaska

Wilderness is someplace that hasn't been cluttered up with people.
Where you are meeting nature on its own terms.

inny Wood and Celia Hunter are familiar names to environmental activ-
ists in Alaska. Many consider them the matriarchs of Alaska conservation. They are credited with starting Alaska's conservation movement in
the 1960s, since they were some of the cofounders of the Alaska Conservation
Society, the state's first conservation organization. They later helped establish the
Alaska Conservation Foundation, a central clearinghouse for funding grassroots
protection and preservation efforts around the state.

Ginny and Celia have each received many accolades and prizes for their
devotion to the environmental movement and for the vast areas of Alaska they
helped preserve. In 1985, Ginny won the Alaska Conservation Foundation's
Celia Hunter Award recognizing an outstanding volunteer in the environmental movement.[1] In 1991, she and Celia Hunter received the Sierra Club's John
Muir Award, which honors a distinguished record of achievement in conservation.[2] In 1993, Ginny was the first recipient of the Alaska Wilderness Recreation
and Tourism Association's Ginny Hill Wood Award for contributions to Alaska
conservation and sustainable tourism.[3] In 2001, Ginny and Celia were honored
with Alaska Conservationist Lifetime Achievement Awards from the Alaska
Conservation Foundation.[4] In 2009, Ginny received the Florence Collins Award
from the Northern Alaska Environmental Center in Fairbanks for her years of
effort to protect Alaska's wild places. And to help mark the fiftieth anniversary
of the Arctic National Wildlife Range (Refuge), the US Fish and Wildlife Service
honored Ginny on August 12, 2010, with their Citizens Award for Exceptional
Service. This award recognizes private citizens and organizations for their contributions to the mission and goals of the service, and was given to Ginny in thanks
for her dedication and lifelong contribution to wilderness and wildlife conservation in northern Alaska.

Despite this legacy, Ginny views her contributions humbly. She is quick to say that there were many other people involved and that she does not deserve to be singled out for recognition. People such as Bob Weeden, Les Viereck, Olaus and Mardy Murie, Adolph Murie, Jane Williams, Richard Cooley, Fred Dean, Will Troyer, and Ed Wayburn were all also committed to protecting Alaska in the early years.[5] They too deserve praise and thanks for their hard work, but Ginny and Celia have become iconic folk heroes of the movement.

Celia was an outspoken leader and advocate. She did not shy away from the limelight. She diligently wrote letters to legislators. She calmly testified at public hearings. From 1972 to 1980, she served on the Federal-State Land Use Planning Commission[6] and traveled around Alaska for the D-2 land hearings held to collect testimony about land selections for the Alaska National Interest Lands Conservation Act (ANILCA), which ended up setting aside one hundred million acres as national parks, preserves, monuments, and wildlife refuges.[7] In 1977, Celia served as executive director of the Wilderness Society in Washington, DC, for a few years, making her the first woman to head a national environmental organization. In 1980, Denny Wilcher founded the Alaska Conservation Foundation to help bring financial resources to Alaska's conservationists, and Celia served on their board of trustees for the next eighteen years. She also was a board member for the Alaska Natural History Association, the Nature Conservancy, Trustees for Alaska, and the Wilderness Society. Finally, starting in 1979, Celia made her environmental and liberal voice heard through a column she wrote in the *Fairbanks Daily News-Miner* newspaper for the next twenty years.[8]

In comparison, Ginny played a less visible but equally vital role. She worked behind the scenes. She wrote to legislators and testified at hearings. She wrote articles for national magazines and organization newsletters, and submitted letters to the editor. From 1960 to 1967, she was the editor, off and on, of the Alaska Conservation Society's newsletter, *News Bulletin of the Alaska Conservation Society*, and from 1967 to 1979 of their magazine, Alaska *Conservation Review*. From 1982 to 2005, she wrote a regular column titled "From the Woodpile" for the Northern Alaska Environmental Center's newsletter, *The Northern Line*. She tried to find common ground and build bridges with diverse organizations to create momentum for a cause. The question is what motivated Ginny to get involved in issues and speak out from a conservation perspective, especially at a time when the majority of people in Fairbanks opposed this view.

I don't think it was one particular incident. I always just grew up in a small town where right next door was wilderness. Or sagebrush. And I didn't think about it as an issue or a movement. Where I grew up in rural Washington, you didn't set aside things to be in national parks, or have environmental protection, that's just where you lived. That's where you ran around as a kid. You never thought about having to have something special designated just for recreation or for its biological reasons.

Coming to Alaska is where I became aware of the importance of wilderness and the need to protect the environment. Before, I just went on adventures. In Alaska, I was motivated to protect the environment because it became important to protect where you lived and how you lived. I thought about the difference development would make up here. How it was a threat. It was new country, and you realized how it was being changed. One of the first environmental hearings I went to was about building a road to Nome. In Fairbanks, the concern was that everyone from Nome would move here.[9] Oh no, we didn't want development, because it was a delight to find this place as it was. We didn't want it changed.

But I think it was Camp Denali and living in McKinley Park that got me interested, too. You got curious about the critters and their habitat and what's happening and why do they do this here and that there. I think it was a matter of knowing the area up close and personal through my own observations and experiences. Just living out there in that country. Our curiosity had shown us so much about that place. And then you'd take a course at the university—that's what people did in the wintertime—and you learned more. Camp Denali started attracting some very interesting people who were tops in biology, and I started learning from them. I guess I can't say this was my enlightenment, it was something that just sort of grew on you. It was curiosity about what was over the next hill and wanting to know why things we were seeing were happening. Why these little plants that are only about that high are willow trees. Watching what was happening around us. And we had a lot of good friends like Bob Weeden and Fred Dean, who were in it professionally, who influenced us.[10]

I also had done some reading related to wilderness and conservation. Like Aldo Leopold's book, *A Sand County Almanac*. They had a very limited library at Denali Park when Woody and I were living at headquarters, when he was working for them in 1951. They had an old copy of it. So I swiped it and read it for the winter. I was very impressed with Leopold. He was a marvelous writer. He just had a way with words. I could have read the same thing by someone else and it could have been deadly dull. But his writings were so good that I keep reading it over and over again. I think everybody should read it once a year, just to refresh yourself. You find new meanings and new expressions each time you look at it. Just in one paragraph he can say something so succinctly. His wilderness was a little farm up in Wisconsin, except when he was first working for the Forest Service out west, but it was equally important. Everybody remembers that story about when he stopped being a wolf hunter. Seeing the last green light in the eyes of that dying wolf. That's why he became an ecologist. He came to understand that shooting wolves meant there was going to be an overproduction of deer.

My concepts of ecology and the balance of nature started then. I was inspired by Leopold being able to use words so beautifully to describe something. He had such a down-to-earth concept of ecosystems and how they work. So that was my beginning of some formal biology. Then I took a course in ecology at the university. Odom was the textbook.[11] The guy who taught the course was not a very good lecturer, but he did expose me to the "learn-ed" part of biology and ecology. Odom's textbook was excellent on that. I still have it. It was just the fundamentals of looking at how everything is connected to everything else in ecology. That took everything I had read before that had just been philosophical and put it in a background of science.

I had read a lot of Indian lore as a youth. I had read and loved Thoreau. I read Robert Marshall's writing in the winter of 1947 when I was weathered in at Galena with my airplane when trying to get it to Kotzebue, because temperatures were fifty, sixty below zero. They put us up in a house of somebody that worked for the Civil Aeronautics Administration [now the Federal Aviation Administration] who was out for vacation. They asked if we wouldn't mind staying in their house and keep the water running and flush the toilets so the pipes wouldn't freeze. It had a wonderful library. And that's where I first read Marshall's writings. He was a good writer. His first book was the one on Wiseman titled *Arctic Village*.[12] But then, there was another one that he wrote later that told of his travels in the Arctic.[13] That really sparked my interest in wild Alaska. And from just flying over it. The vastness of it. I think Marshall's zest for the wilderness and adventure had quite an influence on me at the time. His desire to see what was over the next ridge, which was just like me. As I've said, my early thing as a kid was an enthusiasm for adventure and seeing what was over the hill. I always had that feeling, and still do. When I would get time off from Camp Denali, I just explored the area and the park. I have been to the head of every river down there. Sometimes I was by myself or with one of the staff. I just wanted to see what was out there. I was curious.

In the 1960s and 1970s, the populace of the United States was becoming increasingly aware of social issues, such as civil rights, women's rights, antiwar efforts, pollution prevention, and environmental protection. As large-scale and highly visible national civil rights and antiwar protests developed, environmentalists took notes from their playbooks. They utilized grassroots organizing techniques to bring their issues to the attention of the public and to the political forefront. This effort culminated in the celebration of Earth Day on April 22, 1970.[14] This massive nationwide demonstration helped push the environmental cause onto the national political agenda. Legislative success soon followed. The 1964 Wilderness Act was major federal legislation aimed at saving vast areas of America in their wild natural condition. In 1969, Congress passed the National Environmental Protection Act (NEPA), which required environmental impact statements for large-scale development projects. In 1973, the Endangered Species Act was established to protect threatened species from disappearing forever. The Clean Water Act of 1972 and the Clean Air Acts (1963, 1967, 1970) were meant to control air and water pollution.[15] This national concern for the environment was also manifested on a smaller, more localized scale. People were doing things to bring awareness to environmental concerns in their own towns, neighborhoods, and backyards. It was under these conditions that the Alaska Conservation Society (ACS), Alaska's first environmental organization, was founded.[16] While Ginny has previously written about ACS's beginnings, goals, and accomplishments,[17] her oral narrative provides a more detailed and personal look at how all this happened.

It started when we testified at a congressional hearing that our first senator, Bob Bartlett, held in 1959, just after Alaska got statehood, about establishing the Arctic National Wildlife Range.[18] I'd never thought before about having to have something special designated just for recreation or for its biological reasons.

Fred Dean, who lived next door to us and who was the head of the university's Department of Wildlife Management, and John Buckley, in the Biology Department and head of the Alaska Cooperative Wildlife Research Unit, told us about this issue that Olaus and Mardy Murie were involved with.[19] I had met Olaus and Mardy just socially, but from being at Camp Denali I knew Olaus's brother, Ade [Adolph], who was a ranger and biologist at McKinley Park. They told us that there was this group of people back east with the Wilderness Society—who I'd never heard of—who were looking for a place in Alaska that hadn't had any development, where they hadn't found any minerals, where there weren't any villages, that could be contained in something bigger than a national park. That you would have the marine, the tundra, the alpine, and then over on the other side would be the boreal forest. It was to encompass more of a whole biome, instead of just a single national park or national forest, which really aren't big enough to have the scope that you need for all the animals and birds and everything. It was referred to as the biome theory of preservation.

Olaus Murie and a guy named George Collins,[20] who worked for the Park Service nationally, and then several other people, like Howard Zahniser, who was with the Wilderness Society,[21] wanted this all connected together in one protected place. They were looking up at the northeast corner of Alaska, where there were no roads, no development, no villages—there was just one small Native village on the coast, Barter Island [now known by its Iñupiaq name of Kaktovik], no mining claims where anybody had ever found any minerals, no timber big enough to cut, and no resources that anybody was interested in. It was a place that would be big enough to be designated as this new type of wilderness.

Fred Dean and John Buckley were asked if they could find some people who might come to testify at Bartlett's hearing. There were about eight of us who testified. There was Woody, myself, Celia Hunter, Bob Weeden, John Thomson,

Ginny in her living room, circa 1980. Courtesy Ginny Wood.

who lived next door then, Les Viereck, Fred Dean, and a few others. Woody, Celia, and I liked the Muries very much, and thought what they were proposing was a good idea, so we testified for it. Senator Bob Bartlett was a miner, but he was a very polite guy when we testified before him. It was very easy to say what you thought and why you felt the way you did about preserving wilderness. Woody had grown up as a kid roaming around in the backwoods of Maine and paddling his canoe, and he didn't know why you set aside anything special, you just went out and did it, but he testified about why it was important to have country to roam in. And Celia had grown up on a farm, and you know, what's so special about that. But we had been here long enough, and both Celia and I had been pilots so we were doing a lot of commercial flying over all that wild country (known as "the Bush"), and protecting that seemed like a good idea.

The only other people at the hearing were a few miners and some businessmen who were against it.[22]

After we gave our testimony before Senator Bartlett, we all kind of gathered out in the hall at the courthouse.[23] We heard over and over from the miners and businessmen who came to talk that they didn't want outside environmental organizations telling us how to run Alaska. The Sierra Club, the Wilderness Society, and the Wildlife Federation were the ones that they mostly knew about. They didn't want those outside people telling us how to run Alaska, which had just become a state. Statehood was a big issue, which side you were on. It was not about whether you were a Republican or Democrat, but there was a concern about a state bringing up lots of laws and regulations. But before statehood, all of Alaska was run by the federal government, and the question was starting to develop about the quality of representation in DC and it being so far away.

I don't know whose idea it was, but someone said, you know what, why don't we organize an environmental club up here where you can be a member and pay your three dollar dues, but you can't be a voting member unless you live in Alaska and have voted here and are eligible to vote here and do vote here.[24] It was a way to say, "This represents our feelings, and it's our land." It was so we could get away from this criticism of, "Oh, you're just from these national organizations." We wanted to show that we were from Alaska. That we knew about the place. We wanted to do things our own way, the Alaskan way. The only conservation movement then was more or less like what the Outdoor Council is. There was a guy named Bud Boddy down in Juneau who was well known.[25] He was beginning to get a little worried about timber cutting where it would bother the fishing, or maybe overshooting game. But wilderness was not a concept.

Then we found that people joined us who had been Sierra Club members before they moved up here, or just who kind of thought this was a good idea, that they shouldn't dig up all of Alaska. Woody and I had been members of the Sierra Club when we lived in California, mainly because we liked to go skiing up at the lodge they had in the Sierra Nevada Mountains. It was more of an outing club when we first joined it. We got their literature, but we decided that we couldn't depend on the Sierra Club and the Wilderness Society, it had to come from inside.

We didn't have any office, we didn't have telephones, and we didn't have any paid staff. We met at the university, in people's kitchens, living rooms, and when the big issues came up we'd really get together. We had our first meeting in my living room.[26] For a while our little cabin was the headquarters. We decided to call it the Alaska Conservation Society, and we elected a president, secretary, and I was the editor of the newsletter. We printed out a little newsletter on the Camp Denali hand-crank Gestetner mimeograph machine that was in our basement. We called it "the subversive press." We used to print everything for environmental issues on it, and there was always some controversial issue brewing at the university and kids would come over and ask if they could print something on our mimeograph machine. They used it for every issue—printing propaganda. And for peace. For any issue we thought we agreed with. When it was time to put the newsletter together, we'd have a potluck. We'd put our babies in packs to keep them up out of the way while we collated by marching around the table and picking up sheets of paper from piles. Then when the kids got older they could lick stamps.

It happened that most of the membership and most of the board members of the Conservation Society were biologists or botanists. Celia and I were some of the few people involved that didn't have a formal degree. We had been exposed to the ideas of ecology, though. When we'd go to hearings, we'd always run our testimony through one of these guys to be sure we had the facts right, so the reaction would be, "Where did these people come from? How do they know that?" When everybody else was going on and on just about absolute greed and were absolutely illiterate as far as ecology was concerned.

Celia became the secretary of the Alaska Conservation Society, because she was good at that kind of thing. She even got paid a little bit for this for a while. We all kept shifting around jobs. We all took turns. We divided it up so I can't remember who was in what position when. We passed the officer jobs around so nobody got an ego from wanting to be in charge all the time. Like when it became so that Bob Weeden couldn't, or Les Viereck couldn't, because of their jobs, Celia and I would step in. Celia and I were able to do things at times because we didn't have jobs. All we had was Camp Denali and it wasn't worth anything in those days, so they couldn't take our job away if we said something controversial. They couldn't fire us if we spoke out, like some of the others who worked at the university or for the Alaska Department of Fish and Game or United States Fish and Wildlife Service. Terry Moore had been president of the university and that was fine. But when they got William Wood [as president of the university], you had to keep your mouth shut if you wanted to keep your job. I was the editor of the Alaska Conservation Society bulletins in the early years. Nobody else wanted the job. But later we would alternate. Les Viereck and Bob Weeden would change out with me. Bob is a beautiful writer. I was never the writer that Bob was. He was a giant both philosophically and in what he wrote and as a person. He was probably an Aldo Leopold in his own right.

With this group, it was not always a normal way of doing business. I remember one time when Bob Weeden was president and there was something important that we needed to make a decision about and Bob was out in the field someplace where you had to ski in. I think Dave Klein was vice president and he also was out in the field.[27] This left me and Fred Dean having to make the decision, which we weren't really comfortable doing. So Les Viereck skied in and got Bob's approval.

Then we had some very good guys from other parts of the state. We had Dixie Baade from Ketchikan, who had always been an advocate for forestry ever since World War II, when she went to live there.[28] And then you had Dick Cooley, who was our representative from Juneau. He ended up being a top professor down at the University of California, Santa Cruz.[29]

We really didn't have too much opposition. We even had members from the hunting and fishing group, the Tanana Valley Sportsmen's Association [TVSA], including Dick Bishop.[30] In fact, at one point he was an officer for us. TVSA was different from us. They were more interested in critters. But they didn't buck us.

Ginny's thoughts about the emerging conservation movement of the 1960s can be seen in an article titled "A Conservation Explosion," which she wrote for the *Alaska Conservation Review* in 1968:

There was a time not so very long ago when conservationists were characterized as "bird watchers", "bleeding hearts", or "little old ladies in tennis shoes." They were targets to poke fun at like prohibitionists or suffragettes; or they were condemned as obstructionists to progress. A few looked kindly on them as nature lovers—something akin to poets or mystics.

Conservation has suddenly become more than a small group trying to keep society embalmed in the 19th century or binocular bedecked "life listers." It has become the business man, the legislator, and the housewife; to those like Charles A. Lindbergh whose life has been devoted to the promotion of aviation. The word ecology is no longer confined to the vocabulary of biologists.

The concept of conservation has changed, too. From one of protecting or preserving one aspect of nature, such as wildlife, wilderness, or natural resources, it has come to mean maintaining the quality of our total environment—water, air, soil, and surroundings, as well as all forms of life.

Some of those concerned would never consider themselves conservationists. Others band together in organizations, feeling there is strength and direction in numbers. The north country, the last outpost of civilization to feel the impact of 20th century technology and commerce, is fortunately experiencing a population explosion of conservationists along with sheer numbers of people.

The Alaska Conservation Society has spread from a nucleus of eleven persons in 1960 to 750 dues-paying members. New chapters have erupted on the Kenai Peninsula, Upper Cook Inlet, and just this month, in Sitka. Down in Whitehorse Canadians have formed the Yukon Conservation Society. An Alaskan chapter of the Sierra Club is undergoing labor pains. Sportsmen's organizations, garden clubs, and mountaineering groups have conservation committees.

However, just belonging to a conservation organization and paying one's dues won't do the job. It's not the body count of card carrying conservationists that matters; it's the number of concerned, involved individuals speaking out and doing something about threats to survival of life and the environment that sustains and enhances it that matters.[31]

Issues: Wolf Bounty

The Alaska Conservation Society grew to become one of the primary groups testifying and working on behalf of the big Alaska conservation issues of the time. And Ginny was there in the thick of it for each one.

The first issue we took on was the wolf bounty.[32] We didn't win it by saving the wolves and stopping the bad people from shooting them. It was more the fact that they were paying fifty dollars a head for the wolves and wondering where the money went and how fair was it. We didn't know who was a Republican and who was a Democrat then, you just elected people you thought were competent. And I think there was one of each that looked it up and said, "She's right. What does this fifty dollars go to?" They found out that the bulk of the bounty payments went to people who were wealthy enough to have their own airplane who would take a couple of weeks off and go up to the Brooks Range or out to the villages and shoot wolves, rather than the Native people who lived out there and who the state claimed the program had been established to help. The Natives knew where the dens were, but they never destroyed a female. They sort of let them grow. They got their fifty bucks but didn't shoot the female.

For me, I couldn't see how come you'd want to shoot wolves—well, this is my own personal thing—because isn't it peculiar that when man became *Homo sapiens* the wolf was the first animal he invited to come in and share his hearth with. That's the ancestor of all your dogs. And why is it that he's a varmint? Of course, up here everybody had a sled dog. Most of them were practically half wolves because they had the stamina and their feet would hold up on the long and rough trail conditions. So I thought, this killing of wolves just doesn't make sense.

I do think there are times when wolves have to be managed. For instance, one time there was a whole pack that was causing trouble here in town. We'd had a very rough winter and the population of caribou and everything else was down. When you have rain in the middle of winter and then it freezes on top of the snow, any critter has a hard time living. They can't get through the ice to their food. So these wolves had come down into what is now the Goldstream Valley. There were only a few people living along it then and there was no road over from Ballaine Road connecting to it. Mary Shields, who is a dog musher, lived over there.[33] And the wolf pack got her puppies. They were coming into dog yards, they were so hungry. They were starving. So people decided to do away with that pack. They never had any trouble since. Now that was a particularly unusual circumstance. The Conservation Society approved of it because people were losing their dogs, and then they started to worry about their kids. Well, we've never had a wolf that ran away with a kid, except in Little Red Riding Hood. But that made me begin to look at why people are so much against wolves. I could see the sense of eliminating that pack in town, because that was a threat. You know, if it had been my dog, I would have wanted the wolves killed, too. I think there are times when measures have to be taken. But the other thing is, we're too impatient to wait for nature to take care of itself. But then again you're not going to wait until nature evens the odds when it comes to your dog.[34]

Issues: Polar Bear Hunting

The next issue was the land and shoot from the air of polar bears by big game hunters.[35] They shoot polar bears from the air, for what? You don't eat them. And you don't eat wolves. Why would you pick on those two? So we stopped the aerial sport hunting of polar bears. That was our second victory. It was easy to persuade the state on this one, too.[36] You couldn't get a lot of money for the bear hides. And it wasn't helping the locals. I didn't like the idea of shooting polar bear. Just the idea was unfair.

Issues: Project Chariot

Project Chariot was the key issue on which the fledgling Alaska Conservation Society cut its teeth. After successfully stopping plans for a nuclear blast in northwestern Alaska, ACS went on to become a powerhouse in Alaska's conservation movement for the next twenty years. Given this importance, the Project Chariot story has been repeated time and time again, and from the varied perspectives of the many players involved. After more than fifty years, it is not surprising that Ginny's 2006 telling might differ from earlier versions, both of her own and of others. I have footnoted instances where her story differs from that presented in the definitive written history of Project Chariot, *Firecracker Boys* by Dan O'Neill.[37]

The next issue was Project Chariot, which was this proposition from the Atomic Energy Commission [AEC] where they were coming up to create a harbor in the Arctic. Well, let's look at it from the standpoint of who thought it up. I think they did this in libraries on maps without even knowing the country. To pick a spot that nobody would ever object to. The story gets into a lot of politics as you get into it and look at who were the heroes and who the enemies were. It was

Edward Teller who was behind it all. He was the father of the H-bomb. So that's what they really wanted it for. The people down in Nevada were complaining about this radioactive fallout, and there were some people that were having reper-cussions from it. They didn't like them blowing it off near them, and then there was this radiation thing they were beginning to hear about. And so they thought they better find another place where they can do the testing. And Teller wanted to put out a bigger bomb. So he would sell the plan as blasting a harbor right where they thought there were all these minerals. The AEC believed there were large deposits of high-grade coal adjacent to Cape Thompson, which they also thought meant there were probably a lot of other minerals there, too. They thought if we build this harbor, then we would have commerce between the Orient with all those rich minerals that are in the surroundings. Well, that was kind of fun, because they came up here and found otherwise. They didn't do their research very well. All they found was low-grade coal.

Teller came up to Alaska, and he stopped at Juneau and talked to the leg-islature down there, and talked money. That this would bring a lot of it to the state. That it would put Alaska on the map and all that stuff. So they thought it was all right. Then Teller came up here to Fairbanks and went to the chamber of commerce and the university and they thought it sounded like a good idea.

Scientists at the University of Alaska Fairbanks said, "Well, aren't you going to do any baseline studies first before you do this? How are you going to know if it's changed if you don't?"[38] The AEC agreed, "Well, yes, all right, we can do that." Of course, the university would get the contract. Teller may have thought it would be good to butter them up by giving them a contract. He thought here was this dinky little podunk university that wasn't much more than an overgrown high school packed full of GIs, and they would lap it up. Then here comes Dr. William Wood as president of the university.[39] He bought it, wanting this to be the Harvard of the North, and they'd get contracts and get all this money for the university.

But then there were several scientists on the faculty, like Les Viereck and Bill Pruitt and two or three others, who said, "We're not so sure about this. I don't like the idea of it being atomic, of using atomic bombs for peaceful uses." They said, "This smells." Les just didn't like the idea of the atomic thing, so was uncomfort-able working on it. But others went out there just because it was a good job. So there were these two factions at the university.

Teller's group was looking for somebody that would go up and live with the Eskimos at Point Hope and study them. They found Don Foote.[40] He was excited to go up and live with the Eskimos and find out about this. It was an adventure. He hadn't had any feelings one way or the other on what the project was about, but he began to be quite intrigued with the Eskimos and how they could live in this harsh climate and exist and had for years and were getting along fine. He just liked them, and he enjoyed their humor and he enjoyed their intelligence. The longer he was up there, he realized that the AEC wanted him to persuade the Eskimos that this project would be good for them.[41] He realized that this area they had just selected for this nuclear project was between villages. That this was an area the people used. The idea had been that the Eskimos would think it was good. That they'd make some money. They could have a job or something. But Don got to really like the Eskimos and said, "This isn't going to do them any good."

Don wasn't a biologist, he was a geographer, but living at Point Hope he began to see that Cape Thompson, where they wanted to do this blast, wasn't only important as hunting grounds for the Eskimos but was biologically important, too. They picked this place on a map without even really ever having been there. They thought it was so remote that nobody would ever object to that. Actually, the Cape Thompson area turned out to be biologically very rich.[42] It's one of the few seabird-breeding places. It's where the Eskimos collect eggs. Also, because of the currents there, that's where the marine life was very rich. That's why they had a village near there. And it was where the caribou came in the winter, because the wind blew and they could get down to the feed beneath the snow. All these things like that. Then biological studies being done out there were showing this.[43]

Don Foote was a good friend of Les Viereck's. They had gone to Dartmouth College together. They began to get suspicious about what this was all about. This was promoted as a peaceful use of atomic energy and it was going to blast this harbor and then that would open up the commerce between the Orient, while they developed all these rich minerals that were around it. Well, what minerals?

Bill Pruitt smelled a rat right away. His studies showed high levels of cesium and strontium in the caribou and the lichen they were eating. He said, "Well, this is what the people eat out there and so if you have that atomic blast that's going to really cause a problem."[44] That was his point of view.

Brina Kessel, who's my neighbor up here, she was the head of the Biology Department and later became dean. Brina was in her twenties, right out of getting her PhD, and she had just been moved up from being a professor because all of a sudden the woman who was head of the department died in an apartment fire downtown. Here was Brina, the only other one in the biology department, so they made her head of it.[45] Brina was involved in getting Les and Bill fired because they were against the project, which they had been paid to work on.[46] Plus, I don't think Brina liked Bill Pruitt.[47] As I said, there were a lot of politics that went with all this.

Dr. Wood was one of the promoters of Project Chariot, and he was firing people at the university who weren't in agreement with him. Fred Dean said, "Let him do it, he can't shut us up if he's going to do all of that!" But Les lost his job at the university.[48] Not only did Bill Pruitt lose his job, but when he was hired at Montana State, before he ever got there, somebody had heard that he had been fired from here because he'd been on the wrong side of the Project

Chariot thing. They canceled his contract.[49] When Bill was leaving town for another job, he and his wife came out to Camp Denali to say goodbye. They were very good friends of ours. He said, "I'm not telling anybody I've got a job now, and I'm not going to tell anybody where it is until I've signed the contract. I already lost one."[50] Later on, there was a guy who came to Camp Denali who'd been on the faculty in Montana when this happened to Bill, and he said he just happened to be in the president's office talking to him when a phone call came through from Fairbanks, and he overheard them say, "Don't hire Pruitt, you can't trust him." So it was interesting to hear that side of the story.

When Don Foote and Les Viereck came to be a little bit suspicious about what this was all about, then we got interested. Celia and I got involved because you got involved in anything the town got involved in. It was a very small town, so of course immediately, if you knew certain people, you knew about things. We'd gotten to know Don when he'd come over to visit Les, and he started writing to Bob Weeden and Les about what was happening up there in Point Hope. Don became very disturbed because of what he was hearing from the AEC back out in the States. How negative they were about the area and the Eskimos, thinking they would embrace it without question. Well, they didn't. That's their meat market. Don was sending stuff over to Fred Dean and us and saying, "I've decided, I'm on the Eskimos' side. It would be a shame to ruin this place. The government is saying this is just a wasteland and they picked it 'cause it wouldn't matter. And then they'd have this harbor for the rich minerals." Don said, "There's no minerals up here. The fact is, this is the Eskimos' home. This project is not going to be an asset for them, it's going to be just the opposite."

So then the AEC started sending guys up to Point Hope on a public relations campaign to tell the people how good this was going to be for them. That they'd all be rich and this would be a big success for them. They wouldn't have to live in these little small houses anymore and could have big houses with running water. Don got tape recorders, not the little ones we have now, but bigger ones. He paid for them out of his own pocket.[51] He told the Eskimos, "Whenever you talk to those government people that come up, you tell them to talk into that machine."[52] Then what they were doing was sending those recorders on up to other villages, just ahead of the AEC, so they'd arrive and these Eskimos that looked so primitive, they said, "You talk in there," pointing to the microphone of the tape recorder. Then one time the AEC went one place and someone said, "You dropped that thing down on those Natives down in the South Seas and some of them died." They were talking about the nuclear testing that the U.S. was doing in the Pacific Islands.[53] The AEC thought, "Where is this coming from? How come they know about this?"

Then there was one time when Don had gone down to Kotzebue to get some groceries and stuff and had to stay overnight. There wasn't anyplace to stay except one room that was over Beulah's Restaurant. There were two beds but one guy was already there, so he asked, "Do you mind doubling up?" "No," the guy said. "That would be fine." The guy introduced himself, and Don suspected he was an FBI or CIA agent. Don thought, "Well, this is interesting." He was carrying in his briefcase all this stuff to give to us that we were then writing up and sending to the Sierra Club. Actually, it turns out that this was an FBI guy who had been sent out to find out where the leaks were coming from.[54] Don thought, "Well, that's the safest place for all this stuff, right here with me."

That was kind of fun to be in on that. I think that had something to do with the way the whole thing worked out in the end. The AEC never said, "I think this is a mistake and we shouldn't do this." They just folded their tents and silently moved away without ever telling anybody. Without ever making a statement that "we've decided we don't think this is advisable." It's interesting that there is no record of them ever changing their minds. Out of all the dirt that we dug up, I didn't know until Dan O'Neill was looking through the records on Project Chariot for his book[55] that the AEC had left some of that buried radiation when they left. They had wanted to find out how far it would creep into the environment. This was something that came out later when Dan discovered it.[56]

ACS was involved in getting information out about what was happening up at Cape Thompson with the scientific research,[57] what the scientists were finding and thinking.[58] It sounds like we were a big organization. We weren't. But we were the only organization.[59]

You have to realize that at that time all of Alaska was a small town on a party line. You kept in touch with everything and everybody. People still keep in touch with things that are going on in Juneau, things that are going on in Anchorage, especially if it's a little bit of a scandal. But it's not like it used to be. It was pretty hard to keep a secret. Or not have it be gossip. If it was an event, somebody you knew probably was right there when it happened, so it would be hard not to know about it.

Issues: Rampart Dam

The next big environmental threat around which Alaska's conservationists rallied was the proposal, in the early 1960s, to dam the Yukon River at Rampart Canyon to generate lower-cost electricity for Alaskans.[60] The Army Corps of Engineers proposed to build a dam with twice the capacity of the nation's biggest dam, the Grand Coulee on the Columbia River, that would flood the two-hundred-mile-long and forty-to-ninety-mile-wide Yukon Flats; it would have created a reservoir with a surface area greater than Lake Erie.[61] Alaska's Senator Ernest Gruening was a strong supporter of the dam and worked hard to obtain funding. Alaskans in favor of the dam organized themselves as "Operation Rampart" to promote the project, later renamed Yukon Power for America (YPA). Opponents, like the members of the Alaska Conservation Society, did everything they could to prove the negative effects the flooding would have on the Native people and the fish and wildlife along the Yukon River, and on the state's economy.

The next issue was Rampart Dam, which would have flooded all those Native villages along the Yukon River. The Yukon River provided people food and transportation, and the dam was going to ruin that. ACS took a lead role in opposing that.[62] That was probably more my pet project. You have to credit Bob Weeden and Fred Dean and about a half-dozen other people on the Project Chariot, but I seemed to pick Rampart Dam as more my own. I don't know why. Maybe because it had to do with rivers? But I think it might have been at a time when the university was getting very worried and saying, "You better be careful or you'll lose your job if you say anything against these types of projects or to defend the critters." So the others were being extra careful about what issues they took on. While it was a thing that I could take on and nobody was going to bother me or threaten to take my job. For me, the big thing was that it was a big lie. Yes, we were concerned about the flooding and the effect on the wildlife loss, and the Native people, and the villages that would be flooded out.[63] But mainly it was I just don't like myths and lies and something that's just a fraud. I don't like something that's being promoted that you know is not true. The myth was being sold that if we had that dam, then we could send all this electricity it would produce down to the States and we'd be rich. We didn't have enough people up here then to be able to use all the electricity.

And the other thing is, I'd been flying to that country enough to kind of like the people that lived along the river. That dam project would flood them, and for what? The lie that they would sell all this energy? The question was, How much would it cost to produce that electricity? And you'd be destroying the homes of people who had lived there for thousands of years and probably do away with their fish. That was their income. Eventually, they would have to move.

The whole state legislature, the city council, the chamber of commerce, everybody was in support of Rampart Dam. We were a small minority. But I wrote a lot of letters and articles to try to stop the dam.[64] ACS leaders who were connected to the Tanana Valley Sportsmen's Association reached out to their members and broadened the group. That helped. Then the Alaska Conservation Society got in touch with this economist from the University of Michigan to do an economic study of the project.[65] He was very well known and had a lot of credibility. He did it beautifully when we had him do the real economics and mathematics on how much a kilowatt-hour of electricity would cost by the time they built this thing and they got electricity down to the States. He showed that it would be the most expensive electricity that anyone had.

We turned to economics instead of ecology and could prove that the project was not economically feasible. Like one time, Celia was testifying about the dam. She talked about the poor economics of it. Her opponent got upset, shook his fist, and said, "You're supposed to talk about ducks and geese and moose, and you're not talking about those things. You're talking about economics! And that's not your field!"[66] She was proving that it was not economical to dam the Yukon River and by the time that power got down to the States, it wouldn't be very cheap! We really broadcast all of this. The economist said the same thing we were saying, but he did it as a scientific economist and not as an environmentalist, and that's what stopped that.[67]

Do you know who was on our side at that time? Who I worked with? Don Young.[68] He lived in Fort Yukon. He was a schoolteacher there and a riverboat pilot for freight. I first met him during that time of the fight over Rampart Dam when I was guiding a ten-day Sierra Club trip down the Yukon River. There were ten of us in our group who were brought together to take a critical look at the area that the proposed dam would inundate. We traveled in two eighteen-foot riverboats piloted by Native guys from Fort Yukon. There was no way we could gather quantitative data or make scientific extrapolations from this cursory cruise down the river, but by obtaining personal acquaintance with the area we were able to give focus and feeling to biological facts and statistics. We could not take a census of waterfowl populations, but we would never forget the sandhill cranes that flew overhead, or the geese that scampered up the riverbank, or the peregrine falcon nest we climbed up a bluff to see.[69]

Our group was walking around town and Don came by on a bicycle and invited us up to his house. He didn't want the dam either. His cabin would go in the drink if they flooded that area, so he was on our side. That kind of started his political career. Don was president of the city council in Fort Yukon. Then he ran for state senate on an anti-Rampart platform. Eventually, he was elected U.S. representative because the guy that was supposed to have won, Nick Begich, was killed in a plane crash.[70] It happened only six weeks before we went to the polls, so his name was already on the ballot. Don Young was running against him and the dead man won. So they had to redo the election after enough time had elapsed that they could establish that Begich wouldn't be alive. Don Young won the second time.

It seemed that at the time all people wanted was growth. I wonder what would have happened if they had built Rampart Dam and flooded all that Yukon River area, and then when they discovered oil up north and wanted to build a pipeline, how would they get it across that flooded area. They'd have to use a ferry to get the oil across all that area.

Rampart Dam was just another one of those projects that a bunch of politicians and chamber of commerce types were promoting as a big lie. Probably that's what bothers me most, I guess. I just don't like fakes.

That was part of it for me with Project Chariot, too—was the idea that this was going to make a harbor that would make us rich. That it would help get out those last minerals. But all they had was low-grade coal, so it was a big lie. And that's what I feel now about the 1002 Area of the Arctic National Wildlife Refuge, where it is being promoted that all we have to do is get in there and drill and then all our energy problems will be solved.[71] The tragedy is that as long as they are peddling this myth and people are buying it, they don't have to do anything about looking for alternative energy. We won't get to work and solve it. And we can. There's no miracle. We don't have to invent an atomic bomb to do it. We don't have to go to war over it. I mean, it isn't something that you have to discover some esoteric Einstein theory. It's just something that makes sense. We can do that. It's just that we're lazy. That's what we do best, is invent and figure out things. For better or for worse. But as long as this myth is what they're putting all their efforts and emphasis on, then that's going to keep them from doing what we need to do. It's not that it has to be so spectacular as trying to find another Prudhoe Bay. I mean, look at how long that lasted. We're almost out of all that oil. I guess I never liked subterfuge or trying to sell something that's just not true. Especially if it's economics or sociological. I just don't like the idea of letting people get away with it.

Issues: Arctic National Wildlife Range/Refuge

Designation of the Arctic National Wildlife Range, the issue that originally brought likeminded folks together in 1959 to testify on behalf of saving wild places in Alaska for the first time, was not easily resolved. In 1960, 8.9 million acres were protected as the range, but the region has continued to be a focal point of Alaska's environmental efforts. In 1980, the range was transformed into the nineteen-million-acre Arctic National Wildlife Refuge. But since the mid-1970s, after a 1968 discovery of oil at neighboring Prudhoe Bay, there has been a strident battle over the possibility of oil development in the coastal plain zone of the refuge. The Alaska Conservation Society continued to be involved in this issue. Debate still rages over differing ideas about use of land and resources, whether we as a society should leave some places wild even if we as individuals will never see the place, what the nature of wilderness is, and how our nation's refuges should be managed.[72] Author, pilot, and wilderness advocate Roger Kaye spoke with Ginny about the effort to establish the Arctic National Wildlife Refuge, protect part as a wilderness, and what wilderness meant to her.

I remember that hearing before Senator Bartlett where we all testified about the Arctic National Wildlife Range. The minutes of it are in the Congressional Record.[73] Bartlett, who was an old miner himself, and pretty much a developer and against protecting the Arctic Wildlife Range, was so polite and cordial. He was very kind. It wasn't like later, when you had to testify in front of Senator Ted Stevens and Representative Don Young. They would just insult you, put you down, or call you an extreme environmentalist.

I remember when I testified before Bartlett, because I had never done anything like that before. I had a written testimony that I read and then he asked me some questions.[74] I remember him saying, "Mrs. Wood, do you know you have given an excellent testimony?" I thought, "Oh my gosh!" Because I didn't know what I had said. I was so nervous. He said, "Mrs. Wood, in my opinion, that was an exceptionally well-prepared and well-presented testimony. Your words are extremely eloquent in describing the values of this place."[75]

And it's not that I necessarily planned to go up to visit the Arctic National Wildlife Refuge. I didn't see how there would be any opportunity. I didn't hanker to be the first one there. No, it was the concept of having someplace that maybe someday you'd get to. But it wasn't one of those places that I had seen from the air and wanted to get on the ground to explore. I was busy exploring in McKinley Park.

I think what appealed to me about protecting this place in the Arctic was the fact that I was beginning to think, without ever really expressing it orally, that we as people were getting too clever, but weren't very smart. We don't have wisdom, but we are very clever, and so our technology is running ahead of us. I think Mardy Murie said that her reason was for someplace where you leave nature alone and it is devoid of technology. After World War II, we began to have all of these mechanical things. Too many people were getting too rich and using technology to either develop resources or for pleasure. But you need some places that nobody has done anything to. The idea that if for nothing else, how are you going to know how to fix something if you don't know what it was like originally and what nature is doing there? We go in and try to fix it, we build roads and people come and throw their garbage around. So pretty soon, you'll never know what your baseline was, what it was like before humans changed it.

When all of us were discussing about what we thought the refuge should be, I remember one of the questions being "Who should manage it?" We were very afraid of it being a national park, because if it were, everybody would want to go there, and then you'd have to have a big hotel and concessionaire. Then there was the issue of having the BLM in charge of it. That would have been the best, because they didn't do that with tourist access. But one branch of them was in the business of disposing of land. They sold land. We were in the business of trying to keep the refuge land intact. So it came down to the Fish and Wildlife Service. The essence of that was not to manage wilderness as far as geography was concerned as much as it was for the protection of the wildlife. I think it was Olaus Murie and Sig Olson who promoted this idea.[76]

The other thing is, when Olaus and Mardy Murie and George Collins were talking with everybody, their concept was to find a place that was big enough so it would have all of the biomes protected in it. From the marine, to the tundra, to the alpine, and to the boreal forest over the hills. When they went up to find the logical boundary for the range, they originally made it a lot smaller than what Olaus had originally wanted. I remember a senator saying that he wouldn't give one bit of money for managing this area. And we said, "Goody, Goody, Goody!" We didn't want it to be overmanaged and have trails and facilities for tourists like happens in some national parks. We wanted it to stay wild.[77]

In pressing Ginny for further reflection during an interview about the history of the Arctic National Wildlife Refuge, Roger Kaye quotes from her 1959 testimony before the Senate subcommittee on the proposal to establish the Arctic National Wildlife Range:

> Wilderness is of the highest importance to science as a standard for reference. It is a laboratory where biologists of today and the future can study to find answers to the reoccurring question, what was the natural order before man changed it? ... It's a psychological lift that the visitor gets just knowing that beyond that ridge, across that valley, behind the mountain, there are no roads, power lines or people, just virgin country.[78]

This prompted Ginny to speak more about the meaning of wilderness:

The concept of wilderness, that of it being someplace where it's just wild, not the European concept of a desolate place, is something that gradually came to me. I realized that I probably had it as a little kid. I liked to be where there weren't a lot of people. But I never was aware of the concept of wilderness. Although I had some concept of wilderness by just being a bush pilot and flying over all of this vastness. I was beginning to get a concept that wilderness is someplace that hasn't been cluttered up with people. Where you are meeting nature on its own terms, whether as a scientist or just as a sightseer.

I always remember Joseph Conrad's writings of the sea, saying that the sea is not for you or against you, it's just very unforgiving of errors. That's what flying is in the North, and that's what mountain climbing is. I had done a lot of mountain climbing and skiing in the Northwest. Whether you are talking about climbing a mountain like Mount Rainier or Mount Baker, or skiing where it was a matter of going cross-country on your skis to the highest mountain you could find to ski down. But it was getting away from tows and from where everybody else was skiing. We didn't say, "Oh, I want to go out in the wilderness."

This brings one particular episode to mind. We visited Les and Teri Viereck when he was working on his PhD in Colorado.[79] They were taking care of a science camp, which was up in the mountains. We had gone Outside to pick up a car for Camp Denali. We went on a ski trip where you climbed the ridges in the Rockies. I had never been in the Rockies before. The trip took all day. We spent the day climbing up and had a run back down. After climbing all day on skis up through

Arrigetch Peaks in the Brooks Range, Alaska, 1971. Photo by Ginny Wood.

and above the timberline, we got up to the crest of the mountains and looked down, and there was a highway. It struck me that we had spent all day to see what's on the other side of this ridge, and when we get over there, there's a major highway with cars going up and down. Still, where we were was great. It was wilderness. But I thought, "When I do that in Alaska, in McKinley Park, you look down and see more and more wild country. You never see any man-made thing."

You could use the term "wild" in lots of different ways as far as the diction-ary goes. But I think in wildness, when you're thinking about the wilderness, it is a concept that means the lack of technological manipulation by man. Wildness does get changed. Like landslides can completely change the scenery in a very short period of time. But the meaning of wildness is something that is hard to describe. It gets to a place where each one of us has something different, and it's something that you can't put into words. It's a feeling. Everybody's feelings are a little different, maybe. Wildness is something to me that hasn't been manipulated by man or any machines. It's like trying to describe to a guy that wants to climb a mountain on a snowmachine why there's a difference between going there on skis or snowshoes or foot and going on a machine. He can't understand what you're talking about because he's trying to see what he can make his machine do. Then he wants to know, "Why do you do it your way?" First, it's a matter of tranquility, sanctuary, and what your body can do, the challenge. It isn't to try to compete, change, or conquer. They use the word "conquer" in mountaineering. Most mountain climbers will say, "The mountain yielded." There's a difference. When you begin to see what has happened by altering things, you reflect back and realize that this wasn't the way it was when you first got here. You get to thinking, "How am I affecting this?"

I also think it's important to still have some nameless places. What happens when the USGS names them, or when we people name them, it's usually named after some political person or somebody's aunt or uncle. Often, I think that it's an ego thing or a political thing. It's just putting man into it. Going around and putting names on something just because there was a politician or somebody's girlfriend or wife or husband who had died is silly. They named one place in McKinley Park after a pilot who crashed and killed himself. He was doing some-thing that was a damned fool thing in the first place, and then he gets a place named after him. That was Scott Peak. It had just had a number before that, like Peak C. I think that the thing about it now, as I realize after being in the Arctic a lot and exploring some of the rivers on foot, is that if you are going to name something, find out what the Native name is first. Give it the Native name because it was on their own maps first. Often the name told you what it was, like, "this is the place where the rivers meet and where there's a lot of fish." That's what the name means in the Native language. There is a roadmap in their names for things like this. It's their guidepost. You can't say that you don't want all places to not have a name, because without it it's pretty hard to navigate. It's like trying to explain how to get to somebody's house if you don't have a street name or a house number.

There's also the notion of the frontier. I guess for some people that's the same as wilderness. But for me frontier means that you came to exploit it. This was not the type of frontier I wanted Alaska to be.

Issues: Alaska National Interest Lands Conservation Act (ANILCA)

The 1980 Alaska National Interest Lands Conservation Act (ANILCA) was one of the most far-reaching pieces of land preservation legislation since the establishment of the country's national park system.[80] In one fell swoop, over one hundred million acres of Alaska were set aside as national parks, preserves, wildlife refuges, wild and scenic rivers, and national forest. This success was the result of a hard-fought, nearly ten-year battle by the conservation community. Not only Alaskans but people from across the United States wrote letters to Congress, testified at field hearings, and educated the public about the beauty of Alaska's wild places and the need to preserve them.

Section 17(d)(2) of the 1972 Alaska Native Claims Settlement Act, which paid Alaska Natives $963 million and gave them title to forty-four million acres of land to settle their land claims, directed the secretary of the interior to withdraw eighty million acres of significant federal lands from development.[81] These lands, referred to as "D-2" lands, were to be reviewed for potential designation as nationally protected areas.[82] Land was only officially transferred and designated for protection with passage of ANILCA. Under the D-2 process, a lot of land was reviewed and investigated.[83] Maps were perused. Acres and acres of land were flown over or walked across. Miles of rivers were floated. With Celia out of town so much as a member of the Joint Federal–State Land Use Planning Commission, Ginny was left to run Camp Denali solo, plus raise a child as a single parent, so she was not able to participate in the D-2 process as much as she had hoped. But she found ways to stay involved.

There was what I call the "Bottoms Up Club." In Anchorage, they referred to themselves as the "Maps on the Floor Society." These were folks working with maps to select boundaries for areas under ANILCA. We met at each other's houses and would lay the maps on the floor and lean over them to talk about places we knew that should be protected. We looked like ducks feeding in a pond, with all our bottoms in the air. Some people were involved because they knew areas through their work in biology or geology. They got out into the country with their fieldwork. Like Will Troyer.[84] I did it because I'd guided some, so I knew those areas. We did a lot of looking at maps for places for protecting them for wilderness, biological reasons, even historical. ACS was very active then. Everybody sent in suggestions for sensitive areas they wanted to see protected. President Carter set aside more acres than we dreamed of.

They were asking people to run the rivers, backpack into the country, to give a sense of what ought to be saved. I was very jealous of people that could go do that. And many of these places they went to ended up being the new national parks and wildlife refuges, and in Southeast the national forest. They were chosen because of the recreational opportunities. I couldn't do any of this; I was tied up at Camp Denali.

As a member of the Joint Federal–State Land Use Planning Commission, Celia was on a lot of the survey trips, on the aerial ones.[85] Agencies like the BLM and the Forest Service and the Park Service were sponsoring these survey trips. If you were young and wanted to do it, they would give you food. And you could paddle the river, go into the country, get a feeling for what it was like. You know, figure out whether the walking was good, or if you could get across this river. This was just because they wanted to know what should be set aside just for its naturalness and wilderness. Or for wildlife. Or for outdoor recreational opportunities.

Celia single-handedly saved the north boundary of Denali National Park. Mount McKinley Park was originally established for the wildlife, and the boundaries were set to where you had a sweeping view of the mountain. It was only set up for tourism. Why would you want more land? Ade Murie was the one who said the existing boundaries were not sufficient from an ecological standpoint for animals who migrated in and out of the park. That it was okay to have an area in the park where there were no roads. ANILCA proposed to expand the park to include these lands.[86] Thanks to Celia's position on the Joint Federal–State Land Use Planning Commission, these lands on the north boundary got included in the final bill. She fought for these places. After these new lands were added to the park it was renamed Denali, the Athabascan name for the mountain.

Issues: Creamer's Field, Fairbanks

Since the 1930s, Creamer's Dairy Farm had been a fixture in Fairbanks. They had 250 acres in the middle of town where they grazed their milk cattle, grew grain to feed them, and raised a large vegetable garden every summer to help feed their milking crews. Creamer's Dairy provided locally produced milk and ice cream, with home delivery in town. By 1966, they could no longer compete with air delivery of dairy products from the Lower 48, so the dairy shut down and the family wanted to sell the property. Fairbanks was growing at an increasing rate, putting pressure on this acreage with threat of development. The farm fields had also become important to the community, as it was where everyone went in the spring to view the first geese returning after a long winter.[87]

In 1966 and 1967, the Alaska Conservation Society and other concerned citizens stepped in to help protect the area as a bird sanctuary and state wildlife refuge. ACS members like Jane Williams, Ginny Wood, Celia Hunter, Bob Weeden, Mary Shields, and Gail Mayo worked tirelessly to convince the state government to purchase the Creamer's Field land. They sponsored a local fundraising campaign to raise five thousand dollars as earnest money to hold the land from public sale until the state legislature passed a bill authorizing state purchase of the property.[88] Creamer's Field Migratory Waterfowl Refuge, which was formally established in 1968, now encompasses two thousand acres and serves as an important stopover for migratory birds in the spring and fall en route to their nesting sites farther north or their wintering grounds to the south, as well as protecting critical habitat for numerous resident bird and wildlife species.[89]

When I first got to Fairbanks, College Road was just a dirt road, with lots of mud puddles during breakup. I can remember having to get out and push once when I was all dressed up to go to a dance out at the university. You wouldn't see any houses after you just turned off Illinois Street. There was just one or two and then you saw this field with the cows in it and barns. It was very nice. Then there were a few more houses just at the foot of the university, but that's all the buildings there were along there. Right after that, of course, Fairbanks started building, with the DEW Line and construction and everything, and the houses started creeping out along there. Creamer's Dairy was a landmark. It was just part of the community. It was such a pleasant place. I don't know, there was something about seeing those cows come out in the spring. Creamer turned the cows out to pasture; he had to keep them in the barn most of the time during the winter. Next to the geese and the ducks that came in, that was kind of one of the signs of spring.

Then we heard that Charlie Creamer was going to go out of business. He was getting older, and milk was being flown in by airplanes then, so they were competing with that. When we got the news that that would go out of business, all we could think of seeing was some of the other things that had developed during the construction era, and we thought, "Oh no, we can't lose that field."

I think that protecting Creamer's Field was one of our most rewarding things that we ever worked on, because usually you have to be against things, you're trying to stop things, like Rampart Dam and Project Chariot and all that. And here's something you could be for. Not only that, but everybody was for it, too. I don't think there were any dissenters. We had the Ladies' Garden Club and the Campfire Girls and just about everybody on our side. Even Governor Hickel, when he was governor in 1966, thought that was a good idea.

The only thing we had a problem with was where to get the money. The thing that saved us was that the banks wanted to be sure it was sold in one piece. They didn't want to have to deal with a lot of little subdivisions—one person buy a few acres and subdivide it and another person and another. They wanted it to go in one piece, and that meant that you'd have to come up with some bucks. The first thing was to get the down payment.

That was a real community effort. Kids were bringing money from their piggy banks to school. One of the stories I like to tell is about Mary Shields. She was a dog musher who lived out in Goldstream Valley. She didn't have much money and she didn't have a car, and there wasn't a road over Ballaine Hill connecting to town at that time, so when she came into town she'd hitchhike back and forth and use a dog with packs to carry her groceries. We picked her up one time, and she had boxes and boxes of cake mix that she'd gotten from some grocery store that had donated it. She was distributing it to people that gave her rides, to bake cakes. Then her Campfire Girls group would sell them. I remember it was snowing down by College Inn and here was Mary set up out in the snow with these little kids selling the cakes that had been brought in for them to sell. There was a grocery store there then and they invited them all to come in where it was warm and sell their cakes. I don't know how much money they raised, but that's just one of the many stories that could be told about how people came together. We also got help from other folks in town. The strongest help was from the Ladies' Garden Club. We would never have expected that.

What we got was the down payment, so we could hold it. This was just before they struck oil [at Prudhoe Bay]. Had it been another two years, the oil companies would have been in and bought that land in a minute to have it as their pipeline yard to store their pipes. After that somebody would have subdivided it. I just think it's really neat that that's still there, that dairy and that field. And that's something Fairbanks has that Anchorage doesn't have anywhere in their city limits.[90]

Bob Weeden provides his perspective on ACS's involvement with protecting Creamer's Field:

Jim King, who worked for the US Fish and Wildlife Service, came and said the Creamer's Field area would make a good refuge. Jim had worked for Charlie Creamer in 1948 as a milk hand. I was working at the Alaska Department of Fish and Game and agreed, and I was in a position to promote it as a state waterfowl refuge. When the proposal then came up for the purchase of Creamer's Field, we needed a community organization to take it over as a project and raise money for it. The state couldn't do it. I was president of ACS then, so Dan Swift took over as president and I moved to VP, so there wouldn't be a conflict of interest. That way, Dan was the front person at all the Creamer's meetings. I found out that John Butrovich,[91] who was somebody with a lot of power, was in favor of a refuge. He was a duck hunter. So he helped us a lot. We would use state and federal money, and all ACS had to do was get option money. Everybody did their part to raise money. Like Mary Shields held cookie sales. And in the end it all worked out. We raised the money and were able to buy the land from the Creamers. It was not good real estate to use for much else, because you'd get water every time you dug a hole. The Creamers got the money they wanted. Kids have a place to watch ducks. Snowmobilers and mushers have a place to go in winter. It's been good for the town.[92]

Ginny plays down her role in the effort to protect Creamer's Field, and gives more credit to others she believes were more influential, such as Jane Williams. Jane Williams was on the board of directors of the Alaska Conservation Society when the group got involved with trying to purchase the Creamer's property. As Ginny explains:

I shouldn't get the credit anymore than anybody else. Like there was Jane Williams. She is a quiet little woman who has done more to protect places and doesn't get recognized for what she's done. She should. She is just a wonderful person. And she has a good sense of humor. She lived out in the Bush for a long time. She and her husband, Red Williams, homesteaded in Central. And she was right in with the rest of us as one of the early members of the Alaska Conservation Society. She was also one of the ones who started the Unitarian Universalist Fellowship group in Fairbanks. In her own quiet way, she has done so much. You could always see Jane Williams at hearings, at events. She's a person that's unheralded.

Issues: Pet Peeves

Then there were the smaller-scale issues that Ginny took on personally as affronts to her value system and to the Alaska lifestyle she had known. They were pet peeves of a sort. She wrote about them frequently. These included road building,[93] the use of snowmachines,[94] and general changes that were making life in Fairbanks too busy and too crowded. For example, when her neighborhood thoroughfare, Ballaine Road, was slated for widening and improvement in 1968, she wrote:

Someone has said that the cloverleaf is fast becoming our national flower. Looking at the sparse web of lines on a map that represents Alaska's highway system there seems at first glance little chance that the forget-me-not will be replaced as our state botanical emblem. However, a closer look at the roads and highways that have been built recently or that are now under construction indicates that our highway program suffers from the same affliction as do those in the smaller states—Bulldozer Blight.

The point is not that highways are Bad Things, but that all roads do not serve the same purpose and need not follow the same construction criteria. Road designers need to be as aware of aesthetics, ecological consequences, and the social benefit component of the cost/benefit ratio as they are of engineering problems.

A case in point is 2.2 miles of road through a rural residential area north of the University of Alaska in the Fairbanks area. When the State Department of Highways revealed plans to re-align and upgrade the roadbed to federal highway secondary road specifications over sixty property owners who used the road to get to their homes objected on the grounds that this construction would be too destructive of natural beauty, put houses built back from the road right on the edge of the new highway, disrupt a cross country ski trail system, encourage higher speeds along a country road that children and commuters to the university liked to walk, and invite commercial development.

Those that question highway design and techniques are tossed off by engineers and the highway lobbyists as nature lovers ignorant of engineering problems and obstructionists to progress. But the signs say, "Your Highway Taxes At Work." We have the right to question whether in all cases of new highway construction—and reconstruction—what we are getting with our money is better than what we are giving up.[95]

Doing environmental work can be exhausting. Especially in Alaska, whose economy has always been based on resource development, where at certain times "environmentalist" was a bad word for a majority of the population, and there always seems to be another big project being promoted. There was Project Chariot in 1958, Rampart Dam starting in 1959, the Susitna Hydroelectric Project in the 1960s and 1970s, nuclear testing on Amchitka Island in the Aleutian Island National Wildlife Refuge in the late 1960s,[96] and the establishment of new parks and refuges in the late 1970s. And today it is the Pebble Mine, a proposed large copper, gold, and molybdenum open pit mine in southwestern Alaska. Then there were the projects that didn't get as far, such as a proposal by the North American Water and Power Alliance (NAWAPA) to dam and reverse the flow of Alaskan and Canadian rivers like the Yukon River to send water to New Mexico and Arizona because they were running out of water.[97] Or the idea resurrected in the 1990s by then-Governor Walter Hickel to ship water via a pipeline from Alaska's coastal glaciers down to California to alleviate their drought conditions. And there is a steady stream of rhetoric promoting new roads or railroads, such as to Nome to better access mineral resources, a road to Juneau so the state capital is less isolated, or a road along the Yukon River to help impoverished villages. Ginny spoke out or wrote about all these issues. It's hard to imagine how someone can stay motivated against such odds to continue to push for conservation and environmental protection. Ginny explains her inspiration:

I think I got involved because up here you found out that everybody matters. That you matter just as much as anybody else. I knew a gal who worked as a waitress at the McKinley Park Hotel and then married a ranger down there, who was just a good simple person without too much education, but who I thought said some very interesting things. She said, "The reason I like Alaska is because up here everybody's important." It's true. And everything that happens up here matters.

I guess the thing is that up here you get involved because it's kind of hard to stay uninvolved. It was very easy to be concerned because there were so few of us. You could be living in a big city like Seattle and all sorts of inequities are happening down there all the time, but you'd think, "It's not my business. It's not my concern," unless it was up on the ski hill I used. Like if they were going to put a road in or something, you might read the paper and think I'm for it or against it, and then you'd turn the page and it would be out of your mind. I think it's hard not to get involved, if you have any sensitivity to something that you think is an inequity. Or that's not going to make the money they think it is. Or it's going to spoil something for me or my friends. Up here, you go to any gathering of any of your friends, and it becomes a topic of conversation. Hearing everybody else talking about it makes you want to get involved. In Seattle, I would have been going skiing and hiking the mountains and exploring to see what was over the hills, but it wouldn't have been done as an environmentalist. I think that up here it was different because my best friends and neighbors were the leaders in biology and the conservation movement.

If you didn't see it, it was always easy to find somebody who had; somebody who was there, lived there, was involved in the issue. It's pretty hard to keep secrets up here. It's very hard for somebody to hide their dirty linen. You always knew who you could talk to, or you'd hear about something at a party.

Like it wasn't hard to find out when a scientist was working on something related to one of our conservation issues. Maybe he couldn't say anything publicly because he'd be fired if he did, but he'd tell you as a friend. And you never betrayed his confidence by giving his name. But if I lived in New York or even Seattle, I would have never done that because I wouldn't have known the people. Like when they were testing for the oil pipeline and they buried it in the permafrost, a guy that I knew real well was there. They dug up a section of it and the pipe was all twisted. They hadn't realized electrolysis would be a factor when they were going to put in that pipe. If they built it how they started to, it would have been just all twisted. It's like in saltwater, when you have to make sure the rudder on your boat is a certain metal so it won't get eaten. It was the same with the soils they were burying the pipe in. It was just one of those things that nobody had thought of. But I knew the guy that did the testing. Proved it. So

I was able to spread the word about the safety of the pipeline because he secretly told me about it.

We may have been in the minority in those early years but it was kind of fun. It was interesting. And I think it was the people. You just met the neatest people. It was because of the quality of the friendships I had with the people that were involved. They were fun. They had a good sense of humor. They didn't take life too seriously, or even their defeats too seriously. If you'd been all by yourself, I think it would have been harder.

There were a lot of other people who were doing this work, too. I shouldn't get the credit anymore than anybody else. I think I get more credit than I should get. But I'm not ashamed of what I did. It was kind of fun to be involved in some of these things. But you probably had to have a bit of ego to do what we did. You didn't do it to be famous, but because you just didn't like the way people were doing things.

ACS won the first three big battles we took on: Arctic Refuge, Project Chariot, and Rampart Dam. But when we started the Alaska Conservation Society, we didn't know where we were going. We just started it over the establishment of the Arctic Range. You know what the secret was? In those days, all these things came one at a time, and they were all black and white. Now, they come in multiples and they're all shades of gray. So, it's easier to be focused on one thing when you know it's a big myth and who's perpetuating it. You look back on things in a perspective that's different from when you're in the middle of them. You knew it in little bites, of little victories here, little victories there. And you didn't really see the whole thing.

Looking back on it, in the first place we weren't a threat to anybody to start out with, you know. Everybody had an opinion then, but people didn't get so angry, like they do now. People might express themselves and you'd think they were going to fight, pull a gun or something, but they'd be having fun with each other the next day. People who went down to Juneau to be in the legislature, you didn't know if they were Republican or Democrat. That wasn't what was important.

Protecting Alaska's wilderness. I didn't know that's what I was doing at the time. You look back in the fabric and some things were just how things happened to be. Like how many environmentalists became active after the 1989 *Exxon Valdez* oil spill?[98] There are things that come along that kind of make people stand up and be counted. Or decide, "Somebody has to do it, so I suppose it might as well be me." It was people like that. And then realizing that Alaska was just growing too fast. I mean, you always thought it would be the way it was when you got here: lots and lots of land and there being plenty of room for everybody. You realized how much Alaska is the land. That you're never away from the environment and it's precious. Every time I went Outside,

I'd think about how lucky I was to get up here and see it when I did. Now there are so many changes.

Alaskans have long prided themselves on independence and the freedom to do as they please. Government rules and regulations, and preserving some lands as wild country, goes against the grain for much of the population. Ginny talks about the social milieu of opposition and support that coexisted at the time when she, Celia Hunter, and the Alaska Conservation Society began their environmental work.

When we first got here Fairbanks was a small town, a very folksy town. As Mardy Murie, who grew up here, would say, "Every spring there was a new scandal."[99] Everybody was taking sides. There were lots of scoundrels. But after a while of living here we began to feel personal about the land. It was not like the head of the Sierra Club coming up here and telling us how to do things. We had debates then and everyone went to them. They don't do that now. We didn't even have radio. You had to go to a hearing to hear about something.

There were folks against us, like Joe Vogler, who was a miner.[100] He always wanted trees cut down. He called them "boreal weeds." Most of the time he and I were against each other. But I do remember a couple of issues where we were on the same side. That sure surprised me. Like at the hearing for the construction of Pearl Creek Elementary School, we both had concerns about Ballaine Road being upgraded. Or the issue of having water piped into our neighborhood by Northern Alaska Development Company. Then I remember another time when I went to a hearing about a proposed road upgrade for a church that was over on Ballaine Road. There was a problem with too many cars. I think they were proposing a parking lot or something like that. Turned out that Joe and I were both against it. He was just a part of the warp and the weave of the fabric that was Fairbanks.

In some things we had the Native people as our allies. Like in the fight for polar bears and wolves. They hunted these animals as part of their lifestyle. They did not come at it from the same perspective as environmentalists, but we wanted the same thing, to stop the aerial killing of these animals. It's amazing how sharp the Native people were and how fast they became politically astute. Before statehood, most of them spoke limited English and they were unsophisticated politically. Project Chariot really sparked it for them. They were like guardhouse lawyers in how fast they became so well versed in politics and in making good speeches. In only a few years, I saw the change from these kids in the villages that I knew when I flew there to becoming these politically astute politicians. Now we have some very outstanding Native leaders. It was interesting to see the transition.

For twenty years, the Alaska Conservation Society and its members were the voices of environmentalism in Fairbanks. They focused their attentions on big and small issues, local and statewide, and their enthusiasm motivated people from across Alaska to add their voices and efforts to the cause. In a June 9, 2006, oral history interview, Bob Weeden, biologist, writer, and cofounder of ACS, explains:

> Our twenty-year run proved that for the first time there was a constituency to speak out for conservation, wild things, nature in Alaska. We also showed that a conservation organization once started will collect friends rapidly if it has a good and strong character. The character of ACS was formed by that first Fairbanks group of scientists and passionate people who understood science. It was a collective of people with the outdoors as the common denominator. And they also had a respect for science or knowledge of what it could do, so that we were forever doomed to want to get some facts about what was going on. That isn't always necessary or done in conservation work. Sometimes you just take a line and pursue it and know you're going to compromise. You begin by being outrageous and then you fall back to something that is where you thought you'd go all along. Instead, the ACS style was to build up slowly, to see all sides. At times it was slow and cumbersome. Like I think we paid for it with the D-2 lands issues when we didn't jump on board with all the national organizations in Washington, D.C. ACS's focus was living in Alaska with nature.[101]

Times changed and the Alaska Conservation Society was not able to keep up. Around 1980, the board of directors decided to dissolve the group while it still had money in the bank and use that money to help some of the smaller organizations around the state get better established. In that same June 2006 interview, Bob Weeden and Ginny Wood converse together about the structure of ACS and its eventual demise, each adding their own perspective to the same story. Bob Weeden begins:

> ACS ended as a collective umbrella organization with eleven chapters around the state. Many of these chapters continue today, because they were incorporated themselves as independent groups who had their own officers and raised their own money. It was a stroke of brilliance that we didn't know about because the umbrella collapsed but the shaft remained and the groups put their own sunshades on. It seemed that local groups organized around a state agency person doing something, like Will Troyer or Dave Spencer, and then others were willing to get involved.[102]

Ginny adds:

Then there were small organizations that were chapters of ours. ACS started out just in Fairbanks. We did not start out to be a chapter-based organization. People have too many organizations to belong to so we never proselytized to form chapters. It's just that people around the state started contacting ACS and asking, "How do you become a member?" The people would write us and say that they had this controversy in their town. ACS started as a homegrown thing, and we felt that's how others should start. We felt like they knew more about their issues than we did, so we told them to start their own group. To organize like we did. We told them to fight, and they did. We'd ask, "What is your issue, what is your community upset about? Start there." Like in Petersburg, logging of Petersburg Creek was their issue. They were going to log their favorite recreational river where everybody went hunting and camping and fishing. They said, "Not in our backyard!" It takes a local issue like that to get chapters started. You know, what's the bonfire in your backyard and people getting together over it. The last group to form was in Anchorage. Sometimes we'd send them some money to help locally.

ACS had been going strong. There were good people in it. Then Celia went back to Washington, DC, to be director of the Wilderness Society. Bob Weeden went to work for Governor Hammond in Juneau. Fred Dean was trying to finish a major grizzly bear research project. Things were getting too fast too quick. There were too few of us left to run it. With all of these satellite groups it just got too big to handle. Before, it was kind of fun. It was kind of like David slaying Goliath. Then, people could hitchhike to a meeting and make a speech. It was so easy to get the facts and know somebody that was there. That had changed.

You can't be effective now—and even twenty years ago—without having more than what we had. We realized we couldn't operate a big conservation movement out of our living rooms or our kitchens. You had to have telephones and an office and people working there. We needed a secretary. We needed staff. We needed salaries. You couldn't do it as just a bunch of volunteers. We needed better equipment—you had to have fax and Xerox machines. We needed a way to produce things besides on Camp Denali's old mimeograph machine. We needed more money. Times changed and we decided to quit while we were ahead. While we still had money and some influence. It was not because we weren't effective. ACS won a twenty-five-thousand-dollar award from someplace back East that thought we were the best small nonprofit conservation organization. So it was not because we didn't have money in the treasury. We'd always done things on the cheap, like one time we sent Gordon Wright down to Kenai to go to a hearing and we asked him how much money he needed.[103] He said, "Fifteen dollars for hamburgers and I'll ride my bike." We decided we didn't want to become a professional group, so we split up the money we had left among other groups.

Also Gordon Wright wanted to start a Sierra Club chapter here. We told him that's fine, but that's not us. We were involved in our own things and didn't want to be involved in a national organization. We just wanted to be Alaskan. Then they struck oil and big money was coming up. We couldn't fight against that with our small amount of money.

Bob concludes the discussion with:

ACS lost out because we decided at the start that there was a joy and a benefit to being a volunteer organization. We paid a half-time secretary sometimes, but we remained volunteers. We just couldn't compete in terms of our public presence and outreach with groups with staff, like the Northern Environmental Center in Fairbanks, the Alaska Center for the Environment in Anchorage, or the Southeast Alaska Conservation Center in Juneau. And then the Alaska Conservation Foundation and Alaska Environmental Lobby began taking over the coordination role that ACS had played and they could get money for conferences and things like that. We lost our key functions to those groups with the power of staffing behind them. There is a danger of staff taking over from volunteers, because they are the ones who spend all day thinking about the issues and it is easy for them to lead others along. There are pros and cons of having a staffed versus a volunteer organization.

Our constitution said that if the group dissolved, any remaining money would be given to like-minded conservation organizations. So we distributed our assets. We turned over the archives of our group to the University of Alaska Fairbanks. We distributed the money to existing ACS chapters. We even helped start the first conservation group in the Yukon Territory. A guy named John Lammers contacted ACS because he and his wife had homesteaded at Pelly Crossing in wild country, and suddenly bulldozers came down the riverbank and showed up in their front yard. It turns out there was a mineral lease there with a difference between surface and subsurface rights. He tried to fight it. He moved to Whitehorse and tried to figure out how to get something local going, and he heard about ACS. He got the Yukon Conservation Society going about seven to eight years after ACS.[104]

The Fairbanks Environmental Center, first established in 1971, was one of these groups that started as an ACS chapter and went on to grow into its own entity, due in no small part to the financial assistance from ACS's dissolution. In 1981, the organization officially changed its name to the Northern Alaska Environmental Center. Ginny explains her involvement with this organization:

The Northern Center went into business as ACS went out of business. There was some overlap. Gordon Wright was one of the first founders. Jim Kowalsky was the first staff member.[105] I was still around when it was being started up. I was one of the few involved in both ACS and the Fairbanks Environmental Center. ACS never had an office. The Northern Center has had a variety of offices in different places. The first one was on Third Avenue—it was a place with lots of cubbyholes. Another was in a private home on Sixth or Tenth Avenue. Then there was the little house by the old train station and the *Fairbanks Daily News-Miner* building. That one had furnace problems. I lent them five hundred dollars to buy that place. They paid me back in small ten-dollar increments. Eventually, it got too small for the operation so they moved to the current building on College Road.

I was on the board of the Northern Center under Jim Kowalsky and under John Adams.[106] I wrote the column "From the Woodpile" for their newsletter sort of as a continuation of the articles I wrote for the ACS newsletter. They changed their name from the Fairbanks Environmental Center to the Northern Alaska Environmental Center under John Adams's leadership, because it had a broader focus than just Fairbanks issues and nobody else was covering the Arctic.

As Ginny Wood says, there were a lot of other people involved in the early days of Alaska's conservation movement. In some cases, there were some pretty well-known public figures at the time. Many are names still known today for their successes and the legacies they left behind: People like Olaus Murie, who served as director of the Wilderness Society from 1950 until his death in 1963, and with his wife, Mardy, was a staunch advocate for national parks and protection of a nine-million-acre Arctic National Wildlife Refuge. Adolph "Ade" Murie, who as a biologist at Denali National Park conducted groundbreaking research on the wolf–Dall sheep relationship, was influential in terminating predator control programs within national parks, and emphasized the need for larger protection zones to compensate for animals' migratory routes. George Collins, who proposed wilderness designation for the Arctic National Wildlife Refuge. Lowell Sumner, whom many considered a visionary in the National Park Service because of his views on wilderness. To current conservationists, these heroes loom larger than life for the struggles they endured and the contributions they made, but Ginny knew all these people as friends and co-activists. They were peers who worked together on campaigns, they stayed at her house in Fairbanks, they visited at Camp Denali, and they created many shared memories together.

Lowell Sumner was a big kid! And he had a very good relationship with George Collins. George called him "Doc" because he had a PhD and I don't think Collins ever had one. Lowell was very funny. At the time, people in the Park Service didn't have planes except Lowell. He had this old Luscombe that always seemed to have problems. I can remember him more than anything else with a wrench working under the hood trying to find out what was wrong with it. Luscombes didn't have too high a rating compared to the Piper Cub and the like. But he loved that plane.

Then there was Ade Murie, who also worked for the Park Service, who had no use for airplanes. He didn't like them. He liked us, but he had to forgive us our sins. I told him that being up in the clouds and the weather was a way of being in another realm of wilderness. I agreed with him in that I would use a plane to find out where I wanted to go on the ground. And then go back later on foot to explore it.

I got to know Ade much more than his more well-known brother, Olaus. Ade and his wife, Louise, whose nickname was Weezie, were living at McKinley Park headquarters when Woody and I first went down there. We just learned so much from him. I can remember Ade saying, "If I had to do it over again, I'd have been an agronomist. You start with the soils, that's the foundation of every-thing." He said that he had gone backwards, beginning with the critters and then going to other things. He was stationed at the Igloo Creek Ranger Station at McKinley Park for a long time. He and Weezie even wintered there one year when their kids were young and raised them out there. We'd run into Ade out there when we were hiking with groups from Camp Denali. I remember one time when we met Ade and Charlie Ott, a photographer from town taking pic-tures in the park. We must have been stopped looking at one of those ponds, or doing birding or something of that sort. They just came hiking over the hills. I don't know what they had been doing, but they looked as if they were just hav-ing fun. Then another time, Mel Lockwood, who was another photographer we ran into, said, "I have a permit to do this." He showed me the permit. It was from Ade. It said, "Mel kin [sic] collect posies in the park." This was the official pass he would show if he ever were questioned by the authorities about what he was doing. See, Mel and Ade were good personal friends. They got along real well.

I think I first met Mardy Murie at a Sierra Club meeting down in Seattle. A friend of mine was hosting it at his house. He introduced me to Mardy. But I'd already known Olaus, because I had met him when he'd come up to Alaska. Of course, he had earlier done a lot of biological work with caribou and in McKinley Park in the 1920's. I also met Olaus when Woody and I were invited to come to an Audubon Society meeting down in California and give a talk on Alaska and show some pictures. Woody and I were out to get a new car to bring back to Camp Denali. Olaus Murie was one of the featured speakers at this meeting.

I guess I really got to know Mardy Murie when the Wilderness Society had their annual meeting in 1963 at Camp Denali.[107] The well-known conservation leaders of the time, like Sig Olson,[108] Olaus and Mardy Murie, and all of those guys were there for a week. We had some interesting conversations and got to

Ginny (L) and Celia (R) with conservationist, Mardy Murie, San Juan Island, circa 1988. Courtesy of Ginny Wood.

know them well. Olaus was very sick. In fact, that was the last year of his life.[109] Olaus and Mardy were staying in the A-frame at the bottom of the hill, and he would not accept a ride in the jeep up to the lodge at the top of the hill, even though he was a sick man. He would get his camera out and take pictures of the moose on the lake and insist on wandering around and hiking a little bit. I first thought of Mardy as just Olaus's wife, but then when Olaus got sick, she started to take over, and I realized that this woman is the one who's always arranging meetings and writing. Her activism was sort of a secret to the Wilderness Society. She always gave Olaus the credit. She was not trying to usurp his authority.

Mardy was a comfortable person—warm, disarming, and attentive to others as she was absorbed in the natural world in which she flourished. And she was fun to be with. Ardent and formidable as she was in the causes she threw herself so effectively into, I don't think either she nor her beloved husband, Olaus, ever offended anyone. She was acute at sizing up others, especially frauds and despoilers of nature, but neither she or Olaus were ever vehement or mean minded. When she gave a speech, she didn't speak to an audience, it was like she was speaking to you personally one to one. And she listened to you intently whether you were an old friend—young or old, or unknown to her before you just met. And up until she was almost one hundred years old, she never forgot a name or a face she had ever encountered.[110]

George Collins referred to me and Celia as "the girls," because he was much older than us. I can remember visiting him and I never laughed so much in my life! He was quite a raconteur and hilariously funny. He had a sense of humor that wouldn't stop. It was a matter of just meeting somebody for the first time in passing and having an interesting conversation with him. George would write letters to me and Celia.[111] It wasn't always about wilderness. Sometimes it was just friends telling stories. Actually, Celia probably knew him better from when she was working for the Wilderness Society. She saw him when he was talking about issues.

We knew Sig Olson very well because he stayed at Camp Denali. Sig was chairman of the board of the Wilderness Society when Celia was the director. I knew him well at Camp by just talking to him. His concept of wilderness was lakes and wildness.[112] But the feeling was that if it becomes just a destination for everybody to go to, it loses what you set it aside for. I remember sitting down in the sun under the windows of the lodge at Camp with Sig and discussing philosophical things. I really can't remember any one thing that he said. But I do remember that he was rather wise. He was talking about his feelings about canoeing and paddling. I remember another time that he was at Camp when the Wilderness Society was having their annual meeting there. Sig and I mostly discussed the problems in McKinley Park at that time. Sig's son, Sig Jr., was one of our first board members of the Alaska Conservation Society. He lived in Juneau so I didn't get to know him like I knew the people who lived in Fairbanks.

One of the other people I got to know was John Reed, who was head of the United States Geological Survey.[113] I flew him from McKinley Park back up to Fairbanks. He was the one who said, "I told the Muries that they should stay east of the Canning River for the boundary of their proposed Arctic National Wildlife Range, because right there, there's a big disconnect in the geology, and they'll find oil." They hadn't even found Prudhoe Bay then. But he said that they were going to find oil, and in pretty good amounts. But to the east he said there were entirely different structures so they'd only find little seeps. He explained it to me geologically and why the chance of finding any big amount of oil there was minimal. It was not very much later that they made the big oil discovery at Prudhoe Bay.

Ginny's effort on behalf of environmental issues in Alaska has been underlain by a personal philosophy about nature and wild places. It is a perspective based upon enjoying the great outdoors, being curious about how it all works, and appreciating natural places that still exist without the influence of humans. However, she deflects the labeling when asked point-blank, "How did you become an environmentalist?"

Well, how I became an environmentalist was just from being out in it. I didn't even know the word—what an environmentalist was—when I first came to

Alaska. I had had experience with horses and sailboats and hiking and outdoor things, but I didn't think about it anymore than I suppose Lewis and Clark did when they were exploring country. They didn't feel that they were environmentalists, but they brought back knowledge of stuff that's amazing. The journals that they had and what they noticed and what sketches they made. I guess, what you see when you get up in what's truly wilderness, where there's no technology or any manipulation by man, is just there's an economy of nature that is amazing. It's tooth and claw and dog eat dog. Or wolf eat wolf. But there is an organization, a rhythm. I would say just like there are laws of the economy, there are laws in nature that work themselves out. It's just amazing. I don't know why, whether it's if you believe in God or something did it that way. It's a system where everything's recycled. Then humans come along and completely upset the balance. That doesn't mean you all have to get in caves and live like an animal to make it work, but you can learn a lot.

I don't fight for environmental causes. I get involved sometimes. A lot of the time I wanted to be out skiing or hiking. I wanted to be out smelling the flowers, instead of writing about them. But Celia loved being so involved and being a leader. So I got involved, too.

As a wilderness lover and conservation activist, Ginny Wood has tried to live her life in concert with the natural world around her. She believes in sustainability. She strives toward living a simple life; using as few resources and leaving as small a footprint as possible.[114] She never felt drawn toward the consumerism of modern American society. As she says, "You can't spend money you haven't earned." She has lived a frugal life. She tends a large vegetable garden every summer to fill her pantry. Reuses plastic bags, aluminum foil, nails, rubber bands, and twist ties with a vengeance. And buys only what she feels she needs. She has never wanted the latest model of car or newest technogadget. She is not a fashionista who felt obligated to keep up with current trends. The clothes in her closet suit her just fine. Upon turning ninety, Ginny said, "The best that I can do when I die is to have left as small an imprint as possible, so I'm a cheapskate. I don't buy new clothes. I turn off lights to use less energy." Ginny's philosophy of what it means to live a good life is something that we can all learn from, especially as our resource-consumptive lifestyles are threatened by depletion of the very thing that sustains us.

The lifestyle that I lead developed because we started Camp Denali without any money and we came to Fairbanks needing to find ourselves a place to live. We didn't have much money. But we never were in debt. You couldn't do that now. Our lifestyle wasn't that different back then. It was more like how everybody else was living when we first got up here. We didn't have electricity or running water. We didn't have telephones. We didn't have television. We didn't have mail service. We built a little cabin as our first place.

But I think because we are a consumer society a lot of people are stuck with being poor. They're the ones that are having a hard time hacking it and are on relief. Then you have the people that have to keep up with the Joneses and the fact that there's always somebody that's richer than they are. They're in another world. Their thinking is that, "Well, next year we'll get that thing or do that," or else they buy all this stuff to show that they can afford it. That they've made it. It's a measure of their success.

You know a number of years ago there started to be some planes from here that would fly over to Siberia and sometimes Aeroflot would bring a plane full of people over here. They were doing all these exchanges. Like if they were Eskimos and they had relatives over there, they could now go and visit. This was after it was no longer the Soviet Union but was Russia again.[115] My friend John Lyle was a guide for a group that came to Fairbanks, and he told me this story. When they first started coming, that's when we were pretty oil rich, so the chamber of commerce gave every passenger on the plane a hundred dollars to spend here. Because the Soviet money wasn't worth anything anymore. John took them into Fred Meyer. One woman who could speak English said, "How do you people use all these things?"[116]

I think that's a commentary that really shows our society. You look at it and think about who buys all this stuff. And if this isn't bought, where does it end up? The trash pile? Somebody's junk pile? And they're changing everything every year. It's out of style, there's a new version out, so you get a new one. Or it breaks down, so you buy more. We have this problem where consuming is one of the symbols of our economy, it's considered a good thing. What the consumer index is. Whether we're in a depression or not. But on the other hand, one of the biggest decisions our nation now faces is what to do with our garbage.[117] You can't burn it because that pollutes the air. We bury it and then it pollutes the water. It just keeps expanding. It's so funny if you just sit back and listen to this. And then you want to know about simple living. I don't call this very simple.

I don't feel that living the way I have was trying to prove something. It wasn't a movement. It wasn't an "ism." It wasn't a back-to-the-earth type of thing. It's just that I feel more comfortable when I look at nature. I hope I never have to open my door and step outside on cement. I want it to be dirt. But I'm awfully glad I don't have to go to an outhouse at fifty below zero temperatures anymore. But if the power goes off or the septic system fails, I still could. We didn't take our old outhouse down, just in case we ever needed it.

I'm pretty pessimistic about the outcome of the human race. But, you know, it could change very fast. Everything changes too fast. But it could change for the better, too. There'll always be ups and downs. I think the human race was an experiment and we flunked the test. But hasn't it been fun! Or interesting? Or worthwhile? I don't know. I'm sort of pontificating here, but certainly I don't think I have any words of advice or wisdom or any recipe. You're born with what you're given. You're born with drawbacks and assets and you accumulate some along the way. I was born, I think, at a time when it was the height of opportunity, even for women. And enough wild country so you could always get away from it all, and enough so that you didn't have to go with a crowd if you didn't want to. I never wanted to start a revolution or an "ism." Or be someone to say, "Follow this and all will be okay." No, I think it's a learning experience and I suppose you'll still have it until the day you die. There will be something that you learned and something that you mucked up, failed at.

I think that the two main problems are that there's too many of us and we're too dependent on too few resources. Both material and natural. We're running out. And we've become too greedy and too fat and want to go too fast. We reap what we sow. I don't think it's a done deal, though. Lots of things can still happen. In the cosmic sense, one of those little asteroids or something, all it has to do is hit the earth, which has happened three or four times before, and just about wipe out all life. I don't think it's all over, unless the sun dries up and we no longer have that energy. Then the world would become just a lifeless hunk of rock spinning around with a lot of other planets. It just goes to show you that you can't tell. I mean, it's hard to know what is supposed to happen in the cosmic sense. If there's design or intelligence or a superplanner somewhere? If you want to get spiritual about it, I'm not sure. I'm not sure enough to even say no there is or there isn't. It's a big mystery. And we're all part of it. And to what extent it's preordained and in another sense it's not, who knows?

If I were to distill it down to basics, my overall interpretation right now would be that where it used to be growth equals prosperity, that's not working anymore. We're just too many people and we can't possibly keep dividing the resources—whether the resources are clean water, clean air, soil to grow stuff on, or even where we're going to put our garbage. We're running out of everything. There's just no answer.

So I think the next thing is not this prosperity goal but sustainability. And sustainability is like the way I live. Well, not totally. I'm still utterly dependent on the power line at fifty degrees below zero. But for deeper survival, that you're self-sufficient.

Well, you couldn't do that now. We're living too high off the hog. Too many people with houses that are too big, so if you don't have any power, you can't exist. When I first came up to Alaska, most people's economy was that you had summer jobs and in the wintertime you lived off the moose you shot, the berries you'd picked, and what you grew in your garden, and waited for spring to come when the jobs opened up again.[118] And that just solved itself because enough people that didn't like it or couldn't make it, they went back home. It kept the population smaller. If you didn't have any power, well, you had a woodstove and you had firewood. Nobody starved to death, because there were enough plant and animal resources. But there isn't that now.

I see it now as almost like the spaceship, completely dependent on what gets sent up to them. They can't possibly survive if they didn't have that. If our supply line to Alaska was cut off, no airplanes or no boats coming in, no train, we wouldn't last very long. We couldn't live off the land. We couldn't do like the Natives did. I think we shoot for sustainability, and we're somehow or other going to have to limit our reproduction because there are too many of us.

I think that if we forget about who can get richest and which corporation can get bigger and take over the other one, which is what our economy is based on now, then we'll be better off. Big corporations running things is wrong. I'm not talking about socialism. Russia's tried that and that didn't work. And we can't go backwards to a frontier society. So what do we do instead? I'm talking about sustainability. You don't have to starve to death in the darkness to do it. It can be a very rewarding, pleasant life with enough to eat and be warm. I was just as happy when I lived in a cabin that didn't have anything like electricity or running water. We thought it was just great. It was warm, and it was our house! If we start now to shoot for sustainability and not for prosperity, we can still have a good, high standard of living, a high standard of life, and have a very high well-being index, which should be the real judge of your economy anyway. This would be better than what it is now, where them that has, gets, and for the others that's tough. Let them eat cake! In any case, that's the way I see it now.

If we overshoot and we don't do that, then we're going to be on a pure survival path. It will be every man for himself, and that's not going to very pretty. But I'm not going to be around to find out how it all comes out.

Our Wall Street society isn't going to solve our present environmental problems. Look at all the things that are problems. Like right now there's not even enough water alone as to where we're not going to have enough to live on. I'm not talking about swimming pools and big lawns, I'm talking about just enough water to grow food. And enough soil that's rich enough to produce crops. We're using up soil faster than it's being made. And garbage, they don't really know where to put all these commodities that everyone throws away. But this doesn't mean you have to go to socialism or go to just a meager life, just barely surviving. But if you don't do something, you will be on a survival path, which a lot of the third world countries are on.

I don't think there's anything wrong with our mercantile economy, but it has to be fair. And it certainly now seems like the goal is greed, growth, and fraud. It's turned into corporate feudalism. I just shake my head and think, "You guys just don't get it." We're getting so that there isn't enough food to even feed the rich people unless we make a change. We have to think about what is sustainable and what isn't. We have brains, we can figure it out.[119]

I think Barbara Kingsolver put it very well in her book *Small Wonder*.[120] She said, If it's a race to see how fast we can use up our natural resources, who's going to be the winner? You can't have any winners. You have to think back and say, "How will this work, what can we do?" We don't have to go back and live in caves. We don't have to give up music or art or literature or learning. What's wrong is the measuring stick that we use to measure our economy. It's based on how much we buy—consumerism. The Dow Jones Average. The gross national product, or gross domestic product. All these things don't measure the well-being factor. Now that's kind of hard to measure, because it's not as simple. When you look at all the things that are wrecked just by people shooting and messing up and destroying them, it seems that we've become a nation of small terrorists within our own borders. It's almost that it's a disease. The way to cure it is to realize it's not going to get us anywhere.

I suppose all through civilization and man's recording of it, there have been ups and downs. You would think after the Black Plague or after the Thirty Years' War things would have changed. But the thing is, our technology has expanded so much faster than our collective wisdom. We sort of are victims of our own cleverness. Of the things that we've invented. Before, these things happened to whole societies. Bad things always were happening. From the fall of the Greeks and the Roman Empire and so forth, but always there was somewhere else to go or more resources to get from someplace else. I think historically that's what happened with the United States. Everybody that was a mess in Europe, they came over here. Then they came all the way west and then they came north. Now there's no place else to go. Even Antarctica's not going to last long.

The question is what is going to happen. That's when you have to do what other societies have done. To live within your income. Like you do individually. Tear up your credit card, and don't use more of your income than you know you have. In society, you don't spend your capital. You aim to live off your interest, and don't ever destroy your capital. We think of capital as money, but capital is your natural resources. There have been books written about this. There's a wonderful one by Lester Brown, who is head of the Earth Policy Institute, called *Eco-Economy*.[121] Brown points out that the measuring sticks that we use and the symbols that we go by are the problem: the stock market, the gross national product, how much people are spending. How it's a commodification of everything. But he says the answer isn't socialism, because that didn't work either. The nearest thing is a system of cooperatives, instead of the big corporations. If we don't do something about it, it's going to be hard times. And maybe the end of the human race. My own personal philosophy is that I'm not sure the human race is going to make it.

Ginny backpacking in Denali National Park, circa 1960. Courtesy of Ginny Wood.

18

Tundra Treks: Guiding Wilderness Trips

Everywhere you are, you're somewhere.

B y the time Ginny Wood was a teenager, her summer jobs included leading backcountry horseback-riding trips. It is here that she developed talents as a skillful and knowledgeable guide, and learned the basics of how to outfit a group trip with sufficient food and supplies. In today's world of high-tech equipment and gear (waterproof and breathable fabrics like Gore-Tex; lightweight insulation like Thinsulate; self-inflating padded air mattresses; GPS navigational aides; or sturdy hiking boots), we would not recognize some of the equipment Ginny used in those early years. As she explains:

I began my guiding career back in the middle ages. At age sixteen, I was put in charge of a group from Campfire Girl camp for a five-day hike up to the base of Glacier Peak in the Cascades. In those days, for sleeping bags we carried two blankets arranged into an envelope and rolled up like a sausage with both ends tied together. This we looped over the shoulder and wore across the chest. We called it a bedroll and it also served as our pack. You put your extra clothes in one end—I think this consisted of a sweatshirt and a wool jacket—and the grub in the other.

Grub, as I remember it, consisted of a Hershey bar and a disk of pilot bread for lunch. For breakfast—eggs, bacon, and Bisquick. You fried the eggs on a flat hot rock heated in a campfire with a fifty percent chance of them running off onto the ground and a ninety percent chance of them being seasoned with sand. You wrapped the Bisquick dough around a shaved green stick and baked it over the coals. I seem to remember that what you ate was burned crust on the outside and raw dough in the inside when you slipped this creation off the stick. Butter and jam made it palatable. For supper we usually had pork and beans heated in the can and potatoes baked—well, half baked, anyway—in hot ashes. Then of course there was the usual burned-to-a-crisp marshmallow squashed between two graham crackers.

If this sounds like pretty cumbersome supplies and equipment, remember, we weren't burdened down in those days with all these handy-dandy two-ounce items that you just can't be without nowadays. They didn't make them then.

I was twenty-seven before I owned my first tent and over thirty before I began to use an air mattress. If the weather was bad when it came time to camp, you cut down a few saplings, lashed them to trees, and constructed a lean-to with fir boughs and your poncho for a roof. If you wanted comfort, you made a bough bed. The art of making a proper bough bed has died out with the advent of the air mattress, the foam pad, and environmentalism.

I climbed Mount Rainier in 1940 wearing mountain boots cleated with Tricouni nails before the days of Vibram soles. We roped up with a double bowline harness, and carried ropes with Prusik knots[1] instead of Jumars[2] for self-rescue if we fell in a crevasse. Everything we thought we needed for scaling a fourteen-thousand-foot peak fitted into a Bergen rucksack the size of a present-day day pack. We slept on our packs and the climbing rope for protection from the snow. And—well—you wouldn't believe our crampons!

All this gives you a rough idea of my vintage and where I have come from. Recent technology has given us frame and soft packs, ripstop nylon, Gore-Tex, polypropylene, MSR primus stoves, and freeze-dried prepackaged meals. It has also given us air transportation that makes wilderness trips to the most remote areas of the world available, affordable, and possible for the many instead of the few.

It also means that post–World War II generations of backpackers, moun-taineers, and river runners have substituted lightweight, more efficient, and less cumbersome equipment for a knowledge of wood lore and the wilderness skills of the backwoodsman. How to cook over a campfire and craft bough beds is no longer a necessary know-how for the backcountry traveler. In fact, the practice of this lore has become undesirable and downright anti-environmental, simply because there are too many of us invading the backcountry and the high places for us to make use of nature's bounty for our needs and comforts. Living off the land by use of the axe, the sheath knife, and the rifle have given way to new skills—that of how to travel gently over the land, leaving as few traces as pos-sible behind.

I must admit that I mourn a bit the passing of the old ways. I still feel that camping without a campfire has no soul. One doesn't have the same camaraderie gathered around a primus stove. And I find much of the new way a bit too gadgety, trendy, and commercial. One is tempted to have to have the latest in boots, packs, tents, stoves—and specialized clothing to match each outdoor activity.[3]

World War II gave us all these machines, airplanes, and money to buy tents and packs. And then all the sporting good shops started carrying all this army surplus equipment. My first sleeping bags were army surplus ones. And so you had this equipment that you never could have bought when I was a little kid.

I wouldn't think I needed it. I think it was the technology becoming affordable and vacations becoming longer after the war that changed things. Life looked pretty good and was more promising for jobs. That started more people going out camping and backpacking.

I bought my first real hiking boots and tent at REI. When I first belonged to REI, it was just a little shop in Seattle. It was two stories upstairs in a building with three rooms. You went in there and they just had a list of things you could buy through them as a co-op. All that they had was what was on that list. They didn't have all the variety they do now.

After Ginny and Celia sold Camp Denali in 1975, Ginny had to find another way to fulfill her passion for outdoor adventure. She had led trips at Camp Denali, and while still running Camp had already started periodically outfitting and guiding Sierra Club groups coming to Alaska.

At Camp Denali, we had an outdoor program called the Wilderness Workshop, which was more emphasizing natural history, and then another one called Tundra Treks, where we did multi-day backpacking trips. In the meantime, I had done a couple of trips for the Sierra Club back up in the Brooks Range. At their request, I'd been an assistant guide. Then I decided the Sierra Club and Wilderness Society were sending too many people on their trips. I thought there should be less.

One year, Woody and I were Outside visiting and David Brower, who was an early Sierra Clubber, heard we were there and he asked us into his office.[4] He said that he wanted to have a hike up in Alaska in McKinley Park. They wanted to know if we'd run it. He wanted it for seventy-five people! Woody and I said, "Not with seventy-five people!" He said, "You don't know how well organized we do our trips." They didn't even understand the situation. We said that you can't have seventy-five. That's just a convention!

Ginny first worked as a guide for other folks, but it was a natural progression for her to expand her operation and start her own guiding business.

The next summer after we sold Camp Denali, I had a chance to go up into the upper Shungnak area with a friend, Deborah Voight, who had staked some land up there because she wanted to do this wilderness trip thing. That would be the head-waters of the Shungnak River, where the Gates of the Arctic National Park is now. She wanted to have a base camp up there from which to lead hikes. I was asked to come on up, and while they were building the first cabin I was supposed to just wander around and scout out the territory. Do a lot of hiking around for possible places for them to take people out on trips. They were looking around for other rivers and other places that nobody else was on. Only it snowed and it blowed and it rained and you couldn't see more than two hundred feet high. I wanted to go over the pass and down into the next drainage, but it was zero, zero ceiling, so I never did get up in the mountains. All I did was peel logs. We cut logs and peeled them, and got them all ready for them to be put into the cabin. And then another guy went in and finished the cabin in the wintertime. That was my first time in that part of the Brooks Range. I had been farther west before when I had been flying up there and getting weathered in at villages, but this was the first time that I had been on the ground out in the country. And in that particular area.

I ended up doing some guiding for Deborah Voight and her boyfriend, Bob Waldrup. Deborah wanted to go to law school and he wanted to be a business-man down in southeastern Alaska, so she wanted to know if I wanted to take over their trips. And so I did that for a while. The only problem with Bob was he was a nut on equipment. Just take as little as possible. So he'd take the primus stoves and completely tear them apart to save weight. And then you'd inherit it and you had to try to figure out how to make it work. He liked to take the guys that did really, really tough trips. I mean really "he-man" stuff. So I never did any trips with him, just with Deborah. I ran their business for a couple of years and then finally, they just decided to pull out. They went on to other things.

I just took over their trips, but not their equipment. They would come out from a trip and just throw all the gear in a trailer. And then when you needed something the next time, you were supposed to find the parts and put everything back together again. I didn't like that, so that's when I just went on my own, to do my own trips. I had all the equipment—tents, sleeping bags, packs, stoves—from my Camp Denali trips, so I just started doing it. Since I had the name, I started calling my guiding business Tundra Treks. I just started guiding. There weren't regulations about it back then.

Then the Sierra Club, the Wilderness Society, and some of the other envi-ronmental organizations were running pack trips and river trips and horseback trips with the idea of getting more people into the backcountry, so then you'd have more people who would be fighting to save it. But what was happening there was it was getting overcrowded. So there were several Wilderness Society trips that were sent up here to Alaska and I was their outfitter and guide up in the Brooks Range. I told them I would meet some of their groups, not very often, but every once in a while. They were sending up trips of fifteen to twenty-five people. Plus they had their own leader, too. It was better than when they would send seventy-five people, but it was still too many. I said I would not take that many people on a trip.

I told Celia, who was living in Washington, DC, and was the interim direc-tor of the Wilderness Society, that I was embarrassed to have that many people up in the Brooks Range. I said, "I don't like to come in at Kaktovik with such a large group. I am embarrassed to come in with that many people. The last time they'd come in, they couldn't put all of the camping gear and food on the first flight that we'd been waiting for." I said, "Celia, this is crazy." That's too many people to have in the wilderness! Not only for what it does to the physical land-scape, but it becomes a social occasion, rather than it being about the wilder-ness there. I found as soon as you get a large group of people they just have a lot of fun talking to each other. It shouldn't be just yak, yak, yak all of the time and you don't even notice where you are. You miss wildlife because you're too busy yakking to each other to notice much. Or they don't feel like they're exploring as much. And then I felt that it was bad publicity for the very environmental organizations that were fighting to save these places, if they were the ones that were mucking it up by having too many people in one spot.

Keeping our groups small is a good way to disperse our impact. Wear and tear on the wilderness appears to take place in geometric proportion to the number in your party. Size contributes to other problems—air charter logistics, the diminished opportunities to observe wildlife, finding a suitable campsite for more tents, keeping track of a strung-out party, and large-quantity cooking.

Minimum impact is not just an ethic of environmentalism, it is an impera-tive if wilderness is to survive, and for us as outdoor recreational professionals to survive. Wilderness is our resource, and it is even more finite and irreplaceable than oil or minerals. When wilderness vanishes, our way of life as a means of making a living vanishes—or at best is diluted.

Minimum impact has several aspects and components. My consideration of it came about not out of any environmental concern, but because of the impact on me. It was during the early years of the war. I had a summer job herding people on horses for afternoon rides at a dude ranch in the Sierras. The draft began to take its toll on the cowhands who handled the horses and pack trips. In desperation, the job was offered to me and another girl. The way the back-country trips had been operating was that the management scheduled the trips, the cookhouse crew made up the menus and put up the grub, and the cowboys packed the horses and took out the dudes.

When we took over the latter operation, we discovered we were loading one packhorse for every two persons. For ten people for three breakfasts, the cook house sent out a No. 10 tin of jam, a three-pound can of coffee, and a gallon of syrup. Other meals were proportional. We soon streamlined that operation by taking charge of the menus and putting up the grub ourselves. Not only did we reduce the number of horses we needed to pack and take care of at night, but we practically eliminated hauling back or disposing of leftovers.

And then one summer in the late 1970s, I had occasion to be just a guide, not an outfitter, for a Mountain Travel base camp trip to the Arctic Wildlife Range. The equipment was furnished by them for eleven people. It included regular kitchenware that didn't nest and had little to do with menus. The proce-dure had been for guides of Mountain Travel trips to buy their grub at Safeway en route to the Arctic. They would be set down in the bush with their food in paper bags and cardboard boxes unsorted, quite often in the rain. Even though this was a base camp trip with just day hikes, which assumes (erroneously) that weight is not a consideration, I did my usual thing of repackaging, measuring out exact portions, and combining ingredients as much as possible. And I substituted my own lighter-weight nesting cook gear. Even so, I was embarrassed by the pile of equipment we unloaded at Barter Island. I felt a bit better when Walt Audi, the bush pilot there then,[5] remarked that this was about half the amount Mountain Travel groups usually brought.[6]

Then I met Ramona Finnoff, and she guided for me. Later Ramona and I and three guys—Steve Hackett, Brian Okonek, and Bob Jacobs—thought that as a group we could pool our guiding experiences, so we joined together and called our business Alaska Backcountry Guides.[7] Some were mountain climbers, some were backpackers, some were good at kayaking water, and some were good at all three. I was the backpacking one, mostly. Insurance was so expensive, and you just couldn't guide that much to make enough money to pay for it, so what we wanted to do was combine our resources. Our idea was that we could get an insurance policy to cover all of us that would be cheaper than each of us getting single coverage. We thought, "Why don't we call ourselves a cooperative?" What we would do was each have our own guiding service, but we would pool our equipment and borrow each other's equipment, and we would guide for each other. Whoever needed an extra guide, you know, back and forth. One time somebody that you were working with, well, that was his trip and you were the assistant. And the next time he was your assistant. We'd take turns shifting around. But we each guided separately. We each did our own thing. Also, we were just starting to get into rafting besides hiking and climbing, and none of us had the equipment to outfit for all types of trips, to have everything that was needed. So by borrowing and trading each other's equipment around, we didn't have to outfit ourselves with all these rafts and other gear. But we were still able to expand our operations. There were very few people doing it at that time. Rarely did you see any other party, either on the rivers or hiking. When I quit, more and more people were just starting to get into guiding and doing these types of trips.

Well, this cooperative looked good on paper. And it worked fine for several years. But then the insurance started getting where you couldn't do this. The National Park Service, the Forest Service, and the others wouldn't accept that we could be insured this way. We also realized that with the insurance that we had to have, whatever happened to one of us, the other ones would be liable for it. Each one of us could be sued individually. When we started, nobody thought about liability. People didn't sue. But we had one guy who we thought was a hazard, and with this setup we worried about how that could affect the rest of us. He was not irresponsible. He was a charming guy, an awfully likeable guy. But he just wasn't the safest. That made us think that maybe it wasn't such

Being dropped off in a floatplane, Brooks Range, 1971. Photo by Ginny Wood.

a good idea to all be together in a business like this. We didn't want him on our team.

Our main thing was when we decided that this rafting thing was some-thing, then we started to get a lot of people on raft trips. These were people that probably were capable of climbing Mount McKinley and maybe did, they were responsible, they knew how to camp, but they were in their sixties and didn't want to carry sixty-pound packs anymore. So you got some really neat people who knew how to pitch a tent, and where to pitch it, and were sure to close it up when you left so it didn't get rain inside, or dumb things like that. But they just were not up to something more strenuous than a float trip.

For a guide it was complicated to get up there to the Brooks Range. You had the problem of flying in using commercial operators to Kaktovik or Bettles, and then you had to go by small three-passenger planes to land on a lake or the tun-dra or a gravel bar on a river where you began your trip. Like Wien Airlines was running daily flights that got you to Kaktovik and then you had to get Walt Audi or somebody to fly you back up into the mountains for the trip. Your problem was always the logistics, because you would have to send people out two by two because usually it was a small plane. You just can't have big planes up there. You have to divide up the people and they have never even been in the area before. You had to be sure that everybody that went out had tents, grub, primus stove and gasoline for the stove, and everything they needed so they could be independent in case bad weather prevented the next plane from getting out there. You had to be sure that everyone could be self-sufficient for a couple of days if you, as the guide, didn't get out there with them. Then you had the other ones left behind at the airstrip, so you had to have enough for them, too. Pretty soon, you've got more of your people out there than you've got in the village, but you've got to be sure that everyone has what they need. So as people kept going out, you had to keep readjusting the logistics to be sure that no matter what happened, if you can't do all the flights in one day or even if it took two or three days to get everyone out there, each group could be independent. Otherwise, you have people stuck. And that's a pain in the neck. You didn't want to show your apprehension about maybe getting stuck, because you don't want your clients worrying about that. The more people you have, the more chances this can happen. The lesson is, if you're going to have a group, then don't have too many people. Then you can all do the same thing.

And there are the problems you lay on your bush pilot as well as yourself that are directly proportional to the size of your group and the amount of your gear. The more trips he has to make to relay you in and out, the more chance there is that weather can interfere. This can result in the pilot having to take risks.[8]

And then there is the packaging of the food you carry. For my convenience, I like to prepackage, portion out, and combine as many ingredients as possible in my kitchen rather than do it out on my trip—like when it is raining or so cold you have to do it with mittens on. It's amazing how much bulk you can eliminate by combining the milk and the sauces with whatever glop that's on the menu, and leaving the tinfoil, the cellophane, and the plastic at home instead of having to pack it out.

Eventually I got out of the guiding and outfitter business. I decided that I was getting too old, and if I had an accident, what could I do? Could I get the person out? Clients might start to think, "She's a woman and she's old." So they wouldn't sign up for my trips. And I could be sued if something happened on a trip. Even though I was very careful and I'd never had any problems, all it would take was to have something happen once. You know, when you're on rivers in the backcountry things happen in boats. And it can happen on just a little simple hike. Somebody can stumble and fall. And there's bears. The chance of somebody getting hurt or dying is pretty high. All you had to do was have an accident and get sued. I couldn't afford that. When I first came up here, you didn't have to worry about being sued. Nobody sued in Alaska because there weren't any insurance agents to insure with up here. Anybody who wanted to sue would have to bring up their own lawyers. And what could they get from me? My guiding business? My house? The property I still owned at Denali National Park? Well, none of that was worth very much back then.

So I quit being a guide outfitter, and just guided for other people running guiding businesses.[9] I was available for anybody that needed an extra guide or an extra boatman for rafting trips. I was for hire, whoever wanted me. I guided for Ramona Finnoff, who owned ABEC's Alaska Adventures. She guided for me when she was first starting out, so we turned it around. I guided for Jim Campbell and Carol Kasza, who own Arctic Treks. I guided for Alaska Discovery and some of the other outfitters. There was always somebody who needed an extra guide or an extra boatman. By that time I was doing more raft trips than I was hiking trips. After doing it for so long and after running Camp Denali for twenty-five years, I didn't want to guide at the pace and the amount of time that was necessary to keep a business going. So it worked out fine. The last time I was actually an official guide was for Alaska Discovery up on the Kobuk River. That would have been about 1990, maybe.

I learned all my water skills from Ramona. I'd always been around water and I'd always been in canoes, but not kayaks, and I'd never done rafts. So I learned it all from Ramona, who's tops. Of all the guides that I guided for, or with, I kind of liked her style the best, and I liked her. Ramona has a quality that you wouldn't know unless you've guided with her. I don't think she's aware of it herself. She always senses the person that's being left out in a group. Instinctively she brings that person into the group. It's very subtle, but I sensed it right away. Realizing that she was not out in the front leading the group, but instead she was back hiking with the slowest person. Or she'll say after supper, "Do you want to go for a little midnight stroll?" Ramona is a wonderful person for empathizing with the other person. She doesn't kowtow to them or pamper them, but she makes them feel comfortable. There's always an oddball in the group that doesn't seem to fit in. Or maybe they're shy. Or maybe they're scared and afraid they aren't keeping up with everybody. And Ramona always brings them into the group.

The other thing, she very much had a feeling that you don't want to be an impact on the environment. We both kind of developed that. It was a feeling that you keep your groups small. That you are careful what you do with your garbage to keep the bears away and to not leave a trace. And that you don't want to stay in one place and trample it. You get to learn that the tundra is a very fragile ecosystem. That if you have a small enough group you realize what you're doing, that you're out there. You listen to the wilderness. You're observing, you're learning. You're part of it and you don't spoil it.

And that of course you pack out all your garbage! I must say that I recall with shame those days when I was a good little Girl Scout if I buried or burned my refuse—tin cans and all. Now we know that even in temperate climes, buried cans, plastic, and tinfoil heave up to the surface with the passage of time. Up here, permafrost and seasonal frost can do it in a year, and ground temperatures in Alaska embalm your trash instead of decaying it. Then there is always that client who, if you have a campfire, assumes that anything they put in it will burn, tinfoil and all. You can reduce the bulk of your refuse and certainly eliminate odors if you burn it, but if you do, you need to be sure to rake the coals for the remnants and carry them out.

If this sounds pretty purist, consider that in most parks and wilderness areas in the States, campfires are no longer allowed—period. It's not just the attrition of firewood, but with all the use the backcountry is getting nowadays, the wilderness is getting pockmarked with fire pits and smoke-blackened rocks. So what's repulsive about that? Well, when others see the remains of a campfire, most assume that this must be the place you are supposed to camp, and they do, thus concentrating more trampling, firewood gathering, unburned garbage in the fire pits, and toilet paper. For others, it dilutes the wilderness aesthetically to come onto fire rings, for it just says that the masses have been here before you. It's like the difference between when I first saw the Arrigetch Peaks country in 1971 and when I next returned in 1979. The grandeur of the peaks was intact, but everywhere I hiked during our six-day stay, I saw the imprint of Vibram soles or a twist tie. One delightful knoll that I remembered ankle deep in reindeer moss was now bald and studded with fire pits and ditches around old tent sites.

We can't erase our footprints, and I leave just as many as anyone else, but we can help keep that pristine feeling of Alaska's wilderness extant a little longer if we destroy all evidence of our campfires and camping spots by dismantling our fire rings and covering our ashes. Changing from lugged boots to softer-soled footwear can reduce that rumpled look the tundra gets when you camp with a group, especially for more than one night. Another thing I try to do is not use the same campsite each time I use the same route or destination year after year. Some areas need a rest, so vegetation can recover from over use.[10]

I think the thing that I liked about exploring the tundra and the guiding and our experience in Katmai, in McKinley Park, and in the Brooks Range was that there weren't any trails except for animal ones. And they go across the water where you can't wade like they can, so that's the end of the trail. The thing about exploring in a trail-less place is that there wasn't some sign that said it was so many miles to Lost Lake or Cloudy Pass. There isn't a destination. You're not sure where you're going and you don't know where you're going to camp, because there isn't a trail, so everywhere you are, you're somewhere. In big groups, folks would always say, "Well, when are we going to get there?" I said, "Where's there?" And they said, "Well, where are we gonna camp?" And I said, "Well, I don't know. When we find a good place, and we're tired. We'll see where we are when it's time to make camp. We have twenty-four hours of daylight, so we can pick any part of it to be camp time." It isn't like when you are hiking in the States where in your mind, yes, you notice things along the way and you know it's a good hike, but you don't feel like you're there until you get to the sign that says where you were going. Up here in Alaska there are no signs. You're exploring all the time, trying to find the best place to cross the river, finding your way as you go. I think the concept that we have to get "there" or "we haven't arrived" is bad.

Then you learn to prospect your route because you get to know the foliage. You learn which vegetation is easy walking and which isn't. I used my

A hiker scans her surroundings, 1961. Photo by Ginny Wood.

binoculars as much for looking for routes as I did for seeing wildlife. Binocs are the best guide you can have. Sometimes they can be more important than a compass. By looking at a slope, you can tell by the vegetation that it's going to be easy walking in one place or that it's going to be tough in another. Like if there are lots of obvious bushes in a hollow or a gully, you know that's going to be trouble walking through it. Your pack will catch on all that thick brush. Or you look at the type of tundra. If it's wet tundra that looks swampy, you want to avoid that. That's where your feet get wet between all the tussocks. It's easier walking on the drier tundra that's more solid and which often is higher up or on the tops of ridges. Sometimes you don't always have a choice or you misjudge, but it's that awareness that keeps you always part of it. You're just always aware of what the plants are and where they are. You're also aware of wildlife and what to do around bears and how to handle them. And how to observe them so that you watch them and what they're doing, but you don't disturb them.

The wildlife you see adds another dimension to the total wilderness experience. As the late author Lois Crisler said, "Landscapes without wildlife is only scenery." Most people on trips will carry a camera, and everyone is a trophy hunter or a collector of some sort. The art of simply appreciating wildlife by just observing it died out with the invention of the Kodak Brownie camera. Wildlife can be captured on film without harassing it. This way you are sharing the wilderness, not invading it. A stampede to get a good picture before someone else does not only spooks the animal for others, but can separate mother from offspring, interrupt feeding, and if it's a bear or a moose with young, may add to the cumulative irritation that animal has about encounters with mankind. One day they take this irritation out on someone—perhaps you.[11] I always say if you can take a picture of an animal—whether it's a bear or a moose or even a squirrel—and you get your picture and he goes on doing whatever he was doing when you first saw him, then you're a photographer. Otherwise, you're just harassing animals and you're just a picture snapper. You're like a tourist with a camera that just runs up to get the picture. Like with moose. A moose is in the pond and he puts his head down because he likes to eat that grass under water. So you move up to get a closer picture. I'd say to people, "The minute he starts to put his head up, everybody just stand still. Absolutely stop. When he puts his head down again, move up. And if he gives any indication of being perturbed, just retreat."

And then there is always the person who wants to feed a cute little critter, either from a misguided welfare concern or to get a closer picture. Most don't realize the consequences, and you have to point them out. First, feeding an animal people food is not doing them a favor, especially the young. They have the summer to learn to fend for themselves or they die. Learning to cadge crumbs from campers isn't going to do them any good come winter. The other point is that beasties learn quickly to associate people with food if you are careless with it. So don't give them a chance by allowing others to feed them or by leaving food or scraps around for them to sample. I have found that putting mothballs around my grub bags either disguises the smell or repels the animal. The critter that chewed into your tent to get a candy bar or the peanuts left there learned to do this from careless campers before you, if not from your own group. If the critter is a bear or a wolverine that associates packs and tents with food, the situation can get grim.[12]

You had your sleeping bag and your tent and your grub with you, and you realize that the people that first came in there didn't have those things. They had to live off the land. We can't do that anymore, because there wouldn't be anything left if everybody was doing it. Now there are just too many people in the backcountry. When we had Camp Denali, I had all of McKinley Park to myself. In 1960, when I first started Tundra Treks in connection with Camp, we hardly ever saw anybody in the backcountry, except for an occasional seasonal ranger on his day off. We had the valleys, ridges, and the tundra expanses all to ourselves, and we felt our mission was to proselytize to others to get out and see, feel, and experience what encountering the wilderness on foot was all about. It wasn't until the early 1970s that we began to meet other hikers. By 1974, backpacking had become so popular that the Park Service was forced to put a quota on the number of backcountry users who could be in any one area at any time.

Young Romany hikes behind Celia, circa 1960. Photo by Ginny Wood.

This was done not only to protect the environment, and the impact on wildlife, but also to preserve a wilderness experience for the user. Yet by the very act of rationing wilderness by decree, necessary though it was, the essence of wilderness was diluted philosophically for me.[13]

In my going to the Brooks Range, I was able to get that same feeling of wilderness and being alone that I'd found early on in McKinley Park. But what you're afraid is that something like Princess Tours or a West Tours or someone will want to put a lodge up there. And then they would be able to run backcountry trips from there and do just what they've done to the Colorado River. You pay a lot of money to get a permit on the Colorado River, and then you have to buy somebody else's who's quitting and not using theirs. Like they do for fishing or something like that. A quota system. It would be just terrible. Although I do realize that in my doing trips in the Brooks Range I might have become part of the problem that could result in a quota system in the Gates of the Arctic National Park. If we ration ourselves, perhaps we can be part of a solution to forestall this dreadful day.[14] As long as there aren't any roads, I don't think we have to worry. I think it can be preserved, if you just keep it the way it is and you don't do any roads. If people have to walk, I don't think it's going to get too crowded. Or if you don't find oil on it.

One of my favorite things about doing these kinds of trips was just being in that country. And I enjoyed the people. Sometimes you had some duds, but usually that was a very small number. It was more like just having good companions on a trip. It was a social thing. And quite often you had very interesting people who were very well known in their own field. Especially when I started to do the rafting as a boatman, you had lots of people in their fifties and sixties for whom carrying a sixty-pound pack wasn't doable anymore. When backpacking, you almost had to have at least fifty pounds or you weren't pulling your weight when you've started with sharing the food and everything. You needed to be self-equipped for all the changes in weather with your tent and so forth. So rafting meant that people who were older and may have been active throughout their lives but now they didn't want to or couldn't carry their stuff but who liked wilderness—who had been mountain climbers, had done a lot of backpacking, or maybe a lot of canoeing and stuff—they could still come on a trip. Our rafting trips were really not just boat trips but were more of what I call floating base camps. We would camp someplace for a couple of days and then everybody would day hike. But they didn't have to carry the heavy loads of backpacking. A lot of people can hike for a long time with a little pack with their lunch in a bag and their raincoat, but they don't want to carry sixty pounds anymore. Mainly it was on those hikes where you got to talk with people and get to know them. It was very interesting to hear places other people had been and what they had done.

I got a certain sort of satisfaction of introducing people to the tundra biome. And to the wildlife. You know, you do a lot of hiking in the States before you ever see a bear, and you probably will never see a wolverine or a caribou. I think that was a big thrill for people coming to Alaska. Especially if you see a whole bunch of caribou at once. Often I would get everybody to bed at night because they were pooped, and so was I, but then I hiked until three or four in the morning. I'd go off exploring on my own and cover a lot of ground. You could almost always count on it raining, so you had to have a layover day when the weather was bad, and that's when I figured I could catch up on a little sleep, too.

We never planned our itineraries so closely. Usually there were reasons for taking an extra day at some campsite. Sometimes it was because of bad weather. Or maybe it was just that the water was too high to cross a side creek, because it had been raining in the hills, and it got a little too dangerous. And you'd have to camp an extra day until it went down. Or everybody said, "Hey, could we stay here another day? I want to do this. I want to do that." We didn't necessarily all do it together. A lot of them were so experienced, they went off on their own.

We used to have three-week trips and we got resupplied with airdrops. They don't do that anymore. Now, you take it all with you. But when we did have airdrops, I had to stay in camp until we'd gotten our airdrop. While everyone else was out hiking, I had to go find where the stuff landed. There were sometimes when the airdrop might not get there until six o'clock at night. In order for things to survive being dropped from an airplane, you had to pack it for that. You really have to have somebody there when it drops, both for the pilot and also for yourself. When he flew over, it was good if you were up waving something like a red tarp, so he could see you better. Then you had to be there so you could see where things landed, like one piece here and another that went a little bit over there. It was easier to go retrieve everything if you saw where it landed.

A few words on airdrops in general from out of my experience, both on the delivery and the receiving end. It does have a bearing on minimum impact, because sloppy packaging can result in your groceries being splattered all over the landscape or your being delivered packaging you can't burn and have to carry out. There are still some five-gallon tins sitting on the upper Arrigetch Creek that one party had dropped to them. The plane and pilot can also be impacted fatally trying to deliver your provender to a spot you picked for the drop that was hazardous to their health. You should pick a place that is convenient for the pilot, not just for you, preferably with good approaches and with soft tundra where the drop packages won't be smashed by rocks and trees. And don't put strike-anywhere matches in the drop! We had one package burst into flames on impact because someone packed kitchen matches in it.[15]

People would come back to camp after being on their day hike and tell me about their neat hikes and this wonderful place where they'd been and so forth. So I'd feed everybody and after supper I would take off on my hike. I'd hike all night just to see what they'd seen. Sometimes I'd come back in around four in the morning. Or sometimes just in time to get breakfast started. I did this just because I wanted to see, you know. I wanted to go over in that drainage or I wanted to see what was on the other side of that ridge or whatever. I would do it at "night" because otherwise I wouldn't get to see all that neat country. And you were young and you had all this energy that you'd get in the summertime when there was so much daylight. It's just sort of like your energy seems to match the sun's.

We usually had to get to a certain spot at the end of the trip for an airplane pickup on a particular date. It was not the kind of trip where on Thursday we do this and Friday we do that. You could do whatever you wanted with the time. But you had to get to your take-out point, where the plane was supposed to pick you up. It worked out because you just allow that in your schedule. But there were times where we just had to keep paddling. All day. And other times when we could be more relaxed. But you went on the trip knowing what could happen, so you'd just plan for having three or four layover days in a ten-day trip.

When I started, we used to take three-week trips. That was a normal trip then. People stayed longer in Alaska, because it took longer to get here. What has happened now is that everybody mostly gets a two-week vacation where mama wants to do this and dad wants to do that. So we started having two-week trips. Then it got down to where we found out that the ten-day ones sold the most. Where they'd use the two weekends so they only had to take a week's vacation time from work. One weekend to get here and another week to get out in the wilderness. They have a trip begin on a weekend, where they get themselves to Alaska and leave the next morning to go out into the wilderness without getting to catch up on sleep or anything. So you're actually only on the trip ten days. And then they can get other vacations too, to go somewhere else or go where the wife wants to go or where they can get someone to take care of the kids, or whatever. That's the tourist business now. But in the old days, tourists came up to Alaska for three months at a time. By the time they came up on the boat and took the train, then they'd go by horseback for three weeks back into McKinley Park. People took time back then. Some people, I don't know how they have their vacations now. They must go home exhausted.

While Ginny thoroughly enjoyed being a guide and sharing her love of Alaska's wild places with visitors from around the world, it was not always easy. Travel in Alaska can be difficult. Sudden weather changes can quickly destroy even the best-laid plans. Being a good guide meant being prepared for the unexpected, being flexible, and remaining calm in what others might consider to be disastrous or dangerous circumstances. Ginny had her fair share of difficulties, but she always retained her fortitude and took her responsibility as a guide seriously so that all her clients made it home safely.

Some times things didn't go as scheduled. Going up to the Arctic or into the Brooks Range, you'd go up on a scheduled flight, then you would have to go with Walt Audi, two by two in a small plane, back up into the mountains to the headwaters. And then you'd either be in the mountains hiking around or else you'd get there, launch your boat, and float it back out to the Arctic Ocean.

What's really interesting is that when you'd first go in, everybody wanted to be the first one in. Usually it was a guy, and he'd say, "So, is there any chance of me being the first one in the plane?" When you got there, they'd say, "Oh wow, this place is fantastic. I could stay here forever. I don't care if the plane never comes back. Can I be the last one out?" Then after you've had your trip and they've been very good sports and good people, it's really funny when they get to the last day. You break camp and you have to roll up all the tents and the sleeping bags and you sit there on your baggage waiting for the airplane to come in. When it gets time for the plane to come in, each one wants to be the first one out, even if before they were the one that was going to stay there forever. They say, "Well, I've got a board meeting to go to on Monday." Or "I've got an important business meeting that I can't miss." Or "I have our babysitter just hired until today." All these things they now suddenly have to be back for. And then if the plane is late in coming in, they start to get antsy. They'll pace, wondering why the pilot wasn't there. I'd say, "It's probably because he's busy somewhere else." Or else you could look at the weather and say, "I wouldn't want to go back with him, even if he came. It's bad weather." You know, they fly twenty-four hours a day in the summer, so if they get a mechanical problem or the weather is bad, they will just come when they can, even if it is the middle of the night. People would get so they'd say to me, "Well, what are you going to do if the plane doesn't come?" And I said, "Well, I guess we'll just have to cross that bridge when it comes, huh? We've still got plenty of grub." It was funny to see this in people.

There was this one time when we had a bunch of wheels from the Wilderness Society on a trip. They were city boys. So while we were waiting for a plane to come in, they would just walk and pace the tundra, pace the beach, the sandbar. And finally they said, "Well, shouldn't he be here by now? Well, what if ...?" I said, "Look, why don't you just look at your watch and go out one direction and walk for half an hour and sit down. And stay there for half an hour. Then you come back and tell me what you saw." Because, you see, to them the trip's over. They're not taking anything in anymore. The feeling of "Oh my gosh, I could stay here forever" had worn off. So I'd make them do that and they'd come back and say, "I see what you mean. We feel like there's nothing here because we are already back home in our minds." It was always interesting to see how people that wanted to be the first in, and then wanted to be the first ones out, reacted. It wasn't that they hadn't had a good time, but in their minds now it had ended. The trip was over. And the plane should come. It's just funny to see how that happens if you have to wait for the plane. The plane usually came within twenty-four hours, because they can fly all night.

As Ginny explains, being a guide is not just a matter of being able to read a map, use a compass, and get from Point A to Point B. It is also people management. Individual personalities and group dynamics always come into play on multiperson trips. Keeping everyone happy and having fun is the goal, but it often can be challenging.

The group dynamics that happens with trips is as much of the guiding as anything else. Quite often groups gel. They find partners. Or quite often you have one that's a pill. On a trip where there is such a person, it brings everybody else together because they don't like this one person. And they usually aren't bad people, they're just kind of annoying. Or they're picky. Or they're difficult. But it's amazing how most of them shape up by the time it's over.

There's a time when your group sort of gels, and then you don't have to worry about anything. They may be skeptical at first. Sometimes they're testing you to see if you really know what you're doing. Especially if you're a gal. Then it usually becomes nothing. It's just the funniest thing. Sometimes on the second day, the third day, or maybe even the fourth day, they become comrades. They become a group. Then there's chatter back and forth among themselves and they're having a good time and they're getting used to that you aren't on a trail. That every place is open so you can go any direction you want. It's interesting watching a group come together. And then the little in-jokes that come whenever you're with a group. Kidding and laughing and talking. Talking about their kids, maybe, whatever. And then when you find them after we've made camp, they'll say, "Well, I'm going to go off in that direction for a while. I'll be back in two hours." I told people they didn't have to go in lockstep with each other, but I encouraged them to go off, preferably by twos, so if somebody gets hurt the other one can come back for help. I would say, "Just tell me which direction you're going and the estimated time you'll be gone."

The group dynamics are interesting to see develop. And there's always somebody—often a woman—who is not sure they wanted to come on the trip. They wanted to see the North, but they're not sure they can measure up, because they've never climbed Mount McKinley or done something like that. And so you find out very subtly something that they've done or a place that they've been that you can bring out. You just walk with them for a while and get to know them. Make them feel comfortable. Or after everybody's in bed, say, "Hey, do you want to go out for a little stroll?" You know, give them a little bit of extra attention to make them feel special. It's something that comes from somebody that is conscious of the people around them and does this without letting them know that you're doing this.

Then there comes a time when you're at your wit's end. Some of the times are worst on the river where it's been high water and you can't find a good beach to take out at for a camping spot. Everybody's hungry and tired and you just have to find something. You have to decide. So you say, "Well, I think this will do." Or, "Oh, I think this will do fine." It isn't very good, but it's all there is. By that time no one wants to be the poor sport. So they all put up with something and that becomes part of the adventure.

The most memorable trip I was on was this one Sierra Club trip. That was the first time I was in the Brooks Range. I was asked to be a co-leader. And there were sixteen people on it. I think the reason I was asked to be an assistant guide was because the Sierra Club wanted to use my garage for assembling all their food to prepare for the trip. See, they shipped it all up in boxes, and then in Fairbanks they had to break it down into bags by days, and so forth. I knew the guy who was the trip leader, Doug Powell. He'd been around before. He used to come into Camp Denali sometimes, scouting it out for a place for a possible future trip, I think. He was a good guy, an interesting guy. He was a geologist. He never got his PhD, because if he did he wouldn't get to do what he liked to do in the winter. That was, he worked for a government agency and skied the whole crest of the Sierras to calculate the amount of potential spring water runoff from the snowpack, because they get all their water from that. Eventually, he traveled all over the world doing that in any country where they get all their water from runoff from the mountains and they needed to calculate and predict it.

Anyway, Doug had planned this trip down the Alatna River, putting in way up at the headwaters. He was the leader and got me to be the outfitter. So we were flown in to the headwaters, two by two in a small plane. The pilot's name was Shanahan. He was quite a character. On the way flying up with him, he told us the day he'd come and pick us up and where, and where the places were for the airdrops that we were planning. He said, "Well, I have to write this down. I'm notorious for forgetting. When I get home, I give it to my wife and then she puts it on the blackboard." He said, "Well, you know, last year I was taking a bunch of hunters out during the hunting season. I put them down and then I had one after another of hunter groups that I was flying around after them." Then he said, "My gosh, I forgot where I put that first group of people, and what date I was to go get them, and which group they were. And I wasn't even sure which lake I had put them on." Well, this guy's flying twenty-four hours a day sometimes.

We were flown up to Gaedeke's cabins up there at the head of the Alatna River. Gaedeke said we could stay in his tent cabins up there. And he had one real cabin. I don't remember how I met him. But he said we could use his cabins. Doug had planned that we would all get into rafts there and go down the river. When we got there, we discovered there was so little water that you could jump across it. So we stayed there at the headwaters for almost a week. I was in charge of the food. That meant a lot of the cooking, too. I found out that I didn't like how the Sierra Club organized the food on their trips. They divided the group up in fours and then divided the food up in rations for four people. And then you had to share with the four in your group. The problem was, if you got a bunch of heavy eaters in one group, they never had enough, and the other group might be light eaters and they'd be throwing away food. This was crazy. I said, "Look, this is ridiculous, because some people aren't getting enough and other people are throwing it out. Why don't we just eat all together? We'll just put it all in one pot and everybody take what they want. Then it will even out and we don't have to worry about it and we won't waste any food." Well, Doug, who was the leader, he said, "Well, that's not the way we do it." I said, "Well, I'm doing it that way!" So we did that. I mussed up their whole system, which some of them were quite unhappy about. Another thing they did was that after breakfast everybody would put out their lunch stuff and let everybody get it. There was the usual stuff you had, including Wyler's grape juice crystals. Then they would start bargaining. Two of this is worth one stick of jerky or one piece of cheese. That Wyler's, you could give it away. Nobody wanted it. They weren't worth anything.

Well, anyway, Shanahan was supposed to come in and bring two days of grub and pick up extra things that you wouldn't need for two days, and then drop it at the next camp that Doug had picked. It was just beyond where you see the first spruce trees as you're hiking down the Alatna River. While we were up there waiting and eating up some of our food, Shanahan hadn't come, and he hadn't come. Doug finally said, "Well, I want to take half the group down to where the first spruce trees are. I'll take enough grub for two days. Then when Shanahan comes, tell him to drop everything down there. 'Cause we want to get going. Then you can come down with the rest of the group." Well, off they went. Three days and Shanahan still hadn't come to carry a few days of our grub and extra gear down ahead for us. In the meantime, Doug had said for everybody to go through their gear, and anything you don't need for two days for the walk down—any clothing you won't need, or any extra things you're carrying with you—should be put in a separate duffel bag and it will go with the airdrop that Shanahan would make to us. We knew where that drop would be. We'd picked out the spot when we were flying in with him. It was supposed to be where the first spruce forest started on the way down. Well, finally I realized Doug's group would be out of grub. It had been one day over what they had planned for. So, one guy in our group, who was one of the real old hands, Dave—he was a really neat older guy who'd been out hiking for years—said he'd stay up there waiting for the airplane and I would take down the rest of the group and everybody would carry as much grub as we possibly could down to Doug and the first group. Dave would wait until Shanahan came and have him make all the drops down from there. So we had to hike all night, getting down. And it was pouring rain. Everybody was bitter cold. We decided we'd just keep hiking. It was too wet to make camp. We got down there to rescue these people that were out of food with two days' supply of food for everybody. Then we waited another two or three days, still no Shanahan. The only thing that everybody had to eat was the Wyler's grape drink packets and this one kind of candy bar that nobody liked. We used to trade food. It was like a market day in some third-world country. Everybody trading. The Wyler's and this one type of candy bar were left because they were what nobody wanted. And it was August, so I said, "Look, everybody go out and pick lots of blueberries. Lots of them. And then bring me the grape Wyler's and those candy bars. I'm going to make a big stew out of that because there's lots of sugar and at least your tummy will feel full." I put that all in to sweeten the berries. That's what we had to eat that day.

In the meantime, I and another gal decided to hike up on the mountains back of us. Just a quick trip. I wanted to go someplace where I wasn't thinking about food all the time. While we were up there, we watched Shanahan fly over and drop our gear. But the last bag didn't drop. He was dropping it, kicking it out from the plane, and it got hung up on his rudder. We saw it dangling behind. He tried diving and trying to get it loose. But it didn't work. Then he flew off, hoping that maybe it would be there when he landed. But it wasn't there when he landed back in Bettles. If it had been, he would have come back up with it.

Inflating and repairing the rafts, Alatna River, 1971. Photo by Ginny Wood.

So anyway, we had a missing bag. It's up there in the mountains somewhere. It was the one bag with everybody's extra stuff in it. Along with my camera. Then, finally, down came Dave, who we'd left up top. He hiked down with all the food he could put in his pack.

When they got all the bags open and took the rafts out, they discovered that several of them were ripped, had gotten torn in the airdrop. Doug had just gone to the grocery store or something and gotten these little rubber rafts for $10.98 or whatever. They were just these cheap old things. One of the gals had been a home economics major so she was in charge of mending the rafts. She was a good sewer. So we stayed up all night patching them. We had needles going back and forth.

The plan had been that one group would raft one day, and then hike the next. And then switch. That's how we'd get down the river. Given the condition of our rafts, instead we decided that anybody that had any experience in boats or paddling anything was a boatman, and they would take half of the group in the rafts down to a spot that we picked out. It was to a stream that came in downstream a ways. Then the other half would walk, and we'd all meet down at that next place. So I became the leader of the boatmen, because I had had more experience in a boat than anybody else, which wasn't that much. Most of my boating experience had been sailing. And I'd canoed and I'd paddled before a little bit, so I was in charge of that. We took all the food we could carry.

By this time we had tons of food. We had too much food! Everybody had to carry as much as they could in the boats. And then we would start eating up the food, so it would get lighter. Well, we started off.

I at least had enough sense not to put anything in the bottom of my raft, like my crampons, that would bump against the rocks. You see, we were going to do some climbing in the Arrigetch Peaks country so we all had climbing gear with us. There still wasn't much water. You'd be walking a lot. Pretty soon, I started passing everybody 'cause everybody else's bottom of their rafts came out. As they came downriver, there would be the bottom of the raft coming first, floating by. Nobody's raft still had the bottom. The tubes were all right but the stiff floorboards had come out. It was like floating down the river in donuts! The only one that had a bottom was mine. So I could go faster than anybody else.

At one point, I came around the corner and here was this gal in the water up to her neck. She had been dumped from her boat after having gotten caught in a logjam. She was pulled underneath a bunch of driftwood and had fought her way out. Through just sheer brute strength, she'd gotten herself out and was keeping her head above water. We didn't have life jackets. Nobody had life jackets back then. And we were wearing hiking boots in the boats, too. In doing all this, she wrenched her knee badly. When I came around the corner, she was hanging on to her raft but I could tell that she was in great pain. She was in trouble. She was in shock and hypothermic. So I just got her ashore and quickly gathered a bunch of leaves together and made a little fire. The place where I'd taken her ashore was a good spot, because there was timber there and you could get a fire going. But it wasn't a place to camp. I got my sleeping bag out and put it over her. I realized that she was in no condition to walk. Then it started to rain. Then down came everybody else, people and rafts separate. In the meantime, when Doug came by, he said, "Well, there's a good place to camp across the river." So everybody went over there. We had to put the injured gal in my raft and tow it across the river so we would all be together at the campsite.

Then, Shanahan came. He wasn't supposed to drop for three more days, but he decided because he'd been so late before he'd give us another drop earlier. We camped there in the rain with all this food that we couldn't possibly get on rafts that didn't have any bottoms. And everybody was wet. I have one picture in my scrapbook where we're all sitting around a campfire. Everybody's got their socks on a stick trying to dry them over the fire. Everybody's looking pretty glum. They've got their sleeping bags around them. Trying to keep dry and get warm. And there's Doug looking a bit embarrassed and everybody looking at him as the leader and saying, "Who thought this trip up, anyway?" And we were wondering how badly this woman was injured. I mean, we were miles away from anything. We were up at the head of the Alatna River and we weren't supposed to be down for two weeks. We were going down to Takahula Lake.

Drying out along the Alatna River, 1971. Photo by Ginny Wood.

The next morning was bright and sunny. It was very warm. And we had beautiful weather for the next ten days. Everybody got very ingenious about their raft. The guys all went out in the woods and cut poles to put across the rafts so then they could carry everything on top of that. This would have been before that area was established as the Gates of the Arctic National Park, so you could still cut trees down. As the trip went on, people kept embellishing their boats. They ended up having one advantage over me, who still had the original bottom in my raft. When you're trying to get a raft ashore alone, there's nobody there to catch you if you're in moving water, so you try to go into an eddy. But you don't always have that choice. So it can be challenging. Well, anyway, I was the only one that had any trouble. They could just jump into the water and carry their rafts ashore. I couldn't do this with mine that still had the bottom. It was too heavy to pick up and it would scrape things along the shore, like sticks and rocks, so I couldn't drag it.

The plan was that we were supposed to trade off between rafting and hiking. The next night, the people who were hiking said, "No thanks. I don't want any of that rafting business. We'll all walk, thank you." Those of us who had taken rafts, we were already one day experienced, so nobody else wanted to be a boatman. All these people who thought they were going to sit in a raft and float down to Takahula Lake and hike up to Arrigetch Peaks and spend a week climbing, we thought, "Well that's out. This is a survival thing now just to see if we can get down to where we're going to be picked up."

When I first saw this group I thought, "Oh my gosh, am I going to spend three weeks with these guys?" I was about to say no to going on the trip. And this idea of there being three guides. I wasn't sure how that was going to work. Well, anyway, I never saw a group that got closer together. It was survival. Nobody complained. And how those guys decided they wanted to walk. They didn't want to be in those boats. And no one was wearing life vests. We didn't have room for them. And a lot of them were wearing their mountain boots 'cause we were going to go climbing for a month. And that's what got them in trouble. They put their ice axes and their crampons in the bottom of the boat, so when it bumped on the rocks, the bottoms collapsed. I didn't do this, I put my climbing gear on the top.

We had all kinds of adventures getting down. Luckily, we had very good weather. We got down to the Arrigetch only one day late. We only had six days down there instead of a week. We got down to Arrigetch Creek and left the rafts there. In the meantime, we got another airdrop from Shanahan. As planned, we went on up on the glacier in the Arrigetch Peaks. That was fantastic. It was beautiful. Nobody had been in there before that we knew of. There wasn't a sign of a person. That was probably one of my favorite or the most beautiful places. It was very hard getting up there, though. We went right up along the riverbank. We had to bash our way into it. We pushed our way through. I've been up there since and discovered there's a better way to go up than what we did. You think you can go along Arrigetch Creek and it will be easier. It isn't. So you think to go up high where it looks green, that will be better, and that's not it either. You have to thrash your way in. It was every man for himself to find the best route. There was none. Some would go high, and say, "It's better up." And some would go low and say, "No, it's better down." You just kept going up. Once we got above timberline it was easier. It wasn't easy getting there, but once you got up there it was wonderful. We made it up into this fantastically beautiful place. These fantastic granite spires. It was different than anything else I'd experienced before. And some of them were even glaciated. We made a base camp there and stayed for about five or six days. We had a wonderful time there climbing. There were no footprints. I don't think anybody else had been up there before us.

I almost stayed there for good. I was climbing a peak and a guy who was down below me suddenly told me to look up. There was a big boulder up above me that was slowly making its way downhill. It would roll a little ways and stop. Then it would start coming again. I leapt backwards and landed on a rock and

Admiring the view, Arrigetch Peaks, Brooks Range, 1971. Photo by Ginny Wood.

sort of crushed myself in order to get out of the way of that boulder. After that my back hurt the rest of the trip. The boulder stopped about five feet from me. I figured a bum back was better than being dead.

From there on, the river was pretty calm. There weren't any rapids or anything to deal with. So all those that had been hiking finally traded with the rafters. Except me. There was a beautiful walking trail, game trail, that went along the river. It was a wonderful trail. The next time I went down, maybe six years later, you couldn't do that anymore. It was all brush. We just waltzed down the river to Takahula Lake.

I have to tell you about the first other people we saw on the whole trip. We came around a corner and here were three guys lining a canoe upriver stark naked. Boy, I've never seen people put their pants on so fast! They were surprised, that's for sure! They had taken their clothes off to try to keep them dry, since they had to be walking in the river. Later on I met them with their clothes on, and their story was that they had gone from Fairbanks and were headed for Kotzebue. They had sent their canoe over to Dawson the year before, because there was a commercial freighter that went up to the headwaters of the Yukon River. They had gone down the Yukon and then lined up a river, down another river. They had portaged into the Ray River, over the headwaters and into the Bell River. Finally, they had gotten on the Alatna River and were lining their canoe up. They were pretty sharp about it. For lining up the canoe, they would use their paddle to push the bow to keep it away from the bank and to help keep them moving forward upstream, taking advantage of the current. They were going to take the canoe over the mountains across Portage Pass where they would be at the headwaters of the Noatak River. They were then going to float down the Noatak to be in Kotzebue before the snow flew. We found out later they did it. People do all kinds of crazy things.

They told us something that saved our lives. They said, "You've got to be careful up ahead, because just this spring during breakup the river changed its course. It's going right through the woods. If you ever got in there, you'll never get out because it's just full of logs. If you got swept in there, you'd just get swept under them. It's going fast." They said, "You'll know it when you see it." But they explained to me some little signs to look for that might help me know that it was coming up ahead. They told me because I was ahead of the rest of our group. I was not planning to be the first one through there, but I was because my raft was faster. I just happened to notice it just in time. I realized, "Oh my gosh, this is it!" And I barely got myself ashore and stopped everybody else. It's hard to describe how I could tell so that nobody got swept into that. We would have been dead, all of us. It was just full of logs, so full of brush. So we portaged that.

We only lost one raft completely. We had one seventeen-year-old kid and he was kind of macho. Well, I came around the corner and here he was sitting on a bank with his head in his hands and his raft in shreds. So we burned it on site.

I mean, what could we do? It wasn't Gates of the Arctic National Park yet, so we could do this type of thing, like burning. So, I guess I put him on my boat. I don't remember.

We did have some hair-raising adventures. The whole trip really was just a survival thing. After the first catastrophe we thought, "We're lucky if we get to Takahula Lake in time to get taken out. And will our rafts last? And how many of us will make it? And if we all end up walking, can we carry enough grub?" It was survival, but at the same time everybody got very ingenious and nobody was a poor sport. And that group just clicked. Even the guy that was a pill. He was just one of these guys who was just obnoxious. We all hated him. And that brought us together. He wasn't a bad guy. You know, you always have somebody that just rubs you the wrong way. But we decided he was our salvation because everybody bonded against him. He was everybody's fall guy. He never noticed. You could say anything to him, and he wouldn't get it. So we got to know each other very well. And people who had no idea they weren't going to be sitting in rafts the whole time, walked the whole time. None of them had thought in the world they'd have gone on a trip where they weren't going to sit in a raft and go downriver. They just wanted to see the country. These were people in their sixties, which I thought was terribly old then. And the woman who hurt her knee, it got good enough so that she could go do some of the hiking and climbing. It just got better every day. But first we wondered, "Oh my gosh. All we needed was a basket case on this trip." But she was a wonderful person. A very good sport.

Since then, I've had letters from people in the group. They always said it was the best trip they ever took. One guy I still write to said, "Well, of all the adventures I've ever had, that one stands out." Everybody agreed that they'd never had a trip that had more adventures, more highlights to it, more thinking about how we were going to get out of this, and more fun and more tales and more people whittling themselves spoons because they'd lost the ones they'd brought. Or like the airdrops where the cornmeal mixed up with the powdered lemon drink. They'd smashed on landing, so you couldn't separate them. Or the one time when some of the group didn't ever show up for the evening. So Doug, the leader, and I hiked all night trying to find out what had happened to them. They overshot us, so were downriver, and had started to come hiking back up. So we found them. But we just felt so proud of ourselves for surviving. We just thought we were pretty good by the time we got down to be picked up.

That was probably the most exciting, the most hilarious, the most ingenious, the most adventurous trip I've been on. It was definitely the most challenging one. And it was probably the most fun. Nothing happened like it was supposed to. But we didn't lose anybody.

I think that the Brooks Range is not the most spectacular mountain range compared to either the Cascades or even the Sierras in many ways, but there is an ambience. My mother used to say it's the sky. There's so much sky up here. And other times it's just you're sitting there eating and all of a sudden, someone says, "Hey, look." And here you see a wolf come over. Or sometimes it's a herd of musk ox. One time we were rafting the Kongakut River and we went ashore to go to the potty, and we had seen in the distance large groups of caribou, but we hadn't gotten close to them yet. And all of a sudden, over the hill came a little band of caribou, and another little band, and another little band. And pretty soon there were thousands of them. They came right down to us. By this time we were all sitting in the raft. We were just about to shove the raft off. But we were waiting for the last person. When we saw this, we said, "Come on, get in the boats fast and we'll just watch them from there." We watched several thousand caribou come over the hill. It was a ridge they'd come over in the distance. Then, almost as if somebody had blown a whistle, they came running down the slope. Right down to the water. And then swam all around us. The calves were only about four weeks old, and they make a barking sound. It was quite swift where they were crossing the river. This one little calf was being swept down by the current, and it was going right next to our boat. Our boat was sitting with the tail end in the water and the bow still on shore. Three-fourths of it was in the water. We were all sitting in the boat, and I said, "Don't anybody help. Stay absolutely still. Don't anybody try to touch it." The mother came down and she was so close to the boat you could have reached out and petted her. She just herded that little guy back into the current and they went downstream together. Then she got out and she and the calf walked way back up on the other side to catch up with the rest of the herd and find a better place to cross. They just hadn't allowed for the current or for us being there. But if any of us had touched that calf, then I think the mother might have tried to get away. The calf might have drowned because it was getting pretty frantic. Well, you know, you just thought about that for a long time. Where else could you have been able to watch a little drama like that?

I remember a trip where John Adams was hired by the Wilderness Society or the Sierra Club to be the guide. He was this kid that came up with the group as their leader. And I was the outfitter. He was kind of green, but an awfully nice guy. We flew in with Walt Audi. Oh gosh, that place where we landed, I'll never forget that. You couldn't believe it. I said, "You mean, you're going to land there?!" He dumped us at the head of the Canning River. We stayed there for about four days. We had to wait three days for our food, so while we were waiting for our airdrop we all went hiking. We did a lot of day hiking out of there. We made the first ascent of Peak 700. It was a beautiful climb. You looked down on Carnivore Creek.

We had this very hot weather while we were waiting for our grub to be airdropped. It was so hot we were just melting. Then I led the group down to what we call the Franklin Mountains and over to Carnivore Creek. I knew about this pass where you drop down into Carnivore Creek, because I had been up there with another trip the year before with Deborah Voight. I'd been up on a point in Carnivore Creek, and I had looked at this route and thought this would be fun to hike. Well, unfortunately, I let one of the guys lead who said he'd been up the day before scouting around the area while the rest of us were climbing up that mountain, and he said, "I know the way up there. I know the route." I just didn't think he was right, but I didn't challenge him. Until he finally said, "I don't know where I am." That day we started hiking it was foggy and raining. So I said, "Well, we'll drop down in this valley to camp because there is a chance it could turn into snow up here."

The next day, I knew that if I could get on that ridge I'd know how to get down to Carnivore Creek. I knew coming down that route if there was a caribou trail that led between the rocks and down to Carnivore Creek, then you could jump the creek because there were some rocks you could hop on. But that next day, it was still zero-zero visibility. I was on instruments. I said, "I will lead this time." The day before, the guy that said he knew the way obviously didn't. I walked in the middle of the group so I could sort of keep track of people behind me and ahead of me. And we got down to Carnivore Creek. But that nice place that you could hop across on the rocks was now under water because of all the rain. So we had to wade it. Gosh, it was cold! The wind was blowing, it was pelting rain. It was part hail, part rain. And I thought, "I've got to get these people down." A lot of them had thrown their sleeping bags out of their tents in the morning to air them out without thinking about it. It had been so warm so far. I thought, the sleeping bags are now wet and they'd all just stuffed their clothing any old place. They weren't prepared for the weather. This was the first day of bad weather we'd had, so they thought it was always sunny and warm up there. I had to keep that bunch going. I just had to keep them moving. I knew some of them were getting close to hypothermia, their lips were getting blue. There was water running everywhere. The whole thing was a sheet of water. All these beautiful spots I'd picked to camp were too wet. The last time I'd done this route we'd taken two days to do it. But I knew the only thing I could do now was to keep these people moving. It was fourteen miles. But it was downhill. So I just kept them walking until we got down to Peter's Lake.

On the trip before, we didn't like seeing all those Quonset huts at Peter's Lake.[16] We said, "Oh, this is hideous. We aren't even going to camp here. We don't even want to look at that stuff." But on this trip, when we got down, if I hadn't gotten to those huts and gotten inside, I would have had trouble. Because people's lips were blue, their teeth were chattering. That was the only thing that saved us. Once we got in the huts, it was still cold, but we were out of the wind and rain. Without that, I might have lost somebody. Fortunately, I never had to make a choice. Nobody said, "I don't want to go. I want to die here." If they had, I would have had to be an old meanie and have said, "No, get on your feet." Fortunately, everybody just kept going.

I went on my last trip into the Brooks Range when I was seventy years old.[17] That was with Jim Campbell and his wife, Carol Kasza.[18] We were being filmed by a group from Salt Lake City who were doing a story about the Arctic National Wildlife Refuge for a PBS documentary.[19] We took them down the Hulahula River. They did interviews with us and then they filmed us doing things. It was hilarious, because they staged things for the camera and we'd have to do the same thing over and over again. Like at one place, they had us rafting and then made us carry the boats back up to do it again so they could get their perfect shot. We really were in empty boats since we were doing it over and over again, but we had to fake it to look like we had a fully loaded boat, so we put a tarp in to look like it was covering gear. They weren't bad guys, but they didn't know much about camping. I remember they didn't even tie their tent down. And one guy never looked at the scenery around us, he only looked straight ahead.

One of the last times I was on a river was with Michio Hoshino, the Japanese wildlife photographer.[20] We were friends, and he always said, "Ginny, I want to go on a trip with you." And I kept putting it off and putting it off, and then finally decided, "Hey, now's the summer." That was 1995. Michio invited me and Celia to accompany him and another photographer on a rafting trip in late June down a section of the Sheenjek River that flows southward through the Brooks Range of the Arctic National Wildlife Refuge to the Yukon River flats. It was an idyllic interlude of good fellowship, easy paddling, emerging wildflowers, tasty Japanese cuisine, and quiet communion with the wilderness. A special treat was the visit of two beautiful wolves to our campsite one morning. We saw nary another human being until a small floatplane flew in to pick up us and our gear.[21] The next year Michio was dead.[22]

The last time I was in the Arctic was in 2003 with Carol Kasza, with some Japanese people who were making a movie about Alaska. I'd met the guy that was kind of behind all of it in Japan. They were doing a documentary and they wanted me to be in it in a raft. I tried getting out of it. I said, "I won't do it. I can't do what you want me to do. I don't like doing it." But they were very persistent. So finally I said I wouldn't do it unless Carol Kasza could be the outfitter, would be the guide and run the trip. They didn't know much about this stuff, and I knew Carol did. I said, "Well, if I'm going to be up there with you, I can't be your movie star and feed you, too. And take care of all the things that come up." I knew I didn't want to try cooking for them and being a guide. I'd quit doing that. I was getting older, when you begin to realize that you're not up to what you once were, and you're always going to have emergencies. You're always going to have a time that's going to call for you to do a little bit beyond what you thought you could do, even if it's just psychologically having to handle a situation.

We flew up to the coastal plain of the Arctic National Wildlife Refuge for the Japanese guys to get video footage. Carol was doing most of the cooking and kind of running the base camp. After a lot of back and forth with them in terms of planning, it ended up being just camping on the tundra, instead of a real float trip. But they wanted to be sure there was a boat in the film, so we had to lug this raft with us. This was an expensive trip because every day Carol and I and one of the cameramen with loads of camera gear would get into this four-place Cessna airplane of Walt Audi's and fly around looking for places to film, to get the perfect picture that they wanted to take. But we could never get up into and land at any of the places that we were hoping to get to because the weather was so bad. Here we were in this plane with all this camera gear and I thought, "Oh gads, if we crash that's the end of us." But we were never above fifty feet; we never had more than a fifty-foot ceiling. We tried for four days in a row to get into someplace for a base camp, until finally we asked Walt if there was anyplace he knew where you could always get in, no matter what the weather. It was an old DEW Line camp, but the buildings were not there anymore. We landed on their old fifteen-hundred-foot runway. It was still a good solid runway with no obstructions. It wasn't very scenic, but it worked. We walked out on the tundra on day trips and never once did we find something that had been left behind from the DEW Line camp. There was not a junk pile, they'd cleared it, but we were never out of sight of a manmade object.

Fortunately, one of the crew spoke English very well. Since we couldn't get to where they wanted to go for their shots, they took the boat with them out on the tundra. They wanted us to pump it up and sit in it. It was raining and blowing and snowing. Carol and I felt this was ridiculous. So we said, "No way." It turned out that we had terrible weather the whole trip, so we never got the boat out. They weren't bad guys, and we did get paid well for the trip. But it was hard. The weather was lousy and I was older. But Carol and I had fun together. This was the last year that Walt Audi flew. He cracked up his plane at the end of that season. He did some amazing flying for us. He was quite a pilot.

The one good thing on this trip was in all my trips to the Arctic I'd never seen an arctic fox. And there was one with a den, with babies, that was only about half a mile from our camp. So that was really neat. That saved the day. The Japanese guys got to take pictures of that, even though we wouldn't let them get as close as they wanted to. The mother had obviously had enough of kids. She was sleeping on a bench about fifty feet away from the den, and the young ones would get out and play and play. I wouldn't let anybody get any closer because I was worried about us disturbing her. Finally, she got used to having us around. If she was disturbed a bit, we stopped. The idea was for us to leave them doing the same thing, playing with each other, as if we hadn't been there. She'd look up every once in a while to see if everything was going okay. But as she got comfortable with us, I think she finally said, "Okay, you watch them for a while." She and the pups were brown. They turn white in the winter for camouflage.

Well, isn't it amazing that we all survived these trips? I don't remember worrying much about it ahead of time. We had all these people that we'd taken out to learn about it that we were responsible for and they all made it out alive. Each trip you do can be different, even if it's to a place where you've been before. People might ask you about a river trip that you've been on because they're planning their own trip and want to know what to expect. They say, "How was it?" And I say, "Well, I can only tell you how it was when I went down it last." A river can change completely, depending upon the breakup. And from one winter to the next. It can be utterly different from a winter and breakup to when you go up there, especially if you are the first ones on it in the spring.

As with other parts of Ginny's life—flying an airplane, bicycling through Europe, or taking an extended sailboat trip—being a wilderness guide and leading trips in the Brooks Range put her in a man's world at a time when there were few other women compatriots. Ginny always says that she was not a feminist. She was not doing these things to make a statement. She just did what she enjoyed. Mostly, she claims that she had few problems as a woman. Although sometimes she ran into opposition or had to work harder to prove herself in these settings.

Very rarely did I feel I had to prove myself as a woman being a guide. Maybe for a while they're testing you a little bit, but I found that even the people that are very experienced, they're up in country they've never been in before. They've always had a little sign that says it's eight miles to the next thing. It's different to be out where you're going cross-country and you know you have to look out for bears. You need to know that when you see bears, you quite often have to get your group together and just everybody stay here. Don't anybody go anywhere, you all sit right here. We'll out-bluff him. All those things are new to these people, and they aren't prepared or aren't experienced. Like being in the fog for three days down in Lake Clark country when we were just on a compass course. "Are we lost?" "No, I just don't know exactly where we are." "Well, where are we going to camp?" I said, "I don't know, because I've never been here before. But we aren't lost. I can always do a 180. I know if we don't find where we're going or can't get across the river, I always know how to do a 180 degrees and follow the compass back to where we started from." I think that's why they have to trust you. A lot of them who have done hiking before, they realize that they depend on you. I think most of the times you're equals. It was just that it was more convenient to have somebody arrange a trip when coming up into new country. It takes a lot of living up here before you can know about logistics for places like the Brooks Range—such as which company to use for renting an airplane and good drop-off and pick-up locations. It's a little different than when you just get things in a car and there's a trailhead and you follow the trail.

The only time I remember having trouble as a woman guide was when we had a couple of yuppies on a trip on the Kongakut River that were giving me a hard time, because they'd been there before and acted like they'd done everything. They just

Ginny guiding a hike in the Brooks Range, 1988. Courtesy of Ramona Finnoff.

were pills. I can remember they just were challenging me all the time. These guys were in my raft. I was doing the trip with Jim Campbell. I guess it was his trip and I was his assistant. I think it was the second trip I had done with Jim. Jim was raised on the wrong side of the tracks and ended up in Vietnam in combat when he was nineteen, with only one month of training. He decided, "I don't know what I am doing here, but I'm not going to die here." So he survived. He had this most wonderful outlook on life: "Wow, I'm alive and I'm out here and isn't this wonderful!" He had not had much education, but he was a diamond in the rough.

One night I was in my tent, which I was sharing with another woman. We had gone to bed. But the guys were standing around the campfire and they were bragging about their conquests with women. Of course we could hear this all from our tent. It was just horrible. And Jim says, "You guys don't know what it is to love a woman. If you love a woman, you don't talk about her that way." He was just telling them off. Then he said the most wonderful experience in his life was when his daughter had been born and he got to help deliver her. He was telling this, you know, splitting infinitives and not using the best language, but he said, "Uh—I—my daughter. And I picked her up and I handed her to my wife. You don't know what that's like to catch your first child when she's being born and hand her to your wife. That's love." It was neat to see just the warmth and that feeling that Jim had compared with these two yuppies who were so "been there and done that"—always sarcastic about everything, and who couldn't be enthusiastic because that wouldn't be cool. You get so you just sort of look at this people stuff as another part of the adventure of a trip, the adventure of human relationships.

I think the best thing you can do as a guide is not be too much of a guide. Let people lead, or go off by themselves. You can have good guides that are very good at what they do, and could probably climb Mount McKinley backwards in wintertime, but there is more to guiding than that. It involves people skills. You sometimes get a group that becomes very much of a group except for one person that's maybe quite often a woman who is a little bit afraid that she might not be up to it. Or a guy who is a loner. Or doesn't feel that she fits in. As the guide, it is your job to try to bring her into the group. And you usually can find some occasion or some skill that she has—maybe it's just cooking—where she can feel confident. Or something that happens that everybody can laugh at and have an adventure with together. Like somebody falls in the water, I don't know. That person is now accepted and they feel comfortable. And this is the most wonderful thing that's ever happened to them because they were apprehensive to start with, and I think that having a woman guide made them feel a little more at ease than if it had been a guy. So as a guide, you have to, one, make decisions when it's very important that you have to. But also let others make the decisions when possible; to trust other people's experience and know-how. And to try to find some occasion when they know something about something that somebody else doesn't. To help give them confidence and make them feel important, whether it's just where the bird is. It's a matter of finding out about everybody's life experiences. You find out when you get some stories in the cook tent at night. You hear some very interesting stories from other people.

You also have the environment that you are trying to not leave footprints on and wanting your group to behave properly in the wilderness. You walk that line between safety and always saying, "Oh, don't do this, you might get hurt." Trying not to take the adventure out of it, or that feeling of being the first in a place.

Let everybody experience it. Especially on the layover days, letting them explore and feel that they were just the first ones to discover something. Although it was an outfitter that made it possible to make the arrangements for this trip, you didn't want people to feel like they are at Boy Scout or Girl Scout camp. It's a matter of trying to be a guide, but not a group leader. You want to make it feel more like you're a fellowship. Combining your skills and your knowledge and enjoying each other. And helping out, whether it's hauling water or taking a turn at cooking or whatever you feel good at.

Most of the time when you're hiking you didn't go in lockstep. You'd say, "Well, we're going here and you can go where we're going or you can go another route." People that know how to read a compass and have a lot of savvy, you don't worry about them. They even may go a different route. They go higher, you go lower. Other times you'd just say, "Well, we'll meet again over at that area." So it wouldn't necessarily be all of us walking together. You didn't walk in a line, everybody walking in time with each other. Very often when you had layover days, everybody picked a different place to go explore. One would say, "Well, I'd like to try that peak." Another, "I think I'd just like to go over and sit in the woods and catch up in my journal." Or, "I'd like to go birding." So you'd go off, just, you know, wherever you wanted. They just had to tell us what area they were going to and we never had any problems. Although sometimes they were a little late getting back to camp. But everybody had a chance to go off and experience the wilderness, the sanctuary part of wilderness, the solitude, that feeling of aloneness. It wasn't as if you were on top of each other all the time. A lot of these people were very experienced hikers and backpackers. They would just go with a group because it's too hard to come up here and then try to hire an airplane, and it costs more because you have to pay by the hour flying no matter what's in the airplane. The splitting up the gear and everything made it cheaper and easier with a group. A group can carry a lot of the kitchen stuff if you have it distributed. You can do it alone. A lot of people do. You just do not have quite as varied a cuisine and you need a stronger back.

I think that one of the major considerations that those of us who are guides and outfitters need to remember is the influence we have on our clients as role models, especially on those who will be forming their wilderness ethics, environmental awareness, and minimum impact habits from emulating us on their future wilderness trips on their own. Being a guide should carry more responsibility than just leading a group from here to there and providing logistics. We are responsible for the safety of our clients and to a large extent for the kind of experience they get from our trips. We are also responsible for the impact we make on the wilderness, and we have the responsibility to ourselves to make wilderness and mountain guiding truly a profession to be proud of.[23]

Often I had thought during my long career as a backcountry guide how much fun it would be to take wilderness trips with just a few friends. All I'd be responsible for was taking care of my self and my own gear. Well, I found out that since I've hung up my pack and paddles as a professional guide and outfitter that clients accept and follow your rules on minimum impact, safety (like wearing a life preserver when afloat) and disposing of waste (including human), but not your friends! They take offense, tell you to stop acting like a Scout leader, or just flat out tell you to go to hell.[24]

Through years of experience, Ginny developed into a skilled outdoorswoman. She was meticulous with packing and organizing gear. She kept notes on weight to keep her pack from getting too heavy. Her Tundra Treks office in an outbuilding on her property was stuffed full with dry food, containers and bags for repacking, and extra tents, packs, stuff sacks, and replacement parts. She had a reputation as a good guide and others were eager to go on trips with her. Plus, she gave back to the profession by serving on the boards of the Alaska Wilderness Recreation and Tourism Association and the Alaska Wilderness Guides Association.[25] A number of Alaska's backcountry guides today were inspired by or learned from Ginny. Jim Campbell, of Arctic Treks, is one of them. He credits Ginny with teaching him about wilderness adventuring and guiding. They remain close friends to this day. He clearly remembers his first wilderness experience with Ginny and how this solidified his respect for her:

> The first river trip I did with Ginny was on the North Fork of the Koyukuk River. The upper section of the river was skinny and bouldery and full of debris. It required having to do some maneuvering with the rafts. At the beginning of the trip, Ginny was in my boat. I remember coming around a corner to suddenly find a full-on logjam ahead. I quickly called to stop the boats. You have to pull over by nosing the boat towards the bank, hit the bank, and then swivel before continuing down in the current. This means that someone in the bow of the boat has to jump out and hold the bowline to keep the boat from going downriver. Ginny jumped out and she held that boat. I thought, "Wow!" She was a hero before that, but that really made an impression on me. I don't know what she weighed, but it couldn't have been more than 120 pounds or something. And she held a fully loaded boat. And there was a good current. It was flood-stage conditions. She jumped out and did exactly what she'd told everyone to do in the instructions. She put the rope around her back and was in a position that was like belaying someone in climbing. She just planted herself and held the boat. I had not one bit of doubt or fear that we weren't going to stop.[26]

Ginny remembers other things about this and other early trips she did with Jim Campbell:

I remember the first trip I did with Jim Campbell. It was on the North Fork of the Koyukuk River with lots of people. Jim was in charge and I was his assistant. There was one eighteen-year-old guy who'd been in the army who ate a lot. Jim was new to trip planning, so he had not taken the possibility of a big eater into account, so there was not enough food. This guy would eat his first bowl of food while he circled around and got back in line for seconds before others had gotten their firsts. We had to tell him he couldn't do that. There were other trips I've been on where we got low on food, but on this one I was actually hungry. Jim learned his lesson. He has never run out of food on a trip again.

The next trip was on the Kongakut River in 1985. Jim sent me up to where we were going to start floating the river with all the gear a day early. We landed up at a certain place almost at the head of the river where they can land you. And then he was coming in with the people the next day. That was quite a trip, because what happened is, they had a very late season and it hadn't all thawed up in the mountains. When we flew in, the guy that flew me in never looked out the window. He just had a radio on his plane and he just went by his radio. I would look out and say, "I don't see that there's water. The river doesn't go all the way through yet. There's places where I don't see a river, I think it goes underneath the ice." So I told this guy, "Well, I'd like to check that out. I want to see the river, because we're going to raft it. I want to see if it's open yet." He was on his way to Kaktovik and all he wanted to do was fly in and out quickly. He didn't even look down. When we were milling around once in bad weather, I said, "Do you have a map?" He said, "I never use them. I got a radio." I still wonder how we got in and out of there safely and without getting lost.

That year it was a very late breakup, so we weren't sure that the river was even flowing the whole way. Jim and I would go out every night after everybody else had gone to bed. We would walk on the shore ice, which was very fast walking because it wasn't like going over rocks and under branches and stuff, and we would hike almost all night as far as we knew we'd go the next day in the rafts to scout our route. I remember that was probably one of the best things on that trip. It was so beautiful at night. We did this because we weren't sure that the river wouldn't go underneath the ice someplace. From the plane, it had looked okay, but all it had to do was for the ice to slough in and you'd just get sucked right underneath it. It was a pretty fast river. Unless some ice sloughed in overnight, which it could have, at least we knew it was open water. There were some house-size blocks of ice in the middle of the river, though.

We finally got down to what we called the canyon, and it had a lot of very fast water and about twenty-foot-high banks of ice along it. Once you get in there, you're not going to get out. By that time, Jim and I pretty much trusted each other. So we would take two passengers through at a time on a raft. I'd be in the bow and Jim would be in the stern because he was stronger and could give it more oomph. The other people were paddling, too. We'd go so far, leave the people, and then hike back up and come down again with the others. Then finally we took all the gear through. We did it this way instead of with fully loaded boats, because if we'd been dumped, we'd all have just been swept underneath all that ice.

On these trips, we get into being on Brooks Range time. You stay up late because it is light all night long, and that can be the best time for hiking or viewing wildlife. So then you get up late. I might be out hiking all night long, but as the guide I would still get up early to help those people in the group who were early risers. It was kind of mysterious at night. Especially when you can smell a bear. It is possible to smell a bear. And I was kind of able to sense them. I don't know why. I feel them. Sometimes I would wake up out of a sound sleep knowing that there was a bear outside of my tent. It's like I sense them and I look and sure enough there are bear tracks.

Backcountry guiding is a young person's profession. Even if you are just sitting in a raft floating down a river, it is physically and mentally demanding. For most people, the physical signs of aging—bad backs, sore knees, stiff hips—force a shifting of roles. The nature of having assistant guides on many trips provided an opportunity for someone like Ginny to teach younger, newer guides and slowly turn over leadership.

You have an accumulation of knowledge from having done this. It's kind of a wisdom that isn't because you're so smart, it's just because you're used to doing it. There comes a time when you realize you're not as sharp as you used to be. You don't have the physical strength, or the best judgement anymore. If you can't carry sixty pounds, that's what stops you from being a guide.

The good thing about when you're rafting is that you always have to have a boatman for each raft, and that boatman has to be more than just being along for the ride. So you always have an assistant. You're never leading a trip alone. So leading rafting trips when I was older worked out well. I wasn't alone. And I could teach someone else what I knew.

There is always the chance that you're going to have an emergency on water, and as you get older you realize that if you fall in you're just not going to last as long in cold water as you could have before. But on the other hand, you've picked up other knowledge. I call it wisdom. You just decide that you don't want to be sued if there's an accident because you were too old and something went wrong. You can't afford to be sued. You don't want to think that if I was just a little younger or stronger or wiser, that person wouldn't have died or something.

It's been a wonderful experience doing all these trips. It was fun. Every trip is different. The people are different. The weather is different. And with the river trips, they are never the same twice because rivers change. They can be very calm and a bore, or they can be too exciting. Or they can be a pain in the neck depending on the people on the trip. Times that were not as fun were part of it, too. Instead of saying these were bad times, we'd just say there's some times that are peculiar.

Ginny skiing at Mount Baker, Washington, circa 1939. Courtesy of Ginny Wood.

19

Breaking Trail

A trail includes the whole area you're going through,
not just the two feet of the trail you're walking on.

One of the wonderful things about Fairbanks is an extensive backcountry trail system that winds through town and nearby surroundings. Many of these trails are well known and popular, like the multiuse one along the old Tanana Valley Railroad bed in the bottom of Goldstream Valley. Others are more secretive, privately threading their way through a neighborhood, only used by the local residents. While many of these trails are mostly used in the winter by skiers, dog mushers, and snowmachiners, some are also enjoyed in the summer months by walkers, runners, and bikers. Many people who enjoy these trails probably do not know how they came to be—the hard work that went into cutting them, the persistent advocacy that went into getting land set aside for public recreation. Ginny Wood is one early resident who felt the need for trails. Eventually, she became an avid trail builder and promoter, but it all started for very personal reasons.

I think I got involved in all this trail work because I first made them for skiing near my house. I had always been a skier. A downhill skier. I was one of the first women on the national ski patrol. I got on sort of by accident. I skied at Mount Baker when it would have been classified more as ski mountaineering than downhill runs on slopes surrounded by ski lifts. Using the single rope tow to ski Austin Pass soon dulled compared to the long run one could achieve after a few hours' climb on seal skins. We often referred to these climbing aids that we were seldom without as our "Mount Baker Ski Lifts."

One day, when I was skiing with my boyfriend, Otto Trott, who was already on the ski patrol,[1] I had just begun skiing up the valley towards the ski tow when I saw Otto followed by several ski patrolmen pulling the first aid toboggan below, headed toward Table Mountain in the opposite direction. Otto had my lunch and we were supposed to meet on the top of Paradise Dome. I waved for him to bring it to me. He waved, "No, you come over and get it." He said, "Gin-nee, yoo have to come. This guy has a broken leg up on Table Mountain Glacier. We might need you too." This was the way he pronounced things because of his German accent. I was on the local Mount Baker ski patrol, but not part of the national one. I was not on duty then, and climbing up on top of Table Mountain was not a climb that I had wanted to do that day—it would require more side-stepping than skiing—but one didn't argue with Otto. So I went over there.

My contribution to the rescue was minimal. The guys splinted the man's badly shattered leg, lowered him down off the steep face of the glacier, and dragged him back to the first aid room, where he was transferred by station wagon to the hospital at Bellingham, sixty miles away. All I did was carry out his skis as they brought him down the hill in the rescue toboggan. I think his poles were used as part of the splinting on his leg.

The ruggedness of the terrain, the popularity of the victim—one of the regu-lars at the Mount Baker ski area—and the effort involved to bring him down off Table Mountain attracted the attention of most of the guests staying at the lodge, among them Minoh Dole, the original organizer of the National Ski Patrol from New England. He approached me as we were all being treated to a hamburger and milkshake by the lodge after we got off the mountain. He said to me, "I see you have the woman's patrol badge. Do you have your advanced first aid card?" "No, just the first one," I replied. I didn't add that it was out of date. "Well," he said, "I'd like to see you are awarded a regular one. Send me a copy of a cer-tificate of having passed the advanced first aid course and you'll get the second patrol badge we have ever awarded to a woman." Unfortunately, by the time I got around to completing the course, I was number 30 instead of being the second woman inducted. I suppose it was worth the effort. It got me a lot of free passes at ski areas all over the world. The funny thing is that I didn't do much of anything on that rescue,[2] but because I'd come down with the guys off the mountain they wanted to induct me into the National Ski Patrol and give me a patch. All that just because I wanted my lunch!

I only took up cross-country skiing once I moved to Fairbanks. It was not really a downhill ski kind of place. We don't really have downhill ski country here, really, compared to Seattle or someplace like the Cascades. There were some old dog-team trails around Dogpatch[3] when we moved here in 1952, so I started using my downhill skis with the uphill hitch, where you can undo and loosen the heel. Later I started using cross-country skis.

I think I bought my first pair of cross-country skis in Seattle. The problem was that there wasn't any place that you could buy cross-country ski equipment here in Fairbanks. Most people in the United States downhill skied. You didn't cross-country ski unless you were Norwegian. Celia Hunter started importing skis from Germany and Sweden and sold them out of her house. Eventually, she didn't want to do that anymore.

Ginny on her cross-country skis, circa 1955. Courtesy of Ginny Wood.

Then Clem Rowert, who was a German who had come up here, said he could handle it. He was an upholsterer by training. We first met him when he came to McKinley Park. He came out hitchhiking to Camp Denali. It was pouring rain, so we invited him to stay overnight in our basic wall tent that we called "Bedrock." He chopped wood to pay his way, and then we kept him for the whole summer. He had connections in Germany that could export cross-country skis, so he knew he could get stuff. He first had an upholstery shop in town and then he began to import skis, then kayaks, then other equipment. It became our main sporting good shop—Clem's Backpacking Sports.

I'm the one that cut all the trails in Dogpatch to start with. When I first started skiing in Fairbanks, there were a lot of old dog-team trails out in Dogpatch, and then I started making loops out of them. I was putting in ski trails to hook up with the dog-team trails. And there were other trails to connect to that had been made when that was just farming country. Then I would run into old trapping trails. We were the only ones living out in this area then. Nobody was living on the other side of Goldstream Valley, because at that time you couldn't get across Goldstream Creek in the summertime. There was no road across yet. It was just a network of old trails.

Then one time when I was out cutting trail, I came up on these "blazes," big swaths cut through the woods, and I thought, "Oh, they're getting ready to put a road here, so why am I spending all my time cutting a trail?" Then I ran into Fred Boyle, an early ski coach at UAF,[4] and he said, "Are you blazing a road?" I said, "No. Are you?" He said, "No, I'm making a ski trail for the university."[5] Then we found out we were both doing the same thing. We both just wanted ski trails. So he started enlarging his area to connect with the ones that I had been constructing.[6] This connection between the university trails and Dogpatch's trails is what became the Skarland Trail. I used this to ski to the university from home. Ballaine Road wasn't much more than a dog-team trail then, and we couldn't always be assured our jeep would start or make it through the rough conditions. At the time, there were a lot of other people who skied to campus, too. I also remember the Skiathons we used to have on those trails.[7]

When you're putting in a trail, it tells you where to go. You may put in a trail in one place because there's someplace you want to get to in the country. Or in other cases, it's where there is a wonderful view. Or sometimes it's a popular route, so you put in a trail to make it easier for everybody or it just becomes a trail because of the heavy usage. When you're cutting a trail, though, you have to include a wide enough easement on either side. A trail needs a twenty- to fifty-foot right of way, because the trail includes the area you're going through, not just the two feet you're walking on. Some people don't like trails close by their house, so a big easement like this acts as a good privacy buffer, too.

Clem, Celia, myself, and Doug Bingham, we tried to get cross-country skiing going in the grade schools. We started weekend ski meets. Bill Page, who was a teacher, also helped us put on the ski meets.[8] The trouble was they were using old downhill skis with an uphill hitch. Parents would buy their kids a car when they got to be sixteen, but they wouldn't buy them a pair of cross-country skis. Finally, we got a hold of army surplus skis and Doug adapted them for kids by cutting them down. Celia and I also helped organize the Nordic Ski Club.

Jim Mahaffey started competitive skiing at the university. He was teaching PE classes and then he became the ski coach.[9] To show you how primitive it was back then, anybody that was going to race had to come out and groom the trails. Now, you wouldn't ever ask a competitive skier to have to work for it. To cut trail. And then neighborhoods came out to help. Whole families would come out. We would come out and just make a family ski day of it. We'd do things like connect up places that had been trapping trails, which were no longer being used. Or sometimes when we had heavy snowfall, it would bring down branches everywhere and we'd clean that up. Then we'd all go to somebody's house and have soup and sandwiches. It was just something that everybody did. This was a time when everybody went out and did things like that. The whole community would join in. Like when they had the Glacier Stampede[10] and the Tanana River Raft Race[11] and everybody just went out and participated. We were more of a community then.

Cutting brush to maintain the local ski trail, circa 1970. Photo by Ginny Wood.

The same was true for the Equinox Marathon Trail. Nat Goodhue and Doug Bingham founded the race.[12] But those who wanted to race had to help cut trail. I cut trail and ran the first race. I was cutting trail one day and the next day I was racing on it.

The first trail that was made an official borough trail with ink is the Skarland Trail.[13] When I was on the North Star Borough's Trails Advisory Commission, there were only three or four trails that we got passed by the borough to be designated as official trails. The full name is the Skarland Memorial Trail. We named it after Ivar Skarland, a Norwegian, because he had recently died, had brought cross-country skiing to the University of Alaska Fairbanks, and was well liked in the community.[14] Besides just honoring him, we thought it would give the trail a little bit of extra protection, because people wouldn't do anything against the trail because that would be desecrating his name. Ivar was just a fixture when I got here; everybody knew him. He was a good friend of naturalist and conservationist Olaus Murie and his wife, Mardy, and of Chuck Keim, who was a journalism and English professor and dean at the university and a hunting guide and adventurer.[15] Ivar was a very likeable guy.

I'll back up a little bit and tell you the background of Ivar Skarland. Grant Pearson always told this story from when he was a ranger at McKinley Park starting in the late 1920s. Somebody told him that there was a funny guy with a thick accent who was from Healy, the coal mine down there, and he wanted to come out and go through the park. They said, "But he doesn't know anything about traveling around here in the winter. He doesn't even have snowshoes. He has these funny long wooden things. We know those won't work out there." The superintendent said, "I'll send the chief ranger out with him, because they usually do patrols all the time anyway. We'll just make an official patrol out of it and just see if he knows what he's doing." And so Ivar went out on his skis and Grant had the dog team. They got out to where Eielson Visitor Center is now and stopped to spend the night. Ivar said, "I tink [sic] I go back and get the train tomorrow." He said, "I want to go up to the university and see if I can go to it." He didn't come up through scholarship, you know, like most Europeans. You know how they divide up what type of schooling you will get and whether you go to college or not based upon who you were born to and what their economic class was. The ones that don't go to college get a trade. Ivar had come over to America from Norway and had been working at the coal mine at Healy. He was an amazing skier. From Mile 66 on the park road where he and Grant had spent the night, he got to the train station at the headquarters end of the park in time for the train the next day at four o'clock in the afternoon. He came up to Fairbanks and talked Judge Bunnell, president of the university, into letting him go to the university even though his English wasn't that good. Eventually, he went to Harvard and got his PhD.[16]

When we became the Fairbanks North Star Borough, they started selling land because they wanted to raise money. You've got to have money to run a borough. They didn't want to spend any money in doing anything with trails, though. We thought, "Wow, there go our trails." Including what is now the Skarland Memorial Trail. In 1979, we spontaneously established the Tanana Trails Council, which was a bunch of people that were interested in trying to show that there's an advantage to having trails. To show that people will buy land because there are trails there. There were about thirty of us in the group, and we elected Edwin "Rocky" Rhoads as our first chairperson and he served for about ten years. We started to plot any trails still in use by any means other than automobile. We also got help from the Alaska Trail Riders Association, especially Dorothy Wilde and Barbara Buck, who had ridden many of the trails in competitive horseback-riding events.[17] But we weren't getting anywhere other than just being a little club. Someone suggested that we should be attached to the borough's Land Office and Planning Department. That would get us heard more. It took a couple of years to get them interested. You'd have years where it was all against you. Then all of a sudden, everything would kind of fall in place. I had to go to meetings and meetings and meetings to try to get us officially recognized as a commission within the borough's Planning Department. Unless we were an official commission, we weren't going to get anywhere; nobody would listen to us. There was one guy who didn't want that. He said, "No, that's not what we do." He wanted us to go to the borough's Parks and Recreation Department. But we didn't want to go to there, because creating trails was an official designation and preservation was a land-use issue. It was not just a matter of having recreation. It took a year to convince a very reluctant borough assembly to accept all this. So we went from just being a citizen's thing to being part of the borough, where we could hold meetings in a borough office, use one of their tape recorders, and have one of their secretaries transcribe the minutes of the meeting for the record. For a while, they'd have a very good guy that was in the land office whose business it was to work with us on trails. Then they'd have this other fellow come on as the head cheese and he'd abolish it. But we did keep it going. One of the times the Trails Commission was eliminated was because there was a mayor who got elected who said, "I don't walk and I don't ski. And I don't intend to." So he didn't care whether we had trails. But those of us on the commission just kept meeting anyway.

That became what is now the borough's Trails Advisory Commission.[18] It is advisory. It makes recommendations to the borough assembly. It is all politics. The Planning Commission decides what land is used for. But I was very glad to sit in when I was invited to a meeting a few years ago when they honored me for my contributions to Fairbanks's trails.[19] I looked around, and listened to their meeting, and I thought, "Wow, have you come a long ways." Because nobody's telling you that we don't want that. It was hard when we first started, because anybody that got land, if you were a landowner, you didn't want one inch of it to go to anything except into your own coffer. The borough would say, "Well, nobody is going to buy land out here if they have a trail running right by there." I said, "You will find that if it's laid out and done properly, people will buy land because of the trails." Every once in a while someone would jump in and say, "She's right." But you sure had to fight it. It is different now with the borough's land regulation than when I first arrived in Alaska and we just went out and found land. You can't do this anymore. There are too many people here now. But there are still people who don't want regulation. They feel this is Alaska and they have the right to do what they want. But getting our trails protected has been a good thing.

One of our accomplishments was to get the Planning Department to run all proposed borough land disposals through the Trails Planner and the Advisory Commission to note any trails that should be dedicated in the plat before these parcels were presented for public sale. We convinced the Borough Planning Department that trails would be an asset if they ran along the backs of lots instead of crossing driveways, and would be a desirable amenity to prospective land buyers.[20] The borough's Trails Advisory Commission also established a working relationship with the Department of Transportation in planning for bicycle and snowmachine trails. A comprehensive borough-wide Trails Plan was created and accepted by the borough assembly, and a process for nominating future trails and route systems was developed.[21] It was a bewildering setback in 2000 when the borough assembly voted, not unanimously, to eliminate the position of trail coordinator from the Planning Department.[22] Those of us on the commission tried to fill in, but we served as volunteers and there was just too much to do. Several commission members resigned, but the rest of us "old hands," with some energetic and enthusiastic new members, voted to keep trying.[23] We shared a dedication to try not to lose the progress made in the past, which resulted in a borough-wide trail system that provides so much pleasure, recreation, and a sense of well-being, both physically and mentally, in the Fairbanks greater community. In 2001, I testified before the assembly asking that they and a new mayor take a second look to see about providing a trail coordinator[24]—even if just part-time—to work with the commission to maintain an exceptional trail system which has much use during all seasons.[25]

One of the first land sales that the borough had was of the four quarter-sections that surround Dogpatch.[26] They started putting in subdivisions around us, and this one big one south of us in particular was part of our trail system around Dogpatch. We had to go fight that because they were going to make half-acre lots. We told them if it's a half-acre, then somebody's going to have land that's where all the water runs during breakup. Or it's all hummocky. I said, "If you make big lots, people will buy three acres." And if you have a gully on one acre, then that's kind of nice, but it's not your whole lot. If it's only a half-acre, that gully would be in the way of where you need to build. So we established a loose organization of people who lived around here to fight to protect our neighborhood and the trails we'd put in. We would meet three times a year or something. We thought to give it a name, so we could be somebody. We called it the Pearl Creek Neighborhood Trails Committee.

When they wanted to put Pearl Creek Elementary School out here, those of us living in the neighborhood weren't at all happy. We thought, "Well, you know what happens around a grade school? Somebody's going to put up a little hamburger joint or someplace to get candy bars to go to during recess. Then people will buy land along there because it's near the university. And there goes our neighborhood. There goes our trail system." We had a big fight about that.

We said we'd quit fighting it if they put twenty acres for the school and the rest of it would go into an adjoining park for us. So because of our efforts, we got the borough to put our trails into a designated recreation area. So the four quarter-sections that run up three sides of Dogpatch was another of the first borough designated trail systems. It's about one hundred acres of land that's got trails all through it and lots of wildlife. And nobody living there. It is now known as Pearl Creek Park. Originally, the land belonged to Judge Bunnell. He had all the land around here. It was farms. That's why it's called Farmer's Loop Road. It was still farmland up here when I first came to Fairbanks in 1947.[27]

I guess I was behind that idea of getting our Dogpatch trails put into a community park under the borough's Parks and Recreation Department. It's because I'd been around enough to know that when we organized, we could be successful. We decided that we had to have a club in order to apply for some money to buy the land where our trails were. It was land that Natco owned. It was Bunnell's daughter and her husband who inherited all the judge's property. She didn't much care about the land, but her husband was a developer. We were trying to get some sort of official designation there. It was the last time that the state had a lot of money from oil. And the neighborhood raised several thousand dollars to hold it and apply that towards the purchase. We did not go through the borough land office, because all they do is want to make money for the borough. Instead, we thought we will get this through the Parks and Recreation Department, because that's the department where they designate all these little pocket parks for the kiddies to play in. A park for kids to play in has its own set of rules. It does not come under the same regulations as property that is controlled by the land office. We thought, if this area came under the rules of the parks, then the snowmachiners couldn't say, "Well, it's got to be multiple use." So I'd go down and tell any new guy that was head of Parks and Rec that we wanted our trail area under the same regulations that govern all these little pocket parks around the schools. And we wanted to keep it that way. Well, it was not brilliant, it just was my backyard, my playground. It was very selfish, for me.

After this early success of getting her neighborhood trails protected, Ginny continued to be active in trail development and protection efforts around the Fairbanks area. Others began to recognize her knowledge of the issues and her ability to persuade the powers that be about the need for trails. She worked tirelessly on behalf of trails. One of her next big trail campaigns was establishment of the North Star Borough's Birch Hill Recreation Area. She explains the unique circumstances surrounding this effort:

This was after we got our borough trails commission established. Most of the people on the commission then were horseback riders. They were just as interested as skiers and hikers were that they had places where they could ride their horses that was more than just around the block. They were being cut off from being able to have meets because it was on somebody's land. A lot of people that own horses are in high places. You have to have money to have horses. So they got some money through Juneau, from the state, to buy and set aside some land for their twenty-five-mile ride that they had as a competitive thing. It was not a meet for racing, but just a way to be able to do some long-distance riding on your horse. Then they decided that for some reason they didn't want to do this. I talked to a woman who was a big wheel in that group, and she said that they didn't really want that particular area that was being offered to them. So they said they'd throw it back in the pot for a trail. It included the land that is now part of Birch Hill Ski Area. So a bunch of us that were on the Trails Commission who were skiers said, "Well, we'd like to have it." It was one of those things that starts as an idea, then you get a few people backing it, and then it grows into something with everyone saying, "Yeah, that seems like a good idea." That's how it all started. There were already some trails up there used by the military and by locals. Just like around Dogpatch. But they didn't have a spot that they could really develop for a warming hut. Like you do for downhill skiing.

Then we told Jim Whisenhant about it. He taught in the school system and was getting cross-country skiing going in the grade schools and in the high school. Having little competitive meets. You know, people like races and ribbons. And parents like to have their kids in sports.

Right after we'd gotten the land at Birch Hill and started using it, John Estle, who was then coach for the university, had gone back to the Olympics that were held in Yugoslavia, I think. Afterwards, they had a meeting to decide where they were going to have the next national races.[28] It had been given to New England. It only comes about once every ten years to different countries, so it's quite an honor to be chosen. But New England said they didn't want it. It was too much work, and they couldn't depend on the weather and if they'd have snow. It had to be someplace that was below four thousand feet, otherwise the altitude would make a big difference in terms of where the athletes came from and how well they performed. If they were used to altitude or not. So John called up the Nordic Ski Club and said, "Do you guys think you can put on the nationals for the cross-country ski races?" They said, "I guess so. What do we have to do?" He said, "Well, I don't know, but you've got one month to do it in." They said, "We could try."

The ski club had just acquired the land from the horseback riders who decided they didn't want to ride there, so we had just started to kind of scratch a little trail here, and another one there. It's so near Fort Wainwright, the army base, that there were some skiers from there already coming over and using it. But there wasn't much of a trail system. So the Nordic Ski Club said, "Hey, anybody, bring up your axe, bring up your saws, and let's see what we can do to get ready for this big race event." So we did, and they had it all ready in one month.

It seemed like we got it done because no one ever knew who was in charge. The Nordic Ski Club was just a name. It was your friends and neighbors that you went skiing with. Like anything that starts in Fairbanks, they hadn't gotten around to really being organized. We didn't know what we were supposed to do, but we got everybody that had a pair of skis or had ever skied to come on out and we'd find out. So you'd go up there with your axe and your saw, and you'd say, "Who's in charge?" Somebody would reply, "Well, I don't know, but it sure needs some work down there." Everybody knew someplace that needed a tree cut or trimmed or a little roadwork done. So you'd go down to that spot on the trail and just do the work. Then somebody else comes up to help. Or somebody else would do another part. They had to cut brush and stuff, because there were specifications from the race about what the trails were supposed to be like. That's how it got done.

We put on the national races and it went beautifully. It was March when they had the race. We had plenty of snow. It was a beautiful day. We had skiers from all over the world. They came from all nationalities. Especially the Scandinavians. There was one professional guy that travels around to these meets and orchestrates them. He brings along this little tower that you put up. It's probably over six feet high. While he's up there, he directs the races. So he was up on his little stand and he said, "I want to make an announcement. I want to congratulate you people of Fairbanks." He said, "I've done this all over the world, and we've never put on one of these international races that the hosts didn't know a year ahead of time that they were going to be doing it." He said, "Here, you've done a great job, and I couldn't even find out who was in charge." We didn't know either. What he would do was, when people came out to help, he'd say, "Okay, now everybody over here take two steps forward. The other ones take two steps backward." He always found a spot for someone to step in and help. He just directed and told us what to do. Nobody knew anything different, so we just did it. He said, "I've never had such a delightful audience, people that really came together."

One of the things we did was, when they did the relays, we had to change the whole track in the trail. The snowmachines had to go out and redo the thing because the racers were coming in the same way they had gone out. You had to change the track for the different direction of the skiers coming back along the same trail. The snowmachines that were out making the trail had to be done while the skiers were out and before they came in, because they had to come in on the same trail they went out on. That was, what, forty-five minutes? And we did it. But to get that all done, everybody just did what needed to be done. The way it was so successful is because nobody was in charge.

The first snowmachine I heard about in Fairbanks belonged to Rudy Billberg.[29] He made the first trip from way out, maybe from Nome. I knew him. He was a pilot for Wien Airlines. They had come all this way on this little machine. When we first started having competitive skiing, we couldn't use snowmachines for putting in the trail system around the university. They didn't have any oomph at all. And they were always breaking down. Dave Norton made a little platform turned upside down, with two hunks of railroad track on it to weigh it down, that he pulled behind the snowmachine to make the tracks for the races. It didn't work very well. He was always making something, always dreaming up things. Sometimes they were good ideas and sometimes they didn't work. But he had so much fun trying.

I don't like snowmachines.[30] They are noisy and smelly. And they don't have courtesy for other users on the trails. I was nearly knocked down by some snow-machiners coming fast along the walking trail along Ballaine Road. I had to jump over the berm into the ditch to get out of their way. I don't know if they ever even saw me. I can understand that they can be useful transportation, but the noise is like a rock concert disrupting you when you're listening to a symphony. If you're out walking or skiing, you want to listen to the sounds around you. The silence is the noise. That is the noise I want to hear. I want to hear the birds. I want to hear the breezes in the trees. That is the music.

Ginny's views on snowmachines are made clear in her 1971 article in the *Alaska Conservation Review*, where she states:

> The snowmachine has burst on the winter scene like a plague of locusts. The most considerate operators of this sub-species of the all-terrain vehicle merely shatter the winter's stillness with incessant noise and pollute the air with carbon monoxide. The worst wipe out ski trails, mutilate shrubbery on private property, run down dog teams, play "chicken" with cross country skiers, harass and destroy wildlife, and use the machines to vandalize remote cabins.
>
> Thus, like so many of our technological innovations, the handy-dandy mechanized sled that has liberated so many from ennui by the fireside in the winter has become pestilence to many others—sometimes even to the drivers themselves. The time has come, in fact is long overdue for snowmachine control.
>
> Boon or blight, unless a way is discovered to abolish winter, the snowmachine is here to stay. As well as regulations to restrict abuse, there is also needed provisions for their safe use.
>
> The problem, as with so many mechanical threats to our environment and quality of life, is not one of machines but of people who operate them. And people behaving as they do, laws and limitations must be legislated to control the use of the "abominable snowmachine."[31]

Ginny became an advocate for trails both in Fairbanks and around the state.[32] After protecting Creamer's Field as a wildlife refuge in 1968, Ginny got involved with development of its trail system. She wanted to ensure that a useful trail system was put in place and tried to find ways to avoid conflicts between the allowable mixed uses, such as walking, skiing, dog mushing, and snowmachines. By the 1980s, Ginny's interest in land management issues expanded to the Fairbanks North Star Borough's Trails Commission, which she officially joined in 1980, to serving on the Alaska State Parks Citizen Advisory Board and a state committee working on possible development on the south side of Denali in Denali State Park.[33] She served on the board of the Alaska Natural History Association from 1980 to 1986, and was active with the Alaska Boreal Forest Council, Denali Citizens Council, and Great Old Broads for Wilderness, which uses the voices and activism of elders to preserve and protect wilderness and wild lands.[34]

In 1996, Ginny's role broadened even further when she was appointed by Governor Tony Knowles to his newly established statewide Governor's Trails and Recreational Access for Alaska Citizens' Advisory Board (TRAAK Board). The purpose of this eleven-member body was to encourage development of new trails and recreational resources around Alaska. Specifically, they focused on tying neighborhoods, parks, and commercial areas together, and highway projects that included bike and pedestrian trails, trailheads, pullouts, and picnic areas. Money for these projects was available because all federally funded highway projects in the state were required to put aside ten percent of their budgets for trails and associated public facilities.[35] TRAAK also nominated, evaluated, and recommended routes for inclusion in the Alaska Trails System, a statewide network of land and water trails recognized for their recreational, scenic, and historic value.[36] Ginny expresses both pride in having served on this board and frustration with the government process, having to sit through long meetings four times a year and trying to convince transportation authorities who are only focused on roads about the importance of trails.[37] She considers the construction of the walking trail and bridge alongside the Parks Highway outside the entrance to Denali National Park the biggest accomplishment while she was on the TRAAK Board. This offset path separates pedestrians from car traffic in the congested Glitter Gulch area, thereby making it safer for everyone. Ginny's terms on the TRAAK Board ended in 2004. In October 2004, Governor Frank Murkowski signed Administrative Order 222, which eliminated the TRAAK Board and replaced it with his own Outdoor Recreation and Trails Advisory Board (ORTAB), "to serve as the state trails recreational access and other outdoor recreation activities advisory board."[38]

Ginny and Celia in Ethiopia, 1968. Courtesy of Ginny Wood.

20

Traveling the Globe

I just had a curiosity. I was always interested in new things.

Fom a young age, Ginny had a natural curiosity about the world around her. That included far-away places—other cultures, other countries.

Curiosity is what enticed me to go traveling. I just liked foreign countries and was interested in how people lived. As a little kid, probably I was in the third grade, in school I had a book that was called *The Food We Eat*. It was a story of where our food comes from. It was a way of teaching geography and about all the different countries, just using food as the theme. That fascinated me, and learning about all these countries and the funny foods they ate. I just was always interested in new things. I liked history and I loved geography. Those were my favorite subjects. I got As in those.

Ginny transformed this thirst for discovery into a lifetime of adventure travel. Despite a busy schedule running Camp Denali or leading guided trips in the wilds of Alaska, she always found time for extended trips to what some would consider exotic locales. In May 1954, Ginny, Woody, and five women floated down the Yukon River from Whitehorse, Canada, to Eagle, Alaska, in their folding kayaks on a two-week trip they jokingly dubbed "Squaws Along the Yukon."[1] In May 1960, it was a month-long trip on a boat—the MV *Expansion*—from Seward down along the Aleutian Islands in southwestern Alaska that stopped in every village to deliver mail and groceries, and where the only other passenger was Joan Terry, a woman from Juneau who was visiting each village school to interview the principal.[2] In 1968, Ginny hiked in Greece[3] and visited her friend Dr. Libby Hatton, who was working for the World Health Organization in Gander, Ethiopia.[4] In 1969, Libby and Ginny traveled together again, this time trekking in Nepal.[5] In 1973, Ginny went on a safari in Kenya and Tanzania to view the wildlife and scenery in Africa's greatest national parks.[6] Later, she bicycled in

Ginny and Joan Terry enjoy their Aleutian Island cruise, May 1960. Courtesy of Ginny Wood.

Dr. Libby Hatton, Gander, Ethiopia, 1968. Photo by Ginny Wood.

New Zealand in 1977 with her daughter and Libby Hatton,[7] explored America's hiking trails, and relaxed amidst the peace and quiet and natural beauty of San Juan Island, where she and Celia owned property and a small cabin.[8]

Nowadays, all this might seem commonplace to world travelers, but Ginny did it when "adventure tourism" was still relatively unknown. In some cases, she traveled with close friends. At other times, as a single woman she joined an organized group trip, like in the winter of 1973 when she went on a hiking and camel trek in Algeria. As Ginny explains, "You hardly go as a single woman and just bat around Africa on your own, like I always had done on my trips to other places." She tells what happened on this trip in a story she humorously titles "Committing Malaria."[9]

I decided the big expense of going to Africa is getting there, so I might as well take two trips while I was over there. So I took a back-to-back trip. I left the wildlife safari in Tanzania and Kenya on February 3 to fly to Rome, Italy, to meet up with the group for the next trip, which was going to the Hoggar Mountains in Algeria [Ahaggar Mountains on current maps]. This isn't a place that a woman goes alone just hiking across country. It was supposed to be ten days of hiking and then one week riding on camels. The group leader was a Dutchman by the name of Tom de Booy who was a geologist that taught at a Dutch university until he was kicked out for being a Marxist. But the trip was operated by a French-man, Jean Louis Bernezat, who operated a company in Algeria called Hommes et Montagnes du Sahara. He only spoke French.

To get to the Hoggar Mountains you start in Algiers, then you fly nine hundred miles south to Tamanrasset. And then you get in a jeep that takes you cross-country over the desert on the Trans-Saharan Highway. When you come to this little village called Mertoutek, you leave all your stuff there except your sleeping bag and a change of clothes. There were about eight of us in the hiking group. We saw some animals, but I'd just spent a whole month going through Kenya and Tanzania by jeep, so it wasn't quite as dramatic. The Tuareg people live in the Hoggar Mountains. They're desert people, Arabs kind of. They live in tents.[10]

The Hoggar Mountains are noted for these cave paintings of life back three or four thousand years ago. We had been out for almost a week, and we had just gone up into some boulder country. It was desert, but it's rock desert, not sand. There are lots of rocks.[11] I liked the challenge of finding a route and holds and jumping from rock to rock. I found that I was able to stay up with the leader with no effort. Then you boulder up to where there is this cave with all these wonderful paintings—carvings in the walls—of what it was like thousands of years ago. They were really interesting, because what you saw in these carvings were animals that I'd seen in southern Africa—elephants and lions and tigers and things like that. Animals that didn't live in northern Africa anymore. You also saw pictures of people tossing hay. This meant that probably the climate there used to be different. That it might have been grasslands before it was desert, and that that's where these animals were before. These cave paintings were made by a culture that farmed and grazed when the country was fertile and moist.

At this one spot, we had just made camp and left our sleeping bags and our tents and climbed three or four hours up in these boulders, and I was just looking at one of the best paintings. I was about to snap a picture, feeling on top of the world and in time with myself and life, and the axe fell. There was a call, "You have a message." I thought to myself, "A message? Way out here—a three-day walk into the middle of the Hoggar Mountains?" I looked around and here was a Tuareg youth. He had a piece of paper for Madame Virginia Wood. The French ambassador said I had a telegram in Tamanrasset and I must come get it. A Land Rover would be waiting at a spot which was a three-hour walk from here, and I must pay for it. Tamanrasset was the closest big town. It's not very big, maybe three or four thousand people. But first I had to get to the little village of Mertoutek, which was the last place where we had been. It was where we had left our gear, our extra clothing, our passports, and our money in a locked building, and had gone out from almost two weeks before. I only had my sleeping bag and pack of what I needed for the hiking with me.

But I didn't want to go back. I was supposed to go on a camel trip next. I'd bought clothing and everything for it. But the Tuareg man said, "You are supposed to report to the police in Tamanrasset. There will be a jeep waiting for you down on the river." This really was just a dry riverbed. It had been seven years since they'd had any water in it. To get there from where we were meant dropping off of this sort of escarpment, going through the boulders, and back down to the desert and over to where the river would have been at one time.

Well, so that was about three o'clock in the afternoon. And it gets dark at night. There was this Tuareg who was supposed to be my guide. There were Tuaregs who cooked our meals and were kind of guides, but this one I had never seen before. He didn't speak any English. The Dutch leader, Tom, offered to come with me, but in our group there was this young Frenchman, Robert Meunier, who was a schoolteacher living in Tamanrasset, and he said, "Ginny, I better go with you. You'll get nowhere as a single woman. They may not even talk to you." He spoke Tuareg and French, and very good English. And he knew people in Tamanrasset. He said, "I have to be back at work in two days anyways, so I'm not going on the camel trip part. I'll just go with you now."

The way we had walked in, the village was about ten days away, because we'd been going up here and everywhere in a circuitous route. Going back we would take a shortcut down to the riverbed, which was sand. This would take us right back to the village. We had until just about six o'clock that night to get down to the river before it got dark. We really hurried. Mostly, it was downhill. Down through these boulders and rocks and everything. And as it got dark we could see a campfire in the distance. I kept thinking that must be where the jeep will pick me up. It was about dark when we got down to the river and to the campfire.

Well, we went over there and it was just some people—a group of Tuaregs—and they didn't speak English or anything. There was no jeep. They didn't have anything to do with this. So I said, "How far back to the village where I've left my suitcase, my passport, and my money locked in a stone building?" The Frenchman translated, and he said, "Well, they said if we just drop down into the riverbed and keep walking then we come within about a half mile of that village." I said to the Frenchman, "How far?" He said, "All night." So we hiked all that night. We stopped at seven thirty p.m. to eat a few dates and an orange. We couldn't eat the pork sausage since we didn't want to offend our Muslim guide. As we started out, I asked, "How much water do we have with us?" I had the only canteen that was full of water. I also had the only sleeping bag. I said, "Well, we better get started because as soon as the sun comes up we're going to get very thirsty." As long as it was night it was cool. In daytime, it would be very, very hot: 110, 112 degrees. We only had a quart of water between the three of us and we'd never last very long on that. So we started walking. Robert got terrible blisters and was very tired. I was fine. And the Tuareg just walked steadily on.

The thing that I remember is hiking all night. That is one of the most awesome and weird experiences I had. As the sun set there was an orange glow over the mountains to the west and the different shades gave it a three-dimensional effect. I'll never forget that beautiful moonlight. It was a full moon, which made it a very fascinatingly beautiful atmosphere. Where going along you could see these mountains, which are just rock. And then desert. And I thought, "What am I doing here? I'm with a Frenchman I hardly know and a Tuareg who doesn't speak a word of English. And I'm hiking towards this village where I hope that somebody—the mayor or the head of the village—has a key and will open up that stone building where all my stuff is." I was thrilled by the beautiful setting, but my stomach was sick from the apprehension of why I was supposed to report to the police. I could only think that the only reason somebody would be trying to get in touch with me was that something happened to Romany or Celia or Libby. There was fear and anxiety, yet mixed with this fantastic experience and landscape it was the most awesome, beautiful night I've ever spent.

So we got to the village around midnight. I was very weary—not tired—weary and sleepy and anxious about what the message might be. Robert and I installed ourselves in two rooms at the zeribas "motel" where we had stayed before. A zeribas is a square yurt-type straw hut.[12] In the morning Robert said, "You just stay in this hay hut." He said, "I'll talk to them to see if they'll open up that building." The chief was not supposed to let anybody in that building. It was locked. But I had to have my stuff. The Frenchman said, "Don't try to get into this. They won't bother with a woman." The chief had been told under no circumstance to open that door until the guide and our group got back. So I thought, "Then what do I do?"

As a woman, I was an "it." You're not even a person. I mean, if you're a woman, you have no status whatsoever in that type of country. These were all Muslims. That was hard, because I'd always gone everywhere on my own. In a country like that, you realize that it's best not to be conspicuous. If you're supposed to wear something over your head if you go into a church, you do it. Put a handkerchief or something over yourself. Or, if you're supposed to wear a skirt, you do it. I always had a little skirt that I had in my pack that I could put on if I was wearing shorts. You don't argue and say, "I'm an American and I can do what I want." You just don't want to stand out like that. You don't want try to be a Muslim if you aren't a Muslim. But you show respect by following the rules. When I was out hiking in the desert, I wore shorts. Everybody did. But that was because it was a guided trip.

So Robert and I went to find out about the key to the "hotel" so I could get my bag and passport. While he was trying to get them to open the building up, I had to sit through a tea ceremony for four hours in this hut while the four men squatted around a fire. Then women appeared with broken trinkets to sell. We said we had no money. The man said, "No buy—no key." But I had to have my passport and plane ticket. Finally, they relented and opened the place up and I retrieved my bag.

The jeep that was supposed to be up at the head of the river but was not was in the village. So we got in the jeep to go to Tamanrasset. Right away, I noticed that the red light kept blinking over the oil temperature. Blink, blink, blink. But we just kept going. We started back overland and I noticed this was not the way we had come before. I said, "I don't know where we are, but that surely is not the route that we took coming in." It turned out the driver was doing this illegally. He didn't have a license and he didn't want to meet anybody else, so he was going a back route, off the beaten path, which was a different way than we'd come originally. I kept thinking, "Why is that red light going blink, blink, blink over the oil temperature?"

Well, we finally got back to Tamanrasset. And I went to the police. They only read the telegram to me in French. It said something about taking a malaria pill and that I must telegram the American Embassy. Robert made out a message saying I had taken the treatment. We figured this meant that I would then be able to rejoin the group. But no. The Tuareg guide of Jean Louis said that the police said I must go to Algiers to get the proper paper saying I do not have malaria, even though they had to ask me what that was. It was not enough to have said I took a malaria pill. Well, Algiers was nine hundred miles away. Robert was weary of this stupidity, so we decided to just tell them I would go by plane, but really I would go back to meet the group instead. He said, "Look, I know this country pretty well. Just come to my house and tonight after dark I'll find somebody to take you back up to intersect with your group." I liked that idea because the next part of the trip was going to be camels! I'd already bought my camel outfit and everything.

But at nine o'clock that night somebody came to his door and said, "That woman that you have is wanted by the police. She is not to leave this town, except on a plane back to Algiers." We tried to see the police chief but couldn't even get by the guards. Ugh, it was final! You see, when I got to the police, I was trying to tell them that I had reported to the police as I had been asked to do, but they said, "No, you are to leave the country because you committed a crime." They didn't know what the crime was, but they knew that if the police were looking for me, then I must have done something. It's one of those things that you get trapped in. So I had to fly back to Algiers. I was heartsick. I kept thinking, "here I was halfway around the world and only three days in the Sahara and now it was spoiled." I read Newsweek far into the night to keep myself from bawling.

The next day Robert took me to the airport office in downtown Tamanrasett. Our plane tickets had all been put in a drawer of the travel agent there, or the guy that handled that type of thing. I had an interesting and difficult time trying to get my ticket. The agent would not accept my ticket. He said part was missing. I thought, "Now what? I must buy another?" I figured that Tom must have done something with the ticket when he made the reservations. Finally, Robert said, "Bernezat." The man got out a sheaf of tickets. We were able to convince this bewildered and obdurate man that the SAS one was mine. That I was Va. Wood. You see, everybody else on the trip had come together from the States and had a standard airline ticket, except me. I had come on Scandinavian Airlines. So my ticket looked different. The guy would look through everything and say, "No ticket. No ticket." I said, "There's my ticket." He said, "No, no, no." In his mind, they all had to be the same color because that was the group. Even though I knew my original ticket I'd used to fly from Algiers to Tamanrasset was there with everyone else's. Finally, he issued me a boarding pass.

The thing was, I got caught in this trap. The trouble was, you see, the Algerians had just gotten their freedom from France.[13] They had just changed over to running their own government. Everybody who was in a position of authority had never had that before. They didn't know what they were doing. It wasn't like in Kenya, where the British, for all their stuffiness, still would allow the natives to rise high in the civil service. They couldn't run things, but they did know how to run the civil service. In Algeria, which had been French, nobody knew how to do anything. They didn't know beans. But they couldn't let anybody know that. So that's what I ran into. What a country, stupidity combined with a military dictatorship and bureaucracy.

I eventually unraveled this after finally getting all the way back up to Algiers. I thought to myself, "I must track down the source of that silly telegram and the cause of the finish of my Sahara trip. Shall I get the hell out of here and back to

Alaska—or wait three days in Algiers for the plane to Palma and ten days more for Libby?" The plan had been that after my camel trek I was going to meet Libby and we were going to go through Spain together, and on the way home stop over at one of those nice tropical islands out in the Atlantic that's Spanish. The Azores. I decided that I needed to trace the telegram first. I went to the embassy for help. It was the Swiss Embassy, because Algeria broke off relations with the US in 1967, which meant there was no longer an American embassy there. The Swiss had agreed to help Americans. I found a guard who took me to "his leader." Another man was called in, and at last someone got me the actual telegram. It was from Libby. Celia had gotten a message from Mountain Travel—the group I'd gone to Kenya and Tanzania with. They were trying to get a message to me to tell me that the American leader of the group, Smoke Blanchard, had gotten a very serious and often fatal type of malaria. He had been mountain climbing in Nepal before he met us in Africa. I knew that he had been having headaches. One day he was fine and the next day he was just out of it.[14] Evidently it had really settled in. He was sent back to the United States and they met him at the airport and he was in a coma. Since he had something that was very contagious, Mountain Travel sent word to all the people that had been on our trip about what had happened. They told us that we were to take a pill and to get to a hospital if we got sick or got a headache. But because I wasn't home in Alaska, Celia had got the message as my emergency contact. Celia called Libby, because she was a doctor and had lived and worked in Africa and knew her way around North Africa. So they said, "Oh my gosh, we've got to get word to Ginny that if she gets a headache, if she gets sick, she should immediately go to someplace where they know tropical medicine. They won't know about this where she is in the desert. They won't have ever heard of this tropical disease." Celia and Libby just wanted to get this message to me, and they wanted me to report back to them that I was all right. But I didn't know this until I got to Algiers. I found out that all the embassy wanted was to relay the message and for me to acknowledge it. And for that my whole trip was aborted.

Mountain Travel goofed, because they had told the French guy that they worked through that I was wanted. And then there's this message for me that comes through the Algerian police that's telling them about malaria. Since they didn't know what malaria was, they thought I was wanted for a crime. That's why the Algerian police said I was under arrest. They thought, "Oh, she's committed malaria." So that was pretty funny. I just got caught in the bureaucracy, and the language differences, and mistranslation, too. My crime was I was wanted for committing malaria!

The guy I talked to at the embassy was American, and his name was David Gwinn. It turned out that his wife was a college chum of Libby Hatton's. So they invited me to come to their house while I tried to get a ticket to fly out of Algiers. He was a dope. He had a big picture of Richard Nixon over his kid's bed. But his wife was nice. You know, I didn't have money to go stay in hotels and stuff, so it was helpful to have a place to stay. I don't know what I would have done without this sanctuary.

I sent a telegram to Libby telling her that I was aborting the trip to Spain and was going straight home if transportation was available. God, I was weary of it all! I never did get to ride a camel and this was no women's world. I was weary with fatigue, anxiety, frustration, and disappointment. I had to get my ticket changed, because I now wasn't going on the date or to the destination that was on the original ticket. I had trouble finding anybody that would change my ticket. A Swiss lady who worked at the embassy helped me, and I thought it was figured out, but when I went to pick up the ticket I got the same Algerian cold reception. They would not honor the ticket. It was issued by SAS and I was trying to fly out with Air France, so they wouldn't do anything without permission from the airlines. In those days, you could go anywhere on your ticket as long as it didn't exceed the original mileage to the farthest point you were going to. But they didn't know that in Algiers. You went to anyplace that handled tickets and they said, "No. That's not right. You can't do that. It's going on a different day and a different route." I even went to the airport to try to get on the flight and they said no dice and sent me to Air Algiers. The man there not only would not exchange my ticket but said I had to go through Madrid as on my original ticket, and I could not get off. What a country!

Finally, after three days of trying to figure out how the hell I was going to get home, I finally found a place where they would accept my ticket. I found a woman, the only woman in Algiers that worked in a travel bureau. I said, "Go ask your boss if you can have a ticket change like this. That I can change my routing as long as it doesn't exceed the mileage I bought to start with." This agent took my ticket and issued a new one with no hassle. By this point, I really just wanted to get out of there as quickly as possible. I was so tired of the lack of compassion, stupidity, and obdurate stonewall attitude of the Algerians. I was beginning to dislike them intensely. I was now so frustrated and having such a horrible time that I forgot the beauty of the desert I had just been in.

And of course the flight home did not go as planned. The flight I was supposed to catch in Paris for Anchorage went on to Tokyo, but passengers were not allowed to disembark in Anchorage. So Algeria still reached out her tentacle to trip me. After two hours, a gal got me a seat on a KLM flight from Amsterdam the next day. I spent the night in a hotel in Paris. I was lonely, restless, and defeated—the whole magic mood of Africa dissolved in defeat and weariness. I had been en route from Tamanrasset for so long, it was like each step was like going through a lock towards home and away from the trap of Algeria. I breathed a bit freer with each step.[15]

The sad part was that I missed the camel part of the guided trip that I'd already paid for, and already bought the costume for. It was a big turban that went around your head. And then a scarf to go across your face, because you'd get a lot of sand. Then you had kind of these bloomers that you wore for pants. I think I finally wore that outfit to a Halloween party once.

Age never seemed to slow Ginny down. She kept hiking, biking, skiing, and traveling well into her eighties. In the spring of 1986, at age sixty-nine, she and Celia Hunter hiked across northern England to prove "that there was life in the old gals still."[16] And from June 19 to July 2, 1991, she and Celia joined a tour of Siberia organized by the Alaska chapter of the Sierra Club when Alaska Airlines first obtained permits and authorization to fly scheduled flights to Magadan and Khabarovsk. Ginny described the trip in a May 1991 letter to her friend Connie Barlow: "I don't like guided tours but this is limited to 15, mostly Alaskans and we will be camping with a group of Soviets interested in the ecology and preservation of Lake Baikal. How else can one travel in Siberia? This might be my only chance to see life as it is lived and the natural world of our neighbors across the Bering Sea."[17]

The last international adventure trip Ginny made was in March 1995, at age seventy-eight, when she and Celia went on a cross-country-ski vacation to Norway with an Elderhostel group.[18] Ginny describes the trip in her 1995 Christmas letter:

> I escaped the coldest month that Fairbanks had this year by spending March in Norway; two weeks on an Elderhostel trip that featured cross-country skiing; another two visiting friends in Bergen, then as their guests at a ski cabin near the summit of the Bergen/Oslo railroad.
>
> Participants in the Norway Elderhostel program consisted of my good Alaskan friend, Celia Hunter, and 27 other hearty, interesting, senior citizens (our average age was 69) from all parts of the USA. There was no common denominator, except a shared passion for Nordic skiing. The first week took place outside the small village of Skogn north of Trondheim; the second at a remote working farm in the Trollheimen mountains.
>
> In addition to almost daily vigorous ski tours, each evening included lectures, discussions, and visual immersion in Norwegian history, arts, economics, politics, and lifestyles. Their cultural values include a deep respect for their natural surroundings that Americans might well heed—no urban sprawl, litter or junk. It might be condensed in two words, "Good taste." Cross country skiing and hiking seem an intrinsic way of life. A network of trails and overnight huts radiate from most cities and throughout their mountains, unmolested by snow machines or off road vehicles. "How come?" we asked. "We just wouldn't," they replied.[19]

Ginny exploring sand dunes in the Lower 48, 1992. Photo by Celia Hunter. Courtesy of Ginny Wood.

Although Ginny's age increased and she slowed somewhat, she continued to travel out of Alaska every year (often with Celia) to visit family and friends in the Lower 48 and find new country to hike in. She never lost her curiosity, her sense of adventure, or her excitement for exploring new places.[20]

Celia Hunter, 2001. Courtesy of Ginny Wood.

21

The Loss of a Friend

Celia was a born leader.

A fter more than five decades of friendship, Ginny Wood and Celia Hunter were a nearly inseparable team. They flew airplanes together, explored Alaska's great wilderness, established and operated Camp Denali, fought to protect Alaska's wild beauty and bounty, and did bike trips and hikes around the world. They created a lifetime of shared memories.

When Celia returned to Fairbanks after working for the Wilderness Society in Washington, DC, for a few years, Ginny offered her the basement apartment in her home. Celia had sold her house next door, but wanted to retain her membership in the Dogpatch neighborhood. Ginny was divorced and her daughter was grown up, so she had extra space, and was glad for the company and the help with managing and paying for an Alaskan household.

In their later years, it seemed as if Ginny and Celia were never apart. They came together to community lectures, public hearings, and parties. They held activist meetings at their house. They sat side by side in the dim light of the living room writing letters to congressmen and senators asking for permanent protection from oil development for the Arctic National Wildlife Refuge. They supported each other in their political and environmental work, and with daily chores of life. They had different personalities and were perhaps a bit competitive with each other, so they also fought, interrupting each other and disagreeing about how something happened in the past or what to do about a household issue.

Celia passed away in 2001. A candlelight memorial was set up in her room and a public gathering was held to honor her. Obviously, losing such a close friend would be deeply emotional, but typical of Ginny, she was guarded when she talked about it on the fifth anniversary of Celia's death.

Celia loved this work, fighting to protect the environment. But me, oh gad, I would rather be outside in it instead of sitting inside writing about it. But I have spent from 1960 to—what is it now—almost 2003 working on environmental issues.

L-R: *Celia and Ginny enjoying Alaska's great outdoors, circa 2000. Courtesy of Ginny Wood.*

It started with testifying to protect the Arctic National Wildlife Range, and I am still sending letters and working on that.[1] In fact, that was the last thing that Celia was doing before she died on December 1, 2001. She was eighty-two years old. She'd been on the phone with Debbie Miller, who had just been back in Washington, DC. Celia was asking her which senators were on the fence about the bill to protect the Arctic National Wildlife Refuge. Celia made a list of the names, and we were writing our little notes to send to them. I was writing mine, and she was writing hers. She said that she would type mine up. I can't spell very well. And I purposely haven't learned how to use a computer. I don't want to spend my life down there in the basement on the computer with email. Regular mail is bad enough. We were going to go next door to our friend Sam Deshevsky's, who is a geologist and has an office there, and use his fax machine to send our messages to the senators. It was getting to be eleven o'clock at night, so we said, "Why don't we knock it off and go to bed? We'll go over in the morning and send them." It was a weekend anyway so they weren't going to get to the senators any faster by us staying up all night. So we stopped for the night. Celia went downstairs to her apartment.

The next morning, I got up and Celia was not upstairs yet. Usually she was the first one up. She was always hungry early and wanted to eat. Sometimes we ate together and sometimes we didn't. It depended on when we each got up and what we were each doing that day. She'd just gotten back from a trip Outside for a month and then had gone to an Alaska Conservation Foundation meeting down in Anchorage, so I thought she wasn't up yet because she must've been extra tired. We'd kind of been fighting the night before while working on those letters and I felt bad, so I thought I'd fix her a nice breakfast. Not just oatmeal, but something special. I'd make her an omelet, because we didn't do that very often. I kept pounding on the floor—which was our usual way of me telling her to come upstairs—and still no Celia. I thought she was probably on the computer and couldn't hear me.

Finally, I went down at about ten o'clock, and there she was, dead on the floor! Just looking like she had laid down to sleep! Her face was calm, and she had her clothes on. Her grubbies. I don't know if she slept in them or whether it was a sweat suit. She had her bunk up high so she could see out the window, so she had to go down a little ladder to get out of bed. She had gone down that ladder and was on the floor. There was no anguish or anything like she had choked on something or had a stroke or anything. It wasn't as if she had collapsed. She may have gotten up to do some exercises or some meditation. She had mentioned earlier how she felt out of shape and that she had better start doing some exercises. So she could have not felt well or got tired and thought, "Well, I'll just lie down for a minute." But who knows?

Her death sure was a shock for me! We had been out cross-country skiing together just a couple of days before. We didn't have much snow yet that year,

Ginny (L) and Celia (R) on one of their final skis, 2001. Courtesy of Ginny Wood.

but we could go down to Smith Lake on the university trails and ski around there. So that's what we'd done. We had made one ski trip earlier in the season on our trail by the house. We'd gone up around Les Viereck's land and decided that there were too many roots and things sticking up. We said, "Let's not do this anymore." We agreed that unless we got more snow, we'd better ski together, because you could trip on those roots and fall and break something and be out there for who knows how long. We'd gone to Smith Lake, because there was enough snow to make a good trail on the smooth lake.

As it turned out, we never did send those notes to the senators about the Arctic Wildlife Refuge legislation.

After Celia's death, Ginny wrote the following tribute to her in *The Northern Line,* the newsletter of the Northern Alaska Environmental Center:

> Farewell, old buddy. You were my companion of our ski trails, of the skies in our respective cockpits ferrying airplanes, as business partners establishing and operating Camp Denali in Kantishna for 25 years, electrician and chain sawyer around our Fairbanks home.
>
> We lived interdependent yet separate lives, each adding further elements to the other's quality of life. We argued some, we laughed a lot, shared much, and accomplished goals we couldn't have achieved on our

own. You used to say we could do anything I thought up. Lately it's been more like I could do anything you would help me do—spelling words I wrote incorrectly and transferring my illegible scrawl to print on your computer which I refused to master.

I am missing you in many ways and places I could not have imagined, each of us savoring our individuality as we did. I miss your laughter bursts; your insufferable cheerfulness so early on dark, bleak days; your willingness to tackle any problems—mechanical, societal, or environmental—undaunted.

We had a relationship unusual for women in our younger days. More like the comradeship of soldiers in combat, mountain climbers and shipmates where one's life depends on the skill, endurance, and judgement of the other.

Today, I found the last loaf of bread you baked and put in the deep freeze. I'm savoring it as a last sacrament. I don't know what Valhalla you envisioned as an afterlife—"reincarnation as a bird," you once said? So perhaps you'll have wings but not with the angels. I'd like to think there is a special place for Earth/Nature/Wilderness lovers where you are joining Donella Meadows and David Brower, and our recently departed neighbor, Gordon Herreid. Save a campsite for me.

Skol! Ginny[2]

Ginny enjoying summer on her deck, Fairbanks, July 2010. Photo by Amy Johnson.

22
Reflections

Life is what happens to you while you're making other plans.

Ginny Wood has approached her own aging process head-on, with humor, stubbornness, and now, at age ninety-three, with grace. As she has said, "Like a roll of toilet paper, the nearer one gets to the end of one's life, the faster it goes! And after age ninety, the more inept one becomes at doing the things that need to be done."[1] As her mobility and mental acuity declined, this previously fiercely independent pioneer accepted help from care-givers and friends with less argument than expected. She is polite and thankful to all who help her remain living in her own home. She has proven to be an example of how to age well.

As one ages, it is not unusual to reflect back on the meaning of one's life. While Ginny loves to tell stories from her past, she is not prone to self-reflection. She is interested in the present—in discussing politics, the latest environmental issue, or commenting on the state of our society. Ginny only takes a step back to reflect when prompted by a question, such as: "What has given you the most satisfaction in life?"

At this stage at the end of my life, I'm trying to figure out what I thought about when I was younger. When you are looking at it in retrospect, you get mixed up with how you feel now and how you felt then. How I feel now is that I'm just glad I was born when I was.

What makes me feel contented with my life is not the same thing every day. If you were to take your temperature for your well-being factor, it would go up and down with the events of the days. Like, I don't think any of us felt very happy about the outcome of the elections in 2002 when we were in the middle of President George W. Bush's first term and the Republicans won control of Congress.[2] Or when Bush got us into war.[3] We weren't going to feel any safer, I tell you. What's the world coming to? We as a species had over three million years since, as far as we claim, to attain civilization. When are we going to be and act civil?

Or there's the fact that I'm not skiing anymore so I no longer can get the satisfaction of putting on my skis and going fifteen to twenty miles in one day, just roaming. I can't put my pack on my back and be completely self-sufficient for a month in the Brooks Range. I have withdrawal symptoms about that. But once in a while I get flashbacks of just a scene that I can remember on a hike up in the Brooks Range or at McKinley Park, and it feels like I'm right back there. That makes me feel good. It's wonderful to be able to have memories like that. As the Pete Seeger song says:

> How do I know my youth is all spent?
> My come up and go has come up and went.
> But in spite of it all, still I can grin.
> To recall the places my come up has been.[4]

I feel fortunate to be living where I do and that gives me satisfaction. You know, a lot of people would spend a lot of money just to come to a place like this. With trees and a view and to be able to put your skis on right outside your door and just go. And the great neighborhood that I'm in. This community that we have here.

I'm not sure that I had a grand plan for my life. You know, I'm not a guru or anything. I wouldn't say that this is what everybody should have done. I just have found that it worked for me. One thing that makes me feel good about my life is that I don't have a mortgage. I don't own a credit card. I've never paid on credit. I've always paid cash for everything. It's just simpler not to be in debt. I've never been broke and I've never been rich. I always figured somewhere along the line that what you didn't spend, you didn't have to waste a lot of time earning. I know how much money I have available to spend, and then when I don't have it, I don't spend it. That doesn't mean that a lot of people don't get their satisfaction out of their career. But up here it's easier to just sort of become a jack of all trades. It's sort of interesting to ask people what they got their degree in. People will surprise you. You'd never know that someone living in a tent somewhere has a PhD from Harvard.

I always had dreams. I was a great dreamer. Oh my goodness, one time I made a list of all the things I wanted to do. I think I was twelve or thirteen or maybe I was even fourteen. I don't remember anymore what all was on it, but I do know it contained sailing a boat around the world and driving a dog team. Both of which are things I've kind of done. I don't know that it was list of things that would make you a better person or citizen, it was just adventures.

I'm not sure whether my life has turned out the way I thought it would. But it's been a great adventure. It's had some ups and downs. And there are some things I would like to have changed. But you never know where the road not taken would have taken you. Where you thought at the time something was a big tragedy or a wrong turn, you'll never really know what else might have happened because you didn't take that other road. You only know the ones you traveled.

And looking back on it, I just say thank god I was born in the last century. Because I see lots of things now where there's more and more of what are considered "the good things in life"—if you mean good things as being more things to buy. More things at the stores. The roads are paved. They don't get dusty. We don't get stuck as often. So that's nice. But it means we just go faster and hit each other. We used to just have fender benders. Nobody got hurt. You just couldn't go that fast. But now everybody can go sixty miles an hour and if you have an accident it's serious. Quite often someone dies. Or if you're going any slower than that you get arrested for going too slow, for holding up traffic. That's the law now. Having worked on the TRAAK Board, I've listened to the Highway Department say over and over again how the aim of roads is to get the biggest volume of traffic fastest over a given segment of road. But that's what I think leads to road rage.

I wouldn't say I'm satisfied with the way my life has been. I'd say I'm very grateful. There have been ups and downs, sorrows and disappointments, and I don't think I've achieved much. I haven't invented a cure for cancer. But I think I was a person who was endowed with very good health and with curiosity and with a certain number of basic values. I was born into a family that gave me enough good values and a sense of responsibility for myself and for others without making it a law or enforcing it. And hopefully enough empathy to put myself in another person's place. I think that makes me lucky. But I haven't really accomplished much. Now, what's accomplished? A lot of people, they could look at my life and analyze it, and by their measures they would think I'm sort of a failure. You haven't done this or done that. I don't have a PhD. I don't have a trade. My marriage broke up. I have one daughter who didn't always think I was the best mother in the world. But it's been a great adventure.

The human race was a great experiment and I'm awfully glad I got in on it.

Notes

Prologue

1. This prologue is a combination of a piece handwritten by Ginny Wood found in her personal collection (green notebook titled "The Book (That is not)," undated, Ginny Wood Personal Collection) with revisions and additions she made in response to the original being read to her in 2010. The original writing and the notebook in general are not dated, but amongst the loose papers in the front of the notebook there is one sheet dated "10/19/2000." The fact that she says "three-quarters of an extraordinary century" in the original text instead of "the greater part of an extraordinary century," which we revised it to, leads me to speculate that she might have been about seventy-five when writing this passage. This would mean it could have been written around 1992.

2. Throughout her narrative, Ginny uses the term "air force" when discussing flying during World War II. I have left this terminology since it is her wording, despite the fact that at the time the United States did not yet have a separate officially named air force. The US Army Air Forces was created from the Army Air Corps in June 1941 and put under the command of Hap Arnold (Vera Williams, *WASPs: Women Airforce Service Pilots of World War II* [Osceola, WI: Motorbooks International, 1994], 20). The US Air Force (USAF) was officially declared a separate branch of the military in 1947, with implementation of the National Security Act of 1947, which created the US Department of Defense, composed of three branches: Army, Navy, and a newly created Air Force (Bernard C. Nalty, *Winged Shield, Winged Sword: A History of the United States Air Force*, Vols. I & II [Washington, DC: Air Force History and Museums Program, 1997]).

3. When I read this piece to Ginny in 2010 as part of our manuscript review, she answered the questions in this section as if I was really asking her them. Ginny said the following:

> When I think about these questions today, the answer is that I've discovered meaning and importance in my daughter and her husband, spending time in the wilderness, coming to Alaska where I became aware of the importance of wilderness and the need to protect the environment, my roamings abroad, and my curiosity and desire for adventure. Today, I see the establishment and running of Camp Denali, leading trips in the Brooks Range, and the people I encountered doing these things as my legacy; my marriage and my daughter as my triumphs; my divorce as a disappointment. And one of my greatest sorrows was the death of my close friend, Celia Hunter.

1 Introduction

1. Roger Kaye, *Last Great Wilderness: The Campaign to Establish the Arctic National Wildlife Refuge* (Fairbanks: University of Alaska Press, 2006).
2. Others have used a similar metaphor of life and story, but in a different sense than Ginny. In Julie Cruikshank's book *Life Lived Like a Story* (Lincoln: University of Nebraska Press, 1990), Tagish/Tlingit elder Angela Sidney from Yukon Territories, Canada, says, "I've tried to live my life right, just like a story" (20). As someone who mixes traditional Native stories with her own life experiences to represent the story of her life, Mrs. Sidney regards the lessons of story as critical to shaping one's life. Ginny does not use story in this way. Her stories are what define her, are what create the image and identify of who Ginny Wood is. So for her, living life like a story has a different meaning. For more about the use of story to create identity and how stories can gain meaning and significance in repeated performances, see William Schneider, *Living with Stories: Telling, Re-telling, and Remembering* (Logan: Utah State University Press, 2008).
3. Barbara Allen, "Oral History: The Folk Connection," in *The Past Meets the Present: Essays on Oral History,* eds. David Stricklin and Rebecca Sharpless, 15–26 (Lanham, MD: University Press of America, 1988): 21.
4. David William Cohen, *The Combing of History* (Chicago: University of Chicago Press, 1994).
5. For more about the influence of setting and audience on storytelling, see Schneider, *Living with Stories*; William Schneider, "Lessons from the Storytellers," in *Resilience in Arctic Societies: Papers from the Third IPSSAS Seminar,* eds. Larry Kaplan and Michelle Daveluy, 111–18 (Fairbanks: International PhD School for Studies of Arctic Societies, 2005); and William Schneider, *So They Understand: Cultural Issues in Oral History* (Logan: Utah State University Press, 2002).
6. Isabel Allende, *Portrait in Sepia* (New York: Harper Collins, 2001), 303–4.
7. Elizabeth Tonkin, *Narrating Our Pasts: The Social Construction of Oral History* (Cambridge Studies in Oral and Literate Culture, 22. Cambridge, UK: Cambridge University Press, 1992).
8. Schneider, "Lessons from the Storytellers," 113–14.
9. R. Weeden, pers. comm.
10. From Alfred Lord Tennyson's "Ulysses" as written in "A Part of All That I Have Known," p. 4. Handwritten essay about her childhood by Ginny Wood, probably written for her book about her life. In binder titled "A Part of All That I Have Met," Ginny Wood Personal Collection.
11. Alessandro Portelli, "Oral History as Genre," in *Narrative and Genre,* eds. Mary Chamberlain and Paul Richard Thompson, (London: Routledge, 1998), 23–45; Ron Grele, *Envelopes of Sound: Six Practitioners Discuss the Method, Theory, and Practice of Oral History and Oral Testimony* (Chicago: Precedent Publications, 1975); Valerie Yow, "'Do I Like Them Too Much?': Effects of the Oral History

Interview on the Interviewer and Vice-Versa," *Oral History Review* 24, no. 1 (Summer 1997): 55–79; Tracy E. K'Meyer and A. Glenn Crothers, "'If I See Some of This in Writing, I'm Going to Shoot You': Reluctant Narrators, Taboo Topics, and the Ethical Dilemmas of the Oral Historian," *Oral History Review* 34, no. 1 (Winter/Spring 2007): 71–93; Schneider, *Living with Stories;* Schneider, "Lessons from the Storytellers"; Schneider, *So They Understand;* William Schneider and Phyllis Morrow, *When Our Words Return: Writing, Hearing and Remembering Oral Traditions of Alaska and the Yukon* (Logan: Utah State University Press, 1995); Ruth Finnegan, *Oral Traditions and the Verbal Arts: A Guide to Research Practices* (London: Routledge, 1992).

12. David Mandelbaum notes that life histories often are framed in terms of turning points that resonate through the rest of a person's life ("The Study of Life History: Ghandi," *Current Anthropology* 14, no. 3 [June 1973]: 177–96). I did not adhere to this approach with Ginny's storytelling sessions, instead focusing on themes or small pieces of her life we knew about. However, to form a coherent narrative I wove her stories together in chronological order. In so doing, one comes to see her life's turnings and intellectual and emotional shifts.

13. Michael Frisch, *A Shared Authority: Essays on the Craft and Meaning of Oral and Public History* (Albany: State University of New York Press, 1990); Michael Frisch, "Sharing Authority: Oral History and the Collaborative Process," *Oral History Review* 30, no. 1 (Winter/Spring 2003): 111–13; and Linda Shopes, "Commentary: Sharing Authority," *Oral History Review* 30, no. 1 (Winter/Spring 2003): 103–10.

14. For discussion about how connections like this may affect the interviewer, the interviewee, and the interview itself, see Yow, "'Do I Like Them Too Much?,'" 55–79.

15. Some women's life histories with discussions of women's traditional or domestic roles include: Cruikshank, *Life Lived Like a Story;* Esther Burnett Horne and Sally McBeth, *Essie's Story: The Life and Legacy of a Shoshone Teacher* (Lincoln: University of Nebraska Press, 1998)*;* Margaret Blackman, *During My Time: Florence Edenshaw Davidson, a Haida Woman* (1982; repr., Seattle: University of Washington Press, 1992); Margaret Blackman, *Sadie Brower Neakok, An Iñupiaq Woman* (Seattle: University of Washington Press, 1989); and Ruth Behar, *Translated Woman: Crossing the Border with Esperanza's Story* (Boston: Beacon Press, 1994).

16. For example, California Women Political Leaders Oral History Collection, The Regional Oral History Office, Bancroft Library, University of California, Berkeley, Berkeley, California. Finding aid and transcripts available online at http://bancroft.berkeley.edu/ROHO/collections/subjectarea/pol_gov/ca_women_pol.html, accessed February 12, 2011.

17. September 22, 1980, interview by Maria Brooks (Tape No. ORAL HISTORY 93-01-65); March 10, 1984, interview with Patty Kastelic for KUAC's *Homefires* radio series (group interview also including Celia Hunter, Nancy Baker, and Florence Weber) (Tape No. ORAL HISTORY 90-10-02); July 20, 2000, interview with Karen Brewster (Tape No. ORAL HISTORY 2000-07-03); and November 13, 2002, interview with

Karen Brewster (Tape No. ORAL HISTORY 2000-07-11). Plus a November 10, 2002, interview by Roger Kaye that is not archived.

18. "A life history account obviously involves some kind of selection, since only a very small part of all that the person has experienced can possibly be recorded. Certain salient facts about a person are likely to be recorded by any narrator, but much of any life history has to be chosen for inclusion according to some principles for selection. Often enough, such principles as are used are unstated or unwitting or inchoate" (Mandelbaum, "The Study of Life History," 177).

19. David Dunaway, "The Oral Biography," *Biography* 14, no. 3 (Summer 1991): 256–66.

20. There has been much discussion in the field of oral history about the role of the interviewer and how much he or she should or should not be present in the retelling. I believe it is important to represent myself as part of the life history, since I was part of the process and my presence influenced the stories that Ginny shared. For more on this, see Karen Brewster, *The Whales, They Give Themselves: Conversations with Harry Brower, Sr.* (Fairbanks: University of Alaska Press, 2004); Schneider, *So They Understand*; Blackman, *During My Time*; Blackman, *Sadie Brower Neakok*; and Behar, *Translated Woman*.

21. K'Meyer and Crothers, "'If I See Some of This in Writing, I'm Going to Shoot You,'" 90.

22. Ibid., 92.

23. In 1991, author and friend Connie Barlow encouraged Ginny and Celia to do a book of their stories and thoughts to inspire older women (Letter to Celia Hunter and Ginny Wood from Connie Barlow, New York, New York, February 17, 1991. Loose pages stuck into green notebook titled "The Book (That is not)," Ginny Wood Personal Collection). Connie Barlow was a science writer and the editor of *From Gaia to Selfish Genes, Selected Writings in the Life Sciences* (Cambridge, MA: The MIT Press, 1991). In 1997, Ginny and Celia were approached by the University of California Press, and then again in 2000 by the Alaska History Association, to write up their experiences and adventures in Alaska, including their conservation activities, and the concepts and ideals that were most important to them (Letter from Celia Hunter and Ginny Wood to Doris Kretschmer, University of California Press, July 9, 1997, in folder "Man for Alaska Book—Ginny Wood," Ginny Wood Personal Collection; Letter to Ginny Wood and Celia Hunter from Charles Money, executive director of the Alaska Natural History Association, October 11, 2000, in file folder titled "Correspondence on 'The Book,'" Ginny Wood Personal Collection). Ginny began to outline the book by themes: bears, wolves, Dall sheep, caribou, dogs, horses, adolescence, Waterville, climbing, working for Wien Airlines in Kotzebue, travels in Algiers, Greece, and Ethiopia, Camp Denali, trips with the Sierra Club and in the Brooks Range, rafting trips, Europe in 1938, flying—WASP and to Alaska, sailing, airdrops, marriage/motherhood, environmental awakenings, trails and TRAAK board, 1989 *Exxon Valdez* oil spill, and the fight to protect the Arctic National Wildlife Refuge. I also ran across an unpublished

manuscript written by Ginny Wood titled "Alaska" in the Ginny Wood Personal Collection. It describes Alaska's physiographic characteristics (climate and weather, permafrost, earthquakes, floods, volcanoes, fire, and glaciers), regional geography (Southeast, Southcentral, Southwest and Aleutians, Interior, and Brooks Range and Arctic) with related economies, cultures, and histories, and public land management system. It is unclear for whom or what purpose this was written.

24. Celia also started to write her memoirs for a book project as well as for a radio series she was doing with local broadcaster Amy Mayer. In 2002, Amy Mayer of KUAC FM produced a CD titled *Celia's Alaska: Pioneer Stories of Denali* that contains excerpts of the August 1999 to November 2001 public radio show *Alaska Edition*, which featured Celia as a Fairbanks pioneer. Celia wrote about such things as: arriving in Fairbanks, beginning tourist operations in Kotzebue, how sightseeing tours began in Fairbanks, founding Camp Denali, Fairbanks community events like the Equinox Marathon, the skiathon, and the Great Tanana River Raft Race, and the dogs in her life. These drafts can be found in various places in the Ginny Wood Personal Collection. For instance, a folder titled "From the Moles Den—Celia's Journal."

25. Handwritten draft in green notebook in folder titled "Correspondance [*sic*] on 'The Book,'" Ginny Wood Personal Collection.

26. K'Meyer and Crothers, "'If I See Some of This in Writing, I'm Going to Shoot You,'" 83; Valerie Yow, "Ethics and Interpersonal Relationships in Oral History Research," *Oral History Review* 22, no. 1 (Summer 1995): 57–59.

27. For a similar friendship-based life-history project, see Brewster, *The Whales, They Give Themselves.*

28. For discussion about oral histories with women who diminish their contributions, see Kathleen Ryan, "'I Didn't Do Anything Important': A Pragmatist Analysis of the Oral History Interview," *Oral History Review* 36, no. 1 (Winter/Spring 2009): 24–44.

29. With the previous life history I did with Harry Brower Sr. of Barrow, Alaska *(The Whales, They Give Themselves),* Harry died before we finished the project. This created challenges for me when trying to retell his stories. I did not want a repeat performance with Ginny.

30. Horne and McBeth, *Essie's Story,* xv.

31. K'Meyer and Crothers, "If I See Some of This in Writing, I'm Going to Shoot You," 84.

2. Childhood: The Foundation of an Adventurous Life

1. This was the Sherman Branch Experiment Station. In 1909, the Oregon state legislature passed a law establishing experiment stations "to investigate and demonstrate the conditions under which useful plants may be grown on dry, arid, or nonirrigated lands of the State of Oregon, and to determine the kinds of plants best adapted for

growth on these lands" (W. E. Hall, "50 Years of Research at the Sherman Experiment Station," Miscellaneous Paper 104, June 1961, Agricultural Experiment Station, Oregon State University, Corvallis, Oregon: 4). The Sherman Branch Station at Moro was established in 1911 and was operated by the Oregon Agricultural College (now Oregon State University) and the US Department of Agriculture.

2. When originally talking about her mother in 2007, Ginny did not mention the name of her mother's hometown, and in 2010 when putting these stories together, Ginny could no longer remember the name of the town. Not remembering was upsetting to Ginny, so she was trying very hard to figure it out. By looking at a map with a friend and trying to remember things from her own childhood memories of visiting the place, they guessed that the town might have been Marlborough, Massachusetts, which is almost due west of Boston.

3. This story of Ginny's childhood has been compiled from two sources: the oral history interviews conducted with her from 2006 to 2008, and her own writings in preparation for an autobiography. I have integrated the two to create the best possible telling with the least redundancy. I use notes to indicate the original source for particular sections.

4. From "Although my grandfather…" through "…Denver Museum of Natural History" was handwritten by Ginny Wood in a green notebook titled "The Book (That is not)," undated, Ginny Wood Personal Collection.

5. From "My grandfather did not marry…" through "…nonconformists in our family tree" was handwritten by Ginny Wood in a green notebook titled "The Book (That is not)."

6. Parts of this paragraph are from Ginny Wood's handwritten notes in a green notebook titled "The Book (That is not)."

7. Edwin Hill was hired as a soil erosion specialist for the Department of the Interior and assigned to the Northwest Soil Erosion Project under the direction of W. A. Rockie, whose headquarters were in Pullman, Washington ("C. Edwin Hill Gets Federal Position," newspaper article in scrapbook in Ginny Wood Personal Collection, unknown date and newspaper). The experimental farm in Waterville, Washington, was a branch station of the Washington Agricultural Experiment Station operated by Washington Agricultural College (now Washington State University-WSU) in Pullman. The main station, opened in 1892 on a farm near Pullman, was the site of agricultural instruction and experimental work conducted by the staff of the station and the faculty of the College of Agriculture. Similar work occurred at the various branch stations around the state. In 1946, the Washington Agricultural Experiment Stations were made a part of the Institute of Agricultural Sciences, which included the WSU College of Agriculture, the College of Veterinary Medicine, and the Agricultural Extension Service. The Institute and experiment stations throughout the state existed until 1965, when they were integrated into the Agricultural Research Center of the College of Agriculture (Agricultural Research Center Office Files, 1901–1948, Archives 20, Finding Aid Collection Description,

Washington State University Libraries, Manuscripts, Archives, and Special Collections, Pullman, Washington, http://www.wsulibs.wsu.edu/masc/finders/ua20 .htm, accessed February 12, 2011).

8. From "Waterville was in the high plateau..." to "...wheatfields and livestock pastures" is from a handwritten document by Ginny Wood, titled "Memoirs," p. 3, on loose-leaf pages stuck into green notebook titled "The Book (That is not)."

9. Ginny says that her father developed summer fallow and planted other crops to build up the soil lost to erosion, but according to Andrew Duffin in his article "Vanishing Earth: Soil Erosion in the Palouse, 1930–1945" (*Agricultural History* 79, no. 2 [Spring 2005]: 173–92), the traditional wheat-farming technique of letting some acreage lie fallow was believed to be one of the contributors to extensive soil erosion in the region and was why the government promoted planting "soil conserving crops" like legumes and grasses in non-wheat-producing fields to replenish the ground, hold the soil in place, and reduce erosion. It may be possible that Ginny misspoke about her father developing summer fallow and that his efforts to collect seeds and test their productivity was in line with the government programs mentioned by Duffin.

10. Wheatgrass grows tall, covers the entire surface of the ground, and comes up perennially from its own seed. Edwin Hill's experiments with crested wheatgrass led to the discovery of a new forage crop and was found to be effective in checking soil erosion. It was especially adapted to marginal lands and was suitable for regular agriculture but also could be utilized for grazing ("Its Work Still Lives," newspaper article in scrapbook in Ginny Wood Personal Collection, unknown date and newspaper).

11. At least one local newspaper article did praise Ed Hill for his work. It said that Hill originated "whisker dams" and applied them successfully at the Wildhorse soil erosion control project around Athena, Oregon. The article explained that whisker dams are used to try to protect gully erosion for Oregon farmers. It consists of using straw to form artificial vegetation on newly graded gullies when natural vegetation has not grown enough. Whisker dams are put in after the soil is soft by using a spade to make a trench that is four inches deep and two to three inches wide. A thin layer of straw is scattered over the opening and forced tightly into the trench. Water running the full width of the dams gave the appearance of water running downstairs as each little obstruction formed a level ("'Whisker Dams' Stops Erosion," newspaper article in scrapbook in Ginny Wood Personal Collection, unknown date and newspaper).

12. From "Much, much later..." to "...compiled for over twelve years" is from a handwritten document by Ginny Wood, titled "Memoirs," p. 3, on loose-leaf pages stuck into green notebook titled "The Book (That is not)."

13. From "The first childhood memory..." to "...scooting maneuver again" was handwritten by Ginny Wood in a green notebook titled "The Book (That is not)."

14. From "And then there was the time…" to "…dastardly prank" is from a handwritten document by Ginny Wood titled, "Memoirs," p. 2, on loose-leaf pages stuck into green notebook titled "The Book (That is not)."

15. From "I must have been of school age…" to "…and auditoriums today" was handwritten by Ginny Wood in a green notebook titled "The Book (That is not)."

16. From "Every adult citizen…" to "…never in our town," ibid.

17. From "Cash was a lean, unshaven man…" to "…with her offspring," ibid.

18. From "What I comprehended…" to "…proper riding lessons," ibid.

19. From "When I became a few years older…" to "…fundraising campaigns," ibid.

20. Albert Payson Terhune, *Lochinvar Luck* (New York: Grosset & Dunlap, 1923).

21. According to Edwin Hill's obituary, he was superintendent of the agricultural experimental station at Waterville from 1919 to 1929, spent three years at Wenatchee, and then three years as chief conservationist for the Oregon soil erosion program at Pendleton, Oregon (Obituary, C. Edwin Hill, newspaper article, Ginny Wood Collection, date and newspaper unknown).

22. This was Dr. Walter Clay Lowdermilk, assistant chief of the US Soil and Conservation Service. In 1938, on behalf of the Department of Agriculture, Dr. Lowdermilk surveyed land use in other countries to compare with American agricultural practices and the conservation of land resources. He surveyed in England, Holland, France, Italy, North Africa, and the Near East. After eighteen months, the project was interrupted by the outbreak of war when Germany invaded Poland in September 1939. The group was prevented from continuing the survey through Turkey, the Balkan States, southern Germany, and Switzerland as originally planned. Lowdermilk published his findings in a report, "Conquest of the Land through 7,000 Years" (US Department of Agriculture, August 1953).

23. *Rolf in the Woods: The Adventures of a Boy Scout with Indian Quonab and Little Dog Skookum* (Garden City, NY: Doubleday, Page and Company, 1911); *Two Little Savages* (Garden City, NY: Doubleday, Page and Company, 1903).

24. Parts of this paragraph are from Ginny Wood's handwritten notes in a green notebook titled "The Book (That is not)."

25. From "On Saturdays…" to "…for participants" and from "The robbers… to "…further competition" was handwritten by Ginny Wood in a green notebook titled "The Book (That is not)."

26. From "The skating rink…" to "…the snow beyond," ibid.

27. From "I don't imagine…" to "…buggy room," ibid.

28. From "Our close companionship…" to "…returned unscathed," ibid.

29. From "Waterville also provided…" to "…only by our imaginations," ibid.

30. From "I don't know at just what age…" to "…Alice in Wonderland one," ibid.

31. From "During our first summer…" to "…local granite," ibid.

32. From "It took about…" to "…rushing against it," ibid.

33. From "For us children…" to "…dead snakes," ibid.

34. From "My formal education…" to "…my entrance examination," ibid.

35. Currently known as Washington State University.

36. In 1937, the Hill family moved to Seattle, where Edwin Hill did real estate work for Continental, Inc. However, he would not sell anything that had an erosion problem or the potential for erosion (Obituary, C. Edwin Hill, newspaper article, Ginny Wood Collection, date and newspaper unknown).

37. This is the 63,690-acre Desolation Wilderness area located within Eldorado National Forest and managed by the US Forest Service.

3. Europe by Bicycle

1. According to Celia Hunter,

   Youth hostelling as such began modestly about 1914, when a German, Richard Schirrman, organized the first hostels in Germany... Richard Shirrman conceived the idea of providing inexpensive lodging places for these students [it was the custom of all university students in western Europe to have a year of travel]—places where they might sleep and eat at minimum cost, and enjoy the companionship of their fellow students... The only real requisite for use of a hostel is that the wanderer be traveling by his own power, either by foot or by bicycle. Train and auto are not acceptable means of transportation, save in Sweden. However, during these days of post-war readjustment, hitchhiking has become almost the favorite means of travel of most students. (Celia Hunter, "Guiseppe and Garibaldi and Some In Decision," *Everett* (WA) *Daily Herald,* May 4, 1948)

   According to the official website of Hostelling International, German schoolteacher Richard Schirrman initiated the youth hostel concept in 1909, when one of his school groups was on an excursion, got caught in a thunderstorm, and took emergency shelter in a nearby school building ("100 Years of Hostelling: How It All Started," *Hostelling International,* http://www.hihostels.com/web/100history.en.htm, accessed February 12, 2011). According to the official website of the UK Youth Hostel Association, the Youth Hostels Association of Great Britain was formed in 1930 ("YHA History," *UK Youth Hostel Association,* http://www.yha.org.uk/about-yha/corporate-information/history_of_the_yha.aspx, accessed February 12, 2011).

2. Unpublished manuscript "Once Upon a Time" by Virginia Hill. All my citations refer to the original manuscript in Ginny's possession. Since completing this book, friends of Ginny's have been developing her original bike trip manuscript for publication under the title *Once Upon a Time: A 1938 European Bicycle Adventure* (Gustavus, AK: Press North America, forthcoming).

3. Ibid., 3.

4. Trooping the Colour is a ceremony performed by regiments of the Commonwealth and the British Army. It has been a tradition of British infantry regiments since at least the seventeenth century. On battlefields, a regiment's colors, or flags, were

used as rallying points. Consequently, regiments would have their ensigns slowly march with their colors between the soldiers' ranks to enable soldiers to recognize their regiments' colors. Since 1748, Trooping the Colour has also marked the official birthday of the British Sovereign. It is held in London annually on the second or third Saturday in June (Helene Henderson and Sue Ellen Thompson, eds., *Holidays, Festivals, and Celebrations of the World Dictionary*, 2nd ed. [Detroit: Omnigraphics, 1997: 346]; and the Official Website of the British Monarchy, "Trooping the Colour," http://www.royal.gov.uk/RoyalEventsandCeremonies/TroopingtheColour/TroopingtheColour.aspx, accessed February 10, 2011).

5. Unpublished manuscript "Once Upon a Time" by Virginia Hill, 21–2.

6. King George V died on January 20, 1936, and his eldest son came to the throne as King Edward VIII. Edward VIII gave up the throne in December 1936 in order to marry the woman he loved, Wallis Simpson, an American divorcée. Upon Edward's abdication, his brother ascended to the throne as King George VI. The current Queen Elizabeth is the eldest daughter of King George VI (Sarah Bradford, *The Reluctant King: The Life and Reign of George VI, 1895–1952* [New York: St. Martin's Press, 1989]). According to Ginny, Mrs. Simpson was considered not of the proper breeding or class to be royalty. Ginny added that King Edward had been quite popular, and King George was not because he got the position by default and was not really who the British wanted as their king.

7. Princess Elizabeth (later to be queen) was born April 21, 1926, and Princess Margaret Rose was born August 21, 1930, thereby making them twelve and eight, respectively, in 1938 when Ginny saw them.

8. Unpublished manuscript "Once Upon a Time" by Virginia Hill, 26.

9. This actually translates as "Thank you for the food" (http://translation.babylon.com, accessed February 12, 2011). It is a common Danish colloquial phrase that would not be surprising for someone to say to non–Danish speakers (L. Kaplan, pers. comm.).

10. Literally, "All standing" (http://translation.babylon.com, accessed February 12, 2011).

11. Unpublished manuscript "Once Upon a Time" by Virginia Hill, 123–26.

12. Ibid., 130–31.

13. Known as the Anschluss, the annexation of Austria to Germany took place on March 12, 1938. Austria did not become an independent country again until late 1945 (H. P. Willmott, *The Great Crusade: A New Complete History of the Second World War* [New York: The Free Press, 1991]).

14. The Munich Agreement was signed on September 29, 1938, by England, France, Italy, and Germany after Hitler occupied the Sudetenland, in Czechoslovakia. Hitler believed this area belonged to Germany and was part of his plan to create *Lebensraum* ("living space") for Germany. The major powers of Europe accepted Hitler's action. After signing the agreement and returning to London, British Prime Minister Neville Chamberlain stated that the agreement created "peace in our time." History has shown this statement to have been premature. Hitler believed

that keeping the Sudetenland allowed him to take over all of Czechoslovakia, which he invaded in 1939. Soon all of Europe was embroiled in war (ibid.). Ginny suspects that Chamberlain made a deal with Hitler asking him not to attack England in exchange for Chamberlain's support of the Munich Agreement. At the time, England did not yet have a sufficient army or air force to defend itself.

15. In 1948, Ginny returned to Europe and spent time working in Finland on a Quaker-led project to rebuild log homes that had been destroyed during the war. She discusses this experience in Chapter 10.

16. See the historical context provided for the Help Finland archival collection at the Finnish American Heritage Center Archive and Museum, Finlandia University, Hancock, MI (http://www.finlandia.edu/V-Series.html, accessed February 29, 2012), for a general overview of Finland's involvement in World War II and fighting with and against Germany and Russia. There were the Winter, Continuation, and Lapland Wars in Finland.

17. Unpublished manuscript "Once Upon a Time" by Virginia Hill, 222–24.

18. Ibid., 145–46.

19. Ginny's discussion of her 1948 trip to Europe appears in Chapter 10.

20. Unpublished manuscript "Once Upon a Time" by Virginia Hill, 253.

21. World War II began on September 1, 1939, when Hitler invaded Poland. France and Britain declared war on Germany as Hitler's army entered Poland from the west and Soviet troops entered from the east to claim their portion of the country (Willmott, *The Great Crusade*).

22. From "I found New York City…" to "…the young in those days" is from Ginny Wood's handwritten notes in her personal collection.

23. Ginny's photo album from this trip indicates that they left New York City on October 3, 1939. The photos and Ginny's verbal descriptions when looking at the album tell us that they first went to New England to visit Mrs. Dunham's older daughter, then to Philadelphia, Washington, DC, and Virginia as they took the southern route across the country. They stopped in New Mexico, the Grand Canyon, and California and eventually arrived in Seattle. Ginny has said they were home by Christmas.

24. From "But I was no longer…" to "…just for a diploma" is from Ginny Wood's handwritten notes in her personal collection.

25. From "I had signed up…" to "…on weekends instead" is from Ginny Wood's handwritten notes in her personal collection.

26. Unpublished manuscript "Once Upon a Time" by Virginia Hill, 198–200.

27. Although "Japs" is now considered a racist term for describing the people of Japan, I did not change it because it is the word Ginny used. She most likely used it because it was a commonly used term during World War II, which is the time period being discussed. Its usage is indicative of the sentiments of World War II; it does not reflect any racism on Ginny's part.

28. The Iron Dog Snowmachine Race is a 1,971-mile cross-country test of endurance for man and machine held each March in Alaska. Teams of two drive their snow-machines as fast as they can across Alaska's wilderness from Big Lake to Nome and finish in Fairbanks. For more information, see the Iron Dog official website (http://www.irondog.org, accessed February 12, 2011).

4. Flying and the Women Airforce Service Pilots

1. At this time, the United States did not have a separate air force; the air corps was part of the regular United States Army. The US Army Air Forces was created from the Army Air Corps in June 1941 and put under the command of Hap Arnold (Williams, *WASPs*, 20). The United States Air Force (USAF) was officially declared a separate branch of the military in 1947 (Nalty, *Winged Shield, Winged Sword*).
2. Marianne Verges, *On Silver Wings: The Women Airforce Service Pilots of World War II, 1942–1944*, (New York: Ballantine Books, 1991), 107.
3. In one place Ginny says it was fall 1941 and in another fall 1940. In another place, she says she was twenty-two years old and in another twenty-three years old. Born in October 1917, she would have turned twenty-four in October 1941.
4. From "My flight instructor…" to "…future flying career" is from a handwritten draft of material in orange binder titled "Ginny's a Part of It All," Ginny Wood Personal Collection.
5. From "Perhaps the most important…" to "…than your instructor," ibid.
6. From "I think my instructor…" to "…straight and level flight" and from "I figured that…" to "…couple more sessions" is from a handwritten draft of material for book in orange binder titled "Ginny's a Part of It All," Ginny Wood Personal Collection.
7. From "Eventually, I began…" to "…normal flying altitude" is from a handwritten draft of material for book in orange binder titled "Ginny's a Part of It All," Ginny Wood Personal Collection.
8. This was Dr. Otto Trott, who came to the Seattle area in 1939 from Germany and pioneered modern mountain rescue and medical treatment. He and Ginny met through the Mountaineers, the mountain-climbing group of the Pacific Northwest. They dated, skied, and climbed together, and remained friends for many years. They climbed Mount Rainier in 1940, the plan being to go on skis up to below Kautz Glacier, then with crampons and minimal gear make a quick up/down climb to the top. However, the trip did not go as smoothly as planned. Due to a late start on the summit climb, misjudging the size of the mountain, and Ginny's altitude sickness slowing her down, they ended up spending the night at the summit. Worried that Ginny might not make it, and having no tent or sleeping bags, Trott got her down into the warm thermals along the crater's brim where she could get warm, rest, and recover from the climb. They descended the mountain early the next morning, but Ginny was skiing on the glacier without

metal-edged skis and nearly slid into a crevasse. Trott was able to rescue her by letting a rope down to her. They finished their descent roped together. For more information about Dr. Trott and this climb, see Nicholas Campbell Corff, *The Making of a Rescuer: The Story of Otto T. Trott, MD, A Father of Modern Mountaineering and Rescue* (Victoria, BC, and Bloomington, IN: Trafford Publishing, 2008). The story and photographs of climbing Mount Rainier with Ginny appear on pages 139–41.

9. From "I have never really…" to "…I replied" is from a handwritten draft of material for book in orange binder titled "Ginny's a Part of It All."

10. For more about the history of the WAFS, see Verges, *On Silver Wings,* and Williams, *WASPs.*

11. For the full story about Jacqueline Cochran and her mission to get the air force to include women as pilots, see Verges, *On Silver Wings.*

12. Verges, *On Silver Wings,* 39.

13. Ibid., 38–39.

14. Ibid., 64.

15. Ibid., 50.

16. For more information about Dr. Trott and his life as a skier, mountaineer, and doctor, including discussion about and photographs of his time with Ginny Hill Wood, see Corff, *The Making of a Rescuer.*

17. Ginny wrote about this for her own book about her life. Handwritten draft on yellow-lined paper and in green notebook in folder titled "Correspondance on 'The Book,'" Ginny Wood Personal Collection. She names some of the others in her Mount Baker ski gang who were there: "Otto, Kurt, Gage, Hank, Esther, Fred and Ellie, Dusty, Bill, Tom—all fellow ski patrolmen" (ibid., green notebook, 1). And in another place Ginny mentions "Gage Chatwood, whose graceful high speed turns made skiing look like ballet dancing; "Rocky" Rhoades who made skiing a comedy act; the Amicks [sp?] whose parenthood hadn't diminished their placing among top finishes in regional downhill competitions" (ibid., yellow-lined paper, p. 1).

18. This same story about skiing Shuksan Arm in December 1941 appears in Corff, *The Making of a Rescuer,* 143. Otto's wartime imprisonment is mentioned on pages 144–45.

19. Ginny uses the terms "air force" and "air corps" interchangeably when referring to the aerial portion of the United States military during World War II.

20. From "Our regime was several hours…" to "…examiner's faith in me" is from a handwritten draft of material for book in orange binder titled "Ginny's a Part of It All," pp. 9–10.

21. From "She was on active duty…" to "…especially the air forces" is from a handwritten draft of material for book in orange binder titled "Ginny's a Part of It All," unnumbered page.

22. From "Love's recruiting…" to "…of military life," ibid.

23. The Women's Auxiliary Ferrying Squadron (WAFS) had been established as a squadron of women pilots within the Air Transport Command and was under the command of Nancy Love. Jacqueline Cochran had always thought the women's pilot program within the air force belonged to her, so she forced the creation of the Women's Flying Training Detachment (WFTD) in September 1942 as a separate program for her to train additional women who would eventually serve in the WAFS (Verges, *On Silver Wings,* 42). All new women pilots in late 1942 and into 1943 were required to enter the Ferry Division through the WFTD school (ibid., 57). On August 5, 1943, this redundancy was eliminated, and the two programs were merged and became the Women Airforce Service Pilots (WASP) (ibid., 103).

24. "1002 WASP were stationed at 120 airbases" (http://www.wingsacrossamerica.us/wasp/resources/texas.htm, accessed May 1, 2011). For a list of bases, see http://www.wingsacrossamerica.us/wasp/baselist.htm, accessed May 1, 2011.

25. Verges, *On Silver Wings,* 85.

26. Ibid., 130.

27. Ibid.

28. Ibid., 43.

29. Ibid., 103.

30. From "Jacqueline Cochran..." to "...devoted marriage" is from a handwritten draft of material for a book in orange binder titled "Ginny's a Part of It All," p. 12.

31. From "Two more opposite..." to "...own flying service," ibid.

32. From "But for the inauguration..." to "...kill both of us" is from a handwritten draft of material for a book in orange binder titled "Ginny's a Part of It All," p. 13.

33. Women pilots could not be legally commissioned into the existing Women's Army Corps (WAC), which meant that General Arnold could not use the available and trained women pilots because there was no authority to commission or pay them. An act of Congress was required to change this, so Love and Arnold instead developed a proposal to hire the women as civil service employees (Verges, *On Silver Wings,* 39).

34. For more information about WASP pilots doing more than just ferrying planes, such as towing targets or being test pilots for jets, see the movie *Fly Girls,* written, directed, and produced by Laurel Ladevich (Boston: WGBH Boston for *The American Experience,* 1999).

35. Marianne Verges also states that thirty-eight women pilots were killed during the war (*On Silver Wings,* 220).

36. Ibid., 214.

37. Ibid., 220.

38. Ibid., 236.

39. The 1977 legislation offered the women nonflying reserve commissions as second lieutenants (ibid., 230).

40. From "Rumbling down a runway…" to "…summit of Mount Rainier" is from a handwritten draft of material for a book in orange binder titled "Ginny's a Part of It All," unnumbered page.

41. The legislation to award a Congressional Gold Medal to the Women Airforce Service Pilots was cosponsored by Senator Kay Hutchison of Texas and Representative Barbara Mikulski of Maryland. The bill passed the Senate on May 20, 2009, and the House of Representatives on June 16, 2009 (http://www.Govtrack. us, accessed February 14, 2011). Mention of this legislation passing and the Alaskan recipients of the award appears in "Fairbanksans Eyed for National Honor," "In Brief" column, *Fairbanks Daily News-Miner,* May 23, 2009.

42. Rena Delbridge, "Fairbanks Pilots Receive National Recognition: WWII WASPs Awarded Medal," *Fairbanks Daily News-Miner,* July 6, 2009.

43. Chris Freiberg, "Two Fairbanks Women Who Flew Airplanes in World War II Honored," *Fairbanks Daily News-Miner,* April 3, 2010.

5. A Lifelong Friendship: Meeting Celia Hunter

1. According to notes found in Ginny Wood's personal collection, "Celia flew P-47's from the Republic Factory in Farmingdale, Long Island which was fifty miles as the crow flies to the docks at Newark, New Jersey." While this seems contradictory to being stationed at Wilmington, Delaware, "Wilmington pilots consistently flew P-47's from the nearby Republic Factory" ("Origins of the WASPS, Ferrying Division Air Transport Command," on the P-38 National Association and Museum website: http://p38assn.org/Personnel/wasps/wasps.htm, accessed May 1, 2011).

2. Jessica Wiles, "Celia Hunter: Life and Leadership," Alaska Conservation Foundation publication, undated, photocopy in possession of the author.

3. According to one of Celia Hunter's writings for the *Everett Daily Herald* in 1948, they flew beat-up air corps trainer planes from the surplus center in Ponca City, Wyoming, to the sales center in Portland, Oregon.

6. A Summer Under Sail

1. Ginny's sailing stories have been compiled from two sources: the oral history interviews conducted with her from 2006 to 2008, and her own writings in preparation for an autobiography. I have integrated the two to create the best possible telling with the least redundancy.

2. Captain Joshua Slocum, *Sailing Alone Around the World* (New York: The Century Company, 1899).

3. From "I had accumulated…" to "…I certainly did!" was handwritten by Ginny Wood in a green notebook titled "The Book (That is not)."

4. From "Previous mentions of…" to "…for my future" was handwritten by Ginny Wood in a green notebook titled "The Book (That is not)."

5. From "As Dad usually did..." to "...pranks again," ibid.
6. From "It became the standard..." to "...the hang of it," ibid.
7. The legend of the *Flying Dutchman* tells of a ghost ship that can never go home and is doomed to sail the oceans forever. In some ocean lore, the sight of such a phantom ship is a portent of doom (John Clute and John Grant, eds., *The Encyclopedia of Fantasy* [New York: St. Martin's Press, 1997: 357–58]).
8. *Der fliegende Holländer* (*The Flying Dutchman*) is an opera with music and libretto by Richard Wagner. Wagner conducted the premiere in Dresden in 1843 (Barry Millington, *The New Grove Guide to Wagner and His Operas* [New York: Oxford University Press, 2006: 50–56]).
9. After graduation from training at Sweetwater, Pete was stationed with the Fifth Ferrying Division at Love Field in Dallas, Texas.
10. The Yuculta Rapids are along the Cordero Channel near the north end of Vancouver Island en route to Queen Charlotte Strait. Cordero Channel is a strait located between the mainland and Vancouver Island, among the Discovery Islands north of the Strait of Georgia.
11. Dodd Narrows is located between Mudge Island and Vancouver Island, just south of Nanaimo, British Columbia.
12. The Malibu Club was a luxury resort for the rich and famous operated from 1945 to 1950 by Tom Hamilton. In 1953, Jim Rayburn of Young Life purchased the abandoned resort for $300,000 to be the organization's next youth camp. It continues to operate today (Young Life Malibu Club, "Malibu Club History," *Young Life Malibu Club*, http://sites.younglife.org/camps/MalibuClub/Open%20Content%20Pages/Malibu%20History.aspx, accessed February 12, 2011). Princess Louisa Marine Provincial Park and Chatterbox Falls are located at the end of this inlet. For a history of the resort and Princess Louisa Inlet, see Charles William Hitz, *Through the Rapids: The History of Princess Louisa Inlet* (Kirkland, WA: Sitka 2 Publishing, 2003).
13. Queen Charlotte Strait into Queen Charlotte Sound.
14. "Following the success of her book, in 1946 June and Farrar bought a surplus Coast Guard lifeboat and began their '100 Days in the San Juans,' traveling around the islands and collecting stories of the islands and their inhabitants that were printed as a column in the *Seattle P.I.* The stories were collected together in 1983, and published as a book by the same name" ("June and Farrar Burn Papers Biographical Note," *Finding Aid to the June and Farrar Burn Collection* [Bellingham: Center for Pacific Northwest Studies, Western Washington University, http://www.acadweb.wwu.edu/cpnws/burn/burnbio.htm, accessed February 12, 2011]).
15. June Burn, *Living High: An Unconventional Autobiography* (New York: Duell, Sloan and Pearce, 1941). For additional information about June and Farrar Burn, see "June and Farrar Burn Papers Biographical Note"; and Noel V. Bourasaw, "*Living High*, an Unconventional Autobiography, and June and Farrar Burn" (*Skagit River Journal of History and Culture*, 2005 [updated 2008],

http://www.skagitriverjournal.com/WA/Library/Burn/Burn01-BookBios. html, accessed Feb. 12, 2011).

16. Their initial island, which is known on maps as Sentinel—and which June called Gumdrop—is a tiny island of fifteen acres just northwest of San Juan Island and south of Victoria, British Columbia. To the east is the larger Spieden Island. For the next two decades they also lived on Johns Island and the much larger Waldron Island (Bourasaw, "*Living High*, an Unconventional Autobiography, and June and Farrar Burn").

17. Virginia Hill, "Three Maids Before the Mast," *Pacific Motor Boat* 39, no. 4 (April 1947): 29–32. Ginny also discusses this trip in "Nostalgic Trip Highlights a Half Century of Change," "In the Woodpile" column, the *Northern Line* 16, no. 4 (December 20, 1994): 10.

18. At 363 miles down the Richardson Highway, Valdez is the closest place to access saltwater from Fairbanks.

7. Alaska: The Early Years

1. Having heard Ginny tell this story about flying to Alaska many times, it was not until a personal conversation on February 14, 2010, that I heard her mention that Celia had a passenger. The passenger was the wife or ex-wife of the mechanic who was flying with Gene Jack in his plane. Since Ginny and Celia never saw Gene Jack's plane again throughout the trip, the mechanic proved of little use to them. Ginny was not sure how much he actually knew about airplane mechanics anyway, or if he even really was a mechanic, since Jack had bailed him out of jail in Seattle so he could fly back to Fairbanks with him. Celia got this woman as a passenger because her plane was bigger and Ginny's plane didn't have room. When asked why she had never mentioned this passenger before, Ginny explained that "she was not our cup of tea. The morning we were supposed to leave, she arrived for the flight to Alaska dressed in a short fur coat." Before they could leave, they had to take her to a store to buy attire more appropriate for the rugged journey. And Ginny said that when they landed every night they did not socialize with her; she did not stay in the same accommodations as them. Once they arrived in Fairbanks, they delivered her to her friends and they never saw her again. Ginny could not remember her or the mechanic's name.

2. Creamer's Field was the dairy farm and creamery in Fairbanks at the time that was located across the Chena River and north of central Fairbanks. In the whiteout conditions of the blizzard, Celia had mistaken their large open fields used for grazing cattle for the open area that would be an airstrip. For a good description and history of the Creamer's Field operation and eventual preservation as the Creamer's Field Migratory Waterfowl Refuge, see Jessica Ryan, "A Place for the Birds: The Legacy of Creamer's Field Migratory Waterfowl Refuge" (master's thesis, University of Alaska Fairbanks, 2003).

3. Weeks Field was the main civilian airfield at that time, located on the southwestern edge of Fairbanks. It was within walking distance of central Fairbanks, where most of the businesses and residences were located. Phillips Field was another small airstrip in Fairbanks, but a bit farther out of town. Ladd Field, now known as Fort Wainwright, was the large military field in Fairbanks, but as civilian pilots it is unlikely that Ginny and Celia would have been allowed to land there, similar to Ginny saying they could not land at Eielson Air Force Base because it was for military only.

4. Archie Ferguson operated Ferguson Airways out of Kotzebue from the late 1920s to the mid-1940s, when he sold the business to Sig Wien. Archie was known for his risk-taking as a pilot and his sense of humor. He arrived in Alaska in 1917 as a boy and lived with his family at gold mines around northwestern Alaska. Before becoming a pilot, he made a living trapping, freighting supplies on the Kobuk River, and operating stores in Kotzebue and in the villages along the river. In 1919, Archie married Hadley Wood, the granddaughter of a Kobuk Eskimo chief, and in 1932, when he and his brother, Warren, started the first radio communication in the region, Hadley learned code and later operated the communication station in Selawik, where Ginny and Celia met her (Jean Potter, *The Flying North* [New York: Ballantine Books, 1972: 190–212]). Archie Ferguson died in 1967. For more about Archie Ferguson, see the Archie Ferguson Oral History Collection (series ORAL HISTORY 95–66, Alaska and Polar Regions Archives, Elmer E. Rasmuson Library, University of Alaska Fairbanks), which includes oral history interviews with people sharing their experiences with and memories of Archie Ferguson.

5. According to Celia Hunter, "While in Kotzebue we made friends with Margaret Peterson, whose husband Bill was a pilot there, and she invited us to join her for a big Eskimo dance at the schoolhouse, which was great fun. The Eskimos even made up a dance and song about 'lady bush pilots' in our honor" ("Celia's Short Vignettes: Start of the Nome-Kotzebue Tours, August 23, 1999" in folder titled "From the Moles Den—Celia's Journal," Ginny Wood Personal Collection).

6. Woody talks about his family background, growing up, joining the Tenth Mountain Division, and being in the Po Valley battle in Italy in World War II in an oral history interview with Karen Brewster on May 23, 2007 (Tape No. ORAL HISTORY 2011-04-17, Alaska and Polar Regions Archives, Elmer E. Rasmuson Library, University of Alaska Fairbanks).

7. At this time, the only bridge across the Chena River between the university and town was at Cushman Street in downtown Fairbanks. The University Avenue bridge was not constructed until 1963 (*Design Study Report, University Avenue Rehabilitation and Widening, Federal Aid No. STP-RS-M-0617(3), State Project No. 63213,* prepared by Russell Johnson [Fairbanks: Alaska Department of Transportation and Public Facilities, Northern Region, July 2010]).

8. Piggly Wiggly grocery and J. C. Penney were in Fairbanks at the time (R. Weeden, pers. comm.).

9. Since the interview when Ginny made this statement, Walmart has come to Fairbanks, and there are two Fred Meyer and two Safeway stores in town.

10. Celia Hunter, "Travel the Tough Way and You Will See More Country," *Everett* [WA] *Daily Herald,* December 8, 1948.

11. Chuck West flew for Wien Airlines until November 1946 and then started his own tourism business. For more information about Chuck West's role in developing tourism in northern Alaska, see his oral history interview with Ron Inouye on February 4, 1985 (Tape No. ORAL HISTORY 85-100, Alaska and Polar Regions Archives, Elmer E. Rasmuson Library, University of Alaska Fairbanks. Audio also available at http://jukebox.uaf.edu/aviators/west_chuck_edited/HTML/testimonybrowseraudioonly.html, accessed February 12, 2011).

12. The 1,522-mile Alaska Highway was built in eight months beginning in March 1942 by the US Army to supply military bases in Alaska needed for the defense of the United States after the Japanese bombing of Pearl Harbor. One-third of the enlisted men working on the construction crews were from the army's black regiments. Control over the Alaska Highway was given to Canada on April 1, 1946, but the previously military-only road was not opened to the public until 1948. Paving of the highway began in the 1960s, but it was not until the mid-1980s that the highway was completely paved from Dawson Creek to Delta Junction (Kenneth Coates, *North to Alaska: Fifty Years on the World's Most Remarkable Highway* [Fairbanks: University of Alaska Press, 1992]; Kenneth Coates, *The Alaska Highway in World War II: The U.S. Army of Occupation in Canada's Northwest* [Norman: University of Oklahoma Press, 1992]). For more about the impacts of the road upon the neighboring communities and people living there, see "Changing Communities—Alaska Highway Project Jukebox" (Oral History Program, University of Alaska Fairbanks, http://jukebox.uaf.edu/ak_highway/html/index.html, accessed February 12, 2011).

13. According to Celia Hunter, the car Chuck bought was a "big DeSoto touring car, dusty and muddy from its journey up the Alcan. He had spotted the car with a 'for sale' sign on it on his way to the bank to apply for a loan for a new car. Chuck got the car for a song and the owner threw in a suit to boot" ("Celia's Short Vignettes: How Fairbanks Sightseeing Tours Began, August 21, 1999," in a folder titled "From the Moles Den—Celia's Journal," Ginny Wood Personal Collection).

14. Chuck West indicates that at least the early flights to Kotzebue with tourists utilized empty cargo planes that he chartered and flew. The relationship with using regular scheduled Wien Airlines flights for the tour groups developed later (Chuck West, oral history interview with Ron Inouye on February 4, 1985. Tape No. ORAL HISTORY 85-100, Alaska and Polar Regions Archives, Elmer E. Rasmuson Library, University of Alaska Fairbanks. Audio also available at http://jukebox.uaf.edu/aviators/west_chuck_edited/HTML/testimonybrowseraudioonly.html, accessed February 12, 2011).

15. This story about the tourist operation is a combination of what Ginny has told and what Celia has written in "Celia's Short Vignettes: Start of the Nome-Kotzebue

Tours, August 23, 1999," in a folder titled "From the Moles Den—Celia's Journal," Ginny Wood Personal Collection, and in "Kotzebue—The Last Resort," a typed manuscript by Celia Hunter submitted and rejected for publication in *Travel* magazine in January 1951 in a folder titled "Unpublished Manuscript on Kotzebue and 'Last Resort,'" Ginny Wood Personal Collection.

16. The Distant Early Warning Line, known as the DEW Line, was a series of military radar stations along the arctic coast of Alaska, Canada, and Greenland that were built in the late 1950s to monitor and track Soviet activities during the Cold War. For more information about the DEW Line, see "The Distant Early Warning (DEW) Line: A Bibliography and Documentary Resource List," prepared for the Arctic Institute of North America by P. Whitney Lackenbauer, Matthew Farish, and Jennifer Arthur-Lackenbauer, October 2005. Available at http://pubs. aina.ucalgary.ca/aina/DEWLineBib.pdf, accessed October 19, 2011.

8. Returning to Europe

1. The GI Bill of 1944 was an omnibus bill that provided funding for college or vocational education for returning World War II veterans as well as one year of unemployment compensation.

2. See Ginny's discussion of WASP pilots not getting the GI bill in Chapter 4.

3. Letter from Celia Hunter to Mr. A. M. Glassberg, February 24, 1948, Ginny Wood Personal Collection.

4. Letter from Celia Hunter to Percy and Edith Richards, January 29, 1948, Ginny Wood Personal Collection. Percy Richards helped Celia get the job writing the column for the *Everett Daily Herald* newspaper. Perhaps he was a personal family friend?

5. For example, Celia mentions some of the more mundane details of their everyday life in Stockholm that Ginny does not discuss, such as their eating habits and dealing with the rationing of food. For breakfast, they ate bacon and eggs or oatmeal, toast, and hot cocoa. For lunch, it was usually cheese sandwiches. And they'd complete the day with a hearty dinner. Celia states that despite rationing they were still able to eat meat five times a week without much difficulty. They ate a lot of bread because it was "just so delicious." It was hard to find fresh vegetables, except cabbage, carrots, rutabagas, and beets, and they ate a lot of potatoes because it was the cheapest and most plentiful vegetable they could find. There were hothouse-grown tomatoes, but they were very expensive and Ginny and Celia were on a very limited budget. Lettuce was just plain hard to find. In her column of February 16, 1948, Celia even specifically mentions a shortage of eggs at Christmas (Celia Hunter columns, *Everett Daily Herald*).

6. According to Celia Hunter's writing, they sailed out of New York City on September 5, 1947, on the ship *Gripsholm*. The whole trip included flying from Fairbanks to Seattle, taking a "day coach" to New York, sailing across the Atlantic to

Gothenburg on the western coast of Sweden, and then taking the train across the country to Stockholm on the east coast.

7. According to Celia Hunter, they lived with host families whom they were "auctioned off to" (*Everett Daily Herald*, February 16, 1948).

8. According to Celia Hunter, the woman's name was Fru Giesecke, and she left in December 1947 to work in England and let Ginny and Celia use the apartment for the same price she paid until her return in April. So they both lived there instead of spread apart with different host families (ibid.).

9. According to Celia Hunter, she had been living in a suburb of Stockholm called Djursholm, and it took forty minutes by bike to get to school (ibid.).

10. According to Celia Hunter, it was two hours of Swedish language every morning and a two-hour lecture three afternoons a week on Swedish history and geography (*Everett Daily Herald*, November 19, 1947).

11. Celia's columns indicate that the first semester ended in January, and they used their remaining $500 cash to see the rest of Europe instead of staying in school.

12. According to Celia Hunter's column, they had trouble in Sweden getting visas to other countries. There were also difficulties with transporting goods out of Sweden. Ginny and Celia had brought items with them from the United States that they knew would be hard to get in postwar Sweden with its rationing, such as soap, cocoa, coffee, sugar, tea, and canned butter, which they had not declared upon their entry into the country. Now they were not supposed to leave the country with these items without first getting a permit, and getting this permission was a challenge. You were not allowed to transport rations from one country to the next. As Celia stated, "Sweden is so strict now about taking anything out of the country" (Letter from Celia Hunter to Percy and Edith Richards, January 29, 1948, Ginny Wood Personal Collection). Sweden was rich compared with its neighbors. In postwar Norway, there was no butter, little bread, no sugar, bad coffee, few cars, shabby clothes, and an electricity shortage (Celia Hunter column, *Everett Daily Herald*, January 19, 1948). Denmark suffered with strict coal rations, a lack of hot water, and a fertilizer shortage that led to poor agricultural production (Celia Hunter column, *Everett Daily Herald*, February 5, 1948). There were also up to 250,000 German refugees in camps in Denmark whom the government had to support (ibid.). The German refugees were slowly being repatriated back to Germany, but Denmark still was required to support them for six months after their return (ibid.). Sweden's strict border control was a way to protect itself and keep its resources from being stripped away by neighboring countries (Letter from Celia Hunter to Percy and Edith Richards, January 29, 1948, Ginny Wood Personal Collection).

13. The train was the North Express from Copenhagen to Basel, Switzerland, which took thirty-two hours. They spent the night in Basel and took a train across Switzerland to Davos. There was no drinking water on the North Express train or in any of the stations they passed through (Celia Hunter column, *Everett Daily Herald*, March 11, 1948).

14. Celia Hunter, "Celia Hunter Writes That One Has to See the Ruined Cities of Germany to Appreciate the Damage Wrought There," *Everett Daily Herald,* March 11, 1948.

15. Celia Hunter column, *Everett Daily Herald,* March 23, 1948.

16. Celia describes such a scene in Collioure, France, where she takes off her old ski pants and cuts off the legs to use the pieces to patch the worn-out seat of the pants, thereby changing them into knickers (Celia Hunter, "Deep Pessimism Is Revealed on Part of French People," *Everett Daily Herald,* May 27, 1948).

17. Celia provides the itinerary of Salzburg to Spittal to Lienz, crossing the border into Italy between Sillian and San Candido, then on to Cortina in the heart of the Dolomite Mountains, Venice, Milan, Lake Como, and Lugano, Switzerland. She says they confined their travel to northern Italy because they had limited time and finances (Celia Hunter column, *Everett Daily Herald,* April 12, 1948).

18. Celia Hunter, "Guiseppe and Garibaldi and Some Indecision," *Everett Daily Herald,* May 4, 1948.

19. Celia Hunter, "Nothing Romantic About Venice and Its Canal," *Everett Daily Herald,* April 29, 1948.

20. Celia Hunter, "Work Camps Aiding Finns Repair Damage From War," *Everett Daily Herald,* August 18, 1948.

21. "The Finns and the Germans fought a pitched battle at Kemi, and then as the Germans retreated slowly across Finnish Lapland to Norway, they conducted the most devastating and thorough 'scorched earth' campaign of the war. From the city of Rovaniemi, then a thriving town of perhaps 10,000 people, they blasted and burned every single building in every town, village, and farmstead, no matter how lonely and remote" (ibid.).

22. "Among the groups which came in to assist in the emergency was the American Friends Service Committee. They helped administer the first relief, and in the summer of 1946, they organized the first voluntary work camps in Finland. The object of these camps was to perform actual reconstruction work on homes, for people who otherwise couldn't afford to rebuild. The campers volunteered their services and in return received food and lodging, and general transportation expenses within the country in which they worked. The camps from the very first were planned to be as international in makeup as possible, in the hope that through working together at manual labor in the rebuilding of homes damaged in the war, people of many nations and creeds and beliefs could find better understanding and good will" (ibid.).

23. Celia states that Pat Dunham was "co-director for all work-camp projects in Europe" (Celia Hunter, "Favorable Report on United Nations in Action at Paris," *Everett Daily Herald,* November 12, 1948). American Friends Service Committee offered aid as part of the Help Finland campaign promoted throughout the United States after the war. For further explanation, see the historical context provided for the Help Finland archival collection at Finnish American Heritage

Center Historical Archive, Finlandia University, Hancock, Michigan, http://www.finlandia.edu/V-Series.html, accessed February 29, 2012.

24. Celia states that the tiny of village of Lokka had fewer than a dozen houses and was located several hundred kilometers north of the Arctic Circle. It was in Finnish Lapland. She also says they got their assignment from the office of KVT, the Finnish Work Camp Committee in Helsinki, when they went in to ask if they had a place for them to work in any of their camps. In the summer of 1948, "after consultation with local relief authorities, it was decided that Lokka needed a work camp, so in June the campers arrived. They included young people from six countries: Finland, Sweden, Denmark, Austria, France, and the U.S." (Celia Hunter, "Work Camps Aiding Finns Repair Damage from War," *Everett Daily Herald*, August 18, 1948).

25. According to Celia Hunter, "The camp set-up was strictly international: they lived in tents supplied by the Finnish army, and wore work clothes donated by the Swedish Navy; the common room, which doubles also as kitchen and dining room will one day be a Finnish cowshed. The food was donated by many countries, and includes fish from Norway, knaeckebrod from Denmark, butter and powdered milk from the U.S., meat paste from Canada, and lots and lots of Finnish potatoes and oatmeal" (ibid.).

26. *Sisu* is a noun that translates as "perseverance, grit, guts, plunk or spunk" (http://translate.google.com, accessed February 12, 2011). Celia described *sisu* as follows: "The Finns have a word that expresses the spirit of this country in a nutshell: that word is 'sisu.' Sisu is that something inside one which enables a person to go on in the face of overwhelming odds when physically every resource has been exhausted. Only 'sisu' could account for the way in which tiny Finland has faced up to the loss of her richest farmland, the Karelian Isthmus, and to staggering indemnity payments [postwar reparation payments demanded by Russia]" (Celia Hunter, "Metal Seems Soft Behind Iron Curtain in Finland," *Everett Daily Herald*, August 19, 1948). Apparently, Finnish people still use the word frequently to show that "they are a people with guts" (S. Baldridge, pers. comm.).

27. Celia explains, "Before we arrived, the group had already completed foundations for three new homes, and were mixing and pouring cement for a fourth, had made the shingles and then shingled another house, and were busy finishing up chinking the logs on a third and digging a cellar for still another.... We spent most of our time helping the cement gang mix and pour cement foundations" (Celia Hunter, "Work Camps Aiding Finns Repair Damage from War," *Everett Daily Herald*, August 18, 1948).

28. Celia said, "We work a seven-hour day five days and no loafing. Shifts are constantly changed, so that the girls get a breather between sessions on the cement crew, which can be heavy work" (ibid.).

29. In her columns, Celia comments on the Finnish hospitality and how they were invited to people's homes for visiting, eating cake, and drinking coffee, were offered the use of their saunas, and participated in folk-singing sessions and dances.

30. From "The sound of the music..." to "...among the dancers" is a piece Ginny Wood wrote titled "Finnish Nocturne" by Virginia Hill. From undated typed document in folder titled "Unpublished Manuscript" in Ginny Wood Personal Collection.

31. Celia mentions meeting a Dutch woman at the youth hostel in Lucerne in May 1948 who was the first woman hitchhiking alone that they had met so far (Celia Hunter, "It's Difficult to Break Away from Switzerland," *Everett Daily Herald*, May 13, 1948).

32. Celia Hunter, "German Youth Finding Out What Outsiders Think," *Everett Daily Herald*, May 5, 1948.

33. Celia states that "we had come abroad to live Europe, not merely to look at it. We had come to be with Europeans, not other Americans" (Celia Hunter, "Recalling Good Deeds From Strangers in All Countries," *Everett Daily Herald*, December 10, 1948).

34. As Celia explains, she learned about more than just European culture and history: It isn't the goal that's important to the traveler—it's the business of getting there. Once you have stepped out of the familiarity of routine and surroundings, packed your bags (or a rucksack) with a few essential possessions, and have actually departed on the first lap of the journey, you enter a different world. Removed from the identity you have assumed in your common, everyday life, you become a different person. From the vantage point of your transciency, you survey people and events with new eyes. No one is quite so wrapped in anonymity as the traveler—nothing is known which he chooses not to tell, not where he came from, why he's here, or where he's going, and this anonymity flavors all existence, giving a glamour impossible among familiar things. (Celia Hunter, "It Isn't the Goal That's Important to Travelers," *Everett Daily Herald*, April 13, 1948)

35. Celia made the following comment about the roads in Finland: "We found the highways in sad shape, washboard gravel roads thick with dust—a torturous jaunt for cyclists" (Celia Hunter, "Finland Gives Impression of Being in Pioneer Era," *Everett Daily Herald*, August 17, 1948).

36. As Celia explained:
    Once in London, we decided to give our battered bicycles a well-deserved rest and overhauling so we took to the road with our thumbs, a method highly recommended by most of the students we had met.... We wandered through Kent, Sussex, Hampshire, Devon and Cornwall in the south, then up through the Wye valley to Wales, with a side trip through the Bala Valley and the Snowdon mountains. From Holyhead, we took the boat for Dublin and spent ten happy days roaming through Ireland. (Celia Hunter, "More Fun to Travel by Bike or Thumb, Writer Declares," *Everett Daily Herald*, December 9, 1948)

37. Ginny probably is referring to the Riffelalp Grand Hotel. It was built over a six-year period from 1878 to 1884. It burned in 1961, but was rebuilt and renamed the Riffelalp Resort Zermatt (Durant Imboden, "Riffelalp Resort Zermatt," *Switzerland and Austria for Visitors, Europe for Visitors*, http://europeforvisitors .com/switzaustria/articles/riffelalp_main_a.htm, accessed February 12, 2011).

38. The railroad, called the Gornergratbahn, was started in 1898 and travels from Zermatt to Gornergrat through the scenic backdrop of the high Alps, including the Matterhorn. Gornergrat is at 10,272 feet, and the railroad is the highest open-air railroad in Europe (Zermatt Matterhorn, "111 years Gornergrat Bahn," *Zermatt Matterhorn official website*, http://www.zermatt.ch/en/page.cfm/ zermatt_matterhorn/zermatt_stories/111_years_gornergrat_bahn, accessed February 12, 2011).

39. Celia describes this same scene as follows: "We started walking up the railway tracks at 5 a.m., choosing to save the 22 franc fare. We suspicioned this wasn't exactly approved by the authorities but the only ones who questioned us during the 3½ hour climb were two workmen, who insisted it was 'Verboten' to walk the tracks. We pretended ignorance of both German and English and talked Swedish to them until they simply shrugged their shoulders and waved us on" (Celia Hunter, "Down the Rhone Valley to the Castle of Chillon," *Everett Daily Herald*, May 13, 1948).

40. Celia Hunter, "Franco's Men Trail Visitors Around in Lliva Border Town," *Everett Daily Herald*, June 10, 1948.

41. They took a truck to the border town of Kilpisjärvi, then bicycled to Tromso, Norway, where they caught the coastal freighter *Kvalo* to Narvik, Norway. They left Narvik on September 9, 1948, on the ore boat *Herra* going to Antwerp, Belgium (Celia Hunter Columns, *Everett Daily Herald*).

42. Woody explains his time in France: "I was a student at Grenoble in France because I was determined to relearn the French language which I'd known as a child. Very small, but had lost because my parents didn't keep it up. Neither of them was French speaking. But somehow I kept a love of the language or something. So I actually bicycled through Europe alone that summer. That was a lonely time. And I remember having a French dictionary in my little basket on my handlebars and trying to figure out this language. That would have been 1947, I believe. And then I stayed at Grenoble that winter and went to the university" (oral history interview with Karen Brewster on May 23, 2007. Tape No. ORAL HISTORY 2011-04-17, Alaska and Polar Regions Archives, Elmer E. Rasmuson Library, University of Alaska Fairbanks).

43. Woody remembers: "We went up to Wengen and the Kleine Scheidegg in Switzerland, which was a fascinating, beautiful country in the Bernese Oberland. I remember we stayed in youth hostels there and hiked around. Kind of bumming the way young people do" (ibid.).

44. They managed to hitch a ride on a truck all the way across Germany to Copenhagen. They then canvassed the docks of Copenhagen, Stockholm, and Oslo

looking for a ship to bring them to the United States (Celia Hunter Columns, *Everett Daily Herald*).

45. Indian Rock Park was a gift to the City of Berkeley from Mason-McDuffie Real Estate Company during its development of the Northbrae area. It was dedicated for park purposes in 1917. Dick Leonard, the "father of modern rock climbing," and noted environmentalist David Brower, founder of Friends of the Earth, learned rock climbing and developed their mountaineering techniques at Indian Rock. The large rock outcrop provides great views and is a good place for beginning rock climbers to practice their skills (City of Berkeley, California, Parks, Recreation and Waterfront Department official website, "Indian Rock Park," http://www.ci.berkeley.ca.us/ContentDisplay.aspx?id=12614, accessed February 12, 2011).

46. The University of Alaska Fairbanks did not have a forestry program at the time.

47. Nancy Baker had been in the same WASP training class (W3–43) as Ginny at Sweetwater, Texas, and they'd even been suite mates in the living quarters. They developed a close friendship and stayed in touch after the war. To hear Nancy talk about her own life and her memories of working in Palm Springs and coming to Alaska to take Ginny's place in Kotzebue, see Nancy Baker's oral history interview with Karen Brewster on December 1, 2007 (Tape No. ORAL HISTORY 2011-04-21, Alaska and Polar Regions Archives, Elmer E. Rasmuson Library, University of Alaska Fairbanks).

48. See Nancy Baker's oral history interview with Karen Brewster on December 1, 2007, to hear her talk about her experiences working and living in Kotzebue (ibid.).

49. Tom Stewart came to Juneau, Alaska, in 1919 as a baby, then left to earn a bachelor's degree from the University of Washington, a master's degree in international studies from Johns Hopkins University, and a law degree from Yale Law School. He also served in the Tenth Mountain Division during World War II. He returned to Juneau, where he worked as a lawyer, was the secretary for Alaska's constitutional convention held prior to statehood, served as a territorial representative and state senator, and was a Superior Court judge from 1966 to 1981. Tom Stewart passed away in December 2007.

    Alaska officially became the forty-ninth state on January 3, 1959. Delegates from around the state met at the University of Alaska Fairbanks campus from November 8, 1955, to February 5, 1956, to carve out the main provisions of an Alaska state constitution. For more about statehood and Alaska's Constitutional Convention, see Victor Fischer, *Alaska's Constitutional Convention* (National Municipal League, State Constitutional Convention Studies, Number Nine. Fairbanks: University of Alaska Press, 1975); Claus-M. Naske and Herman E. Slotnick, *Alaska: A History of the 49th State* (Grand Rapids, MI: William B. Eerdmans Publishing Company, 1979: 133–165); John Whitehead, *Completing the Union: Alaska, Hawaii, and the Battle for Statehood* (Albuquerque: University of New Mexico Press, 2004); *The 49th Star: Creating Alaska*, VHS, produced by Michael Letzring (Fairbanks: KUAC-TV, 2006); Dermot Cole, *North to the Future: The Alaska*

Story, 1959–2009 (Fairbanks: Epicenter Press, 2008); and Terrence Cole, *Fighting for the Forty-Ninth Star: C. W. Snedden and the Crusade for Alaska Statehood* (Fairbanks: University of Alaska Foundation, 2010).

50. The job was for the State Division of Forestry located at Demming, Washington, on the way up to Mount Baker (oral history interview with Morton "Woody" Wood with Karen Brewster on May 23, 2007. Tape No. ORAL HISTORY 2011-04-17, Alaska and Polar Regions Archives, Elmer E. Rasmuson Library, University of Alaska Fairbanks).

51. For a related story about fire lookouts at North Cascades National Park, see Kevin Grange, "The Art of Mountain Watching," *National Parks* 83, no. 4 (Fall 2009): 25–30.

52. Henry David Thoreau, *Walden; or, Life in the Woods* (Boston: Ticknor & Fields, 1854).

53. Woody has a slightly different perspective on this experience of having Ginny teach him to fly: "One of the worst mistakes I ever made was having Ginny teach me to fly. So, to save a few bucks she was going to teach me how to fly. Well, she was a flight instructor. She'd taught dozens of people to fly. I was the worst student she ever had. Why? Not because I was inherently a bad pilot or a bad student. It's because I was married to Ginny. And it's something you don't ever want to do. Lots of husbands can't teach their wives to drive. Same sort of thing. Eventually, I went on to learn to fly fine. Got my commercial license in Fairbanks from a woman instructor. No problem. We'd go up and fly around the pylons and she wrote it off and checked it. But I wasn't married to her. Something that got in the way of learning. It was just a real bad mistake, but we lived through it. But flying was fascinating, too. I loved it the same way Ginny did" (oral history interview with Karen Brewster on May 23, 2007. Tape No. ORAL HISTORY 2011-04-17, Alaska and Polar Regions Archives, Elmer E. Rasmuson Library, University of Alaska Fairbanks).

54. According to Woody, "This was an unusual type of airplane. It had a metal body and fabric wing and Noel Wien was the only other person I knew who had this type of plane" (ibid.).

55. Grant H. Pearson was superintendent of Mount McKinley National Park from 1945 to 1956. He was first hired as a temporary ranger in 1926, and remained with the park until his retirement in 1956, serving as ranger, chief ranger, and superintendent (Frank Norris, *Crown Jewel of the North: An Administrative History of Denali National Park and Preserve*, vol. 1—*General Park History to 1980* [Anchorage: US Department of the Interior, National Park Service, Alaska Regional Office, 2006]). Grant Pearson died in 1978. More about his life can be found in his book, *My Life of High Adventure* (Englewood Cliffs, NJ: Prentice-Hall, 1962).

9. Exploring Katmai National Park

1. For more about the history of the landscape, exploration, and formation of Katmai National Park, see Ken Ross, *Pioneering Conservation in Alaska* (Boulder: University Press of Colorado, 2006: 154–75); Frank Norris, *Isolated Paradise: An*

Administrative History of the Katmai and Aniakchak National Park Units (Anchorage: National Park Service, Alaska System Support Office, 1996); and Janet Clemens and Frank Norris, *Building in an Ashen Land: Historic Resource Study of Katmai National Park and Preserve* (Anchorage: National Park Service, Alaska System Support Office, 1999 [2nd printing, 2008]).

2. Les Viereck became a boreal plant ecologist who defined the roles of wildfire, flooding, and glaciers in plant succession and the patterns of community diversity that develop in response to these disturbances. He also helped write the classic book *Alaska Trees and Shrubs* (1972; repr. Fairbanks: University of Alaska Press, 1986). He is also known for his outspokenness against Project Chariot, which would use nuclear bombs to create a year-round ice-free harbor in arctic Alaska, over which he lost his university faculty appointment (Dan O'Neill, *The Firecracker Boys: H-Bombs, Inupiat Eskimos, and the Roots of the Environmental Movement*, rev. ed. [1994; New York: Basic Books, 2007]). Les later went on to do significant work for the US Forest Service in Fairbanks. In particular, he experimented with planting various species of nonindigenous trees in interior Alaska to see how they would survive. Les Viereck passed away in 2008. For more information about Les and his career, see his obituary in *Arctic* 61, no. 4 (December 2008: 451–52) or at http://pubs.aina.ucalgary.ca/arctic/Arctic61-4-451.pdf, accessed February 21, 2011.

3. Les helped construct buildings at Camp Denali, and he and his wife, Teri, built their home in the same Fairbanks neighborhood as Woody and Ginny. In 1954, Les and Woody survived a harrowing expedition on Mount McKinley together. They were members of a team that made the first successful climb of the South Buttress and south-to-north traverse of Mount McKinley. Elton Thayer, the expedition's leader, was killed in a fall on descent of the mountain. Fellow climber George Argus dislocated a hip in the fall and had to be left with dwindling supplies while Woody and Les made a dangerous two-day trek down the Muldrow Glacier to the Park Road in search of help. Woody wrote up the expedition for the American Alpine Club ("The First Traverse of Mt. McKinley—A First Ascent of the South Buttress," *American Alpine Journal* 9, no. 2, issue 29 [1955]: 51–69). An article about the climb and rescue appeared in *Life* magazine: "On Mt. McKinley; Rescue After Victory," June 14, 1954, 28–34.

Woody also tells the story of this expedition in an oral history interview on May 6, 2000, conducted by David Krupa of the University of Alaska Fairbanks Oral History Program (Tape No. ORAL HISTORY 2000-17-03, Alaska and Polar Regions Archives, Elmer E. Rasmuson Library, University of Alaska Fairbanks, available for listening at http://jukebox.uaf.edu/denali/html/mowo.htm, accessed February 15, 2011).

As a pilot and worried wife, Ginny took to the air in search of the missing climbing party. See chapter 20 for Ginny's description of the expedition and her involvement with the search-and-rescue operation.

4. According to Bill Nancarrow, he was in Katmai the summer of 1950 and early summer of 1951: "There were only two of us up at McKinley Park, two rangers, and I still had to go down to Katmai for the start of the season. I went down there, I think it was about the first of June, and opened up our camp down there and was starting work with the people down there at the fishing camp at Brooks River. In about July, I was relieved by Ginny Wood and her husband, Woody, who was a new ranger here at McKinley Park. We spent a week together down there while he got acquainted with the place, then I came back to Park headquarters" (oral history interview with Karen Brewster and Susan Grace on February 3, 2007. Tape No. ORAL HISTORY 2011-04-12, Alaska and Polar Regions Archives, Elmer E. Rasmuson Library, University of Alaska Fairbanks).

5. Ginny also discusses parts of this trip in a 1983 interview with Bill Tanner (Transcript Accession No. KATM-00284. Anchorage: US Department of the Interior, National Park Service, Katmai National Park and Preserve, Archives).

6. "On June 29, 1951, Park Ranger William Nancarrow was promoted to park naturalist, the first permanent naturalist appointed in Mt. McKinley National Park" (Norris, *Crown Jewel of the North*, vol. 1, 145). This information is also stated in Pearson, *History of Mount McKinley*, 88.

7. More about Nancarrow's work at Katmai can be found in Norris, *Isolated Paradise*, 80–84; and Clemens and Norris, *Building in an Ashen Land*, 177.

8. Woody's presence as a ranger at Katmai in the summer of 1951 is mentioned in Norris, *Isolated Paradise*, 84–85.

9. According to an article Ginny wrote in 1953, the National Geographic Society sent in expeditions between 1915 and 1919 (Ginny Hill Wood, "Valley of Seven Smokes," *Alaska Sportsman* 19, no. 1 [January 1953], 6–11, 29–33).

10. From 1915 to 1919, the National Geographic Society sponsored research expeditions to the Katmai area led by botanist Robert F. Griggs (only two people, not including Griggs, were on the 1918 trip) (Norris, *Isolated Paradise, 21–33, 39*). Griggs also visited Katmai in 1930 to investigate plant succession (Norris, *Isolated Paradise, 45*). More about Griggs and the National Geographic research expeditions can be found in Clemens and Norris, *Building in an Ashen Land, 50–57*.

11. Ginny is most likely referring to Robert F. Griggs, *The Valley of Ten Thousand Smokes* (Washington, DC: National Geographic Society, 1922). However, other articles by Griggs of the same title were published in the January 1917 and February 1918 editions of *National Geographic* (Norris, *Isolated Paradise*, 26–27). In addition to his scientific accomplishments, Griggs promoted the idea of Katmai becoming a national park, as seen by his article "Our Greatest National Monument" (*National Geographic* 40 [September 1921], 219–92). For more about Griggs and his role at Katmai National Park, see Norris, *Isolated Paradise*.

12. "Beyond the falls we came to the fish weir which the Fish and Wildlife Service had built across the mouth of the river at Brooks Lake. Hal and Dick, stationed here for the summer, were counting the fish that swam through the gates into

the lake. A tally would show what percentage of fish were getting back to their spawning ground from Bristol Bay and just how much commercial fishing could be allowed" (Wood, "Valley of Seven Smokes," 8).

13. Grant Pearson and Alfred Keuhl, a landscape architect with the National Park Service's Alaska regional office, visited Katmai in August 1945 (Norris, *Isolated Paradise*, 69). This story of Pearson's experience and advice to Woody and Ginny appears in Ginny's *Alaska Sportsman* article (ibid., 11).

14. The story about this climb can be found in Corff, *The Making of a Rescuer*, 139–140.

15. For more details about this trip, see Ginny Hill Wood, "Valley of Seven Smokes," 6–11, 29–33.

16. This was likely one of the cabins belonging to Roy Fure, a trapper in the Katmai area during the early 1900s (Clemens and Norris, *Building in an Ashen Land*, 121; Morton Wood, *Report of Exploratory Trips in Katmai National Monument*, summer 1952 [Anchorage: US Department of the Interior, National Park Service, Katmai National Park and Preserve, Archives]).

17. This was Coville Camp, established by Northern Consolidated Airlines executive Raymond Petersen, as a tourist accommodation. In 1950, Petersen signed a five-year concession contract with the National Park Service to operate a tourist business in and around Katmai National Monument. He established five tent camps to appeal to fishermen: Brooks Camp, Coville Camp (later renamed Grosvenor Camp), Battle Lake Camp, Kulik Camp, and Nonvianuk Camp (Clemens and Norris, *Building in an Ashen Land*, 176–77).

18. For a more detailed explanation of this attempt to get up the Savonoski River by motorboat, see Ginny Hill Wood, "Valley of Seven Smokes," 6–11, 29–33.

19. George L. Collins was an early conservationist, promoter of protecting Alaska's wild places, and a planner who worked for the National Park Service. Sharing an enthusiasm for preserving Alaska, George and Ginny remained friends and colleagues for many years. For more about George Collins, in particular his role in preserving Alaska's Arctic National Wildlife Refuge, see Kaye, *Last Great Wilderness*.

20. Pam Miller, arctic issues specialist with the Northern Alaska Environmental Center in Fairbanks, thought this might have been part of a larger Park Service recreation study that also included the Arctic Refuge (P. Miller, pers. comm.). Collins oversaw the National Park Service's Alaska Recreational Study where from 1951 to 1953 a survey team "examined a wide spectrum of areas throughout Alaska with special potential for recreational use, historic preservation, or scientific research" (Kaye, *Last Great Wilderness*, 15). In 1955, a comprehensive report came out titled *A Recreation Program for Alaska* (Washington, DC: National Park Service, Alaska Recreation Survey).

21. Ginny Hill Wood, "Valley of Seven Smokes," 6–11, 29–33.

22. Morton S. Wood, *General Photographic Report for Katmai National Monument*, summer 1952; and *Report of Exploratory Trips in Katmai National Monument*, summer 1952. Both reports available at the archives of Katmai National Park and Preserve, Anchorage, Alaska.

10. Finding a Place to Call Home

1. For more on the history of dog teams at Mount McKinley/Denali National Park, see Grant Pearson oral history interview with W. Verde Watson on October 17, 1962 (Tape No. ORAL HISTORY 90-46-01, Alaska and Polar Regions Archives, Elmer E. Rasmuson Library, University of Alaska Fairbanks, available for listening at http://jukebox.uaf.edu/akmushing, accessed October 18, 2011) and Norris, *Crown Jewel of the North*, vol. 1.

2. Woody refers to Bill Nancarrow as the park's naturalist and believes he was the first naturalist hired by Mount McKinley National Park (oral history interview with Karen Brewster on May 23, 2007. Tape No. ORAL HISTORY 2011-04-17, Alaska and Polar Regions Archives, Elmer E. Rasmuson Library, University of Alaska Fairbanks). According to Park Service history, Bill Nancarrow was appointed the park's first permanent naturalist on June 29, 1951 (Norris, *Crown Jewel of the North*, vol. 1, 145).

3. These were army-surplus "late-model M-7 snow-tractors (also called snow jeeps, Snow Tracs, or 'Sno-Cats')" (Norris, *Crown Jewel of the North*, vol. 1, 200). Photos of these snow tractors prior to their 1952 expedition into the park (DENA 29–13 and DENA 29–12, Denali National Park and Preserve Collection) appear in Norris, *Crown Jewel of the North*, vol. 1, 201.

4. By 1946, the NPS started to use snow tractors for regular patrol, replacing the previous use of dogteams. "Grant Pearson—who drove one of the vehicles—was so convinced of its utility that, by 1945, he 'believe[d] the dog team is a thing of the past, except for use in connection with winter sports'" (ibid., 200); and see Pearson, *My Life of High Adventure*, 192. It also is noted that "dogs were apparently not used for park patrols between the early 1940s and the early 1950s and the park had no dog teams between 1945 and 1947 and between 1948 and 1950" (Norris, *Crown Jewel of the North*, vol. 1, 201).

5. "In April 1952, however, park naturalist William J. Nancarrow took a dog team on a 13-day patrol after the park's snow tractor was immobilized" (ibid.).

6. Interestingly, dog patrols continued until 1960, when a Bombardier snowmachine was introduced. But by 1963 the snowmachine proved too unreliable and not suited for the park's need. It was surplused and dog patrols were reinstated (ibid., 200–1). In the winter months, the wilderness backcountry of Denali National Park is currently patrolled by dog team.

7. In 1947, a regulation about aircraft landings within Mount McKinley National Park was introduced, which stated that airplanes were not allowed to land on park lands, except on Wonder Lake and at the entrance-area airstrip. During this period, the NPS itself was even known to land ski planes on Wonder Lake in winter, when they would change out crews working as dog mushers and patrolling out of the Wonder Lake Ranger Station. However, in 1960, a national regulation was established that removed the option to land planes off of established airstrips in

national parks, so landings on the lake were prohibited. In 1980, when the Alaska National Interest Lands Conservation Act changed the park's boundaries with the new additions, the old park area came under new park rules and the landing of airplanes was allowed within what had been the former Mount McKinley Park. Nevertheless, the NPS frowns on the landing of planes on Wonder Lake, and some level of peer pressure has limited it, except for emergencies (Steve Carwile, National Park Service, email messages to author, January 27 and February 8, 2011).

8. Woody Wood talks about this same trip in an oral history interview with Karen Brewster on May 23, 2007. Tape No. ORAL HISTORY 2011-04-17, Alaska and Polar Regions Archives, Elmer E. Rasmuson Library, University of Alaska Fairbanks.

9. Bill Nancarrow talks about this same dog-team trip with Woody in an oral history interview with Karen Brewster and Susan Grace on February 3, 2007. Tape No. ORAL HISTORY 2011-04-12, Alaska and Polar Regions Archives, Elmer E. Rasmuson Library, University of Alaska Fairbanks.

10. In contrast to this, Ginny wrote in a 1953 article that "Woody was ordered to Katmai National Monument, where he had been a ranger before. We had to make the decision of whether to leave the Park Service and a life we both enjoyed, or stay with the service and leave McKinley Park. We had liked Katmai, but our hearts were in McKinley Park. Perhaps on his own, Woody could do more to develop the park than he could do as a ranger" (Wood, "Wilderness Camp," *Alaska Sportsman* 19, no. 11 [November 1953]: 23). It is hard to know now where Woody was really being sent, but that is less important than the fact that this possible move instigated his leaving the Park Service.

11. Oral history interview with Karen Brewster on May 23, 2007 (Tape No. ORAL HISTORY 2011-04-17, Alaska and Polar Regions Archives, Elmer E. Rasmuson Library, University of Alaska Fairbanks).

12. Gordon Herreid (October 21, 1924–December 22, 2001) was a mining geologist. He graduated from the University of Alaska Fairbanks in 1951, and earned a master's in geology from the University of California, Berkeley in 1958 and a PhD from the University of Washington. In 1961, he helped start the geology section of the Division of Mines for the State of Alaska. He did geological work in southeastern, northwestern, and interior Alaska. He retired from the Alaska Division of Geological and Geophysical Survey in 1973.

13. Charles E. Bunnell came to Alaska in 1900 as a teacher after earning his master's degree in law from Bucknell University. He passed the Alaska bar and became a practicing attorney in Valdez. In 1914, President Woodrow Wilson appointed him US District Judge of the Fourth Division. At thirty-seven, he was the youngest man ever to be appointed to such a high judicial position in Alaska. Bunnell was president of the University of Alaska from 1921 until 1949. He passed away in 1957.

14. This cabin has been modified since its original construction, with a second story, kitchen, and running water added.

15. Dogpatch is the small neighborhood in west Fairbanks where Ginny and Woody built their first cabin and where Ginny continues to reside. It is bounded by Ballaine Road to the west, Red Fox Drive to the north, the undeveloped lands of Pearl Creek School and recreation area to the south, and bisected by Wolverine Drive, a short gravel road. According to Ginny, Celia came up with the name when she was a ham radio operator in search of a handle and enjoyed the fact that they all had dogs in the neighborhood.

16. In his oral history interview, Woody Wood goes into great detail about the construction of these buildings, including putting in the basement in the early 1960s. He also mentions how they built a larger cabin (known as "the middle cabin") around 1955, when they were about to have a baby and needed a place larger than the original sixteen-by-sixteen-foot cabin (oral history interview with Karen Brewster on May 23, 2007. Tape No. ORAL HISTORY 2011-04-17, Alaska and Polar Regions Archives, Elmer E. Rasmuson Library, University of Alaska Fairbanks).

17. Ginny said she and Woody did these recreation programs for the military in the winter of 1953–1954. In contrast, Frank Norris states in his administrative history of the park that the military left in the early spring of 1953, but the Alaska Railroad, which owned the park hotel, kept it open to civilian use for the upcoming winter and the National Park Service cobbled together a visitor interpretation program. The hotel then remained closed during the winters that followed (Norris, *Crown Jewel of the North: An Administrative History of Denali National Park and Preserve*, vol. 2—*General Park History Since 1980, Plus Specialized Themes* [Anchorage: US Department of the Interior, National Park Service, Alaska Regional Office, 2008: 142). However, Norris does acknowledge that the military used the park for winter activities in the 1950s: "In winter, activities surrounding the hotel during the early 1950s took on an entirely new cast because of its role as an army and air force recreation camp. As in World War II, military authorities created a diversified recreational program; activities included skiing, skating, and tobogganing" (ibid.).

18. Woody Wood also briefly talks about this winter program in an oral history interview with Karen Brewster on May 23, 2007 (Tape No. ORAL HISTORY 2011-04-17, Alaska and Polar Regions Archives, Elmer E. Rasmuson Library, University of Alaska Fairbanks).

19. On June 13, 1953, the National Park Service awarded a twenty-year contract to McKinley Park Services, of which Lauesen was a partner, to operate the hotel and associated services (Norris, *Crown Jewel of the North,* vol. 1, 124). "During the summer of 1953, military officials approached the new concessioner and discussed the idea of operating the hotel during the upcoming winter. Perhaps due to the end of the Korean War, however, they decided not to exercise that option" (ibid., 125). According to Norris, the hotel was in fact open the winter of 1953–1954, but not just for the military as Ginny suggests, and that visitation was low, averaging from four to fourteen guests per night (ibid.). It seems that Ginny has mixed things up with the hotel's earlier role as a military rest camp. McKinley Park

Services was in such financial trouble, and did such a poor job running the hotel, that their contract was terminated before it even got started (ibid).

11. Establishing Camp Denali: Alaska's First Wilderness Camp

1. John Rumohr retired from Mount McKinley Park on July 13, 1951, after working there for twenty-one years. He was first hired as a ranger in 1930 and retired as chief ranger (Norris, *Crown Jewel of the North,* vol. 1, 77, 144).
2. According to Celia Hunter, this happened over the Fourth of July weekend, 1951 (KUAC Radio, *Homefires* radio series, March 10, 1984 [Fairbanks: KUAC FM/ TV], Tape No. ORAL HISTORY 90-10-02, Alaska and Polar Regions Archives, Elmer E. Rasmuson Library, University of Alaska Fairbanks).
3. In her 1953 article "Wilderness Camp," Ginny tells a different version of finding the spot for Camp Denali: "It all started in the fall of 1951, when Celia Hunter came down from Fairbanks to visit Woody, my husband, and me at McKinley Park. Woody was a ranger, in the National Park Service. That week-end we flew our Cessna 170 out to the airstrip at Kantishna....Leaving our 'snow goose' tied down on the field, shouldered our rucksacks and set out to explore the surrounding country....After hiking a mile and a half from Kantishna, we left the road and began climbing up a ridge that rises above Moose Creek. As we ascended, the full drama of the Alaska Range, culminating in majestic 20,300-foot Mount McKinley, or Denali, as the Indians call it, came into full view.... Half an hour of walking from the road brought us to a plateau where tundra cradled a small tarn whose waters reflected the glaciers of Denali.... While we drank in the beauty of the sub-Arctic scenery that stretched all about us, the idea began to take form" (20–21). I have heard Ginny tell the story of hiking in the rain with Les Viereck and receiving the "Wow" postcard so many times and in different settings that I chose to include this version here. The variety in her tellings shows her emphasis on the weaving of a good yarn rather than the accuracy of the facts. This written version may have worked better for the audience at the time.
4. In an oral history interview, Les Viereck mentions hiking up the ridge with Woody, Ginny, and Celia and that he was asked to go back and check the spot for the view (oral history interview with David Krupa on May 23, 2000. Tape No. ORAL HISTORY 2000-17-06, Alaska and Polar Regions Archives, Elmer E. Rasmuson Library, University of Alaska Fairbanks; available for listening at http:// jukebox.uaf.edu/denali/html/levi.htm, accessed February 15, 2011).
5. Celia Hunter started to work for Wien Airlines and run their Kotzebue tourist operation and roadhouse in 1949. Ginny mentions elsewhere that she and Woody met George Collins in the summer of 1951, when they were living at Katmai National Park, and that he had just come from meeting Celia in Kotzebue.
6. The Homestead Act of 1862 granted title to up to 160 acres of undeveloped public land to individuals. Alaskans were restricted to only eighty acres (Naske and

Slotnick, *Alaska*, 78). The act required that once a claim was filed, the applicant had five years to develop the property and "prove up on it" to gain full title of ownership. The Homestead Act was repealed by Congress in 1976, except in Alaska, where homestead claims continued for another ten years.

7. On May 14, 1898, a provision for trade and manufacturing sites was added to the Homestead Act of 1862. The law allowed for the purchase of up to eighty acres of public land as a trade and manufacturing site for $2.50 per acre with occupancy required for no less than five months each year for three years in order to be able to purchase it (*An Act Extending the homestead laws and providing for right of way for railroads in the District of Alaska and for other purposes*, Chapter 299, Section 10, 55th Congress, 2d sess., US Statutes at Large 30 [1899]: 413).

8. The original Mount McKinley National Park, established in 1917, encompassed almost 1.6 million acres (Norris, *Crown Jewel of the North,* vol. 1, 22). In 1963, naturalist Sig Olson and park planner Ted Swem recognized what biologists like Adolph Murie had been saying for years, that the park was too small from an ecological standpoint. By 1965, the public was pushing for expansion, and nine thousand acres of BLM land in the Kantishna area that was considered to have recreation potential was withdrawn for possible future inclusion in the park. Ginny and Celia were opposed to this withdrawal because they did not want Camp Denali to be within the park boundaries where they would be faced with stricter regulations (William E. Brown, *Denali, Symbol of the Alaskan Wild: An Illustrated History of the Denali–Mount McKinley Region, Alaska* [Denali National Park: Alaska Natural History Association and Virginia Beach, VA: The Donning Company, 1993], 211), but they supported "a modest buffer to protect Wonder Lake's biological and viewshed values" (ibid., 210). In 1980, with passage of the Alaska National Interest Lands Conservation Act, four million acres were added and the park was renamed Denali National Park and Preserve. The old McKinley Park area became the park's wilderness and wildlife core and the lands around the edges were designated as national preserve (ibid., 209–13). As a preexisting business on private land, Camp Denali was allowed to continue its operations despite now being within a national park, where such a commercial operation might not otherwise be allowed. For a comprehensive history of Mount McKinley/Denali National Park, see Norris, *Crown Jewel of the North,* vol. 1 and vol. 2; and Brown, *Denali, Symbol of the Alaskan Wild.*

9. "By July 1951 Ms. Hunter had decided to stake the site with the Bureau of Land Management, and on October 29 she applied for a trade and manufacturing site" (Norris, *Crown Jewel of the North,* vol. 1, 136). "More than twelve years after she applied for the land, January 31, 1964, Ms. Hunter received patent to 67.306 acres surrounding her camp" (ibid., 152 and footnoted from BLM, "Case Abstract for AKF 009215" for US Survey 4003, from BLM Alaska State Office, Anchorage).

10. Joseph Conrad (1895–1924) wrote a number of stories and novels with nautical or sea-based themes, such as *The Nigger of the 'Narcissus'* (1897), *Youth, a Narrative,*

and Two Other Stories (1902), *Nostromo* (1904), *Victory* (1915), and *Suspense* (post-humously in 1925).

11. According to historian William E. Brown, Dan Kennedy originally ran horse pack trips and a primitive tent camp at Savage River in 1923–1924. In 1925, Savage Camp was taken over by the Mount McKinley Tourist and Transportation Company under the management of Robert Sheldon, and by 1928 they had expanded to establish camps at Igloo, Polychrome, Toklat, and Copper Mountain (near where Eielson Visitor Center is now) (Brown, *Denali, Symbol of the Alaskan Wild,* 135). In 1939, when the Alaska Railroad opened the McKinley Park Hotel and became competition, Mount McKinley Tourist and Transportation Company shifted its main operation from Savage Camp to Eielson Camp, sixty-six miles into the park (ibid., 187; Norris, *Crown Jewel of the North,* vol. 1, 89–90). A detailed history of these camps, and the park's tourist operations and concessionaire relationships, is presented in Norris, *Crown Jewel of the North,* vol. 1, 47–96. More about Kennedy, the camp, and early park concessionaires also appears in Pearson, *History of Mount McKinley National Park, Alaska,* 63–68.

12. KUAC Radio, *Homefires* radio series, March 10, 1984 (Fairbanks: KUAC FM/TV), Tape No. ORAL HISTORY 90-10-02, Alaska and Polar Regions Archives, Elmer E. Rasmuson Library, University of Alaska Fairbanks.

13. "The road did not open until June 12, one of the latest dates on record" (Wood, "Wilderness Camp," 23).

14. There is variation to this story in Ginny's 1953 article: "Celia and I arrived at Camp Denali, as we now called it, right behind the snowplow. Junior, our jeep station wagon, was jammed with supplies. Woody followed the next day with Jeeper, the military-type jeep, and Creeper, the trailer, loaded with lumber. Ted had hiked on ahead of the plows to set up one tent. For a few days we were able to drive the four-wheel-drive jeep up over our bulldozed road and beyond over the tundra to camp, but as the frost came out of the ground, even the indomitable Jeeper bogged down" (ibid.). It is possible that the different years of Camp are getting mixed together either in the written version or the storytelling Ginny did for this project. It is hard to know which one. However, it is certainly understandable that the years would blur together after so many trips back and forth on the road to Camp, and hard to keep track of details of what happened in a specific year, especially when trying to recall it over fifty years later.

15. According to Les Viereck, this was Castle Rock Lake. For more about Les Viereck and his role in helping to build Camp Denali, see oral history interview with David Krupa on May 23, 2000 (Tape No. ORAL HISTORY 2000-17-06, Alaska and Polar Regions Archives, Elmer E. Rasmuson Library, University of Alaska Fairbanks; audio available at http://jukebox.uaf.edu/denali/html/levi.htm, Section 14, accessed February 15, 2011).

16. "Late in August we saw a weary, bearded figure limping up the trail toward us. It was Les Viereck, clothes ragged, feet blistered, rifle over his shoulder, stumbling in

after hiking sixty miles over the tundra hills and wading countless streams from Castle Rock. Having worked like a slave to help us open camp, he had walked all the way back to help us close it" (Wood, "Wilderness Camp," 24).

17. For more about Grant Pearson's life, see his book, *My Life of High Adventure*.

18. Ginny also said: "Over the years, we had people come to Camp who had been kids there [Kantishna] with their dad, when there were about twenty or thirty people living down there, and they had come back to visit and see the old cabins. When we staked our land, there was only one full-time person who still lived in Kantishna year-round. That was Johnny Busia. He died in 1957." See Chapter 14 for more about Johnny Busia.

19. Gold was first discovered at Kantishna in 1903 by Judge James Wickersham. By 1905, the stampede was on the upswing, and Joe Quigley and Jack Horn filed Discovery Claim on Caribou Creek (Jane Haigh, *Searching for Fannie Quigley: A Wilderness Life in the Shadow of Mount McKinley* [Athens: Swallow Press/Ohio State University Press, 2007], 53). But by late 1906, the rush was over (ibid., 58). By 1942, Fannie Quigley and Johnny Busia were the only residents left at Kantishna because of President Roosevelt's Executive Order E-208, which shut down all gold mining that was not essential to the war effort (ibid., 145 and 148). For more about the history of mining in Kantishna, see Thomas K. Bundtzen, "A History of Mining in the Kantishna Hills," *Alaska Journal* 8 (Spring 1978): 150–61; Brown, *Denali, Symbol of the Alaskan Wild*, 63–77; Norris, *Crown Jewel of the North*, vol. 1, 6–7. For a history of Kantishna and all mining in the park, see Norris, *Crown Jewel of the North*, vol. 2, 325–401.

20. According to Woody Wood, the miner's name was Bill Julian (oral history interview with Karen Brewster on May 23, 2007. Tape No. ORAL HISTORY 2011-04-17, Alaska and Polar Regions Archives, Elmer E. Rasmuson Library, University of Alaska Fairbanks).

21. According to Ginny's 1953 article about Camp Denali, the miner bulldozed the road "within 400 yards of our campsite before he took his equipment out of the park for the season" (Wood, "Wilderness Camp," 23).

22. Woody Wood remembers: "I remember carrying a bunch of two-by-fours with Celia and we'd put them under our straps. Sixteen-foot two-by-fours, we'd put them under our pack straps in the front and the person in back would get the other end and put them under their arm and the pack straps and you'd walk up the hill carrying these things. Usually, with stuff piled on top. And we didn't think much of it" (oral history interview with Karen Brewster on May 23, 2007. Tape No. ORAL HISTORY 2011-04-17, Alaska and Polar Regions Archives, Elmer E. Rasmuson Library, University of Alaska Fairbanks).

23. From "The boys devised..." to "...two at a time" is from Wood, "Wilderness Camp," 23.

24. Oral history interview with Karen Brewster on May 23, 2007. Tape No. ORAL HISTORY 2011-04-17, Alaska and Polar Regions Archives, Elmer E. Rasmuson Library, University of Alaska Fairbanks.

25. In an August 2007 interview at Camp Denali conducted by Oregon Public Broadcasting for the series "Great Lodges of the National Parks," Woody Wood states:

    We had a very simple little military jeep of the type from World War II. It had a winch on the front of it with a 150-foot long cable. We made many trips up over this spongy tundra with that jeep, just pulling it with that winch very slowly. We buried what I call a dead man, where you dig a hole in the tundra and bury this log underneath where you can fasten a cable, or something, on the middle of it that you can hitch onto. And the problem with this tundra, of course, is that once you have driven over it you can't drive over that same spot very many times, because it immediately compresses the sphagnum moss, which loses its insulation and the permafrost underneath it will start to melt. When it melts, it sinks and it turns into a mud pie. So, pretty soon you have a ditch instead of a road and all this tundra is saturated with water, because when it's over permafrost the water can't penetrate any deeper and it can't drain. So that just runs off very quickly and pretty soon you've got a little river. So you've got to figure a way to fill that and ditch it, which we eventually did. And then we were able to drive up to the top with a jeep, but it was rather marginal in those early years. (Transcript_Camp Denali_#8A6, 5–6, electronic document in possession of author)

26. Wood, "Wilderness Camp," 21–22.
27. Ginny's 1953 article gives June 19 as date of first guests (ibid., 24).
28. Woody Wood remembers the details of these events slightly differently: "I remember we were exhausted, dead tired one night. We must've gone to bed around midnight, maybe. The sun was still pretty bright. I mean, it was still fairly light. And a plane came flying over. It was Bob Rice with a passenger and he dropped a note tied to a wrench or something, which we went and found in the tundra. It said come down to Kantishna and pick up your first guests. So, I'll never forget that. We all had to get out of this one little cabin which we had finally completed and put our sleeping bags out on the tundra, I guess, to accommodate the two people, I think, that Bob Rice had brought in. One of them was a schoolteacher from Homer or Anchorage" (oral history interview with Karen Brewster on May 23, 2007. Tape No. ORAL HISTORY 2011-04-17, Alaska and Polar Regions Archives, Elmer E. Rasmuson Library, University of Alaska Fairbanks).
29. From "Woody and Les…" to "…in business" is from Wood, "Wilderness Camp," 24.
30. "By mid-July we had erected four ten-by-twelve housekeeping tent-cabins and a fourteen-by-sixteen main tent-cabin" (ibid.).
31. "Thus ended the first season for Camp Denali. Almost a hundred persons had signed our guest book" (ibid.).
32. Red Top Mine in the Kantishna Mining District developed starting in 1935 and prospered between 1939 and 1944. The Red Top Mining Company was formed by

Ernest Fransen, Clifton Hawkins, and Fairbanks businessman A. Hjalmer Nordale, who purchased the claims from Joe and Fannie Quigley (Haigh, *Searching for Fannie Quigley*, 144–45; Norris, *Crown Jewel of the North*, vol. 2, 332).

33. From "We pitched…" to "…from the elements" is from Wood, "Wilderness Camp," 24.

34. At this time, the only option for driving from Fairbanks to McKinley Park would have been to take the Richardson Highway south from Fairbanks to Glennallen, go west on the Glenn Highway to Palmer, and then drive back north up to the park—a distance of over five hundred miles. This was many miles out of the way and very time-consuming, especially in the 1950s when the roads were not in as good condition as they are today. The 120-mile direct route from Fairbanks to Denali Park on the George Parks Highway was not available until 1971, when the road between Anchorage and Fairbanks was completed.

35. Construction of a road from Paxson Roadhouse on the Richardson Highway to McKinley Park Station began in 1950 with progress being made from both directions every year thereafter. Finally, it was predicted to open June 1, 1957. But typical of any road construction project, it got behind schedule and the two ends of the road were finally linked in August 1957. "The first motorists drove the length of the highway, however, on August 2, and the first auto arrived at the park on August 4; it was a 1957 Ford sedan owned by Mr. and Mrs. P.B. Johem of Los Angeles" (Norris, *Crown Jewel of the North*, vol. 1, 157). The impact of increased motorists arriving at Camp Denali wouldn't have been felt until the 1958 summer season.

36. The park's system of providing bus service along the park road instead of using private vehicles was inaugurated in 1972 (Brown, *Denali, Symbol of the Alaskan Wild*, 202–3). "The NPS began its new shuttle bus system when the park opened on June 1 [1972]" (Norris, *Crown Jewel of the North*, vol. 1, 221).

37. In an August 2007 interview conducted at Camp Denali by Oregon Public Broadcasting for the series "Great Lodges of the National Parks," Ginny states: "It was Brad Washburn that said, you know, what you guys need here is a permanent building that you can eat in and gather in at night. And you can then build one fire that heats everybody instead of trying to bring firewood to each cabin" (Transcript_Camp Denali_#59C, electronic document in possession of author).

38. Oral history interview with Karen Brewster on May 23, 2007. Tape No. ORAL HISTORY 2011-04-17, Alaska and Polar Regions Archives, Elmer E. Rasmuson Library, University of Alaska Fairbanks.

39. Woody Wood recalls, "It was getting cold. And pretty miserable. In fact, I remember Ginny nicknamed the place 'Misery Manor.' Which was a pretty apt description" (ibid.).

40. Woody Wood says it was "an old Sears Roebuck chainsaw which didn't work very long" (ibid.).

41. August 2007 interview with Morton "Woody" Wood conducted at Camp Denali by Oregon Public Broadcasting for "Great Lodges in the National Parks" series, Transcript_Camp Denali_#8A6, 3, electronic document in possession of author.

42. In an August 2007 interview conducted by Oregon Public Broadcasting for the "Great Lodges of the National Parks" series, Woody Wood explains another interesting detail about the new warehouse's construction:

> We had to replace that warehouse, so I built it out of logs that were sawn on three sides. And it's still up there today with a big heavy door, like a portcullis that we lower down in winter. We were limited in the space, so it had a loft that was used for storing all of our supplies. While I was working on it, this gentleman visiting from California said, 'Hey, you know how to make a stairway that's a lot steeper, that you could still use?' And I said, 'No, how would that be?' So he showed me. He actually helped me build a stairway of a different type, which had instead of a riser on the left hand and on the right hand with a step all the way across in between, he had a riser in the middle, with a half a step on the right and then one step higher a half a step on the left. And it's tricky to use. You've got to think about it when you walk on this, because there's only one place you can step, but it works fine. This allows you to have a much steeper angle than you could have with an ordinary staircase. And it saved space. That staircase is still up there today. (ibid., 8)

43. Ibid.

44. After working at Camp Denali, Nancy Bale stayed in the area and became the president of the Denali Citizens Council, a small nonprofit environmental group focused on conservation and management issues in and around the Denali Park area.

45. Oral history interview with Karen Brewster on May 23, 2007. Tape No. ORAL HISTORY 2011-04-17, Alaska and Polar Regions Archives, Elmer E. Rasmuson Library, University of Alaska Fairbanks.

46. Woody Wood adds: "We worried about cutting the spruce trees up on the hill, and we'd always get the dead ones, if possible. And we'd never leave a hole where you'd actually see a bunch of tree stumps. We'd pick and choose them pretty carefully to not make the forest look bad" (ibid.).

47. Camp Denali newsletter, 1952. Ginny Wood Personal Collection.

48. Oral history interview with Karen Brewster on May 23, 2007. Tape No. ORAL HISTORY 2011-04-17, Alaska and Polar Regions Archives, Elmer E. Rasmuson Library, University of Alaska Fairbanks.

49. Construction of the Trans-Alaska Pipeline system began in late March 1975, and the first oil moved through it on June 20, 1977. For more about the history of oil development in Alaska, the construction of the pipeline, and the political and environmental controversy that accompanied it, see Naske and Slotnick, *Alaska*, 233–66; Mary Clay Berry, *The Alaska Pipeline: The Politics of Oil and Native Land Claims* (Bloomington: Indiana University Press, 1975); Peter Coates,

The Trans-Alaska Pipeline Controversy: Technology, Conservation, and the Frontier (Fairbanks: University of Alaska Press, 1993); Jack Roderick, *Crude Dreams: A Personal History of Oil and Politics in Alaska* (Fairbanks: Epicenter Press, 1997); and Roxanne Willis, *Alaska's Place in the West: From the Last Frontier to the Last Great Wilderness* (Lawrence: University Press of Kansas, 2010), 113–31.

12. Driving the Denali Park Road

1. The NPS–Alaska Road Commission Road Construction Agreement was signed in 1922. The Alaska Road Commission began construction of the park road in 1923 and completed it in 1938 (Brown, *Denali, Symbol of the Alaskan Wild*). Also see Norris, *Crown Jewel of the North*, vol. 1; Haigh, *Searching for Fannie Quigley*, 63. From the viewpoint of the National Park Service, the road was "primarily a visitor access road. Only incidentally, in that view, was it a link in an industrial transportation system" between the railroad and Kantishna (Brown, *Denali, Symbol of the Alaskan Wild*, 109). In contrast, the miners at Kantishna considered it mainly an industrial road (ibid.).

2. Through the years, improvements were made to the road, including the National Park Service's Mission 66 project to widen, straighten, and pave it. Due to opposition that stopped construction, widening and paving was only completed to Savage River (Mile 14), and widening and graveling reached the Teklanika River, thirty miles into the park (ibid., 197–203). Overall, the park's single road remains a one-lane wilderness road without guardrails or other safety measures. For more about park road construction history, see Haigh, *Searching for Fannie Quigley*, 132–34; Brown, *Denali, Symbol of the Alaskan Wild*, 104–9; and Norris, *Crown Jewel of the North*, vol. 1, 32–84. For more about the overall history of the park road, see Jane Bryant, *Snapshots from the Past: A Roadside History of Denali National Park and Preserve* (Denali National Park, AK: National Park Service, Center for Resources, Science and Learning, 2011).

3. In June 2007, Susan Grace and I drove Ginny to Camp Denali, stopping at particular places along the park road to record her talking about them, such as Igloo Creek, which was used as a base camp for Camp Denali excursions; Quake Lake, where a landslide blocked the road and created a temporary lake; Stoney Pass, where she witnessed large-scale caribou migrations; and Eielson Visitor Center, where she talked about hiking the surrounding hills, valleys, and on to Muldrow Glacier (Tape No. ORAL HISTORY 2011-04-18, Alaska and Polar Regions Archives, Elmer E. Rasmuson Library, University of Alaska Fairbanks).

4. "McKinley Park, Alaska. Scenic Wonders of America," submitted to John Baker, senior editor/general books, *Reader's Digest* on August 14, 1972. In folder titled "Unpublished Manuscripts by Ginny. Backpacking McKinley Park," Ginny Wood Personal Collection.

5. This same incident is mentioned in Camp Denali's 1952 Christmas newsletter: Ginny started toward the station in Jeeper. Two miles before reaching Camp Eielson she turned back to Wonder Lake—the road was blocked by drifts. For three days she and Elton Thayer, the ranger, waited for the snow plows to reach them. For awhile it looked as though Jeeper would remain at Kantishna and Elton and Ginny be evacuated by air for the snow was piling up faster than the plows could remove it. But on the fourth day the plows pushed through and they drove out" (1952 Camp Denali Newsletter, p. 2. Ginny Wood Personal Collection). A slightly amended version of this story appears in Ginny's 1953 article about Camp Denali, with Woody and Les flying to Fairbanks on September 3, Ginny driving their newly acquired surplus truck Jumbo back to camp facing snowdrifts building up on the road, Celia and the Collinses flying out upon Ginny's return, and Ginny driving the jeep back to Fairbanks: "I started back with Jeeper toward the railroad station. Thirty miles out, I was turned back by snowdrifts. For four days I waited at the Wonder Lake ranger station until plows cleared the road. (Wood, "Wilderness Camp," 24).

6. Oral history interview with Karen Brewster on May 23, 2007. Tape No. ORAL HISTORY 2011-04-17, Alaska and Polar Regions Archives, Elmer E. Rasmuson Library, University of Alaska Fairbanks.

7. This same incident is mentioned in Norris, *Crown Jewel of the North,* vol. 2: "Heightened awareness of the park's landforms did not take place until July 1953, when an earthquake, combined with heavy rainstorms, caused a major landslide in Stoney Creek Canyon, between Highway Pass and Stoney Hill overlook. The slide, approximately one mile north of the park road, dammed the creek bed with a 200-foot berm, and within a month, a mile-long lake had formed—complete with a thriving grayling population—that reached to within 150 feet of the park road. But erosion soon began to wear down the huge earthen dam, and during the next three years the newly designated 'Bergh Lake' diminished to about half a mile in length" (203).

8. "On July 2, 1968, thirty-three years after the lake was formed, rain-swollen waters dug through the berm and the lake disappeared" (ibid.).

9. Ginny wrote about Denali Park Road management and policy issues a number of times, such as: "McKinley Park: The Summer of '72," *Alaska Conservation Review* 13, no. 3 (Fall 1972): 4–6; "When Is Enough, Enough?" "From the Woodpile" column, the *Northern Line* 16, no. 2 (August 5, 1994): 10–11; "Beware of the Hydro-Ax Along the Denali Park Road," "From the Woodpile" column, the *Northern Line*, 19, no. 2 (July 29, 1997): 14–15.

10. "McKinley Park—1973," unpublished and undated manuscript in folder titled "Unpublished Manuscripts by Ginny Backpacking in McKinley Park," Ginny Wood Personal Collection.

11. Ginny and Celia sold Camp Denali to Wally Cole in 1975.

13. Exploring Mount McKinley's Backcountry

1. Louise Potter, *Roadside Flowers of Alaska* (Thetford Center, VT, 1962).

2. Louise Potter, *Wildflowers Along Mt. McKinley Park Road and to Westward* (1969; repr., McKinley Park, AK: Camp Denali Publishers, 1979).

3. Adolph "Ade" Murie was sent to Mount McKinley National Park in 1939 to study predator-prey relationships after working there on caribou studies with his brother, Olaus, in the 1920s. His groundbreaking work, first published as *The Wolves of Mount McKinley* in 1944 (reprinted in 1985 by University of Washington Press), led to the termination of the park's wolf control program that had been in effect since 1929. Ade's "reports on McKinley mammals, birds, and ecological studies number in the scores, with many of them published in popular form. These, plus his periodic evaluation of the wolf-sheep status during the '30s and '40s, and his many letters and comments on the park's evolving development exerted a force both spiritual and scientific" (Brown, *Denali, Symbol of the Alaskan Wild,* 149). For more about Ade Murie's work in the park and the park's wolf control policies, see Norris, *Crown Jewel of the North,* vol. 2, 192–97. Ade Murie retired in December 1964, having spent the summers of 1955 and 1956, and from 1959 on, mostly home-based at the Igloo Creek cabin studying the park's caribou, sheep, and other wildlife (ibid., 205).

4. The formal common name for these mountain animals is Dall's sheep (*Ovis dalli dalli*) but many people call them Dall sheep.

5. The arctic ground squirrel (*Spermophilus parryii*) is a common species found throughout Alaska. It used to be referred to colloquially as "parkie squirrel" because Native Alaskans used their skins to make beautiful and warm fur parkas.

6. Ginny only mentioned Wilderness Workshop and Tundra Treks. Mention of Shutter Safari and details of seasonal availability of the trips is from a biography of Ginny Hill Wood by Celia Hunter, February 23, 1993, that appears in a press release from the Alaska Wilderness Recreation and Tourism Association regarding the first annual Ginny Hill Wood Award being presented at their annual meeting in Anchorage, Alaska, February 23, 1993. In folder titled "Ginny's Resume and Awards (Her Life History)" in Ginny Wood Personal Collection.

7. According to Barbara Powell, this bear incident probably took place in the summer of 1974 (B. Powell, pers. comm.).

14. Camp Denali Staff and Friends

1. In an article written in 1953, Ginny says this was "the Harvard mountaineering party" (Wood, "Wilderness Camp"). In our oral history interview, she said they were a group from California. I chose to use the written reference, since it was produced closer to the actual event.

2. Elizabeth "Liz" Berry married wildlife artist Bill Berry, came to Alaska and worked at Camp Denali, settled in Fairbanks, and became one of Ginny's close friends. Liz was known around Fairbanks for her handcrafted pottery and the wood-fired kiln she built in her yard and made available to university classes. Bill Berry died in 1979 and Liz Berry died in 2006. For information about their artwork, see the Berry Studios official website (http://www.berrystudios.biz/, accessed February 15, 2011).

3. Bill Berry became quite well known around Alaska for his wildlife drawings, often with comedic or cartoony overtones. His final work was a large wall mural in the children's section of the North Star Borough's Noel Wien Library in Fairbanks. He was working on this mural when he was killed in 1979. The reading room is now known as the Bill Berry Room.

4. Oral history interview with Karen Brewster on May 23, 2007. Tape No. ORAL HISTORY 2011-04-17, Alaska and Polar Regions Archives, Elmer E. Rasmuson Library, University of Alaska Fairbanks.

5. As previously mentioned, Les Viereck was a boreal plant ecologist who defined the roles of wildfire, flooding, and glaciers in plant succession and the patterns of community diversity that develop in response to these disturbances. His wife, Teri (Eleanor), studied populations of small mammals and got her PhD in zoology from the University of Colorado. She later taught in the biology department at the University of Alaska Fairbanks, and did research on cold weather acclimatization in pika at the Arctic Aeromedical Laboratory at Ladd Field in Fairbanks, and at the Institute of Arctic Biology at the University of Alaska Fairbanks. She often accompanied Les in the field, such as the year they wintered together with their children at Dry Creek in interior Alaska. Eventually, Teri left science and spent the next forty-two years as a yoga instructor in Fairbanks (T. Viereck, pers. comm.).

6. "Les Viereck, from the University of Colorado, spent the summers of 1956 and 1958 collecting mosses, lichens, and vascular plants near Mount Eielson, and Eleanor Viereck (Les' wife) studied the park's small mammal populations" (Norris, *Crown Jewel of the North*, vol. 2, 206).

7. Published references to Johnny Busia (Norris, *Crown Jewel of the North*, vol. 1, 158; Norris, *Crown Jewel of the North*, vol. 2, 335; and Haigh, *Searching For Fannie Quigley*) spelled his name "Johnny," so that is the spelling I've used. There is a discrepancy in the pronunciation of Busia's name: "Longtime park employee John Rumohr, who knew Busia over a number of years, pronounced his name BOO-see-a, while Bill Brown states that boo-SHAY was correct" (Norris, *Crown Jewel of the North*, vol. 2, 391). Ginny pronounces it BOO-see-a, perhaps having learned it initially from John Rumohr, whom she knew when she first arrived at Mount McKinley National Park in 1950.

8. According to Frank Norris, Johnny Busia moved to Kantishna in 1918 (ibid., 335).

9. In the interview, Ginny also said:

He lived in a cabin that was given to him by some old miner. He had another cabin that went with it that he called his junk cabin. And he had still another cabin that had been bequeathed to him and over the years he'd been using that, too." In a court document, she wrote: "Johnnie had two cabins: one in which he lived ('Busia Cabin') year round, and a cabin he referred to as the 'Drunk Cabin' next door. The Drunk Cabin is where visitors would stay when they got inebriated on Johnnie's home brewed beer. I am very familiar with the Busia Cabin, as I visited Johnnie there often. It was a solid cabin built out of native spruce logs and contained one large room with wood plank floors, a cooking stove, a table, a cupboard, a bunk bed, and many shelves. There was also a cellar beneath the cabin where Johnnie stored beer, food and other supplies year-round. Although the Busia Cabin was not new, it was always well maintained and in very good condition during the time Johnnie lived there. (Declaration of Virginia Wood for United States Bankruptcy Court, District of Alaska, Case No. F95–00795-DMD, Re. Daniel E. Ashbrook, Debtor, Signed by Virginia H. Wood, 18 October 2004, Ginny Wood Personal Collection)

The above is quoted directly from Ginny's declaration, where she spells his name Johnnie.

10. According to Woody Wood:

Johnny pretty much lived on his homebrew beer, which he kept stored in a dug-out little cellar under his cabin. He was a character. He had never been part of the modern world. He didn't want to go Outside. He didn't want to go to town. He didn't feel he could survive there. He was a great storyteller if you could understand him. He did have quite a strong accent. He called himself a 'bohunk.' A bohunk, I believe, was what the miners were called mostly from Yugoslavia, Eastern Europe, Bulgaria, too, and Romania, maybe. And the old Yugoslavia. He was a friendly guy. He loved company. We used to go over and visit him and spend time with him when we could. When we could take time from the work. And off season. Early and late in the season we could go over. (oral history interview with Karen Brewster on May 23, 2007. Tape No. ORAL HISTORY 2011-04-17, Alaska and Polar Regions Archives, Elmer E. Rasmuson Library, University of Alaska Fairbanks)

11. In *Searching for Fannie Quigley*, author Jane Haigh states that Johnny Busia accompanied Fannie Quigley's body to Fairbanks in August 1944 (xvii).

12. "The miner with the most extensive NPS contacts during this period was Johnny Busia, who seldom if ever used the park road. By the late 1940s, the lone sourdough was a well-known figure, both locally and throughout Alaska, and NPS staff stayed in contact with him by radio throughout the year via periodic weather and wildlife reports" (Norris, *Crown Jewel of the North*, vol. 2, 337). Park superintendent Grant

Pearson was especially fond of Johnny and in 1948 wrote an article about him titled "Little Johnnie of Kantishna" (*Alaska Sportsman* 14, no. 7 [July 1948]: 6).

13. "Johnny Busia died on August 20, 1957, just two weeks after the Denali Highway made Kantishna easily accessible to the motoring public" (Norris, *Crown Jewel of the North*, vol. 2, 337). The date of August 1957 also was obtained from Declaration of Virginia Wood for United States Bankruptcy Court, District of Alaska, Case No. F95–00795-DMD, Re. Daniel E. Ashbrook, Debtor, Signed by Virginia H. Wood, 18 October 2004, Ginny Wood Personal Collection. Johnny's death also is mentioned in "Camp Denali, Tundra Telegram," vol. VI , Kay Kennedy Collection, Alaska and Polar Regions Collections, Elmer E. Rasmuson Library, University of Alaska Fairbanks.

14. When he was one of the last remaining residents at Kantishna, "Park personnel dubbed Johnny Busia the mayor, and did what they could to assist him" (Norris, *Crown Jewel of the North,* vol. 2, 335).

15. Ginny also has said Johnny was sixty-nine when he died. According to Jane Bryant, cultural anthropologist, Cultural Resource and Subsistence Division, Denali National Park and Preserve, Johnny was sixty-six years old when he died on August 20, 1957, and is buried in Kantishna (email message to author, January 26, 2011). Her source is Camp Denali's *Tundra Telegram*, vol. 6, Kay Kennedy Collection, Alaska and Polar Regions Collections, Elmer E. Rasmuson Library, University of Alaska Fairbanks.

16. "Ted Lachelt, a University of Alaska graduate student, spent several months in the field on a wolverine study" (Norris, *Crown Jewel of the North,* vol. 2, 205).

17. Woody recalls, "When Romany was about to be born, I had to drive Ginny from the cabin out to our car in the tractor [parked at the bottom of Ballaine Hill near where the golf course is]. We had a little Oliver crawler tractor. Because you couldn't drive in during that particular time of year, which was breakup. I guess it had been bulldozed as a road but it wasn't in very good shape. Especially in the spring. The rest of the time you could drive it" (oral history interview with Karen Brewster on May 23, 2007. Tape No. ORAL HISTORY 2011-04-17, Alaska and Polar Regions Archives, Elmer E. Rasmuson Library, University of Alaska Fairbanks).

18. Herb Crisler made his first motion picture, *From the Mountains to the Sea*, in 1924. In 1949, Walt Disney purchased his film *The Olympic Elk* and released it for big-screen viewing in 1952. After this, Disney Studios contracted with Crisler for other wildlife footage. In 1958, Walt Disney distributed Herb and Lois Crisler's film *White Wilderness* (distributed by Buena Vista Film Distribution). Also in 1958, Lois Crisler published a book, *Arctic Wild* (New York: Harper and Brothers). For more about the Crislers, see F. E. Caldwell, *Beyond the Trails, with Herb and Lois Crisler in Olympic National Park* (Port Angeles, WA: Anchor Publishing, 1998); or the Herb Crisler Papers, Special Collections, University Libraries, University of Washington, Seattle.

According to Ginny,

Herb Crisler was up here two years. He was filming wolves for Walt Disney. We first met him in 1952. He and his wife, Lois, were in the park doing a lot of hiking and camping and stayed in several places in the park taking pictures of wolves, and we'd run into them. He came out to Camp later to help us with our jeep pulling lumber and stuff.

Later, they stayed with us in Fairbanks. That was in the wintertime. Previously, the Crislers had lived in the Arctic, where he was filming his documentary about wolves. They adopted two puppies from these wolves. They knew those puppies wouldn't be able to survive on their own if they left them behind in the wild at their young age. They were bringing the pups from the Arctic to Colorado, where they lived in the mountains, and they had to put them someplace while they waited to ship them out. They kept the wolves with us because our cabin was a bit out of town and the pups would be safer than where they staying in town. There were two puppies and then all of a sudden one of them disappeared. Woody and Herb spent a day trying to follow the tracks in the snow that led into Goldstream Valley. They couldn't see the wolf, only its tracks. We were afraid if anybody heard about a loose wolf they'd try to capture it for the bounty. One night we had the Crislers over for dinner and I went out to get the pie I'd left outdoors in a box to cool, and I saw these eyes glaring at me in the dark. It was the missing wolf. He knew Herb was there, so was hanging around the cabin. I went back inside and told Herb, 'Your wolf knows you're here and is hanging around outside.' Herb went out to try to get the wolf, but it disappeared. Eventually, Herb caught that wolf by putting food out and was able to get close enough to grab it. The tracks indicated that that wolf was coming back for his buddy. After he was captured, that wolf was put on a leash where our sled dogs were tied up.

19. *News Bulletin of the Alaska Conservation Society* 4, no. 2 (April 1963): 15.

15. *Flying Search and Rescue*

1. Parts of the following story about the Collinses' airplane crash and rescue mission is excerpted from a speech by Ginny Hill Wood at the Alaska Association of Mountain and Wilderness Guides Annual Meeting in Fairbanks on December 5–6, 1981. (Typed speech text found in files of Ginny Wood Personal Collection.) Given the quality of the writing in this speech and the detail missing from her verbal telling, I integrated the two into one presentation of the story.
2. From "It was for an expedition…" to "…they arrived there" is from Ginny Hill Wood's speech at the Alaska Association of Mountain and Wilderness Guides annual meeting in Fairbanks, December 5–6, 1981.

3. From "Dick had advised..." to "...Peters Basin," ibid.

4. From "On the fourth day..." to "...load of groceries," ibid.

5. From "McLean had marked..." to "...ripped it off," ibid.

6. Florence Rucker became Florence Collins when she ended up marrying Dick Collins after his first wife, Jeanne, died.

7. From "Both plane and pilots..." to "...approaching storm" and from "With the wind..." to "...flapping tent," ibid.

8. From "They retrieved..." to "...base camp," ibid.

9. From "While grounded..." to "...buttress could begin," ibid.

10. From "Dick lost his plane..." to "...allow for a storm," ibid.

11. This is Ginny's perspective on this climb, as an anxious wife who waited at home and then searched when the climbers were overdue. For Woody's perspective on this climb, see Wood, "The First Traverse of Mt. McKinley—A First Ascent of the South Buttress"; "On Mt. McKinley; Rescue After Victory," *Life*, June 14, 1954, 28–34; and an oral history interview with Morton Wood with David Krupa on on May 6, 2000. Tape No. ORAL HISTORY 2000-17-03, Alaska and Polar Regions Archives, Elmer E. Rasmuson Library, University of Alaska Fairbanks, available for listening at http://jukebox.uaf.edu/denali/html/mowo.htm, accessed February 12, 2011. Les Viereck provides his memories of the climb in an oral history interview with David Krupa on May 23, 2000. Tape No. ORAL HISTORY 2000-17-06, Alaska and Polar Regions Archives, Elmer E. Rasmuson Library, University of Alaska Fairbanks, available for listening at http://jukebox.uaf.edu/denali/html/levi.htm, acessed February 12, 2011. George Argus provides his memories from the climb and rescue in an oral history interview with Karen Brewster, July 7, 2011. Tape No. ORAL HISTORY 2011-25, Alaska and Polar Regions Archives, Elmer E. Rasmuson Library, University of Alaska Fairbanks. For more about the climb and rescue, see "Alaska: Single Slip," *Time*, vol. LXIII, No. 24 (June 14, 1954): 28–29; Dougald MacDonald, "Band of Brothers—Remembering Denali's Greatest Rescue," *Climbing* 233 (September 2004): 64–71.

12. See note 3 above.

13. This was probably John McCall, glaciologist at the University of Alaska Fairbanks, who was part of the team that went in to help rescue George Argus.

14. This was University of Alaska Fairbanks glaciologist John McCall, who had previously climbed Mount McKinley, and anthropologist Fred Milan, with the US Air Force Arctic Aeromedical Laboratory in Fairbanks, who was experienced in cold weather survival (Mike Dunham, "Survivor to Recall Deadly '54 Denali Climb," *Anchorage Daily News*, June 26, 2011, http://www.adn.com/2011/06/25/1936465/survivor-to-recall-deadly-54-denali.html, accessed June 28, 2011). For more about McCall and the rescue operation, see John G. McCall with Jim Rearden, "Rescue on Mt. McKinley," *Saga*, March 1955: 24–29, 64–67.

15. The climb was from April 15 to May 30, 1962. It was Garry Kenwood's second attempt to climb the mountain, and Anore's only attempt (Anore Jones, email message to author, January 27, 2011).

16. In June 1947, Barbara Washburn accompanied her husband, Brad Washburn, and became the first woman to summit Mount McKinley. For more about her, see Barbara Washburn, *The Accidental Adventurer: Memoirs of the First Woman to Climb Mount McKinley* (Kenmore, WA: Epicenter Press, 2001); and the Bradford and Barbara Washburn Papers, Alaska and Polar Regions Collections, Elmer E. Rasmuson Library, University of Alaska Fairbanks.

17. Bradford Washburn (1910–2007) was an explorer, mountaineer, photographer, and cartographer. He pioneered and mapped the now popular West Buttress route for climbing Mount McKinley. He pioneered aerial mountain photography; his black-and-white photos are known for their detail and artistry. He also established and served as director of the Boston Museum of Science. For more about him, see Bradford Washburn and Lew Freedman, *Bradford Washburn, An Extraordinary Life: The Autobiography of a Mountaineering Icon* (Portland, OR: West Winds Press, 2005); Dr. Bradford Washburn, edited by Lew Freedman, *Exploring the Unknown: Historic Diaries of Bradford Washburn's Alaska/Yukon Expeditions* (Kenmore, WA: Epicenter Press, 2001); Michael Sfraga, *Bradford Washburn: A Life of Exploration* (Corvallis: Oregon State University Press, 2004); and the Bradford and Barbara Washburn Papers, Alaska and Polar Regions Collections, Elmer E. Rasmuson Library, University of Alaska Fairbanks.

18. The book Ginny most likely is referring to is *Glacier Ice* by Austin Post and Edward R. Lachapelle (Seattle: University of Washington Press, 1971). Austin Post was a glaciologist with the University of Washington and the US Geological Survey who studied and photographed small glaciers in Alaska. In 1960, he planned the logistics for the American Geographical Society's Glacier Mapping Project (part of the 1957 International Geophysical Year), whose purpose was to prepare precise maps, on large scales, of selected small glaciers to form a permanent record of the condition of these glaciers as a baseline for future comparison. From 1960 through 1983, Post conducted annual aerial photographic missions to document changes in glaciers. It is possible that Celia could have been the pilot for him on any of these projects. For more about Post and his glacial photography, see Bruce F. Molnia, "Glaciers of North America—Glaciers of Alaska," US Geological Survey Professional Paper 1386-K, Part of the series *Satellite Image Atlas of the Glaciers of the World*, edited by Richard S. Williams Jr. and Jane G. Ferrigno, US Department of the Interior, US Geological Survey (Washington, DC: US Government Printing Office, 2008), 45 and 50.

16. Selling Camp Denali

1. This led to a sentimental attachment to the old couches that Woody had built (August 2007 interview with Ginny Wood at Camp Denali conducted by Oregon Public Broadcasting for the "Great Lodges of the National Parks" series, Transcript_Camp Denali_#59C, electronic document in possession of the author).

2. Oral history interview with Karen Brewster on May 23, 2007. Tape No. ORAL HISTORY 2011-004-17, Alaska and Polar Regions Archives, Elmer E. Rasmuson Library, University of Alaska Fairbanks.

3. In 1971, Congress passed the Alaska Native Claims Settlement Act (ANCSA) to settle the Native populations' claims to land, which was preventing development of the newly discovered vast oilfields at Prudhoe Bay in northern Alaska. Under ANCSA, Alaska Natives were paid $963 million and received title to forty-four million acres of land. This led to the identification of land that would be transferred to the newly formed Native corporations and the state of Alaska, and what land would be retained by the federal government and for what purposes. Section 17(d)(2) of the act directed the secretary of the interior to withdraw eighty million acres of significant federal lands from development for consideration as national parks, wildlife refuges, wild and scenic rivers, or national forests. The "D-2 lands" were not officially transferred and designated for specific purposes until passage of the 1980 Alaska National Interest Lands Conservation Act (ANILCA). As a member of the Joint Federal–State Land Use Planning Commission, Celia Hunter was involved in the D-2 hearings held in towns and small villages around Alaska taking testimony for what lands to include or exclude.

4. Wally and Jerryne Cole talk about their relationship with Ginny, their experience with Camp Denali, and the purchase of it from Ginny and Celia in an oral history interview with Karen Brewster and Susan Grace on February 2, 2007 (Tape No. ORAL HISTORY 2011-04-11, Alaska and Polar Regions Archives, Elmer E. Rasmuson Library, University of Alaska Fairbanks).

5. Ginny believes this migration pattern has changed because of improvements to the park road that have allowed for more vehicles and increased noise and dust (G. Wood, pers. comm.).

17. Preserving Alaska

1. Ginny was given this award because she "has spent a lifetime becoming informed, concerned and truly dedicated to making change…. Whatever she undertakes, she does so with spirit, dedication and a big heart. She is one of the rare breed that does not demand nor expect recognition and thanks for her efforts. What she does, she does because she sees a need and because she finds great joy in her work" (Kate Pendleton, "From the Woodpile," the *Northern Line* 7, no. 5 [November–December 1985]: 8). Also see *Fairbanks Daily News-Miner*, "Ginny Hill Wood wins Celia Hunter Award," December 8, 1985: A-1, 7; and "From the Woodpile," the *Northern Line* 8, no. 1 (January–March 1986): 6.

2. "Fairbanks Duo Receives Sierra Club's Highest Award," the *Northern Line* 13, no. 2 (June 14, 1991): 11.

3. "The Alaska Wilderness Recreation and Tourism Association (AWRTA) is a members-driven trade association formed to be a collective voice for

wilderness-dependent businesses. We advocate for the sustainability of Alaska's natural and cultural resources, responsible tourism and tourism planning for communities" (http://www.awrta.org, accessed February 12, 2011).

4. "Each of these women epitomize, in their own way, the best of Alaska's conservation movement. They overcame substantial challenges to create a life in Alaska that is respectful of the natural environment. They've dedicated their lives to environmental justice and protecting Alaska's wild places. Their unique contributions of activism and stewardship are an inspiration for us all" ("Alaska Conservationist Lifetime Achievement Award Ceremony Program," August 15, 2001, Alaska Conservation Foundation. Copy in possession of author).

5. These are some of the major players in the history of Alaska's conservation movement. Les Viereck, Olaus Murie, Adolph Murie, Bob Weeden, Fred Dean, and Will Troyer were all biologists. Richard Cooley was a geographer and economist. Jane Williams was a local citizen concerned with protecting her community. Mardy Murie was born in Fairbanks and, with her husband, Olaus, became an iconic figure in the national effort to protect the Arctic National Wildlife Refuge. And Edgar Wayburn was a devoted Sierra Club activist in San Francisco whose main focus was the protection of Alaska lands (see his personal memoir, Edgar Wayburn, *Your Land and Mine: Evolution of a Conservationist* [San Francisco: Sierra Club Books, 2004]).

   For more about the development of Alaska's environmental movement and the fight to retain the state's wilderness qualities, see Roderick Nash, *Wilderness and the American Mind*, 3rd ed. (New Haven, CT: Yale University Press, 1982), 272–315; Ken Ross, *Environmental Conflict in Alaska* (Boulder: University Press of Colorado, 2000); Daniel Nelson, "Idealism and Organization: Origins of the Environmental Movement in Alaska," *Alaska History* 18, nos. 1–2 (Spring/Fall 2003): 12–35; and Daniel Nelson, *Northern Landscapes: The Struggle for Wilderness Alaska* (Washington, DC: Resources for the Future, 2004).

   For more about the evolution of a conservation ethic in Alaska, see Ken Ross, *Pioneering Conservation in Alaska* (Boulder: University Press of Colorado, 2006).

6. The Joint Federal–State Land Use Planning Commission was established in 1972 to review and propose land for possible inclusion in the Alaska National Interest Lands Conservation Act (ANILCA). The final lands selected received federal protection as national parks, monuments, preserves, or refuges when the final bill was passed and signed into law in 1980 by President Jimmy Carter. The commission held hearings in towns and villages around Alaska to learn about local land use and what lands were important to communities. Commission members were selected as representatives for either the state or the federal government. Representation shifted over time, but in addition to Celia Hunter, some of the other members included Dr. Richard Cooley, Joseph H. Fitzgerald, Jack O. Horton, Walter B. Parker, Joe P. Josephson, Burt Silcock, and Esther Wunnicke.

7. In 1971, Congress passed the Alaska Native Claims Settlement Act (ANCSA) to settle the Native populations' claims to land, which was preventing development

of the newly discovered vast oilfields at Prudhoe Bay in northern Alaska. Under ANCSA, Alaska Natives were paid $963 million and received title to forty-four million acres of land. This led to the identification of land that would be transferred to the newly formed Native corporations and the state of Alaska, and what land would be retained by the federal government and for what purposes. Section 17(d)(2) of the act directed the secretary of the interior to withdraw eighty million acres of significant federal lands from development. These lands, referred to as "D-2" lands, were for potential designation as national parks, wildlife refuges, wild and scenic rivers, or national forests. Land was not officially transferred and designated for specific purposes until passage of the 1980 Alaska National Interest Lands Conservation Act (ANILCA).

For more about ANCSA, the land issues, and the politics of the time, see Berry, *The Alaska Pipeline*; Naske and Slotnick, *Alaska*, 195–232; David S. Case, *Alaska Natives and American Laws* (Fairbanks: University of Alaska Press, 1984); Donald Craig Mitchell, *Take My Land, Take My Life: The Story of Congress's Historic Settlement of Alaska Native Land Claims, 1960–1971* (Fairbanks: University of Alaska Press, 2001); and Robert Lind Gilbert, "Dividing Alaska: Native Claims, Statehood and Wilderness Preservation" (PhD diss., University of North Carolina, 2002).

For more about ANILCA, see Berry, *The Alaska Pipeline*; Nash, *Wilderness and the American Mind*; Case, *Alaska Natives and American Laws*; Nelson, *Northern Landscapes*; George Frank Williss, *Do Things Right the First Time: The National Park Service and the Alaska National Interest Lands Conservation Act of 1980. Administrative History: The National Park Service and the Alaska National Interest Lands Conservation Act of 1980* (Anchorage: US Department of the Interior, National Park Service, 2005); and Roxanne Willis, *Alaska's Place in the West*.

8. For more about Celia Hunter and her conservation work and philosophy, see Jessica Wiles, "Celia Hunter: Life and Leadership," Alaska Conservation Foundation publication, undated, photocopy in possession of author; and "Celia Hunter: An Alaskan Preservation Pioneer" on Wilderness.net (http://www.wilderness.net/index .cfm?fuse=feature1207, accessed February 13, 2011), a website designed to connect federal employees, scientists, educators, and the public with their wilderness heritage.

9. Ginny's longtime friend Bob Weeden noted that "Ginny is reversing the true concerns of Nome residents who were not anxious to be connected to the big city" (R. Weeden, pers. comm.).

10. Bob Weeden was a wildlife biologist who, starting in the late 1950s, worked for the Alaska Department of Fish and Game, and in 1970 became a professor of wildlife management at the University of Alaska Fairbanks, where he felt he "could think about a broader range of things and it meant I could be freer to speak out" (oral history interview with Roger Kaye and Karen Brewster on June 9, 2006. Tape No. ORAL HISTORY 2011-04-06, Alaska and Polar Regions Archives, Elmer Rasmuson Library, University of Alaska Fairbanks). In 1975, Governor Jay Hammond

appointed Weeden director of the state's Division of Policy Development and Planning. As an environmental activist, Weeden was outspoken and a prolific writer. He was editor of the Alaska Conservation Society newsletter off and on for years, and in his book *Alaska: Promises to Keep* (Boston: Houghton Mifflin, 1978) he was one of the first to present the state's environmental, economic, and social conditions from an integrated and conservation perspective. For more about Weeden's role in Alaska's environmental organizations, see Daniel Nelson, "Idealism and Organization: Origins of the Environmental Movement in Alaska," 12–35; and Nelson, *Northern Landscapes*.

Fred Dean was a professor in the department of wildlife management at the University of Alaska Fairbanks. His research was focused on brown bears, and starting in 1957 he conducted long-term studies of the Toklat grizzly bear in Mount McKinley National Park documenting aspects of bear biology and behavior that were not previously well understood.

11. Eugene P. Odum, *Fundamentals of Ecology*, 1st ed (Philadelphia: Saunders, 1953).

12. Robert Marshall, *Arctic Village* (1933; repr., Fairbanks: University of Alaska Press, 1991).

13. Robert Marshall, *Alaska Wilderness: Exploring the Central Brooks Range* (Berkeley: University of California Press, 1970).

14. For a brief history of the first Earth Day from the perspective of its founder, Senator Gaylord Nelson, see "How the First Earth Day Came About" at http://earthday.envirolink.org/history.html, accessed February 13, 2011.

15. In 1972, there also was the Marine Mammal Protection Act and the Coastal Zone Management Act.

16. For more about the history of the Alaska Conservation Society, its administrative workings, and its efforts on behalf of environmental issues, see Betty Cornelius, "The Alaska Conservation Society: A Brief History," *Alaska Conservation Review* 14, no. 1 (Spring 1973): 4–5; Alaska Conservation Society Papers, 1960–1993, Alaska and Polar Regions Archives, Elmer E. Rasmuson Library, University of Alaska Fairbanks; Ross, *Environmental Conflict in Alaska*, 291–316; Nelson, "Idealism and Organization"; and Nelson, *Northern Landscapes*.

17. Ginny Wood, "The Greening of Alaska: A Retrospect," "From the Woodpile" column, the *Northern Line* 12, no. 2 (April 22, 1990): 4 and 6; "From the Woodpile" column, the *Northern Line* 7, no. 4 (September–October 1985): 8; *News Bulletin of the Alaska Conservation Society* 1, no. 1 (March 1960).

18. For more about this US Senate hearing, see Kaye, *Alaska's Last Great Wilderness*, 169–99; and US Congress, Senate, Committee on Interstate and Foreign Commerce, Subcommittee on Merchant Marine and Fisheries, Hearings, S. 1899, *A Bill to Authorize the Establishment of the Arctic National Wildlife Range, Alaska, and for other purposes*, 86th Congress, 1st Sess. Records of the US Senate (Washington, DC: Government Printing Office, 1960).

NOTES TO PAGES 285–287

19. Olaus Murie was a biologist who, under the employ of the US Biological Survey starting in 1920, conducted caribou research, studied waterfowl, and led biological surveys around Alaska and Canada. He eventually became an outspoken advocate for ecology-based environmental protection and wilderness preservation and was a leader in the efforts to establish the Arctic National Wildlife Range, amongst other campaigns of the 1950s and early 1960s. (For more about Murie, see Kaye, *Last Great Wilderness*, 68–76.) Olaus Murie married Margaret "Mardy" Thomas of Fairbanks in 1924. In 1956, the Muries, along with fellow biologists George Schaller and Brina Kessel, spent the summer on a scientific research expedition on the Sheenjek River. (For more about this trip, see Kaye, *Last Great Wilderness*, 81–111.) The Muries published extensively on this experience, including articles in *Alaska Sportsman, Animal Kingdom, Audubon, Living Wilderness, National Parks,* and *Outdoor America* (Kaye, *Last Great Wilderness*, 83); and Mardy's book, *Two in the Far North* (1962; repr., Seattle: Alaska Northwest Books, 1997).

20. George Collins worked for the National Park Service as chief of the state and territorial division, in region four (Kaye, *Last Great Wilderness*, 14–18).

21. Howard Zahniser was a wilderness advocate whose orientation toward wilderness "was more spiritual than scientific" (ibid., 67–68). At the time of the struggle to protect the Arctic National Wildlife Range, Zahniser was the Wilderness Society's executive secretary based in Washington, DC, where he was known for developing congressional contacts, coordinating strategy, and giving persuasive testimony (ibid., 66).

22. The State of Alaska also was opposed to it (R. Weeden, pers. comm.).

23. Roger Kaye says they organized their testimonies prior to the hearing (Kaye, *Last Great Wilderness*, 173–74).

24. According to *Last Great Wilderness*, Ginny suggested the idea of an Alaska conservation organization as early as 1957 in a letter to Olaus Murie (Kaye, *Last Great Wilderness,* 173; Margaret Murie Papers, Box 2, Folder 18, Alaska and Polar Regions Archives, Elmer Rasmuson Library, University of Alaska Fairbanks. Also cited in Nelson, *Northern Landscapes*, 54). For more about the original formation of an Alaskan conservation organization, see Ginny Wood, "Stubborn Ounces," "From the Woodpile" column, the *Northern Line* 20, no. 2 (June 19, 1998): 8–9.

25. Bud Boddy was president of Territorial Sportsmen, Inc., a group based out of Juneau, and executive director of the Alaska Sportsmen's Council, an umbrella organization of thirteen territorial clubs affiliated with the National Wildlife Federation. The council's membership was local hunters mostly lobbying the Alaska Department of Fish and Game about seasons and bag limits (R. Weeden, pers. comm.). Boddy sought support for Arctic National Wildlife Range from Alaska sportsmen, and testified at the Bartlett hearing about the moral obligation to protect an area of national significance (Kaye, *Last Great Wilderness*, 128–29).

26. Bob Weeden remembers being at this first meeting, along with his wife, Judy, where "my perch was the upper bunk of an over-and-under" (R. Weeden, pers. comm.).

27. Dave Klein is a biologist with advanced degrees in wildlife management, zoology, and ecology. Since coming to Alaska in 1947, he has worked for the Alaska Department of Fish and Game and the United States Fish and Wildlife Service, spent over thirty years as the leader of the Alaska Cooperative Wildlife Research Unit, and taught in the Department of Biology and Wildlife Management and Institute of Arctic Biology at the University of Alaska Fairbanks. Much of his research has focused on herbivores in northern latitudes, as well as on management of human use of fish and wildlife resources. He obtained professor emeritus status in 1997. Klein's involvement as an environmental activist began with the Alaska Conservation Society and has continued with terms on the board of the Northern Alaska Environmental Center (David Klein's webpage, http://users.iab.uaf .edu/~dave_klein/dklein.html, accessed February 13, 2011; and Ann Swift, "Then and Now: Profile of David Klein," the *Northern Line* 26, no. 3 [Fall 2004]: 17).

28. Dixie Baade passed away on September 21, 1991. Ginny wrote a biographical tribute to her in "From the Woodpile" column, the *Northern Line* 13, no. 4 (December 20, 1991): 11.

29. Dick Cooley helped start the Environmental Studies Department at the University of California, Santa Cruz, in 1970. He had an academic background in geography, political science, and economics. He also served on Alaska's Joint Federal–State Land Use Planning Commission helping to identify lands for inclusion in ANILCA, and later was a board member for the Alaska Conservation Foundation. Dick passed away in 1994.

30. Dick Bishop was a game biologist with the Alaska Department of Fish and Game from the 1960s until his retirement in 1989. He was the McGrath-area biologist for three years, and lived a subsistence lifestyle at remote Lake Minchumina for several years. Over the years, he has served in various leadership capacities with the Alaska Outdoor Council, a statewide sportsmen's group.

31. Ginny Wood, "A Conservation Explosion," *Alaska Conservation Review* 9, no. 2 (Summer 1968): 12.

32. For more about the wolf bounty, see *News Bulletin of the Alaska Conservation Society* 1, no. 3 (August 1960): 5–6; Celia Hunter, *News Bulletin of the Alaska Conservation Society* 2, no. 3 (May 1961): 9–10; Ginny Wood, "From the Woodpile" column, the *Northern Line* 15, no. 1 (March 26, 1993): 14; and Ross, *Pioneering Conservation in Alaska*, 282–300.

33. Mary Shields is a dog musher who in the 1970s was the first woman to finish the Iditarod Trail Sled Dog Race. A longtime conservation activist in Fairbanks and the author of many books, Shields currently serves on the board of the Northern Alaska Environmental Center in Fairbanks.

34. For more from Ginny about wolf control, see Ginny Wood, "From the Woodpile" column, the *Northern Line* 7, no. 2 (April–May 1985): 9.

35. For more about the issue of polar bear hunting, see *News Bulletin of the Alaska Conservation Society* 1, no. 2 (May 1960); Ross, *Environmental Conflict in Alaska*, 1–15.

36. Part of the success of ending aerial polar bear hunting was also due to the state losing management control of polar bears with passage of the federal Marine Mammal Protection Act in 1972 (R. Weeden, pers. comm.). The US Fish and Wildlife Service was given oversight of polar bears, and hunting was restricted to Native subsistence hunters only, provided the population is not depleted and that the harvest is done in a nonwasteful manner. The law allows non-Natives to shoot polar bears only in emergency situations where there is a threat to life or property. In 1994, the Alaska Nanuuq Commission was formed to represent Native villages in northern Alaska on matters concerning the conservation and sustainable subsistence use of polar bears, and in 2001, they signed a co-management agreement with the US Fish and Wildlife Service (for more information, see http://www.nanuuq.info/index.html, accessed February 14, 2011). In 2008, polar bears were listed as threatened under the Endangered Species Act based on evidence of them being in danger of going extinct due to global warming and loss of habitat. This decision remains controversial and is being challenged in court by the State of Alaska (Dan Joling, "Alaska Files Suit Against Feds over Polar Bear Habitat Status," *Anchorage Daily News,* March 10, 2011; Joling, "State Will Sue over Polar Bear Listing, Palin says," *Anchorage Daily News,* May 22, 2008).

37. Ginny also discusses Project Chariot in an oral history interview with Dan O'Neill on November 8, 1988 (Tape No. ORAL HISTORY 88-69, Alaska and Polar Regions Archives, Elmer E. Rasmuson Library, University of Alaska Fairbanks). The transcript is available in Dan O'Neill, *Project Chariot: A Collection of Oral Histories* (Fairbanks: Alaska and Polar Regions Collections, Elmer E. Rasmuson Library, University of Alaska Fairbanks, 1989).

38. According to O'Neill, biologist Al Johnson is the one who initially asked about comprehensive environmental studies (O'Neill, *The Firecracker Boys,* 66).

39. William R. Wood was president of the University of Alaska Fairbanks from 1960 to 1973.

40. Don Foote was born in New York City in 1931 and graduated from Dartmouth College in 1953 with a deep interest in the Arctic. He worked on a research study on the Russian-Norwegian border, which led to him studying at the University of Oslo in Norway. After service in the army, he earned a master's degree in geography from McGill University in 1958. In the midst of his PhD work, he decided he wanted to go to Alaska and began looking for job opportunities. He heard about the Atomic Energy Commission's regional study in the Point Hope area and applied for the job, even though he did not really know the study's purpose or about the AEC's Project Chariot plan. He was given $50,000 to document the Eskimos' hunting and use of the land. He arrived in Point Hope in early September, 1959 (ibid., 98–102).

41. "Then the AEC wrote him asking for his immediate assistance, to meet with the village council and 'allay the anxiety of the natives'" (ibid., 105).

NOTES TO PAGE 293

42. While the AEC made public statements about the lack of impact a blast would have and that there were no biological objections to it, Don Foote's research was showing the importance of the caribou for the nearby Iñupiat people and the environmental studies were documenting the biological diversity in the area (ibid., 168–78). It was just this manipulation of data that concerned University of Alaska Fairbanks scientists such as Les Viereck, Bill Pruitt, Al Johnson, and L. Gerard Swartz (ibid., 162).

43. Norman J. Wilimovsky, ed., *Environment of the Cape Thompson Region, Alaska* (Oak Ridge, TN: United States Atomic Energy Commission, Division of Technical Information, 1966).

44. For more about these studies and their results, see O'Neill, *The Firecracker Boys*, 209–13.

45. In an oral history interview, Brina Kessel tells this same story of arriving at the University of Alaska Fairbanks in 1951 just after earning her PhD in ornithology (when she would have been twenty-six years old), being the second person in the biology department, becoming head of the department in 1957 when the existing department head, Druska Carr Schaible, died in a fire, and then becoming the dean of the College of Biological Sciences and Renewable Resources in 1960 when William R. Wood arrived as the new president and reorganized the university (oral history interview with Karen Brewster, January 9, 2001. Tape No. ORAL HISTORY 2000-07-07, Alaska and Polar Regions Archives, Elmer E. Rasmuson Library, University of Alaska Fairbanks).

46. Per O'Neill, *The Firecracker Boys*, in March 1961 Brina Kessel received the thirty-page ACS newsletter, which was a summary of the Cape Thompson research to date. She believed Pruitt and Viereck publicizing their data and findings in this way was a breach of protocol. Viereck had already tendered his resignation because of concerns about manipulation of his data (pp. 180–183) and because he had been informed by Kessel that working on the AEC contract as the only opportunity for him to work in the department (p. 180). Pruitt's full contract was not renewed and he was phased out (pp. 187–203).

47. Pruitt says he was told, "I was guilty of being biased, untruthful, using data without permission… Brina informed me that my contract was not being renewed with the University because of a long list of grievances. These ranged from 'not working hard enough,' 'uncooperative,' to 'wearing a lab coat of the wrong color' (honest this was actually said)" (O'Neill, *The Firecracker Boys*, 195). Ginny said Bill wore a gray coat instead of the more common white coat.

48. After losing his university job, Les went on to work for the US Forest Service in Fairbanks. While Ginny has said that Les never worked at the university again, he did later become an affiliate professor of forest ecology, where he worked on projects for several of the university's research institutes (O'Neill, *The Firecracker Boys*), was an adjunct curator at the University of Alaska Museum of the North's herbarium, and served on students' master and PhD committees (T. Viereck, pers. comm.). According to his wife, Teri, Les never taught (ibid.). For more information about

Les and his career, see his obituary in *Arctic* 61, no. 4 (December 2008): 451–52 or at http://pubs.aina.ucalgary.ca/arctic/Arctic61-4-451.pdf, accessed February 14, 2011.

49. More detail about this appears in O'Neill, *The Firecracker Boys*, 258–59.

50. Pruitt not telling anyone where he was going is also mentioned in ibid., 260.

51. O'Neill indicates that Foote did not purchase tape recorders for people in Point Hope, since the Eskimos already had tape recorders that they were using to record songs and stories. They were sending tapes, like audio letters, back and forth to family members in different villages (O'Neill, *The Firecracker Boys*, 112–13).

52. In his Project Chariot research, O'Neill found no evidence that Don Foote directed the Eskimos to record the meetings (D. O'Neill, pers. comm.). He believes they did it on their own, given their familiarity with making recordings (O'Neill, *The Firecracker Boys*, 112).

53. The US detonated a total of sixty-six nuclear bombs at Bikini Atoll and Eniwetok in the Marshall Islands, including the 1946 Baker Shot and the 1954 Bravo Shot on Bikini Atoll. The Bravo Shot is where the AEC tested a prototype of the first aircraft-delivered H-bomb (ibid., 132–37).

54. According to O'Neill, Don Foote wrote to his friend Alan Cooke, who was assistant librarian in the Stefansson Collection at Dartmouth College, about his suspicion. Cooke confirmed that this was the same man who had been at Dartmouth showing interest in Point Hope collections and alumni records of Foote and his research assistant, Tom Stone. Everyone in the Records Office, where the man was known for his inquiries about Hungarian students, knew him to be an FBI agent (ibid., 203–4).

55. O'Neill, *The Firecracker Boys*. Also Dan O'Neill Collection, Alaska and Polar Regions Archives, Elmer E. Rasmuson Library, University of Alaska Fairbanks.

56. In 1992, O'Neill discovered records indicating nuclear waste had been buried at the Project Chariot site as part of a radioactive tracers study in 1962. "The purpose of the study was to determine the extent to which water passing through irradiated soil would dissolve the fallout radionuclides and transport them to aquifers, streams, and ponds" (*The Firecracker Boys*, 279). He shared this information with the people of Point Hope, where their feelings of having been the unwitting victims of a radiation experiment and their grave concerns about the health risks led to their demands for site cleanup. For more about these events, see O'Neill, *The Firecracker Boys*, 277–85. Subsequent reports related to the buried material and site remediation include: *Aerial Radiological Survey of the Chariot Site Surrounding Area, Cape Thompson, Alaska by EG&G Energy Measurements,* The Remote Sensing Laboratory operated for the US Department of Energy by EG&G/EM, Date of survey: July 1993 (Las Vegas: US Dept. of Energy, Nevada Operations Office, 1994); *Project Chariot Site Assessment and Remedial Action: Final Report* (Las Vegas: Environmental Restoration Division, US Dept. of Energy, Nevada Operations Office, 1994); and Bernd Franke, *An Estimation of the Level of Radiation Exposure and an Assessment of the Risks to the Health of the People of Point Hope, Alaska, as*

a Result of Project Chariot Activities (Review conducted by North Slope Borough Science Advisory Committee, Barrow, Alaska, 1996).

57. ACS was opposed to Project Chariot, and there were numerous articles in the ACS newsletter about the issue, from periodic updates on the project's status and ACS's opposition to a whole edition devoted to the topic (*News Bulletin of the Alaska Conservation Society* 2, no. 2 [March 1961]).

58. As O'Neill explains, scientists such as Les Viereck, Bill Pruitt, Al Johnson, and L. Gerard Swartz had concerns that their data were being misrepresented by the AEC (*The Firecracker Boys*, 162). The ACS helped make their original research findings more public (*News Bulletin of the Alaska Conservation Society* 2, No. 2 [March 1961]).

59. For more about ACS's role in Project Chariot, see ACS news bulletins and O'Neill, *The Firecracker Boys*.

60. For more about the Rampart Dam proposal and controversy, see Stephen Spurr, *Rampart Dam and the Economic Development of Alaska*, 4 vols. (Ann Arbor: University of Michigan, Ann Arbor, School of Natural Resources, March 1966)*;* John Corso, "Benefit-Cost Consideration in the Decision Against Rampart Dam, A Public Policy Analysis" (MA thesis, Master of Public Administration, University of Alaska Southeastern Senior College, May 1974); Naske and Slotnick, *Alaska*, 211; Nash, *Wilderness and the American Mind*, 289–91; Coates*, The Trans-Alaska Pipeline Controversy*, 134–61; Ross, *Environmental Conflict in Alaska*, 121–134; Alaska Conservation Society Papers, 1960–1993, Alaska and Polar Regions Archives, Elmer E. Rasmuson Library, University of Alaska Fairbanks; and Willis, *Alaska's Place in the West*, 94–112.

61. Coates*, The Trans-Alaska Pipeline Controversy*, 134.

62. Articles about Rampart Dam appeared frequently in the *News Bulletin of the Alaska Conservation Society*, such as: Robert Weeden, "Conservation and Kilowatts," *News Bulletin of the Alaska Conservation Society* 2, no. 3 (May 1961): 1–7; Representative Jay S. Hammond, "Rampart Dam—Some Rude Questions," *News Bulletin of the Alaska Conservation Society* 3, no. 1 (January 1962): 2–4; Terry Brady, "Rampart Dam—Not Black, Not White," *News Bulletin of the Alaska Conservation Society* 4, no. 1 (February 1963): 2–5. Originally published as "Rampart Dam: Millions of Kilowatts," Terry Brady, *Fairbanks Daily News-Miner*, November 28, 1962; and *News Bulletin of the Alaska Conservation Society*, "Recent Progress in Biological Studies of Rampart Dam," *News Bulletin of the Alaska Conservation Society* 4, no. 1 (February 1963): 5–8.

63. According to Bob Weeden,

> In the 1940s and '50s, the Yukon Flats was well recognized nationwide as prime waterfowl habitat. But when the dam was proposed, Warren Taylor, who was a judge and a biologist in Fairbanks, had written 'ducks don't drown,' so he suggested flooding of the Flats wouldn't be a problem. I said, 'No, they don't drown, but they also don't nest well in 100

fathoms of water.' That was the first biological thing I thought of to use against the dam. Later, I learned from fisheries biologists that the salmon run would be impacted. The dam was going to create a 200-mile-long still lake that young salmon would have to navigate through downstream and they wouldn't do it. There was nothing in the project to protect fish. It was going to be a dead lake from all the decaying vegetation that got flooded and iced over from November until July. Also people began to realize that this lake covered good ground for hunting and trapping, so those activities would be stopped. No moose or caribou would be there. So this was going to be a biological disaster, as well as laughable on economic grounds. (oral history interview with Roger Kaye and Karen Brewster on June 9, 2006. Tape No. ORAL HISTORY 2011-04-07, Alaska and Polar Regions Archives, Elmer E. Rasmuson Library, University of Alaska Fairbanks). Weeden wrote about the effect the dam would have on ducks for the *News Bulletin of the Alaska Conservation Society* 4, no. 4 (December 1963): 7–8)

64. Ginny Hill Wood, "The Ramparts We Watch," *Sierra Club Bulletin* 50, no. 3 (March 1965): 13–15; Ginny Wood, "Big Dam/Big Threat," *Animals* 6, no. 8 (April 20, 1965): 198–203; Ginny Hill Wood "Rampart—Foolish Dam," *The Living Wilderness* 88 (Spring 1965): 3–7.

65. This would be Stephen H. Spurr, who produced the report *Rampart Dam and the Economic Development of Alaska*, a four-volume report with portions authored by other study team members: Robert August, William Spurr, Ernest Brater, A. Starker Leopold, Justin Leonard, Michael Brewer, Gunter Schramm, Gardner Brown, and Betty Bordner. The report indicates that "in July 1964, a grant was made by a group of organizations under the auspices of the Natural Resources Council of America to The University of Michigan to investigate both the ecological and economic consequences of the proposed Rampart Canyon Dam on the Yukon River in central Alaska" (vol. 1, p. 1).

   While Ginny says the Alaska Conservation Society got in touch with Spurr, ACS is not listed in the report's acknowledgments as one of the groups who contributed to the project. Perhaps ACS initiated contact but did not provide funds, or since it was a complicated issue with many partners working together, perhaps Ginny has blurred the lines between which group was doing what.

66. According to historian Peter Coates, this incident occurred during a television debate in April 1965 in Fairbanks between Yukon Power for America and the ACS. Thomas K. Paskvan, a Fairbanks businessman, spoke in support of the dam, defending how the waterfowl would not be impacted. "Ed Merdes, the organization's vice-president, expressed astonishment that Hunter had ignored the ducks. He believed that this was the only issue which she, as a conservationist, should have addressed, besides being the only one she was qualified to discuss" (Coates, *The Trans-Alaska Pipeline Controversy*, 150).

67. The May 1965 issue of the *Sierra Club Bulletin* reported that the Department of the Interior had released their field reports from each agency about the Rampart Dam project and that it "would result in enormous losses of fish and wildlife resources. The final conclusion is that the dam should not be authorized for construction" (William Zimmerman Jr., "Washington Office Report," *Sierra Club Bulletin* 50, no. 5 [May 1965]: 11). The article goes on to state that a bill in the Alaska State Legislature to establish a Yukon Power Authority that would be authorized to issue bonds for financing the dam had failed to pass. These are strong indicators of the demise of the project and the success of the environmental community to stop it.

68. Since 1973, Republican Don Young has served as Alaska's sole congressman in the United States House of Representatives. He has consistently opposed environmental protection and conservation legislation.

69. Wood, "Big Dam/Big Threat," 198–203.

70. Democrat Nick Begich, an Anchorage teacher and state legislator, became Alaska's single member of the United States House of Representatives in 1971. While Begich was campaigning for the 1972 election, the plane in which he was flying from Anchorage to Juneau on October 16 disappeared and supposedly crashed. Representative and House Majority Leader Hale Boggs of Louisiana also was in the plane. No traces of the men or plane were ever found. Given the closeness to the November election, ballots went out with their names on them; both men were reelected. After the men were officially declared presumed dead, special elections were held in March 1973, with Boggs's wife succeeding him and Republican Don Young being elected to replace Begich (Whitehead, *Completing the Union*, 347–48).

71. In 1980, ANILCA doubled the size of the original Arctic National Wildlife Range, renamed it the Arctic National Wildlife Refuge, and designated most of the original acreage as wilderness. The part of the original range that was not designated as wilderness was "addressed in Section 1002 of ANILCA, and is now referred to as the '1002 Area.' Section 1002 outlined additional information that would be needed before Congress could designate the area as Wilderness, or permit oil development. Studies of the 1002 Area included a comprehensive inventory and assessment of the fish and wildlife resources, an analysis of potential impacts of oil and gas exploration and development on those resources, and a delineation of the extent and amount of potential petroleum resources" (US Fish and Wildlife Service, "Potential impacts of proposed oil and gas development on the Arctic Refuge's coastal plain: Historical overview and issues of concern," web page of the Arctic National Wildlife Refuge, January, 17, 2001, available at http://arctic.fws.gov/issues1.htm, accessed February 15, 2011). A national environmental campaign ensued to keep this part of the refuge free from oil development and protect the calving grounds of the Porcupine caribou herd. Development promoters argue the need for the oil in order to reduce America's dependence upon foreign oil. The highly politicized debate still rages on. For more detail about the

controversy, refer to "Arctic Refuge drilling controversy," http://en.wikipedia.org/wiki/Arctic_Refuge_drilling_controversy, accessed February 15, 2011.

72. For more about the history of the Arctic National Wildlife Refuge, see Ross, *Environmental Conflict in Alaska*; Kaye, *Last Great Wilderness*; Ross, *Pioneering Conservation in Alaska*, 413–26; Nelson, *Northern Landscapes*; Alaska Conservation Society Papers, 1960–1993, Alaska and Polar Regions Archives, Elmer E. Rasmuson Library, University of Alaska Fairbanks.

73. US Congress, Senate, Committee on Interstate and Foreign Commerce, Subcommittee on Merchant Marine and Fisheries, Hearings, S. 1899, *A Bill to Authorize the Establishment of the Arctic National Wildlife Range, Alaska, and for other purposes*, 86th Congress, 1st Sess., Records of the US Senate (Washington, DC: Government Printing Office, 1960). There also were House of Representative hearings: US Congress, House of Representatives, Committee on Merchant Marine and Fisheries, Subcommittee on Fisheries and Wildlife Conservation. Hearings, H.R. 7045, *A Bill to Authorize the Establishment of the Arctic National Wildlife Range, Alaska, and for other purposes*, July 1, 1959. 86th Congress, 1st Sess., Records of the US House of Representatives (Washington, DC: Government Printing Office, 1959).

74. Ginny's specific testimony is in US Congress, Senate, *A Bill to Authorize the Establishment of the Arctic National Wildlife Range, Alaska, and for other purposes*, 335–339.

75. Also stated in Kaye, *Last Great Wilderness*, 196.

76. For more about the discussion about the management of the Arctic National Wildlife Range, see Kaye, *Last Great Wilderness*, 116–19.

77. For more of Ginny's thoughts on and role in protecting the Arctic National Wildlife Range, see Kaye, *Last Great Wilderness*, 62–64; 144–45; 165–66; 173; 184; 186; 195–96; 207; 220.

78. Oral history interview with Roger Kaye on November 10, 2002. Recording in possession of Roger Kaye. The transcript is available at Fish and Wildlife Service's National Digital Library website (http://digitalmedia.fws.gov, accessed February 14, 2011). Also US Congress, Senate, *A Bill to Authorize the Establishment of the Arctic National Wildlife Range, Alaska, and for other purposes*.

79. Les Viereck was working on a doctoral dissertation at the University of Colorado on the revegetation of glacial moraines, when he returned to Alaska to accept a job at the University of Alaska to work on Project Chariot's environmental studies at Cape Thompson (O'Neill, *The Firecracker Boys*, 86).

80. For more about ANILCA, see Berry, *The Alaska Pipeline*; Nash, *Wilderness and the American Mind*; Case, *Alaska Natives and American Laws*; Ross, *Environmental Conflict in Alaska*; Nelson, *Northern Landscapes*; Williss, *Do Things Right the First Time*; and Willis, *Alaska's Place in the West*.

81. For more about ANCSA, the land issues, and the politics of the time, see Berry, *The Alaska Pipeline*; Naske and Slotnick, *Alaska*, 195–232; Case, *Alaska Natives and American Laws*; Mitchell, *Take My Land, Take My Life*; and Gilbert, "Dividing Alaska."

82. "An early proponent of the notion that, if undesignated federal land in Alaska was going to be divided up, conservation ought to be in line along with Natives and the State, was Arlon Tussing. A resource economist at ISEGR at UAF since the late 1960s, Arlon loved political maneuverings, was clever, outspoken, and had connections with Senator Henry 'Scoop' Jackson and staff, and the Federal State Land Use Planning Commission. I remember him talking up the idea in 1970" (R. Weeden, pers. comm.).

83. Video of some of these D-2 land hearings held in villages such as Anaktuvuk Pass and Allakaket is available at the Alaska Film Archives, Alaska and Polar Regions Department, Elmer E. Rasmuson Library, University of Alaska Fairbanks. Portions are available online at the Alaska Digital Archives website (http://vilda.alaska.edu/) or the Gates of the Arctic Research Portal website (http://jukebox.uaf.edu/gatesportal/index.html).

84. Starting in 1951, Will Troyer worked as a biologist for thirty years with the US Fish and Wildlife Service in Alaska, including as fish and game warden and manager of the Kodiak Island Wildlife Refuge and the Kenai National Moose Range (now Kenai National Wildlife Refuge). As a biologist, he pioneered early research techniques on the large coastal brown bears of Kodiak Island. Later, he was heavily involved with the land selection process for ANILCA, and helped the Alaska Conservation Society make recommendations for lands they wished to see protected. He has written about his experiences in such books as *Bear Wrangler: Memoirs of an Alaska Pioneer Biologist* (Fairbanks: University of Alaska Press, 2008); *Into Brown Bear Country* (Fairbanks: University of Alaska Press, 2005); and *From Dawn to Dusk: Memoirs of an Amish-Mennonite Farm Boy* (La Vergne, TN: Lightning Source, Inc., 2003).

85. In the mid-1970s, while surveying land that ANILCA might include in the Arctic National Wildlife Refuge, Celia Hunter and Magaret Murie were in an airplane crash in the foothills of the northern Brooks Range. Their pilot was Averill Thayer, who was the first manager of the refuge. He was able to land the plane on the tundra in such a manner that they all survived unscathed and were able to be rescued (A. Thayer, pers. comm.).

86. For more about Denali National Park's shifting boundary, see Norris, *Crown Jewel of the North*, vol. 2.

87. For a good description and history of the Creamer's Field operation and eventual preservation as the Creamer's Field Migratory Wildlife Refuge, see Ryan, "A Place for the Birds"; Mike Spindler, "Creamers Field History," *Alaska Conservation Review* 20, no. 1 (Spring 1979): 13; and Tape No. ORAL HISTORY 2008-10, Alaska and Polar Regions Archives, Elmer E. Rasmuson Library, University of Alaska Fairbanks, recorded in 1993, in which Ginny Wood, Dick Bishop, Gail Mayo, and Laurel Holmes talk about how ACS got Creamer's Field protected.

88. Ryan, "A Place for the Birds," 54–58.

89. For more information about the Creamer's Field Migratory Waterfowl Refuge, see the Alaska Department of Fish and Game, Creamer's Field Migratory Waterfowl Refuge website (http://www.adfg.alaska.gov/index.cfm?adfg=creamersfield.main), and the Friends of Creamer's Field website (http://www.creamersfield.org/Welcome.html).

90. Ginny's discussion about Creamer's Field was put together from a combination of my 2006–2008 oral history recordings with her and Tape No. ORAL HISTORY 2008-10 from the Oral History Archives, Alaska and Polar Regions Collections, Elmer E. Rasmuson Library, University of Alaska Fairbanks (see note 87 above). In this recording, Dick Bishop provides a good description about the financial and political aspects of getting Creamer's Field protected and its management as a refuge, as does Bob Weeden in an oral history interview with Roger Kaye and Karen Brewster on June 9, 2006 (Tape No. ORAL HISTORY 2011-04-07, Alaska and Polar Regions Archives, Elmer E. Rasmuson Library, University of Alaska Fairbanks).

91. John Butrovich (1910–1997), a native-born Fairbanksan, was an accomplished politician who was committed to creating a better life for Alaskans. He served as a Republican in the Alaska territorial senate from 1945 to 1958, was a candidate for governor in 1958, and was a member of the Alaska state senate from 1962 to 1978. He served on every committee of the Alaska senate and was senate president from 1967 to 1968. Butrovich was a strong proponent of statehood and played a pivotal role in developing Alaska from a neglected territory to a vibrant and productive state. In fact, he was speaker of the delegation sent to the White House to persuade President Eisenhower to sign the statehood bill. In 1980, he was named Alaskan of the Year and awarded an honorary doctor of law degree by the University of Alaska.

92. Oral history interview with Bob Weeden and Ginny Wood with Roger Kaye and Karen Brewster on June 9, 2006. Tape No. ORAL HISTORY 2011-04-07, Alaska and Polar Regions Archives, Elmer E. Rasmuson Library, University of Alaska Fairbanks.

93. For some of Ginny's writings about roads, see "From the Woodpile" column, the *Northern Line* 14, no. 1 (March 12, 1992): 14–15; "From the Woodpile" column, the *Northern Line* 14, no. 2 (June 22, 1992): 15; "From the Woodpile" column, the *Northern Line* 20, no. 3 (October 1, 1998): 9, 18; and "Requiem for a Road," *Alaska Conservation Review* 9, no. 3 (Fall 1968): 12.

94. For another of Ginny's writings against snowmachines, see "From the Woodpile" column, the *Northern Line* 21, no. 1 (February 16, 1999): 12–13.

95. Ginny Wood, "Bulldozer Blight, Some Causes and Cures" (*Alaska Conservation Review* 9, no. 3 [Fall 1968]): 1–4.

96. Ginny Wood, "A.E.C.—A Camel in the Tent?" *Alaska Conservation Review* 8, nos. 3 & 4 (Fall/Winter 1967–1968): 1–2.

97. For more background on this project, see Lyndon H. LaRouche, "The Outline of NAWAPA" (Washington, DC: The Schiller Institute, January 1988), available at http://www.schillerinstitute.org/economy/phys_econ/phys_econ_nawapa_1983.html, accessed February 14, 2011.

98. On March 24, 1989, the fully loaded oil tanker *Exxon Valdez* hit Bligh Reef in Prince William Sound after departing from the port of Valdez. Approximately eleven million gallons of crude oil leaked from the vessel, making it the largest oil spill in US waters at the time. For more information, see Art Davidson, *In the Wake of the Exxon Valdez: The Devastating Impact of the Alaska Oil Spill* (San Francisco: Sierra Club Books, 1990).

99. See Margaret Murie, *Two in the Far North*.

100. "A gold miner, merchant and developer by trade, and a lawyer by education, Joe Vogler was born in 1920 in Kansas and migrated to Alaska in 1942. Known as a 'man of principles' who taunted National Park Service officials and gave speeches in -40F weather, Vogler became a mythical figure after a lifelong battle with the federal government to gain an independent Alaska. In 1974, he formed the non-partisan Alaskans for Independence (AFI) as an offshoot of the Placer Miners Association, and later founded the Alaskan Independence Party (AIP) which became the third officially recognized party (with the Republicans and Democrats) in the state in 1986—after Vogler's own gubernatorial campaign attracted 5.6% of the vote. Altogether, Vogler mounted three campaigns for governor in 1974, 1982 and 1986. He served as chairman of the AIP from its founding until 1993, when he mysteriously disappeared from his Fairbanks home. After a sixteen month search that captivated Alaskans and drew nationwide media attention, state law enforcement officials determined that Vogler had been murdered during a robbery attempt" (Alaskan Independence Party website: http://www.akip. org/introduction.html, accessed February 14, 2011). "Joe stressed in his political debates that he believed the biggest problem with the federal government was that they have overstepped the bounds of the Constitution. Vogler challenged the federal government's practice of owning land in Alaska or any other state outside the original limits of the United States Constitution. Vogler believed that federal claims of land for preserves and parks is outside of the original intent of the framers of the Constitution and that the federal government has no right to own land in the western states except for "forts, arsenals, dockyards and other needful government uses" (Memorial Proclamation, 19th Alaska State Legislature, March 14, 1995, website for the Alaskan Independence Party, http://www. akip.org/joe.html, accessed February 14, 2011).

101. Oral history interview with Bob Weeden and Ginny Wood on June 9, 2006, with Roger Kaye and Karen Brewster (Tape No. ORAL HISTORY 2011-04-07, Alaska and Polar Regions Archives, Elmer E. Rasmuson Library, University of Alaska Fairbanks).

102. Ibid.

103. Gordon Wright came to Alaska in 1969 from Wisconsin and taught music at the University of Alaska Fairbanks. He conducted the Fairbanks Symphony Orchestra and the Arctic Chamber Orchestra in Fairbanks for twenty-five years. He also was an accomplished musician and composer. As an environmental activist, he led a Sierra Club chapter in Fairbanks and helped found the Fairbanks Environmental

Center in 1971 (now the Northern Alaska Environmental Center), served on its board, was actively involved in many of the key struggles to protect Alaska, and was on the national board of Friends of the Earth ("Then and Now: Gordon Wright," the *Northern Line* 27, no. 2 [Summer 2005]: 15–16). Gordon Wright passed away in 2007. For more about Wright's role in Alaska's environmental organizations, see Nelson, "Idealism and Organization"; and Nelson, *Northern Landscapes*.

104. Oral history interview with Bob Weeden and Ginny Wood with Roger Kaye and Karen Brewster on June 9, 2006. (Tape No. ORAL HISTORY 2011-04-07, Alaska and Polar Regions Archives, Elmer E. Rasmuson Library, University of Alaska Fairbanks). John Lammers modeled his group in Whitehorse on how ACS had done things. As of April 2011, Lammers was living on Salt Spring Island, British Columbia (R. Weeden, pers. comm.).

105. Jim Kowalsky was an environmental activist who was a graduate student friend of Gordon Wright's at the University of Wisconsin. In 1971, Jim came to Alaska and became the first executive director of the Fairbanks Environmental Center. He was known for being a passionate defender of wilderness values. As a trumpeter, he played in Gordon Wright's Fairbanks Symphony Orchestra and Arctic Chamber Orchestra. For more about Kowalsky's role in Alaska's environmental organizations, see Nelson, "Idealism and Organization"; and Nelson, *Northern Landscapes*. Jim also has had a long career as an educator working with rural students as program director for the Rural Alaska Honors Institute at the University of Alaska Fairbanks and with the Adult Learning Programs of Alaska.

106. John Luther Adams is a former executive director of the Northern Alaska Environmental Center. He also is a musician and composer who obtains inspiration from the natural world. For more about the life and music of John Luther Adams, see his website (http://www.johnlutheradams.com, accessed February 14, 2011); and Alex Ross, "Song of the Earth: A Composer Takes Inspiration from the Arctic" (the *New Yorker* 84, no. 13 [May 12, 2008]: 76–81.

107. *News Bulletin of the Alaska Conservation Society* 4, no. 2 (April 1963): 15.

108. Sigurd Olson was a biologist and prominent advocate for wilderness. In 1953, he became director of the National Parks Association. He served as director of the Wilderness Society from 1968 to 1971. He was a key player in passage of the 1964 Wilderness Act, in protecting wild places in Alaska, and in the establishment of Voyageurs National Park in northern Minnesota and wilderness designation for Boundary Waters Canoe Area. Among his many writings are: *The Singing Wilderness* (New York: Knopf, 1956); *Listening Point* (New York: Knopf, 1958); *The Lonely Land* (New York: Knopf, 1961); and *Runes of the North* (New York: Knopf, 1963). For more about Sigurd Olson, see David Backes, *A Wilderness Within: The Life of Sigurd F. Olson* (Minneapolis: University of Minnesota Press, 1997); Olson's last book, *Of Time and Place* (New York: Knopf, 1982); David Backes, ed., *The Meaning of Wilderness: Essential Articles and Speeches* (Minneapolis: University of Minnesota Press, 2001); and Kaye, *Last Great Wilderness*, 116–17.

109. Olaus Murie died October 21, 1963, at the age of seventy-five (Greg Kendrick, "National Park Service Biography: Olaus J. Murie," National Park Service: The First 75 Years, Biographical Vignettes, http://www.nps.gov/history/history/online_books/sontag/murie.htm, accessed February 14, 2011).

110. From "Mardy was a comfortable…" to "…ever encountered" is from a speech given by Ginny Wood on the occasion of Mardy Murie's one-hundredth-birthday celebration, August 19, 2002. In folder titled "Unfinished Manuscript on Kotzebue and "Last Resort," Ginny Wood Personal Collection. Mardy Murie died in 2003 at age 101 (Kaye, *Last Great Wilderness*, 227).

111. For example, in a letter dated June 26, 1977, from Celia to George Collins, she writes about her new job as director of the Wilderness Society in Washington, DC: "Since receiving your letter, I have taken another fork in that meandering path I call my life. This one has removed me from the place I know as home temporarily, and I am adventuring in a way new for me, trying to adjust to urban living, and to being the head honcho in an operation a good bit bigger than any I have heretofore been associated with…. I have somewhat a sense of destiny, since this post seems to come as a culmination of many other episodes in my existence—bringing together my knowledge of Alaska at a time when that issue is crucial in Congress, and having led me along through a whole series of evolutions of my position within the Wilderness Society Council and now as leader of the staff. I hope I can measure up—I have lots of support from everyone involved" (typed letter in Ginny Wood Personal Collection. Photocopy in possession of author).

112. For more on Olson's wilderness philosophy, see Olson, *Singing Wilderness*; Kaye, *Last Great Wilderness*, 116–17; Backes, ed., *The Meaning of Wilderness*; and Backes, *A Wilderness Within*.

113. John C. Reed was staff geologist for territories and island possessions for the United States Geological Survey and helped oversee the USGS's geological research program during the navy's postwar oil exploration in the Naval Petroleum Reserve No. 4 (PET-4) in the late 1940s and early 1950s (*Exploration of Naval Petroleum Reserve No. 4 and Adjacent Areas, Northern Alaska, 1944–1953*, Part I, *History of the Exploration*, John C. Reed, Geological Survey Professional Paper 301 [Washington, DC: US Government Printing Office, 1958]). All the technical results from this project were published in USGS Professional Papers 301–306 (1958–1964). By 1959, Reed was a senior scientist with the Arctic Institute of North America (Coates, *The Trans-Alaska Pipeline Controversy*, 185). He served as executive director of the Arctic Institute from 1961 until 1968 (John C. Reed, "Reminiscences: The Arctic Institute in the 1960s," *Arctic* 40, no. 4 [December 1987]: 244–48).

114. Ginny wrote about her recycling-based way of life in "From the Woodpile" column, the *Northern Line* 12, no. 1 (February 28, 1990): 18.

115. On June 14, 1988, an Alaska Airlines jet flew from Nome to Provideniya, a port city in Chukotka. It was the first direct passenger flight to the Russian Far East in decades. This "friendship flight" was led by Alaska Governor Steve Cowper

and Senator Frank Murkowski to promote cooperation between these two similar parts of the Arctic. The flight included eighty Alaska Natives, politicians, businessmen, and journalists (Hal Bernton, "Alaskans Fly to a Celebration in Siberia," *Anchorage Daily News*, June 14, 1988; and Hal Bernton, "Flight Offers Hopes for New Beginnings, Long Closed Doorway to Soviet Far East May Open for Old Friends, Businessmen," *Anchorage Daily News*, June 15, 1988). In 1991, Alaska Airlines began regular flights between Alaska and the Russian Far East, but stopped the service in 1998 following the Russian financial crisis.

116. For a related story, see Sheila Toomey, "Soviet Visitors Try American Shopping," *Anchorage Daily News*, September 8, 1988.

117. See Ginny Wood, "From The Woodpile" column, the *Northern Line* 10, no. 2 (April–June, 1988): 9.

118. For discussion about traditional berry-picking grounds, see Ginny Wood, "From the Woodpile" column, the *Northern Line* 6, no. 4 (September–October 1984): 9.

119. Ginny has expressed this same perspective on this and similar topics in some of her writing. For example, "In the Woodpile" column, the *Northern Line* 21, no. 2 (April 1, 1999): 14.

120. Barbara Kingsolver, *Small Wonder* (New York: Harper Collins Publishing, 2002).

121. Lester Brown, *Eco-Economy* (New York: W.W. Norton Publishing, 2001).

18. Tundra Treks: Guiding Wilderness Trips

1. A Prusik is a friction knot used to put a loop of cord around a rope (Don Graydon and Kurt Hanson, eds., *Mountaineering: The Freedom of the Hills*, 6th ed. [Seattle: The Mountaineers, 1997: 121]).

2. A Jumar is the brand name of a mechanical device used for ascending on a rope. Ascenders offer similar functionality to friction knots like Prusiks but are stronger, faster, safer, and easier to use. An ascender employs a cam that allows it to slide freely in one direction on a rope but to grip tightly when pulled in the opposite direction. Ascenders also have a locking mechanism or trigger to keep them from accidently coming off the rope (ibid., 252–53, 270–71, 418).

3. From "I began my guiding career..." to "...outdoor activity." is a combination of excerpts from the text of two speeches made by Ginny Wood found in the files of the Ginny Wood Personal Collection. One speech was given at the Alaska Association of Mountain and Wilderness Guides Annual Meeting in Fairbanks on December 5–6, 1981, and the other was to the Alaska Outdoor Education Conference in Sitka on March 27, 1993. The 1993 speech appears to be a revision of parts of the 1981 speech.

4. David Brower (1912–2000) was an accomplished outdoorsman and mountain climber who turned his love of nature and a desire to protect wild places into a successful career as an environmental activist. Many consider him to be the father of the modern environmental movement. He founded conservation organizations

including the Sierra Club Foundation, Friends of the Earth, the League of Conservation Voters, and Earth Island Institute. He served as the first executive director of the Sierra Club between 1952 and 1969 and served on its board three times between 1941 and 2000. For more about David Brower and his legacy, see David Brower biography on the website of the David Brower Center (http://www.browercenter.org/node/179, accessed February 14, 2011); Joan Hamilton, "Passages," *Sierra* 86, no. 1 (January/February 2001, http://www.sierraclub.org/sierra/200101/brower2.asp, accessed February 14, 2011); John McPhee, *Encounters with the Archdruid* (New York: Farrar, Straus, and Giroux, 1971); and John McPhee, "Farewell to the Archdruid," *Sierra* 86, no. 1 (January/February 2001): 8–9.

5. Walt Audi was a bush pilot based out of Kaktovik (Barter Island) who spent many years flying across the North Slope and into the Brooks Range. He originally came to Kaktovik as a pilot for the DEW Line in the late 1960s, eventually starting his own flight service and later the Waldo Arms Hotel. He was one of the pilots most frequently hired by groups hiking or rafting in the Brooks Range.

6. From "Keeping our groups..." to "...usually brought" is from a speech by Ginny Hill Wood at the Alaska Association of Mountain and Wilderness Guides Annual Meeting in Fairbanks on December 5–6, 1981. Typed speech text found in files of Ginny Wood Personal Collection.

7. In another telling of this story, Ginny says there were seven original owners of Alaska Backcountry Guides, but two of them dropped out the first year to do guiding on their own. One of them just offered guiding services on Mount McKinley, which was very specific, so the pooling of equipment and staff was not doing much for him. And then the remaining group decided they didn't want to guide with the other guy because he was doing things that they didn't like and which they thought might cause them liability problems on their group insurance.

8. From "And there is the packaging..." to "...take risks" is from a speech by Ginny Hill Wood at the Alaska Association of Mountain and Wilderness Guides Annual Meeting in Fairbanks on December 5–6, 1981. Typed speech text found in files of Ginny Wood Personal Collection.

9. According to one version of Ginny's résumé, Tundra Treks operated from 1976 to 1992. In folder titled "Correspondence on 'The Book,'" Ginny Wood Personal Collection.

10. From "And of course you pack..." to "...from over use" is from a speech by Ginny Hill Wood at the Alaska Association of Mountain and Wilderness Guides Annual Meeting in Fairbanks on December 5–6, 1981. Typed speech text found in files of Ginny Wood Personal Collection.

11. From "The wildlife you see..." to "...perhaps you," ibid.

12. From "And then there is always..." to "...can get grim," ibid.

13. From "In 1960..." to "...philosophically for me," ibid.

14. From "Although I do realize..." to "...dreadful day," ibid.

15. From "A few words..." to "...matches in it," ibid.

16. In 1960, the Naval Arctic Research Laboratory (NARL) built Quonset huts and a collection of smaller wood buildings as a field research station at Peter's Lake. For a description of working as a carpenter there, see Brewster, *The Whales, They Give Themselves,* 87–88. The US Fish and Wildlife Service is now in charge of the facility and uses it as a research base camp.

17. Carol remembers the date of this trip as 1989. Ginny would have turned seventy-two in October 1989, so she was seventy-one on the trip (oral history interview with Jim Campbell, Carol Kasza, and Ginny Wood with Karen Brewster, Susan Grace, and Keith Pollock on April 27, 2007. Tape No. ORAL HISTORY 2011-04-16, Alaska and Polar Regions Archives, Elmer E. Rasmuson Library, University of Alaska Fairbanks).

18. Jim Campbell and Carol Kasza own the guiding business Arctic Treks (http://www.arctictreksadventures.com, accessed February 14, 2011).

19. *Arctic Wars,* VHS, produced by John Howe and Jeff Elstad (Salt Lake City: Public Broadcasting Service, KUED Broadcasting, University of Utah, 1990).

20. Michio Hoshino was an expert wildlife photographer and author of many books, including: *Moose* (San Francisco: Chronicle Books, 1988), *Grizzly* (San Francisco: Chronicle Books, 1987), and *Hoshino's Alaska* (San Francisco: Chronicle Books, 2007). Originally from Japan, Hoshino moved to Fairbanks in 1978 to explore and photograph Alaska's wild places. He was killed by a grizzly bear on August 8, 1996, while on the Kamchatka Peninsula in eastern Russia as part of a team making a documentary film about brown bears for a Japanese television network (*New York Times,* "Michio Hoshino Dies While Filming Bears," September 22, 1996, http://www.nytimes.com/1996/09/22/world/michio-hoshino-dies-while-filming-bears.html, accessed February 14, 2011).

21. From "Michio invited…" to "…and our gear" is from "Wood Cuts 1995," Ginny Wood's annual Christmas letter, January 1996, Ginny Wood Personal Collection.

22. Ginny wrote about Michio, their friendship, and his death in "Ode to Michio Hoshino," "In the Woodpile" column, the *Northern Line* 18, no. 3 (October 25, 1996): 6–7.

23. From "I think that…" to "…be proud of" is from a speech by Ginny Hill Wood at the Alaska Association of Mountain and Wilderness Guides Annual Meeting in Fairbanks, Alaska, on December 5–6, 1981. Typed speech text found in files of Ginny Wood Personal Collection.

24. From "Often I had thought…" to "go to hell" is from a speech made by Ginny Wood at the Alaska Outdoor Education Conference in Sitka, Alaska, on March 27, 1993. Handwritten text found in the files of the Ginny Wood Personal Collection.

25. "Ginny Hill Wood wins Celia Hunter Award," *Fairbanks Daily News-Miner,* December 8, 1985.

26. Oral history interview with Jim Campbell, Carol Kasza, and Ginny Wood with Karen Brewster, Susan Grace, and Keith Pollock on April 27, 2007. (Tape No.

ORAL HISTORY 2011-04-16, Alaska and Polar Regions Archives, Elmer E. Rasmuson Library, University of Alaska Fairbanks).

19. Breaking Trail

1. For more information about Dr. Otto Trott and his life as a skier, mountaineer, and doctor, including discussion about and photographs of his time with Ginny Hill Wood, see Corff, *The Making of a Rescuer.*
2. From "…classified more as ski mountaineering…" to "funny thing is that…" is a combination of what Ginny said in her oral interviews and her personal writings in preparation for an autobiography.
3. Dogpatch is the name of the neighborhood in the hills about ten miles northwest of downtown Fairbanks where Ginny Wood has lived since 1952.
4. "Fred Boyle was the first real ski coach hired by UAF. He arrived here in the fall of 1958. In 1960, Boyle was made head of the P.E. Department and Athletic Director. Boyle set a standard for his skiers. Before they were allowed to attend Outside competition, they had to beat their coach" (Jane McNeely Parrish, "Respecting Our Routes…," undated paper written for NORS 600 course—Perspectives of the North, taught by Professor Terrence Cole, University of Alaska Fairbanks, 14).
5. "At the time Boyle arrived, the trail network did not fulfill the needs of his team. He believed the university skiers needed more of a challenge. So, he and his team introduced technical difficulty to old trails and created new ones. They upgraded existing trails to better accommodate racers and created a five-mile circuit.… Boyle wanted to add a three-mile segment off campus to the 9-mile trail. This would establish one 20-kilometer race trail, an Olympic distance. At the same time, Ginny Wood wanted to connect campus trails to hillside trails. One afternoon Wood was cutting above Dogpatch when she 'accidentally bumped' into Boyle and his team" (ibid., 15).
6. "Boyle, his team and Ginny Wood linked the trails on the east side of Ballaine to Turner's 9-mile trail. This created a 12-mile trail which would be the course for the popular Skiathon races of the 1970s" (University of Alaska Fairbanks Master Planning Committee, "A Brief History of the UAF Skarland Trail System: The First Eighty Years," North Campus Subcommittee, Skarland Trail System Management Plan, History of UAF Trails, http://www.uaf.edu/mastplan/committee/subcommittees/north-campus/skarland-trail-system-man/history-of-uaf-trails/, accessed February 13, 2011). For more about the history of skiing and the ski trails at the University of Alaska Fairbanks, see Parrish, "Respecting Our Routes."
7. Jim Whisenhant started the Skiathon in 1967, as a vernal equinox counterpart to the popular Equinox Marathon running race held in September. The Skiathon used trails on and off the University of Alaska Fairbanks campus and was a popular community event. The last Skiathon that included off-campus trails was held in 1979. It was abandoned because there were too many road crossings and the

trails were too narrow to handle the faster skis (University of Alaska Fairbanks Master Planning Committee, "A Brief History of the UAF Skarland Trail System"). The Skiathon has been revived in recent years with a twelve-kilometer course that only uses the trails on campus.

8. Bill Page was a teacher in Fairbanks in the 1970s and also was involved with running the cross-country ski program in the schools, particularly at Pearl Creek Elementary School (B. Page, pers. comm.)

9. Jim Mahaffey was hired by UAF ski coach Fred Boyle in the spring of 1962 to serve as the assistant ski coach (Steve Bainbridge, "Equinox Marathon History. The first years…1963–1966," Equinox Marathon, Fairbanks, Alaska, Running Club North, Fairbanks, Alaska, November 21, 2009, http://www.equinoxmarathon.org/index.php?option=com_content&task=view&id=45&Itemid=37, accessed February 14, 2011; and Parrish, "Respecting Our Routes," 16).

10. "In the spring of 1969 the Alaska Alpine Club started another great tradition to introduce members of the Fairbanks community to the mountain environment. This was the Great Cantwell Glacier Stampede which drew an unexpected 101 people between 7 and 57 years of age to the lower Cantwell hut in its first year. Participants, who had to carry their own food and camping equipment, skied to the hut at their leisure or entered into a ski race…. Participation rose from 101 in 1969 to 243 in 1971…. In its haydays [sic], the Stampede drew people not only from Fairbanks, but from Anchorage, Valdez and other communities as well. To deal with the masses of skiers, many of them new to the mountains and to winter camping, the Alpine Club worked together with the Nordic Ski Club of Fairbanks for several years to coordinate logistics for this annual event.

"In 1983, due to concerns over sanitation and clean-up, the Glacier Stampede was discontinued. It was replaced by a scaled-down version for club members and their guests, the Glacier Rendezvous. The Rendezvous was held every spring at different glaciers in the eastern Alaska Range until at least 1987" (Franz Mueter, "Alaska Alpine Club History," Alaska Alpine Club History page, Fairbanks, https://sites.google.com/a/alaska.edu/alaska-alpine-club/history, accessed February 14, 2011). Ginny has fond memories of the Glacier Stampede and describes it as one big community camping trip with tents scattered everywhere, and people visiting and comparing equipment. It is one of the events she uses in her stories to compare how Fairbanks is different now, and how it used to be much more community oriented.

11. The Tanana River Raft Race was held annually in Fairbanks from 1968 to 1972. People built rafts from old barrels and whatever scraps of lumber they could find and floated approximately eighty miles down the Tanana River from Fairbanks to Nenana. Although it was officially dubbed a race, it was more a community celebration and a challenge to see which ramshackle rafts would make it. Merritt Helfferich, one of the race's founders, describes the mass start in Fairbanks where captains and crews had to run down the riverbank and across the beach to launch their rafts, the fun everyone had, and the hot dog roast and champagne at the

end (Merritt Helfferich, oral history recording about Tanana River Raft Race, March 2, 1996, Tape No. ORAL HISTORY 2008-04-02, Alaska and Polar Regions Archives, Elmer E. Rasmuson Library, University of Alaska Fairbanks). Also available at the Fairbanks Communities of Memory Project Jukebox, at http://jukebox.uaf.edu/comfbks/Helfferich_Meritt/HTML/testimonybrowser.html, accessed February 14, 2011). The race was discontinued after four years when two people drowned after being swept into a logjam because of high water. Also see Merritt Helfferich's account of events surrounding the first race, "Fairbanks Spring Hysteria: The Great Tanana Raft Classic," the *Ester* [AK] *Republic* 10, no. 2 (February 2008), available at http://www.esterrepublic.com/Archives/springhysteria.html, accessed February 14, 2011.

Ginny also wrote an article about the first raft race: "The Great Raft Race," *Alaska Sportsman* 34, no. 9 (September 1968): 24–26.

12. For a brief history of the beginning of the Equinox Marathon, which was first run on September 21, 1963, see Bainbridge, "Equinox Marathon History;" and Parrish, "Respecting Our Routes," 17–21. Doug Bingham is not mentioned in either of these historic overviews of the race. It is unknown whether only Ginny considers him one of the early race founders or if she confused his name with someone else because she had been talking about Doug in reference to ski trails and getting skiing programs started in the schools.

13. "In 1982, the Skarland and Equinox Marathon Trails were the first to be dedicated to the public in the Fairbanks North Star Borough's (FNSB) recreational trail program" (University of Alaska Fairbanks Master Planning Committee, "A Brief History of the UAF Skarland Trail System"). For more about history of the Skarland Trail, see Parrish, "Respecting Our Routes," 21–23; and Parrish, "UAF Campus Trails on the Skarland Trail System."

14. Ivar Skarland was born in 1899 in Norway and died in January 1965 of a heart attack. He attended forestry school in Norway and arrived in Alaska in 1928. While an undergraduate student at the University of Alaska, Ivar became interested in archeology after having met Otto Geist and working with him on an excavation at Kukulik, St. Lawrence Island.

15. Chuck Keim is the author of a biography of well-known arctic archeologist Otto Geist, titled *Aghvook, White Eskimo: Otto Geist and Alaskan Archaeology* (1969; repr., Fairbanks: University of Alaska Press, 2008).

16. Ivar Skarland received his bachelor's degree in anthropology from the University of Alaska Fairbanks in 1935, and went on to earn a master's in 1942 and doctorate in 1949 from Harvard University. With some interruption for military service during World War II, Skarland taught archeology and anthropology at UAF from 1942 until his death in 1965. He was recognized as a world leader in northern archeology, having worked on excavations at famous sites such as St. Lawrence Island, Point Hope, Kobuk River, Cape Denbigh, Anaktuvuk Pass, Onion Portage, and Kachemak Bay. He also was able to show traces of an unexpected ancient population

south of the Alaska Range. (University of Alaska, "Ski Trails and Ivar Skarland Hall Named for Professor," Stories, Electronic Info Spots, http://www.alaska.edu/opa/eInfo/index.xml?StoryID=242, accessed February 14, 2011; and Laurence Irving, "Obituary," *Arctic* 18, no. 2 [June 1965]: 147–48, available at http://pubs.aina.ucalgary.ca/arctic/Arctic18-2-147.pdf, accessed February 14, 2011).

17. From "There were about…" to "…horseback-riding events" is from "The Metamorphosis of the Fairbanks North Star Borough Trails Commission" by Ginny Hill Wood, April 10, 2001, in folder titled "Unpublished manuscript on Kotzebue and 'Last Resort,'" Ginny Wood Personal Collection.

18. In 1980, the Fairbanks North Star Borough established an advisory trail commission, chaired by Bill Stringer, to replace the Park and Recreation Commission. The commission's purpose was "to guide the establishment and management of the recreation trail system" and to develop a Comprehensive Trail Plan to recommend to the mayor ("Resolution 80-9: A Resolution Establishing Policy for Creation and Management of a Recreation Trail System in Fairbanks North Star Borough," adopted February 28, 1980). The borough's Comprehensive Recreational Trail Plan was adopted by ordinance in 1985 (Chapter 2.62). In 1986, the borough's present Trails Advisory Commission was established (T. Hancock, pers. comm.). Administratively, it currently resides within the Parks and Recreation Department and meets quarterly. According to the North Star Borough, the purpose of the commission is "to be the advisory body to borough government on matters relating to trails within the borough, especially relating to the comprehensive recreational trails plan, a component of the Comprehensive Plan of the Fairbanks North Star Borough. This commission replaces the duties of the Parks and Recreation Commission in regard to trails and the borough trail system. It is supported administratively by the Parks and Recreation Department. This commission is up for reauthorization every six years, by ordinance" ("Trails Advisory Commission listing," Boards and Commissions, Fairbanks North Star Borough official website, http://www.co.fairbanks.ak.us/Boards/#trailscomm, accessed February 14, 2011).

19. Ginny's work to protect trails in Fairbanks started in 1979, with the establishment of what she calls the Tanana Trails Council. In May 1980, she joined the North Star Borough's newly established Trails Advisory Commission and served as a member until 2006. On October 26, 2006, Jim Whitaker, the borough's mayor, issued a proclamation honoring Ginny Wood for her twenty-six years of service on the Trails Commission (Fairbanks North Star Borough commission records; and J. Bouton, pers. comm.).

20. The protection of trails is part of the Fairbanks North Star Borough's Regional Comprehensive Plan, adopted on September 13, 2005 (Ordinance No. 2005–56). Being part of the comprehensive plan ensures that the borough makes trails a priority and has to take action to maintain and protect them. The Planning Department made sure that all known trails at the time were included in the Comprehensive Recreational Trail Plan, so that if a trail listed in the plan is on a piece of

property that the owner wants to subdivide or develop, the trail cannot be eliminated. Efforts have to be made to protect and keep the trail (T. Hancock, pers. comm.; and North Star Borough's Comprehensive Plan Advisory Board, Notes from October 8, 2008, meeting, pp. 3–4, available at http://www.co.fairbanks. ak.us/CommunityPlanning/ComprehensivePlanAdvisoryBoard/Meetings2008/ CPABMeeting_100808.pdf, accessed February 15, 2011).

21. Fairbanks North Star Borough, "Guide to Nominating Trails Into the Fairbanks North Star Borough Comprehensive Recreational Trail Plan," Fairbanks North Star Borough, October 9, 2008, http://www.co.fairbanks.ak.us/ParksandRecreation/Forms/Trails/GuidetoNominatingTrails.pdf, accessed February 14, 2011.

22. The Trails Planner position was reduced to half-time. The trails program was not funded by the North Star Borough Assembly and so was reduced to almost nothing. There was some minimal grant money available, but mostly that was used for trail grooming (T. Hancock, pers. comm.).

23. During the late 1990s and early 2000s, the borough's Trails Advisory Commission tried to remain active, but they did not always have a quorum of its fifteen members to be able to hold an official meeting because only six people would show up, or because only seven or eight seats were filled due to a lack of community interest in being on the commission. Eight members were needed to have a quorum (T. Hancock, pers. comm.).

24. Either Ginny has the incorrect date of her testimony or this was an early effort to regain a trails coordinator position that did not succeed, since the job did not return to the borough until 2007. According to current trails coordinator Tom Hancock, in late 2005–early 2006 people in Fairbanks started to show a renewed interest in trails. A variety of local groups concerned about trails saw the need for more involvement from the borough in their protection and management, so they asked the commission to lobby the borough assembly to hire a trails coordinator. Luke Hopkins was on the assembly and was their liaison to the Trails Advisory Commission, and he advocated for the position (Luke also was the North Campus manager for the University of Alaska Fairbanks, where part of his job was to oversee and manage their trail system). Mayor James Whitaker supported the idea and requested funding as part of the normal fiscal process in 2007. The assembly approved it and the full-time position restarted on July 1, 2007. At this time, Mayor Whitaker also moved the trails program from the Planning Department to the Parks and Recreation Department because Parks deals with all trails for all purposes and the borough's 2005 Comprehensive Plan recommended the administrative shift (T. Hancock, pers. comm.).

25. From "One of our accomplishments..." to "...during all seasons" is from "The Metamorphosis of the Fairbanks North Star Borough Trails Commission" by Ginny Hill Wood, April 10, 2001, in folder titled "Unpublished manuscript on Kotzebue and 'Last Resort,'" Ginny Wood Personal Collection.

26. Ginny wrote about this in "Subdivider, Spare Our Ski Trail," *News Bulletin of the Alaska Conservation Society* 4, no. 2 (April 1963): 7–8.

27. For more about the history of farming in the Fairbanks area, see Josephine Papp, *Like a Tree to the Soil: A History of Farming in Alaska's Tanana Valley, 1903 to 1940* (School of Natural Resources and Agricultural Sciences, Alaska Agricultural and Forestry Experiment Station, University of Alaska Fairbanks, 2007).

28. According to the history section of the official website for the Nordic Ski Club of Fairbanks, the Birch Hill trails were originally created by the late Jim Whisenhant and the Lathrop High School Ski Team (of which he was coach). His trail clearing began in 1975 and these trails were then the site of the USSA Junior National Championships in March 1977, the first major national event held in Fairbanks (Nordic Ski Club of Fairbanks, "NSCF History—Birch Hill Recreation Area," http://www.nscfairbanks.org/new/index.php?option=com_content&view=article&id=40:nscf-history-birch-hill-recreation-area-&catid=53:history&Itemid=100012, accessed February 14, 2011).

29. To learn more about the life and flying career of Rudy Billberg, see Rudy Billberg, as told to Jim Reardon, *In the Shadow of Eagles: From Barnstormer to Alaska Bush Pilot: A Flyer's Story* (Anchorage: Alaska Northwest Books, 1998).

30. For another of Ginny's writings against snowmachines, see "From the Woodpile" column, the *Northern Line* 21, no. 1 (February 16, 1999): 12–13.

31. Ginny Wood, "The Abominable Snowmachine," *Alaska Conservation Review* 12, no. 4 (Winter 1971): 12–13.

32. See Ginny Wood, "Save the Trails!" the *Northern Line* 5, no. 2 (April–May 1983): 5, 9.

33. "Ginny Hill Wood Wins Celia Hunter Award," *Fairbanks Daily News-Miner*, December 8, 1985.

34. For more information about Great Old Broads for Wilderness, see their website at http://www.greatoldbroads.org/, accessed February 14, 2011.

35. See State of Alaska Administrative Order No. 161, February 14, 1996, for full description of the TRAAK Board's mission, organization, and member duties, available at http://gov.state.ak.us/admin-orders/161.html, accessed February 14, 2011.

36. See the website of the State of Alaska, Department of Natural Resources for more information about the Alaska Trails System: http://dnr.alaska.gov/parks/aktrails/ats.htm, accessed February 14, 2011.

37. Ginny expresses some of this frustration in "Access or Excess?," "From the Woodpile" column, the *Northern Line* 22, no. 2 (July 12, 2000): 12–13.

38. See State of Alaska Administrative Order No. 222, October 21, 2004, available at http://www.gov.state.ak.us/admin-orders/222.html, accessed February 14, 2011. One difference between these two boards is that TRAAK had eleven members, met four times a year, and was administered by the Department of Transportation and Public Facilities. The new ORTAB has only nine members, meets twice a year, and is administered by the Department of Natural Resources. Other possible differences are the composition of the board, with the degree of representation

from motorized versus nonmotorized groups, the types of issues discussed and recommendations made, and the level of authority given the board within the state's administration.

20. Traveling the Globe

1. The other members of this expedition were Celia Hunter, Florence "Ru" Rucker (later Collins), Florence "Ro" Robinson (later Weber), and Susan Hull and Muriel Thurber, whom they'd met earlier that spring at the Washington Folbot Club. Ginny published articles with photos in *Alaska Sportsman* and later in *National Geographic* detailing the adventures of the trip (Ginny Hill Wood, "Squaws Along the Yukon," *National Geographic* 112, no. 2 [August 1957], 245–65; "Squaws Along the Yukon," *Alaska Sportsman* 20, no. 4 [September 1954]: 6–11, 36–40). Florence Collins shared her memories of this river trip in an oral history interview, where she says one of the gals from Seattle came down with pneumonia, ended up in the hospital in Dawson City, and hitchhiked back to Fairbanks instead of finishing at Circle. Florence also remembers either flying or getting a ride back to Whitehorse to retrieve her station wagon, which the group had driven over and left there (oral history interview with Florence Collins and Ginny Wood with Karen Brewster, Susan Grace, and Keith Pollock on November 3, 2006. Tape No. ORAL HISTORY 2011-04-08, Alaska and Polar Regions Archives, Elmer E. Rasmuson Library, University of Alaska Fairbanks).

2. While doing final book edits, I realized that while I had heard Ginny talk about this Aleutian Island boat trip in the past, it was not included in the book. It must never have been mentioned during our formal recording sessions whose transcripts were the basis for the book. So on January 16, 2011, I asked her about it and took notes during our conversation. Unfortunately, by this time her memory had slipped to the extent that she was no longer able to provide the same level of detail or dates. In June 2011, when looking through Ginny's photograph collection, I discovered a box of photos from this trip. It is here I learned that the trip was in 1960, her traveling companion's name was Joan Terry, they departed from Seward, and they traveled on the ship MV *Expansion*. Ginny's photo of boys on the beach at Akutan village reading the funny papers appeared in *Alaska Sportsman* 30, no. 4 (April 1964): 6.

3. From this trip, the main things Ginny talks about are how she and Libby would take a ferry to an island, hike across the island, than catch another ferry to another island; and looking for a cheap hotel at Christmas, realizing the expensive one was only five dollars, celebrating the holiday with a good meal and a bottle of wine, giving each other little presents made from the tinfoil of chocolate bar wrappers, and enjoying the beautiful sunlight and sea view from their balcony. She also kept a journal and took many photos on her Greece trip (Ginny Wood Personal Collection).

4. Libby Hatton was born and grew up in Massachusetts, went to college in Rhode Island, earned a master's degree from UCLA, and in 1964 graduated from medical school with a specialty in pediatrics. Libby met Ginny Wood when she first came to Alaska in the summer of 1957 when she and coworkers from a Girl Scout camp at Harding Lake vacationed at Mount McKinley National Park and rented a cabin at Camp Denali. She later returned as a staff member, and eventually settled in Anchorage, first working at Providence Hospital and then helping start the Children's Clinic. She and Ginny became close friends and often traveled together: cross-country skiing and hiking together in Alaska's backcountry; hiking in Greece; trekking in Nepal; and bicycling in New Zealand. Libby was in Ethiopia from 1968 to 1970. In an oral history interview, Libby mentions that Ginny was sick much of the time she was visiting Ethiopia, so she didn't get to see or do much. Perhaps this is why Ginny does not share many stories from this trip (oral history interview with Karen Brewster on June 27, 2010. Tape No. ORAL HISTORY 2011-04-26, Alaska and Polar Regions Archives, Elmer E. Rasmuson Library, University of Alaska Fairbanks). In this interview, Libby also talks about concerns she had about the use of baby formula and famine developing in Ethiopia, her friendship with Ginny, and other travel they did together.

5. Libby Hatton talks about this trip in an oral history interview with Karen Brewster on June 27, 2010. Tape No. ORAL HISTORY 2011-04-26, Alaska and Polar Regions Archives, Elmer E. Rasmuson Library, University of Alaska Fairbanks.

6. The trip was organized by Mountain Travel Adventure Company. They visited Lake Nakuru National Park, Masai Mara National Reserve, the Great Rift Valley, Ngorongoro Crater, Serengeti National Park, Olduvai Gorge, Mount Kilimanjaro, Arusha National Park, and Amboseli National Park. Ginny kept a detailed diary of her safari, where she writes about her guides, Smoke Blanchard and Jack Hopcraft; the different parks they visit; the wildlife and unique landscapes they see; and the tough road conditions they face (Africa Travel Journal, Ginny Wood Personal Collection).

7. Libby Hatton mentions this trip in an oral history interview with Karen Brewster, June 27, 2010, Tape No. ORAL HISTORY 2011-04-26, Alaska and Polar Regions Archives, Elmer E. Rasmuson Library, University of Alaska Fairbanks.

8. In 1983, Ginny and Celia, with the help of Woody, Libby, and friends Jim Meredith and Eileen Long, built a small, rustic cabin without electricity or running water on property they owned on the west side of San Juan Island. They named it "Topside." They'd visit for a week or two every spring and fall, driving down from Fairbanks and taking their car on the ferry from Anacortes, Washington. They hiked, biked, kayaked, and visited with friends who came to visit, like Eileen and Bill Long, or others who lived nearby, like Susan and Jim Meredith in Roche Harbor, Rosemary and Neil Davis on the east side, and Mardy Murie at her cabin at Hannah Heights. As time passed, their isolated island began to attract more people and become built up with "trophy homes." It no longer provided the solace

it once had. In hopes of protecting one last little bit of the island in its original state, in 1993 Ginny turned over her eleven acres to the local land trust—San Juan County Land Bank—with a conservation easement.

All of the above information comes from the Topside Cabin Logbook, Ginny Wood Personal Collection. The entries construct a rich memoir of their visits, activities on the island, and their love of the place. October 1999 is the last entry in the logbook; it was written by Celia. Eventually, Ginny's daughter took over the properties.

9. Ginny's 2008 verbal telling of this story on tape lacked detail and the pizzazz that friends who had previously heard the story were expecting. I was ecstatic when I found Ginny's 1973 trip journal. It gave me the chance to fill in missing details that were key to understanding the story, and allowed Ginny's personal style to shine through. I integrated pieces from the 2008 verbal telling and 1973 journal writings into one flowing story and resorted to footnotes only when I could not find another way to integrate the two forms.

10. The Tuareg are a nomadic pastoralist people living in the Saharan interior of north Africa. They are Muslim and are known for the blue robes they wear. For more about the Tuareg people, see Karl-G. Prasse, *The Tuaregs: The Blue People* (Copenhagen: Museum Tusculanum Press, University of Copenhagen, 1995); Francis James Rennell Rodd, *People of the veil. Being an account of the habits, organisation and history of the wandering Tuareg tribes which inhabit the mountains of Air or Asben in the Central Sahara* (London: MacMillan & Co., 1926).

11. See "Ouest Hoggar," a personal site of Jean Bellec, a retired computer engineer, at http://www.kerleo.net/voyages/sahara/ouest_hoggar.htm (accessed February 14, 2011), for photos of the Hoggar Mountains and the area where Ginny was hiking taken around 1960. To read the account of another traveler in the Hoggar Mountains, see Kenneth and Julie Slavin, *The Tuareg* (London: Gentry Books, 1973).

12. A *zeriba* (or *zereba*) is a round stockade-type structure constructed of thornbushes or bulrush. It is used by pastoralists in the desert region of Africa to protect their campsites, villages, or livestock overnight. See photo in Slavin, *The Tuareg*, 26. According to Wiktionary, *zerebas* have been used for defense purposes in parts of Africa, and *zereba* also refers to a village protected by such a structure (http://en.wiktionary.org/wiki/zareba, accessed February 8, 2011, s.v. "zereba").

13. France made Algeria one of its colonies in 1830. The Algerian War of Independence began in 1954 and was a grueling seven-year guerrilla campaign to take the country back from the French. Algeria gained its independence in 1962. Algeria broke relations with the United States in 1967 over Israel. However, by 1980, relations began to warm under a new Algerian presidency (John Ruedy, *Modern Algeria: The Origins and Development of a Nation* [Bloomington: Indiana University Press, 1992]; Benjamin Stora, *Algeria, 1830–2000: A Short History* [Ithaca, NY: Cornell University Press, 2001]).

14. There are entries in Ginny's Kenya and Tanzania travel journal where she mentions Smoke Blanchard not feeling well: "January 27: Smoke laid low. January 29: Smoke must be sick—he slept rather than eating and has been pretty silent all day. January 30: Smoke still sick. Stayed home and slept all day. February 2, Nairobi: Smoke Blanchard sick again. He should see a doctor" (Africa Travel Journal, Ginny Wood Personal Collection).

15. From "This agent took…" to "…freer with each step" is from Ginny's 1973 Africa trip journal, Ginny Wood Personal Collection.

16. "Bits and Pieces of My Life" by Ginny Wood, p. 5, attached to "An informal biography of Ginny Hill Wood," in folder "Ginny's Resume and Awards (Her Life History)," Ginny Wood Personal Collection. For a description of this trip, see Ginny Wood, "From the Woodpile" column, the *Northern Line* 8, no. 3 (May–July 1986): 11.

17. Photocopy of handwritten letter by Ginny Wood in green notebook titled "The Book (That is not)," undated, Ginny Wood Personal Collection. This is a response to a typed letter from Connie Barlow, February 17, 1991, also in this notebook. For a description of this trip, see Ginny Wood, "From the Woodpile" column, the *Northern Line* 13, no. 3 (September 30, 1991): 16–17.

18. Ginny describes this trip in "A Lesson From Norway," "From the Woodpile" column, the *Northern Line* 17, no. 2 (June 22, 1995): 12.

19. "Wood Cuts 1995," Ginny Wood's annual Christmas letter, January 1996, Ginny Wood Personal Collection. Celia also wrote about this trip in her 1995 Christmas letter: "We flew to Seattle then on via SAS to Copenhagen, Oslo and Trondheim. We spent nearly a week at a folk high school in Skogn, where we had good skiing right out the door, and did a lot of sightseeing, attending lectures on Norwegian culture and economic and music, etc. Then were bussed into the Trollheimen Mountains south of Trondheim to a delightful rustic farmstead at Storli, where we went out on ski trips daily (and ate gourmet food in beautifully decorated rooms—part of the farmhouse dated back to the 1700s)" (Celia Hunter's annual Christmas letter, January 1996 Ginny Wood Personal Collection).

20. Celia Hunter made her final trip to the Lower 48 in the fall of 2001, just prior to her death on December 1, 2001. Ginny did not accompany Celia on this trip. Therefore, 2000 was probably Ginny's last trip, since I do not think she wanted to travel alone and she has not traveled out of Alaska since I got to know her in 2006.

21. The Loss of a Friend

1. For years, Ginny has written letters and articles about the Arctic National Wildlife Refuge, ranging from having it protected as official wilderness to the connections between oil development in the refuge and our country's energy use and policies. For example, on February 18, 1961, she wrote a letter to Urban Nelson, the regional director of the Bureau of Sport Fisheries and Wildlife, United States Fish

and Wildlife Service, commenting on the wilderness recreational use of the Arctic National Wildlife Range (photocopy in possession of the author). Or on February 3, 1987, she submitted a letter to the Fish and Wildlife Service commenting on the Arctic National Wildlife Refuge Coastal Plain Resource Assessment, stating a personal emotional attachment to the refuge and her opposition to legislation that would open up the coastal plain to the oil industry for oil and gas development. Or her letter to the US Department of Energy about the need for a US energy policy that appeared in "From the Woodpile" column, the *Northern Line* 12, no. 3 (October 4, 1990): 17. Other "From the Woodpile" columns on this topic include: the *Northern Line* 9, no. 1 (January-February 1987): 9; the *Northern Line* 10, no. 1 (February–March 1988): 11, 14; the *Northern Line* 22, no. 3 (November 20, 2000): 14–16; and the *Northern Line* 23, no. 2 (April 16, 2001): 14–15. Or articles in the *News Bulletin of the Alaska Conservation Society*: "Editorial," *News Bulletin of the Alaska Conservation Society* 1, no. 3 (August 1960); *News Bulletin of the Alaska Conservation Society* 1, no. 4 (November 1960): 3–4.

2. Ginny Wood, "So Long, Celia," the *Northern Line* 24, no. 1 (January 27, 2002): 11.

22. Reflections

1. Scribbled on a piece of scratch paper, undated, found amidst papers in the Ginny Wood Personal Collection.
2. This was a mid-term election where the party in control of the White House gained congressional seats and solidified their majority.
3. The war in Afghanistan began on October 7, 2001, in response to attacks on the United States on September 11, 2001. The invasion of Iraq officially began in March 2003. Both offensives were initiated by President George W. Bush as part of his war on terrorism.
4. "Get Up and Go" by Pete Seeger (http://www.peteseeger.net/getupgo.htm, accessed February 14, 2011).

Bibliography

Adams, John Luther. Website of John Luther Adams. www.johnlutheradams. com, accessed February 14, 2011.

Agricultural Research Center Office Files, 1901-1948. Archives 20. Finding Aid Collection Description. Washington State University Libraries, Manuscripts, Archives, and Special Collections, Pullman, Washington. http://www.wsulibs.wsu.edu/masc/finders/ua20.htm, accessed February 12, 2011.

Alaska Conservation Society Papers, 1960–1993. Alaska and Polar Regions Archives, Elmer E. Rasmuson Library, University of Alaska Fairbanks. Collection description and finding aid online at the Northwest Digital Archives website: http://nwda-db.wsulibs.wsu.edu/findingaid/ark:/80444/xv58835, accessed February 13, 2011.

_____. *News Bulletin of the Alaska Conservation Society* 1, no. 1 (March 1960).

_____. *News Bulletin of the Alaska Conservation Society* 1, no. 2 (May 1960).

_____. *News Bulletin of the Alaska Conservation Society* 1, no. 3 (August 1960).

_____. *News Bulletin of the Alaska Conservation Society* 2, no. 2 (March 1961).

_____. *News Bulletin of the Alaska Conservation Society* 4, no. 2 (April 1963).

_____. *News Bulletin of the Alaska Conservation Society* 4, no. 4 (December 1963).

Alaska, State of. Administrative Order No. 161, February 14, 1996. Mission, organization, and member duties of the TRAAK Board. Available online at http://gov.state.ak.us/admin-orders/161.html, accessed February 14, 2011.

_____. Administrative Order No. 222, October 21, 2004. Updated mission, organization, and member duties of the TRAAK Board. Available online at http://www.gov.state.ak.us/admin-orders/222.html, accessed February 14, 2011.

Alaskan Independence Party. *Official website.* http://www.akip.org/introduction.html, accessed February 14, 2011.

Allen, Barbara. "Oral History: The Folk Connection." In *The Past Meets the Present: Essays on Oral History*, edited by David Stricklin and Rebecca Sharpless, 15-26. Lanham, MD: University Press of America, 1988.

Allende, Isabel. *Portrait in Sepia.* New York: Harper Collins, 2001.

Argus, George. Oral history interview with Karen Brewster, July 7, 2011, Fairbanks, Alaska. Tape No. ORAL HISTORY 2011–25, Alaska and Polar Regions Archives, Elmer E. Rasmuson Library, University of Alaska Fairbanks.

Bainbridge, Steve. "Equinox Marathon History. The first years…1963–1966." *Equinox Marathon, Fairbanks, Alaska.* Running Club North, Fairbanks, Alaska, November 21, 2009. http://www.equinoxmarathon.org/index. php?option=com_content&task=view&id=45&Itemid=37, accessed February 14, 2011.

Baker, Nancy. Oral history interview with Karen Brewster, December 1, 2007, Fairbanks, Alaska. Tape No. ORAL HISTORY 2011-04-21, Alaska and Polar Regions Archives, Elmer E. Rasmuson Library, University of Alaska Fairbanks.

Behar, Ruth. *Translated Woman: Crossing the Border with Esperanza's Story.* Boston: Beacon Press, 1994.

Bernton, Hal. "Alaskans Fly to a Celebration in Siberia." *Anchorage Daily News,* June 14, 1988.

____. "Flight Offers Hopes for New Beginnings, Long Closed Doorway to Soviet Far East May Open for Old Friends, Businessmen." *Anchorage Daily News,* June 15, 1988.

Berry, Mary Clay. *The Alaska Pipeline: The Politics of Oil and Native Land Claims.* Bloomington: Indiana University Press, 1975.

Blackman, Margaret. *During My Time: Florence Edenshaw Davidson, a Haida Woman.* 1982, Reprint, Seattle, WA: University of Washington Press, 1982.

____. *Sadie Brower Neakok, An Iñupiaq Woman.* Seattle: University of Washington Press, 1989.

Bourasaw, Noel V. "*Living High,* an unconventional autobiography, and June and Farrar Burn." *Skagit River Journal of History and Culture,* 2005 (updated 2008). http://www.skagitriverjournal.com/WA/Library/Burn/Burn01-BookBios.html, accessed February 12, 2011.

Bradford, Sarah. *The Reluctant King: The Life and Reign of George VI, 1895–1952.* New York: St. Martin's Press, 1989.

Brady, Terry. "Rampart Dam—Not Black, Not White." *News Bulletin of the Alaska Conservation Society* 4, no. 1 (February 1963): 2–5. Originally published as "Rampart Dam: Millions of Kilowatts." Terry Brady, *Fairbanks Daily News-Miner,* November 28, 1962.

Brewster, Karen. *The Whales, They Give Themselves: Conversations with Harry Brower, Sr.* Fairbanks: University of Alaska Press, 2004.

British Monarchy. "Trooping the Colour." Official Website of the British Monarchy. http://www.royal.gov.uk/RoyalEventsandCeremonies/TroopingtheColour/TroopingtheColour.aspx, accessed February 10, 2011.

Brown, William E. *Denali, Symbol of the Alaskan Wild: An Illustrated History of the Denali–Mount McKinley Region, Alaska.* Denali National Park, Alaska Natural History Association and Virginia Beach, VA: The Donning Company, 1993.

Bryant, Jane. *Snapshots from the Past: A Roadside History of Denali National Park and Preserve.* Denali National Park: National Park Service, Center for Resources, Science and Learning, 2011.

Bundtzen, Thomas K. "A History of Mining in the Kantishna Hills." *Alaska Journal* 8 (Spring 1978): 150-161.

Burn, June. *Living High: An Unconventional Autobiography.* New York: Duell, Sloan and Pearce, 1941.

Burn (June and Farrar) Collection. "June and Farrar Burn Papers Biographical Note." *Finding Aid to the June and Farrar Burn Collection.* Bellingham: Center for Pacific Northwest Studies, Western Washington University. http://www.acadweb.wwu.edu/cpnws/burn/burnbio.htm, accessed February 12, 2011.

Campbell, Jim, and Carol Kasza. Oral history interview with Jim Campbell, Carol Kasza, and Ginny Wood with Karen Brewster, Susan Grace, and Keith Pollock, April 27, 2007, Fairbanks, Alaska. Tape No. ORAL HISTORY 2011-04-16, Alaska and Polar Regions Archives, Elmer E. Rasmuson Library, University of Alaska Fairbanks.

Case, David S. *Alaska Natives and American Laws.* Fairbanks: University of Alaska Press, 1984.

City of Berkeley, California. "Indian Rock Park." Parks, Recreation and Waterfront Department official website. http://www.ci.berkeley.ca.us/ContentDisplay.aspx?id=12614, accessed February 12, 2011.

Clemens, Janet and Frank Norris. *Building in an Ashen Land: Historic Resource Study of Katmai National Park and Preserve.* Anchorage: US Department of the Interior, National Park Service, Alaska System Support Office, 1999 (2nd printing, 2008).

Clute, John, and John Grant, eds. *The Encyclopedia of Fantasy.* New York: St. Martin's Press, 1997.

Coates, Kenneth. *The Alaska Highway in World War II: The US Army of Occupation in Canada's Northwest.* Norman: University of Oklahoma Press, 1992.

____. *North to Alaska: Fifty Years on the World's Most Remarkable Highway.* Fairbanks: University of Alaska Press, 1992.

____. *The Trans-Alaska Pipeline Controversy: Technology, Conservation and the Frontier.* Fairbanks, AK: University of Alaska Press, 1993.

Cohen, David William. *The Combing of History.* Chicago: University of Chicago Press, 1994.

Cole, Dermot. *North to the Future: The Alaska Story, 1959–2009.* Fairbanks: Epicenter Press, 2008.

Cole, Terrence. *Fighting for the Forty-Ninth Star: C. W. Snedden and the Crusade for Alaska Statehood.* Fairbanks, AK: University of Alaska Foundation, 2010.

Cole, Wally, and Jerryne Cole. Oral history interview with Karen Brewster and Susan Grace, February 2, 2007, Deneki Lakes, Alaska. Tape No. ORAL HISTORY 2011-04-11, Alaska and Polar Regions Archives, Elmer E. Rasmuson Library, University of Alaska Fairbanks.

Collins, Florence. Oral history interview with Florence Collins and Ginny Wood with Karen Brewster, Susan Grace, and Keith Pollock, November 3, 2006, Fairbanks, Alaska. Tape No. ORAL HISTORY 2011-04-08, Alaska and Polar Regions Archives, Elmer E. Rasmuson Library, University of Alaska Fairbanks.

Corff, Nicholas Campbell. *The Making of a Rescuer: The Story of Otto T. Trott, MD, A Father of Modern Mountaineering and Rescue.* Victoria, BC, and Bloomington, IN: Trafford Publishing, 2008.

Cornelius, Betty. "The Alaska Conservation Society: A Brief History." *Alaska Conservation Review* 14, no. 1 (Spring 1973): 4-5.

Corso, John. "Benefit-Cost Consideration in the Decision Against Rampart Dam, A Public Policy Analysis." Master's thesis, University of Alaska Southeastern Senior College, May 1974.

Cruikshank, Julie. *Life Lived Like a Story.* Lincoln: University of Nebraska Press, 1990.

Davidson, Art. *In the Wake of the Exxon Valdez: The Devastating Impact of the Alaska Oil Spill.* San Francisco: Sierra Club Books, 1990.

Delbridge, Rena. "Fairbanks Pilots Receive National Recognition. WWII WASPs Awarded Medal." *Fairbanks Daily News-Miner,* July 6, 2009.

Duffin, Andrew. "Vanishing Earth—Soil Erosion in the Palouse, 1930-1945." *Agricultural History* 79, no. 2 (Spring 2005): 173-192.

Dunaway, David. "The Oral Biography." *Biography* 14, no. 3 (Summer 1991): 256–66.

Dunham, Mike. "Survivor to Recall Deadly '54 Denali Climb." *Anchorage Daily News,* June 26, 2011, http://www.adn.com/2011/06/25/1936465/survivor-to-recall-deadly-54-denali.html, accessed June 28, 2011.

Fairbanks Daily News Miner. "Fairbanksans Eyed for National Honor." "In Brief" column, May 23, 2009.

_____. "Ginny Hill Wood Wins Celia Hunter Award." December 8, 1985.

Fairbanks North Star Borough. "Guide to Nominating Trails Into the Fairbanks North Star Borough Comprehensive Recreational Trail Plan." Fairbanks: Fairbanks North Star Borough, October 9, 2008. http://www.co.fairbanks.ak.us/ParksandRecreation/Forms/Trails/GuidetoNominatingTrails.pdf, accessed February 14, 2011.

_____. "North Star Borough's Comprehensive Plan Advisory Board (CPAB), Notes from October 8, 2008 meeting": pp. 3–4. Available at http://www.co.fairbanks.ak.us/CommunityPlanning/ComprehensivePlanAdvisoryBoard/Meetings2008/CPABMeeting_100808.pdf, accessed February 15, 2011.

_____. "Trails Advisory Commission listing." *Boards and Commissions,* Fairbanks North Star Borough official website. http://www.co.fairbanks.ak.us/Boards/#trailscomm, accessed February 14, 2011.

Ferguson (Archie) Oral History Collection. Series ORAL HISTORY 95–66, Alaska and Polar Regions Archives, Elmer E. Rasmuson Library, University of Alaska Fairbanks. Twenty-eight oral history interviews by Steven Levi conducted from October 1989 to March 1992.

Finnegan, Ruth. *Oral Traditions and the Verbal Arts: A Guide to Research Practices.* London: Routledge, 1992.

Fischer, Victor. *Alaska's Constitutional Convention*. National Municipal League, State Constitutional Convention Studies, Number Nine. Fairbanks: University of Alaska Press, 1975.

Freiberg, Chris. "Two Fairbanks Women Who Flew Airplanes in World War II Honored." *Fairbanks Daily News-Miner*, April 3, 2010.

Frisch, Michael. *A Shared Authority: Essays on the Craft and Meaning of Oral and Public History*. Albany: State University of New York Press, 1990.

_____. "Sharing Authority: Oral History and the Collaborative Process." *Oral History Review* 30, no. 1 (Winter/Spring 2003): 111–113.

Gilbert, Robert Lind. "Dividing Alaska: Native Claims, Statehood and Wilderness Preservation." PhD diss, University of North Carolina, 2002.

Grange, Kevin. "The Art of Mountain Watching." *National Parks* 83, no. 4 (Fall 2009): 25–30.

Graydon, Don, and Kurt Hanson, eds. *Mountaineering: The Freedom of the Hills*. 6th ed. Seattle: The Mountaineers, 1997.

Grele, Ron. *Envelopes of Sound: Six Practitioners Discuss the Method, Theory, and Practice of Oral History and Oral Testimony*. Chicago: Precedent Publications, 1975.

Griggs, Robert F. *The Valley of Ten Thousand Smokes*. Washington, DC: National Geographic Society, 1922.

Haigh, Jane. *Searching for Fannie Quigley: A Wilderness Life in the Shadow of Mount McKinley*. Athens: Swallow Press/Ohio State University Press, 2007.

Hall, W. E. "50 Years of Research at the Sherman Experiment Station." Miscellaneous Paper 104, June 1961. Corvallis: Agricultural Experiment Station, Oregon State University.

Hammond, Representative Jay S. "Rampart Dam—Some Rude Questions." *News Bulletin of the Alaska Conservation Society* 3, no. 1 (January 1962): 2–4.

Hatton, Libby. Oral history interview with Karen Brewster, June 27, 2010, Fairbanks, Alaska. Tape No. ORAL HISTORY 2011-04-26, Alaska and Polar Regions Archives, Elmer E. Rasmuson Library, University of Alaska Fairbanks.

Helfferich, Merritt. Oral history recording about Tanana River Raft Race, March 2, 1996, Fairbanks, Alaska. Tape No. ORAL HISTORY 2008-04-02, Alaska and Polar Regions Archives, Elmer E. Rasmuson Library, University of Alaska Fairbanks. Also available at the Fairbanks Communities of Memory Project Jukebox at http://jukebox.uaf.edu/comfbks/Helfferich_Meritt/HTML/testimonybrowser.html, accessed February 14, 2011.

Helfferich, Merritt, and George Cresswell. "Fairbanks Spring Hysteria: The Great Tanana Raft Classic." *Ester [AK] Republic* 10, no. 2 (February 2008). Available online at http://www.esterrepublic.com/Archives/springhysteria.html, accessed February 14, 2011.

Help Finland Archival Collection. Finnish American Heritage Center Historical Archive, Finlandia University, Hancock, MI. http://www.finlandia.edu/V-Series.html, accessed February 29, 2012.

Henderson, Helene, and Sue Ellen Thompson, eds. *Holidays, Festivals, and Celebrations of the World Dictionary*, 2nd ed. Detroit: Omnigraphics, Inc., 1997.

Hill, Virginia. "Once Upon a Time." Unpublished manuscript, first written in 1939. Copy in possession of author. (Forthcoming as: Virginia Hill Wood. *Once Upon a Time: A 1938 European Bicycle Adventure.* Press North America, Gustavus, AK.)

_____. "Three Maids Before the Mast." *Pacific Motor Boat* 39, no. 4 (April 1947): 29–32.

Hitz, Charles William. *Through the Rapids: The History of Princess Louisa Inlet.* Kirkland, WA: Sitka 2 Publishing, 2003.

Horne, Esther Burnett, and Sally McBeth. *Essie's Story: The Life and Legacy of a Shoshone Teacher.* Lincoln: University of Nebraska Press, 1998.

Hostelling International. "100 Years of Hostelling: How It All Started." *Hostelling International.* http://www.hihostels.com/web/100history.en.htm, accessed February 12, 2011.

Hunter, Celia. Recurring column in the *Everett (WA) Daily Herald.* Various dates, 1948.

_____. *News Bulletin of the Alaska Conservation Society* 2, no. 3 (May 1961): 9-10.

Imboden, Durant. "Riffelalp Resort Zermatt." *Switzerland and Austria for Visitors.* Europe for Visitors. http://europeforvisitors.com/switzaustria/articles/riffelalp_main_a.htm, accessed February 12, 2011.

Irving, Laurence. "Obituary." *Arctic* 18, no. 2 (June 1965): 147-148. Available at http://pubs.aina.ucalgary.ca/arctic/Arctic18-2-147.pdf, accessed February 14, 2011.

Joling, Dan. "Alaska Files Suit Against Feds Over Polar Bear Habitat Status." *Anchorage Daily News*, March 10, 2011.

_____. "State Will Sue Over Polar Bear Listing, Palin Says." *Anchorage Daily News*, May 22, 2008.

Kennedy (Kay) Collection. "Camp Denali, Tundra Telegram," Vol. VI. Alaska and Polar Regions Collections, Elmer E. Rasmuson Library, University of Alaska Fairbanks.

Kaye, Roger. *Last Great Wilderness.* Fairbanks: University of Alaska Press, 2006.

Kendrick, Greg. "National Park Service Biography: Olaus J. Murie." *National Park Service: The First 75 Years, Biographical Vignettes.* http://www.nps.gov/history/history/online_books/sontag/murie.htm, accessed February 14, 2011.

Kessel, Brina. Oral history interview with Karen Brewster, January 9, 2001, Fairbanks, Alaska. Tape No. ORAL HISTORY 2000-07-07, Alaska and Polar Regions Archives, Elmer E. Rasmuson Library, University of Alaska Fairbanks.

Klein, David. "Personal Profile." *Institute of Arctic Biology, University of Alaska Fairbanks.* http://users.iab.uaf.edu/~dave_klein/dklein.html, accessed February 13, 2011.

K'Meyer, Tracy E., and A. Glenn Crothers. "'If I See Some of This in Writing, I'm Going to Shoot You': Reluctant Narrators, Taboo Topics, and the Ethical Dilemmas of the Oral Historian." *Oral History Review* 34, no. 1 (Winter/Spring 2007): 71–93.

KUAC Radio. *Homefires* Radio Series, March 10, 1984. Fairbanks, AK: KUAC FM/TV. Topic: Women Flyers. Host: Patty Kastelic. Guests: Florence Weber, Nancy Baker, Ginny Wood, Celia Hunter. Tape No. ORAL HISTORY 90-10-02, Alaska and Polar Regions Archives, Elmer E. Rasmuson Library, University of Alaska Fairbanks.

Ladevich, Laurel. *Fly Girls.* A video production of WGBH Boston for *The American Experience.* Distributed by PBS Home Video/WGBH Educational Foundation, Boston, 1999.

LaRouche, Lyndon H. "The Outline of NAWAPA." Washington, DC: The Schiller Institute, January 1988. Available at http://www.schillerinstitute.org/economy/phys_econ/phys_econ_nawapa_1983.html, accessed February 14, 2011.

Letzring, Michael, prod. *The 49th Star: Creating Alaska.* Video documentary. Fairbanks, AK: KUAC FM/TV, 2006.

Library of Congress, Manuscript Division. *Great Aviation Quotes.* http://www.skygod.com/quotes/highflight.html, accessed February 13, 2011.

Life. "On Mt. McKinley; Rescue After Victory," June 14, 1954: 28–34.

Lowdermilk, Walter C. "Conquest of the Land through 7,000 Years." Washington, DC.: US Department of Agriculture, August 1953.

MacDonald, Dougald. "Band of Brothers—Remembering Denali's Greatest Rescue," *Climbing* 233 (September 2004): 64–71.

Mandelbaum, David. "The Study of Life History: Ghandi." *Current Anthropology* 14, no. 3 (June 1973): 177–196.

Mayer, Amy. *Celia's Alaska: Pioneer Stories of Denali.* Audio CD of excerpts from *Alaska Edition* radio show, August 1999–November 2001. Fairbanks: KUAC FM/TV, 2002.

McCall, John G. with Jim Rearden. "Rescue on Mt. McKinley." *Saga* (March 1955): 24–29, 64–67.

McPhee, John. *Encounters with the Archdruid.* New York: Farrar, Straus, and Giroux, 1971.

_____. "Farewell to the Archdruid." *Sierra* 86, no. 1 (January/February 2001): 8–9.

Mercer, Berle. Oral history interview with Jarrod Decker, September 18, 2000, Healy, Alaska. Tape No. ORAL HISTORY 2000-17-29, Alaska and Polar Regions Archives, Elmer E. Rasmuson Library, University of Alaska Fairbanks. Also available for listening at http://jukebox.uaf.edu/denali/html/beme.htm, accessed February 13, 2011.

Millington, Barry. *The New Grove Guide to Wagner and His Operas.* New York: Oxford University Press, 2006.

Mitchell, Donald Craig. *Take My Land, Take My Life: The Story of Congress's Historic Settlement of Alaska Native Land Claims, 1960-1971.* Fairbanks: University of Alaska Press, 2001.

Molnia, Bruce F. "Glaciers of North America—Glaciers of Alaska." US Geological Survey Professional Paper 1386-K. Part of the series *Satellite Image Atlas of the Glaciers of the World.* Edited by Richard S. Williams, Jr., and Jane G. Ferrigno. US Department of the Interior, US Geological Survey. Washington DC: US Government Printing Office, 2008.

Mueter, Franz. "Alaska Alpine Club History." Alaska Alpine Club History page, Fairbanks. https://sites.google.com/a/alaska.edu/alaska-alpine-club/history, accessed February 14, 2011.

Murie, Margaret. *Two in the Far North,* 5th ed., Seattle: Alaska Northwest Books, 1997. First published 1962 by Knopf.

Nalty, Bernard C. *Winged Shield, Winged Sword: A History of the United States Air Force, Vols. I & II.* Washington, DC: Air Force History and Museums Program, 1997.

Nancarrow, Bill. Oral history interview with Karen Brewster and Susan Grace, February 3, 2007, Deneki Lakes, Alaska. Tape No. ORAL HISTORY 2011-04-12, Alaska and Polar Regions Archives, Elmer E. Rasmuson Library, University of Alaska Fairbanks.

Nash, Roderick. *Wilderness and the American Mind,* 3rd ed. New Haven, CT: Yale University Press, 1982.

Naske, Claus-M., and Herman E. Slotnick. *Alaska: A History of the 49th State.* Grand Rapids, MI: William B. Eerdmans Publishing Company, 1979.

Nelson, Daniel. "Idealism and Organization: Origins of the Environmental Movement in Alaska." *Alaska History* 18, nos. 1-2 (Spring/Fall 2003): 12–35.

_____. *Northern Landscapes, The Struggle for Wilderness Alaska.* Washington, DC: Resources for the Future, 2004.

News Bulletin of the Alaska Conservation Society. "Recent Progress in Biological Studies of Rampart Dam." *News Bulletin of the Alaska Conservation Society* 4, no. 1 (February 1963): 5–8.

Nordic Ski Club of Fairbanks. "NSCF History—Birch Hill Recreation Area." *Nordic Ski Club of Fairbanks History.* http://www.nscfairbanks.org/new/index.php?option=com_content&view=article&id=40:nscf-history-birch-hill-recreation-area-&catid=53:history&Itemid=100012, accessed February 14, 2011.

Norris, Frank. *Crown Jewel of the North: An Administrative History of Denali National Park and Preserve,* vol. 1—*General Park History to 1980.* Anchorage: US Department of the Interior, National Park Service, Alaska Regional Office, 2006.

_____. *Crown Jewel of the North: An Administrative History of Denali National Park and Preserve,* vol. 2—*General Park History Since 1980, Plus Specialized Themes.* Anchorage: US Department of the Interior, National Park Service, Alaska Regional Office, 2008.

_____. *Isolated Paradise: An Administrative History of the Katmai and Aniakchak National Park Units.* Anchorage: US Department of the Interior, National Park Service, Alaska System Support Office, 1996.

Northern Line. "Then and Now: Gordon Wright." *Northern Line* 27, no. 2 (Summer 2005): 15–16.

O'Neill, Dan. *The Firecracker Boys.* New York: St. Martin's Press, 1994.

_____. *The Firecracker Boys: H-Bombs, Inupiat Eskimos, and the Roots of the Environmental Movement,* rev. ed. New York: Basic Books, 2007. First published 1994 by St. Martin's Press.

_____. *Project Chariot: A Collection of Oral Histories.* Fairbanks: Alaska and Polar Regions Collections, Elmer E. Rasmuson Library, University of Alaska Fairbanks, 1989.

O'Neill (Dan) Collection, Alaska and Polar Regions Archives, Elmer E. Rasmuson Library, University of Alaska Fairbanks.

Parker, Harriette. *Alaska's Mushrooms: A Practical Guide.* Anchorage: Alaska Northwest Books, 1994.

Parrish, Jane McNeely. "Respecting Our Routes . . ." Undated paper written for NORS 600 course, Perspectives of the North, taught by Professor Terrence Cole, University of Alaska Fairbanks. Copy in possession of author, received from Fairbanks North Star Borough, Parks and Recreation Department.

_____. "UAF Campus Trails on the Skarland Trail System of the Fairbanks North Star Borough." Trail map and guide, December 1997. Copy in possession of author, received from Fairbanks North Star Borough, Parks and Recreation Department.

Pearson, Grant H. *History of Mount McKinley National Park, Alaska.* Washington, DC: US Department of the Interior, National Park Service, March 15, 1952.

_____. "Little Johnnie of Kantishna." *Alaska Sportsman* 14, no. 7 (July 1948): 6.

_____. *My Life of High Adventure.* With Philip Newill. Englewood Cliffs, NJ: Prentice-Hall, 1962.

Portelli, Alessandro. "Oral History as Genre." In *Narrative and Genre,* edited by Mary Chamberlain and Paul Richard Thompson, 23–45. London: Routledge, 1998.

Potter, Jean. *The Flying North.* New York: Ballantine Books, 1972. Reprint from the original, Philadelphia, PA: The Curtis Publishing Company, 1945.

Potter, Louise. *Roadside Flowers of Alaska.* Thetford Center, VT, 1962.

_____. *Wildflowers Along Mt. McKinley Park Road and to Westward.* McKinley Park, AK: Camp Denali Publishers, 1979. First published 1969 by Thetford Center, VT.

Prasse, Karl-G. *The Tuaregs: The Blue People.* Copenhagen: Museum Tusculanum Press, University of Copenhagen, 1995.

Reed, John C. "Reminiscences: The Arctic Institute in the 1960s." *Arctic* 40,
no. 4 (December 1987): 244–248.

Rodd, Francis James Rennell. *People of the veil. Being an account of the habits,
organisation and history of the wandering Tuareg tribes which inhabit the mountains of Air or Asben in the Central Sahara.* London: MacMillan & Co., 1926.

Roderick, Jack. *Crude Dreams: A Personal History of Oil and Politics in Alaska.*
Fairbanks: Epicenter Press, 1997.

Ross, Alex. "Song of the Earth: A Composer Takes Inspiration from the Arctic." *New Yorker* 84, no. 13 (May 12, 2008): 76–81.

Ross, Ken. *Environmental Conflict in Alaska.* Boulder: University Press of Colorado, 2000.

_____. *Pioneering Conservation in Alaska.* Boulder: University Press of Colorado,
2006.

Ruedy, John. *Modern Algeria: The Origins and Development of a Nation.*
Bloomington: Indiana University Press, 1992.

Ryan, Jessica. "A Place for the Birds: The Legacy of Creamer's Field Migratory
Waterfowl Refuge." Master's thesis, University of Alaska Fairbanks, 2003.

Ryan, Kathleen. ""I Didn't Do Anything Important": A Pragmatist Analysis of
the Oral History Interview." *Oral History Review* 36, no. 1 (Winter/Spring
2009): 24–44.

Schneider, William. "Lessons from the Storytellers." In *Resilience in Arctic
Societies, 3rd IPASSAS Seminar,* edited by Larry Kaplan and Michelle Dav-
eluy, 111-118. Fairbanks: International PhD School for Studies of Arctic
Societies, 2005.

_____. *Living with Stories: Telling, Re-telling, and Remembering.* Logan: Utah
State University Press, 2008.

_____ *So They Understand: Cultural Issues in Oral History.* Logan: Utah State
University Press, 2002.

Schneider, William, and Phyllis Morrow. *When Our Words Return: Writing,
Hearing and Remembering Oral Traditions of Alaska and the Yukon.* Logan,
UT: Utah State University Press, 1995.

Seeger, Pete. "Get Up and Go." Words collected, adapted, and set to original
music by Pete Seeger (1960) TRO (c) 1964 (renewed) Melody Trails Inc., New
York http://www.peteseeger.net/getupgo.htm, accessed February 14, 2011.

Shopes, Linda. "Commentary: Sharing Authority." *Oral History Review* 30, no.
1 (Winter/Spring 2003): 103–110.

Slavin, Kenneth, and Julie Slavin. *The Tuareg.* London: Gentry Books, 1973.

Slocum, Captain Joshua. *Sailing Alone Around the World.* New York: The Century Company, 1899.

Snyder, Louis. *The War: A Concise History, 1939–1945.* New York: Julian Messner, Inc., 1960.

Spindler, Mike. "Creamers Field History." *Alaska Conservation Review* 20, no. 1 (Spring 1979): 13.

Spurr, Stephen. *Rampart Dam and the Economic Development of Alaska.* 4 vols. Ann Arbor: University of Michigan, Ann Arbor, School of Natural Resources, March 1966.

Stora, Benjamin. *Algeria, 1830–2000: A Short History.* Ithaca, NY: Cornell University Press, 2001.

Swift, Ann. "Then and Now: Profile of David Klein." *Northern Line* 26, no. 3 (Fall 2004): 17.

Terhune, Albert Payson. *Lochinvar Luck.* New York: Grosset & Dunlap, 1923.

Time. "Alaska: Single Slip." Vol. 63, no. 24 (June 14, 1954): 28–29.

Tonkin, Elizabeth. *Narrating Our Pasts: The Social Construction of Oral History.* Cambridge Studies in Oral and Literate Culture. Cambridge, UK: Cambridge University Press, 1992.

Toomey, Sheila. "Soviet Visitors Try American Shopping." *Anchorage Daily News*, September 8, 1988.

UK Youth Hostel Association. "YHA History." *UK Youth Hostel Association.* http://www.yha.org.uk/about-yha/corporate-information/history_of_the_yha.aspx, accessed February 12, 2011.

University of Alaska. "Ski Trails and Ivar Skarland Hall Named for Professor." *Stories, Electronic Info Spots.* http://www.alaska.edu/opa/eInfo/index.xml?StoryID=242, accessed February 14, 2011.

University of Alaska Fairbanks. Master Planning Committee. "A Brief History of the UAF Skarland Trail System: The First Eighty Years." *North Campus Subcommittee, Skarland Trail System Management Plan, History of UAF Trails.* http://www.uaf.edu/mastplan/committee/subcommittees/north-campus/skarland-trail-system-man/history-of-uaf-trails/, accessed February 13, 2011.

_____. Oral History Program. "Changing Communities—Alaska Highway Project Jukebox." *Oral History Program, University of Alaska Fairbanks.* http://jukebox.uaf.edu/ak_highway/html/index.html, accessed February 12, 2011.

US Congress. *A Bill to Authorize the Establishment of the Arctic National Wildlife Range, Alaska, and for other purposes.* US Congress, House of Representatives. Committee on Merchant Marine and Fisheries, Subcommittee on Fisheries and Wildlife Conservation. Hearings, H.R. 7045, July 1, 1959. 86th Congress, 1st Sess. Records of the US House of Representatives. Washington, DC: Government Printing Office, 1959.

_____. *A Bill to Authorize the Establishment of the Arctic National Wildlife Range, Alaska, and for other purposes.* US Congress, Senate. Committee on Interstate and Foreign Commerce, Subcommittee on Merchant Marine and

Fisheries, Hearings, S. 1899, 86th Congress, 1st Sess. Records of the US Senate. Washington, DC: Government Printing Office, 1960.

US Statutes at Large. *An Act Extending the homestead laws and providing for right of way for railroads in the District of Alaska and for other purposes.* Chapter 299, Section 10. 55th Congress, 2d sess. Vol. 30, 1899: 409–413.

US Fish and Wildlife Service. "Time Line: Establishment and Management of the Arctic Refuge." *Arctic National Wildlife Refuge* website. http://arctic.fws.gov/timeline.htm, accessed February 14, 2011.

_____. "Potential Impacts of Proposed Oil and Gas Development on the Arctic Refuge's Coastal Plain: Historical Overview and Issues of Concern." Web page of the Arctic National Wildlife Refuge, Fairbanks, Alaska. January 17, 2001. http://arctic.fws.gov/issues1.htm, accessed February 14, 2011.

Vansina, Jan. *Oral Tradition as History.* Madison: University of Wisconsin Press, 1985.

Verges, Marianne. *On Silver Wings: The Women Airforce Service Pilots of World War II, 1941–1944.* New York: Ballantine Books, 1991.

Viereck, Leslie. Oral history interview with David Krupa, May 23, 2000, Fairbanks, Alaska. Tape No. ORAL HISTORY 2000-17-06, Alaska and Polar Regions Archives, Elmer E. Rasmuson Library, University of Alaska Fairbanks. Audio also available for listening at http://jukebox.uaf.edu/denali/html/levi.htm, accessed February 12, 2011.

Washburn, Barbara. *The Accidental Adventurer: Memoirs of the First Woman to Climb Mount McKinley.* Kenmore, WA: Epicenter Press, 2001.

Washburn, Dr. Bradford. *Exploring the Unknown: Historic Diaries of Bradford Washburn's Alaska/Yukon Expeditions.* Kenmore, WA: Epicenter Press, 2001.

Washburn, Bradford, and Lew Freedman. *Bradford Washburn, An Extraordinary Life. The Autobiography of a Mountaineering Icon.* Portland, OR: West Winds Press, 2005.

Weeden, Robert. *Alaska: Promises to Keep.* Boston: Houghton Mifflin, 1978.

_____. "Conservation and Kilowatts." *News Bulletin of the Alaska Conservation Society* 2, no. 3 (May 1961): 1–7.

_____. *News Bulletin of the Alaska Conservation Society* 4, no. 4 (December 1963): 7–8.

_____. Oral history interview with Bob Weeden and Ginny Wood with Roger Kaye and Karen Brewster, June 9, 2006, Fairbanks, Alaska. Tape No. ORAL HISTORY 2011-04-07, Alaska and Polar Regions Archives, Elmer E. Rasmuson Library, University of Alaska Fairbanks.

West, Chuck. Oral history interview with Ron Inouye, February 4, 1985, Fairbanks, Alaska. Tape No. ORAL HISTORY 85–100, Alaska and Polar Regions Archives, Elmer E. Rasmuson Library, University of Alaska Fairbanks. Full audio and transcript available at http://jukebox.uaf.edu/aviators/west_chuck_edited/HTML/testimonybrowseraudioonly.html, accessed February 12, 2011.

Whitehead, John. *Completing the Union: Alaska, Hawaii, and the Battle for Statehood.* Albuquerque: University of New Mexico Press, 2004.

Wiles, Jessica. "Celia Hunter: Life and Leadership." Alaska Conservation Foundation publication, Anchorage. Undated photocopy in possession of the author.

Wilimovsky, Norman J., ed. *Environment of the Cape Thompson Region, Alaska.* John N. Wolfe, associate editor. Oak Ridge, TN: United States Atomic Energy Commission, Division of Technical Information, 1966.

Williams, Vera S. *WASP Women Airforce Service Pilots of World War II.* Osceola, WI: Motorbooks International, 1994.

Willis, Roxanne. *Alaska's Place in the West: From the Last Frontier to the Last Great Wilderness.* Lawrence: University Press of Kansas, 2010.

Williss, George Frank. *Do Things Right the First Time: The National Park Service and the Alaska National Interest Lands Conservation Act of 1980. Administrative History: The National Park Service and the Alaska National Interest Lands Conservation Act of 1980.* Anchorage: US Department of the Interior, National Park Service, 2005.

Willmott, H. P. *The Great Crusade: A New Complete History of the Second World War.* New York: Free Press, 1991.

Wood, Ginny. "A.E.C.—A Camel in the Tent?" *Alaska Conservation Review,* Fall/Winter 1967/1968: 1–2.

_____. "The Abominable Snowmachine." *Alaska Conservation Review* 12, no. 4 (Winter 1971): 12–13.

_____. "Access or Excess?" "From the Woodpile" column. *Northern Line* 22, no. 2 (July 12, 2000): 12–13.

_____. "Beware of the Hydro-Ax Along the Denali Park Road." "From the Woodpile" column. *Northern Line* 19, no. 2 (July 29, 1997): 14–15.

_____. "Big Dam/Big Threat," *Animals* 6, no. 8 (April 20, 1965): 198-203. Magazine published in London, England.

_____. "Bulldozer Blight, Some Causes and Cures." *Alaska Conservation Review* 9, no. 3 (Fall 1968): 1–4.

_____. "A Conservation Explosion." *Alaska Conservation Review* 9, no. 2 (Summer 1968): 12.

_____. "From the Woodpile" column, *Northern Line* 6, no. 4 (September–October 1984): 9.

_____. "From the Woodpile" column, *Northern Line* 7, no. 2 (April–May 1985): 9.

_____. "From the Woodpile" column. *Northern Line* 7, no. 4 (September–October 1985): 8.

_____. "From the Woodpile" column, *Northern Line* 8, no. 3 (May–July 1986): 11.

_____. "From the Woodpile" column. *Northern Line* 9, no. 1 (January–February 1987): 9.

_____. "From the Woodpile" column. *Northern Line* 10, no. 1 (February–March 1988): 11 & 14.

_____. "From The Woodpile" column, *Northern Line* 10, no. 2 (April–June, 1988): 9.

_____. "From the Woodpile" column. *Northern Line* 12, no. 1 (February 28, 1990): 18.

_____. "From the Woodpile" column, *Northern Line* 13, no. 3 (September 30, 1991): 16–17.

_____. "From the Woodpile" column. *Northern Line* 13, no. 4 (December 20, 1991): 11.

_____. "From the Woodpile" column. *Northern Line* 14, no. 1 (March 12, 1992): 14–15.

_____. "From the Woodpile" column. *Northern Line* 14, no. 2 (June 22, 1992): 15.

_____. "From the Woodpile" column. *Northern Line* 15, no. 1 (March 26, 1993): 14.

_____. "From the Woodpile" column. *Northern Line* 20, no. 3 (October 1, 1998): 9, 18.

_____. "From the Woodpile" column. *Northern Line* 21, no. 1 (February 16, 1999): 12–13.

_____. "From the Woodpile" column. *Northern Line* 21, no. 2 (April 1, 1999): 14.

_____. "From the Woodpile" column. *Northern Line* 22, no. 3 (November 20, 2000): 14–16.

_____. "From the Woodpile" column. *Northern Line* 23, no. 2 (April 16, 2001): 14–15.

_____. "The Great Raft Race." *Alaska Sportsman* 34, no. 9 (September 1968), 24–26.

_____. "The Greening of Alaska: A Retrospect." "From the Woodpile" column. *Northern Line* 12, no. 2 (April 22, 1990): 4 and 6.

_____. Interview conducted by Bill Tanner, May 10, 1983, for Melgenak Case. Transcript Accession No. KATM-00284. Anchorage: US Department of the Interior, National Park Service, Katmai National Park and Preserve Archives.

_____. Interview conducted by Oregon Public Broadcasting in August 2007 at Camp Denali for the PBS series *Great Lodges of the National Parks*. Transcript_Camp Denali_#59C. Electronic document in possession of author.

_____. "A Lesson From Norway." "From the Woodpile" column. *Northern Line* 17, no. 2 (June 22, 1995): 12.

_____. "McKinley Park. The Summer of '72." *Alaska Conservation Review* 13, no. 3 (Fall 1972): 4–6.

_____. "Nostalgic Trip Highlights a Half Century of Change." "In the Wood-pile" column. *Northern Line* 16, no. 4 (December 20, 1994): 10.

_____. "Ode to Michio Hoshino." "In the Woodpile" column. *Northern Line* 18, no. 3 (October 25, 1996): 6–7.

_____. Oral history interview with Karen Brewster, July 20, 2000, Fairbanks, Alaska. Tape No. ORAL HISTORY 2000-07-03, Alaska and Polar Regions Archives, Elmer E. Rasmuson Library, University of Alaska Fairbanks.

_____. Oral history interview with Karen Brewster, November 13, 2002, Fairbanks, Alaska. Tape No. ORAL HISTORY 2000-07-11, Alaska and Polar Regions Archives, Elmer E. Rasmuson Library, University of Alaska Fairbanks.

_____. Oral history interview with Karen Brewster, Roger Kaye, and Susan Grace, March 22, 2006, Fairbanks, Alaska. Tape No. ORAL HISTORY 2011-04-01, Alaska and Polar Regions Archives, Elmer E. Rasmuson Library, University of Alaska Fairbanks.

_____. Oral history interview with Karen Brewster, Pam Miller, and Susan Grace, April 5, 2006, Fairbanks, Alaska. Tape No. ORAL HISTORY 2011-04-02, Alaska and Polar Regions Archives, Elmer E. Rasmuson Library, University of Alaska Fairbanks.

_____. Oral history interview with Karen Brewster, Roger Kaye, and Susan Grace, April 20, 2006, Fairbanks, Alaska. Tape No. ORAL HISTORY 2011-04-03, Alaska and Polar Regions Archives, Elmer E. Rasmuson Library, University of Alaska Fairbanks.

_____. Oral history interview with Karen Brewster, Susan Grace, Keith Pollock, and Pam Miller, April 28, 2006, Fairbanks, Alaska. Tape No. ORAL HISTORY 2011-04-04, Alaska and Polar Regions Archives, Elmer E. Rasmuson Library, University of Alaska Fairbanks.

_____. Oral history interview with Karen Brewster, Susan Grace, and Keith Pollock, May 4, 2006, Fairbanks, Alaska. Tape No. ORAL HISTORY 2011-04-05, Alaska and Polar Regions Archives, Elmer E. Rasmuson Library, University of Alaska Fairbanks.

_____. Oral history interview with Karen Brewster, Roger Kaye, and Pam Miller, May 10, 2006, Fairbanks, Alaska. Tape No. ORAL HISTORY 2011-04-06, Alaska and Polar Regions Archives, Elmer E. Rasmuson Library, University of Alaska Fairbanks.

_____. Oral history interview with Karen Brewster and Pam Miller, November 20, 2006, Fairbanks, Alaska. Tape No. ORAL HISTORY 2011-04-09, Alaska and Polar Regions Archives, Elmer E. Rasmuson Library, University of Alaska Fairbanks.

_____. Oral history interview with Karen Brewster and Roger Kaye, December 1, 2006, Fairbanks, Alaska. Tape No. ORAL HISTORY 2011-04-10, Alaska and Polar Regions Archives, Elmer E. Rasmuson Library, University of Alaska Fairbanks.

_____. Oral history interview with Karen Brewster and Susan Grace, February 15, 2007, Fairbanks, Alaska. Tape No. ORAL HISTORY 2011-04-13, Alaska and Polar Regions Archives, Elmer E. Rasmuson Library, University of Alaska Fairbanks.

_____. Oral history interview with Karen Brewster and Pam Miller, March 10, 2007, Fairbanks, Alaska. Tape No. ORAL HISTORY 2011-04-14, Alaska and Polar Regions Archives, Elmer E. Rasmuson Library, University of Alaska Fairbanks.

_____. Oral history interview with Karen Brewster, Roger Kaye, and Frank Keim, April 11, 2007, Fairbanks, Alaska. Tape No. ORAL HISTORY 2011-04-15, Alaska and Polar Regions Archives, Elmer E. Rasmuson Library, University of Alaska Fairbanks.

_____. Oral history interview with Karen Brewster, May 30-June 2, 2007, Camp Denali, Denali National Park, Alaska. Tape No. ORAL HISTORY 2011-04-18, Alaska and Polar Regions Archives, Elmer E. Rasmuson Library, University of Alaska Fairbanks.

_____. Oral history interview with Karen Brewster, Susan Grace, and Keith Pollock, December 14, 2007, Fairbanks, Alaska. Tape No. ORAL HISTORY 2011-04-22, Alaska and Polar Regions Archives, Elmer E. Rasmuson Library, University of Alaska Fairbanks.

_____. Oral history interview with Karen Brewster and Susan Grace, May 2, 2008, Fairbanks, Alaska. Tape No. ORAL HISTORY 2011-04-23, Alaska and Polar Regions Archives, Elmer E. Rasmuson Library, University of Alaska Fairbanks.

_____. Oral history interview with Karen Brewster, Susan Grace, and Keith Pollock, November 5, 2008, Fairbanks, Alaska. Tape No. ORAL HISTORY 2011-04-24, Alaska and Polar Regions Archives, Elmer E. Rasmuson Library, University of Alaska Fairbanks.

_____. Oral history interview with Maria Brooks, September 22, 1980, Fairbanks, Alaska. Tape No. ORAL HISTORY 93-01-65, Alaska and Polar Regions Archives, Elmer E. Rasmuson Library, University of Alaska Fairbanks.

_____. Oral history interview with Roger Kaye, November 10, 2002, Fairbanks, Alaska. Recording in possession of Roger Kaye. The transcript is available at Fish and Wildlife Service's National Digital Library website: http://digitalmedia.fws.gov, accessed February 14, 2011.

_____. Oral history interview with Dan O'Neill, November 8, 1988, Fairbanks, Alaska. Tape No. ORAL HISTORY 88–69, Alaska and Polar Regions Archives, Elmer E. Rasmuson Library, University of Alaska Fairbanks.

_____. Presentation about history of Camp Denali, June 1, 2007, Camp Denali, Denali National Park, Alaska. Tape No. ORAL HISTORY 2011-04-19, Alaska and Polar Regions Archives, Elmer E. Rasmuson Library, University of Alaska Fairbanks.

_____. Presentation to Ginny Wood of Congressional Gold Medal for WASP Service by Alaska Senator Lisa Murkowski, April 2, 2010, Fairbanks, Alaska. Video recording by Karen Brewster. Tape No. ORAL HISTORY 2011-04-25,

Alaska and Polar Regions Archives, Elmer E. Rasmuson Library, University of Alaska Fairbanks.

_____. Presentation to Ginny Wood of US Fish and Wildlife Service's Citizens Award for Exceptional Service, August 11, 2010, Fairbanks, Alaska. Video recording by Karen Brewster. Tape No. ORAL HISTORY 2011-04-27, Alaska and Polar Regions Archives, Elmer E. Rasmuson Library, University of Alaska Fairbanks.

_____. "Rampart—Foolish Dam." *The Living Wilderness* 88 (Spring 1965): 3–7.

_____. "The Ramparts We Watch." *Sierra Club Bulletin* 50, no. 3 (March 1965): 13–15.

_____. "Requiem for a Road." *Alaska Conservation Review* 9, no. 3 (Fall 1968): 12.

_____. "Save the Trails!" *Northern Line* 5, no. 2 (April–May 1983): 5, 9.

_____. "So Long, Celia." *Northern Line* 24, no. 1 (January 27, 2002): 11.

_____. Speech, Alaska Association of Mountain and Wilderness Guides Annual Meeting, Fairbanks, December 5–6, 1981. Typed text found in files of Ginny Wood Personal Collection.

_____. Speech, Alaska Outdoor Education Conference, Sitka, March 27, 1993. Typed text found in files of Ginny Wood Personal Collection.

_____. "Stubborn Ounces." "From the Woodpile" column. *Northern Line* 20, no. 2 (June 19, 1998): 8–9.

_____. "When Is Enough, Enough?" "From the Woodpile" column. *Northern Line* 16, no. 2 (August 5, 1994): 10–11.

Wood, Ginny Hill. "Editorial." *News Bulletin of the Alaska Conservation Society* 1, no. 3 (August 1960).

_____. *News Bulletin of the Alaska Conservation Society* 1, no. 4 (November 1960): 3–4.

_____. *Once Upon a Time: A 1938 European Bicycle Adventure.* Gustavus, AK: Press North America, forthcoming.

_____. "Squaws Along the Yukon." *Alaska Sportsman* 20, no. 4 (September 1954): 6–11, 36–40.

_____. "Squaws Along the Yukon." *National Geographic* 112, no. 2 (August 1957), 245–265.

_____. "Subdivider, Spare Our Ski Trail." *News Bulletin of the Alaska Conservation Society* 4, no. 2, April 1963; 7–8.

_____. "Valley of Seven Smokes." *Alaska Sportsman* 19, no. 1 (January 1953): 6–11, 29–33.

_____. "Wilderness Camp." *Alaska Sportsman* 19, no. 11 (November 1953): 20–24.

Ginny Wood Personal Collection. Papers, manuscripts, photo albums, and scrapbooks in the possession of Ginny Wood, Fairbanks, Alaska.

Wood, Ginny, Dick Bishop, Gail Mayo, and Laurel Holmes. Oral history recording of a discussion about the efforts to get Creamer's Field protected as Creamer's Field Migratory Waterfowl Refuge, 1993. Tape No. ORAL HISTORY 2008-10, Alaska and Polar Regions Archives, Elmer E. Rasmuson Library, University of Alaska Fairbanks. Original recording from Friends of Creamer's Field.

Wood, Ginny, and Morton "Woody" Wood. Presentation about history of Camp Denali: providing commentary while old films are being shown, August 18, 2007, Camp Denali, Denali National Park, Alaska. Tape No. ORAL HISTORY 2011-04-20, Alaska and Polar Regions Archives, Elmer E. Rasmuson Library, University of Alaska Fairbanks.

Wood, Morton S. "The First Traverse of Mt. McKinley—A First Ascent of the South Buttress." *American Alpine Journal* 9, no. 2, issue 29 (1955): 51–69.

_____. *General Photographic Report for Katmai National Monument,* Summer 1952. Anchorage: US Department of the Interior, National Park Service, Katmai National Park and Preserve, Archives.

_____. Interview conducted by Oregon Public Broadcasting in August 2007 at Camp Denali for the PBS series *Great Lodges of the National Parks.* Transcript_Camp Denali_#8A6. Electronic document in possession of author.

_____. Oral history interview with David Krupa, May 6, 2000, Seattle, Washington. Tape No. ORAL HISTORY 2000-17-03, Alaska and Polar Regions Archives, Elmer E. Rasmuson Library, University of Alaska Fairbanks. Audio also available for listening at http://jukebox.uaf.edu/denali/html/mowo.htm, accessed February 12, 2011.

_____. Oral history interview with Karen Brewster, May 23, 2007, Seattle, Washington. Tape No. ORAL HISTORY 2011-04-17, Alaska and Polar Regions Archives, Elmer E. Rasmuson Library, University of Alaska Fairbanks.

_____. *Report of Exploratory Trips in Katmai National Monument,* Summer 1952. Anchorage: US Department of the Interior, National Park Service, Katmai National Park and Preserve, Archives.

Young Life Malibu Club. "Malibu Club History." *Young Life Malibu Club.* http://sites.younglife.org/camps/MalibuClub/Open%20Content%20Pages/Malibu%20History.aspx, accessed February 12, 2011.

Yow, Valerie. "'Do I Like Them Too Much?'": Effects of the Oral History Interview on the Interviewer and Vice-Versa." *Oral History Review* 24, no. 1 (Summer 1997): 55–79.

_____. "Ethics and Interpersonal Relationships in Oral History Research." *Oral History Review* 22 (Summer 1995): 57–59.

Zermatt Matterhorn. "111 years Gornergrat Bahn." *Zermatt Matterhorn official website.* http://www.zermatt.ch/en/page.cfm/zermatt_matterhorn/zermatt_stories/111_years_gornergrat_bahn, accessed February 12, 2011.

Zimmerman, William, Jr. "Washington Office Report." *Sierra Club Bulletin* 50, no. 5 (May 1965): 11.

Index

Page numbers with an *n* denote an endnote;
f refers to a figure.

modern conveniences, 181–182
money
  Camp Denali woes, 193
  philosophy on, 31
Montana State University, faculty hiring after
  Project Chariot, 293–294
Montreal departure, 49
Moore, Terry (UAF president), 288
Moose Creek (Alaska), 187, 195
Morgan, Mr. (helpful European), 51
Moro, Oregon, as birthplace, 13
mothballs as animal repellant, 336
motion sickness, 76–77
motorboat problems at Katmai National Park,
  166
Mount McKinley National Park (now Denali
  National Park). *See also* Denali Park road
  aircraft restrictions, 431n7
  boundary changes, 235, 304, 435n8
  exploration of, 189
  Ginny backpacking in, 324f
  gravel road, 226f
  map, 228f
  naming of, 302
  photos, 176f, 178f
  winter employment at, 177–183
  winter recreation program at, 183, 433n17,
    433n19
  Woody's employment, 165
mountain climbing
  mountaineering medicine, 412n8
  perspectives on, 60–61
  search and rescue, 77, 263–265, 267–273,
    412n8
Mountain Travel, 329–330, 386, 478n6
movie theater, 22
mukluks, reselling, 158
Munich, Germany, 57–58
Munich Agreement, 57–58, 410n14
Murie, Adolph (Ade)
  about, 316
  as environmentalist, 282, 315, 451n5
  on park boundaries, 304, 435n8
  as park service employee, 285–286
  predator-prey relationships, study of, 242, 443n3
  visitor interactions, 242
Murie, Louise (Weezie), 316
Murie, Mardy
  in airplane accident, 463n85
  on Arctic National Wildlife Refuge, 299
  at Camp Denali, 316–317
  as environmentalist, 282, 285–286, 315, 451n5
  humor of, 183, 311
  on San Juan Island, 317f

Murie, Olaus
  about, 454n19
  at Camp Denali, 316–317
  death of, 467n109
  as environmentalist, 282, 285–286, 299–300,
    451n5
  as Wilderness Society director, 315
Murkowski, Frank, 377, 467n115
music in Finland, 149–150
Mustang, 92

N

naked canoeing, 350
Nancarrow, Bill
  at Camp Denali, 211
  with dog-team patrol, 177, 431nn5–6
  at Katmai National Park, 166, 428n3
  at park cabin, 224
  as park naturalist, 428n6, 431n2
Nancarrow, Ginny, 166, 177
NARL (Naval Arctic Research Laboratory),
  470n16
Natco-owned land, 373
National Environmental Protection Act (NEPA;
  1969), 284–285
National Geographic, 166, 168, 429nn9–10
National Ski Patrol, 366
national skiing races, 374–375
National Wildlife Federation, 454n25
Natives. *See* Alaska Natives
natural history workshop, 244, 326
natural resources as capital, 323
nature as direction definer, 191, 192
Nature Conservancy, Trustees for Alaska, 282
Naval Arctic Research Laboratory (NARL),
  470n16
navigational skills, Woody's, 166
Nazi propaganda, 53–54, 57
NEPA (National Environmental Protection Act;
  1969), 284–285
Nepal, 379
New Year's Eve
  at Mount McKinley National Park, 177
  at Northway, Alaska, 127
New York City, 64–65
New Zealand, 381
newsletter, as advertising, 223
Nifty Theater (movie theater), 22
Nordale, A. Hjalmer, 438n2
Nordale Hotel, 129–130
Nordic Ski Club, 374–375
North American airplanes, 92
North Star Borough
  Birch Hill Recreation Area, 373